\*

## Christianity in Western Europe c. 1100–c. 1500

During the early middle ages, Europe developed complex and varied Christian cultures, and from about 1100 secular rulers, competing factions and inspired individuals continued to engender a diverse and ever-changing mix within Christian society. This volume explores the wide range of institutions, practices and experiences associated with the life of European Christians in the later middle ages. The clergy of this period initiated new approaches to the role of priests, bishops and popes, and developed an ambitious project to instruct the laity. For lay people, the practices of parish religion were central, but many sought additional ways to enrich their lives as Christians. Impulses towards reform and renewal periodically swept across Europe, led by charismatic preachers and supported by secular rulers. At the same time, Christians were often preoccupied and troubled by non-Christians within their own communities and on their borders. This book provides accessible accounts of these complex historical processes and entices the reader towards further enquiry.

MIRI RUBIN is Professor of Medieval History at Queen Mary, University of London. Her most recent publications include *Mother of God: A History of the Virgin Mary* (2009) and *The Hollow Crown: A History of Britain in the Late Middle Ages* (2005).

WALTER SIMONS is Associate Professor in the Department of History, Dartmouth College. He is author of *Cities of Ladies: Beguine Communities in the Medieval Low Countries 1200–1565* (2001) and co-editor of *Ludo J. R. Milis, Religion, Culture and Medieval Low Countries: Selected Essays* (2005) with Jeroen Deploige, Martine De Reu and Steven Vanderputten and *The Productivity of Urban Space in Northern Europe* (2002) with Peter Arnade and Martha Howell.

# CHRISTIANITY

*The Cambridge History of Christianity* offers a comprehensive chronological account of the development of Christianity in all its aspects – theological, intellectual, social, political, regional, global – from its beginnings to the present day. Each volume makes a substantial contribution in its own right to the scholarship of its period and the complete *History* constitutes a major work of academic reference. Far from being merely a history of Western European Christianity and its offshoots, the *History* aims to provide a global perspective. Eastern and Coptic Christianity are given full consideration from the early period onwards, and later, African, Far Eastern, New World, South Asian and other non-European developments in Christianity receive proper coverage. The volumes cover popular piety and non-formal expressions of Christian faith and treat the sociology of Christian formation, worship and devotion in a broad cultural context. The question of relations between Christianity and other major faiths is also kept in sight throughout. The *History* will provide an invaluable resource for scholars and students alike.

LIST OF VOLUMES:

*Origins to Constantine*
EDITED BY MARGARET M. MITCHELL AND FRANCES M. YOUNG

*Constantine to c. 600*
EDITED BY AUGUSTINE CASIDAY AND FREDERICK W. NORRIS

*Early Medieval Christianity c. 600–c. 1100*
EDITED BY THOMAS NOBLE AND JULIA SMITH

*Christianity in Western Europe c. 1100–c. 1500*
EDITED BY MIRI RUBIN AND WALTER SIMONS

*Eastern Christianity*
EDITED BY MICHAEL ANGOLD

# THE CAMBRIDGE
# HISTORY OF
# CHRISTIANITY

*

VOLUME 4
## Christianity in Western Europe c. 1100–c. 1500

*

*Edited by*
MIRI RUBIN
*and*
WALTER SIMONS

**CAMBRIDGE**
UNIVERSITY PRESS

CAMBRIDGE UNIVERSITY PRESS
Cambridge, New York, Melbourne, Madrid, Cape Town, Singapore, São Paulo, Delhi

Cambridge University Press
The Edinburgh Building, Cambridge CB2 8RU, UK

Published in the United States of America by Cambridge University Press, New York

www.cambridge.org
Information on this title: www.cambridge.org/9780521811064

First published 2009

Printed in the United Kingdom at the University Press, Cambridge

*A catalogue record for this publication is available from the British Library*

ISBN 978-0-521-81106-4 hardback

# Contents

Contents

Contents

# Illustrations

# Maps

# Contributors

JOHN ARNOLD, School of History, Classics and Archaeology, Birkbeck, University of London, UK

ALAN E. BERNSTEIN, Department of History, University of Arizona, Tucson, USA

PETER BILLER, Department of History, University of York, UK

ALAIN BOUREAU, École des Hautes Études en Sciences Sociales, Paris, France

SUSAN BOYNTON, Department of Music, Columbia University, New York, USA

MARCUS BULL, Department of Historical Studies, University of Bristol, UK

JANET BURTON, Department of History, University of Wales Lampeter, UK

RACHEL FULTON, Department of History, University of Chicago, USA

KANTIK GHOSH, Trinity College, University of Oxford, UK

KOEN GOUDRIAAN, Vrije Universiteit Amsterdam, The Netherlands

AMY HOLLYWOOD, Harvard Divinity School, Harvard University, Cambridge, Mass., USA

KATHERINE JANSEN, Department of History, Catholic University of America, Washington (D.C.), USA

BEVERLY MAYNE KIENZLE, Harvard Divinity School, Harvard University, Cambridge, Mass., USA

HENRIETTA LEYSER, St Peter's College, University of Oxford, UK

ORA LIMOR, Open University, Tel Aviv, Israel

SARA LIPTON, Department of History, State University of New York Stony Brook, Stony Brook, USA

BRIAN PATRICK MCGUIRE, Department of History, Roskilde University Centre, Denmark

MEGAN MCLAUGHLIN, Department of History, University of Iowa, Iowa City, USA

DAVID NIRENBERG, Committee on Social Thought, University of Chicago, USA

CHRISTOPHER OCKER, San Francisco Theological Seminary, USA

ANTHONY PERRON, Department of History, Loyola Marymount University, Los Angeles, USA

BRIGITTE RESL, Department of History, University of Liverpool, UK

BERT ROEST, Department of History, University of Groningen, The Netherlands

MIRI RUBIN, Department of History, Queen Mary, University of London, UK

ROBERTO RUSCONI, Università degli studi di Roma, Rome, Italy

WALTER SIMONS, Department of History, Dartmouth College, Hanover, New Hamp., USA

*Contributors*

Lesley Smith, Harris Manchester College, University of Oxford, UK
Michael Stolz, Department of German, University of Bern, Switzerland
André Vauchez, 2 rue Alasseur, Paris, France
Anders Winroth, Department of History, Yale University, New Haven, Conn., USA
Joseph Ziegler, Department of History, University of Haïfa, Israel

# Abbreviations

| | |
|---|---|
| *AA.SS.* | *Acta Sanctorum*, 3rd edn, Paris: Palmé, 1863– |
| CCCM | Corpus Christianorum: Continuatio mediaevalis |
| CCSL | Corpus Christianorum Series Latina |
| CFS | Cistercian Fathers Series |
| CSEL | Corpus scriptorum ecclesiasticorum latinorum |
| MGH | Monumenta Germaniae Historica, Hanover *et al.*: Hahn *et al.*, 1826– |
| EPP | Epistolae |
| SS | Scriptores |
| *OED* | *Oxford English Dictionary* |
| *PG* | *Patrologiae Cursus Completus, Series Graeca*, ed. J.-P. Migne, Paris: Migne, 1857–66 |
| *PL* | *Patrologiae Cursus Completus, Series Latina*, ed. J.-P. Migne, Paris: Migne, 1844–64 |
| *SBO* | *Sancti Bernardi opera* |
| SC | Sources chrétiennes |
| SCH | Studies in Church History |

Unless otherwise specified, all biblical references are to the Douay-Rheims version of the vulgate.

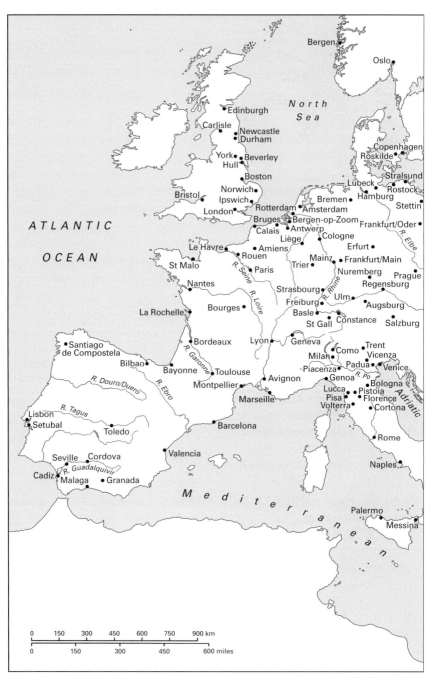

Map 1 Western Europe c. 1100 – c. 1500

Map 2 Universities of Europe

Uppsala

Copenhagen

Greifswald
Rostock

Frankfurt/Oder

Leipzig
Erfurt

Mainz
Würzburg
Heidelberg
Tübingen
Ingolstadt

Prague

Cracow

Vienna Poszony
Buda

Pecs

Treviso
Verona Venice
Pavia Padua
Piacenza Ferrara
Palma Bologna
Lucca
Pisa Florence
Siena Arezzo
Perugia

Rome

Naples
Salerno

Catania

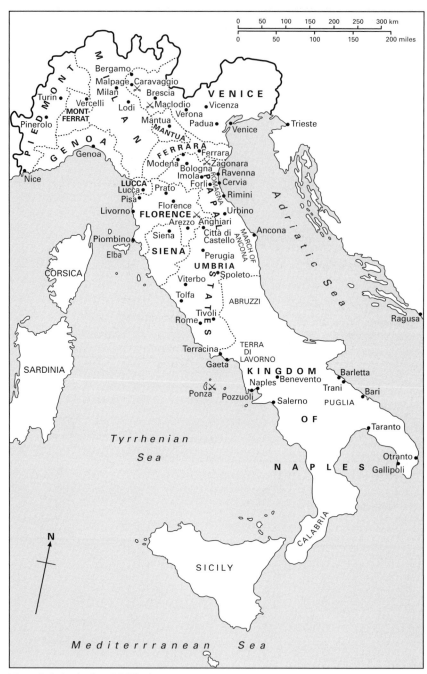

Map 3 Italy in the late Middle Ages

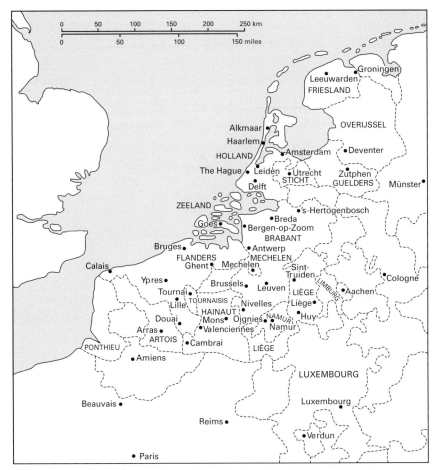

Map 4 The Low Countries c. 1100 – c. 1500

# Introduction

MIRI RUBIN AND WALTER SIMONS

Medieval Christian Europe has long been acknowledged as a place and a time
central to the formation of the Christian heritage. Until recently it was still
described in popular and learned books alike as the 'age of faith', a time of
intense religious feeling and extravagant action in the pursuit of religious
goals: crusade, inquisition, scholastic theology and mysticism. It was an age
characterised by an imposing public Christian art and the institutions of the
papacy in the lead. Until recent decades the study of medieval European
Christianity was based primarily on Latin texts: theological tracts, canon law
and its commentaries, and some devotional tracts. The protagonists of medieval European Christianity were popes, bishops, reforming abbots and activist
preachers; its spaces were envisaged as monasteries, cathedrals and universities. While Europe's tens of thousands of parishes were still in evidence, the
quality of religion in them excited relatively little interest: provision for them
being either sparse, or merely a diluted version of the official and learned
formulations of scholars, popes and bishops.

This volume of *The Cambridge History of Christianity* offers the reader a series
of articles that summarises some of the exciting, imaginative and transformative
historical work on the religious cultures inhabited by Western Europeans
between 1100 and 1500. It cannot encompass all areas of current research but it
offers introductory essays to a vast range of subjects, with the expectation that
the interested reader will go on to pursue more. We have aimed to give an
overview of ideas and theories relating to the Christian life of institutions and
individuals, as well as to provide glimpses of the implementation of such ideas
within the rhythms of life in parishes and religious institutions, on city streets and
along Europe's pilgrimage routes. Every idea and practice discussed here has a
complex history: from a genesis out of traditions patristic, classical or rooted in
earlier medieval centuries, as well as a life within the diverse regions of Europe.

Medieval Christian life was always characterised by uniformity and diversity. Take the central cult of the Virgin Mary, with its spectacular rise in this

period. While Mary was taught at the mother's knee, the forms of address, the shape of her statues, even the variety of feasts celebrated in her honour varied from region to region, as between, say, the emergent group of mother and son in tender embrace in thirteenth-century northern France and the seated, frontal hieratic Mary, of the 'seat of wisdom', as cherished by the Catalan Churches. The central Italian cities developed a rich and resounding vernacular devotional style in celebrating Mary through recitation of her praises – *laude* – in confraternities, a phenomenon unknown elsewhere. Even the rosary, Mary's aid in prayer, created at the end of the medieval period, was a northern product that took long to penetrate the habits of southern Europeans. Even more than was true for their habits in governance, warfare and business, Europeans recognised a family resemblance to others as they travelled Europe for trade, diplomacy or pilgrimage, but there was also a strong local sense, bolstered by linguistic difference and liturgical traditions, in the regional religious cultures of Europe. Belief and practice could show unity in one sense (geographic, social, linguistic) but diversity in another. Both unity and diversity may be perceived but take different forms or manifest themselves differently depending on the subject, place and so on. While institutional centralisation, the spread of the Mendicant orders, the international reach of the great universities and finally the printing press brought uniformity to the world of rules and doctrine, other dynamics in this period worked against uniformity, not least the breakthrough of the vernacular languages in devotional life, powerful 'national' monarchies supporting the salvation of their subjects, or the inexhaustible creativity of devotional life itself.

The beginning of this period coincides with momentous changes in the economic and political structures of Europe and in the quality of life of its people. Between 1000 and 1200 the population of Europe probably doubled. Thousands of new towns – mostly small market towns – developed, and new villages were planted on lands recently brought under plough. Europeans were on the move: trading, travelling on pilgrimage, settling recently conquered lands at the extremities of Europe – in Iberia, in the Baltic region – and their enterprises were facilitated by the organised direction offered by rulers and their officials. The educated men of the church were deeply involved in all these enterprises: they advised kings, managed ecclesiastical estates, negotiated treaties and acted as judges. The leading intellectuals theorised the tenets upon which a Christian society – *societas Christiana* – might and ought to conduct its affairs. The twelfth century saw the seminal formulations of fundamental institutions which were to affect Christian lives for centuries:

the meaning of the sacraments, the just price and reward for labour, the terms of Christian marriage, the nature of clerical celibacy and the appropriate lifestyle for priests.

The co-emergence of ecclesiastical and secular administrations was a battlefield of ideas and personalities. Already in the formative era of the Christian Empire – the fifth century – emperor and bishop of Rome discoursed on the relative weight and honour that each office held. There were complex issues of demarcation to be settled over legal jurisdiction and the right to collect taxes, for both kings and pope claimed the right to do so and depended on the resources raised from the same peoples. So a field of competition as well as emulation developed between the church's bureaucracy, the system through which saving grace was disseminated to Christians, and the states – kingdoms, city-states, principalities – that secured property through justice and protected life and limb. These spheres were intricately linked not least through the powerful institution of sacred kingship, but also in their parallel aims to regulate aspects of family, sexual morality and inheritance. In their mutual commitment to the underlying Christian ethos of the communities they ruled and served, church and state combined in efforts to define and correct religious deviation, and in the related challenge of locating the Jews within Christian polities.

The integrated Europe of the high Middle Ages adhered increasingly to the model of parish Christianity. While the most renowned and well-documented institutions were religious houses of various orders, most Christians experienced religious life within a community of village or urban neighbourhood, a parish into which they were born and with which they were associated for the rest of their lives. All the efforts to expand and deepen Christian teaching and instruction – and this period sees the series of ecumenical councils which defined and disseminated the terms of this project – directed attention to the parish and its servant, the parish priest. Teaching of the basics of faith began at home and continued in the parish; confession, penance and annual communion followed; marriage was directed towards the parish, and at the end of life burial and commemoration too. The priest was charged with the many tasks of celebrating the liturgy, visiting the sick, instructing the young, supporting the poor, ministering to the dying, alongside the maintenance of his parish's income from land, livestock, rents and tithes.

In rural communities the unit of agrarian work, lordship and parish often coincided to create a meaningful space of social interaction through communal religious life. In urban centres, where some 10–15 per cent of Europeans lived, the possibilities for expression of religious interests were more diverse.

Some regions of Europe, like central and northern Italy and the Low Countries, were highly urbanised, and within cities and towns experiments in new forms of religious life for the laity – men and women – took place. From these urban settings emerged a type of female religious, the beguine – a woman committed to religious perfection within the world, in a life that combined prayer, meditation, service and work. The friar was a creation of these cities too: above all the Franciscan model of the poor, begging man, whose personal example was combined powerfully with effective preaching in order to turn Christians into committed Christians, that is, to convert souls. Various forms of confraternal life also transcended the parish, as lay people combined to explore old themes in new ways – the Passion, Mary's life, *Corpus Christi* – with expert guidance in religious poetry, drama and music from the specialists, the friars. This is a period of enormous creativity, as Europe's wealth and inventive energies, its many materials – marble, alabaster, wood, pearls, gold and silver – were worked into visual and tactile representations of the Christian story. This volume includes chapters on the visual arts and music too. The religious life of medieval Europe was full of rhythm and song, light and colour. Since its practices and ideas were mediated through efforts that made them tangible and sensual, some critics – like John Wyclif – considered them to verge on the idolatrous.

The calamities experienced in later medieval Europe, in the wake of the traumatic visitation of famine (1315–22), the Black Death (1347–50) and the recurrent waves of plague in subsequent decades, only served to enhance the intensity of preoccupation with death and the afterlife. It left a depleted European population, but also opened opportunities for those who remained. Polities and communities leapt to associations between disaster and moral danger: the Black Death led to attacks on Jews and to the annihilation of their communities throughout the Holy Roman Empire; a rhetoric grew perched upon the dialectic of purity and danger. A new style of European communication developed through a new type of preacher whose audience was no longer the people of a parish or a city, but whole regions. The papacy – caught up in its own struggles for self-definition throughout the fourteenth and fifteenth centuries – recruited and licensed charismatic preachers from among the ranks of the most enthusiastic and able friars and charged them with the work of reform, correction and exhortation, men like the friars Vincent Ferrer (d. 1419) or Giovanni da Capistrano (d. 1456). Cities and principalities appointed such performers to do the work of social discipline in their piazzas: like Bernardino in the cities of central Italy in the 1420s, or Savonarola in the 1490s. At the same time in the cities of north-west Europe civic authorities tended to prefer bourgeois self-help to public oratory; the more motivated among the literate urban population were served by a rich vernacular devotional literature: the *Mirror, Imitatio Christi*, the books of hours produced in their thousands in the workshops of Bruges, Ghent, Amiens and Antwerp; a somewhat larger group of lay men and women could turn to the dramatic spectacles crafted by chambers of rhetoricians or the mysteries of the Corpus Christi guilds.

Women and men participated vigorously and sometimes differently in the making of European Christianity between 1100 and 1500. A wide range of knowledge – medical, theological, legal – combined to form a robust and commonly held official wisdom about the inadequacy of women to think, to make moral judgements, to endure hardship, to exercise authority, and to lead. In this period, as in earlier medieval centuries, women were excluded from all orders of the church, minor and major, nor did they enjoy access to education within the institutions of learning that were associated with the church. Some women, usually of aristocratic backgrounds, sought religious perfection with nunneries, and a few became extremely distinguished for their mystical insights and exemplary lives: Hildegard of Bingen (d. 1179), Elisabeth of Schönau (d. 1164/65), Marie d'Oignies (d. 1213). As the period progresses, and in keeping with the trends in religious life already delineated, there is a wide diversity of manifestations of religious enthusiasm by women who were or had been married, by mothers with children, by young women of very modest backgrounds. The provision for women's sacramental needs was always a challenge: the priest had to enter their enclosures to hear confession and celebrate mass. Conversely, when women had something important to impart – prophecy, messages for reform, mystical revelations – they had to go about the world in a way that was not considered appropriate for women. Some, like Bridget of Sweden (d. 1373), managed the transition well, others, like Marguerite Porète (d. 1310) did not; she died at the stake as a relapsed heretic.

The very term 'heresy' was refined in this period to new precision. The legacy of early Christian legislation and some early medieval preoccupation with it was overhauled in this period to produce a system that combined identification, examination, attempts at correction, and ultimately punishment of those deemed to be 'heretics'. The task of protecting the faith, by punishing publicly those who knowingly and wilfully deviated from it, was the responsibility of bishops above all. To them parish priests were meant to present cases of people who spread their views and were resistant to correction. The bishop's court dealt with all serious infringements of church law, and they were charged with the protection of true belief. As the system of church law evolved and spread all over Europe, and as it was tightened, made uniform and added to periodically by new papal pronouncements, a whole body of law and practice on heresy grew. Since there was a sense from the twelfth century that in several parts of Europe the challenge was rather more profound, the papacy allowed for the creation of the inquisition in the 1230s, first manned by the recently established order of the Dominican friars. So southern France, Bohemia and northern Italy saw particularly concerted efforts at preaching against heresy and trials of those who persisted. Yet again, the political map of Europe displays variations in the reception of this institution: it never operated in England, and the Iberian monarchs only adopted it in the late fifteenth century. Still, a whole literature on the techniques of identification and interrogation was created by the inquisitors, for the training of future cohorts in the hope of making the system trans-parent, uniform and conforming to the principles of church law.

In this world of vast institutional and intellectual elaboration of the Christian story, where the Christian parish offered the fundamental frame for the lives of Europeans, there was a great deal of preoccupation with those who were not fully part of that world. The amount of imaginative effort and intellectual energy invested in thinking about Jews and Muslims was great, and it was intricately related to the vision of what a *societas Christiana* was and ought to be. Jews played a central role in the narratives of Christ's ministry and became more sharply drawn in this period as the knowing, and thus guilty, agents of the Passion. The traditional formulation of St Augustine, about the value of Jews as witnesses to Christian truth, as a crucial part of the unfolding Christian story unto its ends, was challenged in medieval Europe in towns and cities where Jews were constant reminders of the possibility of doubt. A vast literature of polemic, whose arguments were sometimes rehearsed by preachers from the pulpit, or in staged public disputations (Paris 1240, Barcelona 1263, Tortosa 1410), assisted the birth of elaborate narratives that cast Jews as enemies. Enemies of Christ at the birth of Christianity, they were now imagined as enemies of Europeans too: of their hallowed spaces, their cherished beliefs, and of their innocent children. This period saw the birth of the accusations of ritual murder, the blood libel and the host-desecration narrative too.

In Iberia, southern Italy, in Cyprus and in the Holy Land Christians encountered Jews for periods of time and observed their practice from neighbouring proximity. In Iberia Christian monarchs were conquering lands previously held by Muslims and were confronted with the challenges of ruling truly multi-ethnic communities. Conversion of Muslims to Christianity was actively encouraged and may have been perceived as more easily achievable than the conversion of the Jews. A vast literature cast the Muslim as a figure of romance and of violence. Dozens of stories circulated in Iberia, which involved the encounter between Muslims and the Virgin Mary. The efforts at achieving religious uniformity resulted by the very end of this period in expulsions of Jews and then Muslims from the Iberian Peninsula; by then Jews had been expelled from England, France and cities in Italy and the Empire.

The history of Christianity in Europe between 1100 and 1500 will be the product of several overlapping histories. These took place in parishes and universities, among men and women, learned people and illiterate enthusiasts; these are histories of the eruption of charisma within the routines of daily Christian life, of toleration as well as violent aggression. Everywhere we turn we encounter the efforts by papacy, bishops, theologians, poets and rulers, to define and then maintain the coherence and order of Christian Europe. These efforts coexisted with and even encouraged questions and doubts, as ideas were applied in daily life. The powerful model of sacramental Christianity was delivered to every Christian in Europe by ordained priests, the channels of saving grace. But it also confronted the challenges posed by the claim that matter could bear the divine, that a fallible human could be a channel of grace, that images carved in stone or painted on wood could assist contact with God. These questions were famously asked by Lollards in fourteenth-century England, by Hussites in fifteenth-century Bohemia, and in each case they prompted vigorous political responses from church and state. *Christianity in Western Europe c.1100–c.1500* aims to understand these creative dialectical processes. They shaped the lives of medieval Europe and, when Europeans intervened in the lives of people in the Americas, Africa and Asia, they became part of a global story too.

PART I

*

# INSTITUTIONS AND CHANGE:
## 1100—1200

# Clerical purity and the re-ordered world

## HENRIETTA LEYSER

The Cistercian monk Caesarius of Heisterbach (c.1180–c.1250), scourge of the unchaste, tells the story of a 'libidinous' priest attempting to celebrate mass: at the moment of consecration a snow-white dove flies down to the altar and drinks up the whole contents of the chalice before flying away with the bread in its beak. This happens not just once but at the three consecutive masses the priest tries to celebrate. Terrified, and finally contrite, the priest confesses to his sin – he has had sex with a woman he happened to meet as he set off on his rounds at the start of the day. Once the priest is shriven, the dove returns the three hosts to the corporal and from its throat pours back all the wine into the chalice.[1]

Caesarius combines his relish in telling stories that discomfit priests with a knowledge, even an acceptance of human frailty. For Caesarius celibacy is indeed of paramount importance for both clerks and monks; nonetheless, even those who fail to observe it can count on forgiveness provided they truly repent. Thus a monk who had left his house to become a secular priest and who had taken a concubine 'as is the custom of many' and had had children by her, was led to see the error of his ways; in a state of remorse he asked St Bernard (his former abbot) to re-admit him. Bernard agreed but, since he had a pressing journey to make, he told the priest he must wait awhile. While he was away, the priest died. On his return Bernard ordered the priest's grave to be opened, and 'he appeared to all not in the secular dress in which he was buried but in the tonsure and habit of a monk'. True contrition, observes Caesarius, restores all.[2]

Behind Caesarius' particular mix of scurrility and compassion lie the deeply learnt lessons of the Fourth Lateran Council of 1215; the tale of the dove and

---

* My title is indebted to Gerd Tellenbach's characterisation of the Investiture Contest as 'a struggle for right order in the world'; see his *Church, State and Christian Society at the Time of the Investiture Contest*, trans. R. F. Bennett (Oxford: Basil Blackwell, 1938), 1.

1 Caesarius of Heisterbach, *Dialogus miraculorum*, ed. Joseph Strange (2 vols.; Cologne: Heberle, 1851; repr., Ridgewood, N.J.: Gregg, 1966), vol. 1, distinctio 2, ch. 5, 64–5.

2 Caesarius, *Dialogus*, vol. 1, distinctio 2, ch. 3, 62–3.

the eucharist make very particular sense in the light of the long debate, finally resolved by the Council, about the nature of the mass. Its conclusion reflects the Council's rulings both on the necessity and efficacy of the sacrament of confession and on its insistence on clerical celibacy. 'Chastity and knowledge', for Caesarius, 'were the glory of a priest's life'; and chastity (unlike knowledge) was attainable by all and mattered accordingly.[3] There is more than an echo here of one of Innocent III's sermons to the clergy of Rome:

> we, constituted in holy orders, are necessarily obliged to guard chastity. For it is written that when David fled the persecution of Saul, he came into Nob to Ahimelech the priest, asking that five loaves be given to him to drive out hunger. The priest replied, 'I have no unconsecrated bread at hand, but only holy bread. If the young men are clean, especially from women, they may eat it.' He did not say, if they have faith, hope and charity; if they have the spirit of wisdom and understanding, the spirit of counsel and fortitude, the spirit of knowledge and piety, and the spirit of the fear of the Lord. But he said, 'If they are clean, especially from women, they may eat it', since they can not eat the holy bread worthily unless they are clean from the sexual union with women.[4]

Anxiety that sex polluted and the concomitant insistence on clerical celibacy have, of course, a history that long pre-dates the pontificate of Innocent III; already in the fourth century these were topics that caused impassioned debates in ecclesiastical circles and which opened up differences of opinion between East and West. The East adopted a compromise that demanded a celibate episcopate but that allowed those priests and deacons who were married before ordination to continue thereafter to have marital sex. The West on the other hand, at least after the Council of Elvira c. 325, periodically insisted, even if more often than not in vain, that all married clergy live as celibates. Those who did not were from time to time threatened with floggings and other penalties, but in the main the fulminations of the rigorists had little effect. Until the eleventh century it was therefore quite usual for bishops, priests and deacons to be married and to have children. In turn these children might themselves become ordained and take over their fathers' positions. Such 'hereditary' priests could expect to enjoy positions of considerable honour. But in the eleventh and twelfth centuries all this was set to change.

---

3 Caesarius, *Dialogus*, vol. 2, distinctio 9, ch. 26, 183–4.

4 Innocent III, *Sermones de diversis*, PL 217, cols. 684–5. For the translations of these sermons see Corinne J. Vause and Frank C. Gardiner, *Pope Innocent III: Between God and Man: Six Sermons on the Priestly Office* (Washington, D.C.: Catholic University of America Press, 2004).

The story of Aelred of Rievaulx (1110–67) is but one among many that could be told.

Aelred of Rievaulx came from a long line of priests from the north of England; his great-grandfather had had the responsibility at Durham of looking after the incorrupt body of St Cuthbert, of cutting his hair and nails – and the job of evicting a weasel that had chosen to nest in Cuthbert's coffin; his grandfather and his father had cared for the saints of Hexham. But in 1138 this particular world came finally to its end. In this year Aelred's father Eilaf fell ill. His status in Hexham had already been diminished by the reforming policies of the Norman archbishops of York. Regular (hence celibate) canons had been introduced to Hexham, allegedly to help Eilaf, but effectively minimising his responsibilities. For Eilaf, the writing on the wall was clear. His son Aelred had already given up a promising career at the court of the king of Scotland to join the newly arrived Cistercians at Rievaulx, and Eilaf decided he himself would now renounce all family claims to Hexham and that he would end his days as a monk at Durham. Cuthbert, meanwhile, was no longer the saint he once had been; the days when a married priest had cared for him were past, and Cuthbert had become a notable misogynist, allegedly so opposed in his lifetime to monks enjoying any female company that in death he could not tolerate the presence of women in any of the cemeteries where his body even for a time had lain. The stories of the terrible fates of such women, as reported by Symeon of Durham, raise the question how it was that a saint who in life had asked that he should be buried wrapped in a cloth given to him by a woman should in death have become so obsessed by the need to keep all women at bay?[5] Why had ecclesiastical reformers come to focus with such intensity on issues of sexual pollution?

Eleventh-century ecclesiastical reform was for long associated primarily with the pontificate of Gregory VII. The reasons are not hard to fathom. Gregory's aggressive rhetoric was matched by equally forceful policies. His excommunication of the Emperor Henry IV and the subsequent reconciliation between pope and emperor at Canossa in 1077 provide one of the most dramatic scenes of western medieval history, but it is important to be clear that what was at stake between pope and emperor was a quarrel about power

---

5 For Cuthbert's burial shroud see Bertram Colgrave, ed. and trans., *Two Lives of Saint Cuthbert: A Life by an Anonymous Monk of Lindisfarne and Bede's Prose Life* (Cambridge: Cambridge University Press, 1940; repr. 1985), 272. For Symeon of Durham's tales see his *Libellus de exordio atque procursu istius hoc est Dunhelmensis ecclesie: Tracts on the Origins and Progress of this the Church of Durham*, ed. and trans. David Rollason (Oxford Medieval Texts; Oxford: Clarendon Press, 2000), 104–11 and 174–7.

and authority rather than about clerical morality and reform. Henry IV might dispute Gregory's wisdom in supporting the boycotting of the masses said by unworthy priests, but neither he – nor indeed his anti-pope Wibert of Ravenna – had any doubt that both simony (the buying and selling of office or of the sacraments) and clerical marriage (the two are frequently found linked together) were abuses to be eradicated, 'plagues' which at least in theory ecclesiastical and secular rulers could unite to combat. Henry I of England, for example, however bitter his quarrels over investiture with Archbishop Anselm, had no objection to Anselm's measures forbidding English priests to have wives (especially since on a later occasion, and much to the chagrin of his bench, Henry was able to use the renewal of the prohibition as a way of extorting money from the offenders).[6]

A spotless clergy, freed from the taint of simony and from the lure of the marriage bed: this was an ideal that appealed across the normal divisions of society. For some what seemed an outrage was the sheer cost to the church of clerical families – of the luxuries priests allegedly lavished on their wives and of the privileges they gained for their sons; for others, including those whom the church deemed heretical, the charisma of the chaste exercised a particular fascination, commanding a respect over and above any owed to those in positions of nominal authority. The call to cultic purity became a programme enthusiastically endorsed by the curia, but it is important to note that it had been born elsewhere, in the great peace assemblies of the early eleventh century, its message spread initially not by papal councils and legates, but by wandering preachers and ascetic holy men. Tellingly, one of the first such holy men of whom we know is Romuald, whose *Life*, written by Peter Damian, proclaims that it was Romuald who first identified simony as a heresy and whose ambition, according to Damian, was 'to turn the whole world into a hermitage'.[7] (It was Damian too who popularised the use of the term 'nicolaitism' to apply to married clergy after the heretical sect of Rev. 2.6 and 2.14.) Values which formerly had seemed appropriate only for the cloister were now to be held up for emulation by all. The enormity of this programme is hard to grasp, and its implications were not worked out until the Lateran Council of 1215. To understand how revolutionary it was we must consider first how problematic had been the chances of salvation for laymen and women before the pastoral revolution of the twelfth and thirteenth centuries.

---

6 Henry of Huntingdon, *Historia Anglorum: The History of the English People*, ed. and trans. Diana Greenaway (Oxford Medieval Texts; Oxford: Clarendon Press, 1996), bk. 3, 484.
7 Peter Damian, *Vita Beati Romualdi*, ed. Giovanni Tabacco (Fonti per la storia d'Italia 94; Rome: Istituo Storico Italiano, 1957), ch. 37, 78.

In the tenth century, the key to salvation was held by monks: there was little hope of reaching heaven except by becoming a monk or by arranging for the prayers of monks on one's behalf. How any layman could lead a virtuous life was far from clear. Gerald of Aurillac (d. 909) did his best, allowing himself to be robbed, refusing to spill human blood and steadfastly guarding his chastity – when he was laid out after his death his hand refused to stay on his breast and insisted on moving so as to cover his private parts – but Gerald was an exception, and tellingly he crowned his quasi-monastic way of life by tonsuring himself (though this was a fact he kept secret by wearing a little hat).[8] More usual was the course chosen by the knight Ralph of Noyon. The year is 1092; Ralph had been ill and had become worried about the state of his soul. The monk whom he consulted was unequivocal: 'as long as you live in the world as you have been living up to now, I don't see how you can be saved. If you truly want to be saved, give up the world and embrace the monastic life.' Ralph shares his concern with his wife Mainsendis who turns out to be as anxious as he: 'I fear for my soul just as you are afraid for yours', but she is pregnant so neither feels they can immediately leave the world. For the next eighteen months they continue to live together but 'for all that they did nothing carnal'. When the time comes for them to take their vows they offer to the monastic life not only themselves, but also their sons including the baby, placed in his cradle on the altar, not wanting to leave them 'in the hands of the devil'.[9]

By 1215, the year of Lateran IV, the world of Gerald, of Ralph and of Mainsendis had all but disappeared. A knightly class had emerged whose weapons and way of life the church was ready to bless; the crusades had legitimised warfare; marriage had been declared a sacrament; child oblation was out of fashion, the new orders notably refusing to accept any but adult vocations. The world, it now appeared, was not intrinsically evil; all baptised Christians could be saved: 'not only virgins and the continent but also married persons find favour with God by right faith and good actions and deserve to attain eternal blessedness'.[10] Human nature being what it was, men and women would still sin, but regular confession could restore anyone who

---

8  Odo of Cluny, *Vita Sancti Geraldi Auriliacensis Comitis*, PL 133, cols. 639–704. See in particular bk. 1, chs. 8 and 26; bk. 2, ch. 3; bk. 3, ch. 10.

9  *Herimanni liber de restauracione monasterii Sancti Martini Tornacensis*, ed. Georg Waitz, MGH SS 14, 274–317. Ralph and Mainsendis' story comes in chs. 61–3. The text is available now in translation by Lynn H. Nelson, *The Restoration of the Monastery of Saint Martin of Tournai* (Washington, D.C.: Catholic University of America Press, 1996).

10  Norman Tanner, ed., *Decrees of the Ecumenical Councils*, vol. 1, (*Nicaea 1–Lateran V*) (Washington, D.C.: Georgetown University Press, 1990), ch. 1, 231.

was truly penitent to a state of grace. The chasm between heaven and hell was bridged by purgatory – a place which the very brave might visit on pilgrimage (Lough Derg in Ireland provided a favoured entry point) but from which even those of lesser courage could in the hereafter be rescued by the prayers of the faithful and by masses offered on their behalf.

The Lateran Council of 1215, and the subsequent dissemination of its canons, set the seal on this new order in the Christian world. It turned out to be a world made up not, as had once been thought, of three groups, of clerks, monks and laymen, but only of two: the clerical and the lay. The distinction between the two was to be absolute; it was to be clear at a glance who was, and who was not, a clerk:

> Clerks should not practice callings or business of a secular nature, especially those that are dishonourable. They should not watch mimes, entertainers and actors. Let them avoid taverns altogether, unless by chance they are obliged by necessity on a journey. They should not play at games of chance or of dice, nor be present at such games. They should have a suitable crown and tonsure and let them diligently apply themselves to the divine services and other good pursuits. Their outer garments should be closed and neither too short nor too long. Let them not indulge in red or green cloths, long sleeves or shoes with embroidery or pointed toes, or in bridles, saddles, breast-plates and spurs that are gilded or have other superfluous ornamentation. Let them not wear cloaks with sleeves at divine services in a church, nor even elsewhere, if they are priests or parsons… They are not to wear buckles or belts ornamented with gold or silver, or even rings except for those whose dignity it befits to have them. All bishops should wear outer garments of linen in public and in church, unless they have been monks, in which case they may wear the monastic habit; and let them not wear their cloaks loose in public but rather fastened together behind the neck or across the chest (c. 16).

Clerks should 'abstain from gluttony and drunkenness' (c. 15); they were not 'to hunt or to fowl' (c. 15); they should not stay up late, feasting and indulging in 'forbidden conversation'; they must not neglect liturgical duties in order to listen to 'conversations of the laity' (c. 17); they are to have nothing to do with any sentence that involves the shedding of blood; nor should they be 'put in command of mercenaries or crossbowmen or suchlike men of blood'; they must not practise 'the art of surgery' nor should they take part in ordeals (c. 18); they are to keep their churches 'neat and clean' and never to 'deposit in [them] their own or even other's furniture, so that the churches look like lay houses rather than basilicas of God' (c. 19); but above all, first and foremost, they must be chaste: clerics are 'to live in a continent and chaste way'; God must be served with 'a pure heart and an unsullied body'; anyone caught 'giving way to the vice of incontinence' was to be punished 'according to canonical sanctions, in proportion to the seriousness of their sins...such sanctions [are] to be effectively and strictly observed, in order that those whom the fear of God does not hold back from evil may at least be restrained from sin by temporal punishment' (c. 14).

The decrees of Lateran IV in effect secured the monasticisation of the clergy. There were to be no new actual monastic orders, not only for the stated reason that 'too great a variety of religious orders leads to grave confusion in God's church' (c. 13), but also because such orders were no longer needed. Laymen and women were mandated to look after their own salvation, aided by their priest (c. 21) and, notably as the following decades would show, by the new figure of the friar, harbinger and deliverer of the pastoral revolution. As leaders of the laity, the behaviour of priests must be exemplary. A sinful clergy, insisted Innocent III, is the root of all evil – 'faith decays, religion grows deformed, liberty is thwarted. Justice is trampled underfoot, heretics emerge...'[11] Heresy had long been of particular concern to Innocent, and he had opened the Council with a solemn declaration of faith followed by a condemnation of particular heresies and of heresies in general: 'we condemn all heretics, whatever names they may go under' (c. 3). But heretics apart, anyone who could subscribe to the Council's creed could be saved, but they needed the support of a righteous clergy, 'For all corruption in the people comes first from the clergy'.[12]

Innocent's programme for the church was not only a response to the immediate circumstances of his pontificate; it also sought to provide solutions to the turmoil of the eleventh and twelfth centuries. The spiritual hunger manifested in the crowds who had gathered at the turn of the millennium around the shrines of saints and at the feet of itinerant preachers had to some extent been assuaged by Gregory VII's reforms, but only at a price. Gregory, with good reason, was known as a 'holy Satan' and 'a dangerous man'.[13] In his conflicts with the emperor he had not hesitated to mobilise the crowd. The distinctions between clergy and laity which Lateran IV was to take such pains to safeguard had been in danger of being overthrown by Gregory's demagogic

11 Innocent III in his sermon on the occasion of the convening of Lateran IV, *Sermones de diversis*, col. 673.
12 *Sermones de diversis*, col. 673.
13 Peter Damian calls Gregory his 'holy Satan', Peter Damian, *Die Briefe des Petrus Damiani*, ed. Kurt Reindel, MGH, EPP, no. 107, 3.185; the epithet 'periculosus homo' comes from Archbishop Liemar of Bremen, *Die Hannoversche Briefsammlung*, ed. C. Erdmann, in *Briefsammlungen der Zeit Heinrichs IV* (MGH, EPP, Briefe der deutschen Kaiserzeit V; Weimar: Böhlau, 1950), no. 15, 3–5.

instincts. His support of the Patarenes of Milan, those radical opponents of clerical marriage, who believed not only in the boycotting of the masses of incontinent clergy, but also in taking direct action against them, is but one instance of his readiness to ally with the laity against any priest or bishop who did not seem to him to be sufficiently committed to reform. To the chronicler Sigebert of Gembloux (c.1030–1112) it was precisely these tactics which were so shocking; fighting simony and clerical marriage was one thing – what indeed could be 'more lovely', asked Sigebert – but Gregory's methods undermined all his objectives: 'if you look for the fruit, you see the Lord's flock miserably scattered and their shepherds inciting the wolves against them'. The doctrine of the reformers that the sacraments of married priests had no validity was 'lethal poison'; 'who does not grieve', concluded Sigebert, 'at so great an upheaval in the Church. Which Christian does not, if he has any compassion, feel full of sorrow on seeing Christianity trampled underfoot…and all this backed by authority, by those who are called the leaders of Christendom.'[14]

It fell to the popes of the twelfth century and above all to Innocent III to attempt to set the seal on the new order in the world, and as far as possible to resolve the rifts opened up by previous conflicts. The problem of lay investiture, which had seemed such a stumbling block in the eleventh century, proved after all amenable to compromise – England, France and finally the Empire each found solutions; simony, while it might still be a matter for concern, no longer caused 'moral panic';[15] it was quite simply accepted as wrong. In theory, at least, elections to ecclesiastical office could now proceed freely without undue influence from lay patrons and without money passing hands. Canon lawyers meanwhile satisfactorily established that the validity of masses was in no wise dependent on the moral health of the celebrant. The one issue that remained much less tractable was that of clerical celibacy, demanding time and again the reiteration and tightening up of papal condemnations accompanied by continuing appeals to the laity not to attend the masses of any priest known to have a wife or a concubine. Callixtus II, at the Council of Rheims of 1119, repeated Urban II's 1095 threats of deposition to any priest, deacon or subdeacon found living with his wife or with a concubine; the First and Second Lateran Councils respectively went further, announcing

---

14 Sigebert of Gembloux, *Apologia contra eos qui calumniantur missas coniugatorum sacerdotum*, ed. E. Sackur (MGH, Libelli de Lite Imperatorum et Pontificum 2; Hanover: Hahn, 1892), 438.

15 'Moral panic': see Timothy Reuter's 'Gifts and Simony', in Esther Cohn and Mayke B. de Jong, eds., *Medieval Transformations: Texts, Power and Gifts in Context* (Leiden: Brill, 2001), 160.

in 1123 that the marriages of priests, deacons, subdeacons and monks be held as void and in 1139 demanding the separation from their partners of married clergy – that is, of 'bishops, priests, deacons, subdeacons, canons regular, monks and professed lay brothers' on the grounds that such marriages ('such outrageous behaviour') were against ecclesiastical law and therefore illegal. At the Third Lateran Council of 1179 married clergy are no longer mentioned, suggesting the efficacy of the 1139 decree, but concubinage evidently remained a problem: 'clerics in holy orders who in open concubinage keep their mistresses in their houses should either cast them out and live continently or be deprived of ecclesiastical office and benefice'.[16]

In this new world order it was essential that the men with the power to bind and to loose, and who alone could turn the bread and wine of the eucharist into the body and blood of Christ should be demonstrably separate from the laity, even though chastity, the touchstone of this difference, would always be difficult to enforce, as Innocent III himself recognised, as Caesarius of Heisterbach's stories make plain, and as many a noisy demonstration of married priests proved. Henry of Huntingdon's gleeful telling of the tale of Cardinal John Crema – 'discovered after vespers with a whore' when on that same day he had held a council at which 'he dealt most severely with the matter of priest's wives, saying it was the greatest sin to rise from the side of a whore and go to make the body of Christ' – would have been greeted by sympathetic audiences across Europe.[17] Even as late as 1215 theologians could be found who were uneasy about the wisdom and stringency of the new policy. Thomas of Chobham, for instance, in his *Summa confessorum* composed at about that time, was prepared to argue that it was a lesser sin for a cleric to marry secretly than it was for him to have extra-marital sex and to express in more general terms doubts about the legitimacy of enforcing clerical celibacy. But nonetheless Thomas accepted that Rome had spoken and that to all intents and purposes the matter by now was closed.

To understand the determination behind Rome's stance it may be helpful to consider the insights of social anthropology. The work of Robert Just on late twentieth-century Greece is pertinent here. According to Just the village priest in Greece will be a married man, usually coming from the village where he was born. The system has perceptible weaknesses:

---

16 For the relevant decrees of the Lateran I, II and III, see Tanner, ed., *Decrees* 191, c. 7; 194, c. 21; 198, c. 6; and 217, c. 11.

17 Henry of Huntingdon, *Historia Anglorum: The History of the English People*, ed. and trans. Diana Greenaway (Oxford Medieval Texts; Oxford: Clarendon Press, 1996), bk. 7, 473–5.

on the one hand, the Church as a whole is seen as remote, aligned with the rich and the powerful, part of that envied and inaccessible world whose very success is evidence enough of its corruption, while on the other hand, at the local level, the human failings of the priesthood (real or imagined) are only too intimately known and discussed.

It is a situation in which the village priest loses all ways. He is a servant of the Church which is fabulously wealthy, politically conservative, remote from 'the people'; at the same time he is just another villager, somebody's brother, somebody's husband, somebody's father, somebody's son...who would trust a man who, like everyone else, must seek his advantage where he may? Who would confess his secrets or his problems to a man who also has a daughter to wed and a field he must water? And yet they must call him 'Papas' and have him baptise their children, celebrate their marriages and bury their dead.[18]

Only minor adjustments are needed to make such scenes a fit description of early eleventh-century Europe. The way out chosen by the West brought in its wake hardship, both for clergy and for their discarded women, as well as the occasion for many a ribald joke at the expense of those who failed to live up to the new demands of the celibate life (the thirteenth-century ditty 'Priests who lack a girl to cherish/Won't be mindful lest they perish/ They will take whom'er they find/Married, single – never mind' is but one example[19]). Nonetheless, the imposition of clerical celibacy cannot be seen simply as an indication of misguided puritanism on the part of the reformed papacy, nor as a sign of 'zealous sacerdotalism or unreasoning bigotry'; nor its influence 'one of almost unmixed evil' as the Victorian historian Henry Lea would have it in his monumental work *The History of Sacerdotal Celibacy*.[20] Undoubtedly the system claimed its victims, the most famous of all being Heloise and Abelard, caught as they were by the new ruling of 1123 forbidding the marriage of all clerks in higher orders and which forms the backdrop to Heloise's arguments as Abelard reports them:

What honour could she win, she protested, from a marriage that would dishonour me and humiliate us both?... Think of the curses, the loss to the

18 Robert Just, 'Anti-clericalism and National Identity: Attitudes towards the Orthodox Church in Greece', in Wendy James and Douglas H. Johnson, eds., *Essays in the Social Anthropology of Religion Presented to Godfrey Lienhardt* (Oxford: Jaso, 1988), 27–8.

19 From 'De concubinis sacerdotum', in T. Wright, ed., *The Latin Poems Commonly Attributed to Walter Mapes* (London: Camden Society, 1841) quoted by James Brundage in 'Sin, Crimes and the Pleasures of the Flesh', in Peter Linehan and Janet L. Nelson, eds., *The Medieval World* (London: Routledge, 2001), 298.

20 Henry C. Lea, *History of Sacerdotal Celibacy in the Christian Church* (3rd edn; London: Williams and Norgate, 1907), 410, 430.

Church and grief of philosophers which would greet such a marriage! Nature had created me for all mankind – it would be a sorry scandal if I should bind myself to a single woman and submit to such base servitude...in every people, pagan, Jew or Christian, some men have always stood out for their faith or upright way of life, and have cut themselves off from their fellows because of their singular chastity or austerity...if pagans and laymen could live in this way...is there not a greater obligation on you, as clerk and canon, not to put base pleasures before your sacred duties, and to guard against being sucked down headlong into this Charybdis, there to lose all sense of shame and be plunged forever into a whirlpool of impurity?[21]

However much we may lament the outcome of Abelard and Heloise's affair, it is not for us to question the arguments by which Heloise tried to dissuade Abelard from marriage but to listen to their force and to try to understand their history.

---

21 Peter Abélard, *Historia Calamitatum*, ed. J. Monfrin (Paris: Librairie Vrin, 1959), 75–8. For the translation see Betty Radice, *The Letters of Abelard and Heloise*, rev. edn, M. T. Clanchy (London: Penguin, 2003), 13–16.

# 2

# The bishops of Rome, 1100–1300

ANTHONY PERRON

The history of the bishops of Rome in the twelfth and thirteenth centuries is inseparable from their often bitter conflicts with lay rulers. The era, after all, commenced with the last phase of the Investiture Controversy and witnessed continuing quarrels with the Hohenstaufen emperors and other princes in England, Hungary, Norway, Denmark, France and Iberia, involving not only church–crown disputes, but problematic royal marriages as well. Yet, while the rhetoric of Roman supremacy over the secular state was often shrill (and never more so than in the fight with Frederick II), popes of this period were forced to accept the growing power of monarchs, whose ideological standing was considerably improved both by the study of Roman law in the twelfth century and the translation of Aristotle's *Politics* in the thirteenth. Despite Gregory VII's claim that kings were not latter-day Melchizedeks but merely 'men of this world ignorant of God', until Boniface VIII (c. 1294–1303) and Giles of Rome (c. 1243–1316) such strident claims were usually exchanged for compromise, a spirit already evident in the Concordat of Worms in 1122. In attempting to establish universal papal power over the *regnum*, the 'Gregorian' programme of the 1070s and 1080s by no means became a reality in the succeeding two centuries.

Turning to Rome's relationship with the wider *sacerdotium*, on the other hand, Gregory's legacy is somewhat clearer, for while the papacy was troubled by a pair of schisms in the twelfth century and two lengthy vacancies in the thirteenth, the era can justifiably be seen as the implementation of Gregory VII's vision of Petrine supremacy within the Western church. The particular ideas that lay behind his convictions were themselves old, many formulated already by the great popes of the fifth century (Innocent I, Leo the Great and Gelasius I), for example that Peter's special relationship with Jesus warranted a papal *plenitudo potestatis* over the wider church. But the larger programme of ecclesiastical power into which they were fitted was new and constituted a thorough revision of the early medieval church. In the imperial church organised by the Carolingians in the eighth century, under heavy Anglo-Saxon influence, Rome was the home of the apostles and the source of 'correct' law, liturgy and rule, but effective ecclesiastical jurisdiction was in the hands of bishops and their mighty archiepiscopal supervisors. The popes of the twelfth century and their supporters transformed Gregory's passionate identification with Peter, who sanctified all occupants of his *cathedra*, into Innocent III's vicariate of Christ, which raised the apostolic pontiffs above man, if not to God.

To assert such grand claims is a simple matter. To make good on them requires institutions, and the high-medieval papacy was especially successful in uniting ideology and practice. This chapter discusses the principal components of papal overlordship in the High Middle Ages and the criticisms levelled against overweening Roman might, and briefly considers the apostolic see's relationship with peoples on the expanding Latin-Christian periphery and beyond between 1100 and 1300.

## Councils

The twelfth century witnessed the first large 'general' synods since the seminal councils of the fourth to the ninth centuries. Most notable are the four Lateran councils (1123, 1139, 1179 and 1215) and the two Lyon councils (1245 and 1274), the largest of them attended by over a thousand prelates from throughout the Latin Church and beyond, though representation from each country was by no means proportional, and observers from the Byzantine sphere were rare.[1] Important as the example of the great congresses of the late Roman era was, the medieval councils grew immediately out of the Lenten synods held by popes of the eleventh century, especially Gregory VII, to which bishops from outside Italy might be called.[2] Moreover, while the earlier ecumenical councils showcased the power of the emperor in collaboration with the patriarchal bishops of the East, the dominant power in the twelfth- and thirteenth-century councils was unquestionably the pope. The decrees of Innocent III's Fourth Lateran Council, for example, were regularly referred to simply as the 'constitutiones Innocentii' or the 'constitutiones domini pape'.

---

1 Achille Luchaire discovered and printed a list of attendees to Fourth Lateran in his article 'Un document retrouvé', *Journal des savants* n.s. 3 (1905), 557–68. See also Georgine Tangl, *Die Teilnehmer an den allgemeinen Konzilien des Mittelalters* (Cologne: Böhlau, 1969).

2 I. S. Robinson, *The Papacy 1073–1198: Continuity and Innovation* (Cambridge: Cambridge University Press, 1990), 122–3.

Such gatherings served a number of purposes. Foremost, they were often a show of unity after a time of division. The First Lateran Council took place at the close of the Investiture Controversy. The Second Lateran Council put to rest the Anacletan schism, and the Third came at the end of the schism of Octavian (Victor IV). The First Council of Lyon aimed to consolidate resistance to Frederick II, who was deposed at the meeting. Finally, the Second Council of Lyon followed a long (nearly three-year) and bitter vacancy in the papal office. The papacy also used councils to thunder against those perceived by clerical elites to be enemies of the church, such as Cathars (at the Third Lateran), Greeks (at the Fourth Lateran) and Saracens (Fourth Lateran and Second Lyon both called for crusades). At the same time, the councils of the twelfth and thirteenth centuries laid out clear directions for ecclesiastical reform; they prohibited clerics from engaging in sex (all four Lateran councils) or the shedding of blood (Second and Third Lateran), restricted pluralism (Third Lateran and Second Lyon), insisted upon an educated and 'suitable' clergy (Third and Fourth Lateran especially), mandated poverty and enclosure for monks (Third Lateran) and outlawed new regular orders (Fourth Lateran and Second Lyon). Matters directly affecting the laity were less evident, but by no means absent. Second Lateran, for example, forbade tournaments; Fourth Lateran prescribed annual confession and communion and issued new regulations governing the prohibited degrees of marriage (down from seven to four); Second Lyon even addressed rowdy behaviour in church. Many historians have questioned the degree to which these provisions were implemented,[3] but merely by expressing such standards, synodal decrees helped mould notions of virtue for both priest and parishoner alike. Nor did conciliar legislation ignore key matters of procedure and church administration, such as prelatial elections (Third Lateran), papal appeals and delegated jurisdiction, the latter two covered by First Lyon, the most legalistic of all the high-medieval councils, governed by perhaps the great jurist pope, Innocent IV.

The Lateran and Lyon councils naturally attract the most attention. These six are today among the ecumenical councils recognized by the Catholic Church. Yet, they were only part of a larger wave of papally directed synodal activity, particularly evident in France. The Council of Clermont (1095) famously inaugurated the crusades, while Rheims was the site of three

---

3 For example, Marion Gibbs and Jane Lang, *Bishops and Reform 1215–1272, with Special Reference to the Lateran Council of 1215* (Oxford: Oxford University Press, 1934), 131–79, and more recently Paul B. Pixton, *The German Episcopacy and the Implementation of the Decrees of the Fourth Lateran Council, 1216–1245: Watchmen on the Tower* (Leiden and New York: Brill, 1995).

councils in the twelfth century. The second of these was held by Innocent II, who also presided over meetings at Clermont, Piacenza and Pisa before the Second Lateran Council. Alexander III called a council at Tours fifteen years before Third Lateran, and between Fourth Lateran and First Lyon, Honorius III convoked the Council of Bourges. These councils dealt with many of the same issues as their more famous counterparts at the Lateran and in Lyon.

## Appeals

Rich in liturgical solemnity, councils offered a fitting ceremonial occasion to showcase the pope's growing legislative role, as well as his judicial power, since disputes were aired on these occasions (the question of primacy in Spain, for instance, between Toledo and Compostela at Fourth Lateran, or the complaints raised at First Lyon over the flood of Italian providees in England and other perceived abuses inflicted on the English church by Rome[4]). They were, however, a cumbersome tool for exercising regular jurisdiction, occurring, as they did, only once every decade or two. A more effective means by which the popes of this period functioned as the judges and, by creating precedents, the lawgivers of the Latin West, was by opening the doors of apostolic justice to cases from every corner of Europe. This practice had deep roots. The notion that *causae maiores* belonged to the Roman see can be traced back to Innocent I, and among the Carolingian popes, Nicholas I stands out as a busy *iudex*, for example in the case between Archbishop Hincmar of Rheims and Bishop Rothad of Soissons or the dispute between the churches of Hamburg and Cologne over control of the diocese of Bremen.[5] These causes were undeniably 'major', involving not only bishops, but metropolitan power as well. But what distinguished the popes of the twelfth and thirteenth centuries from earlier pontiffs like Nicholas was both the vast increase in the volume of judicial activity at the curia and the extent to which it involved litigants whose ranks and cases were far more humble. Most of these came to the curia on appeal from lower ecclesiastical courts, though some plaintiffs preferred to skip the intermediate jurisdictions available to

---

4 For the Spanish question, see the Giessen Anonymous description, Stephan Kuttner and Antonio García y García, 'A New Eyewitness Account of the Fourth Lateran Council', *Traditio* 20 (1964), 124. The complaints of the English in Lyon are related by Matthew Paris, *Chronica majora*, ed. Henry Richards Luard, Rolls Series 57:4 (London: Longman and Co., 1877), 440–5.
5 On Nicholas I's adjudication of the case between Hincmar and Rothad, see *Le liber pontificalis*, ed. L. Duchesne, vol. 2 (Paris: E. de Boccard, 1955), 162–5. For his decision in the matter of Bremen, see Rimbert, *Vita sancti Anskarii*, PL 118, cols. 959–1012.

them and head directly to the papal curia. As jurists asserted, while Roman law demanded that a suit first be heard by the proper lower court before being brought before the prince, canon law had no such restriction; anyone might seek the pope at any time.[6]

The number of litigants submitting cases to papal jurisdiction increased rapidly in the second half of the twelfth century, when the era of the 'lawyer popes' begins, particularly during the pontificate of Alexander III. Indeed, so overwhelming had the judicial side of papal business become that some popes sought to restrict the number of cases inundating Rome, as when Alexander tried to eliminate fraudulent or frivolous appeals and when Gregory VIII, complaining he was 'unable to endure the shouts and murmurs of those crowding together from all directions' at the curia, attempted to restrain 'trivial business', that is, cases involving fewer than twenty marks.[7] Gregory's solution was to hand supervision of lesser disputes over to metropolitan bishops. In other matters, however, the papacy assumed exclusive control of certain 'reserved cases' at the expense of archbishops and regional instances, cases that only added to the overwhelming mass of suits at the Lateran. Cases such as grave violence against clerics, as well as episcopal resignations, translations and depositions were thus arrogated to the papacy.[8] Disputed episcopal elections were added to this list by Alexander IV in 1257.[9]

The growth in papal justice, historians often point out, was largely a passive phenomenon.[10] The curia did not so much demand recognition of its claims as litigants chose to seek curial attention. This was particularly true when it came to the use of papal provisions. Responding to the entreaties of petitioners, popes of the twelfth century sometimes requested that local churches install needy clerics in vacant posts. In the thirteenth century, this swelled into an

---

6 See Ricardus Anglicus' gloss to the *Compilatio prima* decretal 'Vel ex malitia' (lib. 2, tit. 20, c. 47) (Vatican City, Biblioteca apostolica vaticana, Pal. lat. 696, fol. 44v): 'secundum leges pretermisso medio non appellatur ad principem, secus secundum canones, nam ab omnibus appellatur ad papam, de aliis secus nisi gradatim procedatur'. Laurentius Hispanus explained further in his gloss to *Comp. I* text 'Cum non ignoretis' (lib. 1, tit. 22, c. un.) (Vatican City, Biblioteca apostolica vaticana, Vat. lat. 1377, fol. 14v) that 'oppressi ad romanam ecclesiam omissis omnibus aliis mediis appellent'.

7 C. 6 of Third Lateran. See Giuseppe Alberigo, ed., *Conciliorum oecumenicorum decreta*, 3rd edn (Bologna: Istituto per le scienze religiose, 1973), 214; and Emil Friedberg, ed., *Quinque compilationes antiquae* (Graz: Akademische Druck- und Verlagsanstalt, 1956 [repr. of Leipzig, 1882]), 24–5 (*Comp. I*, lib. 2, tit. 20, c. 47).

8 See Kenneth Pennington, *Pope and Bishops: The Papal Monarchy in the Twelfth and Thirteenth Centuries* (Philadelphia: University of Pennsylvania Press, 1984), 75–114.

9 C. Bourel de la Roncière et al., eds., *Les registres d'Alexandre IV* (Paris: A. Fontemoing, 1917), vol. 2, 684–6 ('Dilecti filii').

10 For example, R. W. Southern, *Western Church and Society in the Middle Ages* (Harmondsworth: Penguin, 1970), 109.

extensive papal right to bestow benefices throughout the Western church. While the abuses of the provision system (its aggravation of the problem of pluralism, for instance) were serious, the incomes of available prebends proved to be a useful means of supporting the growing cadre of clerics needed to staff the papal administration.

## Canonization of saints

Another procedure that added further to the business of the curia and to the prestige and authority of the papacy involved the canonization of saints. Like provisions, the rise of this institution was passive before it was codified as an exclusive power of the apostolic see. Ulrich of Augsburg is often credited as the first saint canonized by the papacy. In 993 Pope John XV declared that his memory should be revered and 'consecrated to divine worship'.[11] Ulrich's canonization and other early examples of papal saint-making, such as St Knud of Denmark (1096), did not, however, immediately create a binding precedent. Throughout the twelfth century, local saints continued to be recognized in the old liturgical fashion, by the re-interment of the holy man or woman in the sacred space of the church under the supervision of the bishop, accompanied by the composition of hymns and readings for the new saint's feast. Nevertheless, the popularity of papal approbation grew during this time. While the actual number of canonized saints was never very high in the twelfth and thirteenth centuries (on average about one every two or three years starting with Alexander III),[12] control of sanctity became an important symbolic monopoly in the pope's jurisdictional arsenal. When exactly a consensus began concerning the papal right to canonize is a matter of debate among legal historians. Alexander III's decretal 'Audivimus' (1171 or 1172) later became the authoritative basis for the claim that 'without the permission of the pope, it is not permitted to venerate anyone as a saint', as Gregory IX declared in the *Liber extra* of 1234.[13] Yet Alexander's letter seems originally to have implied only that a 'saint' of questionable moral standing should not be revered 'without the authority of the Roman church'. Since 'Audivimus' was included in the *Compilatio secunda* (1210–15), most historians would agree that

---

11 John XV, *Epistolae et privilegia*, PL 137, col. 846.
12 According to André Vauchez, *Sainthood in the Later Middle Ages*, trans. Jean Birrell (Cambridge: Cambridge University Press, 1997), 25 (canonizations under Alexander III, Clement III and Celestine III) and 61 (for canonizations in the period 1198–1431).
13 Emil Friedberg, ed., *Corpus iuris canonici*, vol. 2 (Leipzig: Bernhard Tauchnitz, 1881), lib. 3, tit. 45, c. 1.

by the time of Innocent III, canonization was seen as a prerogative of the pope alone.[14]

In the twelfth century, a variety of tribunals heard evidence of a prospective saint's qualifications, and the final decision might even be handed back to local officials. Under Innocent, a regular procedure for dealing with canonization petitions developed. After an initial request from a local church, often lodged cooperatively by both lay and ecclesiastical leaders, an inquest was authorized by the curia, provided the candidate's case looked promising. Headed by three commissioners, typically including a bishop and a prelate from a regular cloister, frequently in company with the metropolitan, the panel looked into the saint's life (seeking evidence of virtue and, obviously, orthodoxy) and miracles. In proving the latter, it was often necessary to go into graphic detail about the nature of the illnesses and wounds healed by the holy person's intervention, a trait that not infrequently made the resulting dossiers grotes-que reading. When the investigation was complete, an account of the *vita et miracula* was dispatched to Rome, where the final decision would rest with the pope and the cardinals in consistory.

As the process became more systematic, it also became more rigorous. While few petitions were rejected in the twelfth century, of the nearly four dozen processes authorized by Rome from Innocent III to Clement IV, only twenty-three won approval in the end, and six of those were first returned to the local church in need of further evidence.[15] Not surprisingly, political concerns played a large role in determining which requests would succeed and which would fail. While sanctity remained a spontaneous communal phenomenon to the extent that papal canonization was only an official recognition of an already existing cult, those cults that were submitted to Rome and that the apostolic see chose to acknowledge tended to come disproportionately from the ranks of the regular religious and their social networks. The rising prominence of saints from Italian cities, for instance, owed much to the papacy's sponsorship of the mendicant orders that inspired these urban holy men and women.[16]

---

14 At one extreme, Eric Kemp has argued that Alexander III was already 'quite certain of his right to control the veneration of any new saints' in 1171. See his *Canonization and Authority in the Western Church* (London: Oxford University Press, 1948), 98–9. On the contrary, Stephan Kuttner, 'La réserve papale du droit de canonisation', *Revue historique de droit français et étranger* 4.17 (1938), 172–228, asserts that, even after the *Compilatio secunda*, canonists ignored the juridical possibilities of 'Audivimus'.

15 Vauchez, *Sainthood*, 52–3, 61.

16 Donald Weinstein and Rudolph M. Bell, *Saints and Society: Two Worlds of Western Christendom, 1000–1700* (Chicago and London: University of Chicago Press, 1982), 168.

## The rise of universities and the elaboration of the papal bureaucracy

The emergence of papal power as an international force in the twelfth and thirteenth centuries could not have happened without the parallel development of two characteristic high-medieval institutions: the university and the administrative apparatus of the papal curia. Higher learning in the eleventh century was the preserve of cathedral and monastic schools, loosely organized and guided by prominent individual teachers. The articulation of more systematic institutions of higher learning came about gradually through the formation of universities in Bologna and Paris in the twelfth and early thirteenth centuries. Although they owed their existence to royal, not papal, power (Bologna was chartered by Frederick Barbarossa in 1158, Paris by Philip Augustus in 1200), universities, and especially their faculties of law and theology, provided the intellectual ballast for papal supremacy. It was primarily in this learned milieu that notions such as the papal plenitude of power and the vicariate of Christ were formulated and disseminated. Furthermore, popes exercised a controlling hand on these powerful intellectual factories once they were up and running. In 1210, Innocent III sent the *Compilatio tertia*, the first papally authorized book of canon law, to the 'masters and students' of Bologna, with instructions that they were to 'use these [decretal letters] without any scruple of doubt...both in judgments and in teaching *(tam in iudiciis quam in scholis)*'.[17] Some twenty years later, another pope of the Conti family, Gregory IX, recognized the corporate independence of the Paris university, reaffirming the rights of the masters after an ugly dispute with the city's royal officials. University teachers, in turn, influenced generations of students from every corner of Europe, who then carried home ideas of apostolic sovereignty.

As we will see shortly, the universities were by no means monolithic in their support of papal power, but numerous cardinals sprang from the ranks of the masters and scholars, as did many who oversaw appeals to the curia from its outlying regions *partes*.[18] Scholastic education provided not only ideological indoctrination, but also the practical training demanded of both petitioners

---

17 Friedberg, ed., *Quinque compilationes*, 105.
18 John Baldwin's catalogue of masters at Paris between Third and Fourth Lateran lists a total of forty-six masters, of whom four became cardinals and over two dozen prominent cathedral dignitaries. See his 'Masters at Paris from 1179 to 1215: A Social Perspective', in Robert L. Benson, Giles Constable and Carol D. Lanham, eds., *Renaissance and Renewal in the Twelfth Century*, (Cambridge, Mass.: Harvard University Press, 1982), 138–72.

and judges at the papal court. Indeed, the rise of the universities corresponded to a rapid growth in the apparatus of government needed to cope with the increasing volume of business brought before the apostolic see. In the earlier Middle Ages, the papal household had been primarily organized for liturgical duties, though there were officials to handle archival and financial affairs. Substantial changes began in the eleventh century. The cardinals emerged not only as the electors of the pope (starting with Nicholas II's election decree of 1059), but also as his chief advisors and executive aides. The chapel, with its ceremonial responsibilities, remained a key part of the papal household, but its importance was eclipsed by an ever expanding bureaucracy of public administration. The production of documents was handled by the chancery, overseen by the chancellor or, from around 1220, vice-chancellor, and carried out by an army of notaries and scribes. The management of fiscal affairs, including revenues from the Papal States and from traditional payments such as Peter's Pence, not to mention clerical taxes like the crusade twentieth, was overseen by the chamberlain. The most notable *camerarius* was Cencius Savelli, the future Honorius III, who compiled the famous *Liber censuum* (1192), which catalogued the papacy's incomes from throughout Europe.

While the chancery and the chamber each had their own courts (the *audientia litterarum contradictarum* for the former, the *audientia camere* for the latter), the 'supreme court' was the consistory, also known as the *audientia sacri palatii*, presided over by the pope himself. Since the pope could not personally hear all cases, cardinals and other prominent curial dignitaries were assigned as *auditores*, eventually formalized as the *rota*. The decisions of the pope and his justices, copied into the magnificent papal registers along with selected chancery documents, for which the recipients often paid a fee,[19] formed a body of precedents mined by canonists as the living *ius commune* of the Western church. The explosion of chancery letters also provided a lively market for forgers, concerning whom Innocent III was especially anxious.[20] The final significant office, established in the thirteenth century, was the

---

19  With the exception of the registers of John VIII and Gregory VII (only the latter extant in an original manuscript), the series of papal registers begins with the correspondence of Innocent III. See Leonard Boyle, *A Survey of the Vatican Archives and of its Medieval Holdings* (Toronto: Pontifical Institute of Mediaeval Studies, 1972), 103–13. Now-lost registers were in use as early as the fifth century, and certainly during the twelfth century, as discussed by Uta-Renate Blumenthal, 'Papal Registers in the Twelfth Century', in *Papal Reform and Canon Law in the Eleventh and Twelfth Centuries* (Aldershot: Ashgate Variorum, 1998), no. 15.

20  See, for example, Reginald L. Poole, *Lectures on the History of the Papal Chancery Down to the Time of Innocent III* (Cambridge: Cambridge University Press, 1915), 149–51.

penitentiary, empowered to issue routine dispensations such as those for marriage within the prohibited degrees or obstacles to clerical ordination. Navigating this maze was not for the uninitiated, and it involved a corps of professional proctors, some employed full-time by kings and wealthy ecclesiastical individuals and corporations, others hiring out their services to bewildered petitioners, for a fee of course.

The transformation of the papal court into a bustling and cosmopolitan hub was particularly remarkable given that the curia was often itinerant during the twelfth and thirteenth centuries. This nomadism was a seasonal phenomenon in part (popes preferred to spend the summer outside the sweltering *Urbs*), though it also arose from the demands of ruling as the princes of the Papal States, upon whom it was incumbent to supervise the districts of their realm. Flight could sometimes be a necessity when the aristocracy and people of Rome were hostile to their bishop. So while some popes did primarily reside at the Lateran, many spent lengthy periods elsewhere in Italy or abroad. The long sojourns in Lyon during the thirteenth century are especially notable. Although papal peregrinations might have been irksome to appellants and tiring for those in the caravan, it did serve as a visible reminder of apostolic power, and the sites visited by the touring popes fixed a local memory of papal authority for generations.[21]

If central bureaucratic machinery was critical to the successful implementation of Roman jurisdictional claims in the High Middle Ages, no less important was the activity *in provinciis* of papal representatives. These included legates, who might be resident prelates empowered to act on the pope's behalf (later called *legati nati*), usually archbishops (Canterbury and Rheims, for instance), or the more powerful legates *a latere*, typically cardinals sent on specific missions, such as the promotion of crusading, the settlement of political conflicts (typically quarrels between crown and mitre), or the imposition of reform agendas, but simultaneously given wider compass to exercise the papal *vices* while in the legatine field by granting dispensations and indulgences. Though standing legates were not common, *legati a latere* could be plentiful. As many as a dozen such emissaries criss-crossed Germany in just a few years during the 1140s and 1150s.[22] Also increasingly common throughout Latin Christendom was the papal tax collector. Needless to say, such

---

21 Brenda Bolton, 'The Caravan Rests: Innocent III's Use of Itineration', in Anne J. Duggan, Joan Greatrex and Brenda Bolton, eds., *Omnia disce: Medieval Studies in Memory of Leonard Boyle, O.P.* (Aldershot: Ashgate, 2005), 41–61.

22 Johannes Bachmann, *Die päpstlichen Legaten in Deutschland und Skandinavien (1125–1159)* (Historische Studien, 115; Berlin: Emil Ebering, 1913), 67–100.

officials were not received with enthusiasm. In the Swedish diocese of Skara, deputies of the papal chaplain Bertrandus Amalrici were assaulted by local priests excommunicated for their failure to pay up.[23]

The linchpin of local papal jurisdiction, however, was the judge-delegate. These were generally native dignitaries whom the pope commissioned to hear cases appealed to Rome. As a rule, then, they were not the ordinary judges (bishops and their archdeacons or other subordinates), but individuals selected by the papal court or, more commonly, the plaintiffs, to conduct the trial back in the country of origin. Their collective activity surely outweighed that of the apostolic curia itself. The English prior Richard of Dunstable alone heard nearly four dozen cases as a papal judge-delegate during his more than thirty years in office.[24] Since the party appealing to Rome was normally allowed to select its own judge-delegate, subject to challenge by the opposing party, the institution was, in theory, a check against an unfair ordinary.[25] However, given that the opposing party also had to send a representative to Rome or hire a proctor in order to ensure fair deliberations, delegated papal jurisdiction worked in favour of well-heeled individuals and corporations that could afford the expense of such a trip if it meant getting a sympathetic judge. The overwhelming importance of the *iudex delegatus* and the complexity of his job is suggested by the number of canon-law texts governing his work. The title 'de officio iudicis delegati' in Gregory IX's *Liber extra* (lib. 1, tit. 29) contains forty-three chapters, compared with just twenty for the office of the judge ordinary (lib. 1, tit. 31).

## The papacy and holy war

There were of course other areas in which the power of the papacy was made manifest between 1100 and 1300. One that must not be overlooked was crusading. Though Christian Holy War had roots in the era before the rise of the Gregorian papacy (in the Christian imperial ideology of Charlemagne and his forced conversion of the Saxons, for example, as well as in the Peace of God and Truce of God movements of the tenth and early eleventh centuries),

---

23 See P. A. Munch, ed., *Pavelige nuntiers regnskabs- og dagböger förte under tiende-opkrævningen i Norden 1282–1334* (Oslo: Brögger og Christies Bogtrykkeri, 1864), 149 (no. 17).

24 Jane E. Sayers, *Papal Judges-Delegate in the Province of Canterbury, 1198–1254: A Study in Ecclesiastical Jurisdiction and Administration* (Oxford: Oxford University Press, 1971), 296–301.

25 See R. H. Helmholz, *Canon Law and the Law of England* (London: Hambledon Press, 1987), ch. 2 ('Canonists and Standards of Impartiality for Papal Judges Delegate'), 21–39.

Gregory himself took sacred violence to a new level by vowing personally to lead an army to liberate Christians in the East and reunite the Roman and Eastern churches.[26] Even before that, in 1063, Alexander II had offered remission from sins to those participating in the reconquest of Spain.[27] In the last years of the eleventh century a papally summoned crusade was finally launched, the improbably successful First Crusade. In the next two centuries, proclamation by a pope was a virtual *sine qua non* for Holy War, whether directed against Muslims, Cathars, pagans or the political enemies of Rome. Only the apostolic see could bestow the expansive and much coveted crusade indulgence. Over the course of the twelfth century, this doctrine came to be understood as complete remittance of all penalties owing to sin, on earth and in purgatory. Crusading, in the words of Innocent III, afforded 'full forgiveness of sins'.[28] Once a crusade was launched, however, the pope had very little control over its conduct. Innocent thundered against the misguided holy warriors of the Fourth Crusade who pillaged Christian Constantinople and offered thereby 'only an example of wickedness and works of darkness',[29] even as the crusaders were reassured by their advisors that the war was 'droite et juste'.[30]

## Critique

While the papacy's rise to prominence had deep roots in the late Roman and early medieval church, it was nevertheless a radical change. But it was not greeted with unanimous enthusiasm. Criticism of the monarchical papacy included a barrage of satire. Already around the year 1100, the *Tractatus Garsiae* 'documented' the translation of the 'relics of Sts Silver and Gold' to the shrine of 'St Cupidity' in Rome. 'Those who have their relics', says one cardinal, 'are immediately justified; once earthly, they become heavenly; once impious, they are turned into innocents'.[31] The theme of a corrupt and greedy curia was reprised by the *Gospel of St Mark of Silver*, in which a poor man

---

26 See, for example, Gregory VII, *Das Register Gregors VII*, ed. Erich Caspar, MGH, EPP, Epistolae Selectae, vol. 2, fasc. 1–2, 2.31.

27 S. Loewenfeld, ed., *Epistolae pontificum romanorum ineditae* (Leipzig: Verlag Veit and Co., 1885; repr., Graz: Akademische Druck- und Verlagsanstalt, 1959), 43. Some scholars have argued that Alexander's letter referred not to warriors, but to pilgrims. Against this, see Jean Flori, 'Réforme, *reconquista*, croisade: L'idée de reconquête dans la correspondance pontificale d'Alexandre II à Urbain II', *Cahiers de civilisation médiévale* 40 (1997), 320–1.

28 Innocent III, *Regesta sive epistolae*, PL 214, col. 265.

29 Innocent III, *Regesta sive epistolae*, PL 215, col. 701.

30 Geoffrey of Villehardouin, *La conquête de Constantinople*, ed. Edmond Faral, vol. 2 (Paris: Société d'Edition 'Les belles lettres', 1961), p. 24.

31 Rodney M. Thomson, ed., *Tractatus Garsiae* (Textus minores, 46; Leiden: Brill, 1973), p. 18.

appears before the gatekeepers of the pope, begging for mercy. The courtiers reply, 'To hell with you and your poverty! ... Amen, amen, I say to you. You will not enter into the joy of your Lord until you have given your last penny!'[32] Verses like these played on the irony that a papal reform movement born of a desire to purge the church of the ill effects of wealth (one thinks of Peter Damian's associations of simony with excrement in the eleventh century) had itself grown into a voracious pecuniary beast. Nor was money itself the only target of such satire. Poets also attacked the abuses of papal justice that accompanied this flow of cash. As Walter of Chatillon (c. 1134–1200?) wrote, 'The court of the Romans is nothing but a market. There the laws of the senators are up for sale. In this consistory, if anyone would argue his case or that of another, let him first read this: unless he gives money, Rome will deny him everything; he who gives more money, argues his case better.'[33]

Humorous though such satires were, they reflected a serious concern that the papacy was abandoning its role of spiritual leadership in a pursuit of worldly power. This was the substance of the more sober lament delivered by Bernard of Clairvaux (1090–1153) in his *De consideratione* addressed to Pope Eugenius III. Bernard targeted especially the legalism of the curia, in which the 'laws of Justinian' replaced 'the Law of the Lord', crafty litigants subverted justice through iniquitous appeals, scandalous monasteries were arrogantly removed from the orderly supervision of their bishops, and the attention of the pope was distracted from the core mission of apostolic service.[34] Directly inspired by Bernard, Innocent III attempted half a century later to return the papacy to its pastoral duty, echoing in his sermons the saint's admonition that 'a ministry has been imposed upon us rather than a dominion bestowed'.[35]

Innocent's effort led to the creation of the mendicant orders and the reconciliation of groups like the Humiliati and the Poor Catholics. Yet, plans to renew the priestly vocation of the papal office were only partially successful. Cathars and Waldensians continued to argue that the Roman Church was a Babylon whose faith was dead,[36] pointing particularly to the

32 Text in B. Bischoff, ed., *Carmina burana: Die Lieder der Benediktbeurer Handschrift* (Munich: Deutscher Taschenbuch Verlag, 1979), 118.
33 *Ibid.*, 110.
34 Bernard of Clairvaux, *De consideratione*, in *Sancti Bernardi opera*, ed. J. Leclercq and H. M. Rochais, vol. 3 (Rome: Editiones Cistercienses, 1963), 399, 435 and 442.
35 Innocent said, 'Servum me fateor, et non dominum...et ideo ministerium mihi vindico, dominium non usurpo', *PL* 217, col. 655. Bernard wrote in *De consideratione* (p. 416), 'impositum senserimus ministerium, non dominium datum'.
36 Moneta of Cremona, *Adversus Catharos et Valdenses*, ed. T. A. Ricchinius (Rome: N. and M. Palearini, 1743; repr., Ridgewood, N. J.: Gregg, 1964), 389–408.

union of the papal office with earthly wealth and power at Sylvester I's supposed receipt of the Donation of Constantine (then, of course, believed to be authentic).[37] In response, the mendicants, whose original mission was to preach, were transformed into the shock troops of the papal inquisition. First authorized by Gregory IX, the medieval inquisition was staffed heavily by the friars (a later pun on the Dominicans as 'domini canes' appropriated earlier imagery of the preacher as a 'dog' frenetically sniffing out the heterodox 'little foxes' wherever they may, or may not, be present). Especially active in France and Spain, the inquisitors were empowered by Innocent IV's 1252 bull 'Ad extirpanda' to use torture in carrying out their duties.

The intimate relationship between the friars and the papacy represented by the inquisition led to further criticism, indeed to the most serious challenge mounted to the doctrine of papal sovereignty from within the church before Marsilius of Padua. The setting was the university of Paris, where the Franciscans and Dominicans had risen quickly to prominence through the teaching of such masters as Alexander of Hales (Franciscan (d. 1245)) and Albert the Great (Dominican (1193?–1280)), not to mention their legendary intellectual progeny Bonaventure and Thomas Aquinas. The friars were also highly successful at recruiting members from among the student body. The mendicant masters, however, refused to accept the guild authority of the university faculty, for which they incurred the animosity of the secular masters. This intramural dispute quickly encompassed broader issues, however. The fiery William of St Amour took up the cause not simply of the seculars, but also of the diocesan clergy (bishops and priests) to whose detriment the mendicants leveraged their Roman privileges in preaching and hearing confessions. The 'secular–mendicant conflict' principally revolved around the friars' teachings on apostolic poverty, but it also impinged on the question of the papal *plenitudo potestatis*. Against the claims by propagandists like Gerald of Abbeville and William of St Amour (c. 1200–72) who denied that the pope had the authority to encroach upon a bishop's inviolable jurisdiction within his diocese, Bonaventure and other champions of the mendicants stressed the pope's hierarchical power over the pastorate within the confines of divine and natural law.[38]

---

37 For example, Renerius, *Summa*, in *Thesaurus novus anecdotorum*, ed. E. Durand and U. Martène, vol. 5 (Paris: F. Delaulne, 1717, repr., Farnborough: Gregg International, 1969), col. 1775.

38 See especially M.-M. Dufeil, *Guillaume de Saint-Amour et la polémique universitaire parisienne, 1250–1259* (Paris: Éditions A. et J. Picard, 1972).

## The papacy on the periphery

An aspect of papal power in the High Middle Ages which is often overlooked involves the interactions between Rome and such 'fringe' regions as Iberia, Ireland, Scandinavia and Eastern Europe. Popes of the eleventh century were acutely aware of the importance of cultivating relationships with the expanding periphery. Politically, it was advantageous to encircle the often troublesome realms of Germany and France with sympathetic churches on their borders. Such a policy also continued a traditional association between the apostolic see and the effort to spread Roman Christianity among pagans and 'improper' Christians, visible as early as Gregory the Great's mission to England and especially developed by St Boniface in his evangelising in central Germany. Gregory VII's numerous pastoral letters to the rulers and/or people of Spain, Bohemia, Hungary, Poland, Denmark, Norway and Sweden reflect this continuing papal interest in the Latin-Christian periphery.[39] Popes were especially worried about unusual practices among the faithful along the fringe. Clerical concubinage was a near universal complaint, though local clergy in Scandinavia claimed (unsuccessfully) that they had received papal exemption from this burden![40] Other concerns that prompted papal action included incestuous marriages (Ireland, for one)[41] and irregularities in the mass and sacraments; Gregory VII attacked the use of the Old Slavonic liturgy in Bohemia and the Mozarabic rite in Spain,[42] while popes of the thirteenth century prohibited the use of beer for the eucharist and spittle for baptism in Norway.[43] In many places, such as Poland, the establishment of a fixed parochial structure and the implementation of tithing were of paramount importance.[44] Of course, accommodation might ultimately have to be made to peculiar local circumstances, as when Gregory IX agreed to limit

---

39  Gregory VII, *Register*, 1.17, 38, 58, 59, 61, 63, 64, 78, 83; 2.6–8, 13, 50, 51, 63, 70–3, 75; 3.18; 4.25, 28; 5.10, 12; 6.13, 29; 7.6, 11, 21; 8.11; 9.2, 14.

40  *Diplomatarium danicum*, ser. 1, vol. 5, ed. Niels Skyum-Nielsen (Copenhagen: Det danske sprog- og litteraturselskab, 1957), no. 37 (Sweden); *Diplomatarium norvegicum*, vol. 1, ed. C. C. A. Lange and C. R. Unger (Oslo: P. T. Malling, 1849), no. 19 (Norway).

41  John Watt, *The Church in Medieval Ireland* (Dublin: University College Dublin Press, 1998), 17–24. See also Gerald of Wales (Giraldus Cambrensis), *Topographia hibernica*, ed. J. S. Brewer, Rolls Series 21.5 (London: Longmans, 1867) ('nondum matrimonia contrahunt, non incestus euitant…').

42  Lisa Wolverton, *Hastening toward Prague* (Philadelphia: University of Pennsylvania Press, 2001), p. 135, and Robert Bartlett, *The Making of Europe: Conquest, Colonization, and Cultural Change, 950–1350* (Princeton: Princeton University Press; London: Allen Lane, 1993), p. 249.

43  *Diplomatarium norvegicum*, vol. 1, nos. 16, 26; vol. 6, no. 10.

44  Piotr Górecki, *Parishes, Tithes, and Society in Earlier Medieval Poland, ca. 1100–1250* (Philadelphia: American Philosophical Society, 1993).

death-bed gifts to churches on the Baltic island of Gotland 'owing to the sterility and poverty of the land'.[45]

In governing the fringe, Rome frequently made use of archbishops. Although this institution was under assault by the Gregorian papacy in other parts of Europe, the popes of the twelfth and thirteenth centuries viewed archbishops as partners in the implementation of church reform 'in remotis partibus' rather than as rivals. Numerous metropolitan sees were founded at this time, such as the four Irish provincial centres of Armagh, Dublin, Cashel and Tuam, and the three Nordic archiepiscopal churches of Lund, Nidaros/Trondheim and Uppsala. Metropolitan bishops frequently won the designation of 'native legates', responsible for implementing clerical reform and preaching Holy War against nearby infidels. Legates 'a latere' also played a prominent role in frontier regions. The visitations and councils of emissaries like John of Abbeville (Spain), John Paparo (Ireland), Nicholas Breakspear (Norway), Gregorius de Crescentio (Denmark), William of Sabina (Livonia), James of Liège (Poland) and Jacob of Pecorara (Hungary) created a lasting memory of papal authority on the periphery, even if their specific mandates mouldered from neglect.

Papal attention was also devoted to Christianity's 'others' in the High Middle Ages. Already in the Later eleventh century, Gregory VII sent a remarkable letter to the Muslim ruler of 'Mauretania Sitifensis' (Algeria) asserting that Christianity and Islam worship the same god and are bound together by the tradition of Abraham.[46] Gregory's concern and that of many of his successors was with the welfare of remnant churches under Muslim rule, and while they preached crusade in the Holy Land and Iberia, popes more often counselled patience to Christians in Africa. In the thirteenth century, papal interest was increasingly focused on Asia. In part this was motivated by a desire to make contact with Nestorian churches along the Silk Road, which were not necessarily eager for papal assistance, but it also extended to missionary work among non-Christians. As Gregory IX stated, only when the gospel was preached to all peoples would the 'plenitudo gentium' be achieved and the salvation of Israel commence.[47] Innocent IV and Nicholas IV stand out in connection with the Mongol missions. As a canonist, Innocent elaborated the first coherent theory of Latin relations with the infidel world, accepting the

---

45 *Diplomatarium danicum*, ser. 1, vol. 5, no. 105.
46 Gregory VII, *Register*, 3.21.
47 See the bull 'Cum hora undecima', in *Acta Honorii III et Gregorii IX*, ed. Aloysius L. Tăutu, Pontificia Commissio ad redigendum Codicem Iuris Canonici Orientalis, ser. 3, vol. 3 (Vatican City: Typis Polyglottis Vaticanis, 1950), no. 210.

natural-law rights of non-Christians to property and political power but asserting a papal duty over the souls of all people, including the Mongols.[48] Here too
the friars were unsurprisingly important, though their endeavours under
Innocent met with little success. One reason for the missionaries' difficulty
was the belief among the shamanistic Mongols that they were divinely destined
to rule over all lands, including those of Christians and Muslims, and the
perception in central Asia, based on contact with Nestorian communities, that
Christians were subject and contemptible. Under the Franciscan Pope Nicholas
IV, apostolic interest in the East peaked once again, resulting in the Minorite
mission of John of Monte Corvino, who was dispatched in 1291 and worked as
archbishop with the help of a small group of suffragan friar-bishops in Khan
Baliq (Beijing) until his death between 1328 and 1330.[49]

By the second half of the thirteenth century, the vision of the eleventh-century
reform popes had to a great extent been fulfilled. Forged in theology, under-
girded by law, and implemented in church politics, the ambitious notion that
the pope was not simply the bishop of Rome, but the universal ordinary had
been accepted by most Christians. Such acceptance would not last long,
however. The fight between Philip the Fair and Boniface VIII at the turn of
the fourteenth century demonstrated the power of the incipient nation-state
with its claims to monarchical sovereignty over the church. This was followed
by the Avignon papacy, which, rightly or wrongly, was perceived as unforgiv-
ably decadent and unconcerned with holiness, as seen in John XXII's assault on
the Fraticelli. What confidence people might still have had in the apostolic see
was further eroded by the Great Schism. As the great age of Christian humanism advanced, with its tireless reform efforts on a local level and its powerful
vision of episcopal government in the fifteenth and sixteenth centuries, the
papal church of the 'Gregorian' era receded into the distance.

48 See especially James Muldoon, *Popes, Lawyers, and Infidels: The Church and the Non-
Christian World, 1250–1550* (Liverpool: Liverpool University Press, 1979), 3–71.
49 See Peter Jackson, 'The Mongols and the Faith of the Conquered', in Reuven Amitai
and Michael Biran, eds., *Mongols, Turks, and Others: Eurasian Nomads and the Sedentary
World* (Leiden and Boston: Brill, 2005), 245–90. On the Franciscans in the East, see John
R. H. Moorman, *A History of the Franciscan Order, from its Origins to the Year 1517* (Oxford:
Oxford University Press, 1968), 235–9, 429–32. On the Mongol missions in general, see
Felicitas Schmieder, *Europa und die Fremden: Die Mongolen im Urteil des Abendlandes vom
13. bis in das 15. Jahrhundert* (Sigmaringen: Jan Thorbecke Verlag, 1994), esp. 129–51.

3

# Religious poverty and the search for perfection

## BEVERLY MAYNE KIENZLE

'Our order is abjection; it is humility; it is voluntary poverty, obedience, peace, joy in the Holy Spirit', wrote the Cistercian abbot Bernard of Clairvaux (1090–1153) to the monks of St Jean d'Aulps who had affiliated with Cîteaux. Bernard further explained in a sermon that voluntary poverty, like the fortified city into which Jesus entered (Luke 10.38), defends its inhabitants from envy, within themselves and from others. Advising Atto, bishop of Troyes, Bernard asserted that, 'The reward for poverty is the kingdom of heaven'.[1] The search for the kingdom of heaven through the embrace of voluntary poverty animated not only the great abbot of Clairvaux, but many Christians from the regular and secular clergy as well as the laity throughout the twelfth century.

Poverty implied renunciation of the will as much as rejection of worldy goods. The Guta-Sintram codex depicts St Augustine under a banner reading, 'Let poverty be sweet, the mind chaste, and the will one'. The same codex, the collaborative production of the canonesses of Schwartzenthann in Alsace and the canons of nearby Marbach, contains a sermon on Matt. 5.3, 'Blessed are the poor in spirit', composed by Peter Abelard for the nuns at the Abbey of the Paraclete. He admonishes them that, 'those who imitate the apostolic life, renouncing the world utterly, are more authentically poor and closer to God'.[2] In her visionary treatise *Scivias*, Hildegard of Bingen (1098–1179) depicts Poverty in Spirit receiving an outpouring of golden divine light, so glorious that one cannot look at her face.[3] That brilliant light inspired the gold-filigreed

---

1  *Sancti Bernardi Opera*, ed. J. Leclercq, H. M. Rochais and C. H. Talbot (8 vols.; Rome: Editiones Cistercienses, 1957–77), vol. 7, *Ep.* 142, 340; *The Letters of St. Bernard of Clairvaux*, trans. B. S. James, new introduction by B. M. Kienzle (Stroud: Sutton Publishing, 1998), Letter 151, 220. Translations by B. Kienzle.
2  Fiona Griffiths, 'Brides and Dominae: Abelard's *Cura monialium* at the Augustinian Monastery of Marbach', *Viator* 34 (2003), 28.
3  Hildegard of Bingen, *Scivias*, trans. Columba Hart and Jane Bishop; introduction, Barbara J. Newman; preface, Caroline Walker Bynum (New York: Paulist Press, 1990), *Vision* I.1, 68; *Scivias*, ed. A. Führkötter and A. Carlevaris (CCCM 43; Turnhout: Brepols, 1978), 9–10.

feast-day garments of the virgins at Rupertsberg, whose attire incurred the reproaches of Tenxwind, superior of the women at Andernach. Tenxwind disagreed with Hildegard over the interpretation of poverty and criticised her contemporary for rejecting women of low social rank and wealth.[4]

Beyond the religious houses of established orders, lay people and dissident groups also venerated and debated the apostolic ideal of poverty. Wandering preachers advocated evangelical austerity and relied on donations for their living, much as the mendicants would a century later. Norbert of Xanten (1082–1134) sold his worldly goods and was authorized by Pope Gelasius II as an itinerant preacher before establishing the new community at Prémontré in north-eastern France in 1120. Hermit preachers Robert of Arbrissel, Bernard of Tiron and Vitalis of Savigny all founded monastic houses. Robert of Arbrissel, who preached across the countryside barefoot, dressed in animal skins and a raggedy cloak, gathered followers at Fontevraud in 1101 and influenced many, including the Countess Ermengarde of Brittany (c. 1070–1147), whom he counseled: 'Love voluntary poverty. Amidst positions and honors…sighing along with the prophet say: I am a needy woman and poor…'[5]

Not all preachers who called for conversion to the apostolic life received approval from ecclesiastical authority. Evervin of Steinfeld, in an 1143 letter to Bernard of Clairvaux, decried a 'new' heresy whose followers claimed apostolic descent, called themselves the 'Poor of Christ' and held no property of their own. Around twenty years later Ekbert of Schönau (d. 1184) wrote thirteen sermons against the heretics whom he termed 'Cathars'. He joined his sister Elisabeth (1129–1164) and Hildegard of Bingen to deplore the dissidents' undeniably austere way of life, attempting to discredit it as false and deceptive. A decade later, the desire for apostolic poverty roused the merchant Valdes of Lyon to renounce all his wealth and evangelise. He and his followers, called Waldensians, advocated a life devoted to strict poverty, public preaching and obedience to God alone (Acts 5.29). Similarly, amidst the urban prosperity and religious dissent of northern Italy, the Humiliati sought to live in community and to dedicate themselves to common manual labour, drawing charges of heresy before being reconciled to the church in 1201.

---

4 Letters 52 and 52r, *The Letters of Hildegard of Bingen*, trans. J. L. Baird and R. K. Ehrman (3 vols.; Oxford: Oxford University Press, 1994, 1998, 2004), vol. 1, 127–30. *Epistolarium I*, ed. L. Van Acker (CCCM 91; Turnhout: Brepols, 1991), 125–30.

5 B. L. Venarde, ed. and trans., *Robert of Arbrissel: A Medieval Religious Life* (Washington, D.C.: Catholic University of America Press, 2003), 78.

Poverty, whether spiritual or material through renunciation of wealth, lay at the core of the twelfth century's search for religious perfection and its embrace of apostolic ideals. Monks, nuns, canons, canonesses, lay people and dissidents espoused the same scripture-based ideals. The ascetic spirit that animated the foundation of new religious orders permeated society inside and outside the cloisters as preachers advocated the apostolic life grounded in poverty, penance, and for some, public evangelising.

## The twelfth century

The complex reasons for this religious revival included economic growth, population increase, social change, a widespread ecclesiastical reform movement, the burgeoning of schools and monasteries, and the flowering of literature in Latin and the vernacular. As Herbert Grundmann first observed, an extraordinary religious fervour manifested itself in the search for the apostolic life among increasingly literate groups inside and outside the church.[6] Growth of such magnitude took root in the commercial and industrial expansion of the late eleventh century, with the expanded use of money and the growth of towns and cities and their populations. Gaining in size and influence, cities began around 1100 to assert their autonomy against the authority of the landed nobility. Reactions to this economic transformation divide into two broad categories: the attempt to avoid it, as monks and hermits did; and the desire to confront it, witnessed among the canons and certain lay people, who foreshadowed the thirteenth-century friars. Confrontation resulted, as Lester K. Little noted, in the formulation of a new spirituality for urban life.[7]

The reform movement initiated under Pope Gregory VII (1073–85) had renewed and reformed religious life and institutions while it also promoted the monastic discipline of poverty, chastity, obedience and manual labour as a model for all Christians. This quest to sanctify the world reached from the ideal of the *vita apostolica* to the elaboration of crusade ideology. Gregory VII and his advisers defined a view of Christendom that set all lay persons below

---

6 Herbert Grundmann, *Religious Movements in the Middle Ages: The Historical Links between Heresy, the Mendicant Orders, and the Women's Religious Movement in the Twelfth and Thirteenth Century, with the Historical Foundations of German Mysticism*, trans. S. Rowan, with an introduction by R. Lerner (Notre Dame and London: University of Notre Dame Press, 1995).

7 L. K. Little, *Religious Poverty and the Profit Economy in Medieval Europe* (Ithaca, N.Y.: Cornell University Press, 1978).

the ecclesiastical hierarchy, headed by the pope at Rome but with all the bishops and church leaders under him. The resulting thirst for the *vita apostolica* produced dramatic growth in Benedictine houses while new orders were founded as well: the Cistercians in 1098, the Victorine canons in 1108 and the Premonstratensian canons in 1120.[8]

Lay people also aspired to lead a life marked by poverty, preaching, chastity and manual labour. With the flourishing of scholarship in monasteries and schools, literacy increased overall as clerical and lay 'textual communities' expanded, grounding their spirituality on a common interpretation of Scripture.[9] In a predominantly oral culture, preachers wielded a powerful instrument for teaching and public persuasion, attracting crowds, who listened to exhortations advocating the reform agenda.[10] The reforms had extensive spillover effects, as they sharpened the distinction between clergy and laity, resulting in hostility and mistrust towards the laity on the part of the church hierarchy. As the laity applied the reform ideals to their own lives, they became more critical of clergy who did not live up to the reforming spirit. Some lay people, claiming for themselves the authority to evangelise, breached the rule of obedience which grounds the monastic life.[11]

## Monasticism

Monastic spirituality centres on the struggle for spiritual perfection, as the Prologue to the *Rule of Benedict* reads: 'monks must prepare [themselves] in body and soul, to fight under the commandments of holy obedience'.[12] A life of reading, prayer and meditation aspired to mystical union with God and citizenship among the number of the chosen in the heavenly Jerusalem. In monastic thought, the heavenly city's closest earthly parallel was the monastery, which contained, in so far as possible for a terrestrial place, the dignity and spiritual benefits of the supernal city. Bernard of Clairvaux described the monk as a dweller in Jerusalem, imitating the way of life of the heavenly city.[13]

---

8  See works by G. Constable, B. Kienzle, E. Peters and J. Russell in the bibliography.

9  Brian Stock, *The Implications of Literacy: Written Language and Models of Interpretation in the Eleventh and Twelfth Centuries* (Princeton: Princeton University Press, 1983).

10  B. M. Kienzle, 'Medieval Sermons and their Performance: Theory and Record', in C. A. Muessig, ed., *The Sermon in the Middle Ages* (Leiden: Brill, 2002), 89–124.

11  B. M. Kienzle, 'Holiness and Obedience: Denouncement of Twelfth-Century Waldensian Lay Preaching', in A. Ferreiro, ed., *The Devil, Heresy and Witchcraft in the Middle Ages: Essays in Honor of Jeffrey B. Russell* (Leiden: Brill, 1998), 259–78.

12  *The Rule of St Benedict*, trans. with intro. and notes by A. C. Meisel and M. L. del Mastro (New York: Doubleday Image Books, 1975), 45.

13  *SBO*, vol. 2, Sermo 55.2, 112; *SBO*, vol. 7, Ep. 64, 158; James, *Letters*, no. 67, 91.

Furthermore, the monastery was viewed as the *schola Christi*, with Christ as the master. As such it provided the education necessary for attaining eternal life.

Persevering in the monastic life required discipline: obedience to the *Rule* and to the abbot (or abbess) who governed in accord with its precepts. The *Rule* demanded of each follower the humility to surrender his or her own will in favour of that of the community as represented by the abbot, who holds the place of Christ in the monastery (*RB* 2). The abbot in turn was accountable before God at the judgment for his teaching and for the obedience shown by his disciples (*RB* 2). Hence the supreme and inseparable monastic virtues are obedience and humility.

A further key component of the monastic life is the activity of work, which encompasses both manual labour and prayer, termed the *opus dei*. This notion of work's importance derives from Pauline texts and the early fathers of monasticism: Christians should earn their own bread and also earn through their work the wherewithal to help the needy. Monks were taught to follow the Pauline model, as illustrated in Bernard of Clairvaux's definition of poverty as both denying patronage for oneself and providing it to others.[14]

## The Cistercians

Bernard of Clairvaux stands out as the most prominent monk of the Cistercian order, which had its beginnings when Robert of Molesmes led a group of monks to a new monastery in 1098, aspiring to return to the purity of Benedict's *Rule*, which they felt had been lost with the growth of Cluniac monasticism. The Cistercian Order epitomized the spirit of reform through its emphasis on work, austerity, simplicity and withdrawal from the world. Cistercians revised the daily schedule to allow more time for labour and private prayer. They strove for greater simplicity in liturgy and architecture, and literature written from the Cistercian point of view reprehends Cluniac excesses in these and other areas.

The Cistercians exerted a strong influence on the church hierarchy, and some held positions of ecclesiastical power, working as agents and models for

---

14 *SBO*, vol. 7, Ep.103, 259; James, *Letters*, no. 104, 151. See works by J. Leclercq and M. Newman in the bibliography; B. M. Kienzle, *Cistercians, Heresy and Crusade in Occitania, 1145–1229: Preaching in the Lord's Vineyard* (Woodbridge: Boydell Press; York: York Medieval Press, 2001); B. M. Kienzle, ed., *The Sermon* (Typologie des sources du Moyen Âge occidental, fasc. 81–3; Turnhout: Brepols, 2000), 271–317; Carolyn A. Muessig, ed., *Medieval Monastic Preaching* (Leiden: Brill, 1998).

reform. Their rapid expansion exemplified the upsurge in foundations of religious houses and the aspiration to the *vita apostolica*. They profited from that fervour; among the great numbers of conversions to the Order were numerous men who became lay brothers such as Pons of Léras. Pons renounced the material goods he had acquired as a brigand, placed his wife and children in monasteries, performed public penance and pilgrimage, and then founded the monastery of Sylvanès.[15] Educated men also entered the monasteries, as the Cistercians benefited from the rise in literacy and the growth of the schools. From Bernard of Clairvaux onward, they aided in articulating the perceived need to extend the reform agenda to convert dissidents and non-Christians.

Many monasteries, including houses for women, followed Cistercian usages without being formally incorporated into the Order. In France and Spain, women's houses grew into two congregations: one around Tart, near Cîteaux, founded in 1120 and chartered in 1132, the other under the 1187 royal foundation of Las Huelgas near Burgos. Family connections often played a role in the foundation and governance of women's houses. The Benedictine community of Jully, founded in 1113, was governed first by Prioress Elizabeth, whose husband Guy had entered Cîteaux with his famous brother Bernard, and then by St Bernard's sister Humbeline. Life in monasteries with noble members and dowries contrasted sharply with that of communities who endured hard physical labour to produce food for survival.[16]

The Cistercians' self image as an elite spiritual corps, superior to other monks, provoked antagonism even in the early years, as when the Benedictine Rupert of Deutz criticised various of their practices, such as the insistence on manual labour. The Order's expansion, acquisition of property, and involvement in wool production, notably in northern England, brought economic and social benefits to the areas where monasteries were established. It also resulted in wealth that contradicted the message of simplicity and austerity articulated in the Order's founding. The monks who had denounced the excesses of Cluniac abbeys found themselves the targets of satire against their own wealth and greed.[17]

---

15 B. M. Kienzle, 'Pons of Léras' [introduction and translation] in Thomas Head, ed., *Medieval Hagiography* (New York: Garland Press, 2000), 495–513.

16 See J. Nichols, 'Introduction', and Jean de la Croix Bouton, 'The Life of the Twelfth and Thirteenth-Century Nuns of Cîteaux', in J. A. Nichols and L. T. Shank, eds., *Hidden Springs: Cistercian Monastic Women, Medieval Religious Women*, vol. 3.1 (Cistercian Studies 113A; Kalamazoo, Mich.: Cistercian Publications, 1995), 4–7, 14–25.

17 Kienzle, *Cistercians, Heresy and Crusade* 41.

## The Benedictines and the canons

Bernard of Clairvaux and the Cistercians at times dominate the telling of twelfth-century religious history and overshadow Benedictine monasticism. Some scholars even argued that the black monks experienced a 'crisis', but as John Van Engen asserts, this false perception was based on too literal a reading of the Benedictines' critics without sufficient consideration of the context. The black monks suffered no decline in numbers during the first half of the twelfth century and only later lost their central position in the church.[18] Many reformers came from their ranks, such as William of Hirsau (d. 1091) who spurred the renewal of monasticism in Germany, leading to the foundation of around forty houses between 1080 and 1120. Haimo of Hirsau, William's biographer, credited him with the recovery of monasticism in the Teutonic regions and praised him for exhorting 'by words and deeds the poor of Christ and pilgrims to be content with little and to have the world and all its glory under their feet'.[19] The Cluniac-inspired Hirsau movement encompassed a network of monasteries including Disibodenberg, where Hildegard was enclosed with her mentor Jutta in 1112.[20] Benedictine monasticism saw the material prosperity of their prominent houses and the glorious beauty of their churches as proofs of spiritual success. The new spirituality of the twelfth and thirteenth centuries made them targets of criticism as Cistercians and others emphasised the necessity of material poverty as grounds for spiritual perfection.[21]

While monasticism thrived, the demand for education began to outstrip what monastery schools could supply. In the late eleventh century, increasing numbers of students not intending to become monks gravitated toward the episcopal schools. The clergy who staffed cathedral schools included the 'secular' canons, who continued to live in the world, and the 'regular', who lived according to a somewhat monastic rule, usually that of St Augustine of Hippo. The canons of the abbey of Saint Victor in Paris established a model for the new age, striving to be both monks and scholars. Hugh of St Victor (c. 1096–1141) charted a programme for education in the schools which

18 J. Van Engen, 'The "Crisis of Cenobitism" Reconsidered: Benedictine Monasticism in the Years 1050–1150', *Speculum* 61 (1986), 269–304.
19 Giles Constable, *The Reformation of the Twelfth Century* (Cambridge: Cambridge University Press, 1996), 44.
20 Anna Silvas, trans. and annot., *Jutta and Hildegard: The Biographical Sources* (University Park: Pennsylvania State University Press, 1999), 54.
21 Van Engen, 'The "Crisis of Cenobitism"', 302–04.

would become the basis for study in the nascent universities. His *Didascalion*, inspired by Augustine's *De doctrina christiana*, asserted that the liberal arts were to be taught as the foundation for careful study of the Bible.[22]

## Women's communities

These were initiatives to promote the religious lives of men, and the history of women's communities has been more difficult to document and assess. Bruce Venarde signals an increase from 100 to over 400 nunneries in England and France from around 1080 to 1170. These nunneries included houses affiliated with male orders, but more than half were either autonomous or associated with female-centred orders, namely Fontevrists, named from Fontevraud founded by Robert of Arbrissel, and Gilbertines, called after their founder Gilbert of Sempringham (c. 1089–1189). Among the male orders, the Premonstratensians first founded communities for men and women; however, after Norbert's death in 1134, they began to direct the separation of men and women, and in 1198 the Order decided no longer to accept women.[23]

The Cistercians have been portrayed as reluctant to accept women's communities that desired to affiliate with them, but the situation was more complex. Behind the restrictive Cistercian legislation of the thirteenth century, scholars have uncovered evidence which reveals that Cistercian abbots were assisting nuns to follow the Order's usages as early as the 1120s.[24] Nonetheless, one may conclude that the religious orders overall, including the Franciscans and Dominicans in the thirteenth century, whether at first accepting or hesitant to grant affiliation to women's houses, eventually reacted negatively to the problems of managing men and women together and supporting communities of women vowed to apostolic poverty. Brenda Bolton asserts that the church could and should have approved the creation of a new religious order for women, but instead, at the Fourth Lateran Council (1215), it prohibited the approval of any new religious rules and thereby of new religious orders.[25] Continuing research on the history of religious women will indicate to what degree legislation reflected reality and to what extent

22 See works by J. Longère in the bibliography.
23 See B. L. Venarde, *Women's Monasticism and Medieval Society: Nunneries in France and England, 890–1215* (Ithaca, N.Y.: Cornell University Press, 1997), 7–15, 70–9.
24 See Brigitte Degler-Spengler, 'The Incorporation of Cistercian Nuns into the Order in the Twelfth and Thirteenth Century', in Nichols and Shanks, eds., *Hidden Springs*, vol. 3.1, 85–134, and other articles in the volume.
25 B. Bolton, 'Mulieres sanctae', in S. M. Stuard, ed., *Women in Medieval Society* (Philadelphia: University of Pennsylvania Press, 1976), 141–58.

spiritual, intellectual and institutional collaboration continued between male and female communities.[26]

## The laity

Since Grundmann, historians have acknowledged that lay piety, like clerical, was marked with veneration for the apostolic life.[27] Beginning in the late eleventh century, the growth of cities and literacy both contributed to the need for lay people to have supportive spiritual communities and allowed them to develop those outside the church. André Vauchez notes that monastic reform and heresies of the year 1000 shared the view that the only hope for Christianity resided in separation from the material aspects of the secular church and dedication by communities of faith to bring together believers in a reformed way of life.[28]

Pursuing ideals of poverty and evangelism, however, brought some lay movements into conflict with the church. Once the Gregorian reforms had firmly fixed the clerical perspective, lay religious currents that arose without the direction of the clerical hierarchy came under suspicion. The clergy's distrust of lay religion intensified around the middle of the twelfth century when dissident movements gained strength. Correspondingly, the laity, persuaded by apostolic models of reform, came to value those above the monastic ideal of obedience and began to lose trust in the clergy, especially its upper ranks. Lay people became increasingly aware of the contradictions they saw between the teachings of the Gospels and the lives of the clergy, enriched materially by some of the reform measures.

Wandering preachers advocated the austerity of the apostolic life and relied on donations to make a living. Some found patrons, such as Robert of Arbrissel did in Bishop Hildebert of Le Mans. Arnold of Brescia, on the other hand, carried his decrial of clerical corruption to the point that he started a popular uprising in 1146, drove the pope out of Rome, and declared a republic there. Condemned in 1139 by Innocent II at the Second Lateran Council and at the Council of Sens in 1140, he was finally excommunicated in 1148, arrested and executed in 1155 under orders of Hadrian IV. Also around mid-century, Peter of Bruys (d. c. 1140) and Henry the monk (d. c. 1145)

---

26 See articles by F. Griffiths in the bibliography.
27 Grundmann, *Religious Movements*.
28 A. Vauchez, *The Laity in the Middle Ages: Religious Beliefs and Devotional Practices*, ed. and intro. Daniel E. Bornstein, trans. Margery J. Schneider (Notre Dame: University of Notre Dame Press, 1993), 13.

aroused the indignation of two of the most powerful figures in the Western church: Peter the Venerable, abbot of Cluny, who attacked the Petrobrusians, and Bernard, abbot of Clairvaux, who set out to capture Henry and dissuade his followers. Henry, who eventually died in prison, so aroused the people of Le Mans against clerical authority that they greeted their bishop Hildebert's return by pelting him with mud. Dissident movements continued to gain strength, such that R. I. Moore suggests that between 1179 and 1215 there occurred 'the most rapid diffusion of popular heresy that Western Europe had yet experienced'.[29]

## The Cathars

The Cathars, as criticised by Evervin of Steinfeld and later writers, demonstrated remarkable austerity and command of Scripture. Calling themselves simply 'good Christians', or the 'Poor of Christ', according to Evervin's report, the Cathars constituted a counter-church of believers, clergy and bishops, which shared certain basic elements of belief, organization and ritual with the Bogomils who emerged in Bulgaria in the early tenth century. Western Cathars differed from Rome in beliefs on the nature of Christ (who for the Cathars was not truly human), the structure and role of the church hierarchy, the number and function of the sacraments, the source of evil in the world, and the possibility of salvation for all believers. The *consolamentum*, a laying-on-of-hands modeled on the imposition of hands described in the New Testament, was the only sacrament necessary for salvation. It served as baptism, confirmation, ordination, forgiveness of sins and extreme unction. Neither marriage nor the eucharist was considered a sacrament, but the Cathars shared a symbolic breaking of bread. Cathars and Bogomils alike believed that matter was created by the rebellious angel Lucifer and that the last fallen soul would be saved at the end of this world. Both groups rejected icons and practised a simple repetitive liturgy. Simplicity marked their way of life; once ordained or 'consoled', the Cathar clergy, termed 'perfects', observed celibacy and renounced all ownership of property.

In the West, Catharism was especially strong in southern France and northern Italy, but it took hold in northern France and the Rhineland as well. The Cathars thrived not only in cities, but in small villages, where

---

29 R. I. Moore, *The Formation of a Persecuting Society: Power and Deviance in Western Europe, 950–1250* (Oxford and New York: Blackwell, 1987), 23. See also the other works of Moore in the bibliography.

artisans lived, worked and worshipped together, teaching their faith and their trades, notably weaving and shoemaking. All social classes were represented among the Cathars. In Occitania, Catharism began by being strong in the upper class and then filtered down to other classes because of the unique circumstances of Occitan society, where all its members inhabited the town (*castrum*). Family ties represented an important bond in the Cathar network: Cathar houses, held as common property, played a religious and socio-economic role; people were welcomed there for instruction in artisanry and religion. The Cathar religion placed no economic restrictions on believers and exacted no tithes. The Cathars despised the wealth of the Roman Church and rejected marriage as a material relationship.[30]

Whereas the church took actions to discourage women seeking the religious life, dissident groups tended to accord women more important roles than they could enjoy in traditional religious communities. Cathar women lived in their own houses, teaching and preaching to each other, and ministering to others through teaching, preaching, healing and even laying on of hands to perform the sacrament. The Cathar movement offered women the option for a religious life at home, where aristocratic ladies could serve as spiritual directors for their relatives.[31] The growth of Catharism sharpened the clerical hierarchy's suspicion of apostolic movements and its concern for controlling the authorisation to preach. The failure of preaching missions to Occitania contributed to the church's justification for launching the Albigensian Crusade (1209–29).[32]

## The Waldensians

The Waldensian movement was founded on material poverty in as much as it sprang from the merchant Valdes of Lyon's radical conversion and renunciation of wealth in the early 1170s. Valdes advocated a life devoted to preaching and supported by donations, much like the Franciscans who followed not long afterwards. But the early Waldensians called for preaching by all believers, even women, and had the Scriptures and other works translated into the vernacular. The Waldensians met and preached in private homes and also travelled from town to town preaching apostolic poverty. Eventually they

---

30 See the works by A. Brenon, J. Duvernoy, Y. Hagman, B. Hamilton, L. Kaelber, and M. Lambert in the bibliography, and Chapter 12 in this volume.
31 On Cathar women, see works by A. Brenon in the bibliography.
32 See Kienzle, *Cistercians, Heresy and Crusade*.

formed their own communal houses, including those for the Waldensian sisters.

The Waldensians justified their evangelical call by a reading of Scripture that claimed that the Spirit's calling and Jesus' commissioning (Mark 16.15) did not need to be controlled by the hierarchy and that obedience was owed to God alone (Acts 5.29). The apostles, they said, were not formally educated, and Mary Magdalene and other women spread the good news. Inquisition records evidence Waldensian women preaching in houses and also publicly. They worked as healers and some apparently assumed sacerdotal functions.

Insistence on public preaching led the Waldensians to confrontations with the ecclesiastical hierarchy. In 1179, Pope Alexander III approved the Waldensians' voluntary poverty but refused to allow them to preach without their bishop's permission. That refusal alienated the group from the hierarchy; they continued to preach, nonetheless, and in 1184 the Waldensians along with the Humiliati, the Arnoldists and the Patarenes were condemned in *Ad abolendam*, a decree issued at Verona by Pope Lucius III and backed by Emperor Frederick I. The early Waldensians differed from Rome not because of doctrine, but primarily over the question of obedience, brought to a head in the controversy about preaching.

Innocent III was keen to recruit and authorise preachers faithful to Rome in order to counter the dissidents. A group of Waldensians led by Durand of Huesca sought reconciliation with Rome, and in 1208 Innocent III confirmed the *propositum conversationis* of these 'Catholic Poor' provided that they swore a formula of Catholic belief.[33]

## The Humiliati

Also present with the Waldensians at the Third Lateran Council in 1179 were townspeople from Lombardy who sought permission to preach against heresy and to live in poverty but remain in their homes. The Humiliati attracted followers from various social classes, with a large proportion of women. All shared a spiritually based desire to live in community by their manual labour. They remained mostly in urban settings and sought independence for their way of life but without dissent from the doctrines and practices of the church. Jacques de Vitry reported that groups of Humiliati were living in Milan and its vicinity in the 1170s, but most evidence about them dates from the late Middle Ages. An anonymous chronicler of Laon, writing around 1180, compared the

---

33 See works by P. Biller and G. Audisio in the bibliography and Chapter 20 in this volume.

Humiliati and the Waldensians for their rejection of oath-taking. *Ad abolendam* (1184) grouped various adherents to the apostolic life, including the Humiliati, in its condemnation. However, the Humiliati in some regions continued to obtain support from local clergy and in 1201 received Innocent III's approval for their *propositum*, allowing them to live in evangelical poverty and to engage in preaching. Innocent III delineated three 'orders' among them (clerical, regular and tertiaries) but the reality of their lifestyles held greater complexity. One group, comprising male and female communities, corresponded roughly to the mixed orders of canons and canonesses, another to monastic sisters and brothers, and the third included lay members who lived in their own homes. The Humiliati illustrate markedly how twelfth-century Christians adapted the search for poverty and religious perfection to urban life.[34]

## The early beguines

While most documents pertaining to male or female beguines date from the early thirteenth century onward, evidence for lay claims to the apostolic life date from the eleventh century in the Low Countries, which constituted a centre for religious dissent. Lambert le Bègue, erroneously considered a sort of founder of the beguine movement, rebuked the clergy for greed and simony and was arrested for heresy in 1175, a charge rebutted in 1177 by Calixtus III. Lambert's *apologia* asserted that all Christians held the responsibility for exhorting others through good example, a concept that attracted clerical ire but influenced the beguine movement as it blurred the distinction between clergy and laity.[35]

Walter Simons' study of beguines in the Low Countries signals the region's advanced level of urbanisation and literacy and women's contribution to economic production. During the urban expansion from the eleventh century onward, the increasing population of women moved to cities to work. Moreover, increasing numbers of women sought to lead an unmarried and religious life. The Arrouaisian and Premonstratensian orders initially attracted large numbers of women, as did foundations of regular canons and informal communities. An anonymous treatise from Liège deals at length with the numerous women and men who dedicated themselves to a religious life with an informal structure during the first half of the twelfth century. From the

---

34 See works by F. Andrews and S. Brasher in the bibliography.
35 Walter Simons, *Cities of Ladies: Beguine Communities in the Medieval Low Countries, 1200–1565* (Philadelphia: University of Pennsylvania Press, 2001), 24–34.

lives of the holy women Juetta of Huy and Mary of Oignies, some information can be gleaned on what Simons terms the 'pre-institutional phase' of the beguine movement: the loosely structured communities that sprang up before the turn of the thirteenth century. Juetta served a lepers' house outside Huy, while Mary, after persuading her husband to take a vow of chastity, began working at a leper hospital in 1191 before taking up residence near a monastery of canons at Oignies in 1207.[36]

The eventual exclusion of women by the Premonstratensians (1198) actually gave impetus to the women's movement, because the communities remained after they lost their affiliation and sought a new direction. Furthermore, *mulieres sanctae* living in towns grouped together in houses for women and formed their own communities. They developed community rules of life that mirrored those of the monastics but did not bind participants to vows of obedience and stability. It is probably not mere coincidence that many beguines lived in the area that is now northern France and Belgium, where Premonstratensian houses were numerous.

Most women seeking to live a life of apostolic poverty were apparently affluent, whether from the nobility, lesser nobility or merchant class; the benefits of the new economic prosperity moved them to react strongly against the contradiction between wealth and apostolic ideals. *Mulieres sanctae* grouped together in private houses to lead lives modelled on the Gospel, supporting themselves by assets brought with them and by the trades that they practised. Men followed a similar path but in smaller numbers. Some women also lived solitary religious lives, either in their homes or as itinerants. By the 1230s and 1240s, chroniclers report that numerous women living in urban areas had organised themselves into religious communities, many of which became large, structured beguinages. The *vitae* record a strong distaste and distrust of the new urban wealth, such as Ida of Nivelles expressed about the funds her father provided for her monastic dowry.[37]

The ideals of poverty and religious perfection motivated twelfth-century Christians across Europe. At the turn of the thirteenth century, intellectuals in Paris continued the effort begun by Gregory VII to sanctify society, largely by urging the adaptation of monasticism to the lives of all Christians. Pope Innocent III undertook a sweeping agenda for reform, the elements of which were concretised in the canons of the Fourth Lateran Council (1215). Innocent III targeted dissident movements and recruited preachers to

---

36 Simons, *Cities of Ladies*, 39–40.
37 Simons, *Cities of Ladies*, 63.

persuade them to align with orthodoxy. Preaching also propagated the call for crusade against both heresy in Europe and Muslim domination of the Holy Land, an element on the papal reform agenda since Urban II preached the First Crusade in 1095.

Divergent interpretations of the apostolic life, albeit grounded in monastic ideals, resulted in conflict and crisis. The church asserted its authority to control religious fervour and to define and regulate the pursuit of the *vita apostolica*, intervening when competing definitions challenged established bounds. This assertion of authority produced tension, even competition and crisis, as various groups asserted claims to poverty, religious perfection and preaching. The tension over competing definitions and boundaries of the apostolic life escalated in the following centuries, as demonstrated in the conflict between Observant and Spiritual Franciscans and in the decrees of the Council of Vienne (1311) against the beguines, to cite only two of many examples.

4

# Monastic and religious orders,
## c. 1100–c. 1350

BRIAN PATRICK McGUIRE

## Traditional monasticism

This period in Western Europe brought about a reform of traditional monasticism, with the formation of new orders, both contemplative and pastoral. Military life was combined with the monastic vocation in the foundation of military orders. After 1200 forms of religious life appeared that built on earlier manifestations of pastoral life in community but now reflected the concerns of their founders, especially Dominic and Francis. The twelfth and thirteenth centuries manifest an embarrassment of riches: the number, variety and development of monastic and religious orders in this period is overwhelming, and I will seek only to provide an outline.

Monastic or religious life in the Middle Ages meant living according to a rule of life based on community, prayer and obedience. Traditional monasticism required vows of stability, obedience and *conversio morum* (change in way of life). Practically all those bound to such a life in the West after about 800 followed either the *Rule of Saint Benedict* or the *Rule for Canons* adopted at a synod of Aachen in 816. The first was intended for monks or nuns, the second for regular canons or canonesses. After about 1100, however, a new understanding of the monastic life emerged, especially in the genesis of the Cistercian Order. At the same time canons came to interpret their vocation in relation to the *Rule of Saint Augustine*, which in contrast to the Aachen legislation did not allow for personal property and emphasised more strongly life in community.

Before we consider the changes that came in the twelfth century, it is worthwhile first to look at traditional Benedictine monasticism. Scattered across Europe and especially in or near larger centres of population we find communities of men and women which had been following the *Rule of Saint Benedict* long before 1100. Benedictine abbeys were distinct entities, independent of each other, and so it would be wrong to speak of a Benedictine Order at this time. The abbot of each house was a sovereign lord, only subject to the diocesan bishop if he were found guilty of immoral behaviour.

Each Benedictine house formed a complete community, with servants, labourers, patrons and, of course, the monks themselves. The monastic liturgy or *opus dei* was the main concern of such institutions and provided a sense of continuity in the observance of the year's feasts. The monastery was obliged to its patrons and offered prayers to remember their dead. In Christianity from Late Antiquity there had always been a sense of the usefulness of praying for the dead. With an emerging sense of a place of cleansing in purgatory, monastic prayers became all the more valuable. The monks were linked to each other and to their patrons and thus expressed the living reality of the communion of saints: the unity and interdependability of the militant on earth, the suffering in purgatory, and the triumphant in heaven.

When monks of the traditional mould described their concerns, they usually spoke of privileges and properties. The two depended on each other and could not exist without each other. One of the most articulate spokespersons of this mentality is Jocelin of Brakelond, a monk of the great abbey at Bury Saint Edmunds. Writing at the end of the twelfth century, Jocelin provided an unforgettable portrait of Abbot Samson, who became abbot in 1182. On his election Samson promised to respect the customs of the monastery:

> the abbot said that he desired to keep our ancient customs concerning the entertainment of guests, to wit, that when the abbot was at home, he should receive all guests of every kind saving the religious and secular priests, and their men who invited themselves to the court-gate under cover of their masters; but if the abbot should be away from home, then all guests of every condition should be received by the cellarer, up to the number of thirteen horses...[1]

Jocelin's narrative reveals a nagging discussion at Bury concerning the abbot's economy and the monastery's. The two of them had developed in such a way that they were kept separate, but the monks began to feel that Samson was encroaching on their portion. Such a division of resources has no precedent in the *Rule of Saint Benedict*, but the monks felt they needed the protection of a separate administration so that the abbot did not exploit them.

It would be wrong to reduce the history of monasticism in this period to niggardly disputes, and one must remember that nasty disagreements often

---

1 H. E. Butler, trans., *The Chronicle of Jocelin of Brakelond* (London: Thomas Nelson, 1949), 39.

leave traces in the sources, while the smooth functioning of everyday life does not. To get a sense of what also mattered in traditional monasticism, we can turn to one of the finest monastic historians of our period, Matthew Paris, in his account of the abbots of his monastery, Saint Albans north of London. In summarising the career of William Trumpington, abbot from 1214 to 1235, Matthew Paris described how he decorated the church, obtained a rib of Saint Wulfstan, embellished the altar of Saint Alban, supplied candles for his shrine and for that of Our Lady, established a daily mass to be sung in perpetuity, had an image of Our Lady made, and so on. The list continues with further acquisitions of relics, statues and crosses.[2]

Matthew Paris also praised William of Trumpington for calming disputes inside and outside the monastery, but he mainly remembered him for his material additions. Such descriptions do not mean there was no interior life, but they indicate that the traditional monastic vocation involved the acquisition of wealth, the defence of hard-won privileges, and the repetition of ritual acts meant to obtain God's favour. In this context the transition from Anglo-Saxon to Norman abbots in England in Matthew Paris' account is hardly noticeable: monastic institutions carried on as before, under new ownership, as it were. In both England and France firm alliances grew up between the monarchy and great monasteries. Saint Denis outside Paris was, for example, the royal burial place, and its twelfth-century abbot Suger was the advisor of kings and steward of the kingdom while Louis VII was away on crusade.

Women's houses were not usually as well endowed as those of men. In the Anglo-Saxon period in England, abbesses had taken charge of double monasteries, such as Hilda at Whitby (d. 680). Now in the wake of the Gregorian reform such arrangements came under a cloud, and double monasteries began to disappear. Houses for women, however, are to be found all over Europe, leaving behind few written sources, but playing an essential part in the dynastic plans of the aristocracy. At the same time such monasteries gave a few privileged women an opportunity to become literate and live a life unencumbered by the burdens of marriage.[3]

---

2 Richard Vaughan, ed., *Chronicles of Matthew Paris: Monastic Life in the Thirteenth Century* (Gloucester: Alan Sutton, 1984), 47–55.

3 For a general treatment, see Jo Ann Kay McNamara, *Sisters in Arms* (Cambridge, Mass.: Harvard University Press, 1996), ch. 3. Also Penelope D. Johnson, *Equal in Monastic Profession: Religious Women in Medieval France* (Chicago: University of Chicago Press, 1991) and Sally Thompson, *Women Religious: The Founding of English Nunneries after the Norman Conquest* (Oxford: Clarendon Press, 1991).

A woman's own concerns in monastic life are found in some of the letters Heloise wrote to Abelard. More than a century later we are told how Isabelle of France, sister of King Louis IX, founded a monastery at Longchamp. Her story was told by Agnes of Harcourt, the third abbess (d. 1291).[4] Agnes occupied the very summit of medieval society, but even though traditional monasticism was intended for the most part for aristocratic women (and men), we can nevertheless assume that a few women from more ordinary backgrounds were admitted.

Monasticism at the opening of the twelfth century was a conservative institution intended to stabilise society. There were, nevertheless, a number of reform houses spread across Europe. The best known to us today is Cluny, founded in 909 by Duke William of Aquitaine. He had made certain in his foundation charter that neither he nor his successors would have any rights or prerogatives over the monastery. The bond was to be purely spiritual. Cluny specialised in the liturgy to such an extent that some of its monks had little or no time for manual labour. Later forms of monasticism, such as at Cîteaux, would seek to re-establish a balance.

Cluny was blessed with able abbots who lived long, ruled well and had time to groom their successors. At the beginning of our period there was one abbot, Pons, who apparently was incapable of shouldering the burden of the house. His successor, Peter the Venerable (d. 1156), was among the most brilliant and capable of all the Cluniac abbots. Peter has left the imprint of his abbacy in the collection of letters he made. Here he endowed posterity with a representative sample of his friendships and commitments across Europe.[5]

The Cluniac houses formed what we call a congregation: a loose federation of monastic foundations associated in various ways with the abbey. Many, but not all, were priories and considered the abbot of Cluny to be their abbot. There was, however, no Cluniac Order any more than there was a Benedictine Order at the time. Cluny, like other reform houses, exercised greater or lesser influence over other houses, but there was no administrative apparatus to ensure permanent bonds between Cluny and its priories and associated abbeys. Ultimately it was the person and efforts of the abbot of

---

4 Sean L. Field, ed., *The Writings of Agnes of Harcourt* (Notre Dame: University of Notre Dame Press, 2003).
5 Giles Constable, ed., *The Letters of Peter the Venerable* (Cambridge, Mass.: Harvard University Press, 1967), vols. 1–2. For general background for this period, see also Giles Constable, *The Reformation of the Twelfth Century* (Cambridge: Cambridge University Press, 1996).

Cluny alone that bound the congregation together. Formalised bonds in a clear legal structure would not come until the Cistercians.

## The Cistercian challenge

In 1098 a group of monks left the Burgundian monastery of Molesme in 1098 and established what they called *Novum monasterium*, the New Monastery. Their goal was to follow the *Rule of Saint Benedict* more carefully, but they apparently had no intention of starting what would become the first independent monastic order of their era.[6] By the time the founders in 1119 or 1120 began calling the New Monastery Cîteaux, they had acknowledged that they had done more than found a monastery. In the intervening two decades they experienced the scandal of their first abbot being ordered back by papal decree to Molesme. A number of the original monks followed him, and the remainder had to suffice with the former prior, Alberic, as abbot.

At Alberic's death in 1109 the prior, Stephen Harding, took over. He was an Englishman trained in traditional monasticism at Sherborne in the West Country. He had abandoned this monastery and lived as a wandering scholar before coming to Molesme some time before 1098. Now in the new monasticism Stephen Harding found his true vocation. He became the genius of Cîteaux, even if he is overshadowed in the history books by the person and writings of Bernard of Clairvaux. But if any single person can be called the founder of the Order of Cîteaux, it is Stephen Harding.[7]

From 1112 or 1113 Cîteaux began sending out groups of monks to found daughter houses, the first being La Ferté, Pontigny, Clairvaux and Morimond. It was during this time that the constitution of the new order was drawn up, the *Carta caritatis* or *Charter of Charity*, confirmed by Pope Callistus II at the end of 1119.[8] In an attempt to follow the *Rule of Saint Benedict* to the letter, Stephen Harding established forms of monastic life never anticipated in the Rule, which left the final authority in the monastery to the abbot. Now the abbot of each monastery participated in a network of meetings and contacts which limited his power. All abbots were obliged to attend a general chapter at

---

6 According to the *Exordium Cistercii* it was a desire to follow the *Rule* which was the central motivation for leaving Molesme. See Chrysogonus Waddell, ed., *Narrative and Legislative Texts from Early Cîteaux* (Cîteaux: Commentarii Cistercienses, 1999), 400.

7 Brian Patrick McGuire, 'Who Founded the Order of Cîteaux?', in E. Rozanne Elder, ed., *The Joy of Learning and the Love of God* (Kalamazoo, Mich.: Cistercian Publications, 1995), 389–413.

8 Waddell, ed., *Narrative and Legislative Texts*, 273.

Cîteaux once a year in September. They had to accept disciplinary measures the chapter might impose on them and their monasteries. Abbots thus gave up the sovereignty which the *Rule of Saint Benedict* gave them. In the filiation of Cîteaux, they had to accept visitation by the father abbot of their monastery and also to take care of visitations of their own daughter houses. These bonds were to be based on charity, not on finances: the very first chapter of the *Carta caritatis* specified that a mother house had no right to make collections from its daughter houses.

Cîteaux and its daughters and granddaughters developed after about 1115 a magnificent administrative system with a simple hierarchical structure. The Cistercians at the same time rediscovered the meaning of the *Rule of Saint Benedict*: 'Finding no evidence in the Rule or in the life of St Benedict that he, their teacher, had possessed churches or altars, offerings or burial dues, other men's tithes, ovens or mills, villages or peasants...they renounced all these privileges.'[9] The Cistercians thus freed themselves from the bonds and obligations that ensnared their brethren in traditional monasteries. A Cistercian author, Idung of Prüfening, summarised his order's superiority to Cluny in *Dialogus duorum monachorum* from the middle of the twelfth century.[10] Cluny and Cîteaux became rivals in asserting the superiority of different kinds of monasticism.

As abbot at Cîteaux until 1133, Stephen Harding was remembered for his fairness and piety. He would touch the door of the church on the way in to the office, thus symbolically leaving behind the cares of the monastery and opening his mind to monastic prayer. He was wise enough to recognise qualities in the young Bernard but also to criticise him for failing to remember prayers for his dead parents. We hear such stories in the great collection of Cistercian stories gathered in the last decades of the twelfth century, the *Exordium magnum cisterciense*.[11] Here it was claimed that the monastic vocation originated with Jesus and the apostles. In this sense the Cistercians thought of themselves as the truest Christians in following Christ. Inspired by Bernard of Clairvaux, they are perhaps the first and last monastic group in medieval Europe who sought to convert the entire world by bringing as many as possible into the monastery.

9 From the *Exordium parvum*, in Pauline Matarasso, trans., *The Cistercian World* (London: Penguin, 1993), 6.
10 Idung of Prüfening, *Cistercians and Cluniacs: The Case for Cîteaux* (Kalamazoo, Mich.: Cistercian Publications, 1977).
11 Bruno Griesser, ed., *Exordium magnum cisterciense sive narratio de initio cisterciensis ordinis* (Rome: Editiones cistercienses, 1961), 82–4.

Wherever Bernard went he left behind Cistercian monasteries. The story is told about him that mothers hid their sons when Bernard was in the neighbourhood.[12] Once the youths heard him preach, they would insist on joining an order that seems to have appealed strongly to members of the lower aristocracy. Such a tale says nothing about the daughters of such families, but in reality many women were joining houses that chose to live according to the Cistercian institutes. No official recognition was given to this allegiance before the end of the twelfth century, and then already in 1220 the general chapter forbade the incorporation of new women's houses into the order.

The care of the spiritual and physical needs of enclosed women, *cura mulierum*, was considered in many cases to be a burden. But there were by now a number of women's houses visited by Cistercian men who came to form close bonds with abbesses or individual nuns. The history of female Cistercian monasticism has been hidden from view for centuries, but in the last decades has begun to get the attention it deserves.[13]

The standard narrative of Cistercian origins has also been challenged in our time, most recently by Constance Hoffman Berman.[14] Her work shows how the monks developed as an order, and thus provides a welcome corrective to the view that the Cistercians were already an order practically from the time the first monks left Molesme. Berman also points out that the standard view of neat filiations with mother houses founding daughters is misleading, for many houses were already in existence before they decided to join the Cistercian Order. The spectacular case of the congregation of Savigny entering in 1147 is well known, but Berman shows how many monasteries, especially in the Midi, had long been in existence before they came to choose the Cistercian way.

Berman claims that there was no order at all before the 1150s, and it is here that I have to dissent. Such a thesis would require that the early constitutions of the Cistercian Order, especially the *Carta caritatis*, are forgeries from a later period. I see no hard evidence for such a claim. Instead I find Bernard of Clairvaux himself writing letters which assume the existence of a Cistercian Order, with authority vested in the general chapter and the abbot of Cîteaux.

---

12 *S. Bernardi Vita Prima* I.3.15, *PL* 185, col. 235: 'Jamque eo publice et privatim praedicante, matres filios abscondebant…'
13 See, for example, 'The Life of Ida the Compassionate of Nivelles, Nun of La Ramée', in Martinus Cawley, trans., *Send Me God* (Turnhout: Brepols, 2003).
14 Constance Hoffman Berman, *The Cistercian Evolution: The Invention of a Religious Order in Twelfth-Century Europe* (Philadelphia: University of Pennsylvania Press, 2000).

Bernard's witness points to the existence of the Cistercian Order from the 1120s onwards.[15]

The Cistercians were one of the great historical enterprises of Western monasticism. They attempted to live out Benedictine monasticism in its contemplative wholeness. In doing so they built buildings whose architecture reflected the simplicity and stability of the Order's identity. Even a century after their foundation, they were still sufficiently admired for their structure to be the model for other orders. The Fourth Lateran Council in 1215 required that Benedictine abbots meet regularly, on the Cistercian model, in a general chapter. Earlier attempts at such regular meetings of Benedictine houses can be seen in Denmark, under Archbishop Anders Sunesen. Even though traditional monasteries generally resisted such attempts at organisation, a process began which led to the formation of the Benedictine Order. The Cistercians can thus be seen as the makers of the Benedictines as an order.

The Cistercians not only provoked their Benedictine brethren into new forms of monastic government; they also made it unthinkable to join monasteries before adulthood. For centuries parents had been offering their sons and daughters as oblates. Now the Cistercians insisted that only an adult could make the decision to join a monastery. The usually accepted age was eighteen, even if occasional miracle stories showed Mary making exceptions possible. But the general rule for the Cistercians became the fixed norm everywhere.

Recruits to the Cistercian houses could count on the service of lay brothers. Other monastic groups had already welcomed these workers in the eleventh century. They became the first groups of peasants in the West for whom the means of salvation was made easily available. The lay brothers often settled on granges far from the monastery and looked after flocks of sheep or brought in the harvest. Cistercian lay brothers were outstanding in making good use of marginal land and making it profitable. The monks liked to think that they cleared virginal land and made the desert bloom. In reality they often bought up land from peasants or cleared the peasants off land given to the monks. The Cistercians were skilled at idealising their own achievements. Apart from their propaganda, however, the monks and their lay brothers were eminently successful in transforming the countryside in their image and likeness.

---

15 Brian Patrick McGuire, 'Bernard's Concept of a Cistercian Order: Vocabulary and Context', *Cîteaux: Commentarii Cistercienses* 54 (2003), 225–49.

## The Augustinian canons: success in modesty

The *Rule of Saint Augustine* was 'discovered' in the second half of the eleventh century. Various writings about living a monastic life were placed together with a letter of Augustine to some nuns.[16] Even more so than the *Rule of Saint Benedict*, Augustine's recommendations were very general, but they had the prestige of his name and reputation. Augustine's own way of life after he became bishop in common with fellow priests provided a pattern for canons of cathedrals and other churches.

As Richard Southern has pointed out, communities of Augustinian canons could flourish without the huge investments required for making a traditional Benedictine abbey: 'The canons eschewed elaborate buildings and ornaments because they were generally too poor for ostentation.'[17] The Cistercians had turned away from such showiness out of choice, while the Augustinians had no choice. Many of their communities were tiny, with a few canons, and with hardly any worldly possessions.

The *Rule of Saint Augustine*, however, provided the foundation for a successful new form of monasticism. Some communities concentrated on pastoral tasks, while others were more contemplative. The abbey of Arrouaise in the Artois became the head of a congregation inspired by the Cistercians but under Augustine's Rule and emphasising enclosure and austerity of life.[18] In Paris the congregation of Saint Victor also followed the Augustinian way and made itself noticed with a number of outstanding teachers. Saint Victor reformed the secular canons of the Paris church of Sainte Geneviève and brought in Augustine's Rule. William, regular canon of Sainte Geneviève, was called to Denmark in 1165 by his former school friend, Absalon, then bishop of Roskilde. Absalon was concerned about a group of unruly canons living on an island in the Roskilde fjord and holding too many parties. William after his arrival created order and within a few years moved the canons to a less isolated location, Æbelholt.[19]

Here the canons were dangerously close to the Cistercian monks of the abbey of Esrum, fifteen kilometres to the north. William's letter collection, a

---

16 George Lawless, *Augustine of Hippo and his Monastic Rule* (Oxford: Clarendon Press, 1987).
17 R. W. Southern, *Western Society and the Church in the Middle Ages* (Harmondsworth: Penguin, 1970), 251.
18 Ludo Milis, *L'ordre des chanoines réguliers d'Arrouaise* (Bruges: De Tempel, 1969).
19 M. Cl. Gertz, *Vitae Sanctorum Danorum* (Copenhagen: Gad, 1908–12), 300–24.

unique source for medieval Denmark, indicates that differences and disagreements were worked out. There must have been some division of duties: the Cistercians concentrated on the contemplative life, while the Augustinians were pastoral. Written sources provide little information about either, but Æbelholt's role in society has been made evident through archaeological findings. Among the canons were men who were skilled in medicine, for excavations have revealed the care given to wounded warriors or women experiencing difficult childbirths. At the same time the canons would have provided for the spiritual and sacramental needs of the pilgrims who, after Abbot William's death in 1203, began to flock to his grave.

The Augustinians had every reason to emphasise their devotion to *vita apostolica*. They lived together as monastic communities but usually also made themselves available to the laity in dispensing the sacraments and providing acts of charity. The Cistercians chose a select group of peasants and incorporated them into their monasteries as lay brothers. The Augustinians made their spiritual benefits available to all the laity.

The Premonstratensians also belong to the family of Augustinian canons. They were founded by a canon of Xanten in the Rhineland, Norbert, who resigned his benefices and began to live as a hermit preacher. In 1121 he and his followers made a promise to live in accord with the Gospels and the *Rule of Saint Augustine*. In the Augustinian mould the Premonstratensians combined community life with a pastoral mission. At the same time, however, their liturgy borrowed from the Cistercians, and the canons have a similarly contemplative orientation. At first there were a number of double monasteries, but eventually the canons decided not to involve themselves with women. In 1198 the order decided to debar women from entering.

During the second half of the twelfth century the Premonstratensians distanced themselves from their initial missionary form of *vita apostolica*. They became more contemplative. Norbert had been a friend of Bernard, and the two orders considered themselves to be cousins. Another order that had double monasteries was the Gilbertines, which were limited to England. Their founder, Gilbert of Sempringham, asked for his houses to be taken into the Cistercian Order, which refused him.

## Soldier-monks and hermits: seeking the perfect life

The Cistercians were more positive in their dealings with the Templars. In 1119 Hugh de Payns, a knight from Champagne, organised his companions into soldier-monks. Their first duty was to protect pilgrims in the Holy Land, but they also had an office to sing. The Knights of the Temple found their vocation in fighting Muslims by day and praying at night. Bernard of Clairvaux considered them worthy to be celebrated in his *De laude novae militiae* (*In Praise of the New Knighthood*). Here he contrasted the secular knight, caught up in creature comforts, with the slim, spiritually sleek knight dedicated to the defence of Jerusalem.

After the fall of the city to Saladin in 1187, the Templars did their best to find new functions. Their headquarters in London and Paris and other major cities had already begun to function as depositories for the wealth of crusaders. The Templars came to be numbered among the first bankers of Western Europe. In the end the order's undoing was the result of its economic success. King Philip the Fair of France and his henchmen in 1307 trumped up charges against the Templars in order to get hold of their assets. For the first but not the last time in European history false propaganda was used to destroy a monastic movement.[20]

Monks were at risk because society invests its hopes and dreams in their words and actions. One movement which never disappointed its 'investors' was the Carthusians.[21] Their founder Bruno, a teacher at Cologne, was fascinated by the stories of the hermits of the desert in Late Antiquity. In about 1080 he joined a group of hermits in the forest of Colan. From here he found an isolated spot in the Alps for his hermitage. Soon after he left for Calabria, but his successor Guigo, the dean of Grenoble, was elected prior in 1109. The house was moved down the valley after a terrible avalanche in 1132 and became what we know as the Grande Chartreuse. The Carthusians lived in individual cells as hermits and had their food brought to them by lay brothers who inserted the tray in a slot. The monks would meet once a day in church and on Sundays would have more extended contact. Communities remained small: twelve to fifteen brothers, who copied books as a form of manual labour.

The Carthusians came to be known in the later Middle Ages for their mystical spirituality. By the end of the thirteenth century some of them were abandoning their isolated locations and establishing monasteries in the

---

20 Malcolm Barber, *The New Knighthood: A History of the Order of the Temple* (Cambridge: Cambridge University Press, 1996), and Desmond Seward, *The Monks of War: The Military Religious Orders* (London: Penguin, 1995).

21 There are few general treatments in English of the Carthusians, except for Robin Bruce Lockhart, *Halfway to Heaven: The Hidden Life of the Carthusians* (Kalamazoo, Mich.: Cistercian Publications, 1999). The series *Analecta carthusiana*, edited by James Hogg, has published hundreds of works of Carthusian life and spirituality.

midst of cities. Here they managed to continue to live as hermits and to impress their donors with their robust spirituality. The order was little interested in miracles or saints. The one Carthusian saint, Hugh of Avalon, who became bishop of Lincoln, 'thought miracles were the last thing to admire or wish to emulate'. For him 'the mysterious and wonderful works of creation' were 'the one universal miracle'.[22]

## The mendicant orders: the able Dominicans

The foundation of the Franciscans and the Dominicans shortly after 1200 resulted from a new surge of religious feeling and desire for *vita apostolica*, in imitation of the lives of the apostles. The story of Dominic is less extra-ordinary – and thus more easily understandable – than that of Francis. Dominic was a canon who followed his bishop, Diego of Osma, into the Midi, where both of them were shocked by the success of the Cathar heretics. The only opposition to these preachers came from Cistercian abbots commis-sioned by the pope and unable to get their message across.

The Cistercians had never learned to preach, except in chapter, and it is no wonder they were unsuited to the rough and tumble of live confrontation with men whose way of life may have seemed more devout and ascetic than that of pompous abbots. Dominic was much better equipped: he had been living as a canon under the *Rule of Saint Augustine*, and it is this rule which provided the basis of the order that he initiated. The Fourth Lateran Council in 1215 tried to prevent a too rapid growth of monastic orders by requiring that any new foundations make use of an already existing rule. Thus the Dominicans fulfilled the promise first shown by the Premonstratensians as an order of canons dedicated to preaching.

From the start the Dominicans seem to have been at ease with their vocation. We call them mendicants because they, like the Franciscans, begged for alms. But they were primarily, as they called themselves, the Order of Preachers. Everything in their training and convent life was meant to facilitate the ability to make good sermons to convey the Gospel to the laity. As formulated in the constitutions of 1236, nothing was to get in the way of studying and sermonising: 'Let all who have been appointed to preach or study have no duty or responsibility for managing temporal goods, so that they are able better and more effectively to fulfil the spiritual service enjoined

22 *Magna vita sancti Hugonis*, vol. 1, ed. Decima L. Douie and Hugh Farmer (London: Thomas Nelson, 1961), 90–1.

to them.' Similarly, time spent in church was to be cut back in order to leave more time for study: 'They shall be able in their cells to read, write, pray, sleep and even work through the night if they wish, for study's sake.'[23]

Dominic and the first friar preachers were determined to make it possible for the word of God to be preached, heard and understood. Thus many Dominican churches, such as St Catherine's in Ribe in Southern Denmark, have no transept. The simple hall shape was intended to improve acoustics and facilitate the hearing of the sermon. There is no doubt that such architecture was in keeping with the wishes of Dominic. He is often portrayed as rather anonymous, but in the affidavits given about him for his canonisation, he emerges as an affable, passionate man, who believed very much in poverty as a way of life.[24] He lacks the fanatic concerns of Francis, and comes across as a gentle man of organisation: 'I never heard an idle or harmful word from him, whether of flattery or of detraction.'[25]

The Dominican way of representative government was unprecedented in its time. The prior of a convent was directly elected by the brothers in chapter. They also elected a companion, *socius*, to accompany the prior to the annual provincial chapter. A special session of the provincial chapter attended by priors plus two representatives from each priory elected the prior provincial. In order to keep business under control, the Dominicans imitated Cistercian practice and delegated some matters to four 'diffinitors'. The general chapter of the order met yearly, with the master general and one representative sent from each provincial chapter. For two years in a row, elected representatives of each province were in attendance, but in the third year, it was the provincial prior who came. A principle of rotation secured representativity but also guaranteed leadership.

Any new statute had to be accepted by three successive chapters. An enlarged session of the general chapter elected the master-general. This elaborate but still simple form of government was the achievement of Dominic and his successor, Jordan of Saxony. But the Dominicans were more than effective governors of their own affairs. Behind their rational intelligence is also human passion, as can be seen in Jordan of Saxony's description of Brother Henry of Maastricht: 'It was easy for him to touch the hearts of everyone, and he was so affable to everyone that, if you only spent even a little time with him, you would come away thinking that you

---

23  Rosalind B. Brooke, ed., *The Coming of the Friars* (London: Allen & Unwin, 1975), 199.

24  Simon Tugwell, ed., *Early Dominicans: Selected Writings* (New York: Paulist Press, and London: SPCK, 1982), 66–93.

25  'Testimony of Brother Frugerio of Pennabilli', in Tugwell, ed., *Early Dominicans*, 84.

were the friend he loved most in the world.'[26] The same Jordan also expressed his love for Diana of Andalò in her Dominican convent in Bologna.[27] His letters to her indicate that the Dominicans continued the male–female friendships of the religious life that had formerly characterised the Cistercian rapprochement with women.[28]

The Dominicans seemed almost always to do the right thing, and so it is no wonder that they quickly became papal darlings, heading up the new inquisition that was to be set up in dioceses where there was suspicion of heresy. Until now such investigations had been the responsibility of bishops, but once the Cathars had scored their successes, it seemed necessary for the pope to take responsibility in exposing heretical beliefs and practices. By 1230 the Dominicans were taking their place as papal legates to carry out a new and more effective inquisition.[29]

Even the Dominicans could sometimes cause controversy. At the University of Paris they, together with the Franciscans, began taking over chairs of theology. The secular masters, who had succeeded in organising themselves into an academic guild, resented the fact that their own positions were now going to outsiders. At the same time they must have noticed how effective the friars were in their teaching and administration: their life in an order provided a material and spiritual foundation that the secular masters lacked.

Outside the universities the friars caused similar resentment in many town parishes, whose pastors had to put up with Dominicans and Franciscans who were accused of luring away their parishioners. It was bad enough that friars preached at the town square, but soon they were building their own churches. Hearing confessions and administering the oil of the sick, the friars ended up burying the men and women for whom they had cared. This attachment brought testamentary gifts, income that was thus kept out of the hands of parish priests. For all their seeming gentleness the Dominicans could be rough competitors in the university or in the parishes.

---

26 Jordan of Saxony, *On the Beginnings of the Order of Preachers*, ed. Simon Tugwell (Dublin: Dominican Publications, 1982), 19.

27 Tugwell, ed., *Early Dominicans*, 401–8. Also Brian Patrick McGuire, *Friendship and Community: The Monastic Experience* (Kalamazoo, Mich.: Cistercian Publications, 1988), 394–8.

28 'The Cistercians and the Transformation of Monastic Friendships', in Brian Patrick McGuire, *Friendship and Faith: Cistercian Men, Women, and their Stories, 1100–1250* (Aldershot: Ashgate, 2002).

29 Edward Peters, *Inquisition* (Berkeley: University of California Press, 1988), 52–8.

## The mendicant orders: the problematic Franciscans

The Franciscans, like the Dominicans, came to experience problems in university and parish life, but their difficulties were much more fundamental. They had a founder whose words and impact were controversial and disturbing. Everything that Francis of Assisi said and wrote was a challenge to the way the Christian Church had functioned until that time. In marrying Lady Poverty he insisted that the imitation of Christ meant a literal abandonment of all worldly goods. To become a follower of Francis meant leaving everything behind.

The difficulty of capturing the true spirit of Francis and early Franciscan poverty reveals itself in the fact that no one seemed able to write a satisfying life of the founder. There were several attempts to do so. Thomas of Celano made two tries, and then in the 1260s Bonaventure as master-general of the order made his own version and tried to get all earlier ones destroyed. At a general chapter in 1244 the brothers who had known Francis were encouraged to record how they remembered him. One of the stories contributed by the three surviving witnesses (Leo, Rufino and Angelo) tells how Francis once shared some grapes with a friar who was ill. Not wanting the man to be embarrassed by the thought of having a special privilege, Francis ate too so that his companion 'should not be embarrassed at eating alone'.[30] Such a story emphasises an ability to bend rules for the sake of individual needs.

In other situations, however, Francis could feel compromised by the ways of the world. There was a story of Francis angrily trying to destroy the roof of a house built for him by the commune of Assisi. He only stopped pulling off tiles when told that the house belonged to the commune, saying, 'If the house is yours I have no wish to touch it.'[31] Here we have an early instance of what would later be called the *usus pauper*: the friars allowing themselves to use in a modest way what others lent them. This might appear a solution, but for those who insisted on absolute poverty, this device could be seen as a surrender of ideals.

Francis' *Testament* was his attempt to ensure that the friars remained faithful to the Rule he had given them. In forbidding them to gloss over it, he thought he could maintain the purity of the original vocation. The very name of the new order, the little or lesser brothers (*Ordo fratrum minorum*) was meant to

---

30 Rosalind B. Brooke, ed., *Scripta Leonis, Rufini et Angeli Sociorum S. Francisci* (Oxford: Clarendon Press, 1970), 95.
31 Brooke, ed., *Scripta Leonis*, 107.

emphasise the humility and lack of pretension of its members. The name was a direct riposte to the pride of the Italian merchant class from which Francis came. The historian Lester Little has shown how the Franciscans responded to the new profit economy that flourished in Northern Italy from the end of the twelfth century.[32]

As with biographies of Francis, rules for his order went through several versions: the lost *propositum vitae* of 1209/10; the rule given in 1221, *Regula non bullata*; and the *Regula bullata* of 1223, which had to be written a second time after the first version was lost, at least according to Bonaventure.[33] In the *Regula non bullata* as well as in the 'Exhortation to the Praise of God', we find a medley of biblical references. In repeating the praise of God to be found in biblical passages, Francis expressed his own desire to pay homage to the Creator through creation. He did the same when he preached to the birds or lectured the wolf of Gubbio.

Francis is an attractive but difficult person, and his legacy is one of disagreement and division, especially in disputes that continued for a century between conventuals, who accepted poverty as largely symbolic, and spirituals, who insisted on literal observance.[34] Numerous popes made declarations for the one or other interpretation of poverty, while John XXII in 1323 tried to bring the debate to an end, especially in his declaration that Christ and the apostles did not live in absolute poverty.

Franciscan dissension should not distract from the fact that the new order spread all over Europe. We have narratives of the arrival of the first friars in Germany and England. The very first group to cross the Alps knew no German and lacked an interpreter. The brothers discovered that the word 'ja' usually had good results, but when they used it in reply to the question whether they were heretics, they ran into trouble.[35] The next group had an interpreter. The Franciscans trusted their own enthusiasm but could also learn from their mistakes.

Franciscan narratives take us to the ends of Asia, with the missionary brothers who set out to convert the Great Khan. Like Francis, who had preached before a Muslim sultan, the friars took seriously the quest to convert

---

32 L. K. Little, *Religious Poverty and the Profit Economy in Medieval Europe* (Ithaca, NY: Cornell University Press, 1978).

33 Regis J. Armstrong and Ignatius C. Brady, trans., *Francis and Clare: The Complete Works* (New York: Paulist Press, 1982), 107.

34 David Burr, *The Spiritual Franciscans* (University Park: Pennsylvania State University Press, 2001).

35 See the account of Jordan of Giano in Placid Hermann, trans., *Thirteenth Century Chronicles* (Chicago: Franciscan Herald Press), ch. 5, 22.

the infidel. At a time when the Mongols were threatening Western Europe, the Franciscans were heading East. They also could be successful in less dramatic ways, as the brothers established themselves in practically every town in the West. We can see the pattern in the kingdom of Denmark, where the Franciscans arrived in 1232 and within a few decades had established twenty houses for men, while the Dominicans founded thirteen priories.[36] Apparently there was some kind of agreement to avoid excess competition. In smaller towns only one order established a convent. Thus in Western Zealand the town of Kalundborg hosted the Franciscans, while Holbæk about 40 kilometres to the east had a Dominican convent.

The narrative of the Franciscans and Dominicans is incomplete without naming the second and third orders: the nuns and the laity. The friars were the first monastic-religious societies in the Christian West to offer their way of life to lay people, who could remain in the world but find inspiration in a confraternity. Dominican and Franciscan nuns probably outnumbered the friars. Francis himself is incomplete without his Clare. He worried about his bonds with women, but Clare did not allow him to forget her and her monastic experiment. She accepted enclosure as a requirement for women's houses, but her great love seems to have been the call to poverty she had heard in Francis: 'Let the sisters not appropriate anything, neither a house nor a place nor anything at all; instead as pilgrims and strangers in this world who serve the Lord in poverty and humility, let them confidently send for alms.'[37] The Poor Clares became a contemplative and enclosed order.

## An embarrassment of riches: developments to c. 1350

It is traditional in monastic history to consider the question of when and where a decline of standards might have taken place. Well before 1200 the courtier and gossip Walter Map was attacking the Cistercians for failing to live up to their ideals. Some historians would date decadence in this order already from the death of Bernard in 1153. The Franciscans – because of their prominence – have even more been a target for criticism and even ridicule. There is the legend of Robin Hood with the corpulent Friar Tuck. Or we can turn to naughty Franciscans in Boccaccio, as in the story of friar Alberto who seduced

---

36 Jørgen Nybo Rasmussen, *Die Franziskaner in den nordischen Ländern im Mittelalter* (Kevelaer: Butzon & Bercker, 2002).
37 Regis J. Armstrong, ed., *Clare of Assisi: Early Documents* (Saint Bonaventure, N.Y.: Franciscan Institute, 1993), 73.

women by convincing them that they should receive his carnal visitations as manifestations of the Archangel Gabriel.

In savouring such stories, it is important to remember that new forms of monasticism as well as mendicant orders continued to spread right into the fourteenth century. There is no space here for the story of the Carmelites or the Augustinian friars, but churchmen felt so deluged by new orders of monks, nuns and friars that there was a conscious attempt in the later thirteenth century to cut back on recognised orders.[38] It is impressive how many monastic and mendicant institutions medieval Europe could support. Monks, canons and friars continued to make themselves useful by providing for the sick, lodging travellers, dispensing the sacraments, preaching and especially by providing memorials of prayer for patrons rich and poor.

And what about the women? They were present, even if they were theoretically shut off from the rest of society. Francis without his Clare is unthinkable, as is Jordan of Saxony without his Diana. The beguines, dealt with in Walter Simons' chapter, provide another dimension of religious life in community for women (as well as for men).

Wherever there were monks or friars there emerged stories to provide admonition and encouragement. The first edificatory tales were set down by Cluniacs and Cistercians, in the miraculous mould that Gregory the Great had provided in his *Dialogues*. The friars took over many of these tales, sometimes literally, as with the Cistercian story of how Mary hid her monks beneath her cope. Monks became Dominican friars in the mendicant version. Medieval life was rich in the telling of good stories, and monks and friars did their best to keep them in circulation.[39]

There was always a fear of slipping away from the standards of the founders and a desire to return to them. We can see such an effort in the papacy of Benedict XII (1334–42), much maligned as the inquisitor Jacques Fournier. Benedict had first been abbot of Cistercian Fontfroide before becoming bishop of Pamiers and spending his time listening to the endless narratives of the villagers of Montaillou. As pope, however, he devoted himself to reforming monastic orders and especially the Cistercians. His decree, *Fulgens sicut stella*,

---

38 As at the Second Council of Lyon, 1274, nr. 23, in dealing with 'excessive diversity of religious orders'. See G. Alberigo, *Conciliorum Oecumenicorum Decreta* (Basel: Herder, 1962), 302–3.

39 Brian Patrick McGuire, 'Written Sources and Cistercian Inspiration in Caesarius of Heisterbach', in *Friendship and Faith*. Also McGuire, 'Cistercian Storytelling – A Living Tradition: Surprises in the World of Research', *Cistercian Studies Quarterly* 39 (2004), 281–309.

tried to inspire his fellow monks to return to the standards of Stephen Harding and Bernard of Clairvaux.[40]

Anyone who has visited the monastic ruin of Rievaulx, with its graceful arches perched against the Yorkshire hills, or who has attended the monastic hours at a Trappist Cistercian house in any corner of the world can experience something of what once was and to some extent still is in monastic life. The same is the case with the Dominicans and the Franciscans, both of whom continue in their medieval commitment to learning and to preaching. Bare ruined choirs and living communities carry on old values and make them new. Monasticism, unlike so much else from the Middle Ages, is still with us.

40 J.-B. Mahn, *Le pape Benoît XII et les cisterciens* (Paris: Champion, 1949).

PART II

*

# FORGING A CHRISTIAN WORLD,

## 1200–1300

# 5

# The theological framework

LESLEY SMITH

The thirteenth century was one of the most theologically vibrant periods in the history of the Christian church. It was in this period that the subject matter of theology (usually called by contemporaries *sacra doctrina* or *sacra pagina*) was more closely defined, and that theology became a subject for study in educational institutions. Yet the ideas that made up the doctrines of theology were, for the most part, static. How could they, indeed, be anything else? Christian doctrine was largely worked out and agreed upon by the Councils and theologians of the early-church ('patristic') period in the fourth and fifth centuries, which, even as they defined the canon of Scripture, drew out of it the statements of faith that made up the creeds and the fundamentals of sacramental life. The basic structure of creation, sin, incarnation, grace, redemption, Trinity, sacrament and eschaton was in place long before the thirteenth century, and essential change was neither possible nor desirable to a belief system steeped in the concept of the authority of the past.

In this deepest sense of fundamental doctrine, then, the theological framework of the thirteenth-century church was, and could be, no different from that of its predecessors. What changed, however, and what justifies the thirteenth century's claim to reverberate in Christian theological history, was a double evolution: firstly, a refinement of what it meant to study theology; alongside, secondly, an opening up of the arena in which theological thinking might have some practical effect, with a broadening of the recipient constituency for its pronouncements.

It may seem to be a paradoxical, if not impossible, statement that Christian theology had become more comprehensive. How could it reach an area wider than the Christian church? How could its statements encompass more than the meaning and conduct of life in this world and the next? In theory, of course, such questions were merely rhetorical, and there was no wider sphere; but in practice the situation was rather different. Up to the thirteenth century, the church was thought of, and could realistically only think of itself, as little more than one part of that medieval division of society into the triad of those who worked, those who fought and those who prayed; but the thirteenth century saw the confluence of a set of circumstances which allowed this role to change. The expansion of the church's ambitions for its place in the world, which had begun with the aspirations of Pope Gregory VII (1073–85) and were furthered in the twelfth century, was at last able to be realised. The church embarked on an era of 'big government' – the so-called 'papal monarchy' – in which it not only attempted to make its mark on the broad canvas of the international political scene, but also aimed to have effects in depth, reaching down into the lives of the ordinary members of Christendom, and regulating their deeds, words and, if possible, thoughts.

The theological framework of Christianity in the thirteenth century was, then, especially important because it formed the skeleton of a body which was growing, flexing its muscles, and was prepared to fight off whatever, inside or outside the body, it perceived as a threat to its survival. Although the theological answer to the question 'what is church?' was not substantially different from that which Augustine would have given eight hundred years earlier, political, social and cultural realities meant that the reach and scope of the church and its doctrines encompassed the daily lives – literally the hopes and fears – of the population of most of Western Europe.

Why did these changes come about? Were they driven by external forces or by the internal logic of theology itself? A pivotal sequence in these impulses can be discerned in the reforms of the church promulgated by popes Leo IX (1048–54) and Gregory VII. Gregory's determination to have the church recognised as the premier force in the Christian world, along with his attempts to improve the moral standards of the clergy, may be judged to have failed in his own time: for he died after being forced into exile by secular political rivals. But the changes that his ambitions wrought in the longer term have led to their being named after him, the Gregorian Reform. And as we shall see, what Gregory could not himself achieve, his thirteenth-century successor, Innocent III (1198–1216), was to bring to fruition. A lasting effect of Gregorian policies was the increasing clericalisation of the church and the exclusion of lay people from most of its organisation, appointments and decision-making. In time, this had as a partial concomitant the effect of heightening lay people's awareness of their own individual salvation, and their desire to take a greater part in working towards it. Both sides of this clerical–lay divide were strengthened in the century after Gregory's papacy, in the phenomenon known as the twelfth-century Renaissance.

One of the features of this Renaissance was urban life, which experienced a growth and popularity it had not known since the Roman era. New towns grew up on old sites, were promoted as population centres, or simply sprang up spontaneously in favourable positions or on trade routes. The church and theology both affected and were affected by this move from country to town. The church had a somewhat ambivalent theology of town life, for whilst the Bible offered the malignant examples of the cities of Babel or Sodom in this world, its picture of the hoped-for end of human life was the heavenly Jerusalem, the city of peace. Church leaders began to realise that, in the face of a rather feeble system of parishes, monastic communities whose aim was to live outside the world offered inadequate service to the body of Christ. It was no longer sufficient for professional churchmen to pray on behalf of everyone else; intense groups of (mostly) lay believers were springing up like mushrooms after rain, and if their theology was to be kept within the bounds of orthodoxy, they needed education and pastoral care. Towns were places where new ideas might take hold, and the influx of strangers and those with no ties to the familiar could easily threaten to subvert Christian beliefs. The church needed a new ministry to the believing laity and to those who professed other faiths. It must take seriously the religious faith of ordinary people, providing structure and nurture; if it did not, there were others who were all too ready to step in.

In another way, too, the monasteries were losing their dominance. Although, like many creative enterprises, 'regular' life (i.e., life under a religious rule) blossomed during the twelfth century, nevertheless new educational arenas meant that monasteries lost some of the functions and purposes they had made particularly their own. In theology, monasteries had a double disposition: firstly, almost all official theological thinking was done by monks producing contemplative treatises on biblical books or themes, or on aspects of Christian life especially relevant to the cloister, for example, meditations on the Song of Songs, or works on virginity or on spiritual friendship; and secondly, monastery schools provided much of the higher education available for those who might themselves go on to think about or write works of theology. During the twelfth century, both of these roles were opened up to others, so that by 1200 there was a greater variety of actors and, perhaps more importantly, audiences, for the theological stage. New works of theology were no longer mostly produced by monks writing for other monks, as the outcome of a life of ruminative study and prayer; the Bible and theology had become a valid subject for teaching and examination at the new secular schools or universities of urban Europe.

Education had been provided around cathedral cloisters for centuries, but in the late-twelfth century these 'secular' (so-called because their teachers, whilst being clerics, were not monks) cathedral schools came to the fore as providers and regulators of higher education. Some schools in important urban settings became known outside their locality and developed specialities which attracted students from far and wide. For theology, the schools at Paris, clustered around the cathedral of Notre Dame and the abbey of Augustinian canons at St Victor on the Left Bank (still called the Latin Quarter after the language of the schools) were pre-eminent. By 1200, anyone who aspired to the best education in theology made their way to Paris.

By 1200, too, Christendom had a new pope. Innocent III was an Italian who had studied theology in Paris and – perhaps – canon law in Bologna.[1] He combined intelligence and determination with analytical skill, and seeing the dangers and opportunities of the times, he set out boldly to confront them. Circumstances and his own gifts allowed him to come closest to realising Gregory VII's dream of a dominant church. To give his vision of an invigorated and confident church a permanent strength by means of a more controlling central authority, he convened a new Council of the church at the Lateran palace in Rome in 1215. The legislation enacted at Lateran IV, as it is known, deals with relations with the Eastern church, and condemns heretics; but crucially it also lays out the way that clergy and laity should, together, make the body of Christ on earth. Bishops are reminded of their duty, especially with respect to teaching and preaching; and the laity, both men and women, are enjoined to make a private confession to their parish priest and to receive the eucharist at least once every year. Here are recognised in full the consequences and responsibilities of Gregory VII's clerical–lay division of the church, with clergy bound to make serious provision for those in their care, and lay people similarly charged with – or permitted, depending on one's viewpoint – an active contribution to the business of being a Christian.

To make this ideal a reality, Innocent appreciated the need to train existing parish clergy more effectively, and for those clergy to live up to standards of behaviour increasingly expected by the church and by lay people, who saw their own priests often acting more poorly than the leaders of other quasi-Christian sects or those of other faiths. He used bishops and legates who could

---

1 For Innocent, see B. Bolton, *Innocent III: Studies on Papal Authority and Pastoral Care* (Aldershot: Variorum, 1995); C. Morris, *The Papal Monarchy: The Western Church from 1050–1250* (Oxford: Clarendon Press, 1989); J. E. Sayers, *Innocent III: Leader of Europe 1198–1216* (London: Longman, 1994).

act as his lieutenants on the ground; often, like him, they had been students or masters in Paris, and were influenced by a towering figure of late-twelfth-century moral theology, Peter the Chanter. Peter had pioneered the use of biblical interpretation and theological thinking for practical moral purposes in lay contexts, considering such issues as usury, prostitution and the just war. The gifted biblical scholar and preacher Stephen Langton (c. 1155–1228), master in Paris and archbishop of Canterbury, and the teacher and cardinal legate Robert Courçon (d. 1219) were both able to put a theology of pastoral care to work in practice, even before the canons of Lateran IV were framed. They represent Innocent's willingness to use academically orientated theologians to address the practical and moral problems of the church.[2]

When a new group of men appeared, offering to carry the faith to the laity in new ways, Innocent saw a God-given chance: he recognised the mendicant followers of Francis of Assisi (1181/2–1226) and Dominic Guzman (c. 1171–1221) as, in their different ways, the means to spearhead the church's fight for souls. As Stephen Langton and Robert Courçon furthered the aims of Lateran IV in their own ecclesiastical legislation, so two great bishop-theologians of the next generation encouraged the friars working in their dioceses to satisfy the spiritual needs of their people. Robert Grosseteste (c. 1170–1253), bishop of the largest diocese in England, Lincoln, had the burgeoning schools at Oxford under his control. Dominican friars had arrived in Oxford in 1221, Franciscans in 1224, making their way deliberately to the schools there. Grosseteste had acted as tutor to the Franciscans in Oxford before he became a bishop, and he continued to support them and their ministry whilst promulgating legislation concerning the pastoral care of the laity and the training and morals of the clergy. As well, he wrote his own treatises on confession and penance for clergy use. Across the Channel, Bishop William of Auvergne (c. 1180–1249) in Paris was a similar supporter of the mendicants. He was a professor in the schools when he was made bishop, and was also the author of a wide range of theological works, including treatises for the use of clergy on the sacraments, confession and penance, and preaching.[3] Writing on confession, these two secular bishops were drawing on a tradition of works for the use of confessors

---

2 For Peter and his circle, see J. W. Baldwin, *Masters, Princes and Merchants: The Social Views of Peter the Chanter and his Circle* (2 vols., Princeton: Princeton University Press, 1970). For pastoral care more generally, see L. E. Boyle, *Pastoral Care, Clerical Education and Canon Law, 1200–1400* (London: Variorum, 1981); J. W. Goering, *William de Montibus (c. 1140–1213): The Schools and the Literature of Pastoral Care* (Toronto: Pontifical Institute of Mediaeval Studies, 1992).

3 See N. Valois, *Guillaume d'Auvergne* (Paris: Alphonse Picard, 1880).

which had an important revival around the time of Lateran IV. Without the support, approval and encouragement of Robert and William, and bishops like them, the development of practical pastoral theology would have been quite different. And as it turned out, Innocent's seal of approval for the Franciscans and Dominicans was to provide more than simply the stimulus for the evangelical and pastoral momentum of the church; much more fundamentally, the Orders were to set the course for academic theology for the rest of the thirteenth century.

From its inception, Dominic's Order of Preachers was envisaged by him as a group of men trained specifically to teach and preach the orthodox faith. It is no surprise that, in 1218, barely three years after Innocent's approval of their enterprise, the Dominicans had set up a house in Paris and were eager to learn from the schools. Their establishment turned out to be a two-way street, for not only did they want to learn from the best theologians, but the best scholars began to want to learn from them. The Preachers were the first university chaplains: their house in Bologna attracted both students and teachers into the Order, and at Paris they had similar success. In 1230, John of St Giles, master of theology, became a Dominican, whilst continuing his university teaching. The Franciscans were quick to join in, and they too turned heads: around 1235, Alexander of Hales, like John an established academic, took the habit of the Order of Friars Minor mid-sermon, climbing back into the pulpit in a gesture of typical Franciscan theatricality. These were to be the first of a long line; from that time on, the friars began a steady movement towards dominance of the theology faculty and of theological writing. Mendicant scholars coming into the university in the late 1220s and early 1230s were not inventing from scratch. For example, around 1216, the secular master, Thomas of Chobham, had written a very popular *Summa confessorum*, a pragmatic manual for priests needing to fulful their Lateran IV obligations.[4] Rather, the friars grasped the existing situation and used their considerable organisational and distributional powers to stretch their influence far beyond the schools.

Whereas the audience for theology expounded by monks was largely one of other monks, the friars saw their audience as the whole world. The sense of audience is always present in works by mendicants. They developed a new, less formally exegetical preaching style and produced books of sermon *exempla* – stories and jokes intended, in Bonaventure's (c. 1217–74) words, to make the lesson 'stick in your mind'; and they responded to the money

---

4 Thomas of Chobham, *Thomae de Chobham: Summa confessorum*, ed. F. Broomfield (Analecta mediaevalia Namurcensia 25; Louvain and Paris: Nauwelaerts, 1968).

economy of the thirteenth century by incorporating and sometimes parodying its vocabulary of debt and payment, profit and reward into the relationship of God and humankind. When, around 1230, the granting of indulgences became more common, the language used to defend them was of storing up credit in the treasury of merit. The vocation of the laity was increasingly valued. Both orders of friars developed 'Third Orders' – attenuated Rules of life for lay people – and confraternities of laymen were formed to practise the works of corporal mercy. Married life began to be valued as a means to salvation, and an elevated theology of the body was manifested in various ways, from the introduction of the feast of Corpus Christi in 1264 to new interest in religious processions and drama, or the use of the rosary for prayer (erroneously attributed to Dominic) – all ways in which the body, and not simply the mind, might worship.

Although secular clerics continued to teach in the university, the friars very quickly began to dominate professional theology. This did not happen without complaint from secular academics, but scholars of both orders benefited from being part of an international organisation which had a stake in producing an elite of excellently educated teachers whose work would be an engine for the practical ministry of the rest of the Order. The Order could support them materially, and arrange for the copying and distribution of their works, and its missionary needs were the source of innovation and creativity in the types of works produced. In addition, the Order provided them with a steady stream of pupils, successive generations of eager listeners, ready to discuss issues and solutions with the pointed interest of those who would soon be arguing and debating in the outside world. The mendicant ideal of communal poverty, embraced in order to live like Christ and the Apostles and allowing the friars to travel light, proved hugely popular. The best and brightest no longer flocked to join Bernard in Cistercian solitude; they joined the missionary shock troops of Francis and Dominic. The great theological names of the thirteenth century are mendicants: Albert the Great, Bonaventure, Thomas Aquinas. Their works had the lasting advantage over their talented secular contemporaries of being kept 'in print' as, in effect, set texts for their confrères.

Nevertheless, the focus on practical, pastoral theology was not absolute, or rather, it was not separable from more abstract theological thinking. The Dominican Hugh of St Cher (d. 1263) sums up the relationship: 'first the bow is bent in study...then the arrow is loosed in preaching'.[5] The ideas that were

---

5  The phrase is taken from his commentary on Gen 9.13, referring to the rainbow.

taken out from the schools were based on ground-breaking research by the academic elite. They pursued knowledge on a number of fronts. All theology had to be based on the foundation of the Bible and its interpretation; but whereas much patristic and Carolingian exegesis went straight to the discernible moral or spiritual lessons, the twelfth and thirteenth centuries developed a new interest in the literal or historical sense of the text. Without a correct literal foundation, no reliable moral meaning could be expounded. The building of this foundation involved learning biblical languages, or finding those, often Jews, who could interpret, and it meant trying to understand the original context and meaning of biblical geography and customs: Jerome's little works on the interpretation of Hebrew place and proper names became a standard addition to most thirteenth-century Bibles. It also gave rise to careful textual criticism using different versions of Scripture, resulting in *correctoria* – lists of places where the texts conflicted, and variant readings.

Twelfth-century scholars had developed a new respect for the whole created universe, as a beneficent impression of God's essential nature. To this end, theologians began to study natural science, mainly by trying to recover ancient texts about cosmological and physical subjects.[6] The characteristic medieval method of working is always to look for an authoritative text which could be used as a basis for exegesis and commentary. In this way, novelty and change could take place, but always with one foot in something already known. Texts from a wide variety of backgrounds and cultures might be employed, if they seemed to be useful for the understanding of God's work of creation.

It should not be too surprising, then, that the works of Aristotle, an ancient pagan Greek, but a polymath with a comprehensive, systematic and encyclopaedic approach to knowledge, were irresistible to twelfth- and thirteenth-century scholars. Some of Aristotle's works, mostly on logic, were known in their translations by the early-sixth-century scholar Boethius, and were used for teaching the liberal arts. Twelfth-century interest stimulated more translations, either made directly from the Greek, or via a roundabout route of translations from Arabic versions which had travelled from the eastern Mediterranean to Islamic Spain. The textual traditions were not always clear: some of what was transmitted as Aristotle's opinions was commentary or paraphrase made by the Arab scholars Avicenna (Ibn Sina, 980–1037) or Averroes (Ibn Rushd, 1126–98). A citation of 'Aristotle' might mean either a

---

6 See, M.-D. Chenu, *La théologie comme science au XIIIe siècle*, 3rd edn (Bibliothèque thomiste 33; Paris: Vrin, 1957).

genuine text, or an opinion of Avicenna or Averroes, or even a pseudonymous work, especially in the case of the influential *Liber de causis*.

Christian scholars were thirsty for the kind of material that Aristotle could supply. He appealed not only in his attempt to do everything; his work presented the results of observation of the whole of the natural world, animate and inanimate, and he ventured to draw conclusions from nature for the wider realm of ethics (the *Politics* was not translated until the later thirteenth century): in Aristotle's view, what *was* could teach us what *ought* to be. With twelfth- and thirteenth-century scholars themselves attempting encyclopaedic works, and the *Summa* – a title embracing the notions both of summary and summit – as the emblematic treatise of the scholastic community, Aristotle's authoritative display of multiple expertise was bound to be mesmerising; it was, at least, impossible to ignore. Further, he combined the width of his interests with a talent for division and structure, and in this he appealed to the medieval desire for categorisation and taxonomy. Part of his method was to increase and refine knowledge by ever more accurate definitions, and thirteenth-century theologians employed the same technique.

As products of the schools, the theology and theologians of this era are sometimes called 'scholastic', but the 'scholastic method' is more tightly defined than this. It applies to works which proceed by questioning, in breadth and depth. Each question is approached argumentatively, amassing pros and cons drawn from authoritative texts – Scripture, patristic writers, law or selected modern masters in weighted order of importance. To solve the question, each of the opposing arguments must be answered and the individual question takes its place in the accumulated body of knowledge that a *Summa* represents. Drawing on legal practice, the method dates at least to the logician Peter Abelard, and was popularised in the textbook of twelfth-century theology, Peter Lombard's *Sentences*. It was, thus, not influenced by Aristotle directly, and its appeal to authorities was *not* an Aristotelian trait; but the measured progression of its arguments was encouraged by his example.

By 1200 almost all of Aristotle's works were available in translation and were taken up by the Paris arts faculty, which was accustomed to reading his logical treatises. The new works fuelled the expansion of the faculty, over time, into the centre for what we would consider natural and experimental science, and philosophy. The arts faculty was a stepping stone for students going on to higher studies – in Paris, generally to theology – and it was from a training in arts that theologians acquired their knowledge of Aristotle. Arts students were the youngest (around fifteen to twenty-one years old) and arts masters, at barely more than twenty-one, were the least experienced scholars.

They took up Aristotelian ideas with gusto, and developed them with an abandon that left the more conservative theologians reeling. Their reaction was to clamp down: in 1210, Peter of Corbeil, archbishop of Sens and former master in the schools, held a council at Paris at which he condemned and burnt the work of two scholars, Amalric of Bène and David of Dinant, and prohibited public and private lectures on Aristotle's works of natural philosophy.

The ban was renewed in 1215 by Robert Courçon, now papal legate in Paris and charged with organising the curriculum of studies there. Robert allowed the reading of Aristotle's logic and ethics, but not his metaphysics or natural philosophy, including all 'commentaries or summaries' of them, a move which may have been aimed at the work of Avicenna and other Arab scholars. Aristotle's views challenged basic tenets of the Christian creed, and those of the Jewish and Muslim faiths as well. Belief in the eternity of the world was in obvious contradiction of the creation of the world in time by God; and his theories on how we can know things, which for Christians was a matter of divine illumination of the human intellect, had important implications for the possibility of the resurrection of humans as *individual* beings at the Last Judgement. Under Aristotelian influence, it was easy to produce theologies that were pantheistic or subsumed incorporeal individuals into a single undivided intelligence. Most worryingly, from the theologians' point of view, Aristotle's reasoning method had no place for divine revelation; in the long run, the judging of all conclusions by the standard of empirical, rational provability was to be the most damaging legacy of the Aristotelian revival.

The prohibitions seem to have had some effect, if we judge by an advertisement from the newly founded University of Toulouse in 1229, which boasted that it would teach 'the books of natural philosophy banned in Paris'. And yet, although there may have been no lecturing on the natural philosophy, it is clear that theologians were reading it, as we know from the appearance of quotations from banned texts in works by unimpeachable secular masters from about 1220 onwards. That Aristotle was not Christian was not in itself an insuperable problem. Platonic ideas, adapted by Augustine, had a central place in Christian thinking, and Roman poets and authors were often drawn on for examples of right behaviour. As Christian theologians grew more knowledgeable of Jewish biblical interpretation, commentators from that tradition, especially Maimonides and Rashi, were quoted with admiration, and even given preference (for particulars of exegesis, though not, obviously, for their overall understanding) over some Christian readings of texts. The earliest theologians using Aristotle in the schools, masters William of Auxerre, Philip the Chancellor, William of Auvergne and Alexander of Hales (and Grosseteste in England), enlisted Aristotle in much the same way as they did Jewish and Roman ideas – taking what they thought was useful and discarding the rest.

It is unlikely that these masters – all renowned and sophisticated thinkers – did not see the consequences of taking Aristotle on his own terms. But this period was one in which the church was increasingly and confidently defining itself over and against groups of 'others'. It was formulating arguments against the challenges of the beliefs of Jews, Muslims and heterodox groups of various sorts, contending with them and asserting the superiority of orthodox Christian doctrine and practice. Certainly by 1231, Gregory IX (who had himself studied theology in Paris) ordered the offending Aristotelian books to be expurgated of their errors, but he did not ban them outright. By now, it was clear that the tide could not be turned back, or perhaps it seemed better to embrace Aristotle than to oppose him. Mostly, he was simply mined for useful nuggets; there were few who took seriously his complete rational-empirical worldview for the anti-Christian system that it represented. In 1255, the new Paris arts faculty statutes, previously prescribing merely his logical works and *De anima*, included almost the entire corpus of his natural philosophy as set books.

The new statutes seem to have provided an impetus to the arts faculty's sense of itself as different from theology; the masters had developed a self-identity as 'philosophers' (Aristotle was often known simply as 'The Philosopher') which the influx of newly valid material only confirmed. As a term and an idea this was not new – Peter Abelard (1079–1142/3) had referred to himself as a philosopher, but he likewise incurred suspicion from theologians. This time, when the arts masters were spreading their wings, two brilliant mendicant masters were starting their academic careers in theology. The varied responses of the Franciscan Bonaventure and the Dominican Thomas Aquinas reflected and summarised the charisms of their respective Orders, whilst showing how theology could deal with Aristotle and what the future might hold.

Like Aquinas, Bonaventure was an Italian, sent to Paris by the Order which recognised his scholarly gifts. He and Thomas were contemporaries in the schools, serving out the terms of their mastership at the same, turbulent time, when the mendicant masters were in dispute with the seculars and when opposition to the mendicant emphasis on the ideal of poverty was growing. Bonaventure's purely academic career was cut short in 1257 when he was elected master-general of the Franciscans at a time when the Order's persistent civil war over the nature of the poverty to which it was vowed threatened its very existence. Some modern scholars have concluded that Bonaventure's somewhat dismissive response to the challenge of Aristotelian ideas is a product of this curtailed scholarly life and the energy and imagination he was forced to put into the Order's affairs. But his relative lack of interest in the theological problems posed by Aristotle's philosophical formulations is entirely consistent with Bonaventure's own tastes. His clarity of mind was matched by a limpid Latin style which make his academic theology a joy to read; but even aside from the turn of fate that took him away from the schools, his preference seems to have been towards writing that more directly fitted the work of the church.

Bonaventure was not hostile to Aristotle and his methods, but he did not think that reason could solve the deepest problems of theology or bring anyone closer to God. Of course, this is not to say that Bonaventure did not use rational arguments: his apologetic treatise on behalf of poverty written to counter William of St Amour (d. 1272) and the secular campaigners against the mendicants is a classic of exegetical reasoning. But if he does not take on the philosophical challenge to Christian belief, it is because he sees the answers it produces as largely sterile for the building up of faith. Bonaventure does not debate the question of the eternity of the world on philosophical terms; he knows from common Christian doctrine that it is wrong, and judges that the philosophical sphere can remain separate and inferior. Instead, he turned to the writing of practical treatises detailing the process of the contemplative approach to God. Two in particular, *The Soul's Journey to God* and *The Six Wings of the Seraph*, became spiritual classics, leading the faithful believer up the steps towards a closer, mystical union with God. With his mystical theology of contemplation (including an influential treatise, *Meditationes vitae Christi*, which was wrongly attributed to him), Bonaventure presages a situation in which all Christians are confident that, with their own faith and in their own language, they can by grace make their way to God.

Thomas Aquinas (c. 1225–74) chose a different path. Originally, the Dominicans were rather cut off from knowledge of Aristotle: they did not study in the arts faculty before going on to theology, but were taught in their own Dominican teaching centres; and their 1228 Constitutions forbade them to study profane sciences and liberal arts. But it was Thomas' German Dominican teacher in Paris, Albert of Lauingen (known even in his own day as 'the Great'), who mirrored Aristotle's own fascination with the natural world and the possibilities of science. Albert (d. 1280) was alive to all kinds of new ideas. As well as paraphrastic commentaries on virtually the whole Aristotelian corpus, he wrote commentaries on the works of the Neo-Platonist mystic, Ps.-Dionysius. For him, theology could not move forward without addressing and embracing this new knowledge, although not uncritically and certainly not at the expense of faith. His belief that philosophy had to be addressed in its own terms made him fearless as a scholar: his work on Aristotelian science was immensely influential in the arts faculty, and yet Alexander IV (1254–61) asked him to write a refutation of Averroes' theories which contradicted the possibility of the immortality of the individual soul. Nevertheless, his own Order was still dubious, reiterating at General Chapters in 1271, 1278 and 1280 the primacy of theology over other forms of knowledge.

With such a teacher, however, it is no wonder that Aquinas felt he could not turn his back on the problems that Aristotelianism posed. Thomas attempted to produce not merely a refutation of the arguments in philosophical terms, but a new sort of synthetic philosophical theology, still known as Thomism, that conformed to the demands of both disciplines. Nature could take its place alongside grace; reason and revelation were complementary not competitive. As part of the argument, Thomas declared theology, like philosophy, to be a science, that is to say, an ordered body of knowledge accessible to reason. Although he argued, of course, for orthodox Christianity against the Aristotelians, nevertheless on occasion Thomas showed his annoyance with those theologians who did not think that the philosophical argument needed to be addressed, for instance in his short treatise of 1270–1, *De aeternitate mundi contra murmurantes*: the *murmurantes*, or grumblers, in this case are Christian thinkers who do not see the point of arguing. In the 1260s, Thomas found himself faced by powerful opponents in the form of the philosophers Siger of Brabant and Boethius of Dacia and their followers (the so-called Latin Averroists). They espoused – or were thought to – a potent combination of Aristotelian and Averroist views, debating the eternity of the world against Creation and the doctrine of the unity of the passive intellect, which eradicated the possibility of individual resurrection. They were charged with belief in 'double truth', the idea that there was one truth for philosophy, reached by reason, and another for theology, gained by revelation, with primacy given to the former over the latter.

Siger himself seems to have been more radical than revolutionary, quite clear that he was seeking philosophical and not eternal truth; and he moderated his views on reading Thomas' arguments against them. But once again, the more conservative theologians intervened, this time in the form of the bishop of Paris (and former student at the schools), Stephen Tempier. In 1270 and 1277 he issued two lists of propositions whose content was condemned. They comprehensively cover all the disputed issues, so much so that Thomas himself, who had died in 1274, was caught by some of them. Fighting fire with fire had led to his own fingers being burned.

The writings of Siger and the 'Averroists' survive only in part, but it is not clear from what remains that they formally taught any of the opinions condemned by Tempier. It may be that he and the pope took more seriously than the protagonists themselves the heated verbal arguments characteristic of teaching in the schools; or perhaps Tempier judged more accurately than they the fatal blow which rationalism could deal to theology. Although the condemnations caused the two sides to pull back for the rest of the century, the progress of reason and science was ultimately inexorable. Thomas' attempt at synthesis was brilliant but hopeless; even his genius could not hold back the tide. Over time, philosophical theology was confined to an increasingly narrow academic ghetto, and science and rationality moved to conquer the world.

The seeds of the scientific revolution were planted. *Sacra doctrina*, which started the century as queen of the sciences, had seen her upstart handmaiden, philosophy, cheekily rise to claim the throne, with the aid of the infidel Aristotle. Ironically, the queen had welcomed the rascal to her palace and colluded in the *coup d'état*. From her omniscient place at the centre, *sacra doctrina* had become theology, one subject amongst many, just another examination paper in the schools. Ahead of her, a future of arguing for her own relevance, and eventual house-arrest inside the walls of the academy; her claim to comprehensive knowledge could never be accepted again. Within her own walls, as long as certain questions of science and philosophy were ignored, all could seem well. The church was rampant, and the practical theology of pastoral care was expanding into more and more areas of ordinary life. Lay people as well as clergy were recognised as essential members of the Body of Christ, and their private spiritual well-being was the subject of mystical as well as practical theology. Thus, in their own arena, theologians remained essentially united, working towards the single purpose of building up the faith of the people of God. This was also what Aquinas conceived to be his purpose; but his intellectual legacy was to philosophy rather than theology. Once Aristotle had arrived, neither Thomas' embrace nor Bonaventure's reserve could ultimately uphold the supremacy of theology.

# 6

# The legal underpinnings

## ANDERS WINROTH

The legal underpinnings of the Western church experienced a major trans-formation during the twelfth and thirteenth centuries. This was a period in which papal legislation found its stride, in the form of conciliar decrees and papal decisions. Papal jurisdiction was much expanded and produced a rich body of case law which became systematically collected. The law of the church, 'canon law', became a subject of study in the emerging universities of Europe, which produced an expanding and often innovative body of commentary and analysis. As a result, canon law moved towards greater complexity, sophistication and precision. The reasons for this development are to be found in general developments within European government and administration as well as in the history of the high medieval church. The movement to reform the church, which is usually thought to have begun with the German Emperor Henry III's intervention in the affairs of the papacy in 1046, propagated a vision of the church that was firmly rooted in law. The reformers also used law in impressing that vision on clergy and laity. These circumstances gave impulses to both the study of law and renewed vigour in ecclesiastical legislation.

Great efforts to trawl libraries and archives for law and to collect it in useful formats characterised the first century after 1046. Among the discoveries were many canon and Roman law texts, including Justinian's *Digest*. Many authors compiled collections of church law along lines that furthered the goals of the papal reform movement. Notable is the collection (c. 1083) of Bishop Anselm of Lucca, who was a close associate of Pope Gregory VII (1073–85). His work with its insistence on the power and supremacy of the papacy bears out that pope's programme. Anselm was the first canonist to bring a systematic effort to collecting the law concerning just war, a topic of immediate relevance in a time of open war between the German emperor and the papacy, and on the cusp of the crusades. The collection (c. 1087) of Cardinal Deusdedit has a similar tendency, as does the *Polycarpus* (c. 1111) of Cardinal Gregory of St Grisogono.

The French bishop Ivo of Chartres took a more moderate position in his collections (1090s): the *Panormia* was a very influential handbook and the *Decretum*, containing 3,760 chapters, was the largest repository of canon law up to this point. His works covered a greater thematic range than those of his predecessors. Like them, Ivo included only authoritative texts and no commentary in his own voice. He provided, however, a *Prologue* outlining a 'scholastic' programme for reconciling conflicting authorities. Ivo encouraged users of his collections to distinguish between seemingly contradictory canons that might be of different authority, applicability or authenticity. His own opinions on specific legal issues may sometimes be gleaned from the large collection of letters that he left behind, many of which contain legal advice that other bishops had requested.

While Ivo himself did not practise his proposed programme in his canonical collections, other canonists produced a few small monographs treating particular legal issues along such lines in the early twelfth century. Most remarkable is the *Liber de misericordia et iustitia* (before 1101) of Alger of Liège, discussing the problems of the church at the time, including simony and the validity of sacraments administered by unworthy clerics. In addition to the authoritative texts he quoted from legal sources, Alger included (in '*dicta*') his own arguments and conclusions along the lines that Ivo had put forward.

Most of the canon law collections mentioned above included some excerpts of relevant Roman laws. Texts deriving from the *Theodosian Code* (438) had been known and used throughout the early Middle Ages. Much of the *Code* was included in the *Lex Romana Visigothorum* (506), which was used by the Pseudo-Isidorian forger in the ninth century. In the 530s, Emperor Justinian pulled together the products of centuries of Roman legislative and jurisprudential activity into a voluminous legal corpus, which until the twelfth century had only limited immediate influence on Western European legal history. This body of sophisticated law became the subject of systematic study at about the same time as canon law, in the early twelfth century.

Canon law collections provide a window into the rediscovery of Justinian's compilations, because they incorporated snippets of Roman law as it became available. Deusdedit was the first to quote the *Novellae* (in the widespread medieval Latin translation and rearrangement known as the *Authenticum*). In the 1090s the anonymous *Collectio Britannica* and then Ivo quoted passages from the first part (*Digestum vetus*) of Justinian's *Digest*, which was apparently rediscovered piecemeal. Fragments from the last part (*Digestum novum*) followed in the *Polycarpus*. There is no evidence for use of the middle part (*Infortiatum*) until c. 1140.

This collecting activity provides the background for the beginnings of the academic study of law. The first half of the twelfth century was a period when the centres of study that would develop into universities first took shape. The premier site for legal study was Bologna, where a group of teachers were active by the 1130s, at the latest. In Roman law, the 'Four doctors' (*Quattuor doctores*), including Bulgarus (died c. 1166) and Martinus Gosia (died c. 1160), mastered and taught Justinian's works.

The Bolognese teachers included Gratian, who soon after 1139 finished the first recension of his textbook in canon law, the *Concordia discordantium canonum* ('The concord of discordant canons'), also simply known as the *Decretum*. Almost nothing is known about Gratian, except that he was the author of at least one recension of his book. He probably appeared in 1143 as an expert in a court case in Venice, but it remains unclear whether he was a bishop or a monk, as is variably claimed by different later sources.

The first recension of the *Decretum* contained some 1,860 canons. After a long introductory treatise on clerical ordination and life ('the first part'), these canons are organised into thirty-six thematic *causae* ('cases'), each divided into from two to eleven questions. The *De penitentia* – a long treatise on penance – interrupts the thirty-third *causa*. As did his predecessors, Gratian included material from many kinds of sources, including legislation of general and provincial councils, papal decretals, the writings of the church fathers, the Pseudo-Isidorian decretals, penitentials and secular law. Within each section, the canons are put into the framework of Gratian's discussion (*dicta Gratiani*), in which he resolves contradictions among them, using the methods of early scholasticism similar to those that Ivo of Chartres had outlined.

His book was used both as a teaching tool (a reasoned text book of valid law) and as a repository of ecclesiastical legislation from the first millennium. It fell short in the second respect, resulting already in the 1140s in the production of a second recension of double size, containing some 3,800 canons. A notable addition is the entire third part of the *Decretum*, a treatise on some sacraments (especially baptism and the eucharist) known as the *De consecratione*. Otherwise, the additions are spread over practically all sections of the text. The first part became divided into 100 (later 101) distinctions. Among the additions are some 200 excerpts from Justinian's Roman law corpus, while the first recension simply contains excerpts that had already been included in earlier canonical collections, such as Ivo's works and the *Polycarpus*. The second recension became accepted as the definitive collection of earlier legislation (the *ius antiquum*), and later canonists only rarely went back to previous sources. The differences in outlook and methods between the recensions are great, and many scholars believe that they had different authors.

The *Decretum* was fundamental for the teaching of canon law and for ecclesiastical courts during the rest of the Middle Ages and beyond, despite its being the product of private enterprise and never officially promulgated by any church authority. It was included in the *Corpus iuris canonici*, which was valid law in the Catholic Church until 1917. The first generations of teachers using the *Decretum* as a textbook (the 'decretists') noted their interpretations, cross-references and commentaries as glosses in the margins of manuscripts of the text. Many decretists composed sets of glosses extending over the entire *Decretum*, always drawing on previous scholars. Many such compositions are preserved, either in the margins of *Decretum* manuscripts or as separate works. In the 1140s or 1150s, Paucapalea composed the earliest such commentary that is extant. Among later canonists producing influential commentaries on the *Decretum* are Rufinus (c. 1164), Stephen of Tournai (c. 1164–9), Johannes Faventinus (c. 1171), and most importantly, the acute and original thinker Huguccio (after 1188). Johannes Teutonicus summarised this tradition in the definitive collection of glosses on the *Decretum*, its *Glossa ordinaria*, in c. 1216. Bartholomew of Brescia revised the *Glossa* in c. 1240 to take account of the *Liber extra* (see below).

In addition to interpreting Gratian's *Decretum*, teachers of canon law began to collect new legislation. They were particularly interested in papal letters with useful legal content. The volume of such letters grew exponentially throughout the High Middle Ages. While an average of less than fifty letters of any sort are preserved from each year of the papacy of Gregory VII (1073–85), the corresponding figure for Innocent III (1198–1216) is 303 and for John XXII (1316–34) 3,646. Many of these letters delegated the pope's judicial authority in individual disputes and criminal cases to local churchmen, who were charged with finding out whether the facts in the case corresponded to what the pope had been told. If so, the delegated judges were to adjudicate in accordance with the pope's precise instructions. Such letters are called decretals and make up a kind of papal case law. Popes had issued decretals for centuries, but Pope Alexander III (1159–81) led the way in making them a major tool of papal government. More than 700 decretals are preserved from his papacy.

The 'decretalists' began to collect excerpts of decretals soon after the completion of Gratian's *Decretum*. The instructions from the popes might be applied to other cases. The decretals, thus, retained their value as authoritative determinations of valid law after the conclusion of the specific cases they addressed. At first, canonists copied such letters on flyleaves of their manuscripts of the *Decretum* or other law books. In the 1170s, separate collections began to circulate, especially in England. The collectors usually cropped away words in the letters that had no legal value, such as the names of the litigants or of disputed property. At first such collections were without logical order, but they soon became systematic. A path-breaking collection was the *Breviarium extravagantium canonum* (1188) of the Bolognese law teacher Bernard of Parma, which joined Gratian's *Decretum* as a fundamental textbook of canon law in the Bologna law curriculum. Bernard included 912 excerpts from decretals. He designed an organisation modelled on the sources of Roman law, dividing his work into five thematic books (focusing on judges, judgments, clergy, marriage and crimes, respectively, according to an old Latin mnemonic). Each book was divided into titles addressing individual subtopics. Later decretal collections use the same organisation.

The formal authority of such compilations resided in the fact that each individual decretal had been issued by a pope, while law professors selected and arranged the texts. This meant that the papacy controlled imperfectly which recent laws were being taught in the law schools. Furthermore, forged decretals were introduced into some collections. In 1210, Pope Innocent III attempted to remedy this. He reviewed a collection of decretals from the first twelve years of his papacy that the canonist Peter of Benevento had completed. The pope sent it to Bologna with a brief preface instructing the law teachers there to use it in courts and classrooms. Bolognese law professors collected the decretals of the popes immediately before Innocent, as well as his legislation after 1210 in two further compilations, which were not officially approved. In 1226, the canonist Tancred, at the instigation of Pope Honorius III (1216–27), brought together the decretals of this pope in yet another collection. These five works are collectively known as the *Quinque compilationes antiquae* ('The five old compilations'). In addition to papal decretals, they included legislative decisions of church councils, especially the Third (1179) and Fourth (1215) Lateran Councils, as well as a few imperial constitutions.

Pope Gregory IX (1227–41) commissioned the canonist Raymond of Peñafort (d. 1275) to bring together the five compilations and Gregory's own legislation into a single collection, removing superfluous material and adding new laws as needed. The resulting book, known as *Decretales Gregorii IX* ('The decretals of Gregory IX') or *Liber extra*, was promulgated in 1234 as the definitive collection of canon law since Gratian. It contains 1,871 excerpts, as compared to a total of 2,143 in the five *Compilationes*. Later papal legislation appears in other similar collections, including the *Liber sextus* (1298) of Pope Boniface VIII (1294–1303).

Law professors at Bologna and elsewhere lectured on the various collections of decretals, producing commentaries and summas. The former follow and comment on the authoritative text line by line, while the latter summarise topics in the same sequence as the text book, but the organisation within each topic is determined by the author. Pope Innocent IV (1243–54; Sinibaldo dei Fieschi) and Cardinal Henry de Segusio (known as 'Hostiensis', since he was the cardinal bishop of Ostia; d. 1271) compiled the most important commentaries on the *Liber extra*. Hostiensis also wrote a major summa (later known as the *Summa aurea*, the 'Golden summa') on the *Liber extra*, following the model of the *Summa* of Goffredus de Trano (d. 1245). Bernard of Parma summarised the commentary tradition on the *Liber extra* in the *Glossa ordinaria* before his death in 1266.

In addition to glosses, commentaries and summas on the different law books, jurists began to produce monographs during the last decades of the twelfth century, breaking free from the organisation but not the contents of the authoritative law books. The earliest such works were treatments of legal procedure, not surprisingly since the sources of Roman law contain no section devoted exclusively to such law, and its treatment in Gratian's *Decretum* leaves much to be desired. Medieval legal procedure relied heavily on both Roman and canon law and is therefore known as romano-canonical procedure. An important summa on procedure is the *Ordo iudiciarius* (c. 1215) of Tancred, which was followed by the massive *Speculum iudiciale* (completed c. 1271; revised c. 1287) of William Durand (d. 1296). Other summas treated specific areas of church law, such as the election of bishops, marriage and penance. Among the most familiar are the summas on penance (c. 1225) and on marriage law (c. 1235) by Raymond of Peñafort. Bernard of Pavia also produced a summa on marriage law as well as a treatise on canonical election.

The doctrines of canon law developed greatly during the period. Not only did new laws take form, but all law acquired greater precision and complexity. This was a part of the general tendency in the High Middle Ages towards greater administrative sophistication that is often summarised under the label 'from memory to written record'.

With respect to the laws of the church, the move towards complexity was also a product of the encounter with Justinian's Roman law. Its sophistication influenced canon law greatly, lending it structure and intellectual precision. Roman law is conspicuous in the various works of commentary and analysis in canon law, as is evident simply from the large number of references to Justinian's compilations in the writings of medieval canonists. The result was the development in the law schools of a new legal system, the so-called *ius commune*, or 'European common law', which was based on canon and Roman law but which went beyond each of them. The *ius commune* informed practically all European legislation and judicial activity throughout the Middle Ages and beyond.

The thematic scope of canon law was in the main laid down with the second recension of Gratian's *Decretum*, which took its cue from the wide range of matters that Ivo treated in the *Panormia*. In addition to internal church matters (papal authority, ecclesiastical hierarchy and property, monastic life, heresy) and the administration of the sacraments (including marriage), the *Decretum* addresses subjects that a modern reader might think of as secular, such as some economic matters and the law of war.

Central to canon law were rules for handling church affairs. The authority of the pope grew during the Middle Ages so that the constitution of the church certainly by the papacy of Innocent III may be characterised as a sovereign papal monarchy. Secular rulers from emperors to aristocratic Roman families had long had an often decisive say in the appointment of a new pope, but this changed. A Roman council in 1059 laid down a new procedure for electing the pope: the cardinals, in the first place the cardinal bishops, elected him. The role of secular persons was restricted to agreeing to their choice. The Third Lateran Council (1179) revised the rules to specify that a two-thirds majority among cardinals of all ranks is required for election. This rule still applies.

Pope Gregory VII demanded wide-reaching powers through a short text inserted into his chancery register, the so-called *Dictatus pape*, which is a summary of the legal rights he claimed for the papacy. Anselm of Lucca collected legal texts supporting at least some of the claims, which were then accepted or modified by Gratian and the jurists following him.

Among these was the rule that the pope may be judged by no one, while he may judge everyone, clergy as well as laity (including emperors and kings). This claim had often been put forth since the fifth century, without preventing kings and emperors from in fact sitting in judgment over popes. Gregory VII's and his successors' insistence led to the full acceptance of this principle, making the pope a sovereign ruler. It also led to the creation of the large apparatus of papal jurisdiction, including a Roman curial bureaucracy, papal legates and delegated judges.

The pope's jurisdiction over everyone, secular and religious alike, was an aspect of his 'fullness of power' (*plenitudo potestatis*). This concept contrasts the full authority of the pope with the lower 'share in caring' (*pars sollicitudinis*) that he delegated to other churchmen. Pope Leo I (440–61) used the terms in this sense. The second recension of Gratian's *Decretum* quotes him. At the same time, about 1150, Bernard of Clairvaux developed and popularised the idea in his *De consideratione*. The popes, especially Innocent III, appropriated it to justify their claims on supremacy within the church and over secular society. Canonists adopted and refined the concept further in their lectures and publications. They argued that the pope was above human law. He was able to make exceptions from the ordinary course of canon law for the benefit of individual persons and institutions or collectives (such as monastic orders or the clergy in its entirety). Many such 'privileges' are preserved, for instance allowing laymen to listen to mass also during interdicts (when all church services were otherwise suspended within a region), or allowing men born out of wedlock to become priests. Some commentators, but not all, went further and asserted that the pope, as the 'vicar of Christ', could dispense even from divine law. He was, for example, able to free monasteries and even laymen from paying tithes, which God was thought to have instituted. Hostiensis was the strongest proponent for papal power among the canonists. He claimed that the pope could even square circles, although he must always use his power properly, expediently and for the common good.

With the papacy's legally founded claims to power came the religious responsibility of organising the life of the clergy in accordance with Christian ideals, as they were understood in the reforming circles. The papacy sought to impose these ideals on a sometimes remonstrating society.

The reformers sought to separate clearly the clergy from the rest of society. Hence ecclesiastical legislation from the period abounds in rules emphasising the separateness of the clergy. Clerics should be tonsured, not wear elaborate clothing, not participate in typically lay activities, such as war, chess or hunting. They must not be judged in secular courts but only in ecclesiastical courts (*privilegium fori*). They must not buy their offices from laymen ('simony'), and they must not be married. The ideals behind these prohibitions were nothing new but, from the middle of the eleventh century, there was a new sense of urgency. The papacy sought to implement them through legislation, but this was not a quick process.

For instance, even as late a canonist as Gratian hesitated about exactly how the prohibition against clerical marriage was to be interpreted. If a cleric married, the strength of the bond of marriage was such, he argued, that the marriage could not be dissolved. Rather, he had to leave his clerical office. Stephen of Tournai disagreed, stating that such a union was not a marriage. His standpoint set the tone for the rest of the Middle Ages and beyond.

On their side, the popes did not strictly enforce the strictures against clerical marriage either. Alexander III still issued dispensations allowing clerics to remain married, but this became increasingly unusual. By the thirteenth century, many clerics still lived in unions with women, and there were overt protests against a law that some thought too strict. The prohibitions, however, succeeded in establishing such relationships as concubinates and marking children born of them as illegitimate. Measures enforcing clerical celibacy became more effective only in the sixteenth century.

The prohibitions against simony were more successful. Legislation against this abuse was issued repeatedly at councils between 1059 and the First Lateran Council of 1123. Many influential churchmen wrote treatises against simony, including the canonist Deusdedit (*Libellus contra invasores et simoniacos*, finished before 1095). Later in the twelfth century, and for the rest of the Middle Ages, councils and pope more seldom promulgated such legislation, suggesting that simony had become less of a problem.

The procedure for electing bishops was laid down with more rigour, to exclude lay influence. Such rules soon became obsolete, as the papacy took direct control of the appointment of bishops, particularly during the course of the thirteenth century. The rules for canonical elections are still important, because they shaped the practice of secular elections taking form during the later Middle Ages.

Beyond regulating its own affairs, the church claimed and often achieved jurisdiction over several aspects of lay life. The theoretical justification for this was that the church is responsible for preventing sin, so any human action that might lead to sin was subject to canon law.

Marriages fell under canon law and ecclesiastical jurisdiction in most of Western Europe. This was not a foreordained outcome, since secular law had a long tradition of marriage law. At the beginning of the period, there were two competing definitions of how a marriage came about. The coital theory, with roots in Germanic law, considered marriage to start with sexual intercourse between the parties. The consensual theory was based on Roman law and entailed that marriage begins with both parties consenting to marry. Gratian reconciled these theories by arguing that marriage comes about through a two-step process: first consent, then coitus. French theologians argued at the same time for a theory of the formation of marriage more based on consent. The Parisian theologian Peter Lombard (d. 1160) asserted that if the consent was couched in the present, this in itself made a marriage, while if it was formulated in the future tense, subsequent intercourse was required to make a marriage. This inspired canonists active in Paris to adopt a similar stance already in the 1160s. In his decretals, Alexander III followed the French position, rather than Gratian. His stance would be definitive.

The church also regulated some economic matters as opportunities for sin, most famously in prohibiting usury, which it defined as any return in addition to the principal of a loan. Starting in the late twelfth century, canonists worked out exceptions to this general rule to meet the needs of the rapidly expanding European commercial economy.

The papal reform movement culminated with the Fourth Lateran Council (1215), at which Pope Innocent III presided over bishops from all of Europe. Ambitious legislation put in place many of the basic building blocks of medieval Christian life. The council defined, for example, the contents of faith (in opposition to various heretical movements, including the Cathars). It also promulgated legislation stipulating that all Christians at least once a year must take communion after confessing their sins to their parish priest. He is bound by secrecy about the confessions he receives.

The council prohibited clerics from participating at ordeals, where they had used to bless the implements – such as hot iron or boiling water – used to find out the truth. This method of proof was less arbitrary than modern persons may think. It was, however, being replaced by the rules of the romano-canonical procedure in which testimony and confession determined the guilt or innocence of the defendant.

The normal, 'accusatorial', procedure always required an accuser who was a private person bringing charges in front of a judge. During the twelfth century, a new procedure called 'inquisition' came into use, first in prosecuting clerics, at least from the papacy of Alexander III. In the inquisitorial process, no accuser had to come forth but the judge took it on himself to investigate rumoured crimes.

Innocent III laid down rules for this procedure at the Fourth Lateran Council. Gregory IX brought the inquisitorial process to bear on the prosecution of heretics in appointing special judges, 'inquisitors', for the purpose of seeking out and punishing heretics. Innocent III had declared that heresy was equivalent to treason against the emperor, so inquisitors were able to use against heretics the Roman procedural rules for prosecuting treason. This entailed several exceptions from the usual procedural rules, including the option to use torture.

The period c. 1050–c. 1300 represents the apex of medieval ecclesiastical law. This was a defining moment in the church history of Western Europe, when the legal foundations were laid for much that is considered characteristic of the medieval and modern church. The institutions of the church were shaped through papal legislation and the jurisprudence of the law schools, and especially from the interaction between them.

# 7

# Material support I: parishes

BRIGITTE RESL

The thirteenth century saw the triumph of the Gothic style in architecture in the building of great cathedrals all across Europe, a phenomenon much celebrated by modern art historians. 'The Gothic Image' seems to capture the spirit of the 'Age of Cathedrals' with its intellectual ambitions, artistic development and the craftsmanship available in twelfth- and thirteenth-century Europe.[1] But who paid for it all? The material support offered to ecclesiastical institutions is probably most often explored by historians with regard to aristocratic patronage and to donations made in connection with the preparations for a 'Good Death'. Yet the perpetual daily provision of ecclesiastical services to the community, the sustenance and education of the church personnel as well as the construction, daily running and repair of complex and expensive buildings required more and regular provision. From its origins, the church depended on a robust economic foundation and persistent support from the community in order to guarantee its services; this need led to the establishment of a series of practices and rules for both obligatory and voluntary contributions, thus creating a complicated framework of links and interdependences between the laity on the one hand, and the church's many institutions, from cathedrals and parish churches to monasteries or hospitals, on the other.

Many of the features of lay support of the medieval church derived from gradual developments which evolved over many centuries. Yet in the thirteenth century some significant changes in these systems of material support can be observed. The key aspects of this transformation can be considered in part as the legal formalisation of hitherto customary practices, through the impact of the expansion of canon law, and in part as the consequence of new

---

1 E. Mâle, *The Gothic Image: Religious Art in France of the Thirteenth Century* (London: Collins, 1961). G. Duby, *The Age of Cathedrals: Art and Society, 980–1420* (London: Croom Helm, 1981).

trends in both the quality and quantity of donations, a consequence of the broader social and cultural changes taking place at the time.[2]

Accounts of the various forms of material support provided to the church often distinguish between involuntary and voluntary contributions. This differentiation may be helpful for the purposes of general orientation, but the boundaries between the two are always blurred, not surprisingly for an issue that had been largely guided by customary practice for centuries; not even the best efforts of canon lawyers could manage to establish clear and firm rules and formalise conclusively the various payments due to the church. Tithes offer a good example of the ambiguities involved. The giving of a tenth of annual production, based on the Old Testament, began as a voluntary form of support in the early Christian church, but became firmly defined as a compulsory duty from the eighth century onwards, and was subsequently the subject of a series of further regulations. Tithes were mostly derived from agricultural produce, but did not spare any kind of income however small it might have been. Although the basic principles had been long established, various aspects of their application needed constant monitoring and improvement. As with all tax payments, those required to make them often sought opportunities to escape, or to avoid payment of the full amount required, something that was easier to achieve with regard to the profits that could be made by townsmen. Meanwhile, as one would expect in a period of increased activity among legal specialists, throughout the thirteenth century the system was thoroughly monitored for loopholes that could be closed.[3] The Fourth Lateran Council in 1215 decreed that the payment of tithes was to take precedence over any other form of tax (Canon 54). And one particularly obvious weakness in the system was patched: the widespread custom of avoiding payment of tithes by entrusting the cultivation of estates to persons who were exempt from them was no longer tolerated (Canon 53). English statute law provided some fine examples of the refined legal gaze that detected and attempted to clarify the potential confusion or contention that could arise if, for example, sheep were left to graze by day on pastures within the boundaries of one parish and kept in pens by night in another.[4] It is worth mentioning, even so, that despite the efforts of many parishioners to reduce

---

2 For the expansion of papal taxation in the thirteenth century, see, for instance, J. Thomson, *The Western Church in the Middle Ages* (London: Hodder, 1998).

3 J. Moorman, *Church Life in England in the Thirteenth Century* (Cambridge: Cambridge University Press, 1945), 116.

4 C. Deedes, ed., *Registrum Johannis de Pontissara, Episcopi Wyntoniensis, A.D. MCCLXXXII–MCCCIV* (London: Surrey Record Society, 1916), 231; Moorman, *Church Life*, 118.

their annual tithe payments, there was hardly any substantial opposition to the system itself.[5]

The changing practices regarding mortuary or funeral fees serve as an illustration of the fact that many parishioners tried to evade the payment of tithes. The church demanded these payments upon the death of parishioners on the assumption that they needed to make up for arrears of tithe payments built up over their lifetime; in the countryside they usually took the form of an animal, and in towns of a best gown or something similar.[6] But it was not only the laity refusing to pay their dues which posed a significant and constant risk to church funds and especially tithes. Another risk to parish churches came from the fact that lay and ecclesiastical patrons, including bishops, attempted to alienate part of their funds, a custom the Fourth Lateran Council sought to prevent in 1215 (Canon 32). Already the Third Lateran Council of 1179 had decreed that tithes could not be alienated to lay people without the pope's consent.[7]

Apart from tithes, another main source of income, especially at parish level, took the form of fees for essential church services, for example at weddings and christenings, funerals and anniversaries, for observance of the great church feasts of Christmas, Easter and Whitsuntide, and of more specific feast days such as a church's dedication feast or All Saints. However, it was not entirely clear whether these dues were obligatory or voluntary. The Fourth Lateran Council, for example, apparently dealt with the issue by decreeing that all sacraments had to be administered for free, contrary to customary practice. But the same canon stated that the laity was not to refuse the payment of customary offerings (Canon 66). Despite the underlying ambiguity, it is obvious that these fees were essential to the income of clerics and had to be sustained. The Statutes of Winchester, for example, stated that all adult parishioners 'must pay their due and accustomed oblations at the four festivals, namely: Christmas, Easter, the Festival and the Dedication of the Church'.[8] But by doing so, they clearly contradicted the general tenor of church legislation about the free provision of services.

5 G. Constable, 'Resistance to Tithes in the Middle Ages', *Journal of Ecclesiastical History* 13 (1962), 172–85.
6 R. N. Swanson, *Church and Society in Late Medieval England* (Oxford: Blackwell, 1989), 216.
7 For the decrees of the Third and Fourth Lateran Councils, see N. Tanner, ed., *The Decrees of the Ecumenical Councils* (London: Sheed & Ward; Washington D.C.: Georgetown University Press, 1990), vol. I, 206–71.
8 Moorman, *Church Life*, 126.

The papacy not only tried to control lay payments to local churches more vigorously but ecclesiastical expenditure also became the object of scrutiny and legislation in the thirteenth century. Tithes, for example, were initially supposed to be divided in equal parts between the bishop, the poor of the parish, the church fabric and the parish priest or other owner of the benefice. Although the episcopal share of tithes had fallen into abeyance by the thirteenth century, bishops acquired other rights to extract money from parishes, for example via procurations: the right to accommodation for themselves and their entourage on such occasions as visitations.[9] The parishes, on the other hand, had been successful in retaining the biggest share in tithe payments, but now found themselves confronted with strict rules about how they were allowed to spend the money: funds had to be set aside, for example, for the parish church fabric. Again, thirteenth-century statute law supplies many examples confirming the importance of the issue, while the documentation of cases where the rule was broken illustrate, as so often, why the legislators had to renew their claim time and again.[10] The parishioners not only contributed towards the costs for the church fabric through the dedicated proportion from their tithe payments; they were directly responsible for certain elements of the structure of the parish church, as well.[11]

A vast range of other forms of gifts and payments can be listed among the support offered more voluntarily to the church by the laity. Such transfers of money, properties or goods to ecclesiastical institutions were essentially based on reciprocity; the community provided the material basis that enabled the church to supply its spiritual services. Donors hoped through their gifts not only for the spiritual rewards promised by the church, but also to share in a communal identity and enhance their social status thereby. Collections were made during all regular services as well as at major feasts or on special occasions. In order to increase revenue-generating opportunities or enhance the appeal of a specific place, individual institutions introduced additional feasts or acquired new relics. The festival of Corpus Christi is an example of a highly successful liturgical innovation which spread quickly across Europe in the late thirteenth and particularly the early fourteenth century and was

---

9 Moorman, *Church Life*, 120.

10 For examples of Statute Law dealing with the issue, see Moorman, *Church Life*, 126–31. A. Brown, *Popular Piety in Late Medieval England: The Diocese of Salisbury, 1250–1550* (Oxford: Clarendon Press, 1995), 77, quotes two examples of breaking the rule in Salisbury from 1222 and 1224.

11 Swanson, *Church and Society*, 217. K. French, *The People of the Parish: Community Life in a Late Medieval English Diocese* (Philadelphia: University of Pennsylvania Press, 2001).

received enthusiastically by clergy and laity.[12] It also created substantial revenues for the institutions which adopted it. Similarly, pilgrims were accustomed to leave gifts while attending services at the places they visited. The attraction of such pilgrim traffic was therefore highly desirable; so much so, that relics and claims were forged or fabricated. Another method of attracting bigger audiences and thereby increasing the volume of donations was the offering of indulgences. These promised additional deductions in the number of days souls were supposed to remain in purgatory in exchange for attendance at particular services in specified churches. To make sure that churchgoers knew about these premium-carrying occasions, the charters granting the privileges were publicly displayed.

These and most other aspects of lay donations to religious institutions were related to the contemporary concepts of the afterlife. The hope or anticipation of accruing advantages in the afterlife was the main motivating force behind lay support of the Christian church from the outset, yet the thirteenth century saw some important innovations. Jacques Le Goff went as far as to call the thirteenth century 'the triumph of purgatory'.[13] This space, in which souls remained for varied periods of time whilst they were purified, became more precisely defined and visualised in this period. This belief structured patterns of lay donations to ecclesiastical institutions.[14] In order to avoid joining the 'goats' on their way to hell on Judgement Day and follow the 'sheep' into heaven, medieval Christians could also compensate for sins during lifetime by prayer, almsgiving and donations to the church.[15] In the earlier medieval period, monasteries usually were the beneficiaries; by the thirteenth century, friars, parish churches and chantries were popular recipients of such offerings.

These transformations were a direct consequence of the economic changes taking place in Europe at the time. The surge in urban populations and the production of new wealth evident since the eleventh century gave lay donations a new direction. The change could sometimes happen within the space of a single generation, as shown by the practices of wealthy thirteenth-century families of Vienna. Otto vom Hohen Markt, a prominent member of the Viennese elite, had established a sound economic and material footing for

12 M. Rubin, *Corpus Christi: The Eucharist in Late Medieval Culture* (Cambridge: Cambridge University Press, 1991).
13 J. Le Goff, *The Birth of Purgatory* (Chicago: University of Chicago Press, 1984), 235–41.
14 Le Goff, *The Birth*, 209–34.
15 Matt. 25.32–46. Jacques Chiffoleau coined the phrase 'budget de l'au-delà' (budget for the afterlife) in this context: J. Chiffoleau, *La comptabilité de l'au-delà: Les hommes, la mort et la religion dans la région d'Avignon à la fin du Moyen Âge, vers 1320–vers 1480* (Rome: École française de Rome, 1980).

himself and his family by 1250 and invested in provisions for urban religious communities. Yet his favourite institution was the Cistercian abbey of Heiligenkreuz, situated in a valley in the surrounding countryside. Otto's son Greif followed his father's example, but his devotion also displayed significant new tendencies. He favoured the private chapel of St Mary's 'am Gestade', a private chapel in one of his father's townhouses, which became a prominent urban church attracting substantial support by the town's élite. While his father had asked to be buried at Heiligenkreuz, to which he retired, Greif devoted time and money to the city's hospital, an institution actually founded by his more distant ancestors.[16]

This shift from rural to urban institutions, and from monastic to civic institutions, is characteristic of a new trend. People sought to make discretionary donations (as opposed to compulsory parish-bound tithes) to institutions within their communities under their scrutiny. The foundation of private chapels by wealthy townspeople is evident all across late medieval Europe. The earliest English examples show that initially bishops who approved such grants considered them to be temporary and required owners to attend parish services as well.[17] That a variety of institutions were aiming to provide services previously offered by parishes reflects donors' wishes to have closer control over the ecclesiastical institutions which they entrusted with the care for their souls.

The voluntary support of religious institutions did not change only in quality in the thirteenth century, but also in quantity. More people were able to make donations. In England, anxiety arose in royal administration about the amount of land being held by religious institutions. The Statute of Mortmain in 1279 aimed to stem this flow by regulating transfers of land to religious institutions.[18] Similar forms of intervention are documented from most European regions. But the consistently increasing volume of donations cannot simply be interpreted as a consequence of the growing number of people who could afford them; it also reflects the increase of lay involvement in the church in general. This development had begun with the Gregorian Reform and steadily gained momentum throughout the twelfth and thirteenth centuries.

The thirteenth century also saw a growth in the making of wills. These usually included some form of religious donation, sometimes connected with

16  B. Pohl-Resl, *Rechnen mit der Ewigkeit: Das Wiener Bürgerspital im Mittelalter* (Vienna and Munich: Böhlau, 1996), 25–7.
17  Moorman, *Church Life*, 15.
18  Swanson, *Church and Society*, 197.

the funeral or anniversary celebrations. Such donations may appear as a prime example of voluntary support. Unlike mortuary fees, they were not legally required, but donors considered them necessary for the salvation of their souls. The witnesses required to guarantee the legal acceptance of wills may not only have helped to secure the fulfilment of testators' wishes after their death, but could exert pressure on them to conform to expectations. In 1419, when the former mayor of Vienna Rudolf Angerfelder had his will recorded, the three witnesses asked him three times whether he was sure he did not want to make any donations at all to a church institution before accepting his decision.[19] In a similar way, mortuary payments became routine in English wills of the fourteenth century.[20]

Another key aspect of material support offered by the laity to the church, namely their involvement in and funding of charitable practices, also underwent significant transformations in the thirteenth century. Caring for the poor was one of the church's duties, and a part of the tithes was supposed to be set aside for such purposes, but the public also engaged much more directly in helping with poor relief. Charitable bequests formed another essential component of provisions for the afterlife and could take many forms, from donations to religious institutions to endowment of chantries and their associated charitable provisions, to payments towards educational establishments or public works such as bridges. In particular, the thirteenth century saw a huge rise in lay hospital foundations and a diversion of charitable donations from churches to these hospitals. As in the case of the other changes outlined above, what we see here is a difference in the outward form of the practice, rather than in the spiritual intentions behind it, and again the reasons are to be found in evolving economic and social conditions. Hospitals offered more efficient and tangible poor relief, especially in larger settlements, and lay founders could exercise more control over their functioning than over a specifically religious foundation. Looking at it from the point of view of the gift-exchange model, charitable donations made to hospitals may have been particularly appealing for donors because the institutions offered both the enduring and repeated execution of donors' wills, and also a good crowd of people who would pray for their souls. One document from the city hospital in Vienna can illustrate the new directions of material support. In this charter dated 1268 the master and fraternity of the hospital asked the public for

19 Wiener Stadt- und Landesarchiv, Stadtbuch 3, fol. 15v (1419, 22 October. Entry in the register 1419, 10 November).
20 Swanson, *Church and Society*, 216.

assistance with the daily expenses of the institution. Everybody making a contribution was promised indulgences granted by several authorities, from the local bishops and archbishop to the pope. The document is clearly a forgery, but it is well made, and must date from the late thirteenth or early fourteenth century. It even comes with the genuine seal of the town of Vienna attached. Interestingly, its production coincided with the main building phase of the hospital complex including a huge and lavishly decorated Gothic church.[21] Donors would have been able to see what they were getting for their money in stone, as well as in the indulgences' promise of future reward.

Fear of eternal damnation because of sins committed during one's lifetime, or the desire to have a private chapel or chaplain to guarantee one's access to the sacraments, cannot wholly account, however, for the generous support for ecclesiastical institutions. Nor can the idea of conspicuous consumption and the display of individual wealth, especially when it comes to the financing of the great cathedrals and similarly extensive building projects in the thirteenth century. Single donors did make spectacular contributions to such complexes by funding stained-glass windows or donating richly decorated liturgical objects. But much more investment was required to assist deans and chapters with their efforts. In this respect, civic pride, expressed in the creation of a landmark and a symbol for the community, also needs to be taken into consideration. Regardless of the sometimes troubled relationship between a bishop and chapter with a city's population, contemporaries did view cathedrals as signs of communal identity, and contributing towards their building, maintenance and decoration was a highly desirable practice. For the erection of the new cathedral in Salisbury, for example, generous support was offered not just by King Henry III, but also by a substantial sector of the local population who made donations in various forms according to their means.[22] In similar fashion, great cathedrals were completed in the thirteenth century all across Europe.[23] When looking more closely at the material support offered to the church by the community in the thirteenth century, we may as well start with the great works of art.

---

21 Wiener Stadt- und Landesarchiv, Bürgerspitalurkunde 2, 1268 June 29; Pohl-Resl, *Rechnen mit der Ewigkeit*, 15–21.

22 Brown, *Popular Piety*, 49–51.

23 See F. D. Logan, *A History of the Church in the Middle Ages* (London: Routledge, 2002), 251–2, for a list of European cathedrals built or completed in the thirteenth century.

# 8

# Material support II: religious orders

## JANET BURTON

Throughout the Middle Ages the religious orders and the society that they shunned exhibited a mutual dependency. From the early days of Western monasticism, those who entered the cloister spent much of their day engaged in the *opus dei*, the work of God, the continuous, and communal, round of prayer and worship. This not only enabled them to fulfil their own personal spiritual aspirations, but, increasingly, to perform the social function of intercession for humankind. Monks and nuns prayed particularly for the souls of those who provided them with their material support, and the elaboration of the liturgy through the addition of masses and prayers for the dead reached its apogee in the congregation of the Burgundian abbey of Cluny, founded in 909–10. The twelfth and thirteenth centuries, however, saw great changes in the nature of the material support for institutions within the monastic and religious orders.

Early medieval material support for monastic houses came from a number of sources. The mid-sixth-century *Rule of St Benedict* hinted that some of the endowment of a monastery might come from the monks themselves. Chapter 58 laid down that an adult recruit who had goods or property must choose whether to bestow it on the monastery or give it to the poor.[1] Chapter 59, which made provision for the offering of children to the monastery, enjoined the parents of a child oblate to ensure that any means of him inheriting property be closed off. One way to do this was by making a donation to the monastery.[2] Benedict was not concerned to outline anything further about the material basis of the monastery, but he clearly thought that it would enjoy possession of estates that, if the monastery were poor, might have to be worked by the monks themselves.[3] Surviving medieval charters

---

1 *The Rule of St Benedict*, ed. J. C. McCann (London: Sheed and Ward, 1972), 128–33.
2 *Ibid.*, 134–5.
3 *Ibid.*, 111.

bear witness to the desire of those outside the walls of monasteries to make donations to religious houses *pro salute anime/animarum*, for the salvation of their souls. Some went further and through their support for the monastic order entered into fraternity, or confraternity, becoming, as many charters state 'participators in all the prayers and good works (*orationes et beneficia*) that are offered in the house'.

By 1200 much had already changed. For one, under pressure from the reformed orders such as the Cistercians, in which the emphasis was on the validity of the freely made vow of the adult over that made on a child's behalf, the child oblate had all but disappeared, and that staple of early medieval monastic recruitment was becoming a thing of the past. As the great Cistercian, St Bernard, abbot of Clairvaux, asked his nephew who had for-saken Clairvaux for Cluny, claiming that his parents had promised him to the Cluniacs as a child, 'which has the most force: the vow a father makes on behalf of his son, or the vow a son makes on his own behalf?'[4] Further, the grants that accompanied the entry of men and women as monks, canons and nuns were becoming linked to the sin of simony. Councils at Melfi (1089), Rome (1099) and Westminster (1127, 1175, 1200) legislated against the practice of the acceptance of entry fees: 'certain exactions of money for receiving canons, monks, and nuns';[5] and the Fourth Lateran Council of 1215 suggested that nunneries in particular were 'stained by the sin of simony'.[6] The link between the entry of a man and woman into religion and some form of endowment, pecuniary or landed, did not cease – witness the charters that granted land to a house when a son or daughter, or indeed the donor him/herself took the habit. However, monastic institutions could no longer expect this source of income, had to be wary of accepting it, and became, perhaps, more reliant on the material support of their benefactors.

Other aspects of monastic endowments were changing. The twelfth century had seen the religious themselves diverging on the nature of the material endowments that they were prepared to accept. The Benedictines clung to the

---

4 *The Letters of St Bernard of Clairvaux*, trans. B. S. James (London: Burns and Oates, 1953), Letter 1, 1–10 (6).
5 'exactiones certas pecuniarum pro recipiendis canonicis monachis et sanctimonialibus': quoted from the 1127 Council of Westminster, in *Councils and Synods with Other Documents Relating to the English Church, vol. 1, AD 871–1204*, ed. D. Whitelock, M. Brett and C. N. L. Brooke (Oxford: Clarendon Press, 1981), 747.
6 See J. Lynch, *Simoniacal Entry into the Religious Life from 1000 to 1260* (Columbus: Ohio University Press, 1976), 193–5. Lynch suggests that the Council singled out women for special criticism because the economic basis of nunneries tended to be less secure than that of male houses, making nuns more reliant on entry grants.

traditional economic assets given by generations of benefactors: landed estates, manors, rents, churches, tithes, mills, markets and serfs. The early charters of St Mary's Abbey, York, for instance, give a good idea of the nature of the endowments of a prosperous urban Benedictine community.[7] As a result of these grants, the larger monasteries and nunneries became important landowners, controlling often vast estates. Moreover, the nature of their endowments meant that in many ways monastic houses operated in the same way as secular landlords and lords of the manor. From the late twelfth century, as many abbeys and priories took lands previously farmed to tenants for rent back into direct exploitation, the administration of monastic lands was tightened up, with the introduction of central treasuries and regular audits. Such developments are illustrated in the revolution in estate management under Prior Henry of Eastry (1285–1331) at Canterbury Cathedral Priory.[8] In contrast, the new reformed orders such as the Cistercians avoided all revenues associated with the manorial economy, and those that derived from *spiritualia*, that is, churches and tithes, relying instead on their vast army of *conversi* (lay brothers) to administer unencumbered landed estates through a series of granges or outlying farms.[9] The reliance on the order's own workforce, rather than the labour services due to the manor, allowed for the consolidation of monastic estates and revolutionised the economic base of Cistercian houses. In many parts of Europe the Cistercians were at the forefront of the extension of cultivable lands through the clearance of forest and waste land, and the drainage of marshy and low-lying areas. This allowed for both mixed farming and the development of specialised economic activities such as mining. The reality of the Cistercian economy was, naturally, more complex than the paradigm, but it is useful to recall that the twelfth century had seen a radical reassessment of the nature of acceptable endowments received from the laity.

7 See Janet Burton, *The Monastic Order in Yorkshire 1069–1215* (Cambridge Studies in Medieval Life and Thought, fourth series 40; Cambridge: Cambridge University Press, 1999), 39–41.

8 R. A. L. Smith, *Canterbury Cathedral Priory: A Study in Monastic Administration* (repr., Cambridge: Cambridge University Press, 1969 [1943]).

9 The last few years have seen a lively debate concerning the emergence of a distinctive Cistercian attitude to the economy; see especially Constance Brittain Bouchard, *Holy Entrepreneurs: Cistercians, Knights and Economic Exchange in Twelfth-Century Burgundy* (Ithaca, N.Y. and London: Cornell University Press, 1991); Constance Hoffman Berman, *Medieval Agriculture, the Southern French Countryside, and the Early Cistercians* (Transactions of the American Philosophical Society, 76.5; Philadelphia: Diana Publishing, 1986). It is accepted that the picture is not as clear cut as once thought, and that ideas were worked out more gradually than the early Cistercian documents suggest. Nevertheless, whether in 1134 or the mid 1150s, the Cistercians did articulate a particular view of the nature of monastic endowments.

For some religious houses a further source of material support came from pilgrims and visitors to their saints, shrines and relics. Supreme among the English monasteries that boasted their own saint was Canterbury Cathedral Priory, scene of the martyrdom of Thomas Becket. Other houses, too, had relics that drew pilgrims: the Augustinian canons of Waltham, for example, had a fragment of the True Cross. The early generations of Cistercians discouraged visitors to their monasteries, but they too came to see the advantages of having something that would attract pilgrims. Hailes Abbey, founded in 1246 and richly endowed by its founder, was nevertheless in considerable debt by 1261. The monks' financial position improved after 1270, when Earl Edmund of Cornwall presented them with a relic of the Holy Blood of Christ. This transformed the community into one of the foremost centres of pilgrimage in medieval England.

More change was on its way, and the dynamic (as in the twelfth century) came partly from within the monastic order and partly as a result of changing social and economic conditions. From the twelfth century, and increasingly in the thirteenth, the monastic orders, who were once widely seen as the true exponents of the *vita apostolica*, faced challenges for that title from groups with new ideas about how the religious life could be lived. Though women as well as men were affected by these developments, in practice they had more impact on the male monastic life, since social convention and practical considerations dictated that the enclosed life was deemed appropriate for women. For some the emphasis was to be on poverty as a key concept in the religious life. This renewed emphasis on poverty arose in part from an anxiety about an increasingly prosperous and economically complex society, and a desire to reject any role in it. This divorce was something that the monastic order had found it difficult to achieve. Even those monastic groups whose literature emphasised that they sought the 'desert' found that their enterprises in taming the wilderness brought them wealth and commercial success. No single individual exemplifies the new spirit of the age of the thirteenth century better than Francis (1181–1226), founder of the Franciscan friars, himself the son of a rich merchant, who deliberately rejected that wealth. Initially an informal group dedicated to preaching the precepts of the gospel, Francis' ragged band soon grew into an order, which required regulation. The *Regula Bullata*, the final version of Francis' rule, laid stress on the idea of poverty that was the dynamic of the new movement, speaking of the 'eminence of loftiest poverty' and the need to serve God 'in poverty and humility'.[10] The novelty of

10  There is a useful translation of *Regula Bullata* in R. B. Brooke, ed., *The Coming of the Friars* (London: Allen & Unwin, 1975), 120–5.

the order was further demonstrated by the friars' rejection of the world of buying and selling, and their refusal even to handle money.[11] The aim of the friars was to be on terms of equality with the poorest of the poor, and thus they extended their interpretation of poverty by a further rejection of property in which they could live. The friars were wanderers, and they were to be sustained by begging. However, true poverty proved difficult to achieve. The friars came to attract the material support that had hitherto been lavished on the monastic order. The friars who sought poverty – Dominican and Franciscan as well as the smaller orders of the Austin and Carmelites – became popular among benefactors, and much of their history in the thirteenth century is the story of how they tried to accommodate their own desire for 'Lady Poverty', and the desire of their benefactors to relieve that poverty. There can be no doubt that the material support offered by the laity had an impact on the ideals of the orders. In 1230 the pope allowed the Franciscans to have 'spiritual friends' who could hold money on their behalf; this was followed in 1247 by a further provision that the spiritual friend became a legal representative in all business matters.[12]

The reasons for the appeal of the friars are complex – that they represented something novel and fresh no doubt played a part – but their success also owed much to changing social and economic conditions. The friars deliberately sought the towns, where they could more easily maintain themselves by begging, and where they found a ready audience for their preaching among the merchant and urban classes. They became part of a new urban religiosity. In the 'monastic centuries' monastic literature is peppered with military metaphors: the monks were 'fighters' or 'spiritual soldiers' who fought against unseen enemies with their weapons: intercession and the ceaseless round of prayer.[13] Such language appealed to those of the aristocratic and knightly classes who both founded and entered monastic houses. However, such rhetoric meant little to the emerging urban classes of the thirteenth century.

---

11 Such a refusal was radical but not new. It is one of the traits noted in the *vita* of Bernard of Tiron, the monk-abbot-hermit-abbot founder of the house and then the order of Tiron. For the ban on the handling of money by the Franciscans, see *Regula Bullata*, chapter 4, in Brooke, ed., *Coming of the Friars*, 122.
12 D. Knowles, *The Religious Orders in England, vol. 1* (Cambridge: Cambridge University Press, 1948), 142; M. D. Lambert, *Franciscan Poverty: The Doctrine of the Absolute Poverty of Christ and the Apostles in the Franciscan Order 1210–1323* (London: SPCK, 1961).
13 See, for instance, the description by Orderic Vitalis of the foundation of Shrewsbury Abbey, where monks are described as 'Christ's garrisons' and 'cowled champions' engaged in 'ceaseless combat' against the Devil: *The Ecclesiastical History of Orderic Vitalis*, ed. Marjorie Chibnall (Oxford Medieval Texts 3; Oxford: Clarendon Press, 1972), 142–7.

As Lester K. Little has expressed it, they 'wanted to hear speakers; they relished amusement and spectacle; they sought to be convinced and they demanded explanations'.[14] In this lay part of the appeal of the friars: their sermons and *exempla* spoke directly to their audiences by using the language of the market place and the tavern. The material support for the friars came from those who had previously supported monks, such as kings – Louis IX of France and Henry III of England – and aristocracy. However, it was from the urban class that the friars found their most consistent support.[15]

In the face of the challenge of the friars, the endowments to the monastic orders began to fade. They did not disappear, but the friars were in many ways more attractive targets for a wide range of benefactors. The evidence comes not from charters and cartularies, but from wills, surviving in increasing numbers from the late thirteenth century. These indicate that, although testators still remembered monasteries and nunneries in their final bequests, these beneficiaries were likely to be outnumbered by friars.[16] It is possible to overplay the way in which benefactors turned their back on monasteries. Endowments continued to be made, patrons continued to seek burial in monasteries, men continued to become monks and canons, and women nuns. However, a glance at the leaves of medieval cartularies, on the whole, confirms that the days of large-scale benefactions were over; after 1200 there was just too much competition, much land had already been alienated to the monastic order, and in England by 1279 the Statute of Mortmain forbade alienation of land to religious houses without royal consent and payment of a fine.[17] Charters also indicate that those providing material support for the monastic order were now likely to be more demanding in return for their generosity. No longer content to make a gift *pro salute anime mee*, many now granted alms specifying that they should be used for the feeding of the poor, or to purchase wax for candles, or books for the library. Finally, the evidence of cartularies suggests that a greater sense of practical business acumen had crept into donations to monasteries and nunneries, with the provision of corrodies in return for benefactions, that is, insurance against old age or reduced prosperity.

---

14  Lester K. Little, *Religious Poverty and the Profit Economy in Medieval Europe* (Ithaca, N.Y.: Cornell University Press 1978), 198.

15  *Ibid.*, 205.

16  On this theme, see R. W. Southern, *Western Society and the Church in the Middle Ages* (Harmondsworth: Penguin, 1970), 286–92. See also Andrew D. Brown, *Popular Piety in Late Medieval England: The Diocese of Salisbury 1250–1550* (Oxford: Clarendon Press, 1995), 27–33.

17  Sandra Raban, *Mortmain Legislation and the English Church 1279–1500* (Cambridge: Cambridge University Press, 1982).

Much of this betokened a new attitude to the means to salvation. Before 1200 the liturgical round of prayer was the function of the spiritual warriors, the monks in their monasteries. Thus, in the heyday of the monastic order, most of those who sought spiritual benefits for their material support shared their commemoration with all the other benefactors of a monastic house. Theirs might be one name among many listed in a *liber vitae*, or they may be remembered and prayed for generally in the masses for the dead. By the end of the twelfth century, just as benefactors might specify the particular use to which their grant was to be put, so too could they make more specific demands about their own spiritual welfare; they came to want more personal commemoration in the form of obits, anniversaries and masses. From the late twelfth century we begin to find the establishment of chantries within the monastery, in the form of lights before altars, and the provision of obits, in other words the perpetual celebration of masses for the soul. And it is not long before we find the idea of the chantry taking root in other contexts, outside monastic houses, as free-standing chapels or in parish churches. This is the result of a shift in thought about the commemoration of the dead, which was seen as the responsibilities of a social community and not just a religious house. Monks were not the only ones who could pray for salvation.[18] This could be done by a priest or chaplain employed by a family, in a parish church, or for a guild or lay confraternity. The chantry offered a more personal kind of commemoration.

18 For a recent discussion of these themes see Andrew Brown, *Church and Society in England 1000–1500* (Basingstoke: Palgrave Macmillan, 2003), 122–6.

# 9

# The Word and its diffusion

KATHERINE JANSEN

In his *Ars Praedicatoria*, written in the closing decades of the twelfth century, Alan of Lille (c. 1128–1202) summed up the parts of preaching thus: 'preaching is an open and public instruction in behaviour and faith, the origin of which derives from the path of reason and from the wellspring of the "authorities", the purpose of which is the formation of human persons'.[1] As distinct from teaching conducted privately, preaching was a discourse performed publicly, the basis of which was authoritative sources, guided by holy Scripture, which aimed to instill right belief and moral practice in the Christian faithful. Alan's treatise was one of the first salvos fired in a revolution that was to transform the mode in which preaching was delivered to the people in the medieval period. That is, from the twelfth century the art of preaching was fundamentally reconceived, reconfigured and retooled to confront the challenges of a changing world. Adopting a new style called the 'modern sermon', preaching now broached new subjects, and gave rise to a new literature to aid in sermon composition. This new literature was produced in mass quantities to meet the demands of a new professional class of preachers – the friars – who now joined the bishops in bearing the 'good news' to far-flung audiences from Cork all the way to Cathay. Audiences themselves also contributed to the sea-change in the history of preaching. As they became ever more literate and concerned about individual salvation, they created consumer demand – a market – for books of sermon collections, which now became reading material for personal inspiration and reflection. Thus, from the late twelfth century onward, the church formulated a pastoral mission which sought to Christianise Europe anew and, through preaching, to diffuse the word of God to all the lands that lay on Christendom's frontiers and well beyond.

All this is not to say, however, that the early medieval period was indifferent to preaching. Ever mindful of his pastoral duties as bishop of Rome,

---

1 *PL* 210, col. 111.

Pope Gregory the Great (c. 590–604) was himself a great preacher, so great that his *Forty Gospel Homilies*, a gathering of sermons from his stational circuit in and around Rome in the years 591 and 592, was one of the most widely diffused homiliaries throughout the entire Middle Ages, even extending its reach into Scandinavian territories where, in Old Norse, it became the most copied sermon collection after 1150. Athough Gregory I set the example, it was Charlemagne who eventually enacted the law, and as such, the *admonitio generalis* of 789 decreed that every parish should have a priest whose duty was to preach to the people. That same piece of legislation stipulated furthermore that every priest should possess a copy of Gregory the Great's *Forty Gospel Homilies*; subsequent legislation from the southeastern part of the empire decreed that every priest should have at his disposal a collection of homilies in order to preach the gospel on Sundays and all feast-days. Such legislation ensured that Paul the Deacon's homiliary, commissioned by Charlemagne himself, would become the model collection from which sermons were fashioned throughout the Frankish kingdom. The *Homiliary of Paul the Deacon* was written in Latin, but the Frankish councils recognised that for preaching to be efficacious it must be done in the vernacular. Toward that end, in 813, the Council of Tours decreed that preaching was to be carried out in plain and simple language so as to be readily comprehended by the laity. In late tenth- to early eleventh-century England, in the circle of Wulfstan, archbishop of York, the Carolingian decrees on preaching were adapted for local usage. Now priests were compelled to preach on Sundays and feast-days too, and likewise to explain the meaning of the Gospels in English. Medieval preaching from its beginnings, therefore, served as a catalyst, spurring the development of spoken vernacular languages; however, most preaching in its written sermonic form is preserved in Latin. Thus it is important to recognise at the outset the gap that exists between the written record – the sermon collections – and the oral event in which the preacher, as mediator of sacred theology, translated and transmitted scriptural knowledge along with correct religious belief and practice in the vernacular.

Because of the erudition required for such a task, throughout the early and central Middle Ages, preaching to the public remained in the purview of local bishops and canons. But in the twelfth century, as a legacy of the unfinished business of the Gregorian Reform, itinerant preachers, propounding a message of church reform, began to appear wandering throughout the landscape of Western Christendom. Some of them such as Robert of Arbrissel (c. 1047–1117) preached against simony and nicolaitism, abuses which continued to plague the church even after the reform period. Although Robert's practice of allowing female followers raised eyebrows amongst his more conservative colleagues, his preaching seems to have remained above rebuke by the authorities. This was not the case with subsequent charismatic preachers such as Henry of Lausanne (b. early twelfth century). His fiery Lenten sermons in 1116 against the worldliness and lasciviousness of the clergy incited so much outrage among the inhabitants of Le Mans that they attacked their local priests, inflicting damage on both their persons and property. In 1135 the Council of Pisa ordered Henry to cease his rabble-rousing and enter a monastery, but he seems to have done no such thing, since in 1145 we find Bernard of Clairvaux still fulminating against him. A spiritual heir to these charismatic preachers was Arnold of Brescia (1090–1155), who for ten years in Rome preached a combustible mixture of church reform and republican politics. Beginning in 1144, he joined up with the Roman communal movement then in open rebellion against the temporal power of the pope. Arnold's sermons attacked the wealth and hypocrisy of the papacy to whom, he preached, neither obedience nor reverence was due. Arnold was captured and executed by the imperial forces which had marched on Rome to rescue the embattled pontiff; his reforming message, however, remained well alive, taken up by others – heterodox and orthodox alike – it continued to reverberate throughout the medieval period and beyond.

Church reform, then, formed the basis of a preaching tradition which attracted many distinguished proponents, among them the German abbess, Hildegard of Bingen (1098–1179). The polymath Hildegard was, as is well known, a visionary, a scholar, a musician, a playwright and a scientist. Less well known is that she was also a formidable preacher. Driven by the strength of her visionary experiences and strong moral convictions, she denounced the moral failings of both church and state in her day. In 1158, when she was about sixty years old, Hildegard embarked on a series of four preaching tours. Some of her tours – such as the final one in 1170 through Swabia – entailed traditional monastic preaching, visiting different monasteries and addressing the assembled monks or nuns in the chapter house. At other times, she took the more remarkable step of preaching in public to a mixed audience of clergy and laity, as she did in Trier during her second circuit in 1160. Collected with her letters, some of her sermons survive and reveal that she was no shrinking violet when it came to criticising the failings of the clergy. In Cologne, possibly in 1163, she denounced the local clergy thus: 'You ought to be the cornerstones of the Church's strength, holding her up like the cornerstones that sustain the boundaries of the earth', she thundered. 'But you are laid low and do not hold up the Church, retreating instead to the cave of your own desire. And because of...your riches, avarice, and other vain pursuits, you do not properly teach your subordinates.'² Hildegard's visionary authority had endowed her with a *magisterium* such that she could preach publicly without censure and chastise the clergy without fear of reprisal, even though she would have been well aware of the Pauline injunction silencing women's public speech. It is not without interest that a copy of her sermons was found in the medieval library of the Franciscans of Santa Croce in Florence.

The content of Hildegard's sermons reveals her to be more than a routine preacher of reform, she was also an outspoken critic of heresy, a new challenge to the teaching authority of the church, particularly since leaders and members of heretical movements such as Waldes in Lyon, the Humiliati of northern Italy and the Cathars of southern France all claimed the duty if not the right to ascend the pulpit. In making such a claim they both challenged clerical privilege and threat-ened the established ecclesiastical order sanctioned by tradition. And unlike those itinerant preachers who had preceded them, the adherents of these new religious movements were neither ordained clergy nor, for the most part, had they any formal theological training. Some of them may also even have been women, or at least so their ecclesiastical critics claimed. Preaching, then, became the stumbling block which forced many groups into schism and sometimes into outright heresy, since the church forbade their public preaching on the grounds that lay people were not trained for the sophisticated theological task of explicating the Gospels.

Such was the predicament of Waldes, who went to Rome in 1179 deter-mined to plead his case for lay preaching before the Third Lateran Council. His efforts came to naught. In 1182 the Waldensians were excommunicated and expelled from Lyon because of their continued insistence on preaching the Gospels; two years later they were condemned by Pope Lucius III at the Council of Verona. It is important to note that when in 1184 the Waldensians were first condemned, they were not accused of heresy, that is adhering to doctrinal error, rather, they were accused of defying episcopal authority (*contumacia*) in continuing to preach the Gospels without the consent of the local bishop. It appeared that the debate, which turned on the question of who had the authority to mediate the Gospels, had reached an impasse.

Significantly, at that very same council, the Humiliati of northern Italy were condemned for a similar offence. The Humiliati, who sought to live a common life of voluntary poverty, prayer and manual labour while maintain-ing their familial ties, also claimed a vocation to preach. However, unlike the

---

2 Hildegard of Bingen *Epistolarium*, ed. L. van Acker (2 vols.; CCCM 91–91A; Turnhout: Brepols, 1991–93), vol. 1, *Epist. Xvr*, 37; Joseph L. Baird and Radd K. Ehrman, trans., *The Letters of Hildegard of Bingen* (3 vols.; Oxford: Oxford University Press, 1994–2004), vol. 1, x.

Waldensians, whose insistence on preaching the Gospels pushed them over the threshold into heresy, the Humiliati were subsequently reconciled with the church, when in 1201 Innocent III approved their *propositum*, or statement of intent. Among other things, that document gave permission to the Humiliati to assemble to hear sermons from preachers drawn from their own ranks, provided they were qualified and approved by the local bishop, who should not reasonably withhold permission. The Humiliati might preach on moral matters, but never on theology, dogma or the sacraments: the *arcana* of the church continued to be the preserve of the learned clergy. Thus, within a generation, Innocent III (c. 1198–1216) had found a compromise solution for a problem which threatened to rend the fabric of the institutional church. The laity could exhort and teach privately, while the clergy continued to enjoy the privilege of publicly explicating the Gospels.

Innocent's treatment of the Humiliati is but one example of his preoccupation with preaching, a result no doubt of his intellectual formation at Paris. Trained at the university where Alan of Lille had once taught, the young Lothario de' Conti likely studied in the circle of the moral theologian Peter the Chanter, who gathered around him some of the best and the brightest of that generation, Robert of Courson and Stephen Langton amongst them. The ambitious agenda of the Paris circle was to demonstrate the relationship between moral theology and everyday life, bringing their conclusions to the laity through preaching. In their written form, their arguments were often cast as treatises on the virtues and vices. Indeed, both Alan of Lille's *Ars Predicatoria* and Peter the Chanter's *Verbum Abbreviatum* adopted this discursive format.

Two of the greatest preachers of the period – Fulk of Neuilly (d. 1201) and Jacques de Vitry (c. 1170–1240) – absorbed the lessons of the Paris circle and disseminated them to wide audiences in their sermons. Although none of his sermons survive, one of Fulk's most successful preaching events, which took place in the market square of Champeaux on the right bank of the Seine, 'so moved his listeners by his call for repentance that they tore at their clothes and cast themselves at his feet'.[3] His colleague, Jacques de Vitry, was also an enormously popular preacher, perhaps because he was so masterful in sizing up an audience. Among his more than 400 extant sermons, 74 are grouped into *ad status* collections, which are arranged according to sociological typologies such as widows, merchants, judges, scholars, crusaders and sailors. These sermons, also called *vulgares*, survive in fifteen manuscript copies.

---

3 James of Vitry, *The Historia occidentalis of Jacques de Vitry: A Critical Edition*, ed. John Frederick Hinnebusch, O. P. (Fribourg: The University Press, 1972), 95–6.

Paris' most celebrated alumnus, Innocent III, was also a preacher of not inconsiderable oratorical gifts, even his enemies conceded it. His implacable opponent, Giovanni Capocci, once interrupted his preaching shouting out angrily: 'your words are God's words, but your deeds are those of the devil'.[4] A collection of Innocent's sermons preached early in his pontificate survives in eighty-six manuscripts, a forceful reminder of his rhetorical skills. This gathering of sermons was sent to the monastery of Cîteaux, in all likelihood designed to serve as a model sermon collection for the Cistercian Order who, since 1145 had been engaged in an ongoing preaching campaign against the Cathar heretics in southern France.

The Cistercian preaching mission to the Cathars signals a volte-face in the history of monastic preaching, but not one that was altogether unfamiliar. As part of the missionary activities of the early Middle Ages, learned monks such as Willibrord, apostle to the Frisians, had set up convents throughout north-eastern Europe with the express purpose of diffusing the Gospels; but as those conversion campaigns came to a close, monks directed their preaching internally, focusing on the observance of the monastic rule and the spiritual progress of the community. The sermons of Bernard of Clairvaux are prime examples of this genre, as are those by Umiltà of Faenza (1226–1310), whose preaching was directed to her community of Vallombrosan nuns. However, the crisis signalled by the upsurge of religious dissent and heresy in the twelfth century spurred the White Monks to quit the cloister in order to combat heresy with the power of the Word.

The Cistercian campaign against the Cathars in the Midi was not destined for success, but from the ashes of its failure rose the phoenix that embodied a young Castilian canon's vocation. In an epiphany which occurred in 1206, Dominic of Guzmán (c. 1171–1221) realised why the unceasing sermonising against the Albigensian heresy had yielded so little fruit: only true practitioners of the apostolic life could compete with the Cathar priests, known for their austere lives of self-sacrifice. Consequently, with the blessing of Fulk, bishop of Toulouse, Dominic set up a preaching mission which aimed to 'uproot heretical depravity and to expel vices, to teach the rule of faith and to imbue men with sound morals'. These new preachers would perform their mission 'on foot as religious, in evangelical poverty', an implicit critique of ecclesiastical wealth, which the Cistercian mission, with its fine horses and lavish displays, now seemed to embody.[5] The *Ordo Praedicatorum*, the Order of

---

4 Caesarius of Heisterbach, *Dialogus miraculorum*, ed. Joseph Strange (2 vols.; Cologne: J. M. Heberle, 1851), vol. 1, 103.

5 *Monumenta diplomatica S. Dominici*, ed. Vladimir J. Koudelka (Monumenta ordinis fratrum Praedicatorum historica 25; Rome: Institutum Historicum Fratrum Praedicatorum, 1966), no. 63, 57.

Preachers, which Dominic founded in 1215, had at its heart the propagation and defence of Christianity through preaching. Since nothing less than the salvation of souls was at stake, the mission called for preaching suffused in orthodoxy and deep theological learning.

In stark contrast stood Dominic's contemporary, Francis of Assisi (1181–1226), who favoured unscripted spontaneity, preferring that his brethren remain unlettered and improvise their sermons from their own experience. Extemporaneously declaiming on the themes of peace and penance, Francis' own sermons seem to have been quite a spectacle. Thomas of Celano reports that sometimes *il poverello* looked as if he were dancing; at other times he seems to have forgotten altogether what he was saying and so dismissed the crowd with a blessing.[6] Either way, Francis soon drew disciples, and when, around 1209, his motley band of followers reached twelve in number, they accompanied him to Rome to seek approbation from Innocent III, who affirmed their way of life. The pope confirmed for the nascent *Ordo Fratrum Minorum* the right to preach penance – not doctrine – just as he had done a few years earlier for the Humiliati. The clerical monopoly on preaching the Gospels was yet again preserved, though it remained a site continuously contested throughout the medieval period.

Innocent's pontificate was marked by its attentiveness to the laity's need for spiritual nourishment, the ministry of the word through preaching. His concern was enshrined at the first plenary session of the Fourth Lateran Council (11 November 1215) in Canon 10, *inter caetera*, which decreed:

> It often happens that bishops by themselves are not sufficient to minister the word of God to the people... We therefore decree by this general constitution that bishops are to appoint suitable men to carry out with profit this duty of sacred preaching, men who are powerful in word and deed and who will visit with care the peoples entrusted to them in place of the bishops, since these by themselves are unable to do it, and will build them up by word and example. ... We therefore order that there be appointed...coadjutors and cooperators not only in the office of preaching but also in hearing confessions and enjoining penances and in other matters which are conducive to the salvation of souls.[7]

---

6 Thomas of Celano, *Vita prima* in *St. Francis of Assisi: Writings and Early Biographies: English Omnibus of the Sources of the Life of St. Francis*, ed. Marion Habig, 4th rev. edn (Chicago: Franciscan Herald Press, 1983), ch. 27, 65–6.

7 Norman Tanner, ed., *The Decrees of the Ecumenical Councils* (2 vols.; Washington, D.C.: Georgetown University Press, 1990), vol. 1, 239–40.

The proximate beneficiaries of this canon were the new mendicant orders of Francis and Dominic. In the event, they were the 'suitable men' mighty in 'word and deed' who stepped into the void to fulfil the 'duty of sacred preaching'. They were also the ones who accelerated the pace of the preaching revolution begun in the twelfth century: by 1300, the Franciscans alone, who numbered about 30,000, were dispersed throughout Christendom and its frontiers in approximately 1100 foundations. And these men, mighty in 'word and deed', required systematic training and texts in order to 'fulfill the duty of sacred preaching'.

Dominic had seen to it that his friars would be up to the task of sacred preaching by integrating a sophisticated educational programme into his conventual system. As early as 1220 the Dominican constitutions stipulated that no convent could be established without a *doctor* (a teacher) and a master of students, who monitored and guided their training as preachers. By the mid-thirteenth century, the Order had already developed pedagogical techniques and a curriculum to prepare novice preachers for the pulpit. The syllabus included lectures on the study of sacred Scripture, but also a cycle based on the theology text-book of the medieval world, Lombard's *Sentences*, supplemented by the first quarter of the fourteenth century with the work of the Order's newly minted saint, Thomas Aquinas. Lectures were the bedrock of the Dominican course of studies, but disputations and repetitions (tutorials) were also part of the standard curriculum.

It was the task of the master of students to train the students to preach, mostly through imitation of the great masters of the genre. At the more important convent schools the preachers-in-training had the benefit of a conventual preacher *in situ* whom they could imitate; in less prestigious venues they learned from model sermon collections and other preaching aids, produced in mass quantities for the education of preachers. The master of students was responsible for seeing that the shelves of the conventual libraries were stocked with the most up-to-date tools of the trade such as *florilegia*, reference collections of authoritative statements excerpted from 'canonical' texts; *exempla*, collections of instructive, even entertaining tales that served to leaven the weight of the moralising sermon; and the *artes praedicandi*, practical how-to manuals for composing sermons. Most important of all were the model sermon collections, which provided representative examples of the *sermo modernus*, the new sermon type, already in vogue by the 1230s, which came to epitomise the later medieval sermon genre. The *sermo modernus*, also called the 'scholastic sermon', was characterised primarily by its structure around a *thema*, usually a scriptural verse, which was then divided into three or four parts, which each in turn developed an aspect of the theme. The sermon generally signalled at its onset its divisions and how elaboration would proceed. In vernacular modern sermons, such as those in Middle English and Anglo-French, as well as in Latin exemplars, those divisions often rhymed, pointing to their possible usage as mnemonic devices for preacher and audience alike. The preacher's initial broadcast of the architecture of the sermon, its rhymed parts, and its reliance on *auctoritates* and *exempla* for constructing an argument created a familiar structure which assisted audience reception of the message. Indeed, so familiar was the modern sermon's structure that by the end of the medieval period the great Valencian preacher Vincent Ferrer (1350–1419) could playfully inquire of his listeners, 'Do you want the authority now? Do you want the authority now?'[8] Interestingly, the form of the modern sermon made it so ubiquitous, so successful that it crossed religious lines. It has been argued that by the late fifteenth century, the Jewish sermon conscientiously adopted the 'modern method' of sermon making, importing the device of the theme, in Hebrew called the *nosei*.

Modern sermons travelled in model sermon collections, organised according to the liturgical calendar. *De tempore* collections included predominately Sunday sermon cycles (*dominicales*) as well as Advent (*adventuales*) and Lenten (*quaresimales*) cycles, this last probably the most widely diffused type during the medieval period. The popularity of the *de sanctis* collections, cycles of sermons composed for the feast-days of the saints, increased along with the enormous growth of devotion to the cult of the saints, which has been estimated to have expanded by 25 per cent between the eleventh and fifteenth centuries. Jewish sermons circulated in a similar manner to their Christian counterparts; collections for the Sabbath formed one type of collection, while those for specific holy days formed another. Groupings of sermons for diverse occasions, such as the commemoration of marriage or death, developed in both the Jewish and Christian traditions. Political occasions, such as the entry of a monarch into a city, could also be included in such collections; contrariwise, sermons by King Robert of Naples (1275–1343), recording significant events in the fourteenth-century *Regno*, can be categorised as occasional sermons.

This melange of typologies attests the increased production of sermon texts between the twelfth and fourteenth centuries. It has been estimated that of the

---

8 Manuel Ambrosio Sánchez Sánchez, 'Vernacular Preaching in Spanish, Portuguese, and Catalan', in Beverly Mayne Kienzle, ed., *The Sermon* (Typologie des sources du Moyen Âge occidental, fasc. 81–3; Turnhout: Brepols, 2000), 805–6.

60,000 Latin sermons by known authors which survive from the period between 1150 and 1350, only 5 per cent of those texts predate the year 1200, a stunning increase in textual production, driven by the demand of mendicant convent schools and university theology faculties. So momentous was this explosion in the production of preaching-related texts that one scholar has likened it to the printing revolution of the early modern period.

Above and beyond the texts, the neophyte preacher learned by doing. He did so in the privacy of the convent community and under the tutelage of the master of students, who critiqued his written text and commented on his performance in the pulpit. After successful completion of his studies and chapterhouse performances, the friar was deemed ready to preach publicly and, as such, assigned as a companion to an experienced preacher with whom he could apprentice in the field. This was the penultimate stop before the fledgling preacher was licensed by the Order, whose Italian churches hosted between 240 and 250 sermons per year.

Such was the training that the Order of Preachers transmitted through their provincial system which stretched from Britain to the Far East. As the Order clericalised, and the mission broadened beyond penitential preaching, the Franciscans soon adopted a similar but not identical system to train new recruits in theology and homiletics. As such, convent lectors were assigned the responsibility for such a course of studies. After 1260, no Minorite friar could hope to become a lector, bachelor or master of theology without having first received his episcopal licence to preach.

An urban orientation characterised the missions of both Orders. Heretics abided in cities and so did the temptation associated with newly found wealth. Cities proved to be fertile seed-beds for sowing the good word; therefore, early on the Orders organised provincial systems across the urban centres of Europe and into the Middle East to accommodate their phenomenal growth. The Franciscan case alone is instructive. Five provinces had emerged by 1217: Italy, France, Spain (including Portugal), Germany, which included central and eastern Europe, and the Holy Land, including Nicosia. The system was already outgrown when the province of England, which included Ireland and Scotland, was added in the 1220s after friaries were founded in London in 1224 and Cork c. 1229. By 1239 the German province had expanded into eight distinct sub-provinces, which included Germany (the Rhine region), Saxony, Austria, Hungary, Sclavonia (Dalmatia), Cologne to which the Low Countries were amalgamated, Dacia (Scandinavia) and Bohemia, including Poland. By 1263, the Order could count thirty-four provinces in its orbit now including Romania, under which heading fell the Balkan areas and Greece. By 1300, the vicariates of Orientalis, including Constantinople, and Tartaria, the Far East, had been established. (The Order of Preachers' provincial expansion followed a similar pattern both temporally and geographically.)

As the Orders had arrived on the frontiers of Christendom, so now their mission expanded to include the salvation of non-Christian souls through preaching. As early as 1219, on the heels of the Fifth Crusade, Francis had journeyed to Egypt in a failed attempt to evangelise the Muslims. The sultan, Malek-al Kamîl, politely received Francis' preaching, but showed no intention of converting from Islam. Early Dominican missions in the 1220s to the Cumans, a nomadic and 'pagan' people on Hungary's eastern border, appear at first to have fared more successfully. Conversions were made in 1227; however, it seems that they may have been no more than politically expedient gestures as the Cumans were in need of the Christian Hungarian princes – patrons of the Dominican mission – as allies.

By the 1230s the friars had also become crusade preachers, summoned to the duty by papal missives to the provincial ministers: in 1234 and 1235 Gregory IX called up two preachers from each province. Crusade preachers such as Jacques de Vitry often organised their own preaching events with the consent of the local bishop, but they also were known for piggy-backing their recruiting sermons onto other events. John Wildeshausen and William of Cordelle, for example, preached at tournaments, where they hoped to find a receptive knightly audience ready to take up the cross.

As the crusades opened up the Middle East, mendicant missions pushed ever more eastward in the 1240s as Francis' progeny, friars such as Giovanni da Pian del Carpine, William of Rubruck and Oderico da Pordenone, ventured their way into the Far East, following the trade routes through India and China. In that early period, missionaries and merchants travelled side-by-side with the result that wherever a merchant's *fondaco* was established, a Latin chapel sprung up too, served by the mendicant friars.

By the second half of the thirteenth century, it became clear that if souls were to be saved in territories outside Christendom, the friars had to learn the appropriate languages in which to preach conversion. The most ambitious project toward this end was that Raimond Lull (1235–1315), who, in the 1270s, founded the Collegio Miramar in Majorca. Its mission was to promote the study of the Arabic language, preparing friars to evangelise in the Islamic world.

The question of language even 'at home' in Christian territories remains a vexed one. The Franciscan chronicler, Salimbene da Parma, recounts that the great German preacher, Berthold of Regensberg (1220–72), preached 'in lingua theotonica', and scholars agree that sermons were generally delivered in local vernaculars to the laity, even if the majority are preserved in Latin, the language of the learned.[9] At least two reasons can be adduced to explain this situation. First is the internationalisation of the religious orders who, scattered across linguistic frontiers, maintained lines of communication and scholarly transmission of learning in the international language of Latin. Second is that vernacular languages were often suspect, tainted by the faint odour of heresy, particularly so if they were used to convey the meaning of holy Scripture. The Waldensians, and subsequently the English Lollards, were condemned for translating the Gospels into the vernacular for the purpose of lay preaching. As such, Dominican legislation dating as early as 1242 forbade the brothers from editing sermons in the national vernaculars, whilst Arundel's Constitutions of 1409, aiming to combat Lollardy head-on, banned any scriptural translation in the vernacular. Due to this prohibition, Lollard sermons now improbably account for the bulk of extant Middle English preaching texts for the simple reason that orthodoxy forbade translations of scriptural material in the vernacular.

Just as at Pentecost when the disciples, galvanised by tongues of fire, were sent out to preach in diverse languages, medieval preachers – heterodox and orthodox alike – preached in the language their public understood best. Even if not all preachers were multilingual, they nonetheless found ways to impart their message. In 1147, Pedro, bishop of Lisbon, preaching a crusade sermon to an audience of soldiers made up of mixed language-groups, employed translators to render his Latin into the various requisite vernaculars. Three centuries later, in 1451, Giovanni da Capestrano (1386–1456) did much the same. Interpreters in his retinue translated his Latin into the local vernaculars, as he made his way through Bavaria, Saxony and Poland, preaching anti-heresy sermons against the Hussites.

Anti-heresy and crusade sermons were two well-known forms of preaching, each guaranteed to draw large and responsive audiences. Shortly before his death in 1216, Innocent III preached the crusade in Orvieto, where it was reported more than 2000 new crusaders took up the cross. In 1244, Peter of Verona's (1205–52) anti-Cathar sermons at Sta Maria Novella in Florence drew such huge audiences that the Dominicans had to petition the commune to enlarge the piazza in order to accommodate the crush of people, vying for an earful of his inspiring rhetoric. Another type of preaching event, one likely to draw a violent crowd, was anti-Jewish preaching, especially well documented on the Iberian peninsula. In 1328, for example, the incendiary sermon of the

---

9 Salimbene de Adam, *Cronica*, ed. Giuseppe Scalia (2 vols; Bari: Laterza, 1966; repr. CCCM 125–5a; Turnhout: Brepols, 1999), vol. 125a, sec. 813, 840.

Franciscan friar Pedro de Ollogoyen whipped the crowd into such a frenzy that it ended in a pogrom against the Jews of Navarre. Such instances, unfortunately, can be multiplied many times over.

Most sermons, however, aimed simply to 'sow the word of God', in Bernardino da Siena's (1380–1444) phrase.[10] In practice that meant two things: preaching on peace and preaching on penance. Neither of these two subjects required theological training; as such, the early sermons of Francis of Assisi (none of which survive) took up these themes, epitomised in his celebrated phrase, 'pax et bonum'. In a description of Francis' preaching in Bologna in 1222, Thomas of Spalato observed:

> the whole manner of his speech was calculated to stamp out enmities and to make peace. His tunic was dirty, his person unprepossessing and his face far from handsome; yet God gave such power to his words that many factions of the nobility, among whom the fierce anger of ancient feuds had been raging with much bloodshed, were brought to reconciliation.[11]

Peace and reconciliation were also the goals of the 'The Great Hallelujah' of 1233, a pacification campaign of the faction-riven towns of northern Italy undertaken jointly by Franciscan and Dominican friars. Their peacemaking brought concrete results: many long-standing feuds were ended as inveterate enemies exchanged the kiss of peace. The Franciscan preacher, Gerard of Modena, was even drafted by the city of Parma to serve as *podestà*, the chief municipal officer charged with ensuring communal peace.

Later in the century, learned Dominican friars such as Remigio de' Girolami (1235–1319) began confronting the ethical dimensions of peace in their sermons. What did peace between individuals mean for the *bono communi*, the welfare of the community? Here is how Giordano da Pisa, O. P. (c. 1255–1311), presented the problem to his listeners on 20 April 1305:

> Do you want to play lord over your neighbor?... Such was the pride of Lucifer, who wanted to reign over the others; he disturbed the peace of heaven for which he was ejected and chased out of heaven eternally. And from that...root was born...all disagreements, arguments, tensions, and divisions between people. That is, from pride – I want to be lord over you – and you over me: it's one from the other. But if people were humble...there would be peace and prosperity.[12]

---

10 Bernardino of Siena, *Prediche volgari sul Campo di Siena, 1427*, ed. Carlo Delcorno (2 vols., Milan: Rusconi, 1989), vol. 2, no. XXVIII, 803.

11 Thomas of Spalato, trans. Paul Oligny, in *St. Francis of Assisi: Writings*, 1601–2.

12 *Prediche del Beato Giordano da Rivalto dell'Ordine dei Predicatori* (Florence: Pietro Gaetano Viviani, 1739), no. LII, 316.

Particularly in northern and central Italy, where vendetta was still practised regularly, peacemaking sermons were of paramount importance throughout the Italian Middle Ages. By the fifteenth century, the Franciscan Observants had become specialists in the field, so much so that the likes of Bernardino da Siena, Giovanni da Capestrano and Giacomo della Marca (1391–1476) were frequently invited by urban councils to pacify their cities. In the wake of their sermons it was not unheard of for city magistrates then to consult the peacemaking friars on judicial and government reforms to cement the peace.

Bernardino da Siena, a seasoned peacemaker, preached a message of peace that was deceptively simple: inner personal conversion facilitated outer conversion, a peace that would contribute to the common weal. Sermons about peace and concord were entwined with sermons on conversion; that is, conversion to penance, the subject-matter of most medieval sermons. The penitential life was a broad complex of ideas including conversion from sin, accompanied by acts of repentance, expiation, self-mortification and charity, not infrequently held together by the bonds of voluntary poverty. In her dramatic conversion at Christ's feet in the house of the Pharisee, Mary Magdalene was considered the very exemplar of personal penance, thus she was often proposed as a model for such a life in medieval sermons. Preachers envisioned the penitential path as a permanent process, a life's work, which called for constant vigilance and attentiveness to the pitfalls of the secular world. Those pitfalls included vanity, lust, sodomy and usury, along with witchcraft and sorcery, a catalogue made famous by Bernardino da Siena's fire-and-brimstone sermons denouncing them.

Words, even Bernardino's persuasive words, were not always enough to lead the public away from such vices. Audiences needed convincing, and preachers used every resource in their theatrical grab-bag to do so. Sometimes they explicated the frescoes on the church walls, at other times they gestured to the crucifix hanging in the apse to make their point, but preachers could also be far more theatrical when the occasion warranted it. In the thirteenth century, Berthold of Regensberg dramatically lit a bonfire of vanities, encouraging his audience – female members particularly – to stoke the flames with their hairpieces, combs and veils, all vain superfluities. Bonfires were such an effective technique of rousing an audience to repentance that, at the end of the fifteenth century, Savonarola (1452–98) was still using the spectacle of a bonfire for the same ends, but the catalogue of vanities had now grown very long indeed. Among the items cast into Savonarola's fires were paintings by Sandro Botticelli, a devoted follower of the Dominican firebrand. Although bonfires were also amongst the weapons in Bernardino's preaching arsenal, he is most associated with the holy *tavoletta*, a panel inscribed with the YHS, the initials of the holy name of Jesus. The golden monograph set on a blue field, encircled by a radiant sun was designed by Bernardino himself and used theatrically as a talisman to direct audience participation in his preaching events. At the climax of his sermon, Bernardino sometimes brandished the *tavoletta*, at the sight of which his audience knelt down, uncovered their heads, and wept in reverence. Knowing full well that minds often wandered, Bernardino went after the body too, inviting or, better, demanding the active, kinesthetic participation of his audience.

Despite Alan of Lille's advice that preachers should not engage in buffoonery or cheap antics, that counsel sometimes went unheeded, especially by the fifteenth century, the age of the super-star preachers. Vincent Ferrer used tears, pregnant pauses and grand gestures to great effect. He even sang popular songs, if only to denounce them. Ferrer was not alone in using dramatic interludes in his sermons to animate the faith for his audience. During Lent and holy week, the busiest oratorical season of the year, Italian preachers often experimented with a genre known as the 'semi-dramatic sermon'. It was a sermon punctuated by theatrical action, which often consisted of a recitation of vernacular poetry by Dante or Petrarch or *laude* by Jacopone da Todi, the 'Donna del Paradiso' being a favourite text. The preacher used the poetry to act out and give voice to the scriptural figures he was explicating in his sermon. Observant Franciscans such as Alessandro de Ritiis and Roberto Caracciolo were masters of this genre which fused together image, word and gesture in a spectacular new way. Italian communes sometimes associated the friars with other street performers. A statute of 1288 from Faenza forbade the singing of French poems or other songs under the city's arcades while a sermon was being delivered.

As preaching events developed into spectacles, so the theatre of preaching evolved to accommodate the diffusion of the Word. Early on, Berthold of Regensberg festooned his preaching platforms with pennants, which served double-duty as decoration and wind-indicators, informing audience members where to seat themselves for the optimal audio experience. Sensitivity to acoustics was also the binding feature of mendicant architecture, which organised space to privilege the spoken word. The friars' 'preaching barns' of Tuscany testify to the main architectural requirements of preaching. They are often a single wide space whose purpose is to hold a vast crowd, but from any point in that enormous hall the words of the preacher were meant to be heard effortlessly. But of course preachers did not always have the luxury of preaching in acoustically designed spaces, they had to preach wherever an audience congregated and that often meant outdoors in marketplaces, granges, fields and public squares. If the cathedral had an external pulpit, such as the one at Perugia, itinerant preachers might be given permission by the bishop to use it, but most often they made do with portable wooden pulpits and scaffolds, assembled on the spot for the occasion. Heretical preaching such as that done by the Cathars, whose preachers were known to preach on Sundays and feast-days, was carried out covertly, perforce, in out of the way places such as cemeteries, or in the secrecy of private homes.

The average sermon lasted about an hour, though some of the super-preachers spun out their performances to last hours on end. Giovanni da Capestrano, who, early in his career was assigned as Bernardino da Siena's preaching companion, testified that Bernardino could preach for four to five hours at a time. Vincent Ferrer was known to go on for as long as six hours.

Thus, by the fifteenth century, the preacher's props, his dramatic delivery, the venue, and the sermon's extraordinary length, to say nothing of the audience's participation, each contributed to making the diffusion of the word into a sacred performance, even more so when it was accompanied by miracles. In 1372, the sermons of the Carmelite preacher, Frei Afonso Abelho made the rains stop in Évora, while Vincent Ferrer's preaching was so efficacious that it brought an end to drought in Majorca. Late medieval revivalist preachers had so ratcheted up the horizon of expectation of their audiences, that now the public had come to expect thaumaturgy of their super-preachers and seldom did they disappoint. Both Bernardino da Siena and Giovanni da Capestrano were known for producing miraculous healings at their preaching events, the latter even using the relics of the former to effect them. Indeed, sometimes preaching events produced their own relics as audiences carried off pieces of makeshift pulpits as holy objects.

But mostly audiences looked to preaching events as a diversion from everyday life, or at best as a form of scriptural explication and moral guidance. Michel Menot (1440–1518) astutely observed that his audiences were composed of many who came to hear him out of curiosity: 'After they eat supper and their stomachs are full, they say, "Let's go hear that preacher, so that we can hear something that might amuse us."'[13]

Occasionally, sermons did alter the course of individual lives. The Clarissan sister, Camilla Battista da Varano (1458–1524), in her spiritual autobiography, relates how when she was just a girl she heard a sermon that changed her life. That sermon inspired her to take the veil. Of course not all sermons bore such sweet fruit; generally all that a Christian preacher could expect from a stimulating sermon was confession and penance on the part of the audience.

---

13 Michel Menot, *Domenica quarta quadragesime*, in Joseph Nève, ed., *Sermons choisis de Michel Menot (1508–1518)* (Paris: E. Champion, 1924), 421.

Preaching and confession had been linked in Canon 10 of the Fourth Lateran Council, and it is for this reason that preachers often travelled with confessors in their entourages.

Group action could also be mobilised as the result of a rousing sermon. The monte di pietà in Cortona was founded in 1494 by the city fathers after Fra Bartolomeo di Nibia of Novara swept into town spewing anti-Jewish venom. But Jews could and did respond to such preaching. In the late fifteenth century, the Jews of Braga, having been compelled to listen to the insulting sermons of Mestre Paulo, lodged an official complaint with Afonso V. At the same time in Seville, a community of *conversos*, stung by the assault of Hernando de Talavera's (1428–1507) preaching, struck back with a tract, *Herético libelo*, defending the sincerity of their conversion. These of course were measured, considered, even respectful responses; it is likely that the discourteous words of the Jews Jacob and Vidal Struch, critiquing one of Vincent Ferrer's sermons in Perpignan, probably represented the ordinary uncensored Jewish response to Christian anti-Jewish oratory.

Preachers often complained about their audiences, especially their inattentiveness, but listeners were far from indifferent to the contents of the homily, as the case of Jacob and Vidal Struch testifies. It was not unknown for audience members to dispute a preacher's point, or for the sermon's theme to be criticised, as preacher-manqué Franco Sacchetti recounted. It seems that once an Augustinian friar, engaged to preach a Lenten cycle to a gathering of poor Florentine wool-workers at Sta. Reparata, launched into his homily on the topic of usury. After having preached for a couple of evenings to a bewildered audience, one indignant listener finally stood up and told the friar to preach on a topic more germane to the status of his audience. The preacher, realising his gaffe, hastily changed his theme to the blessedness of poverty.

Audience members were also known to walk out on themes of which they disapproved, even if articulated by a star such as Bernardino da Siena. Thus, on one occasion when Bernardino began to preach on the marital debt, he offended the sensibilities of a number of women in his audience by speaking out frankly on sexual practices in the presence of their daughters. Their response was to storm out of the piazza in protest, leaving the desperate preacher to implore them from the pulpit: 'Don't go, don't leave, wait! Maybe you'll hear things that you haven't ever heard before!'[14]

---

14 Bernadino of Siena, *Prediche volgari 1427*, vol. 2, no. XX, 586.

Clearly then, medieval audiences could be discerning audiences, particularly when they themselves were literate. At the end of the medieval period, it was not unheard of for a discriminating listener to record the words of a sermon he had heard in a common-place book for personal reflection, as was the case of an anonymous Florentine auditor who recorded more than twenty sermons in his spiritual diary over a thirty-five year period. Like hagiography, sermons in their written form became devotional material for private reading in the later Middle Ages. Indeed, homilies and hagiography often circulated together as in John Mirk's *Festial* (c. 1400), an assemblage of saints' lives and *de tempore* sermons, produced at the end of the fourteenth century. It survives in Middle English in over thirty manuscript copies.

The passage from preaching event to written devotional text occurred in any number of ways. Sometimes model sermon collections, written in Latin, were adopted wholesale as contemplative material. But lay and religious people were also fuelling the demand for vernacular texts. Female religious, often unlettered in Latin, were particularly avid producers and consumers of vernacular religious literature. Indeed it has been argued that early German-language sermons, those produced between 1170 and 1230, were almost exclusively destined for the *cura monialum*, the spiritual care of religious women. Monastic inventories support this argument. In the fifteenth century, the female convent of Santa Caterina al Monte (S. Gaggio) commissioned translations of St Bernard of Clairvaux's sermons and owned copies of Giordano da Pisa's *Quaresimale*, a vernacular collection of Lenten sermons.

Giordano's sermons, delivered in Italian, were recorded in the vernacular by various hands including confraternity members, notaries and interested lay people. The resulting transcription of sermons, *reportationes*, are the priceless records of sermons performed in front of live audiences that get us as close as possible to the atmosphere of a medieval preaching event. In addition to the text of the vernacular sermon, the reporter often included remarks on the preacher's gestures, the sound of his voice, the audience's response, the location and date of the sermon, and occasionally even the weather. In addition to the *reportationes* of Giordano's sermons, the best studied are those of Bernardino and Vincent Ferrer, whose sermons were recorded in Catalan and Castilian by clergymen and lawyers in his employ. Less known but no less important are those *reportationes* of thirteenth-century Parisian provenance. Significantly, preachers such as Bernardino and Savonarola used their vernacular *reportationes* as guides when collecting their sermons for subsequent transmission in Latin.

With the advent of printing in the fifteenth century, sermon collections – among the first texts to be printed – were initially printed in Latin editions. Indeed, sermon texts comprised a great proportion of the books printed in the incunable period. It has been estimated that 25 per cent of the books printed in Strasbourg before 1500 were sermonaries. The first republic of letters created by printing was predominately a latinate culture, but as demand for printed devotional material increased, sermons made their first printed appearance in the vernacular. In 1474, Roberto Caracciolo (1425–1495) published one of the first sermonaries printed in the Italian vernacular and dedicated it to King Ferdinand of Aragon for 'reading at his leisure'.[15] As had happened in manuscript culture, increased vernacular literacy was creating a market for devotional material in the new world of print. Sermon collections played a prime role in this market in their original format but now also recast as treatises on the virtues and vices and various other *opuscula*. The printed editions of the *Specchio di vera penitenza* of Jacopo Passavanti and Hernardo de Talavera's *Collación muy provechosa* are devotional works which bear the marks of having begun life as preaching material. Now, with the help of the printing press, at the end of the fifteenth century, the vernacular served along with Latin as a vehicle to convey the Word of God to a mass audience. Nonetheless, it should not be forgotten that the oral preaching event was still alive and well at the end of the Middle Ages, and the art of vernacular reform preaching would play a pivotal role in the gathering storm ahead.

15 Roberto Caracciolo, *Quaresimale in volgare*, in Enzo Esposito, ed., *Opere in volgare* (Galatina: Congedo, 1993), 74, 83.

# PART III

*

# THE ERECTION OF BOUNDARIES

# 10

# Christians and Jews

ORA LIMOR

The term 'boundary' in reference to Jews is a complex one. Like Muslims, Jews were outside the Christian faith but, unlike the Muslims, they were present within Christian society. Like heretics, Jews were present in Christian society but, unlike them, they were not perceived as a part of the body of faith. These three groups represent three disparate types of boundaries, each determining a different attitude towards the group defined by the boundary. Yet, the Christian world did not view these groups as completely distinct from one another, and its attitude towards each carried over to its treatment of the other groups. In this way, the crusades, explicitly declared against the Muslims – the enemies of the church in foreign lands – influenced and aggravated the treatment of the enemies within Christian lands – the Jews. Similarly, the intensive campaign against heretical sects initiated in the thirteenth century led to the erection of sturdier barriers between Christians and Jews.

In addition, the Jew figures in the Christian world on two levels – one physical and the other theological – and the two are not fully congruent. The theological (or hermeneutical)[1] Jew is present in Christian imagination and thought; the Jew forms an integral part of the Christian worldview as an internal entity bearing unvarying characteristics, and this perception also dictates the attitude towards living Jews. Moreover, even when 'real' Jews are absent from Christian society, in spite of their absence they continue to function as an internal, imagined 'other'. The concept of boundary and that of the imagined Jew are both keys for deciphering the code of the relations between Christians and Jews in the Middle Ages, particularly in the thirteenth century.

---

1 Jeremy Cohen, *Living Letters of the Law: Ideas of the Jew in Medieval Christianity* (Berkeley, Los Angeles and London: University of California Press, 1999), 1–21.

Whereas in the early Middle Ages the Islamic lands were home to the majority of Jews as well as the seat of the chief Jewish cultural creation, with the advent of the second millennium, the Jews underwent a process of 'Europeanisation'. The Jewish pronouncement '[better] under Edom than under Ishmael' is voiced repeatedly in a variety of Jewish sources, indicating that Jews preferred to live among Christians than among Muslims.[2] Records normally dwell on descriptions of calamities, adversity and deviations from normality, silently passing over routine days of peace and quiet. In spite of this, the sources enable us to infer that by the early thirteenth century Jews were integrated in their environment, their communities flourished, and relations with Christians were by and large neighbourly. For the most part, Jews were practically indistinguishable from Christians in their dress, language and even customs, with the exception of their religious practices. Jews lived mainly in cities, made their living in commerce and financial ventures, and greatly benefited from Europe's increasing urbanisation. It is customary to distinguish between the large concentration of Jewish communities in Germany (including northern France and England) and the Jewish centre in post-Reconquista Spain (including southern France), and a third and separate community in Italy.[3]

As a rule, Jews were the only minority whose existence was permitted in Christian society. Jews lived throughout the Christian West in a state of relative tolerance inspired both by a fundamental Christian theological precept (as formulated by St Augustine) and the understandable desire of the authorities to maintain law and order. This state of tolerance and stability was disrupted by sporadic outbreaks of intolerance, which in extreme cases took the form of violent attacks, in a sort of perpetual pendulum that increasingly swung towards intolerance. The need to mark boundaries became pressing

---

2 Bernard Septimus, '"Better under Edom than under Ishmael": The History of a Saying', *Zion* 47 (1982), 103–11 (in Hebrew).

3 Salo Wittmayer Baron, *A Social and Religious History of the Jews*, 2nd edn (18 vols.; New York: Columbia University Press, 1952–83), vols. 10, 11; Guido Kisch, *The Jews in Medieval Germany: A Study of their Legal and Social Status* (Chicago: University of Chicago Press, 1949); Michael Toch, *Die Juden im mittelalterlichen Reich* (Munich: R. Oldenbourg, 1998); Robert Chazan, *Medieval Jewry in Northern France: A Political and Social History* (Baltimore and London: Johns Hopkins University Press, 1973); Yitzhak Fritz Baer, *A History of the Jews in Christian Spain*, trans. Louis Schoffman (2 vols.; Philadelphia: Jewish Publication Society, 1961–66); Attilio Milano, *Storia degli Ebrei in Italia* (Turin: Einaudi, 1963).

The different communities are distinguished from one another in a variety of aspects. Up until the fourteenth century, the Spanish world was characterized by 'convivencia': a co-existence of Jews, Christians and Muslims in relative harmony and with utmost tolerance, which included cultural openness, a range of economic occupations and inclusion in positions of government, all phenomena unknown in the German world.

specifically in view of the physical, social and cultural proximity between the two groups. The more the concept of the solidarity of the Christian world took hold, the worse the treatment of the Jews grew. The pressing need to delineate clear boundaries, indicating who is in and who is out, and to prevent any possible contact between the groups is the primary feature of thirteenth-century Christian legislation and measures regarding Jews. Whereas the marking of boundaries was an essential need for both parties – Christians and Jews alike – and was intended to preserve the individual identity of each, as of the twelfth century, and to a greater extent as of the thirteenth, it was often attended by restrictions imposed on Jews in various areas of life, as a prime expression of the transformation of Christianity into a 'persecuting society'.[4] This process culminated in the absolute expulsion of Jews from the lands in which they dwelt. Hence, whereas in the early thirteenth century Jews lived throughout Europe, by the end of the Middle Ages (1500), Jews were to be found in Western Europe only in Italy and in a few regions of the German Reich.

Medieval ecclesiastical legislation upheld the rights of Jews to protection and to an existence with a modicum of honour in the Christian world, and several popes issued protective bulls.[5] The theological justification for having Jews remain in the Christian world and for granting them protection is to be found in the verse 'Slay them not, lest at any time they forget your law; scatter them in your might' (Septuagint version of Ps. 58.12). In other words, Jews are the guarantee that Christians will not forget their own faith, which is to be found in Jewish Scripture. Yet the Jews' existence may be tolerated only so long as their servile and inferior status is maintained. This is the basis for their protection, but likewise serves as the grounds for imposing restrictions on them.

The most fundamental and well-known document in this matter is the *Sicut Iudaeis* bull (*Constitutio pro Iudaeis*). The bull was first promulgated in 1120 by Pope Calixtus II and later re-issued by several different popes.[6] It reaffirms the

---

4 R. I. Moore, *The Formation of a Persecuting Society: Power and Deviance in Western Europe, 950–1250* (Oxford and New York: Blackwell, 1987).

5 Amnon Linder, *The Jews in the Legal Sources of the Early Middle Ages* (Detroit: Wayne State University Press, 1997); Solomon Grayzel, *The Church and the Jews in the XIIIth Century* (Philadelphia: Dropsie College, 1933); Shlomo Simonsohn, ed., *The Apostolic See and the Jews*, vol. 1, *Documents: 492–1404* (Toronto: Pontifical Institute of Mediaeval Studies, 1988).

6 Grayzel, *The Church and the Jews*, 92–5; Solomon Grayzel, 'The Papal Bull *Sicut Judaeis*', in Meir Ben-Horin et al., eds., *Studies and Essays in Honor of Abraham A. Newman* (Leiden: Brill, 1962), 243–80.

theological principle of the doctrine of Jewish Witness as the basis for extending protection to the Jews and for the prohibition against abusing them or their rights, despite their obstinacy and refusal to recognise the truth. They must not be forcibly converted, but anyone who has converted to Christianity may not renege and resume being a Jew. Naturally, all of the above is applicable only providing that they do not plot against Christians and Christianity.

An important milestone in the attitude of the church towards the Jews was the Fourth Lateran Council (1215), convened in the Lateran Palace in Rome by Pope Innocent III. The Council addressed the burning issues of the day in the Christian world: the status of the church, the doctrine of transubstantiation, the spread of the Cathar heresy, and the attempts to renew the crusades. The main aim of the Council was to bolster the unity and uniformity in the Christian world and to delineate more sharply the boundaries of Christian society. It is in this broader context of the conciliar legislation (seventy decrees in all), that the four clauses pertaining to Jews should be understood.[7] These four clauses determined ecclesiastical policy and were to have a great impact on the lives of the Jews in Europe: they imposed restrictions on the rate of interest that Jews may charge, barred them from positions of authority over Christians, prohibited the observance of Jewish customs by voluntarily baptised Jews, and attempted to minimise contact between Jews and Christians by distinguishing Jews by their garb. The common features of these decisions are their focus on contacts between Jews and Christians and their aim to limit the interaction between the two groups as much as possible.

The decree on dress is the best-known among the Council's decisions with regard to the Jews. Immediately after the Council, Innocent III wrote to the archbishops and bishops of France, demanding that they enforce the dress code, provided it does not endanger the lives of the Jews. The pope thus validated both facets of the policy of the Christian church: the Jews must be sustained and safeguarded, but at the same time they must be kept as separate as possible from Christians. The repeated petitions to enforce the decree indicate that it was neither immediately nor universally implemented. Nonetheless, the Jewish badge – the identifying mark that all Jews were required to affix to their clothes whenever they went out in public – was a direct outcome of this decree, and the duty to wear it remained in force for many centuries.[8]

---

7 Grayzel, *The Church and the Jews*, 306–13.
8 Guido Kisch, 'The Yellow Badge in History', *Historia Judaica* 19 (1957), 89–146; Alfred Rubens, *A History of Jewish Costume* (London: Weidenfeld and Nicolson, 1973).

A further means of keeping Christians and Jews apart from one another was by setting Jews apart in specially designated quarters. From the outset Jews, as any minority would, tended to reside together in their own neighbourhoods or streets. In the early Middle Ages, when rulers were desirous of Jews settling in the city, Jewish neighbourhoods were established in the better areas, in proximity to the centre of town, the market or the river. This was the case in the cities of Ashkenaz, and also in post-Reconquista Spain. The central location of the Jewish neighbourhood had economic, social and cultural implications. Because medieval cities were small, the synagogue was close to the cathedral or another church, and the two groups – Christians and Jews – were in constant contact. These Jewish neighbourhoods did not have a closed or exclusive character. There were cities which did not have specifically Jewish neighbourhoods, and others in which Jews lived intermingled with Christians. As of the thirteenth century, and even more so in the fourteenth, as part of the attempts to restrict contact between Jews and Christians, the demand began to be voiced that Jews live in separate areas.[9] The process of re-settling Jews in completely separate neighbourhoods, sometimes established in remote and unhygienic locations, gained momentum only in the late Middle Ages, and culminated in the establishment of ghettos, a phenomenon originating in sixteenth-century Italy which played a crucial role in the marginalisation of Jews.

The founding of separate and closed Jewish neighbourhoods was a type of internal expulsion. A more drastic solution was the absolute expulsion of Jews from Christian lands. Although the reasons for expulsion varied and were usually made up of a jumble of religious, economic and political motives, they undoubtedly express the most extreme aspect of Christian–Jewish relations in Europe, more specifically the Christian trend to eradicate completely these relations. Yet many of the expelled Jews remained within the realms of Christian Catholicism, mainly in Italy and Poland.

From the very advent of Christianity, Christians articulated the differences between them and the Jews in written works which were to become a sizeable genre called, as were many of its compositions, *Adversus Iudaeos* or *Contra Iudaeos*.[10] From the second to the sixteenth century some 240 Christian pieces

---

9 Alfred Haverkamp, 'The Jewish Quarters in German Towns during the Late Middle Ages', in R. Po-Chia Hsia and Hartmut Lehmann, eds., *In and Out of the Ghetto: Jewish–Gentile Relations in Late Medieval and Early Modern Germany* (Cambridge: Cambridge University Press, 1995), 13–28.

10 Heinz Schreckenberg, *Die christlichen Adversus-Judaeos-Texte* (3 vols.; Frankfurt am Main: Peter Lang, 1982, 1988, 1994); Samuel Krauss and William Horbury, *The Jewish–Christian*

were composed in this genre, a number which indicates the importance of the topic to Christianity. Many of these works were written by renowned thinkers. A parallel genre developed in the Jewish world, beginning in the ninth century, but more impressively from the twelfth century. Known as 'Victory / *Nizzahon* Literature', dozens of works were written in this genre. It may be viewed as a mirror of the Christian compositions and as an expression of the theological pressure exerted by Christianity.[11] Yet, the polemic with Judaism is not limited to a particular literary genre and is present in nearly every type of work written in the Middle Ages: homilies by clergy, epistles, historical chronicles, poetry, religious drama and above all in commentaries on the Scriptures. Visual art also served as a patently polemical tool.

In the twelfth century the *Contra Iudaeos* genre began to flourish, not only as part of the overall cultural resurgence, but also as a bold expression of the church's vision of a *societas Christiana*. The polemic with Judaism underwent an intensification and systemisation that ought to be regarded as part of the intellectual and missionary trends of the time. Despite the presentation of these polemical works as having been written with a view to persuading the opponent, they are not written in the language of the opponent (the Christian works are written in Latin and the Jewish ones in Hebrew), and many of them are worded aggressively and sometimes even venomously, a doubtful method of engendering trust and understanding. Thus they should be regarded as an internal instrument of persuasion – a means for internally confronting the problem posed by the sister religion – in order to reinforce the faith of the believers.

Up until the thirteenth century, the polemical literature centred mostly on Scripture and its exegesis, seeming to take the form of an internal family debate over the correct understanding of a common text, its stories, protagonists and prophecies. The Christian reading which gave the text a prefigurative and allegorical significance compelled the Jews to insist on a historical reading that adhered to the literal meaning of the verses. However, an openness to the reading and exegesis of the other side may be found on both sides. There were even some Christian scholars like Hugh of St-Victor (d. 1142) and

*Controversy: From the Earliest Times to 1789* (Tübingen: J. C. B. Mohr [Paul Siebeck], 1995); A. Lukyn Williams, *Adversus Judaeos: A Bird's-Eye View of Christian Apologiae until the Renaissance* (Cambridge: Cambridge University Press, 1935).

11 David Berger, ed., *The Jewish–Christian Debate in the High Middle Ages: A Critical Edition of the Nizzahon Vetus* (Philadelphia: The Jewish Publication Society of America, 1979); Robert Chazan, *Daggers of Faith: Thirteenth-Century Christian Missionizing and Jewish Response* (Berkeley, Los Angeles and London: University of California Press, 1989).

Andrew of St-Victor (d. 1175) who considered the Jewish exegesis superior expressly because of its adherence to the Hebrew source, the *Hebraica veritas*.[12]

The debate on Scripture lasted throughout the Middle Ages and into the modern period. However, in the thirteenth century the polemic underwent radical changes as part of the intensive Christian missionary attack against anyone outside the boundaries of its faith, including the Jews. The new missionary and polemical attack was planned and managed largely by the recently founded mendicant orders. The friars acted as missionaries, polemic-ists, itinerant preachers, university scholars and inquisitors, all functions aimed at defending the fortifications of faith and sharply defining its boundaries.[13]

One innovation that the Dominicans instituted was bringing the Talmud into the heart of the debate between the two religions. Even before the birth of the mendicant orders, as early as the twelfth century, Peter the Venerable, the abbot of Cluny, in his book *Adversus Judeorum inveteratam duritiem* (1144), had argued that the present-day Jews are not the same as the Jews of the past, and that therefore the church need not tolerate them.[14] Peter the Venerable drew his portrait of the present-day Jews from the *Dialogi* of Petrus Alphonsi (1108 or 1110), a work that employed talmudic legends to prove the folly of Jewish beliefs.[15] Unlike the Bible, the Talmud was unfamiliar to Christians and had not been translated into their languages. It was an internal Jewish text, and thus far there had hardly been any Christian interference in internal Jewish affairs. The thirteenth-century mendicant mission made the Talmud a central topic for attack, arguing that the Jews do not live according to the Bible, but rather according to the Talmud. They are not the Jews who appear in the stories of the New Testament, but rather 'Talmudic Jews'.[16] At the vanguard

---

12 See among others: Beryl Smalley, *The Study of the Bible in the Middle Ages*, 2nd edn (Oxford: Blackwell, 1952); Michael A. Signer, 'God's Love for Israel: Apologetic and Hermeneutical Strategies in Twelfth-Century Biblical Exegesis', in Michael A. Signer and John Van Engen, eds., *Jews and Christians in Twelfth Century Europe* (Notre Dame: University of Notre Dame Press, 2001), 123–49.

13 Jeremy Cohen, *The Friars and the Jews: The Evolution of Medieval Anti-Judaism* (Ithaca, N.Y. and London: Cornell University Press, 1982); Steven J. McMichael and Susan E. Myers, eds., *Friars and Jews in the Middle Ages and Renaissance* (Leiden: Brill, 2004).

14 Peter the Venerable, *Adversus Iudeorum inveteratam duritiem*, ed. Yvonne Friedman (CCCM 58; Turnhout: Brepols, 1985).

15 Petrus Alphonsi, *Dialogus Petri cognomento Alphonsi, ex Judaeo Christiani et Moysi Judaei*, PL 157, cols. 535–672; Petrus Alfonsi, *Dialogue against the Jews*, trans. Irven M. Resnick (The Fathers of the Church, Medieval Continuation 8; Washington D.C.: Catholic University of America Press, 2006).

16 Alexander Patschovsky, 'Der "Talmudjude": Vom mittelalterlichen Ursprung eines neuzeitlichen Themas', in Alfred Haverkamp and Franz-Josef Ziwes, eds., *Juden in der christlichen Umwelt während des späten Mittelalters* (Berlin: Duncker & Humblot, 1992), 13–27.

of this offensive were Jews who had converted to Christianity. They especially had access to the talmudic texts, and their attack was multi-faceted. One contention against the Talmud was that it is filled with heresy and blasphemy. This was the argument that Nicolas Donin tried to prove in the Disputation of Paris (1240); the argument was accepted to be true and led to the burning of twenty-four cartloads of volumes of the Talmud in France in 1242.[17] Another argument was that the talmudic sages knew Jesus and recognised the veracity of his gospel, and that proof of this is embedded in talmudic legends. That was the strategy that led the architects of the Disputation of Barcelona (1263) and was also the basis for the large-scale work by Ramon Martí (Raimundus Martini), *Pugio fidei* (1278).[18]

The perception of the Talmud as being heretical literature according to which Jews live their lives caused a further deterioration in the image of the Jew in Christian eyes and heralded the end of Jewish cultural autonomy. It may also be seen to contain the seeds of Christian censorship, which would develop and flourish in later periods. In Paris, the Christians implemented against the Jews an inquisitorial system that was intended for the battle against heresy within Christianity. As in the trials of the Inquisition, the prosecution, the testimonies, the proof and the conclusions were in the hands of the clerics, whereas the execution of the verdict was left to the secular authorities.

The religious polemic was not merely a literary phenomenon. The cultural and physical proximity between the two groups made for a persistent and animated dialogue, expressing the vitality of their religious world. Naturally, any spontaneous, chance and popular encounters among minor ecclesiastics or even among laymen hardly left a trace. Information about them may be gleaned indirectly from ecclesiastical rulings forbidding disputations by laymen,[19] and from a few atypical works, such as the Disputation of Majorca (1286), which presents disputations among lay merchants in the thirteenth century.[20]

One thirteenth-century innovation was the formalisation of disputations as public affairs, planned and orchestrated by mendicant friars as a kind of

17 Ch. Merchavia, *The Church versus Talmudic and Midrashic Literature (500–1248)* (Jerusalem: The Bialik Insitute, 1970) (in Hebrew); Cohen, *The Friars and the Jews*, 60–76.

18 Raimundus Martini, *Pugio fidei adversus Mauros et Judaeos* (Leipzig, 1687, repr. Farnborough: Gregg, 1967).

19 Grayzel, *The Church and the Jews*, 300–1, 318–19, 324–5; Solomon Grayzel, *The Church and the Jews in the XIIIth Century*, vol. 2, ed. Kenneth R. Stow (Detroit: Wayne State University Press, 1989), 39, 67, 68.

20 Ora Limor, ed., *Die Disputationen zu Ceuta (1179) und Mallorca (1286): Zwei antijüdische Schriften aus dem mittelalterlichen Genua* (MGH, Quellen zur Geistesgeschichte des Mittelalters 15; Munich Monumenta Germaniae Historica, 1994).

show trial aimed at proving the Christian truth. Among these public disputations were the Disputation of Paris in 1240, the Disputation of Barcelona in 1263 and the Second Disputation of Paris in 1269.[21] These disputations all involved Jews who had converted to Christianity, and all discussed the Talmud in addition to presenting biblical evidence. The most elaborate one was the Disputation of Barcelona, held over the course of four days in July 1263 in Barcelona under the auspices of the king of Aragon. Its elaborateness and sophistication were a function not only of its agenda, but also of the interlocutors. On the Jewish side was Nahmanides, the greatest among the Spanish rabbis of his day, and on the Christian side was Pablo Christiani, a former Jew who became a Dominican friar, along with a battery of scholars from the mendicant orders, headed by the learned Dominican friar Raimundus of Peñaforte, formerly the Master General of the Dominicans. The agenda of the disputation clearly articulated the central topics of controversy between the two religions: has the messiah already come as the Christians believe, or is he yet to come as the Jews believe? Is the messiah God or is he truly human? And is it required to observe the commandments of the Law after the coming of the messiah?[22] The Genoese merchant Inghetto Contardo, who disputed with Jews in Majorca in 1286, summed up the differences between Jews and Christians in a single sentence: 'there is no difference between us and you except regarding the Messiah, whom we say has already come, and you say is still to come.'[23] The theme of the messiah was a connecting thread which links the discussion to other fundamental topics: the Deity (Is God one or is he three?); the virgin birth; and even the historical condition of the Jews, the continuing exile as proof of their error. That said, the first part of the merchant's remark deserves attention as well: that Jews and Christians are alike in all things, except with regard to the messiah. At the end of the thirteenth century such an assertion could still be made in the mixed cities of the Mediterranean, and it was precisely against assertions of this type that the mendicant friars and other representatives of the church wished to erect a barrier.

---

21 Cohen, *The Friars and the Jews*; Chazan, *Daggers of Faith*; Hyam Maccoby, *Judaism on Trial: Jewish–Christian Disputations in the Middle Ages* (London and Toronto: Associated University Press, 1982); Joseph Shatzmiller, ed., *La deuxième controverse de Paris: Un chapitre dans la polémique entre chrétiens et juifs au Moyen Âge* (Paris: Peeters 15, 1994).
22 Robert Chazan, *Barcelona and Beyond: The Disputation of 1263 and its Aftermath* (Berkeley, Los Angeles and Oxford: University of California Press, 1992), 59.
23 'Quoniam inter nos et vos non est dissencio nisi de Messia, quem nos dicimus venisse et vos dicitis venire debet'. Limor, ed., *Die Disputationen*, 257.

The public disputations are an expression of the Christian missionary zeal of the thirteenth century, but the Jewish opponents were still treated in a respectful manner. Such at least was the case in Barcelona, where Nahmanides was granted freedom of speech and even took part in setting the agenda. Other missionary methods were sermons preached coercively in synagogues by Christian preachers, mainly mendicants, including Pablo Christiani and Ramon Lull.[24] Yet, it is noteworthy that the new interest in the Jews and their culture also engendered a new type of Christian scholarship. The voluminous *Pugio fidei* by Ramon Martí was written ostensibly for missionary purposes, but at the same time it also represents a scholarly interest in Jewish literature, and as such it heralds the Christian Hebraism of the late Middle Ages. Despite the polemic's goal, it also has an aspect of exchange and dialogue as expressed also in the ongoing cultural interaction between Jews and Christians, the translations of works from one language to another and from one culture to another, and in the existence of a dialogue in biblical hermeneutics and in philosophy and science.

Whereas the public and written polemic was mainly aimed at learned Christians, its representations in visual art were universally understood and had a wider impact.[25] The artistic depiction of church and synagogue – *ecclesia* and *synagoga* – was prevalent in contemporary sculpture and painting, and expressed a state of simultaneous conflict and complement between the sister religions, whereby the images explain one another and the one cannot exist without the other.[26] In addition to this serene image, there were others that bore a more negative message, such as the image of Cain or Judas Iscariot – the traitorous, avaricious arch-villain who, as his name implies, personifies 'The Jew'. Similarly, exempla that preachers used in church homilies, such as the legend of Judas Iscariot told in *The Golden Legend* of Jacobus de Voragina, painted present-day Jews in extremely negative colours based on traditional attributes of the alleged Jews of the past.[27]

---

24 Jocelyn N. Hillgarth, *Ramon Lull and Lullism in Fourteenth-Century France* (Oxford: Clarendon Press, 1971); Harvey J. Hames, *The Art of Conversion: Christianity and Kabbalah in the Thirteenth Century* (Leiden: Brill, 2000).

25 Heinz Schreckenberg, *The Jews in Christian Art: An Illustrated History* (New York: Continuum, 1996); Ruth Mellinkoff, *Outcasts: Signs of Otherness in Northern European Art of the Late Middle Ages* (2 vols.; Berkeley and Los Angeles: University of California Press, 1994); Sara Lipton, *Images of Intolerance: The Representation of Jews and Judaism in the Bible moralisée* (Berkeley: University of California Press, 1999).

26 Wolfgang S. Seiferth, *Synagogue and Church in the Middle Ages: Two Symbols in Art and Literature*, trans. Lee Chadeayne and Paul Gottwald (New York: Ungar, 1970).

27 Ruth Mellinkoff, *The Mark of Cain* (Berkeley, Los Angeles and London: University of California Press, 1981); Peter Dinzelbacher, *Judastraditionen* (Vienna: Selbstverlag des österreichisches Museum für Volkskunde, 1977); Hyam Maccoby, *Judas Iscariot and the Myth of Jewish Evil* (London: Peter Halban, 1992).

The complex figure of the Jew as a historical and theological being had an eschatological aspect as well. According to deep-rooted Christian belief, the Jews had in fact refused to see the light, but at the end of days they would acknowledge the Christian truth, and their dramatic conversion to Christianity would presage the coming of the kingdom of heaven on earth. The upsurge in messianic tension in the thirteenth century and the expectation of the impending *parousia*, particularly among mendicant circles that were influenced by the teachings of Joachim of Fiore (c. 1135–1202), made the conversion of the Jews to Christianity a pressing matter, and the vigorous mission conducted against them should be understood also in this context.[28]

In the Middle Ages conversion generally operates in a single direction – from Judaism to Christianity – and traditionally the church continued to oppose forced conversions. However, this unidirectional conversion did not cure the deep-rooted Christian fear of Christians being converted to Judaism. Pope Clement IV, in his bull *Turbato corde* (1267), ordered the Dominicans and the Franciscans to investigate reports of Jewish attempts to convert Christians, an order reiterated by subsequent popes.[29] The newly formed Inquisition took steps to prevent Jews from influencing former Jews, now converts to Christianity. Sexual relations between Jews and Christians were considered heresy, and any who took part in them were condemned to burning at the stake. It is reasonable to assume that, like the polemic tracts, the aim of the public disputations was mostly that of internal propaganda, as a means of strengthening believers in their faith. Things would be different at the public Disputation of Tortosa (1413–14) which was conceived as a weapon for converting Jews to Christianity, and indeed in the course of it hundreds of Jews did convert, an expression of weakness and a sense of persecution uncharacteristic of thirteenth-century Judaism.[30]

The growing of an urban mercantile class led – especially in northern Europe – to the Jews gradually being driven out of commercial trade, and many Jews turned to money-lending, an occupation necessary in economic terms, but despicable in both theological and social terms. Over time this occupation became the distinguishing mark of Jews. Money-lending strengthened the

---

28 Richard Kenneth Emmerson, *Antichrist in the Middle Ages: A Study of Medieval Apocalypticism, Art, and Literature* (Seattle: University of Washington Press, 1981); Robert E. Lerner, *The Feast of Saint Abraham: Medieval Millenarians and the Jews* (Philadelphia: University of Pennsylvania Press, 2001).
29 Grayzel, *The Church and the Jews*, vol. 2, 102–4, 122–3, 147, 171–2, 181.
30 Baer, *A History of the Jews*, vol. 2, 170–243.

association between Jews and the sovereigns who needed financial credit, levied high taxes on the earnings of the Jews, and in return provided them with protection.[31] This dependence on the authorities further weakened the status of the Jews and in several cases led to their expulsion from the kingdom once their usefulness had been exhausted.[32] Their despised occupation along with direct ties to the authorities tarred Jews with the colours of sin and exploitation and further augmented the animosity towards them. In addition, the urbanisation, the increased activity in trade and finances in Christian society and the widened gap between rich and poor caused the Christians to lay their sense of guilt at the doorstep of the Jews, thereby turning the Jews into Christian society's scapegoats.[33] Usurious money-lending was added to the satanical image of the Jews as persecutors of Christians and Christ-killers. As of the twelfth century and particularly in the thirteenth century, the image of the Jew grew even more negative, and his satanical aspect became more sharply defined. If up until this point the Jews had been conceived of as blind and therefore acting unknowingly, they now came to be viewed as maliciously evil, with a deeply rooted demonic, perverted and traitorous character.[34] Radical expressions of the demonic image of the Jew were the accusations of ritual murder, ritual cannibalism (the blood libels) and the desecration of the Host, and were frequently followed by violent attacks against the Jews.

The first recorded instance of Jews being accused of the ritual murder of Christians (usually, of Christian children) is in the mid-twelfth century

31 The appellation 'servi camerae' first appears in the twelfth century, and would remain common throughout the Middle Ages. This terminology, which was meant to protect the Jews, ultimately added to their humiliation. Kisch, *The Jews in Medieval Germany*, 143–5; David Abulafia, 'The King and the Jews – the Jew in the Ruler's Service', in Christoph Cluse, ed., *The Jews of Europe in the Middle Ages (Tenth to Fifteenth Centuries)* (Turnhout: Brepols, 2004), 43–54.

32 Robert Stacey, 'Thirteenth-Century Anglo-Jewry and the Problem of the Expulsion', in David S. Katz and Yosef Kaplan, eds., *Exile and Return: Anglo-Jewry through the Ages* (Jerusalem: The Zalman Shazar Center for Jewish History, 1993) (in Hebrew); William Chester Jordan, *The French Monarchy and the Jews: From Philip Augustus to the Last Capetians* (Philadelphia: University of Pennsylvania Press, 1989); Markus J. Wenninger, *Man bedarf keiner Juden mehr: Ursachen und Hintergründe ihrer Vertreibung aus den deutschen Reichsstädten im 15. Jahrhundert* (Vienna: H. Bohlaus Nachf., 1981).

33 Lester K. Little, *Religious Poverty and the Profit Economy in Medieval Europe* (London: Paul Elek, 1978).

34 Joshua Trachtenberg, *The Devil and the Jews* (New Haven: Yale University Press, 1943); Anna Sapir Abulafia, *Christians and Jews in the Twelfth-Century Renaissance* (London and New York: Routledge, 1995); Jeremy Cohen, 'The Jews as the Killers of Christ in the Latin Tradition: From Augustine to the Friars', *Traditio* 39 (1983), 1–27.

(Norwich, 1144).[35] From that time until the expulsion of the Jews from England in 1290, at least fourteen libels are known in England, including the blood libel in Lincoln in 1255, demonstrating the ease with which this idea took root in Christian soil. In the second half of the twelfth century libels appeared on the Continent as well, including the Libel of Blois (1171), which terminated in the burning at the stake of some forty Jews, even though no body of a missing Christian was found.[36] In Fulda, in 1235, the libel of ritual murder was enhanced by a further accusation: the use of Christian blood for ritual purposes, usually for the purpose of baking *matzot*, the unleavened bread of Passover.[37] This elaborated version of the blood libel is undoubtedly the darkest juncture in Christian–Jewish relations in the Middle Ages. The libel garnered believers throughout Christendom, first in northern Europe and later in the Iberian peninsula as well. To be sure, not all Christians believed that Jews murdered Christian children for ritual purposes and used their blood. Kings, popes and Christian scholars spoke vociferously and consistently against the libel and even tried to expose its spuriousness, but did not manage to uproot the belief in it or halt its proliferation.[38]

In addition to the blood libel, the Libel of the Host appeared in the late thirteenth century (Paris, 1290). Its premise was the belief that Jews deceitfully obtained the Host and then abused and desecrated it.[39] The famous libels concluded in miracles effected by the Host, and thus the Jews ended by validating the Christian faith against their will. Both libels, that of the ritual murder and that of the Host, replicate the original and eternal sin of the Jews – the sin of the crucifixion of Jesus. According to the logic of the libels, the Jews murdered Jesus, even while knowing that he was the messiah, and they repeatedly murder his body (the Host) and his believers because their faith commands them to do so. Today, at least 180 blood libels are known to have

35 Gavin I. Langmuir, 'Thomas of Monmouth: Detector of Ritual Murder', *Speculum* 59 (1984), 820–46; Gavin I. Langmuir, 'Historiographic Crucifixion', in David R. Blumenthal, ed., *Approaches to Judaism in Medieval Times* (Brown Judaic Studies 54; Chico, Cal.: Scholars Press, 1984), 1–26.

36 Robert Chazan, 'The Blois Incident of 1171: A Study in Jewish Intercommunal Organization', *Proceedings of the American Academy of Jewish Research* 36 (1968), 13–32.

37 Bernhard Diestelkamp, 'Der Vorwurf des Ritualmordes gegen Juden vor dem Hofgericht Kaiser Friedrichs II. im Jahr 1236', in Dieter Simon, ed., *Religiöse Devianz* (Frankfurt am Main: V. Klostermann, 1990), 19–39.

38 Grayzel, *The Church and the Jews*, index: Ritual Murder; Grayzel, *The Church and the Jews*, vol. 2, index: Ritual Murder.

39 Miri Rubin, *Gentile Tales: The Narrative Assault on Late Medieval Jews* (New Haven, Conn.: Yale University Press, 1999).

been levelled against Jews, as well as approximately 100 Host libels, many of which led to the loss of Jewish lives.[40]

Many explanations have been rendered for the appearance of the libels. Some seek their sources in the Jewish world – in Jewish customs or beliefs that were misconstrued by Christians; others seek them in the Christian world and link them, among other things, to the formulation of the doctrine of transubstantiation and the anxiety aroused by doubts about it.[41] Later these accusations would be joined by others, such as the poisoning of wells (e.g., during the Black Death) or the use of black magic to destroy Christianity. The willingness of the Christian public to accept the accusations against the Jews and their writings is a manifestation of the atmosphere of the time and the nature of Christian devotion which strongly emphasised Jesus' suffering as a man and the worship of his mother, the Virgin Mary.[42] The accusations against the Jews reflect a basic Christian anxiety and an intensification of the irrational element in Christian consciousness. The libels also point to the fact that, although Jews had been a minority for centuries in Christian society, and at times even a persecuted minority, Christian imagination preserved in all its original vitality the original trauma at the basis of Christian faith, the trauma of the crucifixion. In the Christian imagination the Jews were still the persecutors, and the Christians the persecuted. In terms of the Jews, the myriad accusations created impenetrable boundaries between the two religions, and their destructive influence is apparent in the late Middle Ages and into the modern period.

40 Will-Erich Peuckert, 'Ritualmord', in *Handwörterbuch des deutschen Aberglaubens* (Berlin: Walter de Gruyter, 1935–36), vol. 7, cols. 727–39.

41 Israel Jacob Yuval, *Two Nations in your Womb: Perceptions of Jews and Christians in Late Antiquity and the Middle Ages* (Berkeley and Los Angeles: University of California Press, 2006); Rubin, *Gentile Tales*.

42 William Chester Jordan, 'Marian Devotion and the Talmud Trial of 1240', in Bernard Lewis and Friedrich Niewöhner, eds., *Religionsgespräche im Mittelalter* (Wiesbaden: Harrassowitz, 1992), 61–76.

## II

# Christendom and Islam

### DAVID NIRENBERG

Given the great variety of Christian and Muslim cultures in the Middle Ages, it should not be surprising that relations between the two defy synthesis. The relationships to Islam of the many Christians who lived in Muslim lands, for example, were very different from those of Christians living in orthodox Christian Byzantium or Catholic Latin Europe. The word 'Christendom' in the title therefore reflects a sharp but necessary abridgement of the topic. This article will focus only on those lands that came to think of themselves as 'Christendom': that is, Catholic Western Europe, from the Iberian to the Hungarian kingdoms.[1] It will ask three interrelated questions. First, what did Christians know about Islam? Second, how did their thinking about Islam affect the formation of the concept of Christendom itself? And third, how did Islam experience Christendom? For throughout our period there were not only numerous Christian incursions into the lands of Islam (via pilgrimage, trade, crusade and mission), but also many Muslims living *within* Christendom.

The first two questions, of course, are quite different from the third, for they have less to do with the study of historical contacts and relations between Christianity and Islam in the Middle Ages, and more to do with the study of the role that Christian ideas about Islam play in the formation of Christian conceptualisations of the world and Christianity's place in it. The third question, on the other hand, is about historically specific encounters between Christians and Muslims. I will touch briefly upon the best-known forms of these encounters, namely trade and crusade. But I will give more space to the less well-known phenomenon of the practice of Islam in Christian lands. We tend to think of medieval Catholic Europe as a region largely 'Muslimrein'.

---

1 Readers interested in Byzantium may turn to (among others) the work of Adel Théodore Khoury: *Polémique byzantine contre l'Islam (VIIIe-XIIIe s.)* (Leiden: Brill, 1972); *Les théologiens byzantins et l'Islam: Textes et auteurs (VIIIe-XIIIe s.)* (Louvain and Paris: Editions Nauwelaerts, 1969).

Even when we acknowledge the presence of Islam in Christendom, we rarely pause to think about how the Christian context might affect the type of Islam practised within it. But in fact throughout our period Europe contained Islamic communities whose experience of 'being Muslim' was quite different from the experience of Muslims living in more heavily Islamic lands.

I

My first question, 'What did medieval Christians know about Islam and when did they learn it?', is often asked by scholars, but is in at least one sense much less interesting than it seems. Christians knew most of what they felt they needed to know about Islam from the moment it began its muscular journey from the Arabian Peninsula in the mid-seventh century: Islam was not Christianity, and it was mighty in war. From a Christian point of view, the victories of these non-Christians could mean only two things. Either Christianity was an incorrect religion that should be abandoned in favour of Islam, or Christians were indeed correct in their religious choice, but were being punished by an angry God. The first option was taken by the countless Christians who chose to convert to the Islam of their conquerors. Christian writing about Islam, of course, was generally produced by those who opted for theodicy. Preaching on Christmas day 634 in the midst of the invasions, the patriarch of Jerusalem explained to his trembling flock that God had sent 'the godless Saracens' as punishment for 'countless sins and very serious faults'. 'Let us correct ourselves', he exhorted. 'If we constrain ourselves…we would see their final destruction.'[2]

The actual content of the Saracens' faith was irrelevant to Sophronios, who was interested only in elucidating the Muslims' role in Christian sacred history. Nor did penance's failure to stem the invasions incline him more seriously towards ethnography. As the Caliph 'Umar triumphantly entered Jerusalem, the patriarch is said to have proclaimed, 'Verily, this is the abomination of desolation standing in a holy place, as has been spoken through the prophet Daniel.'[3] Maximus the Confessor, writing from Alexandria at much the same time, put it more bluntly. The invaders were 'wild and untamed beasts who have merely the shape of human form'. They were, he added, Jews

---

2 'Christmas Sermon', trans. Walter Kaegi, 'Initial Byzantine Reactions to the Arab Conquest', *Church History* 38 (1969), 139–49.
3 *The Chronicle of Theophanes the Confessor*, trans. Cyril Mango and Roger Scott (Oxford: Clarendon Press, 1997), 471.

and followers of the Antichrist.[4] Muslims, in short, were either Christ's scourge for the improvement of Christendom or the shock troops of apocalypse, related one way or another to other enemies of God (such as Jews, idol-worshippers and heretics). In either case, contemporaries saw no point in studying their religious beliefs or cultural practices except to condemn them or prove them wrong.

As a very general rule, this one holds true throughout the Middle Ages. From the seventh century to the end of the fifteenth, Christian understanding of Islam was predicated on two basic axioms. First, Islam was a false religion. Second, it was a carnal one, glorying in violence and sexuality. It is striking how early these positions crystallised. Already in 634, for example, a Christian author treated Islam's conquests as a sign of its falsity: 'Do prophets come with swords and chariots?'[5] (The same author would, of course, doubtless have interpreted Christian military victories as signs of that religion's truth.) Sexuality too rose immediately to the polemical forefront, with Christians asserting that the religion of Islam had been founded by Muhammad in order to help him satisfy his lusts, and that the afterlife he promised to those who died following him was entirely carnal.

Increasing familiarity with Islam did not alter the tone of these polemics, but only sharpened it. John of Damascus (Yuhanna b. Mansur b. Sarjun), for example, was fluent in Arabic (in fact Greek was for him a second language), and an important financial administrator at the court of the Umayyad caliphs 'Abd al-Malik and Walid I (685–715). His obvious knowledge of Islam did not, however, alter the general lines of the polemic he wrote against it. The Ishmaelites, he wrote, were precursors of the Antichrist. Worshippers of Aphrodite, they were seduced by 'a false prophet Mamed…who, having casually been exposed to the Old and the New Testament, and supposedly encountered an Arian monk, formed a heresy of his own'. According to John, Muhammad's motives were primarily sexual: hence he dwelt extensively on the Qur'anic treatment of polygamy and divorce, and on Muhammad's many wives.[6]

---

4 Maximus the Confessor's complaint in *PG* 91, col. 540 is translated in John Lamoreaux, 'Early Christian Responses to Islam', in John Tolan, ed., *Medieval Christian Perceptions of Islam: A Book of Essays* (New York: Garland, 1996), 3–31, here pp. 14f. For some more positive early Christian appraisals of Islam, see John Tolan, *Saracens: Islam in the Medieval European Imagination* (New York: Columbia, 2002), 45–6.

5 'Doctrina Jacobi nuper baptizati' [The Doctrine of Jacob recently Baptized], trans. Kaegi, 'Initial Byzantine Reactions', 141.

6 John of Damascus, *Liber de haeresibus*, in P. Bonafatius Kotter, ed., *Die Schriften des Johannes von Damaskos* (5 vols.; Berlin: de Gruyter, 1969–81), vol. 4, 19–67, here p. 60. See

These are among the earliest Christian accounts of Islam. They predate our period and are from outside the borders of the region with which we are concerned. But they do not differ substantially from what Christians said about Islam centuries later and further west. All of these themes, from heretical monks to idol worship and rampant sexuality, can be found in Christian writings of every century from the eleventh to the sixteenth. This is not to say that available knowledge about Islam in the West was unchanging. On the contrary, if twelfth-century vernacular poets (like the author of the Song of Roland) and Latinate clerics (like the canon lawyers of the Decretals) alike continued to present Muslims as worshippers of Apollo or Aphrodite, it was not for lack of sources that knew better. But even in the best-informed sources, new learning was only intended to give well-worn polemics a sharper edge. For instance, the author of the *Liber denudationis*, a work written in Arabic by an Iberian Christian in the twelfth century, knew a great deal about Islam, and was clearly familiar with Arabic commentaries on the Qur'an. But he read these sources in order to solidify rather than challenge his prejudices, mining them for evidence to support the ancient topoi of Muslim materialism and hyper-sexuality. Thus he trumpeted with great glee a marginal and esoteric (not to say fantastic) Islamic tradition that in paradise each virtuous Muslim believer will be rewarded by the growth of his penis to such a length that he will need seventy Christians and seventy Jews to carry it before him.[7]

Engagement with Islamic texts did not alter Christian understandings of Islam because (like Islamic engagement with Christian and Jewish texts, or Jewish engagement with Islamic and Christian texts) this engagement was largely structured by polemic.[8] The marginal notes in medieval translations of

also Daniel Sahas, *John of Damascus on Islam: The 'Heresy' of the Ishmaelites* (Leiden: Brill, 1972). Later Christian polemics against Islam written in Arabic, like the ninth-century *Risâlat al-Kindî*, display even greater knowledge both of Qur'an and Sirah (the biography of the Prophet), but deploy that greater knowledge to the same goals of characterising Islam as sexual, and as derivative of Judaism and heretical Christianity. On this polemical tradition, see Samir Khalil Samir and Jørgen S. Nielsen, eds., *Christian Arabic Apologetics during the Abbasid Period: 750–1258* (Leiden: Brill, 1994). On the circulation of such polemics in Christian Spain, see P. Sjoerd van Koningsveld, 'La Apología de Al-Kindî en la España del siglo XII: Huellas toledanas de un "animal disputax"', in *Estudios sobre Alfonso VI y la reconquista de Toledo: Actas del II congreso internacional de estudios mozárabes* (Toledo: Instituto de Estudios, 1989), 107–29.

7 *Liber denudationis* §9.20, in Thomas Burman, ed., *Religious Polemic and the Intellectual History of the Mozarabs* (Leiden: Brill, 1994). On Christian study of Islamic Qur'an exegesis in the Latin West, see also Thomas Burman, 'Tafsīr and Translation: Robert of Ketton, Mark of Toledo, and traditional Arabic Qur'ān Exegesis', *Speculum* 73 (1998), 703–32.

8 This is a sweeping statement, even if 'largely' does not mean 'completely'. The exceptions, however, were few. One of the most interesting comes from Maimonides: 'By no means are Muslims idolaters...they recognize God's unity. Just because they falsely accuse us...we cannot also lie by saying that they are idolaters... If someone were to

the Qur'an, for example, told Christian readers exactly what they should be taking from it, as in this example: 'Note that he everywhere promises a paradise of earthly delights, as other heresies had done before.'[9] Indeed these translations were undertaken, not to increase knowledge of Islam, but simply to reaffirm what every Christian already knew. Peter the Venerable of Cluny, the most powerful churchman of his age and the organiser in the mid-twelfth century of the first translation of the Qur'an and a number of other Arabic texts into Latin, put the point simply in his anti-Islamic manifesto: 'I translated from Arabic into Latin the whole of this sect, along with the execrable life of its evil inventor, and exposed it to scrutiny of our people, so that it be known what a filthy and frivolous heresy it is.'[10]

Modern historians often stress the importance of subtle differences in medieval Christian characterisations of Islam, and are very much on the look-out for evidence of real knowledge about Islamic practice, which they often valorise positively as a sign of cultural engagement and exchange. For the modern critic it makes a great deal of difference whether a medieval Christian author characterised the Muslims as idol-worshippers, as Judaisers, or as monotheistic heretics. (In fact most medieval commentators on Islam presented it as a blend of paganism, Judaism and Christian heresies such as Arianism). But these subtle distinctions miss a basic point: medieval Christians believed that Islam was a false and dangerous belief, and, with very few exceptions, their study of it was aimed entirely at its condemnation and defeat.

This did not stop them from developing a body of knowledge, a 'science of Islam' involving a great deal of gathering and translation of information. The science they developed remained standard until the end of our period, and even transmitted a little of its ideological content to the 'Orientalist' learning of French and British scholars in the eighteenth and nineteenth centuries. Yet the truth-value of this science was measured by the extent to which it

argue that the House [in Mecca] where they praise Him is an idolatrous temple that conceals inside the idol their ancestors worshipped [the Kaaba], [they should know that] those who bow to him now have only God in mind. The rabbis have already explained in Sanhedrin that if one bows in an idolatrous temple but believes it is a synagogue, his heart is dedicated to God.' Moses Maimonides, *Letters and Essays of Moses Maimonides*, ed. and trans. Isaac Shailat (Jerusalem: Maliyot Press of Yeshivat Birkat Moshe Maaleh Adumim, 1987), 238f.

9 John Tolan, 'Peter the Venerable, on the "Diabolical Heresy of the Saracens"', in Alberto Ferreiro, ed., *The Devil, Heresy, and Witchcraft in the Middle Ages: Essays in Honor of Jeffrey B. Russell* (Leiden: Brill, 1998), 345–67; Marie-Thérèse d'Alverny, 'Deux traductions latines du Coran au Moyen-Âge', *Archives d'histoire doctrinale et littéraire du Moyen Âge* 16 (1947–8), 69–131.

10 *Summa totius haeresis Saracenorum*, in Rheinhold Glei, ed., *Schriften zum Islam* (Corpus Islamo-Christianum, series latina 1; Alternberg: CIS-Verlag, 1985), §18.

conformed to and reinforced Christian theology, not by its consonance with the historical and religious experience of Muslims. When a medieval chronicler like Otto of Friesing points out that Muslims revere Muhammad as a prophet, not as a god, he is trying to show how well read he is, not trying to educate his readers about Islam or soften their antipathy toward it. There is no real point, he and his contemporaries would have agreed, in worrying too much about details when writing the history of an error. As Gautier de Compiègne put it in his twelfth-century life of Muhammad, 'One may safely speak ill of a man whose malignity transcends and surpasses whatever evil can be said about him.'[11]

2

The sharp increase in the information about Islam available in Latin Europe across the period from 1000 to 1500 did not substantially redirect the polemical channels through which that knowledge flowed. One reason for this is the increasing importance of the work to which these channels were put over the course of the Middle Ages. Curiously enough, that importance is inversely proportional to the military threat posed by Islam to Latin Europe itself. Before the eleventh century, when the military reach of Islam was longest (the Muslims sacked Genoa as late as 993, for example, and captured Abbot Maiolus of Cluny in the Alps in 972), the polemic with Islam remained relatively unimportant in the core areas of Western Europe.[12] After the year 1000, at precisely the point that Latin Christian power began to extend itself once more into the Mediterranean, that polemic began to become ideologically central. We can see one important example of this centrality in the new role assigned to Islam in Christian thinking about violence and war. The same decades that saw the Christian conquest of southern Italy, Sardinia and Sicily, and of large parts of Muslim al-Andalus, produced the proclamation of Pope Alexander II that, although the shedding of human blood is forbidden to the Christian, it was 'just to fight' against the Saracens, 'who persecute Christians

---

11 Recounted in Guibert of Nogent's account of the First Crusade, *Dei gesta per Francos*, ed. R. B. C. Huygens (CCCM 127A; Turnhout: Brepols, 1996), 94; trans. Robert Levine, *The Deeds of God through the Franks* (Woodbridge: Boydell Press, 1997), 32. See also Jean Flori, 'La caricature de l'Islam dans l'Occident médiéval: Origine et signification de quelques stéréotypes concernant l'Islam', *Aevum* 2 (1992), 245–56.

12 The episode involving Abbot Maiolus is particularly interesting. It is related in Syrus, *Vita Sancti Maioli* (PL 137, cols. 763D–768D), translated and discussed in Benjamin Z. Kedar, *Crusade and Mission: European Approaches towards the Muslims* (Princeton: Princeton University Press, 1984), 42–3.

and expel them from their towns and dwelling places'.[13] This is not a coincidence: in the eleventh and twelfth centuries, ideas about Islam played an important role in the creation of a muscular version of European Christianity, one that increasingly saw itself as united by a common destiny to conquer a wider world imagined as Muslim.[14]

What we today call the crusades are, of course, the most famous example of this process. Though western warriors, merchants and pilgrims had long been present in the Eastern Mediterranean, the unruly progress of French, Norman, Occitan, German and Italian crusaders on their long march to Jerusalem during the First Crusade in 1096 struck observers as something new. The Byzantine Princess Anna Comnena described it as the northern forests suddenly emptying themselves into the Mediterranean. For Muslim rulers in the East, the entry of the crusading armies into their domains was indeed the first significant intrusion of Western Europe into their political consciousness, and the shape of that first impression is interesting. Muslim rulers did not think of the first few crusades as part of a coherent and ongoing Christian attack on Islam: that consciousness took more than a century to emerge. But they did think of the heterogeneous crusading armies as a unified people, and this from the very beginning. Muslims would for centuries call all the members of these armies 'firandj', 'Franks', regardless of their actual provenance. The term came to signify 'European' in Arabic, Chinese, and a good many other languages of Asia and its subcontinent well into the modern age. If the people Columbus famously mistook for 'Indians' in 1492 had in fact been that, they would have doubtless called this Genoese sailing under the flag of Castile a 'Frank.'[15]

Though entirely the product of too crude an ethnography, the Muslim homogenisation of crusading Europe did parallel an explicit goal of the crusade's organisers themselves. For Pope Urban II, the first crusade was as much about establishing peace and unity in the West as it was about giving aid to Byzantium or conquering Jerusalem from Islam. Every report we have of

---

13 *Epistolae et diplomata*, no. 101 (*PL* 146, cols. 1386–7).

14 Two recent studies of this role, from quite different but complementary points of view, are Dominique Iogna-Prat, *Order and Exclusion: Cluny and Christendom face Heresy, Judaism, and Islam (1000–1150)*, trans. G. R. Edwards (Ithaca, N.Y.: Cornell University Press, 2002); and Tomaž Mastnak, *Crusading Peace: Christendom, the Muslim World, and Western Political Order* (Berkeley: University of California Press, 2002).

15 On Islamic reactions to the Crusades, see the works of Emmanuel Sivan, *L'Islam et la Croisade: Idéologie et propagande dans les réactions musulmanes aux Croisades* (Paris: Librairie d'Amérique et d'Orient, 1968); and *Interpretations of Islam Past and Present* (Princeton: The Darwin Press, 1985), ch. 1. See also under 'Crusades' in the *Encyclopedia of Islam*, 2nd edn. On the term 'Frank', see *ibid.*, under 'Ifrandj'.

his preaching stresses the same thing: war against Muslims was an antidote to civil war amongst Christians. The summary of Baldric of Bourgueil, archbishop of Dol, is representative:

> Listen and understand. You have strapped on the belt of soldiery and strut around with pride in your eye. You butcher your brothers and create factions amongst yourselves. This, which scatters the sheepfold of the Redeemer, is not the army of Christ... You must either cast off as quickly as possible the belt of this sort of soldiery or go forward boldly as soldiers of Christ, hurrying swiftly to defend the Eastern Church... You may restrain your murderous hands from the destruction of your brothers, and on behalf of your relatives in the faith oppose yourself to the Gentiles... You should shudder, brethren, you should shudder at raising a violent hand against Christians; it is less wicked to brandish your sword against Saracens. It is the only warfare that is righteous.[16]

Robert the Monk assigned to Urban slightly different words, but the same argument:

> This land which you inhabit is too narrow for your large population; nor does it abound in wealth; and it furnishes scarcely enough food for its cultivators. Hence it is that you murder one another, that you wage war, and that frequently you perish by mutual wounds... Let therefore hatred depart from among you, let your quarrels end, let wars cease, and let all dissensions and controversies slumber. Enter upon the road to the Holy Sepulcher, wrest that land from the wicked race, and subject it to yourselves.[17]

The consequences of such preaching, according to Otto of Freising, were dramatic: 'And so, as countless peoples and nations...were moved to take the cross, suddenly almost the entire West became so still that not only the waging of war but even the carrying of arms in public was considered wrong.'[18] Urban, Bernard, Peter the Venerable, all were able students of Durkheim and Frederick Jackson Turner. They promoted peace and unity at home in Christendom by projecting discord outward towards the 'Gentile frontier': *Intus pax, foris terrores*, 'Peace inside, terror outside'.[19]

---

16 Baldric of Dol, *Historia Jerosolimitana* I.iv, 14–15; trans. Edward Peters, *The First Crusade: The Chronicle of Fulcher of Chartres and Other Source Materials* (Philadelphia: University of Pennsylvania Press, 1989), 9. See also Jonathan Riley-Smith, *The First Crusade and the Idea of Crusading* (London: Athlone, 1993), 149.

17 *Roberti monachi historia Iherosolimitana* I.1–2, 727–29, trans. Peters, *The First Crusade*, 2–4.

18 Otto of Freising, *The Deeds of Frederick Barbarossa*, trans. Ch. Mierow (Toronto: University of Toronto Press, 1994), vol.1, xliv.

19 Hence Joseph Strayer called the First Crusade 'a spectacular advance toward European peace and unity': see 'The First Western Union', in his *Medieval Statecraft and the Perspectives of History* (Princeton: Princeton University Press, 1971), 334. On the

The crusades were designed to give Western Christendom a common project and a shared sense of purpose, as well as to pacify it. They were not the task of just one king, noble, or nation, but a *negotium christianum*, a Christian business. The notion of *christianitas* was expanded through the crusade preaching of popes like Innocent III into the idea of a *populus christianus*, 'a Christian people', and thence into the concept of a 'Christendom' defined collectively by its struggle against all unfaithful foreign nations. Of course from the papal point of view a single entity needs a single leader, and that leader was to be the pope, the vicar of Christ. It is not a coincidence that the same theologians who championed crusade developed this title 'vicar of Christ' (rather than, for example, the older papal title 'vicar of Peter'). Bernard of Clairvaux, for example, was the first to apply it to the pope alone (as opposed to all bishops, or even lay princes), and Innocent III was the first pope to use the title publicly.[20]

In other words, Urban, Bernard, Innocent and other architects of papal power were political theorists as much as sociologists, readers of Carl Schmitt as well as of Durkheim. By emphasising the danger posed by an external enemy and declaring war upon it they sought not only to pacify Latin Europe, but also to strengthen a newly emerging form of sovereignty over it, the sovereignty of the papacy, known amongst medievalists as 'papal monarchy'. This sovereignty was not simply a matter of struggle over titles like 'vicar of Christ'. It was also a matter of building pan-European institutions and wielding pan-European power, and in this construction the crusade against the Muslim 'enemies of God and holy Christendom' played a vital role.[21]

Taxation provides a good example of this role. The need to raise money for crusades (and the possibility of using the crusade to justify the raising of

emergence of the terms 'christianitas' and 'christianissimus' in this period, see Jean Rupp, *L'idée de chrétienté dans la pensée pontificale des origines à Innocent III* (Paris: Les Presses Modernes, 1939); P. Rousset, 'La notion de chrétienté aux XIe et XIIe siècles', *Le Moyen Âge* 69 (1963), 195ff. 'Intus pax, foris terrores' is cited without attribution by Étienne Delaruelle, 'Paix de Dieu et croisade dans la chrétienté du XIIe siècle', in *Paix de Dieu et guerre sainte en Languedoc au XIIIe siècle* (Cahiers de Fanjeaux 4; Toulouse: Édouard Privat, 1969), 51–71, here 61.

20 On the development of these terms see Tomaž Mastnak, *Crusading Peace: Christendom, the Muslim World, and Western Political Order* (Berkeley: University of California Press, 2002), 91–9, 144–6; Agostino Paravicini-Bagliani, *The Pope's Body* (Chicago: Chicago University Press, 2000), 58; Jane E. Sayers, *Innocent III: Leader of Europe (1198–1216)* (London: Longman, 1994), 16. Bernard's uses are in *On Consideration* II.viii.16, IV.vii.23.

21 *Gesta Francorum* VI.xiii: 'Turci inimici Dei et sanctae christianitatis.' As Alphonse Dupront put it in his conclusion to the volume of Paul Alphandéry's lectures that he edited, 'Crusade and Christendom were made together, in a reciprocal creation.' Paul Alphandéry, *La chrétienté et l'idée de croisade*, vol. 2, ed. Alphonse Dupront (Paris: Éditions Albin Michel, 1959), 274.

money) put the papacy in the position of establishing the first regular taxation system in the West. Crusading taxes (or tithes) were raised at the level of the locality (parish church, bishopric, etc.), then passed on to the pope as leader of the crusading movement. The pope in turn distributed the money to those kings or nobles who had entered into an agreement with him to carry out a crusade. It was Innocent III who obtained at least theoretical consensus that all benefices should contribute a percentage of their revenues to the support of papally sanctioned crusades. Later popes refined the system. Gregory X (1271–76), for example, divided all of Christendom into a system of twenty-six collectorates, or tax districts, for the collection of a truly universal tithe. And of course once the system was in place its exactions became regular, so that taxes were collected even when no crusade was being fought, as preparation for the next one. (Indeed in Spain, the tax continued to be collected well into the modern period.)[22]

The tax is one example of what would today be called a 'transnational European institution'. The term is anachronistic for the Middle Ages. But the important point here is simply that the crusades furthered the project of creating pan-European institutions centred around papal authority and control. Another example of such an institution, perhaps the most important one in terms of its implications for the future of European expansion and colonisation, is the very idea of crusade itself, that is, of holy war authorised by papal sanction.

In all these ways, the idea of Christian war against Islam gave medieval Europe a much more unified and self-conscious sense of historical mission.[23] But it would be wrong to exaggerate the dependence of this awakening of an expansionary Western European notion of Christendom on a confrontation with Islam or on the creation of a 'Muslim enemy', although the tendency is understandable in the light of current events.[24] It is certainly true that the

---

22 Sayers, *Innocent III*, 73–4, 188; Ludovico Gatto, *Il pontificato di Gregorio X (1271–1276)*, (Rome: Istituto Storico Italiano per il Medio Evo, 1959), 87–8 ; Jonathan Riley-Smith, *The Crusades: A Short History* (London: Athlone, 1992), 171, 176; William Chester Jordan, *Louis IX and the Challenge of the Crusade: A Study in Rulership* (Princeton: Princeton University Press, 1979), ch. 4.

23 For an example of this self-consciousness see *La chanson d'Antioche*, ed. Suzanne Duparc-Quioc (Paris: Académie des Inscriptions et Belles-Lettres, 1977), 26, IX, lines 170–82, where Jesus predicts on the cross the future birth of the people who will avenge his death, reconquer his land, and restore 'sainte Crestïentés'.

24 See, for an example of such exaggeration, Mastnak, *Crusading Peace*, 115: 'The fact that Latin Christians knew nothing (or next to nothing) about Islam did not prevent them from making Muslims *the* enemy of Christianity and Christendom' (Emphasis in the original).

Muslim strongholds in southern Italy particularly influenced early papal efforts to sanction or direct warfare, because they directly threatened papal territorial interests. It is also true that the earliest justifications of crusading did take aim against Islam. This had, however, as much to do with the geography of the sacred as with Islam. It was only because Muslims were occupying 'Christ's birthplace', 'the land in which his feet had stood', God's 'inheritance', that they needed to be defeated, a defeat that need not extend beyond the Holy Land.[25]

If the crusades began as a project to recuperate God's fief and birthplace in the Holy Land, they quickly came to be understood more generally, as 'God's war for the expansion of Christendom', 'bella Domini...ad dilationem Christianitatis'.[26] This broader expansionary ideology, however, was no longer particularly motivated by confrontation with Islam. It could take aim at any non-Christian or heretic, and was in fact (with significant exceptions) not aimed primarily at Muslim lands. Indeed many theological treatises on crusade do not even mention Islam. St Thomas Aquinas, for example, codified an influential justification of crusade in his *Summa Theologica*: 'Christ's faithful often wage war against the unbelievers, not indeed for the purpose of forcing them to believe (for even if they were to conquer them and take them prisoners, they should still leave them free to believe, if they will), but in order to prevent them from hindering the Christian faith' (II-IIae, Q. X, art. 8). He went on to argue that crusaders had the right to destroy non-Christian governments even when these were sanctioned by human law. Such governments could be 'justly done away with by the sentence or ordination of the Church that has the authority of God: since unbelievers in virtue of their unbelief deserve to forfeit power over the faithful who are converted into

---

25 On the use of these expressions, specific to the Holy Land, in the preaching of crusade, see Ursula Schwerin, *Die Aufrufe der Päpste zur Befreiung des Heiligen Landes von den Anfängen bis zum Ausgang Innozenz IV: Ein Beitrag zur Geschichte der kurialen Kreuzzugspropaganda und der päpstlichen Epistolographie* (Berlin: Ebering, 1937), 51–4. Though the importance of the destination for the early crusading movement is undeniable, some recent historians of the broader crusading movement prefer to stress papal *auctoritas principalis* as a defining principle, since it allows the incorporation into the concept of those many later crusades whose goal was not the Levant. See above all the introduction to Norman Housley, *The Later Crusades: From Lyons to Alcazar 1274–1580* (Oxford: Oxford University Press, 1992). See also Jonathan Riley-Smith, 'History, the Crusades, and the Latin East: A Personal View', in M. Shatzmiller, ed., *Crusaders and Muslims in Twelfth-century Syria* (Leiden: Brill, 1993), 9–10, and more generally C.J. Tyerman, *The Invention of the Crusades* (Toronto: University of Toronto Press, 1998).

26 For these phrases see P. Rousset, *Les origines et les characteres de la première croisade* (Neuchâtel: Baconnière, 1945), 100–1, and his 'La notion', 199; Mastnak, *Crusading Peace*, 123.

children of God' (art. 10). Arguments like these would be of tremendous utility to European expansionists precisely because they were not specifically concerned with Muslims, but spoke rather more generally of *gentiles* and *infideles*.

In short, Islam was only the first, and an increasingly infrequent, target of an expansionary Christendom. Far more land was added to Europe through the German conquests in Eastern Europe that began with the second crusade than in all the wars against Islam put together, Iberian 're-conquest' included. Indeed perhaps the most horrific achievement of the crusades took place not in the Old World but the New, where logic like that articulated by St Thomas justified the destruction of the Aztec, Inca and other native polities, and the subjugation and evangelisation of their peoples.

Nor did the crusades produce a monolithic image of the Muslim as 'enemy' in the Middle Ages. It is true, as Tomaž Mastnak points out, that crusade preaching and propaganda made 'Saracen' an important negative term in the Christian imagination, one that could sometimes be generically applied: Normans, Slavs, east Europeans in general, Saxons, Danes, Scots, Irishmen, Vikings, all are at one point or other in the twelfth century called 'Saraceni', 'Agareni' and so on.[27] Such usage was, however, rare. Unlike 'Jew', 'Saracen' did not become a common insult among medieval Christians. Nor, outside areas like the Iberian Peninsula or the short-lived Crusader States, can we really detect a widespread sense that Islam posed an existential threat to the Christian order itself. For that we must wait until the very end of our period, with the fall of Constantinople (1453) and the beginnings of westward Ottoman expansion.

Moreover, although crusade propaganda could present the Muslim as an almost inhuman foe to be destroyed (the *Song of Roland* provides a good example), such representations were scarcely hegemonic within Christendom. More pragmatically ethnographic views could be found in those regions where interaction with Muslim powers was a fact of life (compare the Song of the Cid to that of Roland). For Christians living in Iberia and the Crusader States, or for anyone desiring to participate in the vast economic

---

27 On the Normans as 'Agareni', see Carl Erdmann, *Die Entstehung des Kreuzzugsgedankens* (Stuttgart: W. Kohlhammer, 1935), 110. For a few thirteenth-century Middle English sources that call Danes, Irish, Saxons and Scots 'Sarazins', see J. Hall, ed., *King Horn: A Middle English Romance* (Oxford: Clarendon Press, 1901), 96–7; Diane Speed, 'The Saracens of King Horn', *Speculum* 65 (1990), 566–7. In 1149 Pope Eugenius III spoke of the unheard of and inhuman invasion of Christian territory in Eastern Europe by 'L. dux Poloniae, collecta sarracenorum multitudine…' See his letter to Bishop Henry of Moravia: *Epistolae et Privilegia* n. 351 (*PL* 180, col. 1385).

networks of the Mediterranean and the Black Sea, the point was not (or rather, not only) to demonise Islam and fantasise its destruction, but also and often simultaneously to engage with it in constructive and profitable ways.[28] For example, among the earliest compendia of Islamic law translated into European vernaculars is a Catalan handbook produced for a Christian lord so that he could maximise his judicial profits from his Muslim subjects, whose transgressions had to be judged by Muslim law.[29] The considerable knowledge produced by such endeavours had no perceptible effect on the representations of Islam articulated by polemicists or preachers of crusade because the two projects took place in different registers of a complex Christian culture.

Another example of a cultural register that yields very different views of Muslims from those of polemicists or preachers is that of the military élites themselves. Despite the harsh polarisation we find in a *chanson de geste* like the Song of Roland, already in the twelfth century new genres of lay literature were emerging in which the crusading ideal could coexist with and even foment the recognition of a common culture uniting Christian knights with their Muslim counterparts. Sometimes this sense of commonality was the product of direct military engagement: thirteenth-century crusaders like Joinville did not hesitate to note the dignity, courage and suffering of their rivals, as well as those of their own co-religionists. But even in regions very far from real Muslims, the image of the Muslim soldier was shaped by an emerging chivalric ideal whose valorisation of violence was predicated on the proper treatment of a worthy foe. The result was that, by the late twelfth century and far beyond the end of our period, readers throughout northern Europe expected to find Muslim knights roaming the landscapes of their courtly romances. In Parzival we even find one (Feirefiz Angevin) who is the piebald offspring of a Christian and a Muslim, his skin mottled white and brown. Such stories betray no real knowledge about Islam. But they do suggest that in courtly literature Islam was not a category of pure enmity,

---

28 There is an endless bibliography on the subject of diplomatic and economic connections between Christian polities and Islamic ones. An interesting recent study of institutions for trade and travel is Olivia Remie Constable, *Housing the Stranger in the Mediterranean World: Lodging, Trade, and Travel in Late Antiquity and the Middle Ages* (Cambridge: Cambridge University Press, 2003). On diplomatic contacts see, inter alia, Michael A. Köhler, *Allianzen und Verträge zwischen fränkischen und islamischen Herrschern im Vorderen Orient: Eine Studie über das zwischenstaatliche Zusammenleben vom 12. bis ins 13. Jahrhundert* (Berlin: Walter de Gruyter, 1991).

29 Carmen Barceló, ed., *Un tratado Catalán medieval de derecho islámico: El llibre de la çuna e xara de los moros* (Córdoba: University of Córdoba, 1989).

and posed no impediment to an imagined solidarity of military elites. It is this solidarity, both imagined and (in the late medieval world of mercenary armies) quite real, that Chaucer represents and criticises through the knight of his Canterbury Tales, a soldier of 'sovereign price' to Christian and Muslim employers alike.[30]

Even at the level of political ideology itself, medieval Christian Europe was capable of imagining pluralist polities: 'A kingdom of one people and one custom is weak and fragile', as a Hungarian cleric put it in the eleventh or twelfth century. In regions like Hungary or the Iberian peninsula, Christian kingship, and even Christendom itself, could be self-consciously understood as depending on the services of non-Christian peoples, and this despite papal objection. As King Béla IV wrote to Innocent IV c. 1250, 'For the good of Christendom...we defend our kingdom today by pagans...and we tread the enemies of the church underfoot with the aid of pagans.' Similarly, in 1266 King James the Conqueror of Aragon ignored (as his successors would do for centuries) the command of Clement IV that he expel all Jews and Muslims from his kingdoms: to have done otherwise would have meant the destruction of his prosperity and his realms.[31]

Such convictions obviously weakened over the course of our period, but they never disappeared, even with the conquest of Granada and the expulsion of the Jews from Spain in 1492. In that very year, for example, an anonymous chronicler completed a 'brief summary' of the history of Spain's kings, beginning with Hercules, addressed to the king of Naples. The chronicler understands Spain's successive incorporation of many peoples as the basis of its strength. And though he everywhere stresses that the re-conquest of the Iberian peninsula from Islam is the most glorious task of a Christian monarch, he also insists that the mistreatment of Muslims or Jews weakens both kingdom and monarchy. The cruelty King Peter displayed toward his Muslim

---

30  Wolfram of Eschenbach, *Parzival*, ed. Karl Lachmann (Berlin: Walter de Gruyter, 1926), lines 57:15–22. Cf. Stephanie Cain van D'Elden, 'Black and White: Contact with the Mediterranean World in Medieval German Narrative', in Marilyn J. Chiat and Kathryn L. Reyerson, eds., *The Medieval Mediterranean: Cross-Cultural Contacts* (Medieval Studies at Minnesota 3; Minneapolis: University of Minnesota Press, 1988), 112–18. For Chaucer's knight, see *The Canterbury Tales*, the General Prologue, lines 64–7.
31  The cleric's claim is in the *Libellus de institutione morum*, ed. J Banogh (Scriptores rerum Hungaricarum 2; Budapest: Academia Litter. Hungarica, 1938), 625. King Béla's letter is discussed by Nora Berend, *At the Gates of Christendom: Jews, Muslims, and Pagans in Medieval Hungary, c. 1000–c. 1300* (Cambridge: Cambridge University Press, 2001), 166ff. Chapter 5 provides an illuminating analysis of the conflict between papal and monarchical visions of what a Christian Hungarian kingdom should look like. For Clement's letter to James, see Santiago Dominguez Sánchez, *Documentos de Clemente IV (1265–1268) referentes a España* (León: Universidad de León, 1996), 224–7.

neighbours in the fourteenth century, for example, helps to explain his subsequent downfall in a bloody civil war. Similarly, the unprecedented expulsion of Jews in his own day, the chronicler implies, can only weaken the kingdom.[32] The point, in short, is that even in those regions most constantly engaged in armed conflict with Islam, and even at a culminating moment of Christian victory in that conflict, Christendom's relation to both Muslims and Islam remains much more than merely one of enmity. For all its current political importance, the critical study of these relations is still a young field. One of its greatest challenges, as it matures, will be to have its account of those relations reflect that complexity.


3


The self-definition of Christendom vis-à-vis Islam that we have focused on thus far has little to do with the presence of real Islam in Latin Europe, though there were in fact populations of Muslims living within Christendom through-out the Middle Ages. Muslims constituted a minority in Hungary, a few parts of southern Italy, and above all in the Iberian peninsula. (There were no Muslims yet in the Balkans, since until the very end of our period Byzantium still stood between Islam and the West.) By far the largest of these commun-ities, and the only one to survive throughout the entirety of our period, was the Iberian one, and its example can give us a sense of the peculiarities involved in being Muslim in medieval Europe.[33]

Iberian Muslims living under Christian rule are called 'Mudejars', and they represent a novel and important phenomenon in Islamic history: 'diaspora' communities of Muslims living willingly in the 'house of war', that is, in a non-Muslim polity. Today millions of Muslims live in non-Muslim countries. Some of these, like the Mudejars of old, live in areas 'reconquered' by Christians from their ancestors (e.g., the Muslims of the former Yugoslavia or the former Soviet Union). Others are emigrants to more prosperous lands. These are all very different historical contexts from the medieval Iberian one. Nevertheless, the questions of acculturation, assimilation and the maintenance of group identity that these Muslim populations face today bear more than a passing resemblance to those confronted by the Mudejars.

32  *Breve compendio de las Crónicas de los Reyes de España*, B. N. Paris. Ms. Esp. 110, folios 4r, 21v, 30r–31v.
33  For other regions a good beginning can be made with James Powell, ed., *Muslims under Latin Rule, 1100–1300* (Princeton: Princeton University Press, 1990).

Mudejars were Muslims *de pacis*, that is, Muslims who had agreed, or more usually whose ancestors had so agreed, to be at peace with Christians and subject to them. In this fundamental way they differed from Muslims *de guerra*, who remained at war with Christians and could therefore legally be killed or enslaved by them. In principle, the rights of Mudejars were stipulated by treaty signed at the time of conquest. Given that the conquest of the Iberian peninsula spanned half a millennium and a number of realms, it is not surprising that these treaties varied. The most important concessions, however, were fairly standard across time and are easily listed. In exchange for their labour and their taxes, Mudejars were to receive: (1) safety and confirmation of property rights; (2) guarantee of the free practice of religion, including the right to pray in their mosques, to teach Islam to their children, and to go on pilgrimage; (3) the right to rule themselves according to Muslim law (Shari-'a), to be judged under it in any case involving only Muslims, and to name their own religious and judicial officials; (4) the confirmation of existing pious endowments in perpetuity; (5) a limitation on taxes, which were to be roughly similar to those paid under Muslim rule.[34]

These privileges are the foundation stones of Mudejar existence, which is not to say that they could not be violated or ignored. Mudejars were not naive on this score: they were aware that, even when they wanted to, Christian kings could not always force their violent subjects to comply with the provisions of treaties they had signed. Nevertheless, these treaties articulated the contractual basis for the continued existence of Muslims in Christian Iberia in formal legal terms that were remarkably stable. The treaty signed at the surrender of Granada in 1492 would have been completely intelligible to those Muslims of Toledo who had surrendered their similarly magnificent city to the Christians some 400 years before.[35]

Such willing submission by Muslims to Christian jurisdiction was controversial among Islamic jurists, who associated it with cultural vulnerability, corruption and decline. The most often cited of these writers is the fifteenth-century North African jurist al-Wansharīsī, whose opinion of the Mudejar was not ambivalent: 'his residence is manifest proof of his vile and base spirit'.

---

34 Compare, e.g., the treaty of Xivert (1234), in M. V. Febrer Romaguera, ed., *Cartas Pueblas de las Morerías Valencianas y documentacion complementaria*, vol. 1 (Zaragoza: Anubar, 1991), 10–16, and the treaty of Granada (1491) summarized in L. P. Harvey, *Islamic Spain, 1250–1500* (Chicago: University of Chicago Press, 1990), 314–23.

35 One fourteenth-century Andalusi imam, Ibn Rabīʿ, wrote explicitly about this danger. See P. S. van Koningsveld and G. A. Wiegers, 'The Islamic Statute of the Mudejars in the Light of a New Source', *Al-Qanṭara* 17 (1996), 19–59.

'To exalt Christian and diminish Muslim authority is a great and disastrous ruination...and he who does this is on the border of infidelity'. The late fourteenth-century mufti (and emigrant from Christian Iberia?) Ibn Miqlash illustrated this cultural vulnerability in an unusual passage which depicts the fate of Islam under Christian rule in sexual terms. The Mudejar, he claimed, mingled with worshippers of idols and lost his zeal. His wife depended upon (and was therefore sexually vulnerable to) his Christian lord. What fate could be worse, he asked, than that of one without zeal, either for his religion or for his wife![36]

Most jurists were less vivid. They stressed, not the debasement of the Mudejar's wife, but of his religious and legal culture. By demonstrating that Mudejars were deficient in legal culture as defined by the Maliki scholars, these jurists argued that they were less than full Muslims. As early as the twelfth century no less an authority than Ibn Rushd (Averroes) ruled that Mudejars were of 'suspect credibility, their testimony in court cannot be accepted and they cannot be allowed to lead prayer'. The legal authority of the Mudejar scholars was doubtful, they asserted, because Mudejar judges were appointed by infidels and because they were ignorant, an ignorance which became something of a topos in the writings of North African and Granadan jurists.

There were, of course, less severe opinions on the Mudejar question among Maliki jurists than the ones just quoted, but these provide a clear example of how a jurisdictional classification could translate into a cultural identity.[37] The problem of Muslims who willingly and permanently resided in the lands of Christian enemies, and who by their labours directly supported these enemies in their long and successful war against Islamic polities, forced jurists to confront the question of what constituted a Muslim, and to use the ensuing characteristics, which they presented as normative, to distinguish the particular, corrupt nature of Islam under Christian rule.

These jurists approached the corrupting effects of mudejarism through two quite different logics. The first was strictly jurisdictional: the Islamic life could not be fulfilled under Christian rule. How could one follow Muslim law if the scholars, judges and officials were appointed by Christian authorities? How, without a Muslim head of state to pay it to, could one fulfil the

---

36 H. Buzineb, 'Respuestas de jurisconsultos maghrebies en torno a la inmigración de musulmanes hispánicos', *Hespéris Tamuda* 26–7 (1988), 59, 63.

37 The Maliki school of law, dominant in the Maghreb and al-Andalus, was in fact the most severe on the issue of Muslim minorities living in non-Islamic polities. K. Abou el-Fadl, 'Islamic Law and Muslim Minorities', *Islamic Law and Society* 1.2 (1994), 141–87.

obligation to pay *zakāt*? The second approach was more explicitly cultural. As Al-Wansharīsī put it:

> One has to beware of the pervasive effect of their [the Christians'] way of life, their language, their dress, their objectionable habits, and influence on people living with them over a long period of time, as has occurred in the case of the inhabitants of Ávila and other places, for they have lost their Arabic, and when the Arabic language dies out, so does devotion to it, and there is a consequential neglect of worship as expressed in words in all its richness and outstanding virtues.[38]

According to this model, the vital Islamic nature of Mudejar culture could be evaluated by measuring it against certain cultural markers drawn from the normative Islam of more central Muslim lands: language, legal procedure, dress, ritual and custom. Ridicule of Mudejar Arabic was one very common strategy within this framework. Criticism of Mudejar legal knowledge was another, as when a Mudejar emigrant to Oran claimed, toward the end of the fourteenth century, that among Mudejars innovation (*al-bidaʿ*) has 'extinguished the light of Muslim law'.[39] We might sum up by saying that for medieval Muslims living in Islamic lands, the idea of 'Islam within Christendom' was something of an oxymoron.

Medieval Muslims living in Christian lands, however, clearly felt otherwise. Certainly most Mudejar scholars felt that theirs was a culture in decline. 'Because of the distance of our dwelling places and our separation from our coreligionists, no one is studying or writing': such laments were common coin among Mudejar scholars, and marked an awareness of the gap they perceived between their textual practice and what they took to be normative. Nor was textual practice the only marker of Islamic identity that required defence and translation in a world ruled by Christians. We have already seen how the Maliki faqihs insisted that Christian domination led to the degradation of a number of specific and indispensable markers of Muslim identity: Arabic, adherence to Qur'anic punishments (*ḥudūd*), inaccessibility of Muslim women to non-Muslim men. To these we might add, as North African muftis did, the inability to identify the start of Ramaḍān, to leave Christian lands on pilgrimage, or to fulfil the obligation of paying *zakāt*, all crucial obligations of the believer according to Muslim law. Yet for all their strong sense of cultural decline, Mudejars worked constantly to maintain the boundaries they thought

---

38 Harvey, *Islamic Spain*, 58.
39 Buzineb, 'Respuestas', 65, lines 1–2.

crucial to the expression of Muslim identity, and in the process forged what we today might call a diasporic Islam.

In the case of some obligations this work was relatively straightforward. Mudejars, for example, tended to replace *zakāt* (which required a Muslim polity) with *ṣadaqa*, charity, and specifically with alms for the redemption of enslaved or captive Muslims. By the Morisco period we even find some North African muftis advocating this solution. Other boundaries required more than reclassification to remain recognisable. Perhaps the one whose defence exacted the heaviest toll was that between Muslim women and non-Muslim men. The argument that under Christian lords Mudejars could not protect Muslim women from sexual advances by non-Muslims was often made by Granadan and North African jurists (like Ibn Miqlash above). Without the power to enforce Islamic legal prohibitions on intercourse between Muslim women and non-Muslim men, or to punish transgression with Qur'anic punishments, how could Muslims in the Diaspora maintain this essential boundary?

This was not a theoretical issue. Christian archives contain references to thousands of Muslim women engaged in sexual relations with Christians and Jews. But these references are the result, less of cultural erosion than of new ways of maintaining boundaries deemed essential. Again and again Mudejar communities purchased privileges allowing them to put to death Muslim women accused of adultery or interfaith sex, though the *ḥudūd* punishment was necessarily commuted to the social death of enslavement to the Crown. Again and again Mudejar fathers accused their own and their neighbours' wives and daughters with transgressing these boundaries, and delivered them up for punishment. The Christian nature of the records that document the legal consequences of these actions should not obscure the fact that behind them lie Muslim communities and Muslim individuals translating Islamic legal prescriptions into Mudejar idioms.[40]

Just as the risk to Muslim women in the House of War stimulated a heightened awareness of the boundary-marking role of women on the part of Mudejars, so the possibility of conversion prompted a heightened sensitivity to markers of religious identity. We might even say that, in the diaspora, the responsibility for recognising Islam and maintaining its boundaries devolved more heavily upon the individual Muslim. This process was crucial to the production of an identity that simultaneously recognised its 'decline' yet

---

40 Cf. David Nirenberg, *Communities of Violence: Persecution of Minorities in the Middle Ages* (Princeton: Princeton University Press, 1996), 139.

resolutely insisted on its Islam. Consider as an example the rise among Iberian Muslims of Aljamiado, that is, of romance languages written in Arabic characters. The increasing use of Aljamiado has often been cited as a sign of cultural decline, a consequence of the erosion of Arabic. But it could equally well be studied as an example of the expansion of Islamic learning among Mudejars as of its contraction. The fact that the peculiar conditions of Christian domination on the Iberian Peninsula made it possible for Muslims to justify an extensive practice of glossing and translation may have meant that knowledge which was increasingly restricted to the 'learned class', the *ulama*, in more central Islamic lands, penetrated further into the 'popular' or 'igno-rant' classes in the peninsula.[41]

The point is movingly illustrated by a recently discovered fatwa written by al-Mawwaq, chief qadi of Granada in its final years. Responding to a question about how a Muslim should behave in the House of War, he replied by fusing, rather than opposing, the status of one learned in authoritative Islamic tradition with that of the individual struggling to make the discriminations necessary to maintain a Muslim identity among infidels. The individual Mudejar, he wrote, should 'be a faqih of himself' (*faqīh al-nafs*). 'He teaches himself, and he should distinguish the good deed which presents itself from the bad one which befalls.'[42] This devolution of the responsibility for the recognition of the boundaries between Islam and other faiths from the learned élite onto embattled individual believers is one of the more remarkable cultural consequences of the Islamic diaspora in medieval Christian Europe.

Judging from manuscript evidence, one of the more important ways in which this devolution was achieved was through religious polemic. Beginning with Ibn Ḥazm (994–1064), who wrote in the wake of the collapse of the Caliphate of Cordoba and the beginnings of Christian expansion, Iberian Muslims seem much more concerned with polemic against Christianity and Judaism than Muslims in more central lands, and this becomes increasingly true as the so-called reconquest continues. Mudejars came to depend on an expanding corpus of polemical texts that they produced, circulated, glossed, and translated. The case of the North African Muhammad al-Qaysī (MS 1557 in

---

41 Here and in the following pages I am reiterating my argument in 'Varieties of Mudejar Experience: Muslims in Christian Iberia, 1000–1526', in P. Linehan and J. Nelson, eds., *The Medieval World* (London and New York: Routledge, 2001), 60–76.
42 The fatwa was discovered by Kathryn Miller. See pp. 51 and 57 of her pathbreaking 'Guardians of Islam: Muslim Communities in Medieval Aragon' (PhD Dissertation, Yale University, 1998), many of whose insights inform my argument here and in 'Varieties of Mudejar Experience'; see Miller's *Religious Authority and Muslim Communities of Late Medieval Spain* (New York: Columbia University Press, 2008), 129.

the National Library of Algiers) provides a good example. A captive in the Crown of Aragon in the early fourteenth century, al-Qaysī offers a moving description of the cultural effects of living among Christians, including the claim that his soul had betrayed him, and his interior and exterior had become un-Arabic. But al-Qaysī also provides the text of what he claims was his disputation with a priest in the presence of the king of Aragon. Entitled 'the Key of Religion [*Kitāb Miftāḥ al-Dīn*], or the Disputation between Christians and Muslims', the text was promptly translated in the first half of the four-teenth century into versions which survive in some four Aljamiado manuscripts.[43]

Al-Qaysī is not unique, nor is the Muslim–Christian frontier the only one polemically policed. A mid-fourteenth-century Arabic polemic written by a Mudejar against the Jews, the 'Defence of the Faith' (*Ta'yīd al-millah*), exists in multiple Arabic manuscripts, some of which contain extensive interlinear glosses in Aljamiado, and others complete translations and adaptations.[44] The multiple survivals of these polemics are very unusual for so fragmentary a record, and attest to their popularity. Moreover, of all genres, these were among the first to be glossed and translated, a process that was well under way already in the early fourteenth century. These translations were not for the learned, but for the broader audience of Mudejars, enabling each to become, in this 'land of polytheism', a defender of his or her own faith.

The importance of polemics to Muslims living within Christendom reminds us of my earlier conclusions about Christian encounters with Islam. Contrary to the expectations of the more naively progressive strands of modernity, increased proximity to and knowledge of other religious com-munities is as capable of heightening the power of polemical forms as it is of effacing it. Like Mozarabic Christians living under Iberian Islam, Mudejar Muslims living in Christendom learned a great deal more about the religions against which they defined themselves than did their co-religionists in more homogenous lands. But as we saw already in the Christian cases we touched upon, that knowledge was (with very few exceptions) not oriented toward the understanding and accommodation of religious difference in heterogeneous societies. Rather, it was used to buttress the structures of one faith against the claims of others.

---

43 P. S. van Koningsveld and G. A. Wiegers, 'The Polemical Works of Muḥammad al-Qaysī (fl. 1309) and their circulation in Arabic and Aljamiado among the Mudejars in the Fourteenth Century', *Al-Qanṭara* 15 (1994), 163–99.

44 Nirenberg, *Communities*, 196–8.

# 12

# Christians and heretics

## PETER BILLER

'The power of the Church ought to be aroused to obliterate the wickedness of various heresies, which in modern times have begun to sprout in many parts of the world.'[1] The opening words of this papal decretal of 1184 articulate a view widely held among churchmen of the decades around 1200 about the danger of heresies, which, combined with pastoral deficiency, constituted an extraordinary crisis for the Latin Church. The groups denoted here by the words *wickedness* and *heresies* regarded themselves as good and Christian. However, they have left virtually nothing of the theological libraries and administrative archives which historians would use to construct accounts of the church or religious orders. When looking at these groups this chapter is therefore forced to adopt much of the language and viewpoint of the church. It has to begin with the principal archaeological remains, namely the large numbers of manuscript books which contain the *church*'s views of the topic, and then ask how these groups were fashioned and reshaped in these texts.

This means looking at the contents of the libraries of cathedral chapters and religious houses, and then the works produced by and for theological and canon law teaching in the schools and universities.[2] Copies of books of the Bible included passages held to denote heretics and their characteristics, such as wolves in sheep's clothing, while there was an older deposit of patristic writing against early church heretics, especially the dualist Manichees, and

---

1 X 5.7.9; *Corpus iuris canonici*, ed. Emil Friedberg (Leipzig: B. Tauchnitz, 1879), vol. 1, 780. Modern general accounts of medieval heresy include Malcolm D. Lambert, *Medieval Heresy: Popular Movements from the Gregorian Reform to the Reformation*, 3rd edn (Oxford: Blackwell, 2002), and Andrew P. Roach, *The Devil's World: Heresy and Society 1100–1300* (Harlow: Pearson Longman, 2005).
2 For the following, see Arno Borst, *Die Katharer*, (Schriften der Monumenta Germaniae Historica 12, Stuttgart: Anton Hiersemann, 1953), 1–26, and Caterina Bruschi and Peter Biller, 'Introduction', in Caterina Bruschi and Peter Biller, eds., *Texts and the Repression of Medieval Heresy* (York Studies in Medieval Theology 4; Woodbridge: Boydell and Brewer, 2003), 3–12.

important definitions of *church*, *sect* and *heresy* in what was the Middle Ages' dictionary, Isidore's *Etymologies*. During the twelfth century the texts proliferate. They combine the older language and themes with the notion that there were *new* heretics and heresies, and some contain the direct description or refutation of a specific new heresy. There are brief references in histories and chronicles to contemporary heresies, and formal letters about heresy from Peter the Venerable and Bernard of Clairvaux. Peter the Venerable also produced a treatise against a contemporary heretic with point-by-point refutation of doctrine, in a revitalised genre (the polemical treatise) which was to have important successors. Bernard also adapted a passage in the Song of Songs, little foxes demolishing the vine of the Lord: the foxes were heretics. There were conciliar decrees dealing with contemporary heresy, and the collection of much material on heresy, dialectically arranged, in Gratian's *Decretum*. During the thirteenth century there is amplification, for example the 1184 decretal forms part of the section on heresy in Gregory IX's *Five Books of the Decretals* (1234). But there were also new genres, the collections of tales (*exempla*) to vivify sermons, sometimes featuring heretics. Direct action against heretics through preaching in southern France was helped by pamphlets listing their errors and Scripture that could be quoted against them, while massive and learned polemical treatises were written to help debating with heretics in northern and central Italy. The rise of formal Inquisition in the 1230s, manned mainly by Dominican and (in fewer numbers) Franciscan friars, brought about the writing of technical literature – manuscripts containing set formulae for heresy suspects to swear to tell the truth, to be questioned and to be sentenced – and records of interrogations and sentences.

Part of heresy's *existence* in the High Middle Ages was precisely this: its delineation in these texts, and its presence in the minds of those who copied, read, discussed and used these texts in teaching, preaching and Inquisition. A general history of this aspect of heresy would need a description of the dissemination and uses of these texts, for example the frequent copying of Bernard of Clairvaux's commentary on the Song of Songs and its penetration into so many Cistercian and other religious houses around Europe, or the lecturing and commenting on the *Decretum* and *Five Books of the Decretals* in schools of canon law, or the closely guarded records of interrogations of heretics, sometimes the objects of plots to steal or destroy them. It would need a description of the varying manifestations of heresies, heretics and the sect present in these texts. One end of the spectrum is dark and vague, the other end glittering and precise – though still distorting. At the murkier end there are texts dominated by the biblical animal metaphors of wolves in sheeps' clothing or little foxes and stock phrases of 'heretical wickedness' and 'walking in darkness'. At the brighter end there are the records of inter-rogations, where the suspect responded to questions derived from an intelli-gent and observant but generalised model of the typical actions an inquisitor ascribed to a legal and penitential category, a 'believer' in heretics. Also at this end are theological refutations. These had to represent heretics' views pre-cisely, but they reduced heretics to a series of theological propositions. The knowledge of a former heretic or someone close to a heretical group was highly valued. The best example is the treatise written in 1250 by Raniero Sacconi.[3] A Cathar for seventeen years and now a Dominican, he produced a crisp and very knowledgeable account. At the same time his treatise was shaped by the (developing) literary conventions of the anatomy of a sect, and it was organised according to one element in the church's typology of sects and the true church, that sects were characterised by division and plurality, the church by unity.

Between the two ends of the spectrum there were many degrees and types of representation, many odd twists produced by the meeting-point of the mind of a cleric, what he read and what he observed. One of the most important features of these texts was the imposition onto heretics of words which were not theirs. In a moment we shall turn to a more direct description of the two major heresies of the period, those of the Cathars and the Waldensians, while continuing to use the church's vocabulary. But it is necessary first to establish the two realities articulated in two different vocab-ularies, the words used by heretics and the words used by churchmen. The elite among Cathars (*Good Men* and *Good Women*) and among Waldensians (*Brothers* and *Sisters*) became *heretics* in churchmen's vocabulary, Waldensian *friends* became *believers*, the Cathar *church* or *churches* and the Waldensian religious *order* became *sects* or *heresies*. There were exceptions. A few writers, like Sacconi, did retain much of heretics' own vocabulary. And the two vocabularies could occasionally coincide, for example in Cathar *believers*, and Cathars, from a Greek word meaning *pure*, a word occasionally but not frequently used by Cathars of themselves,[4] probably deriving from the Greek-speaking Bogomils of Constantinople who will be discussed later. There were also many complexities not fully described here. For example, in Languedoc, Catharism was *the* heresy par excellence and Waldensianism

3 Franjo Šanjek, ed., 'Raynerius Sacconi O.P. *Summa de Catharis*', *Archivum Fratrum Praedicatorum* 44 (1974), 31–60; translated in Walter L. Wakefield and Austin P. Evans, *Heresies of the High Middle Ages* (New York: Columbia University Press, 1969), 329–46.
4 Borst, *Die Katharer*, 240–43.

only a minority. This was reflected in the local usage of Languedoc, where inquisitors simply referred to the former by *heresy* or *heretic*, without further specification, but used the names (*Waldensians, Waldensianism*) to denote the rarer group.

The church's vocabulary manipulated reality in many ways. More obviously it made heretical movements evil. Less obviously and more interestingly it obscured similarities between orthodox and heretical movements. The similarity between Franciscans and Waldensians is thought of easily when the vocabulary is the *Order of the Minors* and the *Order of the Poor of Lyons*. It is cloaked when the latter appear in the church's heresy vocabulary.[5] The vocabulary also provided a framework within which churchmen were encouraged to conceive of a heresy's identity, through its name, history and doctrine. Here the fundamental influence was Isidore's *Etymologies*. This work listed heresies, and provided three things for each heresy. One was the name of the heresy (for example, *Manichaeism*), the source of this name, which was often the name of the originator (in this case, *Mani*), and a few words on the main heretical doctrine. A cleric looked out on a contemporary movement banned by the church, the Order of the Poor of Lyons. He had no problem inserting it into this model, concentrating on the recent founder, Valdes, and imposing the words *Valdenses* or *Valdesia* (*Waldensians, Waldensianism*) on the order and its members. Looking at Catharism, a contemporary movement whose principal doctrine was theological dualism, a cleric might make a quite intelligent comparison with the dualist doctrine of the Manichees, but he had a problem in Catharism's lack of an easily identifiable history. Expecting an originator but not finding one, he still tried to use Isidore's model, hinting at their history and originator by calling them *Manichees*.

Around 1260 in upper and lower Austria, along the banks of the Danube, the Enns and the Ybbs, there were over forty villages in which men and women listened in their houses to the sermons of Brothers who belonged to the Order of the Poor and under their direction learned passages from the Bible; they were still doing so in many of these villages in 1390. Their neighbouring monasteries included many monasteries, like Seitenstetten, St Florian and Klosterneuburg, whose still intact libraries contain copies of an inquisitor's compilation and a polemical refutation, the Anonymous of Passau (c. 1266) and *When Men Were Asleep* (1395), both of which describe these

---

5 In their own texts, male Franciscans and Waldensians were both religious *fratres*. Consistency in modern translation would underline the same point, providing us with both Franciscans and Waldensians as *friars*.

Waldensian heretics, wolves in sheeps' clothing preaching wicked doctrines.[6] The two realities – of these people and of the texts in which they were pejorative words – lived literally next door to each other.

If the real history of heresy has to be written on the basis of such texts, how can we trust them? For example, one set concerns the heresy of the Free Spirit. Their supposed doctrines were listed in the decree *Ad nostrum* of the Council of Vienne (1311). Suspects questioned by inquisitors said that they had believed and practised as adepts of this sect, but it has been shown that they were repeating formulations, based on *Ad nostrum*, put to them by inquisitors. The combination of fear and torture produced assent to leading questions. More broadly, the nebulous basis of the Council of Vienne's decree and the fictional character of these confessions combines to suggest that the heresy of the Free Spirit was more or less dreamed up by the church.[7]

The modern historical demolition of this sect is convincing. But the model does not apply to the larger sects. There is such a variety of evidence relating to the Cathars and Waldensians, assisted by tiny survivals from the groups themselves, that there can be no doubt about their reality. Rather, the lesson is caution about texts which were always positioned at a certain angle in relation to these groups. Accordingly, the next section will rely on these texts to access the two major heretical movements of the High Middle Ages, and the chapter will then conclude with comment on the main distortions of these texts.

*Heresy* was sometimes found and condemned among academic theologians at the University of Paris. The label had various other uses, most notoriously in the papacy's struggle against the emperor Frederick II, who was condemned as a heretic at the Council of Lyons in 1245. But by 'dangerous heresies and sects' the church usually meant what modern historians call 'popular heresies', those of the Cathars and Waldensians. When the famous theologian Alan of Lille composed a four-book treatise around 1200, defending the Catholic faith against its enemies, he devoted one book each to two non-Christian faiths of Jews and followers of Mahomet, and one book each to the two major Christian faiths of the Cathars and Waldensians. Nearly half a century later the opening questions of an inquisitors' manual show inquisitors sharing the same preoccupation with these two groups: 'Did you see heretics (= Cathars) or Waldensians?' Seventy years later, in the trials

---

6 Alexander Patschovsky, *Der Passauer Anonymus: Ein Sammelwerk über Ketzer, Juden, Antichrist aus der Mitte des xiii. Jahrhunderts* (Schriften der MGH 22; Stuttgart: Anton Hiersemann, 1968); Peter Biller, *The Waldenses 1170–1539: Between an Order and a Church* (Variorum Collected Studies Series 676; Aldershot: Ashgate, 2001), chapters 15–16.

7 Robert E. Lerner, *The Heresy of the Free Spirit in the Later Middle Ages* (Berkeley, Los Angeles and London: California University Press, 1972).

and inquisitors' manual of Bernard Gui in the early fourteenth century, the main preoccupation was still with the Cathars and Waldensians, albeit with the addition of smaller movements, such as the Apostles in Italy and the Béguins of southern France, followers of a radical Franciscan theologian.[8] This chapter will imitate the church's long principal preoccupation with just two sects.

The origins of the Order of the Poor of Lyons are described in Chapter 3, and therefore only briefly recapitulated here.[9] The Poor need to be ranged among other contemporary movements aspiring to the apostolic life of wandering and poor preachers, most of which, like the later followers of St Francis, ended up as religious orders within the church. The movement, started by the rich Lyons citizen and businessman Valdes, enjoyed some years inside the church, supported by the cathedral chapter of Lyons and given qualified approval at the third Lateran Council (1179).[10] Its most distinctive feature was the commissioning by its vernacular – but not Latin-literate – founder of a local scribe and cleric to translate into Romance vernacular some books of the Bible and patristic passages. Valdes and his followers began to preach sermons. Their cavalier attitude to a requirement of canon law (the need for lay people to seek local ecclesiastical approval for preaching), together with criticism of the clergy in these sermons, led to difficulties and then excommunication in 1184. Although two groups were reconciled to orthodoxy by Innocent III, thereafter the Order of the Poor became a proscribed heretical sect, whose existence and ramifications are occasionally glimpsed, mainly through inquisitions. A lot of unorganised and miscellaneous information survives in the compilation of the Anonymous of Passau, while an anonymous, *On the Way of Life…of the Poor of Lyons*, possibly from the late thirteenth century and based on the confessions of a renegade priest whom the Waldensians tried to recruit as a Brother, provides a remarkable formal description of the movement after a century or more of existence.[11]

8 Louisa A. Burman, *So Great a Light, So Great a Smoke: The Beguin Heretics of Languedoc* (Ithaca and London: Cornell University Press, 2008).

9 On the origins, see Kurt-Viktor Selge, *Die ersten Waldenser*, 2 vols. (Arbeiten zur Kirchengeschichte 37/1–2; Berlin: Walter de Gruyter, 1967). Modern general accounts: Gabriel Audisio, *The Waldensian Dissent*, trans. Claire Davison (Cambridge: Cambridge University Press, 1999); Euan Cameron, *Waldenses: Rejections of Holy Church in Medieval Europe* (Oxford: Blackwell, 2000); see also Biller, *Waldenses*, and Peter Biller, 'Goodbye to Waldensianism?', *Past and Present* 192 (2006), 3–33.

10 On early support in the Church, see Michel Rubellin, 'Guichard de Pontigny et Valdès à Lyon: La rencontre des deux idéaux réformateurs', *Revue de l'Histoire des Religions* 217 (2000), 39–58, and 'Valdès: Un "exemple" à Clairvaux? Le plus ancien texte sur les débuts du Pauvre de Lyon', *Revue Mabillon* 72 (2000), 187–95.

11 Peter Biller, 'Fingerprinting an Anonymous Description of the Waldensians' and 'Appendix: Edition and Translation of the *De vita et actibus*', in Bruschi and Biller, eds., *Texts and the Repression of Medieval Heresy*, 163–207.

What these texts suggest is essentially a movement produced by the church and still in some ways within it, which existed at two levels. One of these was essentially a clandestine mendicant order. Men and women renounced living in the world to become members of a religious order, formally taking the three religious vows of poverty, chastity and obedience, adopting a habit and thereafter following a timetable of prayer and instruction in a house. The vocabulary was that of religious orders in the church, *Brothers* and *Sisters*, *professing vows*, belonging to an *order*, and having regular *general chapter* meetings, held annually in northern Italy and southern France and bringing together Brothers from both these regions and also Germany. The other level was that of their friends. These were a sub-group of the ordinary lay members of the Catholic Church. Like all Catholic lay people they were baptised in the local church, went to mass, confessed and got married and received their funeral services there, but in secret they received in their houses the Brothers, duplicating in two areas what they received or did in the local church. They listened to the Brothers' sermons and instruction, and confessed their sins to them. (Orthodox laity confessing to their parish priest and *also* to mendicant friars provide an interesting parallel.) While there are references to priesthood among the Waldensians and the commemorative blessing of bread on Holy Thursdays, there was no broad attempt to replace the church's sacraments or remove friends from them. Existing to some extent sacramentally within a church which excommunicated them, a church much of which they in turn criticised or rejected, might well seem an utter contradiction to post-Reformation minds: but it was the reality that was lived out by the Poor of Lyons and their friends.

How rapidly had this movement taken shape? The way of life of men and women who were the earliest followers of Valdes abandoned ordinary life, wandering around preaching, crystallised at some point into a formal order. A clue is provided by the confession of one woman in 1246, who told inquisitors that she had stayed with *Waldensian women* (an early phrase for the Sisters) in Castelnaudary for four years around 1206. She dressed, ate, drank, prayed and did other things as they did, a formulation that suggests that the formal life of a religious house already existed then.[12] Clandestinity came in slowly and patchily, paralleling the advance of effective repression. With it came the decline and disappearance of public preaching, and the adoption of positive measures to remain secret. Brothers travelled in the disguise of craftsmen, German Brothers travelled over the Alps to chapters in Lombardy disguised as

12 Biller, *Waldenses*, 135–7.

pilgrims, and there was an elaborate secret system for the reception of Brothers by local friends, and their safe conduct into safe houses where they preached and heard confessions at night-time. While the Sisters can be glimpsed preaching publicly and in friends' houses up to the 1240s, they become nearly invisible in the texts thereafter. This was most probably the result of the curtailment of their pastoral activities and successful secrecy, not their disappearance from the movement.[13]

Itinerant preaching and conversion produced a movement which spread more widely than any other medieval heresy. By 1218 they were in German-speaking areas. Spreading always with German-speakers, they had reached the Baltic by 1300. While they seem not to have spread in north-west Germany or Scandinavia, they went eastwards into Poland, Bohemia, Transylvania and western Hungary, achieving their strongest penetration in Austria and Bohemia. It is the numbers of Cathars in Languedoc that is lodged most strongly in modern minds. This may be a mistake. It is from Languedoc that most Inquisition trials survive, while there are only fragments from Germanophone areas. A combination of estimates in literary evidence and calculations based on comparing numbers of interrogations and executions found in the fragments still extant of an Inquisition in northern Bohemia 1335–c. 1353 and the executions of heretics tried by Bernard Gui in Languedoc suggests that the numbers of Waldensians in those areas exceeded the numbers of Cathars in Languedoc.[14] Waldensians also spread into Burgundy, northern Spain, the Dauphiné, Piedmont, Lombardy, Tuscany and southern Italy, although, with the exception of Piedmont, not with a comparable density.

Very rarely does evidence illuminate the first mission, the first penetration into an area. Usually Inquisition trials uncover and provide a snapshot of a movement which has existed for some time. Secret affiliation to the Brothers has passed down generations. One of a boy's or girl's parents or a relative or friend tells them about these men who travel the world in secret, and with whom one can be saved, before taking them along to confess to a Brother (probably at roughly the same age as first confession in the local parish

---

13 The glimpse of the rite of their reception into the Order afforded by Strasbourg trials has recently been re-edited in Georg Modestin, ed., *Quellen zur Geschichte der Waldenser von Straßburg (1400–1401)* (MGH, Quellen zur Geistesgeschichte des Mittelalters 22; Hanover: Hansche Buchhandlung, 2007), 93–4, and commented upon in Georg Modestin, *Ketzer in der Stadt: der Prozess gegen die Straßburger Waldenser von 1400* (MGH, Studien und Texte 41, Hanover: Hansche Buchhandlung, 2007), 141–5.

14 Alexander Patschovsky, 'Einleitung', in Alexander Patschovsky, ed., *Quellen zur Böhmischen Inquisition im 14. Jahrhundert* (MGH, Quellen zur Geistesgeschichte des Mittelalters 11; Weimar: Hermann Böhlaus Nachfolger, 1979), 21–4.

church). They are encouraged to marry others within the sect. Affiliation is very much a matter of family – within which the rebellious child may well be the one who wants just to be Catholic – and men's and women's local activities within the sect tend to follow the more general norms for men and women, with men doing more of the safe-conduct work, women more of the hospitality and (sometimes) the local conversion work. Many of the friends live in the country and are at poor to middling levels: farmers, millers, and small to middling craft workers such as cobblers and tailors. But there are also glimpses of friends of greater status and wealth.[15] For example, two friends who came from a solid Waldensian family – three of their siblings became Waldensian Brothers – were sentenced by Bernard Gui in 1319.[16] French royal records show that each of them was worth over 70 Toulouse pounds.[17] Friends gave the Brothers money, *On the Way of Life…of the Poor of Lyons* stated that most of the money brought to general chapters came from Germany, and Inquisition in the decades around 1400 was to uncover rich urban friends.[18] In combination, this comment in *On the Way of Life* and these much later trials suggest the possibility that there were already considerably wealthier urban friends in southern Germany and Austria at the point in the thirteenth century when *On the Way of Life* was written: people who managed entirely to avoid discovery.

Trial records show that in their nocturnal sermons the Brothers taught some heresies, that killing and oath-taking were always sinful (and thus war and criminal justice were sinful too). They said that there was no purgatory and that saints had no power to intercede and should not be invoked. They mainly concentrated on morals, not doctrine: do not do evil unto others, do not sin, do not lie. The memories of particular night-time occasions do not usually include what is emphasised in treatises like that of the Anonymous of

---

15 Jörg Feuchter, *Ketzer, Konsuln und Büsser: Die städtischen Eliten von Montauban vor dem Inquisitor Petrus Cellani (1236/1241)* (Tübingen: Mohr Siebeck, 2007), 246.

16 Annette Pales-Gobilliard, ed., *Le livre des sentences de l'inquisiteur Bernard Gui*, 2 vols. (Paris: CNRS, 2002), vol. 2, 1076, 1078, 1080.

17 Robert Fawtier, ed., *Comptes royaux (1314–1328)* (Recueil des Historiens de la France, Documents Financiers 4; Paris: Imprimerie Nationale, Librairie Klincksieck, 1961), nos. 4319–20, Part 1, 248.

18 Peter Biller, 'German Money and Medieval Heresy: The Wealth of the German Waldenses', in Biller, *Waldenses*, 111–23; for Strasbourg, Modestin, ed., *Quellen*, and Modestin, *Ketzer in der Stadt*; for Fribourg, Kathrin Utz Tremp, ed., *Quellen zur Geschichte der Waldenser von Freiburg im Üchtland (1399–1439)* (MGH, Quellen zur Geistesgeschichte des Mittelalters 18, Hanover: Hahnsche Buchhandlung, 2000), and Kathrin Utz Tremp, *Waldenser, Wiedergänger, Hexen und Rebellen: Biographien zu den Waldenserprozessen von Freiburg im Üchtland (1399 und 1430)* (Fribourg: Universitätsverlag Freiburg Schweiz, 1999).

Passau (c. 1266), the Brothers' passionate concern was with instruction, getting their followers to learn Scripture by heart in order to recite from memory and teach in turn. The Anonymous does describe what begins to appear in trials with Bernard Gui and then Inquisition in Piedmont in 1335, the presentation of the Brothers' mission and identity within a history of the church. Poor and humble in the first stage of its history, with Christ and the apostles, the church declined in its second stage, which began with its reception of wealth at the time of the Donation of Constantine, and Valdes arose in the third stage, reviving or continuing apostolic poverty in humility. A mixture of textual and oral preservation encouraged variety in this history; one version posited a small band of elect connecting the apostles and Valdes.[19] Over the medieval centuries a tiny number of women remembered this history, when interrogated. This suggests the possibility that a small number of women friends played a special role here, preserving memory and supplying local communities with identity.[20]

Though persecuted by the church and labelled heretical, the Cathars were very unlike the Waldensians.[21] Not formed from the Catholic Church, they were a coalescence of favourable spiritual currents indigenous in the West and the successful implantation of a Latin manifestation of an eastern group, the Bogomils. The Bogomils professed a radical view of the divinity and the origin of this material world. Extant in the Byzantine empire and Greek- and Slavonic-speaking milieux, the earlier Bogomils and especially those of Bulgaria held what has been termed a 'mitigated dualist' cosmogony, while another view grew up during the twelfth century, associated with the Bogomils of Drugunthia, which professed absolute dualism – both are defined below.

The first certain dates for the Cathars in the West are the Rhineland around 1140, Languedoc in the 1160s and northern and central Italy around 1170, and

19 Peter Biller, 'The *Liber Electorum*', in Biller, *Waldenses*, 207–24.
20 Peter, Biller, 'Women and Dissent', forthcoming in Alastair Minnis and Rosalynn Voaden, eds., *The Yale Companion to Medieval Holy Women in the Christian Tradition c. 1100-c. 1500* (New Haven, Conn.: Yale University Press).
21 See the general accounts of Malcolm D. Lambert, *The Cathars* (Oxford: Blackwell, 1998), and Malcolm Barber, *The Cathars: Dualist Heretics in Languedoc in the High Middle Ages* (Harlow: Longman Pearson, 2000), and also Bernard Hamilton, 'The Cathars and Christian Perfection', in Peter Biller and Barrie Dobson, eds., *The Medieval Church: Universities, Heresy and the Religious Life. Essays in Honour of Gordon Leff* (Studies in Church History, Subsidia 11; Woodbridge: Boydell Press, 1999), 5–23. On the attempt to dismantle Catharism by Mark G. Pegg, *The Corruption of Angels: The Great Inquisition of 1245–1246* (Princeton and Oxford: Princeton University Press, 2001), see the reviews by Bernard Hamilton in *American Historical Review* 107 (2002), 925–6, and Peter Biller in *Speculum* 78 (2003), 1366–9.

southern Italy in the 1190s. Eastern origins left traces in some of the earliest names in western sources, *Cathars* from the Greek word for pure, probably from the Greek-speaking Bogomils of Constantinople, and various forms of *Bulgars*, indicating origin in and contacts with Bulgaria's moderate Bogomil Church. While the precise dating and origins of the western Cathars cannot be delineated with certainty, they self-evidently pre-date the earliest references to them, and they clearly had eastern origins. Some modern scholars have been very eager to minimise Catharism's eastern origins and its internationalism, and to date its western rise as late as possible. An exception is Bernard Hamilton, whose suggestions are followed here.[22]

A Latin church of Bogomils/Cathars came into existence in Constantinople, constituted by northern Frenchmen who had come there, probably during the military expeditions of 1096–7 or 1101. It was in Constantinople – which was also connected with some of the translation of Greek Aristotle into Latin in the first half of the twelfth century – that the Latin version of the Cathar ritual was probably produced. From Constantinople northern Frenchman went back to France and set up the Cathar Church of northern France, whose first named bishop is encountered in 1167. The obscurity of the missionary activity that followed may well result from the fact that the missionaries, westerners by language and culture and preachers of moderate dualism, did not attract extraordinary attention among the ascetic wandering preachers of early twelfth-century France. Those who spread northwards into the Rhineland were probably the source of an abortive further mission over the sea, to England, in the 1160s. The northern French also missionised in Languedoc and Italy. Piercing light is cast on the movement around 1170 by missions to the west of Nicetas (or Niquinta), the head of the Greek-speaking Bogomils of Constantinople, whose church had been converted to absolute dualism. He presided over a general council in Languedoc in 1167. Nicetas persuaded those present to adopt absolute dualism, as he persuaded some of the Italians in another mission a few years later. The presence at this council of heads of churches from Constantinople, northern France, Languedoc and Lombardy strikingly attests internationalism, while the setting up of two new dioceses in Languedoc suggests the expansionism of Catharism during these years. Absolute dualism made those western Cathars who adopted it stand out

---

22 Bernard Hamilton, 'Introduction', in Hugh Eteriano, *Contra Patarenos*, ed. Bernard Hamilton, Janet Hamilton and Sarah Hamilton (Leiden and Boston: Brill, 2004), 1–102; Bernard Hamilton, 'Bogomil Influences on Western Heresy', in Michael Frassetto, ed., *Heresy and the Persecuting Society in the Middle Ages: Essays on the Work of R. I. Moore* (Leiden and Boston: Brill, 2006), 93–114.

more as radical heretics, and the fact that many in Italy remained mitigated dualists was to be a source of schism and strife during the thirteenth century.

Fierce repression curtailed the presence of Cathars in north-western Europe, and by the middle of the fourteenth century (and apart from a few locations in the hills of Piedmont) most southern Catharism had been extinguished. In between it had flourished – or survived – for over a century and a half in many parts of southern Europe: Languedoc, northern Spain, Lombardy, Tuscany, southern Italy and the Dalmatian coast. Outstanding among the texts which provide glimpses of it during this period are the rich trial records of Languedoc and the descriptive treatise written in 1250 by an Italian Dominican, Raniero Sacconi, mentioned earlier. The Languedoc trials show a movement numerically much stronger in this region than the Waldensians and with a more marked grip among the nobility and urban elites. The memories of old people, whose 1230s–40s interrogations survive, go back two decades into the twelfth century: but not far enough to touch on the early missions. The Catharism of their youth was already settled, often handed down in families. They describe it as open and public until the coming of the crusaders in 1209, and thereafter a progressively clandestine movement. Cathars in depositions were ever on the move, living sometimes in cabins and tents in the woods, flitting from one safe house to another.

These and similar texts depict the theology of mitigated dualism, with one God and his two sons, Christ and the Devil, and the belief that although God created the four elements, it was the Devil that had fashioned this world. In absolute dualism there were two eternal principles, a good God and an evil God, the former the creator of a remote alternate world, the latter the creator of this world. The people in this latter world were composed of bodies, souls and spirits. Souls had fallen from that other world down into this evil world, and the evil God had imprisoned them in the evil material bodies of men, women, birds and animals. The rite of *consolamentum* assured its recipients of the release and return of the soul to that other world at death, provided they had avoided sex, killing, the eating of foods produced by coition and other major sins. These recipients were the Good Men and Good Women of Languedoc, known as *perfects* to many modern historians, who have selected a word that was used rather rarely.[23] Before the arrival of crusade and

---

23 Borst, *Die Katharer*, 205–6. The inquisitor Bernard Gui provided a formal definition of the word *perfect*. He used it in its Latin sense, meaning 'complete' or 'fully-fledged'. In this way it denoted the 'full' heretic of a sect, as opposed to his or her believer, who were 'imperfect', meaning not complete or fully-fledged; Bernard Gui, *Practica inquisitionis heretice pravitatis* iv.3, ed. Célestin Douais (Paris: Alphonse Picard, 1886), 218.

Inquisition, some of these Good Men and Women lived in specific houses. Some resemblance to Catholic religious houses will have been suggested by the co-residence of religious celibates of one sex, wearing distinctive black habits, following a life of prayer and fasting, and having a monthly *service* for the confession of minor sins. And there were a few structural parallels to the Catholic Church, as well as differences, in the system of Cathar churches with territorial boundaries, like dioceses, each with its all-male hierarchy of bishop, elder son (who would succeed the bishop), younger son (who would succeed the elder) and deacons.

Only this hierarchy and the Good Men and Women constituted the Cathar Church. Those among ordinary lay people who believed in them were not part of this church. They had not received the *consolamentum*, and they were still co-operating with this evil world, in marrying, having children, eating forbidden foods and killing. Here there was a fundamental divide. Where a fundamental part of both the Catholic Church and the Waldensian Brothers was the effort to make ordinary people sin less and do good, through exhortation, confession and penance, there was nothing comparable among the Cathars. Of course these extreme and pure Christians did not encourage sin – that suggestion only came from the lies of polemicists. But there was no rationale in their theology for the moral improvement of their flock. Even though believers did not often display (or were not asked to display) a good grip of dualist theology, they were clear on this. Interrogated about what heretics preached to them, they monotonously repeated that Cathars talked doctrine and Waldensians talked morals.

At the heart of Catharism was knowledge. And, as time wore on, while the schools and new universities were producing increasingly scholastic theology in the Catholic Church, something similar though less easily known was happening to Cathar theology. Cathars in Como told one cleric who stayed with them c. 1214/15 that Lombard and Tuscan Cathars sent their good scholars to learn logical sophistries and theological discourse in Paris.[24] In northern Italian cities, where levels of education were high in some lay circles and heretics enjoyed much freedom until the third quarter of the thirteenth century, there was much doctrinal debate. The considerable polemical exchange between different Cathar groups and Cathars and Catholics has left traces in Catholic polemical treatises and one Cathar treatise, the *Book of Two Principles*, works which suggest that in these sophisticated milieux Cathar

---

24 Peter Biller, 'Northern Cathars and Higher Learning', in Biller and Dobson, eds., *The Medieval Church: Universities, Heresy and the Religious Life*, 25–51 (50–1).

theology had been made more scholastic both by new learning in general and through re-armament in the face of Catholic attack. It is a world far removed from the simple moralising of the Gospel-quoting Waldensian Brother.

So far, this chapter has tried to establish the parallel and intersecting existence of *heresies* in the minds and texts of churchmen and the movements of self-describing good Christians which were thus labelled, and this has been an effort of description rather than explanation. 'Why heresies?' was a question most knowledgeable churchmen would have answered by reference to St Paul's providential explanation that 'There must be heresies, that they which are proved be manifest among you' [1 Cor. 11.19]. The Anonymous of Passau's chapter on what occasioned heresy straightforwardly produced a long and miscellaneous list of priests' abuses in the diocese of Passau: taking the eucharist to taverns, denying communion to post-childbirth women and suchlike. The assumption of most churchmen trying to reform the church during the period of the third and fourth Lateran councils (1179, 1215) was that heresies arose because of a deficiency of well-instructed and effective preachers. The origins of the specialist Order of Preachers (the Dominicans) in anti-Cathar preaching in Languedoc is the largest expression of this, while one statement by the anon-ymous author of the 1250s treatise *On the Inquisition of Heretics* is very telling both about circumstantial cause and parallelism: that Waldensians mainly went to people and places where the Franciscans and Dominicans did not go.[25] All this is consonant with modern historians' discussions of the pastoral crisis of the years around 1200 and the church's counter-reforms. Another self-evidently persua-sive point in modern scholarship deserves repeating. The eventual map of heresy in western Europe is in part produced by another map. Heresy was driven out of areas where there was strong central authority and the desire to repress, for example England, Flanders and northern France. And it was to be found for a while where these conditions were absent.

Further patterns and contrasts elude explanation. Cathars were destroyed. Waldensians survived until the sixteenth century. Cathars appealed more strongly than Waldensians to elite groups. Despite early Cathar entry in north-western Europe and Waldensian persistence in parts of southern Europe, Cathars came to be strongest in the Romance vernacular areas of southern Europe, while Waldensians (until 1400) were strongest in German-speaking areas of northern and north-eastern Europe.

---

25  (Pseudo-David of Augsburg), *De inquisitione hereticorum* xv, ed. Wilhelm Preger, 'Der Tractat des David von Augsburg über die Waldesier', *Abhandlungen der bayerischen Akademie der Wissenschaften*, Philosophisch-historische Klasse 14 (1879), 204–35 (213).

The evidence from Cathars' and Waldensians' interrogations tells the historian about already existing and settled heretical communities, not the earlier missions which established them, which therefore elude the historian who is trying to describe and explain. This is the leitmotif for this chapter's final theme. Beyond the elementary transposition of people and movements into *heretics*, *heresies* and *sects*, what can be said about the inadequacies or distortions of the church's textual representation of these people and movements?

The records of interrogations preserve answers to questions put by inquisitors, and at best (which is often quite good) they preserve knowledge of those things in which the inquisitor was interested: actions that denoted degrees of guilt, such as how many times someone had heard a heretic preaching, rather than inner disposition, something not readily provable. It is a partial picture. Most extant records are of interrogations of followers rather than preaching heretics, and their grounding in doctrine was often not as deep. The combination of this – the general loss of heretics' theological books and the representation of heresy as a series of negative points (rather than a whole) in polemical treatises – produces an impression of lack of theological uniformity and coherence. Were the uniformity and coherence of the Catholic Church to be assessed only on the basis of interrogations of Catholic lay people (which we unfortunately do not have) and without the texts of high Catholic theology, its faith also would seem to be a jumble. This is not to deny that the jumble was a part of the 'lived religion' of both Catholics and heretics. But, broadly speaking, we have system and not the jumble in evidence surviving about Catholicism, the jumble and not system in evidence about heresies. The historian should be wary of the false contrasts that result from this.

At least a tiny number of theological or ritual texts survive: nothing archival. We glimpse a boundary commission at work in the acts of the Cathar council of St Félix-de-Caraman,[26] and a polemicist, Salvo Burci, writes that the Cathars spent a lot of money on travel to peace-making councils.[27] A Waldensian letter shows us detailed formal preparations, the appointment of

---

26  A facsimile of the seventeenth-century edition is provided in a volume devoted to a discussion of its authenticity, Monique Zerner, ed., *L'histoire du Catharisme en discussion: Le 'concile' de Saint-Félix (1167)* (Collection du Centre d'Études Médiévales de Nice 3, Centre d'Études Médiévales: Nice, 2001), between pp. 248 and 249. See Hamilton, 'Introduction', 79–87.

27  Salvo Burci, *Liber Suprastella*, ed. Caterina Bruschi (Istituto Storico Italiano per il Medio Evo, Fonti per la Storia dell'Italia Medievale, Antiquitates 15, Rome: Nella Sede dell'Istituto, 2002), p. 5.

delegates and the exchange of written positions in the run-up to the Waldensian council of Bergamo (1218),[28] and we know that Waldensians brought money to general chapters, and formally presented financial accounts.[29] A whole face of these movements as organisations which dealt with money and had written records is missing. The few snapshots we get construct groups that are very concrete and far removed from the nebulous appearance of *sects* in some of the church's texts.

Finally, the danger and its extent. The Anonymous of Passau included in his text a warning. The Waldensians were more dangerous than other sects because more widespread; there is virtually no land without them. It is reminiscent of the note sounded at the beginning of *Ad abolendam* that heresies are sprouting in many parts of the world, and means that we should be aware of geographical exaggeration in texts whose primary purpose is warning. The Anonymous also drove in the opposite direction, building on an old series of contrasts between the church and heresy which had been transmitted to the central Middle Ages most influentially by Isidore of Seville's *Etymologies*. The polarities include the following. The church is long-lived, heresies new-fangled. The church is universal, heretics are in few countries. The church's believers are a multitude, including all estates. Heretics have few believers, and they come from a smaller and lower-ranking range of estates. The Catholic faith is not divided, it is one and integral. Against this, there are more than seventy sects (an approximation based on the sixty-eight listed by Isidore).[30]

The church's texts could both exaggerate and minimise heresy. Here minimisation meant underplaying the coherence, size, power and spread of heresies, and underlining internal divisions. Of the two opposed tendencies, the second has been more insidious because it has joined forces with one characteristic of inquisition and clandestinity and one trend in modern histor-iography. Once persecution started, heretical movements became clandestine. They were noticed: only *sometimes*. The church got to know something about them: only *something*. Modern historians, anxious to see medieval churchmen as exaggerating fantasisers, have paid heed mainly to their exaggeration, not

---

28 *Rescriptum heresiarcharum Lombardie ad Leonistas in Alamania*, in Alexander Patschovsky and Kurt-Viktor Selge, ed., *Quellen zur Geschichte der Waldenser* (Texte zur Kirchen- und Theologie-Geschichte 18, Gütersloh: Gerd Mohn, 1973), 20–43; trans. Wakefield and Evans, *Heresies of the High Middle Ages*, 279–89.

29 Biller, 'Fingerprinting', 173–4.

30 Patschovsky, *Der Passauer Anonymus*, p. 109.

their minimisation. It seems reasonable to suggest that these 'heretical' movements were usually *more* – larger, more coherent and more organised – than what is suggested by the phrases about heresies in the church's manuscripts and the occasional searchlight of Inquisition trials, oh so rarely alighting upon and illuminating a patch of the dark.

# 13

# Women and men

## MEGAN McLAUGHLIN

'There is neither Jew nor Greek, there is neither slave nor free, there is neither male nor female; for you are all one in Christ Jesus' (Gal. 3.28). This promise of equality between women and men, spelled out in an early Christian baptismal formula, and then repeated by Paul in his letter to the Galatians, awoke few echoes in the later Middle Ages. While medieval exegetes sometimes discussed the whole formula, the specific claim that there is 'neither male nor female' received very little attention. In contrast, notions of gender difference and gender hierarchy pervaded mainstream Christianity in the years between 1000 and 1500. In biblical commentaries and pastoral letters, in canon law and scholastic *summae*, the later medieval clergy repeated patristic and early medieval ideas about the distinct natures of women and men, and about the unequal relationship between the sexes, occasionally refining old arguments and addressing new issues as they arose. In homilies and admonitions, preachers retailed many of the same ideas to a broader audience of layfolk. And clergy and laity together performed gender difference and gender hierarchy within the ordinary rituals of parish life.

The consistent, and apparently unassailable, message of these texts and performances was that God had made men and women different in very significant ways, that men were superior to their mothers, sisters, wives and daughters, and that women should accept their divinely ordained subordination. Even female thinkers such as Hildegard of Bingen (d. 1179) accepted and repeated these views, although women generally softened or complicated the message.[1] Yet a closer look reveals how vulnerable the walls of difference and hierarchy really were. For while overt assertions of equality between the sexes were rare, gender hierarchy was often reinterpreted, revalued and occasionally even turned on its head, in medieval texts and in practice as well.

---

1 Barbara Newman, *Sister of Wisdom: St. Hildegard's Theology of the Feminine* (Berkeley and Los Angeles: University of California Press, 1987), 89–120.

Let us begin by examining more closely the liturgical performance of gender, the ways in which the differences between men and women were acted out in the recurrent ceremonies of the medieval church, for it was in the liturgy, rather than in sermons or the confessional, that Christians most often encountered the ideas about women and men that theologians and canonists developed more fully in their written texts. Our most detailed information on these performances comes from the works of liturgical commentators, clerics who described and interpreted the rituals of the church for the use of other clerics. These liturgists drew extensively on the writings of theologians and canonists in their interpretations, so their works remind us of some of the key elements in medieval gender ideology, while at the same time informing us about what was actually done in medieval churches. Their works demonstrate how, in the ceremonies of the parish mass, in the festivals of the parish year, and in celebrations of the life-cycle, gender difference and gender hierarchy were ritually enacted over and over again.

For example, women and men normally stood in separate places during the parish mass, highlighting the distinction between the sexes. In many places, the custom was for women to stand on the north side of the nave, and men on the south side; elsewhere, the men stood in the front, while the women filled up the back of the church. This separation of the sexes could be understood simply as a way of preventing unseemly flirtation during sacred times. However, the liturgists also explained the difference in placement in terms of inherent differences between the sexes. Honorius Augustodunensis (d. c. 1157) associated the south with the 'heat' of temptation. Men were appropriately placed on the south side of the church, because, as the naturally stronger sex, they could more easily withstand such heat. The weaker sex should be placed on the north side, farther away from temptation.[2] Sicard of Cremona (d. 1215) noted that in some places men were placed in front of women. This reflected the belief that man is the head of the woman (Eph. 5.23), and therefore her leader.[3]

A further spatial distinction between the sexes involved access to the altar. In general, the space around the altar tended to be reserved for members of the clergy during this period. Yet laymen might sometimes approach the altar, and even – if they were of sufficiently high rank – have seats in the choir

---

2 Honorius Augustodunensis, *Sacramentarium* 31 (PL 172, col. 763): 'Masculi stant in parte australi, et feminae in boreali: ut ostendatur per fortiorem sexum, firmiores sanctos constitui in majoribus tentationibus hujus mundi; et per fragiliorem sexum, infirmiores in aptiori loco.'

3 Sicard of Cremona, *Mitrale* 1.11 (PL 213, col. 39): 'Secundum alios, viri in parte anteriori, mulieres in posteriori; vir nam est caput mulieris.'

during mass. Women, on the other hand, were forbidden by church law to enter the sanctuary.[4] With a few notable exceptions, even women whose husbands were seated in the chancel had their own seats in the nave.[5] Some monasteries prohibited women from entering their precincts at all – not only the sanctuary, but also the nave of the church, and even the cemetery were closed to the female sex. In the case of the monasteries, these regulations seem to have been symbolic of the struggles saintly founders and members of the community had to maintain their chastity.[6] On the other hand, the sanctuaries of parish churches were probably closed to women because of concerns about cultic purity and fears of female pollution.

The sexes were also distinguished during the liturgy by their head coverings. St Paul had taught (1 Cor. 11.3–16) that men were to wear nothing on their heads in church, while women should pray with veiled heads, for man 'is the image and glory of God', while woman 'is the glory of man' – she was created for man, but man was not created for woman. This custom was preserved in the Middle Ages. Indeed, if a young girl came to church without a veil, her mother 'or another woman' was to cover her head immediately with a piece of cloth.[7] The liturgical commentators' explanations for this distinction played on the common association of women with sin. The Parisian theologian John Beleth (fl. 1160–64) believed that long hair represented a 'multitude of sins'. Hence women, with their long hair, could be seen as the most sinful, and their veils could signify the distance between themselves and God. Laymen, who had shorter hair, fell in between, whereas clerics wore the tonsure so that there would be nothing between them and God.[8] The veil, then, was a marker of difference that for many liturgists indicated moral inferiority.

The moment during the mass specifically devoted to 'union, charity, peace, and reverence'[9] within the Christian community provided another

---

4 Bonizo of Sutri, *Liber de vita christiana* 9.87–8, ed. E. Perels (Texte zur Geschichte des Römischen und kanonischen Rechts in Mittelatter 1; Berlin: Weidmann, 1930), 9.87–8, 275–6; Ivo of Chartres, *Decretum* 2.135 (PL 161, cols. 197–8); cf., O. Pontal and J. Avril, eds., *Les statuts synodaux français du XIIIe siècle*, 5 vols. to date (Collection des documents inédits sur l'histoire de France; Paris: Comité des travaux historiques et scientifiques, 1971–), vol. 4, 65.

5 Margaret Aston, 'Segregation in Church', in W. H. Sheils and Diana Wood, eds., *Women in the Church* (SCH 27; Oxford: Basil Blackwell, 1990), 237–94, at 244–8.

6 Jane T. Schulenburg, *Forgetful of their Sex: Female Sanctity and Society, ca. 500–1100* (Chicago: University of Chicago Press, 1998).

7 John Belethus, *Summa de ecclesiasticis officiis* 39, ed. H. Douteil, 2 vols. (CCCM 41; Turnhout: Brepols, 1976), vol. 2, 73; cf. Sicard, *Mitrale* 3.4 (PL 213, cols. 111–12).

8 Belethus, *Summa* 39, vol. 2, 73; cf. Honorius, *Gemma animae* 1.146 (PL 172, col. 589).

9 William Durandus, *Rationale divinorum officiorum* 4.53.10, ed. A. Davril and T. M. Thibodeau, with B.-G. Guyot, 3 vols. (CCCM 140; Turnhout: Brepols, 1995), vol. 1, 546.

opportunity for the performance of gender difference. In the later Middle Ages, the kiss of peace was increasingly bestowed not on another person, but on a painted tablet or board, which was passed among the members of the congregation. Nevertheless, liturgical commentators remained very concerned about the possibility that the exchange of kisses in church might excite lust rather than reverence. This led them to insist that women and men should not 'kiss one another'.[10] Sicard of Cremona explained that this was why women and men stood in separate parts of the church during the mass: 'let men and women not kiss one another, because of [the possibility of] lust; and this is why they should be set apart, not only in physical kissing, but even in location'.[11] The implication of this 'setting apart', however, would seem to be the denial of 'union, charity, peace, and reverence' between the sexes. While there might be reconciliation and forgiveness among men or among women at this point in the mass, there was no ritual possibility here for the performance of reconciliation or forgiveness between men and women, or for a recognition of their fellowship. The sexes remained alienated during the mass in a profound, if not fully articulated, way.

The order of kissing during the ritual of peace further reinforced notions of social hierarchy within the Christian community. The *pax* descended from the clergy at the altar to the lay members of the congregation in order of social rank, which might lead to courteous wrangles over precedence, or even to outright quarrels over who was entitled to kiss the board next.[12] But regardless of other issues of rank, liturgists often specified that the *pax* should go to the men in the congregation before it went to the women, for 'man is the head of woman'.[13]

Less regularly than in the mass, but still very often, the life-cycle rituals of individual parishioners reinforced notions of difference and subordination. In particular, the rituals surrounding women's fertility and childbearing capacity carried a range of powerful messages about female impurity, which had no male equivalent. At the end of the sixth century, Pope Gregory the Great had assured Augustine of Canterbury (d. c. 604) that a menstruating woman committed no sin in attending church, yet there remained some uncertainty on this point.[14] In the early thirteenth century,

---

10 Belethus, *Summa* 48, vol. 2, 83; Durandus, *Rationale*, 4.53.9, vol. 1, 546.
11 Sicard, *Mitrale* 3.8 (PL 213, col. 140).
12 Eamon Duffy, *The Stripping of the Altars: Traditional Religion in England, 1400–1580* (New Haven, Conn.: Yale University Press, 1992), 125–7.
13 Sicard, *Mitrale* 3.8 (PL 213, col. 140): 'Per hunc descendit pax ad populum, sed primo ad viros, postea ad mulieres; quia vir est caput mulieris…'
14 R. Meens, 'A Background to Augustine's Mission to Anglo-Saxon England', *Anglo-Saxon England* 23 (1994), 5–17.

Sicard of Cremona claimed that it was the 'custom of the Romans' that menstruating women not enter a church 'out of reverence'.[15] The more general consensus was that women could enter a church during their monthly periods, but some clerics were still troubled by the prospect of menstrual blood polluting sacred rituals and spaces, or even other people. Medieval canonists told menstruating women not to make liturgical offerings.[16] And in some places, women who had had sex with their husbands while they were menstruating were obliged to stand outside the church during mass, publicly doing penance for their sin.[17]

If there was some difference of opinion about menstruation, liturgical commentators all agreed that childbirth should be hedged about with taboos, to prevent the pollution of sacred space. William Durandus (d. 1296) urged women, when they felt the pangs of labour, not to enter a church, or at least to take care 'lest they pollute it'.[18] After childbirth, too, women were to stay out of churches, as Honorius put it, 'because they signify that the unclean are excluded from the heavenly temple'.[19] The reference here is to the custom of 'churching' women – excluding them from the church for a set period after childbirth, and then ritually readmitting them once they had been 'purified'. Women required such purification because both the sexual activity associated with conception and the process of childbirth itself were thought to make them 'polluted and sinners'.[20] In clerical discussions of churching, the blood associated with childbirth was sometimes equated with menstrual blood, and evoked concerns about filth and pollution.[21] The blood of childbirth might also be likened to the blood shed through violence. According to Honorius, the body of a murder victim should not be carried into church, lest its pavement be stained with blood, which would require the reconsecration of the building. And he claimed that some people believed that women who died

---

15  Sicard, *Mitrale* 1.11 (*PL* 213, col. 38).

16  Burchard of Worms, *Decretorum libri XX* 19.140 (*PL* 140, col. 1010): 'Mulieres menstruo tempore non offerant, nec santimoniales, nec laicae. Si praesumpserint, tres hebdomadas poeniteant.' Cf. Ivo of Chartres, *Decretum* 15.150 (*PL* 161, col. 891).

17  Honorius, *Gemma animae* 1.146 (*PL* 172, col. 589): 'Propter hanc significationem in multis locis menstruae viris commistae, foris ecclesiam stare solent, et ob hoc poenitentes intrare ecclesiam non debent.'

18  Durandus, *Rationale* 7.7.7, vol. 3, 37–8: 'Verumptamen mulier dum sentit sibi imminere dolores partus non intret ecclesiam vel saltem caveat ne polluat illam.'

19  Honorius, *Gemma animae* 1.146 (*PL* 172, col. 589): 'Mulieres quoque post partum ecclesiam non intrant, quia immundos a templo coelesti excludi designant.'

20  Fulbert of Chartres, *Sermones* 3 (*PL* 141, col. 319).

21  P. Rieder, 'Between the Pure and the Polluted: The Churching of Women in Medieval Northern France, 1100–1500' (PhD dissertation, University of Illinois, 2000), 67–71.

in childbirth should not be carried into church for the same reason – although Honorius himself thought that this was permitted.[22] In short, every time a woman gave birth, the parish community was reminded through her ritual exclusion from and then readmittance to the church building, of the dangers associated with female impurity.

Whether she died in childbirth, through illness or accident, or even from old age, the death of a woman led to a final reminder of gender difference and hierarchy. By the twelfth century, many places followed the custom of ringing the 'passing bell' for the dead, so that their fellow parishioners could pause in their activities and pray for the newly departed soul. However, the knell for women was different from that for men – two rings, as opposed to three rings. Presumably, the intention behind this distinction was to indicate for the listeners the identity of the person who had just died, so that they could pray for him or her in a more personal way. But the liturgists also interpreted this in terms of gender difference: the three rings for a man reflected his resemblance to the Trinity.[23] On the other hand, the bells were rung for a woman only twice, because 'through woman came difference – that is, the separation of humanity from God; and thus she is doubly disgraced, and on that account *she signifies difference (unde binarius infamis est, eo quod alteritatem significat)'*.[24]

Woman, then, 'signifies difference'. Hence the repeated performance of female weakness, sin, impurity and subordination in the most common rituals of the medieval church, and the repeated assertion of female inferiority in the teachings of the medieval church. But hence too the usefulness of gender to medieval theologians and preachers as a signifier of other kinds of difference. Women were constantly invoked in medieval texts as symbols of weakness, imperfection, sensuality, body and humanity, while men represented strength, perfection, rationality, spirit and divinity. And this, in turn, led to the use of women to symbolise particular groups in medieval society who were thought to embody such negative, 'female', characteristics.

---

22 Honorius, *Gemma animae* 1.170 (*PL* 172, cols. 596–7): 'Interfecti ideo in ecclesiam non portantur, ne sanguine pavimentum maculetur. Ob hanc enim causam putant quidam mulieres in partu defunctas, in ecclesiam non esse deferendas, quod tamen licet fieri.'

23 Belethus, *Summa* 161, vol. 2, 317; Durandus, *Rationale* 1.4.13, vol. 1, 56.

24 Peter of Roissy, *Manuale de misteriis Ecclesie*, ed. M.-T. d'Alverny, in P. Gallais and Y.-J. Riou, eds., *Mélanges offerts à René Crozet à l'occasion de son soixante dixième anniversaire*, 2 vols. (Poitiers: Société d'études médiévales, 1966), vol. 2, 1100: 'Pro viro pulsantur ter intercise, quia ymago unitatis primo inuenta est in viro qui primus factus est. Pro femina vero bis, quia per feminam fuit alteritas, id est separatio hominis a Deo. Unde binarius infamis est, eo quod alteritatem significat.'

Heretics were one such group. In his commentary on the Song of Songs, Honorius interpreted the phrase 'O beautiful among women' (Song 1.7) in allegorical terms, to refer to the one who is beautiful 'in faith' among women – 'that is, among heretics'. For 'woman' (*mulier*) is pronounced like 'softer' (*mollier*), and is understood in terms of the multitude of heretics or of the imperfect, who are 'softer, that is, prone to sin'.[25] The association of heresy with softness, weakness and effeminacy dates back to Christian antiquity. In the twelfth and thirteenth centuries, however, as theologians and pastors began to pay greater attention to unorthodox belief, they interpreted more and more biblical references to women in terms of heresy. The rape of Dinah, who 'went out to visit the women of that region' (Gen. 34.1–2), for example, could be taken to refer to simple folk, who are separated from the church because they 'like to listen to the teachings of heretics and philosophers'. Such folk are 'quickly captured and deceived, and join the flock of the heretics'.[26] The 'foolish and clamorous woman' of Prov. 9.13, who calls out to 'the simple', could also be linked to heresy: 'The foolish and clamorous woman is heretical depravity: foolish, because of empty reasoning, and clamorous, because of garrulity.' Such heresy attracted the foolish, those lacking in good sense.[27]

And of course, 2 Tim. 3.6 refers specifically to the wicked men (normally understood in the Middle Ages as heretics) who 'creep into houses and lead captive silly women (*mulierculas*) laden with sin'. *Mulierculas* could be interpreted in general terms as 'foolish and weak and unworthy and inconstant' souls, whether of men or of women.[28] Often, however, the text was taken more literally. It was a commonplace for orthodox writers to accuse heretics of too close an association with women. Heretical preachers, it was said, travelled with women (again, *mulierculas*) who were neither their wives nor

---

25 Honorius, *Expositio in Cantica canticorum* 7 (PL 172, col. 372): 'Mulier dicitur quasi mollier, et intelligitur multitudo haereticorum vel imperfectorum, qui molles sunt, id est proni ad peccandum.'

26 Bruno of Segni, *Expositio in Genesim* (PL 164, col. 216): 'Egreditur autem Dina ad videndas mulieres regionis illius, quoniam simplices viri ab Ecclesia separantur, quos haereticorum et philosophorum dogmata audire delectat. Mox igitur capiuntur et decipiuntur, et in haereticorum gregem transferuntur; unde fit ut anima Deo desponsata scortum diaboli esse incipiat.'

27 Bernard of Fontcaude, *Adversus Waldensium sectam* 7.4 (PL 204, col. 821): 'Mulier stulta et clamosa est haeretica pravitas. Stulta scilicet per fatuum intellectum; et clamosa per garrulitatem...'

28 Hervé of Bourg-Dieu, *Commentaria in epistolas Pauli* (PL 181, cols. 1466–7): 'in captivitatem errorum trahunt insipientes et infirmas ac viles et inconstantes, seu virorum seu mulierum animas.'

their sisters.[29] Some heretical groups even allowed women to preach.[30] Moreover, many of the orthodox clergy asserted that heretics found their most eager audience among women.[31] Bernard of Fontcaude (d. c. 1192) explained that heretics approach women first, because they can be more easily swayed, and can then bring their husbands into the heretical fold with them, just as Eve led Adam astray. Given this close association between women and heresy, it is hardly surprising that men who listened to heretics were said to be acting 'not in a manly, but in a womanish fashion' (*non viriliter, sed muliebriter*).[32]

The identification of women with another despised group in medieval society, the Jews, was more complex.[33] Christian theologians had traditionally associated Jews with stubbornness and 'hardness of heart', which made it difficult to link them with the 'softness' of women. Nevertheless, women continued to serve as useful foils for Jewish 'perfidy' because of their association with pollution. A number of medieval writers associated contemporary Jews with biblical concubines and prostitutes. When Absalom's revolt forced King David to leave Jerusalem, he left behind ten of his concubines to look after the palace (2 Kings 15.16). When he returned, he put those concubines under guard, providing for their upkeep, but never visiting them again; they were 'shut away until the day they died, widows, as it were, of a living man' (2 Kings 20.3). Peter Damian (d. 1072) drew on this text to argue that 'the Jews now are clearly shut away, and living in widowhood, since they don't go in to the husband of Holy Church. Neither does Her heavenly Bridegroom go in to them, since He scorns to live with them, like foolish women prostituted to the devil, and instead gives them a bill of divorce, because they are polluted by adultery.'[34]

29  *Vita S. Norberti* (PL 170, col. 1314); Eberwin of Steinfeld, *De haereticis sui temporis* (PL 182, col. 680); Bernard of Clairvaux, *Sermones super Cantica canticorum*, 65 in J. Leclerq, H.-M. Rochais and C. H. Talbot, eds., *SBO*, vol. 2 (Rome: Editiones Cistercienses, 1958), 172–7.

30  E.g., Stephen of Bourbon, *Tractatus de diversis materiis praedicabilis* 4.7.342, in A. Lecoy de la Marche, ed., *Anecdotes historiques, légendes, et apologues tirés du recueil inédit d'Etienne de Bourbon, dominicain du XIIIe siècle* (Publications de la Société de L'histoire de France: Paris: Renouard, 1877), 291–2.

31  *Vita S. Norberti* 13 (PL 170, col. 1313); cf. Hugh of Rouen, *Contra haereticos sui temporis* (PL 192, cols. 1289–90).

32  Bernard of Fontcaude, *Adversus Waldensium sectam* 7.2 (PL 204, col. 821).

33  See Sara Lipton, 'The Temple is my Body: Gender, Carnality, and Synagoga in the *Bible Moralisée*, in Eva Frojmovic, ed., *Imagining the Self, Imagining the Other: Visual Representation and Jewish–Christian Dynamics in the Middle Ages and Early Modern Period* (Leiden: Brill, 2002), 129–63.

34  Peter Damian, *Epistolae*, 90, *Die Briefe des Petrus Damiani*, ed. K. Reindel, 4 vols. (MGH, *Die Briefe der deutschen Kaiserzeit*, 4; Munich, 1983–93), vol. 2, 579: 'Iudei plane nunc clausi sunt et in viduitate vivunt, quoniam ad virum sanctae aecclesiae non accedunt. Nec ad eos caelestis ille sponsus ingreditur, quia tamquam mulierculis a diabolo prostitutis suum praebere contubernium dedignatur, eisque, quia polluti sunt per adulterium, repudii dat libellum.'

The level of hostility to the Jews in such texts is disturbing, although perhaps not surprising, given the growth of anti-Jewish sentiments among Christian writers during this period. For Peter Damian, the Jews were not only 'prostitutes', but 'prostituted to the devil'. In the same vein, Rupert of Deutz (d. c. 1129) likened the Jews to Jezebel, the wicked queen,[35] whose name was taken to mean 'flow of blood'. This linked both her and the Jews to menstrual impurity,[36] while reminding readers that the Jews had called for Christ's blood to 'be upon us and upon our children' (Matt. 27.25).[37] Rupert also saw the great harlot in the Apocalypse (Rev. 17.1–6), who was 'drunk with the blood of the saints', as a type of the Jews: 'therefore it is certain that the first and foremost part of this harlot is the Israelite race, which killed the holy prophets, and for this reason it received a woman's name and was convicted of having fornicated with the kings [of this earth]'. 'Carnal Israel' was represented as a harlot, Rupert asserted, because it 'raged with feminine lust'.[38]

The common association of women with certain negative traits, then, made them useful for medieval clerics to 'think with'.[39] Nevertheless, it is important not to oversimplify the dichotomy between 'male' and 'female' characteristics in medieval Christian belief, since individual thinkers might play with the usual clerical language of gender, depending on their own particular situations and goals.[40] Normally 'female' characteristics might be used to distinguish between different categories of men.[41] Thus, in some monastic texts, choir monks were described as 'spiritual', while lower class *conversi* were associated with physicality.[42] By the same token, the attribution of characteristics such as

---

35  1 Kings 16–21; 2 Kings 9; cf. Rev. 2.20.
36  W. Johnson, 'The Myth of Jewish Male Menses', *Journal of Medieval History* 24 (1998), 273–95.
37  Rupert of Deutz, *De sancta Trinitate et operibus eius* 26, ed. H. Haacke, 4 vols. (CCCM 21–4; Turnhout: Brepols, 1971–72), 1415.
38  Rupert of Deutz, *Commentaria in Apocalypsim* (PL 169, cols. 1135–6): 'Proinde constat, quia prima et praecipua meretricis hujus portio gens Israelitica exstitit, quae sanctos prophetas occidit. Unde et merito nomina sortitur muliebria et fornicata fuisse convincitur cum regibus …' ; *ibid.*: 'et femineis arguatur insaniisse libidinibus.'
39  Rupert of Deutz, *In librum Ecclesiastes commentarius* 4 (PL 168, col. 1269): 'Si autem vertamus causam mulieris ad allegoriam, tanta figura notanda quanta mulier facit.'
40  C. W. Bynum, '"…And Woman his Humanity": Female Imagery in the Religious Writings of the Late Middle Ages', in C. Bynum, S. Harrell and P. Richman, eds., *Gender and Religion: On the Complexity of Symbols* (Boston: Beacon Press, 1986), 257–88.
41  Sharon Farmer, 'The Beggar's Body: Intersections of Gender and Social Status in High Medieval Paris', in S. Farmer and B. Rosenwein, eds., *Monks and Nuns, Saints and Outcasts: Religion in Medieval Society* (Ithaca, N.Y. and London: Cornell University Press, 2000), 153–71.
42  Barbara Newman, *God and the Goddesses: Vision, Poetry, and Belief in the Middle Ages* (Philadelphia: University of Pennsylvania Press, 2003).

weakness or carnality to women as a group might be complicated by differences among women. In particular, virginity – or even chastity within marriage – might transform the carnal female into a member of the spiritual élite.[43]

The variety of ways in which medieval authors used gendered imagery to reflect on the nature of God is particularly striking. Most often, of course, He was represented as male – the Father in heaven, the Warrior God of Hosts. But sometimes 'He' might be depicted as female, in order to illustrate 'His' maternal love for humanity.[44] And still other writers used a language of paradox, highlighting female difference in order to illustrate divine difference – using the 'otherness' of women to unveil the supreme 'otherness' of God.[45] Peter Abelard (d. 1142), for example, pointed out that God had chosen to be born of a woman – not because women were worthier than men, but precisely because they were less worthy:

> What glory can be compared to that which this sex won in the mother of the Lord? If he had wished, our Redeemer could certainly have assumed his body from a man, as he chose to form the first woman from the body of a man. But he transferred this singular grace of his humility to the honor of the weaker sex. He could have been born from another, worthier part of the female body than other men, who are born from that most vile part by which they are conceived. But to the incomparable honor of the weaker body, he more highly consecrated its genitals by his birth than he did those of a man by circumcision.[46]

This positive reference to women's normally 'dishonourable' parts is surely intended to shock, but it is far from revolutionary. Abelard's goal was less to

---

43  E.g., the *vita* of Frances of Rome, ed. *AA. SS.*, March, vol. 2 (Antwerp: Société des Bollandistes, 1668), 96.

44  C. Bynum, *Jesus as Mother: Studies in the Spirituality of the High Middle Ages* (Berkeley and Los Angeles: University of California Press, 1982), 110–69.

45  M. McLaughlin, 'Gender Paradox and the Otherness of God', *Gender and History* 3 (1991), 147–59. Constance Bouchard, *'Every Valley Shall Be Exalted': The Discourse of Opposites in Twelfth-Century Thought* (Ithaca, N.Y. and London: Cornell University Press, 2003), 28–56.

46  Heloise and Peter Abelard, 'The Letter of Heloise on Religious Life and Abelard's First Reply', ed. J. T. Muckle, *Mediaeval Studies* 17 (1955), 270–1: 'Quae gloria huic poterit comparari quam in Domini matre adeptus est sexus iste? Posset utique, si vellet, redemptor noster de viro corpus assumere sicut primam feminam de corpore viri voluit formare. Sed hanc suae humilitatis singularem gratiam ad infirmioris sexus transtulit honorem. Posset et alia parte muliebris corporis digniore nasci quam ceteri homines, eadem qua concipiuntur vilissima portione nascentes. Sed ad incomparabilem infirmioris corporis honorem longe amplius ortu suo consecravit eius genitale, quam viri fecerat ex circumcisione.'

make his readers look favourably upon women, than to remind them of Christ's supreme humility in the Incarnation.

We should remember as well that, in a religion based on redemption, the 'feminine' can never have wholly negative connotations, for it always evokes not only the Fall – the 'separation of humanity from God' – but also the possibility that love will overcome that separation and restore humanity and God to unity. For medieval Christians, 'woman' symbolised not only what was imperfect in the universe, but also how that imperfection could be brought back into the realm of the sacred. In particular, she represented the sometimes wayward, perhaps even impure, but always beloved church. Just as man and woman became one flesh, a single body, in marriage, so the church was the Bride and the Body of Christ, the difference created by the Fall ultimately erased in the nuptial moment of the Redemption. An anonymous sermon for the Rogation Days tells the story of man whose bride was desired by 'strangers'. They took her by violence and held her for a long time, until finally – after a series of warnings which he sent on ahead – he came and freed her from the hands of her enemies. The man in the sermon was, of course, Christ, who came to earth to free the church from her enemies, 'the demons, who defiled her from top to bottom, that is, polluted her with the sin of idolatry'. Christ cleansed the church and made her pure again, and now the Bride, who had been 'polluted with many lovers', was adorned with ornaments to please her Spouse.[47]

Medieval Christian teachings on gender could, therefore, be quite ambiguous. While medieval clerics generally emphasised the negative associations of femininity in order to reinforce the normal superiority of the masculine, they sometimes did the same thing in order to *question* ordinary categories of authority and status, and to exalt certain women favoured by God. Moreover, positive female attributes – beauty, tenderness, constancy – might be invoked under certain circumstances, especially in writings about the church, the Virgin Mary or other female saints, but occasionally even in discussions of ordinary women.[48] And while there were few advocates for the equality of the sexes in medieval Europe, a number of thinkers emphasised gender complementarity rather than hierarchy. As Hildegard of Bingen wrote:

47 Pseudo-Hildebert of Le Mans, *Sermones de tempore* 45 (*PL* 171, cols. 568–9): 'de manu hostium, id est daemonum, qui eam totam constupraverunt, id est idolatriae reatu polluerunt'; *ibid.*, 'prius cum multis amatoribus polluta.'
48 E.g., Marbod of Rennes, *Liber decem capitulorum* 4, ll. 64–71, ed. R. Leotta (Rome: Herder, 1984), 119.

man and woman are dependent on each other so that each is necessary to the other; because man is not called 'man' without woman nor is woman named 'woman' without man. For woman is necessary to man, and man is the consolation of woman; and neither of them can be without the other.[49]

Male and female could be seen as two different, but equally essential aspects of creation, which together fulfil God's plan for humanity and the world.

The most extreme expression of this viewpoint may be found in the writings and actions of the tiny Milanese sect known to historians as the Guglielmites, after the holy woman who served as its focus. Guglielma, who was probably a member of the Bohemian royal family, arrived in Milan in the 1260s, and began attracting followers because of her simple life, her healing powers and her miracles. How she viewed her own life and work is uncertain, but after her death in 1281, two of her followers circulated the idea that Guglielma had been the incarnation on earth of the Holy Spirit, 'true God and true human in the female sex'. Probably they were influenced by the apocalyptic ideas of Abbot Joachim of Fiore (d. 1202), who had taught that history was divided into three ages, that of the Father, that of the Son and that of the Holy Spirit. At least some of Guglielma's followers seem to have thought that just as the death and resurrection of Christ – a male redeemer – had ushered in the second age, so the death and resurrection of Guglielma – a female redeemer – would usher in the third and final age of the world. In that age the Jews and 'Saracens' would be converted, and the church would be renewed. And in fact the Guglielmites began that renewal in the Jubilee year of 1300, when – in expectation of their redeemer's imminent resurrection – their female 'pope', Maifreda da Pirovano, surrounded by both male and female assistants, celebrated a solemn Easter mass. A few months later, she and several other members of the sect were tried for heresy and executed.[50] The career of the Guglielmites was brief, and their end tragic, but the mere fact of their existence tells us something about the vulnerabilities of the medieval gender order.

---

49 Hildegard of Bingen, *Liber divinorum operum* 1.4.100, ed. A. Derolez and P. Dronke (CCCM 92; Turnhout: Brepols, 1996), 243: 'Vir itaque et femina sic ad invicem admixti sunt, ut opus alterum per alterum est, quia vir sine femina vir non vocaretur, non femina sine viro femina nominaretur. Femina enim opus viri est, et vir aspectus consolationis femine est; et neuter eorum absque altero esse posset'; trans. C. Bynum in *Holy Feast and Holy Fast: The Religious Significance of Food to Medieval Women* (Berkeley and Los Angeles: University of California Press, 1987), 260. Cf., 1 Cor. 11.11–12.

50 Barbara Newman, *From Virile Woman to Woman Christ: Studies in Medieval Religion and Literature* (Philadelphia: University of Pennsylvania Press, 1995), especially 185–95; Janine L. Peterson, 'Social Roles, Gender Inversion, and the Heretical Sect: The Case of the Guglielmites', *Viator* 35 (2004), 203–19.

The research of the last half century has demonstrated clearly the diversity of medieval religious belief. The clergy did not always agree among themselves. And certainly the rest of the population did not always share the views of those with spiritual authority over them, as witness the beliefs and behaviour of Maifreda and her comrades. Instead, like modern individuals, medieval women and men took threads from whatever cultural materials were available, and wove for themselves a pattern of belief that made sense to them and to the people around them. It seems likely that, in the realm of gender ideology, the consensus was higher than in some other areas, for secular law and social practice reinforced the notions of gender difference and gender hierarchy expressed in theology and preaching. Yet even here, as we have seen, there remained ample room for exceptions and inversions.

# 14

# Heaven, hell and purgatory: 1100–1500*

ALAN E. BERNSTEIN

This chapter's story unfolds on many levels: most profoundly, in the individual conscience. Far from existing alone, however, personal feelings about the afterlife fit in a web of societal relationships. Heaven, hell and purgatory certainly involve the dead, but dead souls were not completely absent from earth and continued to haunt their families. As in Roman times, the family included its departed parents and ancestors.[1] Medieval Europeans expressed clan loyalty through 'suffrages', actions dedicated to the dead. Charters recording gifts to churches show donors acted to benefit their own souls and those of their predecessors. Tales relate the visits from purgatory or hell requesting that heirs pay debts or resolve other unfinished business. Revenants also appear from heaven to encourage the pusillanimous. Thus, however pious the language, many charitable actions also comprised a personal interest: a cleansing of conscience, earning of merit, removal of guilt. Gifts to churches were also gifts to ecclesiastics; pious donations created alliances with people influential in the world.

Religious authorities, who were often political powers too, functioned at all levels, from the papacy to the parish, and also shaped personal attitudes towards heaven and hell. Popes and councils intervened with dogmatic definitions and the prosecution of heretics. Theologians articulated reasons for individual doctrinal provisions and offered their conclusions to confessors and preachers in manuals that began to circulate in Latin around 1200, in the vernacular around 1300, and in print around 1450. Public art inside and outside church walls, liturgical drama and guild-sponsored mystery plays involving angels, saints and demons rendered the most potent of religious figures

---

* For their helpful suggestions on this chapter, I wish to thank JoAnne Gitlin Bernstein, Paul R. Katz, Miri Rubin and Jeffrey Burton Russell.

1 Charles King, 'The Organization of Roman Religious Beliefs', *Classical Antiquity* 22 (2003), 275–312. Charles King, 'The Living and the Dead: Ancient Roman Conceptions of the Afterlife', (PhD dissertation, University of Chicago, 1998).

familiar to the people. The literature of visions records (often second or third hand, it is true) dialogues between a penitent soul and 'her' (the word for soul is feminine in Latin) guardian angel. Sometimes mystics report intimate, physical exchanges with Jesus himself, as, in some cases, he descends from a crucifix to bestow his greeting.

The impression of a top-down, authoritative church commanding assent to centrally defined beliefs is misleading. The religious community, whose hopes and fears and calculations are the subject of this chapter, was not altogether cohesive. Popes were not considered infallible. They could only occasionally enforce doctrinal uniformity against particular heresies or heretics. Political manoeuvring shaped doctrinal definitions. Authoritative pronouncements could spur popular resistance. People saw their faith through a kaleidoscope of popular, pastoral, theological, dogmatically defined ideas and visual images concurrently. It is crucial, therefore, to distinguish the personal, psychological, literary, theological and dogmatic levels of perception and expression.

In the centuries from 1100 to 1500, Christian ideas about the afterlife trace three great developments. The first is the democratisation of conscience. Attention to the conscience filtered 'down' from the monastic champions of Late Antiquity and spread to large numbers of ordinary believers in the High Middle Ages, when the systematic examination of conscience became part of penitential discipline for the laity. Second is the increased focus on 'the interim', the time between one's death and the general resurrection and Last Judgement at Christ's Second Coming. When the interim became the field of action where conscience could be appeased, purgatory emerged. Third, as time passed, in the fourteenth and fifteenth centuries, purgatory, suffrages and issues related to the interim became problematic in their own way. The resultant contest between the claims of a temporary purgatory and the eternity of salvation and damnation produced a new phase in the religious development of Western Europe.

The role of the conscience emerged clearly in Late Antiquity. Jerome (d. 420) had opposed Origen's denial of an eternal hell on the grounds that he placed it 'merely' in the conscience.[2] Jerome himself, however, confided a dream in which he suffered the fires of hell in his own conscience.[3] Here, through the conscience, hell invades a living person. Isidore of Seville (d. 636) applied the name *tristitia* (sadness) to these attacks of conscience. His idea was

---

2  *Epistola* 124, *ad Avitum*, §7; *Eusebii Hieronymi Epistulae*, ed. Isidorus Hilberg (CSEL 56.1; Vindobonae: Verlag der Österreichischen Akademie der Wissenschaften, 1996), 104.
3  *Epistola* 22, *ad Eustochium* §30, CSEL 54, 189–91.

that the contemplative should attend to *tristitia* while still alive or it would torment the soul forever in hell. In hell, said Isidore, 'fire burns the body, but *tristitia* burns the mind'.[4] Monastic experience of the Early Middle Ages articulated for Western Europe a link between the conscience of the living and the later pains of hell. I call this foretaste of hell in the living person's guilty conscience 'inner death'.

Suffrages – actions, consisting of prayers, alms or masses dedicated to the dead – also pervaded the emotional life of the early Middle Ages. Augustine (d. 430) discussed the subject in his *Enchiridion*. Prayers for the dead vary in their effect according to how the individual dead person had lived. The very good are beyond the need of prayers; the very bad are beyond their reach. A middle group benefits in one of two ways. The not very good obtain a full release from their sins; the not very bad merely achieve an improved situation (*tolerabilior damnatio*).[5] In the hope of this benefit, Christians subsidised prayers for their parents, but also anticipated their own needs. They made donations to monasteries, convents and cathedrals, which, as prebends, became the landed endowments of influential ecclesiastical corporations over centuries.[6]

Another stabilising influence from the early Middle Ages is an analogy that informs virtually all medieval eschatology. It harkens back to the biblical idea of heaven as a divine kingdom. As political as it is religious, it is the parallel between heavenly and earthly order. In the High Middle Ages, William of Auvergne, theologian and bishop of Paris (d. 1249), used it to argue that there must be a hell, because every well-ordered city has a place to administer justice. The universe is the city of God, and therefore there is a hell, God's place for executing justice.[7] Thomas Aquinas (d. 1274) reasoned in the other direction. He advised kings to rule 'in their kingdoms as the soul in the body and God in the universe'.[8]

The visual representation of the Last Judgement also provided continuity. The composition that would become standard for half a millennium appears first in

---

4 Isidorus Hispalensis, *Sententiae* 1.28.1, ed. P. Cazier (CCSL 111; Turnhout: Brepols, 1998), 86.

5 Alan E. Bernstein, *The Formation of Hell: Death and Retribution in Antiquity and the Early Christian Worlds* (Ithaca, N.Y.: Cornell University Press, 1993), 322–5.

6 For an overview, see Paul Fouracre, *The Age of Charles Martel* (Harlow: Longman, 2000), 137–45. A more detailed picture emerges from Ian Wood, 'Teutsind, Witlaic and the History of Merovingian *Precaria*', in Wendy Davis and Paul Fouracre, eds., *Property and Power in the Early Middle Ages* (Cambridge: Cambridge University Press, 1995), 31–52.

7 Guilielmus Alvernus, *Opera Omnia*, 2 vols. (Paris, 1674; repr. Frankfurt: Minerva, 1963), *De Universo*, 665 (= 673) aD–bA.

8 *Thomas Aquinas*, 'On Kingship, to the King of Cyprus', ch. 12., in A. P. d'Entrèves, ed., *Aquinas: Selected Political Writings*, trans. J. G. Dawson (Oxford: Blackwell, 1959), 66–7.

Fig. 14.1 The Bamberg Apocalypse, Msc.Bibl.140, folio 53r, *The Last Judgement* (photo: Bamberg Staatsbibliothek)

an illumination of about 1000 (Fig. 14.1). The Bamberg Apocalypse depicts the Last Judgement in stark, authoritative terms, stressing the majesty of Christ the Judge, and dividing the scene clearly. Christ presiding from heaven surrounded by his heavenly court, the trumpeting angels, the saints acting as assessors oversee an earthly scene, where one angel displays to the blessed, on Christ's right, the welcome scroll 'Come, blessed of my father [inherit the kingdom prepared for you...]' (Matt. 25.34) and an opposing angel displays to the damned, on Christ's left, the unwelcome news 'Depart from me you accursed, into the [eternal] fire...' (Matt. 25.41). Beneath the damned opens a view of hell, where a grasping demon drags the wicked to join an enchained Satan.

For all the stability they represent, these two examples of standard religio-political expression omit the middle time (the interim), the middle people (Augustine's not very good and not very bad) and the middle space (purgatory). Despite Augustine's categories, apprehension about those who are neither great sinners nor great saints elicited visions of people between their individual death and the general resurrection. Visions from those of Fursey and Barontus (seventh and eighth centuries) to Wetti and Charles the Fat (ninth century) show souls removed from their body before death touring the other world. The visionaries were unable to tell the difference between souls suffering eternal punishment and those experiencing temporary purgation.[9] Sometimes, those torments occur on earth. In a vision of about 1160, Herbert of Torres, in Sardinia, saw a procession of the dead. 'Some of them were to be liberated sooner, others later, but many of them would endure inescapable punishments.' He saw a soul, who had spent the nine years since his death expiating his faults in the catch basin of his house, promoted to heaven by angels in a column of light.[10] The damned and the soon or not so soon to be saved mingle here on earth, enduring a tedious, crepuscular non-death.

Other texts similarly blend temporary and eternal postmortem suffering. In the Vision of Tundal (1148), his guardian angel conducts a prodigal knight brought near death by a seizure, through the otherworld. Tundal samples physical torments in locales resembling industrial sites, a kitchen, a forge, a grill and mythical places (a monster's jaws). Tundal must carry a cow similar to one he had earlier stolen across a bridge planted with upturned spikes that pierce his feet. Halfway across, he encounters another guilty soul coming the other way. Tundal laments, but acknowledges his guilt. Immediately he finds himself safely across. Admission of guilt ends punishment. At the pit of hell,

---

9 For Barontus: J. N. Hillgarth, ed., *Christianity and Paganism, 350–750* (Philadelphia: University of Pennsylvania Press, 1986), 195–204. For Fursey, Wetti and Charles the Fat: E. Gardiner, ed., *Visions of Heaven and Hell before Dante* (New York: Italica Press, 1989), 51–5, 65–79, 129–33.

10 *PL* 185, col. 1376 C-D, 1376-A: 'Quidam ex eis citius, quidam tardius liberandi erant, multorumque nihilominus poenae insolubiles permanebant.' See also Jean-Claude Schmitt, *Ghosts in the Middle Ages* (Chicago: University of Chicago Press, 1998), 93–121.

Tundal sees Satan writhing on a grill as he simultaneously eats, defecates and claws the souls of his victims. (In the *Très Riches Heures* of the Duke of Berry, the Limbourg Brothers have immortalised this image.) Tundal recognises his companions there and renounces these evil associates. The angel praises him and calls him 'a converted soul'. Tundal has 'shed his former *tristitia* and is now filled with joy'.[11] Once Tundal has disowned his evil past, his angel shows him where people who were otherwise good but failed to give alms to the poor are punished or rewarded in proportion (*per aliquot*) to their charity. King Cormac leaves his palace in heaven for punishment fitted to his sexual sins and his perjury, yet the poor whom he had helped in life serve him, in his torments. Tundal's heaven is a walled city suffused by the harmony of a choir made up of the 'consortium' of the saints – a term with important social connotations, as a consortium is a professional association, like a guild or trade group. Concentric walls separate the chaste married, virgins and martyrs. No king is mentioned; in Tundal's vision heaven is a consortium.

Another text, *Saint Patrick's Purgatory*, probably written around 1179–81, relates the experience, dating from about 1151–52, of a knight named Owen. Famous for explicitly naming purgatory as a place, much of this text's drama nonetheless revolves around the confusion between purgatory and hell. The tale begins with a foundation myth. In order to help convert the Irish, Jesus shows St Patrick a cave containing the terrors of hell and the pleasures of heaven. Jesus does not call it purgatory, but says anyone residing in it overnight earns the total remission of his sins. The story begins when Owen, a remorseful knight, tackling his *tristitia*,[12] desires to undertake an unusually harsh penance by visiting the purgatory of St Patrick. Once inside, demons urge him to turn back or else he will suffer the cave's torments forever. They seek to convince Owen that the purgatory is really hell. In the 1220s, Caesarius of Heisterbach will declare to his Cistercian novices that angels punish in purgatory, demons in hell, yet in *Saint Patrick's Purgatory*, it is the 'Tartarean ministers' (referring to the punitive underworld of antiquity) who staff the

---

11 *Visio Tnugdali*, ed. A. Wagner (Erlangen: Deichert, 1882), 40: 'Deposita preterita tristitia anima repleta est gaudio'. Gardiner, *Visions of Heaven and Hell*, 180–1.

12 A range of textual variants illustrate the twelfth-century idea of late antique *tristitia*. Here is how three Latin versions and a French translation of the *Purgatory of Saint Patrick* render the concept. *PL* 180, col. 989B: 'miles multum contristatus' (the knight was greatly saddened). Karl Warnke, ed., *Das Buch vom Espurgatoire S. Patrice der Marie de France und seine Quelle* (Halle: Niemeyer, 1938; repr., 1976), 38–9 'miles graviter indoluit' (the knight grieved seriously within), 'intima contritione cordis ingemuit' (he groaned with an intense contrition of heart), and Marie's Old French reads 'Li chevaliers pur ses pechiez / fu mult tristes e esmaiez' (The knight, because of his sins, / was very sad and fearful).

torture of the fiery wheel. This text propounds a new reading of hell. Understood correctly, infernal wracking is a catalogue of the punishments one deserves. By voluntarily reviewing, while alive, the punishments one deserves in hell, as monks did by means of their *tristitia*, this introspection can be purgatorial. *Saint Patrick's Purgatory* publicises a place to which the penitent might travel in order to structure their repentance.

This link between penance and the other world entered the nascent universities. What exactly is the connection between the guilty conscience, penitential actions and one's eventual fate? If penance can earn one's own remission, what is the status of one's ancestors? Should one pray for the damned? Peter Lombard (d. 1160), theologian and bishop of Paris, whose textbook of theology, *The Sentences*, prevailed in the schools until the sixteenth century, approved prayer for the damned. It will not liberate them from punishment, he admitted, but it will diminish their suffering.[13] For those to be saved through purgatory, suffrages do not effect a fuller absolution, but only speed its completion – that is, entering heaven sooner.[14] These contentions encouraged suffrages and a certain quantification linking suffrages (actions on earth) to results in the afterlife. There was a *de facto* calibration of death, as a 'final reckoning' weighed one's good deeds against one's sins. Peter Lombard's successors, however, rejected his position on prayers for the damned. William of Auxerre (d. 1231) considered suffrages effective only for those 'in whom are found the foundation and root of merit, namely charity'.[15] Some theologians, therefore, resisted the temptation to extrapolate from the diminution of punishment in purgatory to a putative relief in hell.

The art of the period also tackled the right disposition of space in the other world. The tympana of important churches presented the composition of the Bamberg Last Judgement. At Conques, gleeful demons torture victims and eagerly await more. At Autun, they tip the scale that weighs souls' deeds. Along the lintel, resurrected bodies grimace, facing their doom. At Bourges, as on Chartres' south portal's Last Judgement, the mouth of hell has moved onto the tympanum proper. Yet, at Notre Dame of Paris, where it has moved beyond the tympanum to the first archivolt, calm prevails. Devils lead the damned away in chains, but overall, a filial respect for the divine King has displaced the servile fear of hell. The audience for the resultant doctrinal

---

13 Peter Lombard, *Sententiae in IV Libris Distinctae* 4SN d.46 c.1 n 4 (Grottaferrata: Collegium S. Bonaventurae, 1972), vol. 2, 531, lines 11–12.

14 Peter Lombard, *Sententiae*, 4SN d. 45 c.4 n. 2; 526, lines 22–3.

15 William of Auxerre, *Summa Aurea* 4.18.4.1 (Paris: Pigouchet, 1501; repr. 1964), 538.145–9: 'in quo inveniunt fundamentum meriti et radicem, scilicet caritatem'.

lessons grew as these images shifted from illuminated manuscript pages to the public spaces facing the exterior portals of churches. Behind these doors, within the ecclesiastical enclosures, cloisters symbolise paradise.

In the thirteenth century, preachers also expanded the audience significantly. The newly founded Franciscan and Dominican orders trained cohorts of preachers in the new universities or in the schools of their orders under the supervision of university graduates. These teams spread throughout Europe preaching in the vernacular. Their sermons highlight biblical passages supporting the conclusions of theology. To appeal expressly to the unlettered, they include modern parables, *exempla*, drawn from centuries of uplifting literature. Sermon *exempla* illustrate every aspect of religious life. We learn from Stephen of Bourbon about the flaming tree in hell, rooted in the chest of a businessman, who led his sons into usury. Each generation occupies an additional branch. All their sins weigh on the founder, crushing him against the fiery floor of hell. Monasteries offer another way, given perseverance. Stephen tells of the Cistercian novice unhappy with his cell, which he declares 'worse than hell'. His deceased mother appears, as a ghost, to counsel him. She offers him a foretaste of hell's slightest pain, the grunting of pigs; then a sample of heaven's least blessing, birds chirping. The novice endures in salutary discipline.[16]

As preachers disseminated these edifying stories from quasi-authoritative collections and preached from model sermon books, church leaders sensed the power of the vernacular and imagined a new ability to disseminate doctrine to the remotest parish. Without ever achieving full standardisation, these innovations nonetheless energised the grass roots greatly. There would be no comparable jump in the dissemination of religious messages until the invention of printing in the fifteenth century. Women, in particular, benefited from this shift as tradition had largely prevented them from learning Latin, and the clergy closed the universities to them. Some nuns like Hildegard of Bingen (d. 1179) or Herrad of Landsberg (Hohenbourg, d. 1195), writing in Latin, to judge from the surviving records, made outstanding contributions in theology, science, music and art despite age-old prejudices. As women helped make literary vehicles of their vernacular languages, some, like Hadewijch of Brabant (thirteenth century), Mechthild of Magdeburg (d. c. 1285), Marguerite

---

16 For these *exempla*, see: Alan E. Bernstein, 'The Invocation of Hell in Thirteenth-Century Paris', in J. Hankins, J. Monfasani and F. Purnell, Jr, eds., *Supplementum Festivum: Studies in Honor of Paul Oskar Kristeller* (Medieval and Renaissance Texts and Studies 49; Binghamton, N.Y.: M.R.T.S., 1987), 13–54.

Porète (executed 1310) and Julian of Norwich (d. 1413), wrote more frequently – and without necessarily being nuns or being supervised by males.

More effective dissemination of other-world doctrines (or, put differently, a more comprehensive clerical response to popular concerns) entailed behavioural consequences. Many laypeople pursued heaven fervently. Because preachers labelled their sermons the Word of God, simply attending them was considered virtuous. Pilgrimage as penance earned indulgences (diminution of punishment owed for sin), and crusading was a form of pilgrimage. Men and women entered monastic houses. Venerating saints brought supernatural advocates. Public and private rituals from the birthplace to the cemetery linked private meaning to public spectacle, political propaganda and then again to collective sensibilities. Churches, then guild associations, sponsored open-air performances dramatising biblical stories. Some sacraments also evolved. Before the twelfth century, penance had usually been voluntary, but in 1215, Pope Innocent III required annual confession to one's own parish priest. The mendicants popularised this private confession. New forms of religious associations evolved for lay people: the mendicant third orders, confraternities and, mostly for women, beguinages. Rigorous, new observant branches strained the religious orders themselves. From the thirteenth century, founding hospitals spread as a new form of charity. Administered by ecclesiastical institutions, charitable donations of all kinds linked benefits in this world and the next. Indeed, donations to churches profoundly shaped Europe's economy. So also did taxes levelled by ecclesiastical authorities. The hope for heaven and the fear of hell and purgatory augmented the church's economic and political influence, both results of its engagement with the population's view of postmortem punishments and rewards.

Building on their perception of popular involvement, popes used doctrinal definitions in their attempt to standardise the faith. Among their chief concerns was to apportion places, times and destinations in the interim and in eternity. These thirteenth-century declarations intensify supernatural sanctions by initiating reward or punishment at the deathbed rather than postponing them to the Second Coming.

In the creed of 1215, Innocent III declared a judgement according to merit: so that those who have done good 'will receive eternal glory with Christ' and those who have done evil 'will receive eternal punishment with the devil'.[17]

---

17 H. Denzinger and A. Schönmetzer, eds., *Enchiridion Symbolorum*, 34th edn (Barcelona: Herder, 1967), no. 801, 260.

This explanation implies a weighing of both good and evil deeds, with a greater weight or number of merits winning salvation. There is no reference to the interim or to purgatory.

Innocent IV's letter *Sub catholicae professione* of 1254 made repentance the criterion that determines whether, in purgatory, one can expiate one's 'venial and minute sins'. In the absence of penance, one pays the eternal price for dying unconfessed, in hell. 'If anyone should die in mortal sin without penance ... he will be tormented forever by the flames of eternal Gehenna.'[18] Innocent IV defined purgatory as 'that transitory fire [by which] are purged small and tiny sins which burden souls even after death, if they have been released [that is, absolved] during one's lifetime'. In addition to opening up purgatory officially as a destination for the penitent, Innocent IV declared that the souls of those who die 'in charity immediately cross into the eternal home'.[19] In practice, Innocent IV's specification that purgatory could cleanse only venial sins soon yielded to an older tradition claiming that confession makes even 'criminal' or mortal sins venial.[20] In 1274, Gregory X omitted the insistence that only venial sins could be expiated in purgatory, but determined that, like purgatory and heaven, hell, too, begins immediately at death.[21] Thus collapsing eschatological time emphasises individual action and confession by bringing their consequences closer to the present.

Beneath the level of papal declarations, Parisian theologians worked to articulate a consistent afterlife. Difficulties came from institutional demands such as suffrages and crusading. If these deeds affect one's postmortem condition, then at what rate? Europe's leading thinkers strove to avoid the quantification of quid-pro-quo arrangements. It was not always easy. Alexander of Hales (d. 1245) established a scale of offenses (venial sin, mortal sin) and their corresponding punishments (penitential, here on earth, and, in the hereafter, purgatorial and infernal). He reflected on how each might be converted or commuted into the other. He observes: 'Each punishment is commuted into the punishment corresponding to it.'[22] Like it or not, Alexander's metaphor of exchange, commutation, did not limit, but rather fostered what had become a de facto culture of calibrated death.

18 *Ibid.*, no. 839, 272.
19 *Ibid.*
20 *Decretum. De Pen.* d.1 c.88: 'Fit enim veniale per confessionem quod criminale erat in operatione', in E. Friedberg, ed., *Decretum Magistri Gratiani* (Leipzig, 1879; repr. Graz: Akademische Druck und Verlagsanstalt, 1959), vol. I, 1188.
21 Denzinger, *Enchiridion*, nos. 856–8, 276–7.
22 Alexander of Hales, *Glossa in quatuor libros sententiarum Petri Lombardi* 4.18.4, IV.q. (Quaracchi, Florence: Collegium S. Bonaventurae, 1957), vol. 4, 324.

If suffrages can relieve punishments in the other world, can enough of them combine to save even the damned? Medieval biographies of Pope Gregory I relate how the saint interceded to obtain the pagan Emperor Trajan's removal from hell to a second life on earth, where he could die as a Christian and, by the time of Dante, emerge as a star in heaven, saved.[23] Bonaventure (d. 1274) considered the case of Trajan. God could, but does not, save the damned. '[After death] it is not only difficult, but even impossible for someone who died in sin to be saved, not because divine power could not accomplish it, but [because] divine justice has reasonably and justly decreed against it'.[24] This preservation of divine power, usually not noticed until the fourteenth century, would become more and more important as the distinction between God's *potentia absoluta* and *potentia ordinata*.

Thomas Aquinas (d. 1274) followed William of Auxerre's position on suffrages for the damned: 'Charity, which is the bond uniting the members of the church, extends not only to the living, but also to the dead who die in charity.'[25] What characterises the souls in purgatory, then, is not the negative (their mediocrity) but the positive (their possession of charity). Having charity, they are open to suffrages. Lacking charity, the damned, in hell, have closed themselves to suffrages.[26] This reclassification of the dead, even as it put purgatory on a firmer footing, by no means emptied hell. Rather, it strengthened hell by segregating its inmates absolutely from contact with any others, living or dead. Oblivion receded.

Displaying its propensity for these finely honed categories, theological writing can neglect the insistent, autonomous, popular outlook, but sometimes the people's mindset emerges. Around 1220, Caesarius of Heisterbach, writing an introductory theological manual for the novices of his monastery, relates a tale from nearby Liège. The bishop denied a Christian widow the right to bury her non-Christian, usurer husband in the church cemetery. The wife won a judicial appeal and moved into a shed next to her husband's grave, where she prayed for him. After seven years, he appeared to her in half-white half-black clothing, saying, 'I have been drawn out of the depth of hell and from the greatest punishments. And if you devote similar good deeds to me

---

23 E. Gordon Whatley, 'The Uses of Hagiography: The Legend of Pope Gregory and the Emperor Trajan in the Middle Ages', *Viator* 15 (1984), 25–63.
24 Bonaventure, *Commentaria in Quatuor Libros Sententiarum*, 4 d.20 p. 1 a.1 post q.6; dubium 3 (Quaracchi: Collegium S. Bonaventurae, 1889), 527b–8a.
25 P. Caramello, ed., *Summa Theologiae, Tertia Pars, Supplementum*, Q.71 a.2 (Turin, Rome: Marietti, 1956), vol. 3, 254b.
26 Thomas Aquinas, *Supplementum* a. 5; 258a.

for seven more years, I shall be wholly liberated.' The wife complied and, after seven years, her husband appeared in glowing white, thanked her, and declared himself 'liberated'. Caesarius classifies this story under the heading of purgatory, not hell, because, he says, no one can be redeemed from hell. He conjectures an unstated, last-minute contrition.[27] Caesarius' effort to explain away the obvious theological problem (a wife praying a sinner out of hell) in the popular tale circulating in his neighbourhood indicates some contradiction between learned and popular culture. It is an error to assume a uniform theological consistency throughout the whole social fabric. Caesarius' 'correction' notwithstanding, the tripartite structure of this tale suggests that some people believed it possible for one person to pray another out of hell, then out of purgatory and finally into heaven.

Give-and-take on eschatological matters could occur at the highest level, too, as in 1331–32, when Pope John XXII declared that the Beatific Vision, that is the heavenly reward consisting in the direct vision of God, cannot be attained until the body reunites with the soul at the general resurrection. Similarly, the damned, whether humans or demons, do not go to hell until after the Last Judgement for the same reason. His declarations threatened to reverse the trends of the previous century, which had moved the decisive moment up to the individual's death. Faced with immense popular, political and even royal objections, he retracted his opinion on his deathbed. His successor, Benedict XII, restored the momentum towards the immediacy, for those appropriately deserving, of the two final fates: heaven and hell.[28]

Much as theologians shifted rhetorical levels in moving from the university lectern to the preacher's pulpit, or a fresco painter represented ineffable mysteries on church walls, so Dante's *Divine Comedy* addresses both the learned and popular sides of the religious community. Besides being a magisterial exposition of Catholic theology, Dante's masterpiece is a human love story and an occasion for political invective. Writing in Italian verse, the poet recounted his fictional vision to trace the road to God.[29] By the stages of his pilgrimage, Dante embraced the calibration of death. All is measured. In hell,

---

27 Caesarius of Heisterbach, *The Dialogue on Miracles*, 12.24, trans. H. von E. Scott and C. C. Swinton Bland, 2 vols. (London: Routledge, 1929), vol. 2, 313–14.
28 Denzinger, *Enchiridion*, nos. 1000–1, 296–7.
29 Aron Gurevich outlines a convergence of popular and learned patterns of thought in 'The "Divine Comedy" before Dante', in J. M. Bak and P. A. Hollingworth, trans., *Medieval Popular Culture: Problems of Belief and Perception* (Cambridge: Cambridge University Press, 1988), 104–52.

immersion measures guilt; in heaven, the intensity of one's vision of God measures grace.

> e del vedere è misura mercede,
> Seeing measures their reward (*Par.* 28.112).

For him, this measuring explains divine justice.

Yet Dante also doubts these rational devices. In heaven, St Peter asks him to define his faith. Hearing the Florentine exile employ the scholastic terms 'syllogism' and 'quiddity', Peter challenges: 'Why do you take these propositions that close your mind to be the divine spark?' (*Par.* 24.98–9). When Dante calls the Three Persons and the Gospel the burning flame within him, his answer gladdens Peter.

Fire is indeed the organising metaphor of the *Divine Comedy*.

> catun si fascia di quel ch'elli è inceso.
> Each one swathes himself in that which makes him burn. (*Inf.* 26.48)

To burn (*ardere*) in hell causes eternal torment, in purgatory purification, in Paradise eternal light and love. With this love we are all, potentially, 'inflamed' (*incesi*). Thus, ardour itself, whether human obsession, cleansing fire or divine love, pervades the universe. God's return of human love will quench the fire that excites the seekers of heaven. Dante's fictional vision implicitly challenges the inscription on the Gate of Hell. One should not abandon hope, but 'enter' hell while alive, thus, like Owen, confront *tristitia* and review one's faults, cultivate faith, pursue love.

In the *Paradiso*, Peter had not questioned only Dante's faith. In their conversation, the first pope deplored Europe's spiritual decline. Religious authorities, he said, abuse their office for personal profit, theologians vaunt superfluous distinctions, preachers chatter, hawkers of false indulgences take debased coin from the credulous who buy counterfeit promises (*Par.* 29). In the generation after Dante, Francis Petrarch (d. 1374) criticised academics for knowing how to define virtue but not how to love or practise it. The concession Bonaventure granted – that God could save the damned if he chose, but did not – blossomed, among the nominalists, into an effort to bypass the bureaucratic image of a predictable God (confined to his *potentia ordinata*) and remembering the traditional emphasis (in Pseudo-Dionysus, for example) that he is beyond knowing (and therefore free to employ his *potentia absoluta*). Had the rationalisation (and, on an institutional level, the quantification) of faith gone too far?

Some attempted to restore a qualitative focus using mathematical ideas and imagery. Dante's contemporary, the Spiritual Franciscan Ubertinus de Casale (writing in 1305) saw humble self-abasement, the voluntary adoption of spiritual poverty, as a precondition to salvation through his literal interpretation of Matt. 25.40. Ubertinus demanded the soul's conjunction with Jesus through identification with 'the least' of Christ's brethren. This transformation, making the faithful into 'little Jesuses' (*jesunculi*), achieved a state of 'minimacy' (*minimitas*) that, alone, is saving.[30] The contrast and, mystically, the correspondence of the minimum and the maximum informed the studies of Nicholas of Cusa (d. 1464), who explored the coincidence of opposites, thus developing the mathematical idea of infinity as another way to God.

Intense institutional pressures remained. Indulgences for crusade, pilgrimage, attending special events like the Jubilee which Boniface VIII proclaimed in 1300, donations of all sizes; the quid-pro-quo approach to expiation elicited various means of 'measuring' progress through repentance. The quantification of Alexander of Hales' commutations worked its way into popular and institutional practices that outran his sense of the relationship between penitential discipline and the afterlife. Endowing private masses in chantries or at altars in the chapels of side aisles, these broke down the greater tasks of endowing cathedrals and providing prebends, work of the early Middle Ages, into smaller units – each one with corresponding expected credits, whether before or after death.[31] Note that authorities denied that these actions remitted guilt, only the resultant punishment. Yet the distinction was lost on a population anxious about the pains of hell and purgatory. In 1477, Sixtus IV asserted the ability, as pope, to distribute the collective merits 'of Christ and the saints', which he called 'a treasury' on behalf of those in purgatory, in need of suffrages.[32] Relief from purgatorial punishment seemed ever more accessible, sometimes, as in the case that provoked this declaration, in return for a cash donation to construct a church.

Scholars like William of Ockham at Oxford (d. 1349) had long objected that these theologies restrict the power of God to the inferences humans can derive from Scripture. In fact, his followers, the nominalists, insisted God's power is absolute; it is certainly not limited by human reason. Invocation of God's *potentia absoluta* (divine power seen as absolute, unbound) over his *potentia*

---

30 *Arbor Vitae Crucifixae Jesu* (Venice: Andreas de Bonettis of Pavia, 1485; repr. with an introduction and bibliography by Charles T. Davis, Turin: Bottega d'Erasmo, 1961), 490b.

31 R. W. Southern, 'Between Heaven and Hell', *Times Literary Supplement* 4133 (18 June 1982), 651–2.

32 Denzinger, *Enchiridion*, no. 1406, 349.

*ordinata* (divine power limited to what God has revealed) challenged the notions of purgatory, suffrages and indulgences. Critics believed they carried quantification – and human confidence in extrapolation – too far. In 1479, an ecclesiastical court in Mainz forced John of Wesel to retract a treatise he had written against indulgences. Wesel contended that the right to distribute these merits of Christ and the saints could only exist if Christ had made such an agreement with his apostles, but that the Bible reveals nothing of the kind.[33] Though Wesel recanted, his invocation of Scripture to challenge the quantification of merit did not disappear. Scripture, indeed, was to be the rallying cry for the Protestant challenge to these Catholic practices. To heaven, too, the Protestants would bring their levelling eye, de-emphasising ranks and hierarchy, abolishing the cult of saints, for example.

Meanwhile, whatever objections they aroused among theologians, actions to gain postmortem advantage intensified. The attention to conscience, heightened since the requirement of annual confession in 1215, affected personal piety. There was a corresponding democratisation of artistic objects. The monumental compositions of Romanesque and Gothic church facades, uniting heaven and hell at the Last Judgement, proliferated, as in the ceiling of the Florence Baptistery (late thirteenth century). Yet private patronage could personalise them, as in Giotto's Arena chapel in Padua (1305). Smaller altarpieces also appeared in the private chapels of wealthy families. Many of these scenes, too, combined the whole perspective from heaven to hell in a diptych or even a single image. This retailing of art, that is, making objects smaller and less expensive, advanced remarkably with the introduction of printed woodcuts in the early fifteenth century. Presses could reproduce pious images on a single sheet of paper. Communication of religious messages no longer depended on public spaces to reach large numbers. This concentration of audience achieved a particular intimacy in what were called 'books of hours', prayer books of slight dimensions, illuminated to enhance meditation, as text and image united in the laps of private owners.

As the core series of prayers for the book of hours is the Office of the Virgin, many of their illustrations depict heaven in recounting scenes from her story, such as the Coronation and Assumption. Yet heaven never lacked as the setting for the many dramas in the Apocalypse (the woman dressed in the sun, the adoration of the lamb, Christ's appearance with a sword in his mouth, the battle with the dragon, the fall of the rebel angels, the heavenly Jerusalem, the Last Judgement).

---

33 Cited by Heiko A. Oberman, 'Luther and the Via Moderna: The Philosophical Backdrop of the Reformation Breakthrough', *Journal of Ecclesiastical History* 54 (2003), 641–70 at 661.

Fig. 14.2 Illuminated initial from a Book of Hours, folio 197r, manuscript 133 M 131 (photo: Koninklijke Bibliothek, National Library of the Netherlands, The Hague)

Heaven also appears as the place from which Providence oversees the earth. The hand of God or diving angels warn, inspire, protect, expel their human charges. Angels make music or dance as in the Portinari chapel in Milan or in Fra Angelico's 'Christ Glorified in the Court of Heaven' at London's National Gallery. Heaven is the seat of the royal court for the Last Judgement. It is also where Christ hears Mary's intercessions (her appeals to Jesus on behalf of those who pray for her help). With the rise of interest in science in the twelfth century, heaven appears as the scene of creation. God the geometer designs the earth. Heaven frames the zodiac. Secularised, heaven may be the lover's enclosure in the Romance of the Rose or the Cluny museum's unicorn tapestry. It appears in medieval theatre at stage left, whereas the mouth of hell is to the right.

Purgatory makes its appearance in art during the fourteenth century,[34] but later, two particularly majestic representations occur with the coronation of the Virgin by the Trinity of Enguerrand Quarton at Villeneuve-les-Avignon (1454) and by Jean Colombe (c. 1480) in the *Très Riches Heures* of the Duke of Berry. Important quantitative evidence for the widespread acceptance of the doctrine includes the appearances in illuminated initials in books of hours showing two facing souls, kneeling in prayer in purgatorial flames.[35]

The new ability, associated with Renaissance art, to render human bodies in flesh-tones and with naturalistic anatomy makes the eschatological scenes of Signorelli in Orvieto and the early Netherlandish artists Rogier van der Weyden, Hans Memling, Dierk Bouts and Jan van Eyck breathtakingly immediate. A generation later, Hieronymus Bosch set seemingly absurd figures in scenes resembling heaven and hell as symbols of the guilt and fantasy of inner death. These images accentuate dread and fear, hope and longing. These are the inner realities Martin Luther evoked in his ninety-five theses attacking indulgences in 1517. The fulcrum of his critique is contrition, the personal relationship between the sinner and God, where remorse is separate from any priestly function. Only God governs one's soul. Donated coins, pilgrimages accomplished, battles waged avail nothing. This focus on the inner person had its Catholic sympathisers, too. Michelangelo's *Last Judgement* in the Sistine Chapel (1536–41) shows as much fright and hope as awe – strong indications that, for him, psychological realities dominate on Doomsday.

---

34 See Joseph Polzer, 'Andrea di Bonaiuto's *Via Veritatis* and Dominican Thought in Late Medieval Italy', *Art Bulletin* 77 (1995), 262–89; Michelle Fournié, 'La représentation de l'au-delà et le purgatoire à Saint-Just de Narbonne', in *Le grand retable de Narbonne* (Narbonne: Ville de Narbonne, 1990), 45–55.

35 For example, see The Hague, KB, 133 M 131, fol. 197$^r$ by the Master of Zweder van Culemborg (Fig. 14.2).

PART IV

*

SHAPES OF A CHRISTIAN WORLD

# 15

# Sacramental life

## MIRI RUBIN

Some time between 1445 and 1450 the Flemish artist Rogier van der Weyden (b. 1400, Tournai, d. 1464, Brussels) painted three oak panels which have come to be known as the Seven Sacraments Altarpiece.[1] The artist had made a pilgrimage to Rome in the Jubilee year of 1450, and his subsequent work – including this panel – displays a new-found vibrancy and colour. The trip to Rome may have also inspired a state of mind which is evident in the work: for Rogier offers a *summa*, a visual summary, of the Christian life as a sacramental journey from cradle to grave. This was a vision conceptualised and promoted by popes since the twelfth century, one which had become, by van der Weyden's time, the elementary framework for Christian lives.

The history of the sacraments begins, of course, much earlier. Already the second-century Tertullian (c. 160–c. 225) attempted to use the Roman legal term *sacramentum* – oath – to describe religious commitment.[2] He also developed *sacramentum* to mean 'symbol, figure, allegory, symbolic virtue or power, a symbolic order or person'.[3] Sacraments were those gestures or practices which denoted a commitment, or signified events of great importance.[4] The next

---

1 This panel measures 200 × 97 cm (central panel), 119 × 63 cm (side panel, each) and is on display at the Royal Museum of Fine Arts (Koninklijk Museum voor Schone Kunsten) in Antwerp. Dirk De Vos, *Rogier van der Weyden: The Complete Works* (New York: Harry N. Abrams, 1999), 217–25 offers an authoritative discussion of the altarpiece. De Vos suggests an earlier date of 1440–5 and that the commission was made by Jean Chevrot, Bishop of Tournai, who intended the altarpiece for the chapel of the Collegiate church of Poligny in the Franche–Comté, Chevrot's home town. See also Pierre Quarré, 'Le triptyque des Sept Sacraments de Rogier van der Weyden, en Bourgogne', *Publication du centre européen d'études burgundo-médianes* 17 (1976), 85–94. I am grateful to James H. Marrow and Walter Simons for advising me on the literature about the altarpiece.
2 Peter Cramer, *Baptism and Change in the Early Middle Ages, c. 200–c. 1150* (Cambridge: Cambridge University Press, 1993), 63–4.
3 Brian Stock, *The Implications of Literacy: Written Language and Models of Interpretation in the Eleventh and Twelfth Centuries* (Princeton: Princeton University Press, 1983), 256–8.
4 See also Elizabeth Saxon, *The Eucharist in Romanesque France: Iconography and Theology* (Woodbridge: Boydell Press, 2006), 14–15.

Fig. 15.1 Triptych of the Seven Sacraments by Rogier van der Weyden, Royal Museum of Fine Arts, Antwerp

important stage in the discussion was, as is so often the case, the treatment offered by Augustine of Hippo (354–430). As part of his thoroughgoing conceptualisation of a Christian society and polity, of the processes which he witnessed all around him in the regions of the Roman Empire, he explored the nature of sacraments. These were the rituals through which people became Christians and lived as Christians, both individually and in groups. If Christian life was predicated upon the hope for salvation though the saving grace which came to the world with Christ's sacrifice, then sacraments were the channels through which that grace flowed to individuals. First at baptism, for the erasure of original sin, and then, throughout life, grace supported the efforts of a Christian life.

Sacraments made palpable and visible the invisible and mysterious workings of grace. Inasmuch as they were visible signs, they always operated through a material medium such as water, oil or bread. Augustine conceded that some people may be sanctified and touched by grace in other ways too, but for most believers sacraments were utterly necessary. As bishop of Hippo he confronted the Donatist tendency which argued that sacraments were only effective if they were celebrated by a pure priest. This position was rejected by Augustine and was persecuted as a heresy by the Empire. Augustine's position on the sacraments and those who administered them was best suited to the turbulent period of mass conversions in which he lived: how were pagans to be drawn to Christianity if they could not trust that the baptism and the eucharist at the heart of their new lives as Christians were indeed valid, and thus saving?

Sacraments were not only rituals of incorporation which made and sustained Christian lives, they were also links in a chain of succession, re-enactments of the fundamental structure of an evolving, historic church. From Christ's life, through apostles who founded churches, and later through the pope of Rome, Peter's successor, a chain of sacramental action was created. Augustine's understanding of the sacraments was thus linked to his vision of the church as an edifice which contained the legacy of grace and the heritage of teaching and example which emanated from Christ's own life. Thus discussions of the sacraments were always bound to touch upon the status and powers of the clergy, their unique privileges. Additionally, the material aspect of sacraments – their appeal to sense experience – was a bolster against those tendencies within Christianity, to which Augustine had been attracted for much of his life, which espoused a dualist rejection of matter in the conduct of Christian life.

It is important to bear in mind this early Christian legacy when we discuss sacramental life in Western Europe in our period. The early medieval centuries saw relatively little discussion of sacramental theory, although individual sacraments did receive some attention and elaboration.[5] The most striking re-engagement with the subject happened in those centres of theological work and pastoral provision, the schools of Paris in the twelfth century. In his treatise on the sacraments the Augustinian scholar Hugh of St Victor (1096–1141) distinguished between the type of sacrament that prevailed in each phase

5 Arnold Angenendt, *Geschichte der Religiosität im Mittelalter* (Darmstadt: Wissenschaftliche Buchgesellschaft, 1997), 387–404; Philip Lyndon Reynolds, *Marriage in the Western Church: The Christianization of Marriage during the Patristic and Early Medieval Periods* (Supplements to Vigiliae Christianae 24; Leiden: Brill, 1994); Frederick S. Paxton, *Christianizing Death: The Creation of a Ritual Process in Early Medieval Europe*, (Ithaca, N.Y.: Cornell University Press, 1990); Stock, *The Implications of Literacy*, 255–8. I am grateful to Yitzhak Hen for his advice on the early medieval period.

of history: under natural law, under written law and under grace. He also refined the relationship between the external facets of the sacrament and its internal working:

> sacramentum est corporale vel materiale elementum foris sensibiliter propositum ex simili repraesentans, et ex institutione significans, et ex sanctificatione continens aliquam invisibilem et spiritualem gratiam.

> A sacrament is a physical or material element, which represents externally according to the senses by similarity, and which signifies by the fact of its institution, and as to the sacred, contains a certain invisible and spiritual grace.[6]

In the emergent sacramental theology and its pastoral application the issue of appearance was to be enhanced.

Hugh of St Victor's rethinking of the sacraments influenced the great systematiser of sacramental theology, his pupil Peter Lombard. Turning to this most important theological commentary, Peter Lombard's (d. 1160) *Sentences*, we find Augustine's word re-expressed:

> Sacramentum proprie dicitur quod ita signum est gratiae Dei, ei invisibilis gratiae forma, ut ipsius imaginem gerat et causa existat.

> It is proper to name a sacrament that which is a sign of God's grace; in the form of his invisible grace, so that it bears the image of that grace, and is also its cause.[7]

Unlike the rituals of the Old Law, Christian sacraments not only symbolised, but conferred grace *(haec conferunt gratiam)*.[8] Lombard also settled the question of the number of sacraments: Augustine had already differentiated between types of sacraments, but Lombard was definitive about their number, not three or four or twelve, as some would have had it,[9] but seven: baptism, confirmation, ordination, marriage, confession, eucharist, extreme unction.[10]

---

6 Hugh of St Victor, 'De Sacramentis', Book 1, Part IX, c.2; *PL* 176, col. 317 D.

7 Peter Lombard, *Sententiae in IV libris distinctae* (Grottaferrata: Collegium S. Bonaventurae, 1981), IV Sent. D.1, c.2; vol. 2, 232.

8 *Ibid.*, III Sent D.40, c.3; vol.2, 229.

9 N. Häring, 'The Interaction between Canon Law and Sacramental Theology in the Twelfth Century', in S. Kuttner, ed., *Proceedings of the Fourth International Congress of Medieval Canon Law* (Monumenta iuris canonici ser. C, Subsidia 5; Vatican: Apostolic Library of the Vatican Press, 1976), 483–93.

10 Marcia Colish, *Peter Lombard*, 2 vols. (Brill Studies in Intellectual History 41; Leiden: Brill, 1994), 528. For discussion in Paris, see John W. Baldwin, *Masters, Princes, and Merchants: The Social Views of Peter the Chanter and his Circle*, 2 vols., (Princeton: Princeton University Press, 1970).

Van der Weyden's panel shows the sacraments as social events, with all the variety and animation that family celebrations involve. Its composition cleverly conveys the fundamental meaning of sacraments: at the front, above each and all of the sacramental scenes, is the crucifixion – the source of all grace and hope for salvation. Christ's body soars above, even as on the ground John, Mary and the holy women lament his death. Along the same axis, deep within the church, at its east end, there is an altar, with the celebration of the sacrament of the altar. The priest is shown at the moment of the elevation – right after the consecration of the bread and wine and the operation of transubstantiation, by which these were turned into Christ's body and blood – his chasuble facing the viewer with the sign of the cross. The central panel evokes the space of history and its remaking at the altar through the arch-sacrament, the eucharist. A lay person kneels behind the priest awaiting his participation through communion?

The two side panels each contain three sacraments, beginning with baptism at the bottom left and ending with death at the bottom right. Three brightly coloured angels hover over the sacramental scenes of this panel. The baptism is that of an infant – a far cry from the multitude of adult baptisms Augustine had to confront – who is surrounded by godparents as it is dipped in the font. Baptism incorporated the infant into the Christian community, but it was also the sign of the commitment of adults: the biological parents and the baptismal parents promised that they would guide the child towards a Christian life. This was, of course, a serious commitment, animated not only by the hope for salvation, but by hope that the child would survive the dangers of infancy and grow into adulthood.[11] The moment around the font was full of meaning. It is not surprising, therefore, that fonts were often carved with a summary of the faith which those attending promised to secure: in late medieval East Anglia most fonts were octagonal in shape. The panels offered eight surfaces for the depiction of seven sacraments, and of the crucifixion from which the grace they conveyed originated.[12]

Parents feared greatly the possibility that their children would die without baptism, and the church relaxed the condition of baptism so that in the absence of a priest any lay person could pronounce the formula. Midwives, who were often present when a sickly newborn came into the world, were

---

11 Cramer, *Baptism and Change in the Early Middle Ages, c. 200–c. 1150*, 136–55; Shulamith Shahar, *Childhood in the Middle Ages* (London and New York: Routledge, 1991), 45–52.
12 Ann Eljenholm Nichols, *Seeable Signs: The Iconography of the Seven Sacraments, 1350–1544* (Woodbridge: Boydell, 1994). I am grateful to Ann Nichols for an edifying conversation on octagonal fonts.

tested in some dioceses for their knowledge of the baptismal formula. Forced baptism of Jews and Muslims under the threat of violence challenged the sacramental understanding that sacraments were to be freely received. The relative ease with which baptism could be enacted set it apart from most other sacraments. Bishop Bertram of Metz wrote to Pope Innocent III in 1206 with the question about a Jew who, 'Being close to death, had personally recited the baptismal formula and plunged himself into some water in the presence of just other Jews.'[13] The pope required that he be baptised again in a proper manner.

Next follows confirmation, that additional boost of grace which was given to youngsters at the outset of the testing age of adolescence and sexual awakening. The bishop administered confirmation as parents looked on. The child being confirmed is part of a group of youngsters, at the liminal stage between childhood and adulthood. This was also the age of first communion; those deemed able to appreciate its complex truths were ready to receive it.

After confirmation young people were considered responsible for their actions, and able to make moral choices. They now required the guidance and balm of confession, the next sacrament on the left. In the early church, confession was a public ritual, but by the fifteenth century it was a somewhat more private one, though confession boxes were not introduced into Catholic practice until the Counter-Reformation. Confession was guided by the questions of the priest, himself aided by the guidelines of the *Liber poenitentialis*, the penance handbook, a genre which proliferated from the late twelfth century.[14] Confession was elicited through a process of probing, which produced self-knowledge and true confrontation with sin. Priests were instructed to discern the many circumstances of sin – prompted by the alliterative – where? when? how? with whom? how often? Consequently transgression was examined in its full context, leading to a more nuanced meting out of appropriate penance. Penance could take the form of fasts of varying degrees of severity, almsgiving, pilgrimages to shrines near or even very far. The bishop of Cambrai required in his synodal statutes of 1260 that the confessed be exhorted to visit the 'mother church of the diocese, the Cathedral of Cambrai', and attached an

---

13 Paul B. Pixton, *The German Episcopacy and the Implementation of the Decrees of the Fourth Lateran Council 1216–1245* (Watchmen on the Tower; Leiden: Brill, 1995), 141.
14 Robert of Flamborough, *Liber poenitentialis*, ed. J. J. Francis Firth (Pontifical Institute of Mediaeval Studies and Texts 18; Toronto: Pontifical Institute of Mediaeval Studies, 1971). See also Alexander Murray, 'Confession before 1215', *Transactions of the Royal Historical Society*, 6th series 3 (1993), 51–81.

indulgence as a reward.[15] An ethos of responsibility developed around confession: anything heard during confession was to be kept secret, never divulged or even insinuated. A whole new dimension was added to the persona of the priest, as indicated in the statutes of Guiard de Laon, Bishop of Cambrai (1238–48):

> Item nullus sacerdos ira vel odio vel etiam metu mortis in aliquo audeat revelare confessionem confitentis signo vel verbo, vel generaliter et specialiter insinuando ut sic dicendo: 'Ego scio te esse talem qualis es'. Et si revelavit, debet degredare absque miserciordia.[16]

> And no priest should dare, out of anger, hatred or the fear of death, reveal anything of the confessed person's confession, in sign or in word, in general or by insinuation, as in saying 'I know you are such and such'. And if he does reveal, he should be degraded [from priestly status] without mercy.

After confession and contrition, a change of heart and a separation from sin, Christians were allowed to partake in communion. Indeed, the whole thrust of the sacramental package offered and required from Christians by the Fourth Lateran Council (1215) and its national offshoots was to combine the two into a solemn and meaningful annual event. For lay people that would suffice:

> Omnis utriusque sexus fidelis, postquam ad annos discretionis pervenerit, omnia sua solus peccata confietatur fideliter, saltem semel in anno proprio sacerdoti, et iniunctam sibi poenitentiam studeat pro viribus adimplere, suscipiens reverenter ad minus in pascha eucharistiae sacramentum, nisi forte de consilio proprii sacerdotis ob aliquam rationabilem causam ad tempus ab eius perceptione duxerit abstinendum; alioquin et vivens ab ingressu ecclesiae arceatur et moriens Christiana careat sepultura.[17]

> Let [all the faithful of either sex, after they have reached the age of discernment] reverently receive the sacrament of the Eucharist at least at Easter unless they think, for a good reason and on advice of their own priest, that they should abstain from receiving it for a time. Otherwise they shall be barred from entering a church during their lifetime and they shall be denied a Christian burial at death.

The central panel shows the expectant communicant. Everything that had formed the Christian person from baptism, through instruction, confirmation and in the exchanges prompted by confession, should have prepared for the

---

15 *Les statuts synodaux de l'ancienne province de Reims*, ed. Joseph Avril (Collection de documents inédits sur l'historie de France 23; Paris: Comité des travaux historiques et scientifiques, 1997), no. 5, 73.

16 *Ibid*. no.44, 36.

17 Canon 21, *The Decrees of the Ecumenical Councils* I, ed. Norman P. Tanner (London: Sheed & Ward; Washington, D.C.: Georgetown University Press, 1990), 245–245*.

reception of communion, Christ's flesh and blood, confected at the altar by the priest. The centrality of the eucharist in van der Weyden's panel reflects its position in contemporary discussion and debate. Most guide-books and all collections of edifying tales for instruction of the laity contained a particularly long section about the sacrament of the altar.[18] In the eucharist were enfolded so many basic truths, getting it right should lead to a positive disposition and a willing trust in the operation of the other sacraments. Additionally, the theology of the eucharist had developed by the year 1200 into a testing edifice: its keystone was the belief in transubstantiation – a term coined in the 1180s – in the transformation of the bread and wine at the altar into Christ's flesh and blood through the operation of the words of consecration, Christ's words of the Last Supper (Matt. 26.26–8), by a priest. The first clause of the Fourth Lateran Council made belief in transubstantiation – in that particular form of Christ's presence in the sacrament of the altar and no other – a requirement of faith.

Moving to the right panel of van der Weyden's altarpiece, we encounter three sacraments which were not experienced by all, and not utterly necessary for salvation. First ordination, the privilege of the few who chose the priestly vocation. Access to this sacrament was highly restricted, for it was open only to men, of free legal status, born in wedlock, whose body was without blemish, of right age, and who were celibate. In the desire to recruit priests, canon law offered some avenues that allowed those who fell short of these requirements to apply for dispensations, and these were left to the discretion of bishops. Ordination was the end of a long process: a young person began by receipt of the tonsure as a boy, and then could progress through the minor orders, playing various auxiliary roles alongside a priest. These ranged from acolyte (*acolyta*), to reader (*lector*), to helper in exorcism (*exorcista*), or carrier of holy water (*aquabaiulus*). The major orders, which could lead to the pinnacle of ordination, were entered at the age of 25, as subdeacon (*subdiaconus*), then deacon (*diaconus*) and on to priest (*presbiter*). While all clerics below the rank of priest were able to contribute to sacramental celebration, and indeed to administer some sacraments, the sacrament of the altar was to be celebrated by priests alone.

Ordination was a marriage of sorts, a marriage with Christ, and van der Weyden shows the kneeling ordinand dressed in white, like a bride. Ordination conferred a great deal of privilege: proof of a living and suitable income had to be secured in advance, and once ordained the priest enjoyed the

---

18 On the hierarchy of the sacraments, see Saxon, *The Eucharist in Romanesque France*, 45–6.

authority to teach and offer leadership; he answered to ecclesiastical courts and their laws. Be they of dubious character, of little learning, feeble in body or dull in oratory, the ordained were nonetheless effective agents of sacramental action – they made Christ's body at the altar every day of the year and twice on Christmas Day.

Administration of the sacraments was the priestly privilege that represented the church's power to loose and to bind, to manage the treasury of grace, and to offer the unique and sole means for salvation. Since the eleventh century, the church promoted and battled for its freedom – *libertas ecclesiae*.[19] This freedom had to be earned in each polity through struggles with secular rulers, but the struggle was also an internal one: if the church claimed freedoms and privileges, then its members had to undertake the trials of celibacy, and comport themselves in a dignified manner. The exclusive power to mediate grace and to teach the faith was bought at the price of personal sacrifice and endeavour. It was thus important that priests handle themselves well, and appropriately. A twelfth-century bishop of the Norman diocese of Coutances reminded his priests:

> And we advise, that while outside, at home or when visiting your parishioners, you maintain a suitable appearance, be it regarding your tonsure, or your clothes... They should be fastened and should not draw attention for being too long or too short; if that were the case you would resemble archers or prize-fighters.[20]

Like ordination the sacrament of marriage was not taken up by all, but by most people, and it helped order society into Christian units of nurture, work and mutual support. Marriage was a ground for continuous contention between the church and the state; its rules were laid down by both. Inasmuch as marriage was the institution through which property and status were conveyed, it was embedded in regional traditions of great antiquity, ranging from the Roman law which affected marriage customs in southern Europe, to the Germanic codes that informed those of Germany, northern France, England and Scandinavia. By 1100 the church had developed a theology of marriage which defined degrees of consanguinity allowed or prohibited between partners, and which understood marriage as a moral choice, freely taken by individuals.[21] This idea of marriage

---

19 G. Cushing, *Reform and Papacy in the Eleventh Century: Spirituality and Social Change* (Manchester: Manchester University Press, 2005).

20 Edmond Martène, *Thesauram novum anecdotorum* IV (Paris, 1717; repr. Farnborough: Gregg, 1969), c. 18, col. 806.

21 Constance B. Bouchard, 'Consanguinity and Noble Marriages in the Tenth and Eleventh Centuries', *Speculum* 56 (1981), 268–87; Christopher N. L. Brooke, *The Medieval Idea of Marriage* (Oxford: Oxford University Press, 1989), 126–43.

flew in the face of family customs in patriarchal societies in which marriage was an arrangement brokered by heads of families, who determined the future lives of their sons and daughters.

The development of Christian marriage was a lengthy process, all the more complex because of the sometimes conflicting positions which the church maintained towards sexuality.[22] Augustine is again a good example of a seminal thinker who moved from the abhorrence of concupiscence (which he had experienced mightily as a young man) and towards the acceptance of marriage as a framework for the containment of sexual life and the production of Christian progeny.[23] The twelfth century saw intensive discussion and ground-breaking legal formulations particularly on the issue of how marriage was made. If marriage was to be seen as a sacrament, then it had to follow from a moral act, freely made. There was in marriage a mutuality which corresponded to the ideal quality of all souls, the equality of all creatures, so often denied and distorted in practice.

Sacramental marriage gave equal weight to the role of male and female in making the marriage. Twelfth-century theology increasingly insisted that acts were to be judged by the underlying intention that caused them to be; and so an expression of the intention to marry was taken to be binding too.[24] Thus church law recognised marriage contracted by two people even without witnesses, without a public ceremony. At the same time the church also provided a sacramental occasion for the solemnisation of the marriage and encouraged people to use it. Over the centuries, and beyond the Middle Ages, church ceremonies gradually became necessary parts of the age-old traditional celebrations of a marriage within families and communities.[25] As a sacrament, marriage was indissoluble – note the stole with which the priest is shown binding the couple in the Altarpiece. Marriage could be annulled or dissolved, for grounds that rendered the underlying 'freedom' of the marriage choice invalid. Marriage litigation provided much of the business in church courts in the later Middle Ages. Making marriage a sacrament created many complex

---

22 Pierre J. Payer, *The Bridling of Desire: Views of Sex in the Later Middle Ages* (Toronto: University of Toronto Press, 1993).

23 Elizabeth A. Clark, '"Adam's Only Companion": Augustine and the Early Christian Debate on Marriage', in Robert R. Edwards and Stephen Spector, eds., *The Olde Daunce: Love, Friendship, Sex, and Marriage in the Medieval World* (Albany: State University of New York Press, 1991), 15–31; Brooke, *The Medieval Idea*, 54–6. For early medieval discussion, see Reynolds, *Marriage in the Western Church*.

24 Colish, *Peter Lombard*, 473–80.

25 Judith M. Bennett, 'Conviviality and Charity in Medieval and Early Modern England', *Past and Present* 134 (1992), 19–41.

challenges, but it also linked the elementary forms of social life to the liturgical and administrative provision of the church. Marriage, love and sexuality preoccupied all great poets and artists: Dante, Chaucer, Christine de Pizan, and lesser ones too.[26]

The sacraments punctuated the lifecycle and provided the ritual frame for the enactment of rites of passage.[27] The greatest passage of all was, of course, that from this world to the next. The sacrament of extreme unction, the deathbed ritual, aimed to offer a final boost of grace to the Christian about to embark on that most terrifying journey. Death attracted a number of rituals: the bringing of the consecrated Host to the sick- and deathbed became a widespread and regulated ritual in the course of the twelfth century.[28] The Fourth Lateran Council obliged physicians to advise their patients on calling the priest in time for reception of the sacrament.[29] The pastoral provision to the dying was often also linked to the making of a last will.[30] The sacrament of the altar was absorbed into the treatment of the dead: the burial liturgy incorporated a requiem mass; and masses for the benefit of souls in purgatory became the main provision whereby the living could lessen the suffering of dead loved ones, and provide into the future for the alleviation of their own torments.

A vision of a Christian Europe in which lives were guided towards salvation by the clergy within parishes and through the administration of sacraments was becoming a reality in the twelfth and thirteenth centuries. The universal system was finally proclaimed in the Fourth Lateran Council. Faith was grounded and tested in sacramental life, as we have seen above.[31]

---

26 The appearance of these themes in visual imagery merits investigation. See, for example, Jonathan J. G. Alexander, 'Chastity, Love and Marriage in the Margins of the Wharncliffe Hours', in Bernard J. Muir, ed., *Reading Texts and Images: Essays on Medieval and Renaissance Art and Patronage in Honour of Margaret M. Manion* (Exeter: Exeter University Press, 2002), 201–20. See also Christine Peters, 'Gender, Sacrament, and Ritual: The Making and Meaning of Marriage in Late Medieval and Early Modern England', *Past and Present* 169 (2000), 63–96.

27 On rites of passage in the later Middle Ages, see Nicola F. McDonald and W. M. Ormrod, *Rites of Passage: Cultures of Transition in the Fourteenth Century* (Woodbridge: York Medieval Press with Boydell and Brewer, 2004).

28 Rubin, *Corpus Christi*, 77–82.

29 *Decrees of the Ecumenical Councils*, 245–6.

30 Michael M. Sheehan, *The Will in Medieval England from the Conversion of the Anglo-Saxons to the End of the Thirteenth Century* (Toronto: Pontifical Institute of Mediaeval Studies, 1963), chs. IV–VI.

31 Tanner, ed., *Decrees of the Ecumenical Councils* I, 245–*245.

The Council's decrees informed and reinforced the initiatives which bishops were clearly already enforcing within their dioceses.[32] A plethora of statutes emanated all over Europe from diocesan and provincial councils: through them the sacramental system was made real and palpable. The shape of sacramental provision depended not only on theological debate and decrees of councils, but on the continuous dissemination and explication of the ideas and practices involved to the clergy. Several theologians turned their hands to the writing of summaries and handbooks about the sacraments; indeed, a whole genre developed, of *summae de sacramentis*. These were to aid the edification and work of the clergy as they spread knowledge about the sacraments and also performed them. Other tools developed in the thirteenth century for the edification of lay people: handbooks for use in parish teaching.

A long and continuous process of instruction and coexistence between clergy and the religious on the one hand, and the laity on the other, led to the penetration of understanding of the sacraments into the life-worlds of lay people. Alongside the professional handbooks for the use of priests, a world of narratives was also composed and compiled, stories which were aimed at compelling and convincing Christians of the efficacy, necessity and uniqueness of sacraments and their powers. The *exemplum*, a type of short illustrative tale which preachers inserted into their sermons or told as admonitory tales in the course of instruction, often dealt with the sacraments. Certain topics, those probably most puzzling and challenging to believers, seem to have inspired the largest number of *exempla*: transubstantiation, confession and penance, the force of marriage vows, the effect of masses for the dead.

A collection of edifying miracle tales compiled by the Cistercian monk Caesarius of Heisterbach (1170–1240) was much used, copied and translated in the later medieval centuries. Cast as a dialogue between an experienced monk and a novice, the didactic power of the tales is stark. He tells, for example, of a clerk who killed a silversmith and then involved his sister in hiding the crime. Both were caught and condemned to death. On their way to execution, the sister recommended that the clerk confess, but he answered in despair: 'I will not do it; how could so late a confession be of any use to me?' The sister called a priest and confessed with true contrition. When they were tied to a stake, surrounded by piles of fuel,

---

32 For a guide to synodal statutes, see Odette Pontal, *Les statuts synodaux* (Typologie des sources du Moyen Âge occidental 11; Turnhout: Brepols, 1975).

[w]onderful power of confession wonderful mercy of the Saviour! The flames at once devoured the despairing clerk, but the fire neither touched nor injured nor gave any pain to the girl. Only her chains were burnt.

Witnessing the miracle, the judge decided to set her free.[33]

Such stories were compiled and then translated into the vernacular from the thirteenth century on. They were used by friars – Franciscans and Dominicans – in sermons delivered in cities and towns all over Europe. And where there is narrative, visual representations often followed. The Chapel of the Sacrament in Orvieto Cathedral (which houses the cathedral relic) was adorned with miracle tales about the eucharist.[34]

Specialised texts in the vernacular were made first for the more privileged and then for instruction of wider audiences too. Around 1250 Jean de Joinville composed a treatise on the sacraments before he embarked on Louis IX's crusade. The most important events were illustrated: baptism and the eucharist.[35] That multi-tasker, the parish priest, was provided with specialised workbooks aimed at filling in gaps and providing guidelines and answers to the many questions that the sacraments undoubtedly prompted. By the late thirteenth century it was commonly agreed that teaching the sacraments was at the core of instruction to young and old by their parish priests.[36] The curriculum devised by Archbishop Peckham of Canterbury, and disseminated throughout that province in 1281, offered a short summary on the material for instruction: the articles of the faith, the ten commandments, the six works of mercy, seven vices and virtues and the seven sacraments.

> Septem etiam sunt gratie sacramenta, quorum dispensatores sunt prelati ecclesie; quorum quinque ab omnibus debent recipi christianis: utpote baptismus, confirmatio, penitentia, eukaristia suo tempore, et extrema unctio, que tantum illis dari debet qui gravis infirmitatis indiciis videntur mortis appropinquare periculo... Sunt et duo alia sacramenta, ordo et matrimonium.[37]

---

33  Caesarius of Heisterbach, *The Dialogue of Miracles* I, trans. H. von Scott and C. C. Swinton Bland (London: Routledge, 1929), c. 15, 147–8; at 147.

34  Catherine Harding, 'The Miracle of Bolsena and the Relic of the Corporal at Orvieto Cathedral', in H. Weston and D. Davies, eds., *Essays in Honour of John White* (London: University of London Press, 1990), 82–8.

35  *Text and Iconography for Joinville's Credo*, ed. Lionel J. Friedman (Medieval Academy of America Publications 68; Cambridge, Mass.: Medieval Academy of America Publications, 1958), 45.

36  Leonard E. Boyle, 'The Fourth Lateran Council and Manuals of Popular Theology', in Thomas J. Heffernan, ed., *The Popular Literature of Medieval England* (Knoxville: University of Tennessee, 1985), 30–43.

37  F. M. Powicke and C. R. Cheney, eds., *Councils and Synods and other Documents Relating to the English Church II/2* (Oxford: Clarendon Press, 1964), 905.

There are seven sacraments of grace, dispensed by priests of the church; five of them are to be received by all Christians: that is baptism, confirmation, penance, eucharist at the appropriate time, and extreme unction, which is to be given to those who appear to be in danger of approaching death according to signs of grave illness... There are two other sacraments, ordination and marriage.

This system was largely untouched, repeated and reinforced throughout the later medieval centuries, and with some gusto in areas of recent Christianisation, as in some dioceses in Iberia, Pomerania and Lithuania, and by the fifteenth century in north-west Africa too. Since the sacraments were so fundamental to Christian life and belief, on occasion they were re-promulgated on special occasions. At the Second Council of Lyon in 1274 the Byzantine Emperor Michael Palaeologus was converted to the Catholic faith with the following formula:

> The same Holy Roman Church also holds and teaches that there are seven sacraments of the Church: one is baptism, which has been mentioned above; another is the sacrament of confirmation which bishops confer by the laying on of hands while they anoint the reborn; then penance, the Eucharist, the sacrament of order, matrimony and extreme unction which, according to the doctrine of the Blessed James [James 5.14–15], is administered to the sick. The same Roman Church performs the sacrament of the Eucharist with unleavened bread; she holds and teaches that in this sacrament the bread is truly transubstantiated into the body of our Lord Jesus Christ, and the wine into His blood. As regards matrimony, she holds that neither is a man allowed to have several wives at the same time nor a woman several husbands.[38]

The eucharist receives particular elaboration here as this was a ritual understood and performed very differently in the Greek Church. Similarly, in the fifteenth century attempts to unite eastern churches with Rome resulted in other such statements on the sacramental system. In 1439 the Council of Florence published a statement for the benefit of the Armenians on the nature of each sacrament, to facilitate the union which indeed followed.

So far we have traced the development of the sacramental system hand in hand with the implantation throughout the Christian world of a network of parishes and dioceses, which ensured that every Christian belonged to a sacramental unit. Sacraments were understood to be efficacious as and when the priest celebrated them in proper form, but scrutiny of the

---

38 J. Neusner and J. Dupuis, eds., *The Christian Faith in the Doctrinal Documents of the Catholic Church*, rev. edn (New York: Alba House, 1982), no. 28 (p. 19).

beneficiary was also part of the sacramental exchange. We have already noted the coupling of penance and communion. There were other preconditions too. The offering of sacramental comfort to those who made mockery of fundamental beliefs could undermine the balance of faith and trust in the sacraments. For that reason the Fourth Lateran Council required that priests inquire in cases of people suspected of heresy and debar them from participation unless they had made amends.[39] The synod of Liege of 1287 further distanced from the communion – excommunicated – those who breached the social codes of work and cooperation, those who entered into and seized common lands, marsh or forest; they were to be denounced every Sunday and treated as common thieves, since they were thieves of the common good.[40]

A sacramental net of salvation was thus laid upon the Christian continent, and in it was caught every Christian of birth and converts too. Even those who repudiated and rejected it were still caught in its grip. Yet Europeans were often on the move, far removed from their village or town of origin, and their needs challenged the system. Pilgrims received dispensations from parochial participation, soldiers were cared for by their lords' chaplains, royal and aristocratic courts offered private services in sumptuous chapels, and religious houses formed autonomous sacramental units. Merchants *en route* were another vulnerable group. Those who enjoyed a long-standing association with another mercantile community often left in their wills bequests to it too, and instruction on the preferred burial site. Canon law engaged continuously with the many dilemmas raised by parishioners who were in reality often on the move, yet who were still thought of as members of cohesive and intimate parish groups.

Those charged with caring for the sacramental edifice of Christian Europe were constantly alerted to movement and change, to doubt and failure. The sacraments were after all performances, involving thousands of people every single day. There was constant effort to make the sacraments appear as the powerful and reliable saving channels that they were claimed to be. A specialised liturgical literature on the management of the sacraments and other rituals developed hand in hand with the enhancement of sacramental life. More corrective than analytical is the theologian Henry of Langenstein's (c. 1325–97) short practical treatise on celebration of the mass, *Secreta*

---

39 Tanner, ed., *Decrees of the Ecumenical Councils* I, 233–*234.
40 E. Schoolmeesters, ed., *Les statuts synodaux de Jean de Flandre, évèque de Liège* (Liège: Cormaux, 1908).

*sacerdotum que in Missa teneri debent multum utilia.*[41] Flamboyant movements at the altar could cause embarrassing accidents:

> And those things whose effect is evidently good, are not always safe, because at the extension of the arms, the hanging of the alb-sleeve might easily cause the chalice to be overturned.

Visual evidence shows that several practical adjustments were made to the world of sacramental action. The altar was cordoned off to keep parishioners away from the place where the greatest mystery took place. Fonts acquired covers to keep them clean; curtains were erected around the altar lest a draught blow out the candles and torches lit at the moment of the elevation; sweet-smelling herbs were strewn or hung in bunches to ward noxious smells that could be distracting and displeasing. The sacraments appealed to the senses, and were enhanced by them too.[42]

Rogier van der Weyden's altarpiece thus presents a highly evolved, ubiquitous system, one which aimed to reach every Christian. This system was subject to myriad variation dependent on weather and region, taste and enthusiasm, wealth and size of communities. Yet, however varied, the claims resounded similarly throughout Europe: no salvation without the sacraments, no access to grace without the clergy, no amount of virtue or self-help would suffice. There was a great deal of enterprise in seeking religious experiences outside the parish, supplements and adornments to a routine. The arrival of the friars in early thirteenth-century cities marked real competition between the new professional preachers, bound to no parish, nor weighed down by parish duties, and parish priests. People sought to make confession after an engaging sermon, or to be buried in a friary church, all to the detriment of the parish. Canon law protected the parish, but there was significant diversion of resources – benefactions, testamentary bequests – from the parish of sacramental belonging, to the new and exciting houses of friars. A whole network of confraternities was in place by 1350 which offered membership in religious clubs devoted to a particular saint, or associated with a specific craft, or oriented towards a particular devotion (flagellation, the Passion, Corpus Christi).[43] New devotions attracted people into further activities outside the parish: the Rosary fraternities which swept through Europe from 1476

---

41 Augsburg, 1503.
42 In thinking about the senses and liturgical action, I have benefited greatly from reading the unpublished doctoral thesis of Matthew Milner, 'A Sensible Reformation: the Senses and Liturgical Life in Tudor England', University of Warwick, September 2006.
43 Rubin, *Corpus Christi*, 232–43.

onwards were guided and promoted by friars, towards a practice which could be undertaken at home, at work, on the road.[44]

Beyond these enthusiasms of ordinary people there were the attachments of the specialists in religious devotion, among them many women all over Europe, who lived in or in attachment to nunneries. They often rebelled against the deficiency imputed to them by a system handled by men alone. Julianna of Cornillon (1193–1258) was frustrated by the limited access to the sacraments allowed by her confessor. She thus developed practices of savouring meditation during and following each communion:

> After receiving the Body of Christ our virgin liked to remain silent for at least a week. During this period she was upset at the approach of anyone whatsoever... She felt certain there was such strength in the eating of that sacred bread that she did not doubt she could survive for so long, even physically, on the strength of such food... Whenever she received the Body of Christ (and she craved to do so often because of her boundless love), he revealed to her some new secret from his heavenly mysteries.[45]

The northern French beguine Marguerite Porète (d. 1310) developed a contemplative life and theological understanding which dispensed with virtues and other attachments to the practices of Christian life. She expressed her experiences in an allegorical poem composed in the French dialect of Picardie in *The Mirror of Simple Souls* (*Le mirouer des âmes simples*):

> Virtues, I take my leave of you     for evermore
> And so my heart will have more joy   and be more free;
> Your service is a lifelong yoke     as well you see.[46]

Margery Kempe, a laywoman from King's Lynn in Norfolk (1373–1438) left her marital home (in which she had borne fourteen children) because she was no longer fulfilled or consoled by her parish church. She put aside the routines of sacraments and lifecycle and reinvented herself as a pilgrim and as an author. She travelled widely, often a woman alone, and fell foul of preachers and priests. The settled sacramental system held few attractions for her, though

---

44 Anne Winston-Allen, *Stories of the Rose: The Making of the Rosary in the Middle Ages* (University Park: Pennsylvania State University Press, 1997).

45 Barbara Newman, trans., *The Life of Juliana of Mont-Cornillon* (Peregrina Translation Series 13; Toronto: Peregrina, 1988), c.12, 40.

46 Marguerite Porète, *The Mirror of Simple Souls*, trans. Edmund Colledge, J. C. Marler and Judith Grant (Notre Dame Texts in Medieval Culture 6; Notre Dame: University of Notre Dame Press, 1996), 17. See the original in Marguerite Porète, *Le mirouer des âmes simples*, ed. Romana Guarnieri (CCCM 69; Turnhout: Brepols, 1986), 24.

she participated enthusiastically in processions and masses at shrines and pilgrimage centres.

And there were those who found the sacraments to be lacking in justice. The rich seemed to benefit from them more than the poor. The Master General of the Dominicans, Humbert of Romans (d. 1277) was not a disinterested onlooker. In his 'De modo prompte cudendi sermones' (How to sew a sermon quickly) he guided the preacher towards the problems of the poor, to tailor their teachings to the life experiences of the least privileged.[47]

Just a few years later the Statutes of the Synod of Bayeux of 1300 considered it useful to affirm that extreme unction was not reserved for rich people only, who may consider receiving it as frequently as they fell ill, and then return to a normal life.[48] Those who came to be called Lollards in England voiced similar views when interrogated by their bishops: they denied transubstantiation and the pains of purgatory, they rejected the notion that Christians needed sacraments delivered by priests. Margery Baxter was reported in 1429 to have said to her neighbour Joanna Clyfland that

> nullus puer sive infans natus habens parentes Christianos debet baptizari in aqua secundum usum communem quia talis infans sufficienter baptizatur in utero matris.[49]

> No child or infant born to Christian parents need be baptized in water according to common usage, because such an infant is sufficiently baptized in its mother's womb.

She further added that the dipping in fonts, within churches, is simply an idolatrous act devised by priests in order to extort money from people for the maintenance of their own incontinent lifestyles. John Eldon, a glover from Beccles, was similarly interrogated for having expressed the view that no priest had the power to bind or loosen the sins of men and women, and so people were not bound to do penance.[50]

The sacramental system was the basic provision of a vast and ambitious project for the incorporation of a whole continent with all its variety into a single vision of the sacred. It aimed to make routine and accessible the

---

47 Alexander Murray, 'Religion among the Poor in Thirteenth-Century France: the Testimony of Humbert of Romans', *Traditio* 30 (1974), 285–324.
48 Johannes Dominicus Mansi, ed., *Sacrorum conciliorum nova, et amplissima collectio* (Venice: A. Zatta, 1782), ch. lxxiv, col. 73.
49 Norman P. Tanner, ed., *Heresy Trials in the Diocese of Norwich 1428–31* (Camden Society fourth series 20; London: Royal Historical Society, 1977), 46.
50 *Ibid.*, 135.

charisma of grace, the enthusiasm of faith and the desire for transcendence. In the trenchant rethinking of the terms of the enchanted sacramental world, Martin Luther preserved only two sacraments: baptism and the sacrament of the altar.[51] By unmaking the sacraments, Protestants were not only refiguring the rituals of a church, but remaking the rhythms of life, the rituals by which lives and communities had lived for some 300 years.

---

51 Lee Palmer Wandel, *The Eucharist in the Reformation: Incarnation and Liturgy* (Cambridge: Cambridge University Press, 2006), 94–114.

# 16

# Religious soundscapes: liturgy and music

## SUSAN BOYNTON

Music played a crucial role in the world of medieval Christianity. The performance and composition of music not only reflected surrounding historical and theological contexts, but also actively determined liturgical and devotional experience. In the High and Late Middle Ages, musicians continued to cultivate the traditional genres of chant and also created new kinds of music for performance both inside and outside the liturgy. The present chapter aims to show the place of these musical trends in religious culture.[1]

In the period 1100–1500, sacred music took on an ever-expanding range of functions and contexts, including not only the worship of the regular clergy, and those services and processions that were attended by parishioners, but also votive performances specially commissioned by lay and clerical patrons, and communal singing by associations of laypeople. Guilds and other associations were increasingly involved in the patronage and performance of religious music, and the mendicant orders' emphasis on spiritual instruction fostered confraternities of laypeople who sang vernacular songs.[2] The performance of the liturgy remained the cornerstone of the corporate identity of those in religious orders. Not all were equally committed to the priesthood, however; the thirteenth to fifteenth centuries saw the development of institutions for training professional ecclesiastical singers, and many musicians

---

1 For music-historical overviews of the period, see Richard Crocker and David Hiley, eds., *The Early Middle Ages to 1300* (New Oxford History of Music 2; Oxford: Oxford University Press, 1990); Reinhard Strohm and Bonnie Blackburn, eds., *Music as Concept and Practice in the Late Middle Ages* (New Oxford History of Music 3.1; New York: Oxford University Press, 2001); Reinhard Strohm, *The Rise of European Music, 1380–1500* (Cambridge: Cambridge University Press, 1993).

2 On the *lauda* confraternities in ritual and social contexts, see particularly Blake Wilson, *Music and Merchants: The Laudesi Companies of Republican Florence* (Oxford: Oxford University Press, 1992); on a confraternity of the rosary that commissioned liturgical chant manuscripts at the end of the fifteenth century, see Lorenzo Candelaria, 'El Cavaller de Colunya: A Miracle of the Rosary in the Choirbooks of San Pedro Mártir de Toledo', *Viator* (2004), 221–64.

associated with collegiate and cathedral churches remained in minor orders. For the regular clergy, singing the liturgy occupied most of the day and was the essence of life in community, as demonstrated colourfully by monastic writers such as Hildegard of Bingen and Caesarius of Heisterbach.[3]

In the later Middle Ages music played an increasingly important role in devotional and commemorative rituals outside the liturgy of the mass and office as well. These ceremonies were usually associated with particular spaces in the church, such as chantry chapels, lady chapels and side altars. Commemoration of the dead expanded beyond the longstanding traditions of the office of the dead and votive masses for the dead to encompass specially endowed commemorative services designated by donors. Not all such memorials were sung, but the proliferation of those with music attests to a veritable explosion of sacred vocal polyphony in the fourteenth and fifteenth centuries.[4] The first group of polyphonic mass ordinary movements known to be the work of a single composer, the *Messe de Notre Dame* of Guillaume de Machaut (1300–77), is a votive mass for the Virgin Mary that may have been intended for annual performance in his own memory in the cathedral of Reims, where he was a canon.[5] Machaut's mass embodies the intersection of two major forces in the composition of sacred music in the period 1100–1500: belief in the efficaciousness of prayers sung on behalf of the departed, and devotion to the Virgin as a saint uniquely able to intervene on behalf of those who sought her aid. Patrons believed in the power of prayer to diminish the time a soul spent in purgatory, elevating musical prayer to a central place in the culture of intercession.

Music had always been integral to Christian thought, and it acquired continuously enriched theological meaning throughout the High and Late Middle Ages. In the Latin liturgy, the interplay of words and music both new and old, and the interweaving of scriptural with nonscriptural texts, created a

3 On the function of Hildegard of Bingen's musical works in her community, see Margot Fassler, 'Composer and Dramatist', in Barbara Newman, ed., *Voice of the Living Light: Hildegard of Bingen and her World* (Berkeley and Los Angeles: University of California Press, 1998), 149–75; for Caesarius of Heisterbach on liturgical performance, see Susan Boynton, 'Work and Play in Sacred Music and its Social Context, ca. 1050–1250', in R. N. Swanson, ed., *The Use and Abuse of Time in Christian History* (Studies in Church History 37; Woodbridge: Boydell, 2002), 57–79.

4 Barbara Haggh, 'Foundations or Institutions? On Bringing the Middle Ages into the History of Medieval Music', *Acta musicologica* 68 (1996), 87–128.

5 Anne Walters Robertson, 'The Mass of Guillaume de Machaut in the Cathedral of Reims', in Thomas Forest Kelly, ed., *Plainsong in the Age of Polyphony* (Cambridge: Cambridge University Press, 1992), 100–39; see also Robertson, *Guillaume de Machaut and Reims: Context and Meaning in his Musical Works* (Cambridge: Cambridge University Press, 2002), 257–75, 398–406.

mode of performative exegesis in which multilevelled readings of the Bible were articulated in real time and repeated over the course of a single service, day, season and the church year as a whole.[6] Typological, allegorical and eschatological meanings were literally performed through the juxtaposition, entwining and expansion of scriptural texts. Christian typological interpretations of the book of Psalms as prophetic texts, articulated by commentators throughout the history of exegesis, were enacted daily through the chanting of psalms that had pervaded Christian liturgical practice since late antiquity. The musical performance of psalms encompassed a continuum of styles from the psalmody of the divine office (as well as some chants of the mass) in which successive psalm verses were chanted to the same simple, repetitive melody, to settings of single psalm verses or groups of verses (sometimes in combination with other texts) in chants of widely varying length and complexity.

Members of the clergy were required to memorise the psalms for choral performance during the divine office, and thus these texts were thoroughly imprinted in their minds through the repeated act of singing, as well as through frequent reading and reflection. Musical performance endowed the psalms and other scriptural texts with layers of meaning that adhered to their specific liturgical functions, associations that were stored in worshippers' memories and shaped the commentary tradition.

In keeping with this hermeneutic tendency of the liturgy, many new compositions were poems that applied the techniques of scriptural commentary, explicating the meaning of the feast on which they were performed. Sequences – poems in double versicles sung at mass after the alleluia – originated in the ninth century as prose-like compositions, but underwent considerable development in the twelfth and thirteenth centuries. In Germanic regions, new sequences continued to accumulate around a late-Carolingian core repertory, but elsewhere in western Europe, from the twelfth century on, the predominant type of sequence was characterised by short, memorable musical phrases and rhyming texts with infectious rhythms.

---

6 On the notion of performative exegesis, see Susan Boynton, 'Performative Exegesis in the Fleury *Interfectio Puerorum*', *Viator* 29 (1998), 39–64; for hermeneutic uses of biblical texts in the medieval liturgy, see William Flynn, *Medieval Music as Medieval Exegesis* (Lanham, Md. and London: Scarecrow Press, 1999); Susan Boynton, 'The Bible and the Liturgy', in Susan Boynton and Diane Reilly, eds., *The Practice of the Bible in the Western Middle Ages* (New York: Columbia University Press, forthcoming). A useful general introduction to the medieval Latin liturgy can be found in John Harper, *The Forms and Orders of Western Liturgy from the Tenth to the Eighteenth Century: A Historical Introduction and Guide for Students and Musicians* (Oxford: Oxford University Press, 1991), 11–152; for more detail on the musical aspects of the liturgy, see David Hiley, *Western Plainchant: A Handbook* (Oxford: Oxford University Press, 1993).

Religious writers such as Adam of St Victor, Peter Abelard and Hildegard of Bingen created new sequences in this style that reflect the theological discourse of the day, their texts dense with biblical imagery and layers of typology.[7]

Even more exegetical by their very nature were tropes, in which new text and music are added to a pre-existing chant, producing a form of liturgical commentary structurally integrated into the structure of the chant itself. Tropes represent a fascinating dialogue between poet-composers and their musico-liturgical environments, as well as between the scriptural texts of the base chants and their medieval exegetical traditions.[8] Some tropes were even cast in dialogue form, as in the semi-dramatic 'Quem queritis' dialogues performed on Easter morning.[9] By about 1300, most tropes had become rather less common in western Europe, although they continued to flourish in German-speaking areas.[10] Several religious orders excluded tropes from their services, and in many places sequences seem to have replaced the trope as the favoured genre for new composition. Orders such as the Augustinian regular canons and the Dominicans developed their own sequence repertories to project their collective identity as religious communities.[11] Other orders, such as the Cistercians in the twelfth century, revised the melodies of their chants to produce new versions they perceived as more authentic.[12]

7 Chrysogonus Waddell, 'Epithalamica: An Easter Sequence by Peter Abelard', *The Musical Quarterly* 72 (1986), 239–71; Hildegard of Bingen, *Symphonia: A Critical Edition of the Symphonia Armonie Celestium Revelationum*, ed. and trans. Barbara Newman (Ithaca, N.Y.: Cornell University Press, 1988); Margot Fassler, *Gothic Song: Victorine Sequences and Augustinian Reform in Twelfth-Century Paris* (Cambridge: Cambridge University Press, 1993).

8 See Margot Fassler, 'The Meaning of Entrance: Liturgical Commentaries and the Introit Tropes', in Paul Brainard, ed., *Reflections on the Sacred: A Musicological Perspective* (New Haven, Conn.: Yale Institute of Sacred Music, Worship, and the Arts, 1994), 8–17; Fassler, *Gothic Song*, 18–37.

9 For a recent overview of scholarship on Easter drama with bibliography, see Nils Holger Petersen, 'Liturgical Drama: New Approaches', in Jacqueline Hamesse, ed., *Bilan et perspectives des études médiévales (1993–1998)* (Turnhout: Brepols, 2004), 633–44.

10 On late trope repertories, see Andreas Haug, *Troparia tardiva: Repertorium später Tropenquellen aus dem deutschsprachigen Raum* (Kassel and New York: Bärenreiter, 1995); Lori Kruckenberg, 'Some Observations on a *troparium tardivum*: the Proper Tropes in Utrecht, Universiteitsbibliotheek, 417', *Tijdschrift v.d. Kon. Vereniging voor Nederlandse Muziekgeschiedenis* 53 (2003), 151–82.

11 See Fassler, *Gothic Song*, and Fassler, 'Music and the Miraculous: Mary in the Mid-Thirteenth-Century Dominican Sequence Repertory', in Leonard Boyle and Pierre-Marie Gy, eds., *Aux origines de la liturgie dominicaine: Le manuscrit Santa Sabina XIV L1* (Rome: École française de Rome; Paris: CNRS Editions, 2004), 229–78.

12 On the Cistercian chant reforms, see the many studies of Chrysogonus Waddell, 'The Origin and Early Evolution of the Cistercian Antiphonary: Reflections on Two Cistercian Chant Reforms', in Basil Pennington, ed., *The Cistercian Spirit: A Symposium*

The revision and composition of liturgical music continued unabated throughout the period 1100–1500, creating a vast legacy of late-medieval chant that remains largely unexplored by scholars. Much of this activity provided new compositions for the mass and office on new feasts of the church year such as Corpus Christi, and for commemorations of saints or other feast days that had accrued in solemnity. New texts could be fitted to pre-existing melodies, resulting in a type of composition that musicologists term a contrafact (or *contrafactum*). Through textual and musical echoes of the original chant, a contrafact could establish layers of signification beyond the surface meaning of the text performed.[13] For some purposes, however, entirely new sets of chants were created. In particular, versified offices for saints increased, beginning in the eleventh century and became extremely ubiquitous in the thirteenth.[14] In the thirteenth century, the offices of widely venerated saints such as Thomas of Canterbury, Dominic and Francis furnished textual and musical models for other saints' offices. Recently canonised lay saints, particularly royal saints such as Elisabeth of Hungary, Charlemagne and Louis IX of France, were also commemorated with proper offices, often existing in various versions because of the adaptations that were carried out for different institutional settings.[15] Some of these compositions illustrate important historical developments that shaped the medieval world. For instance, the creation and spread of the liturgical office of the martyred Norwegian king Olav Haraldson reflects the Christianisation of Norway through the royal family.[16] Similarly, the acquisition of a relic of the Crown of Thorns for the Sainte-Chapelle in Paris led to the creation of a new office

in *Memory of Thomas Merton* (Washington, D.C.: Cistercian Publications, Consortium Press, 1970), 190–223; see also Waddell, ed., *The Twelfth-Century Cistercian Hymnal* (Cistercian Liturgy Series 1–2; Trappist, Ky.: Gethsemani Abbey, 1984).

13  For an example of particular meaning created by a contrafact of a sequence, see Michael McGrade, 'O rex mundi triumphator: Hohenstaufen Politics in a Sequence for Saint Charlemagne', *Early Music History* 17 (1998), 183–219.

14  For a recent overview, see Andrew Hughes, 'Late Medieval Plainchant for the Divine Office', in Strohm and Blackburn, eds., *Music as Concept and Practice*, 47–96. On Becket offices, see Kay Brainerd Slocum, *Liturgies in Honour of Thomas Becket* (Toronto: University of Toronto Press, 2003).

15  See Barbara Haggh, ed., *Two Offices for St Elizabeth of Hungary: Introduction and Edition* (Musicological Studies 65.1; Ottawa: Institute of Mediaeval Music, 1995); on the Charlemagne office, see Eric Rice, 'Music and Ritual in the Collegiate Church of St Mary in Aachen, 1300–1600' (unpublished PhD thesis, Columbia University, 2002), 85–95; for the most recent discussion of the rhymed offices of Saint Louis, see Cecilia Gaposchkin, 'Philip the Fair, the Dominicans, and the Liturgical Office for Louis IX: New Perspectives on *Ludovicus decus regnantium*', *Plainsong and Medieval Music* 13 (2004), 33–61.

16  For a comprehensive study and edition of this office, see Eyolf Østrem, *The Office of Saint Olav: A Study in Chant Transmission* (Acta universitatis upsaliensis, Studia musicologica upsaliensia, nova series 18; Uppsala: Elanders Gotab, 2001).

that became something of a liturgical status symbol abroad.[17] Unlike the early chant repertory, these new offices were not always anonymous; the identity of composers as individuals, and their status as artists, was becoming increasingly prominent.[18] The vast corpus of late-medieval offices constitutes a form of sonic hagiography comparable to contemporaneous textual hagiography; it has its own conventions and reflects the religious, socioeconomic, and political vicissitudes of the period.

In addition to sets of chants for the liturgies of individual feast days, some entire chant repertories arose to fit the needs of particular communities. In the twelfth century, Peter Abelard compiled a collection of hymns, including many of his own compositions, for Heloise's abbey of the Paraclete.[19] The nuns of the Brigittine (or Bridgettine) order, founded in the mid-fourteenth century by Bridget of Sweden, had a distinctive chant repertory known as the *cantus sororum* that was composed of both newly composed and traditional elements. The Brigittine chant repertory, which travelled from the Swedish mother house in Vadstena to places as far afield as Henry V's foundation at Syon Abbey, reflects this contemplative order's emphasis on simplicity and austerity both in the style of individual chants and in the extensive repetition of material over the course of the weekly liturgical cycle.[20] While the Paraclete and the Brigittines were monastic communities, religious musical repertories, such as the Italian *laude*, were also developed for lay participation in services. The Hussite movement in Bohemia produced Czech translations of the liturgy, as well as some entirely new chants in the vernacular, which appear for the first time in a manuscript from the late 1420s or early 1430s along

17 Judith Blezzard, Stephen Ryle and Jonathan Alexander, 'New Perspectives on the Feast of the Crown of Thorns', *Journal of the Plainsong and Mediaeval Music Society* 10 (1987), 23–47.

18 Rob C. Wegman, 'From Maker to Composer: Improvisation and Musical Authorship in the Low Countries, 1450–1500', *Journal of the American Musicological Society* 49 (1996), 409–79.

19 For an edition of melodies and text with commentary, see Chrysogonus Waddell, ed., *Hymn Collections from the Paraclete* (Cistercian Liturgy Series 8–9; Trappist, Ky.: Gethsemani Abbey, 1987–9). See also David Wulstan, '*Novi modulaminis melos*: The Music of Heloise and Abelard', *Plainsong and Medieval Music* 11 (2002), 1–23; and Marc Stewart and David Wulstan, eds., *The Poetic and Musical Legacy of Heloise and Abelard* (Ottawa: Institute of Mediaeval Music; Westhumble: The Plainsong and Mediaeval Music Society, 2003).

20 On the Brigittine chant, see Viveca Servatius, *Cantus sororum: Musik- und liturgiege-schichtliche Studien zu den Antiphonen des birgittinischen Eigenrepertoires nebst 91 Transkriptionen* (Acta universitatis upsaliensis, Studia musicologica upsaliensia nova series 12; Uppsala: Almqvist & Wiksell, 1990). On liturgy and chant at Syon Abbey, see most recently Anne Bagnall Yardley, *Performing Piety: Musical Culture in Medieval English Nunneries* (New York: Palgrave MacMillan, 2006), 203–27.

with nonliturgical Czech religious songs.[21] Music with both Latin and Dutch texts emanated from the *devotio moderna* movement of the fifteenth century.[22] One of the most significant developments in the period 1100–1500 was the increasing prominence of written polyphony, which developed ever more complex and varied forms and functions, even as simpler oral practices of polyphony continued to flourish.[23] Some of the earliest known written examples of polyphony are settings in eleventh-century manuscripts of the soloists' portions of chants for the mass or office on certain feasts of the church year (particularly the alleluia and gradual of the mass and the responsory of Vespers), and organa based on the proper chants of the mass formed the core of the polyphonic repertory associated with the cathedral of Notre Dame at Paris in the late twelfth and thirteenth century.[24] By the end of the fifteenth century it was polyphonic settings of the ordinary of the mass (Kyrie, Gloria, Credo, Sanctus and Agnus Dei) that had come to predominate. In the second half of the century many masses drew upon the music of secular French songs rather than being based upon traditional chant melodies. One such tune used in dozens of masses from the mid-fifteenth century to the end of the seventeenth is 'L'homme armé' ('the armed man'), which may be linked to a ritual of the 'armed man' commemorating Longinus, or to a theological understanding of the 'armed man' as Christ.[25] Reminiscences of well-known chansons in the mass thus introduced a new set of textual and musical associations into the liturgy. Moreover, the custom of borrowing secular music engendered yet another layer of musical intertextuality: chanson masses were often related to previous masses based on the same song.

The very existence of genres such as the chanson mass confirms that boundaries between secular and sacred music culture were porous when

21 For an edition of part of one manuscript with introduction and commentary in Czech and English, see Jaroslav Kolár, Anezka Vidmanová and Hana Vlhová-Wörner, eds., *Jistebnický kancional, MS Praha, Knihovna Národniho muzea, II C 7, Kritická edice / Jistebnice Kancionál, MS Prague, National Museum Library II C 7, critical edition, vol. 1: Graduale* (Monumenta liturgica bohemica 2; Brno: Marek, 2005).
22 On one manuscript containing such music, see Ulrike Hascher-Burger, *Gesungene Innigkeit: Studien zu einer Musikhandschrift der Devotio Moderna (Utrecht, Universiteitsbibliotheek, ms. 16 H 34, olim B 113), Mit einer Edition der Gesänge* (Studies in the History of Christian Thought 106; Leiden: Brill, 2002).
23 On simple polyphony, see Cesare Corsi and Pierluigi Petrobelli, eds., *Le polifonie primitive in Friuli e in Europa: Atti del congresso internazionale, Cividale del Friuli, 22–24 agosto 1980* (Rome: Torre d'Orfeo, 1989).
24 On this repertory, see the introduction to Edward Roesner, ed., *Le magnus liber organi de Notre-Dame de Paris*, vol. 1, *Les quadrupla et tripla de Paris* (Monaco: L'Oiseau-Lyre, 1993).
25 On the interpretations of the 'L'homme armé' masses, see Craig Wright, *The Maze and the Warrior: Symbols in Architecture, Theology, and Music* (Cambridge, Mass.: Harvard University Press, 2001), 159–205, 282–8, 325–32.

they existed at all, and certainly not all music we would consider religious was intended for performance in the liturgy. Many sung Latin rhythmic poems from the eleventh, twelfth and thirteenth centuries reflect doctrinal concerns of the time such as Marian and incarnational theology; the musical settings aptly convey the ideas in the texts.[26] Some Latin songs have secular texts that offer a glimpse of contemporary religious polemics and can be tied to university milieux.[27] Similarly, medieval song in the vernacular languages offers insight into the religious experience of the laity. Some of this music had specific ritual functions, such as the *laude* performed by Italian lay confraternities.[28] Even music apparently intended for entertainment, such as the songs of the troubadours and trouvères, attest to their creators' ideas about religion and sometimes to their assimilation of ecclesiastical influences. A vast collection of music that seems to combine the functions of lay performance, devotion and entertainment is the vernacular *summa* of Marian miracles, the 'Cantigas de Santa Maria', a thirteenth-century collection of Galician-Portuguese religious songs attributed to King Alfonso X of Castile and Leon.[29]

One of the best examples of cross-fertilisation of liturgical and courtly genres was the motet, a type of composition for multiple voices that emerged in northern France in the thirteenth century and spread throughout Western Europe by the fourteenth.[30] Early motets were fertile sites for the interaction of old and new, for most had tenor voices based on melodies from liturgical chants, but the texts of the other voices were newly composed poems, often in French. In some motets, the assignment of different texts to different voice parts created intertextual references that extended beyond the work itself to other compositions; many thirteenth-century motets in the vernacular shared brief passages of text known as *refrains*, these and other relationships

26 James Grier, 'A New Voice in the Monastery: Tropes and *versus* from Eleventh- and Twelfth-Century Aquitaine', *Speculum* 69 (1994), 1023–69; Rachel Golden Carlson, 'Striking Ornaments: Complexities of Sense and Song in Aquitanian *versus*', *Music & Letters* 84 (2003), 527–56.

27 For a recent study of a 'political' conductus and bibliography on the genre as a whole, see Thomas Payne, '*Aurelianis civitas*: Student Unrest in Medieval France and a Conductus by Philip the Chancellor', *Speculum* 73 (2000), 589–614.

28 On the *lauda* in its ritual and social contexts, see particularly Wilson, *Music and Merchants*.

29 On the music of the 'Cantigas', see Stephen Parkinson, ed., *Cobras e son: Papers on the Text, Music and Manuscripts of the 'Cantigas de Santa Maria'* (Oxford: European Humanities Research Centre, 2000).

30 On the early motet, see Mark Everist, *French Motets in the Thirteenth Century: Music, Poetry and Genre* (Cambridge: Cambridge University Press, 1994); Sylvia Huot, *Allegorical Play in the Old French Motet: The Sacred and the Profane in Thirteenth-Century Polyphony* (Stanford: Stanford University Press, 1997).

engendering a complex web of intertextuality.[31] The origins of the motet are a matter of debate, but right from the start they appear in manuscripts alongside other new types of vocal music both sacred and secular, attesting to the vogue for the genre. In the thirteenth century, motets with French vernacular texts exhibit affinity with trouvère song, but while their French poetic texts represent the courtly-love tradition, they are linked to the chants of the liturgy through their tenor melodies, which are often derived from pre-existing chants. A good example is 'Plus bele que flors/flos filius eius' from the late-thirteenth-century Montpellier Codex (Example 1 at the end of this chapter).[32] In this composition a musical phrase from the source chant, the early eleventh-century Marian responsory 'Stirps Jesse' attributed to Bishop Fulbert of Chartres, forms the basis of the tenor voice but is completely integrated into a polyphonic complex with three other voices, each sung to a different French text. The text of the tenor voice, 'flos filius eius', metonymically evokes the complete responsory text, a Christological reading of Isa. 11.1–12: 'The stock of Jesse produced a rod, and the rod a flower, and on this flower rests the nourishing spirit. The rod is the virgin mother of God, and the flower is her son. And on this flower rests the nourishing spirit.'[33]

In the rich texture characteristic of such pieces, the identity of the individual texts is essentially lost. Yet even though the simultaneous performance of multiple texts prevents each individual text from being continuously audible, distinct vowel sounds and rhythmic patterns project from the mass of sound, and singers and readers of the motet can perceive both the individual texts and their interrelations with one another. The word *flor* appears in all three of the French texts, for example, and links them to the word *flos* in the tenor, signifying Christ. And while generically diverse on their surface, these texts are subtly interrelated. The highest voice (the quadruplum) expresses devotion to the Virgin in the vein of courtly love service that appears also in the text of the triplum voice, which sings of love and the advent of spring. Only

31 See Ardis Butterfield, *Poetry and Music in Medieval France from Jean Renart to Guillaume de Machaut* (Cambridge: Cambridge University Press, 2002), 75–102.

32 Hans Tischler, ed., *The Montpellier Codex*, vol. 1 (Madison, Wis.: A-R Editions, 1978), 39–40. Two widely available recordings that include this motet are Anonymous IV, *Love's Illusion* (Harmonia Mundi, 1994) and Gothic Voices, *The Marriage of Heaven and Hell* (Hyperion, 1990).

33 'Stirps Iesse virgam produxit, virgaque florem, et super hunc florem requiescit Spiritus almus. V. Virga dei genitrix virgo est, flos filius eius. Et super hunc florem requiescit Spiritus almus.'

On this responsory and its theological context, see Margot Fassler, 'Mary's Nativity, Fulbert of Chartres, and the *Stirps Jesse*: Liturgical Innovation circa 1000 and its Afterlife', *Speculum* 75 (2000), 389–434.

halfway through the text does the speaker reveal that the object of his love is the Virgin Mary. The motetus voice also sings of love, but within a narrative framework that begins as a *pastourelle* complete with spring exordium and erotic connotations as the narrator encounters not a shepherdess, but a well-dressed lady who speaks of love's anguish and announces her intention to persist nevertheless. The final two lines of her reported speech take up a well-known refrain found in numerous thirteenth-century French songs. Sylvia Huot has observed that the triplum, musically situated in the thick of the polyphonic complex, mediates textually between devotion to the Virgin in the quadruplum text and the implicitly suggestive encounter with the woman in the garden in the motetus text, echoing the language of the Song of Songs that permeates Marian liturgical texts.[34] Thus a broad network of intertextual references emerges from the combination of texts in the motet, as well as from other external resonances that nevertheless contribute to its effect. In performance, the voices are blended into a smooth aural fabric; from the confluence of diverse genres and images arises a love song both courtly and devotional, as in many other vernacular religious songs of the thirteenth century.[35]

A comparable symbiosis of sacred and profane can be seen in works such as the Beauvais 'Play of Daniel', a music drama of the late twelfth century that offers a panoply of musical and poetic styles, dialogue in Latin and in the vernacular, and vivid characterisations. Margot Fassler has argued that this play reflects the culture of cathedral clergy in northern France, and in particular, the world of the subdeacons also glimpsed in the Beauvais festive office of the Circumcision, which seems to be linked to the Feast of Fools.[36] Some Passion plays of the thirteenth century incorporate vernacular songs that offer early examples of Marian lament.[37]

A particularly vivid example of interaction between sacred, secular, Latin and vernacular is the early-fourteenth-century manuscript of the *Roman de Fauvel* with musical interpolations. This unique, richly illustrated compilation combines and juxtaposes liturgical chant, French songs and polyphony

---

34 Huot, *Allegorical Play in the Old French Motet*, 90–4.
35 See Marcia Epstein, *Prions en chantant: Devotional Songs of the Trouvères* (Toronto: University of Toronto Press, 1997).
36 Margot Fassler, 'The Feast of Fools and *Danielis ludus*: Popular Tradition in a Medieval Cathedral Play', in Kelly, ed., *Plainsong*, 65–99.
37 Susan Boynton, 'From the Lament of Rachel to the Lament of Mary: A Transformation in the History of Drama and Spirituality', in Nicholas Bell, Claus Clüver and Nils Holger Petersen, eds., *Signs of Change: Transformations of Christian Traditions and their Representation in the Arts, 1000–2000* (Amsterdam: Rodopi, 2004), 319–40.

between sections of narrative featuring thinly disguised caricatures of contemporary potentates at the French court.[38] Later in the fourteenth century, the works of Machaut exemplify the fusion of sacred and secular music, in his motets particularly through the combination of tenors based on chants from the liturgy with voice parts in the style of secular French song and Latin poetry. Anne Walters Robertson has recently argued that Machaut's early motets form a coherent cycle reflecting the influence of late-medieval theology, particularly mystical writings such as Heinrich Suso's *Horologium sapientiae*.[39] Individually and as a group, Machaut's motets represent a performative working-out of complex theological, musical and poetic ideas.

One of Machaut's Latin motets, 'Felix virgo / Inviolata genitrix / Ad te suspiramus', demonstrates the intermingling of text and music that was richly productive of meaning in the late-medieval motet (Example 2).[40] The tenor voice is taken from 'Salve regina', one of the four Marian antiphons sung during the daily and weekly commemorations of the Virgin Mary beginning in the twelfth century. Unlike antiphons that were sung with psalms or canticles (such as the 'Magnificat' at Vespers and the 'Nunc Dimittis' at Compline), a Marian antiphon was sung by itself, after a procession to an image of the Virgin following certain services, particularly the hour of Compline at the end of the liturgical day. This ritual of evening devotion to the Virgin became so ubiquitous among the secular, regular and mendicant clergy, as well as the religious confraternities and guilds, that it formed a soundscape common to religious communities throughout western Europe. The Compline procession and other rituals linked to the Virgin's intercessory function gave rise to innumerable polyphonic compositions, many composed on the basis of Marian antiphons. Unlike the other three principal Marian antiphons, the 'Salve' achieved special prominence: it was mentioned by writers such as Chaucer, associated with miracles in the literature of the Dominican order, and developed its own commentary tradition.[41]

---

38 Margaret Bent and Andrew Wathey, eds., *Fauvel Studies: Allegory, Chronicle, Music, and Image in Paris, Bibliothèque nationale de France, MS français 146* (Oxford: Oxford University Press, 1998); Susan Rankin, 'The Divine Truth of Scripture: Chant in the Roman de Fauvel', *Journal of the American Musicological Society* 47 (1994), 203–43.

39 Robertson, *Guillaume de Machaut*, 79–186.

40 Ed. Leo Schrade in Machaut's *Oeuvres complètes*, vol. 2 (Monaco: L'Oiseau-Lyre, 1977), 82–9. A recent recording of this motet is included in the Hilliard Ensemble's *Guillaume de Machaut: Motets* (ECM, 2004).

41 On a 'Salve' miracle, see Fassler, 'Music and the Miraculous', 238–43; for the most recent account of late-medieval commentaries on the 'Salve', see Martina Wehrli-Johns and Peter Stotz, 'Der Traktat des Dominikaners Albert von Weißenstein über das Salve regina (gedruckt: Zürich um 1479/1480)', in Andreas Meyer, Constanze Rendtel and Maria Wittmer-Butsch, eds., *Päpste, Pilger, Pönitentiarie, Festschrift für Ludwig Schmugge zum 65. Geburtstag* (Tübingen: Günter Narr, 2004), 283–313.

Clerical singers, who performed the 'Salve regina' every day, would certainly have perceived the references to it throughout Machaut's motet. The text of the triplum voice, for example, refers to the image of Mary as the 'only hope' (*sola nostra spes*), echoing the antiphon text's phrase 'spes nostra'. In the final strophe of the motetus voice, the phrases 'Eia ergo' and 'et versus nos converte' also refer to the text of the 'Salve regina'. Another Marian chant that is quoted in the motetus text is the well-known hymn 'Ave maris stella', which is probably the textual source of the phrase 'para nobis tutum iter', echoing 'iter para tutum' in the hymn text, and the epithet 'stella maris' at the end of the first strophe of the motetus text may also be an allusion to this hymn. In the first strophe of the triplum voice, the phrase 'sic hereses peremisti', in combination with the words 'virgo' and 'gaudium', may be an allusion to the Marian responsory 'Gaude Maria virgo: cunctas haereses sola interemisti in universo mundo' ('Rejoice, Mary: you alone in the entire world have destroyed all heresies'). In addition to these textual echoes, the motet subtly evokes the 'Salve regina' melody in the upper voices with a melodic phrase from the opening of the Marian antiphon that is not present in the tenor part of the motet, which instead derives from a subsequent phrase of the 'Salve'. Thus, through subtle quotation and elaboration, the absent segment of the melody is rendered present.

Anne Walters Robertson has suggested that the motet's interweaving of references to invasion, torment and persecution by one's enemies with more conventional petitions to the Virgin for mercy and intercession may be allusions to the Hundred Years' War raging at the time this motet was composed, and included the siege of Reims, imbuing the universal plea of the 'Salve regina' with the more immediate concerns of the historical moment. Expanding the network of references even further, Robertson proposes that it was used for the daily commemoration of the Virgin after Compline in the nave of Reims Cathedral, a service established by Charles V in 1380 that included the sequence 'Inviolata, integra, et casta Maria' (which begins with the same Marian epithet as one of the voice parts in the motet), along with a Marian antiphon (probably the 'Salve Regina', which pervades the motet both musically and textually).[42] The intersection of local elements with a widespread form of collective supplication for intercession endows the performance of Machaut's motet with a specific meaning grounded in the ritual life of Reims cathedral.

---

42 Robertson, *Guillaume de Machaut*, 215–21.

Some motets were ceremonial compositions created for specific occasions, but they were also closely bound to the liturgical practices of a specific church while reflecting more universal liturgical traditions. One of the most famous examples is Guillaume Dufay's 'Nuper rosarum flores', composed for the consecration of the cathedral of Florence in 1436. The motet's complex construction constitutes a heightened form of discourse on the theology of the church and its dedication. Its overall temporal structure is based on the numbers associated with the Temple of Solomon in the biblical book of Kings. The melody in its two tenors is the standard introit chant of the mass for the dedication of a church, while the upper two voices sing a text that is specifically bound to Florence Cathedral and is closely related to a sequence created specifically for the consecration.[43] That the northerner Dufay wrote a motet for the dedication of Florence Cathedral attests to the internationalism of music in the later Middle Ages; composers from French- and Flemish-speaking lands worked extensively in Italy, while patrons, performers and manuscripts brought the music of English composers to the Continent. Whatever their geographic origins, composers continued to create music for the liturgy as well as motets, including Marian motets set to an ever-increasing variety of texts.

About a century after Machaut's distinctive allusion to the 'Salve regina' in his motet 'Felix virgo / Inviolata genitrix / Ad te suspiramus', the supplications in three Marian motets of the 1470s and 1480s take on the connotation of intercession for specific individuals in addition to speaking on behalf of a larger collectivity. Loyset Compère's motet 'Omnium bonorum plena', which draws upon the melody of an extremely popular chanson echoed in the motet's title ('De tous biens playne' by Hayne van Ghizeghem) entreats the Virgin's mercy for a series of named singers, including the composer himself. The 'Ave maria gratia plena / Dominus tecum' of Josquin de Pres commemorates the cycle of Marian feasts in the church year and concludes with a strikingly simple musical declamation of the words 'Mater dei memento mei', a text that frequently appeared in votive images of the Virgin in which the donor was also represented.[44] It was precisely such confluences of particular and universal meanings, old and new, vernacular and Latin, courtly and liturgical, that reveal music's central place in medieval religious culture.[45]

---

43 Craig Wright, 'Dufay's *Nuper rosarum flores*, King Solomon's Temple, and the Veneration of the Virgin', *Journal of the American Musicological Society* 47 (1994), 395–441.

44 Bonnie Blackburn, 'For Whom Do the Singers Sing?', *Early Music* 25 (1997), 593–610.

45 On the fifteenth-century motet, see Julie E. Cumming, *The Motet in the Age of Dufay* (Cambridge: Cambridge University Press, 1999).

Example 1. *Paris, BNF, nouv.acq.fr. 13521, fol. 377v, translation by Susan Boynton, modified from Stephen Haynes.*

### Quadruplum

| | |
|---|---|
| Plus bele que flors | More beautiful than flowers, |
| est, ce m'est avis, | is, I believe, |
| cele a cui m'atour. | she to whom I devote myself. |
| Tant com soie vis, | As long as I live, |
| n'avra de m'amor | none shall have |
| joie ne deliz | the joy and pleasure of my love |
| autre mes la flor | save the flower |
| qu'est de paradis: | of paradise: |
| mere est au Seignor | she is the mother of the Lord |
| qui si nous a mis | who put us in this world |
| et nos au retour | and who wants us |
| veut avoir tout dis. | to return to him always. |

### Triplum

| | |
|---|---|
| Quant revient et foille et flor | When both leaves and flowers return |
| contre la saison d'este, | and summer approaches, |
| diex! Adonc mi souvient d'amours | God! Then I remember love |
| qui tot jours | which always |
| m'a courtoise et douce esté. | has been gentle and sweet to me. |
| Molt aim son secors, | I treasure its solace, |
| c'a ma volenté | which contents me |
| m'aliege de mes doulours. | by relieving my suffering. |
| Mout en vient biens et honours | Much good and honor |
| d'estre a son gré. | come from being at its service. |

### Motetus

| | |
|---|---|
| L'autrier jouer m'en alai | The other day I went off to play, |
| par un destor; | taking a byway; |
| en vergier m'en entrai | I entered into a garden |
| por cuillir flor. | to pick flowers. |
| Dame plaisant i trovai, | I found a fair lady there, |
| cointe d'atour; | elegantly dressed, |
| cors ot gai; | she had a lovely body, |
| si chantoit par grant esmai: | yet she sang in great distress: |
| *'Amors ai* | *'I am in love:* |
| *qu'en ferai?* | *what shall I do?* |
| *C'est la fin, la fin,* | *It's the end, the end,* |
| *que que nus die, j'amerai.'* | *whatever people may say, I shall love.'* |

### Tenor

| | |
|---|---|
| Flos filius eius. | The flower is her son. |

Example 2. *Guillaume de Machaut, Motet 23, text and translation from Anne Walters Robertson in* Guillaume de Machaut and Reims: Context and Meaning in his Musical Works *(copyright Cambridge University Press, 2002), 329–31, reproduced with the permission of the publisher and author.*

Triplum

| | |
|---|---|
| Felix virgo, mater Christi, | Happy Virgin, mother of Christ, |
| que gaudium mundo tristi | who has brought joy to an unhappy world. |
| ortui tui contulisti, | By your birth, |
| dulcissima, | sweetest one, |
| sic hereses peremisti | thus you destroyed the heresies |
| dum angelo credidisti | when you believed the angel |
| filiumque genuisti | and bore a Son, |
| castissima. | most chaste one. |
| Roga natum, piissima, | Beseech your child, most faithful one, |
| ut pellat mala plurima | that he might drive away the many evils |
| tormentaque gravissima, | and severest torments |
| que patimur; | that we endure; |
| nam a gente ditissima, | for we are brought down by a most wealthy tribe, |
| lux lucis splendidissima, | [o] most splendid light of the light, |
| de sublimi ad infima | from the heights, |
| deducimur; | to the depths. |
| Cunctis bonis exuimur, | We are stripped of all good things, |
| ab impiis persequimur, | We are pursued by the impious, |
| per quos jugo subicimur | Through whom we are brought under the yoke |
| servitutis, | of servitude, |
| nam sicut ceci gradimur | for we make our way as if blind |
| nec directorem sequimur, | and do not follow a guide, |
| sed a viis retrahimur, | but we are drawn back from paths |
| nobis tutis. | [that are] safe for us. |
| Gracie fons et virtutis, | Fountain of grace and virtue |
| sola nostre spes salutis, | only hope of our salvation |
| miserere destitutis | have mercy on those bereft |
| auxilio, | of help, |
| ut a culpis absolutis | so that, freed from [our] sins, |
| et ad rectum iter ductis | and led to the right path, |
| inimicisque destructis | and our enemies destroyed, |
| pax sit nobis cum gaudio. | we may have peace with joy. |

Motetus

| | |
|---|---|
| Inviolata genitrix | Inviolate mother |
| superbie grata victrix | beloved conqueress of pride |
| expers paris, | having no peer, |
| celestis aule janitrix, | door-keeper of the celestial palace, |
| miserorum exauditrix, | you who hearken the wretched, |
| stella maris. | star of the sea. |
| Que ut mater consolaris | You who comfort like a mother |
| et pro lapsis deprecaris | and intercede humbly on behalf of |

| | |
|---|---|
| humiliter, | the fallen |
| gracie fons singularis | singular font of grace, |
| que angelis dominaris | you who rule over the angels, |
| celeriter | swiftly |
| para nobis tutum iter, | prepare a safe way for us |
| juvaque nos viriliter | and help us with vigor, |
| nam perimus, | for we perish, |
| invadimur hostiliter | we are invaded by enemies, |
| sed tuimur debiliter, | but weakly defended, |
| neque scimus | nor do we know |
| quo tendere nos possimus, | Which way we may go, |
| nec per quem salvi erimus | nor by whom we shall be saved |
| nisi per te; | if not by you; |
| eya! Ergo poscimus | Ah! Therefore we pray |
| ut sub alis tuis simus | that we may be under your wings; |
| et versus nos te converte. | and turn yourself toward us. |

Tenor

| | |
|---|---|
| Ad te suspiramus gementes et flentes | We sigh to you, lamenting and weeping |
| in hac lacrimarum valle. | in this vale of tears. |
| Eia ergo, advocata nostra. | O therefore, our advocate. |

# 17

# Images and their uses

SARA LIPTON

In the first half of the twelfth century, three men, all Benedictine monks, penned defences of Christian art. The first appears in a psalter dated c. 1120–39 and is a French paraphrase of a letter attributed to Pope Gregory the Great:

> It is one thing to worship a picture and another to learn from the story of a picture what is to be worshiped. For what writing conveys to those who can read, a picture shows to the ignorant...and for that very reason a picture is like a lesson for the people.[1]

This prayer book, known as the Saint Albans Psalter, was the first English manuscript in almost two hundred years to contain full-page painted scenes, and its scribe apparently felt that some justification for the lavish decoration was necessary. The second, by Rupert, abbot of Deutz (d. 1129), is a refutation of Jewish charges that Christian veneration of images amounted to idolatry. Rupert's response was to emphasise the emotional impact and devotional efficacy of images: 'While we externally image forth [Christ's] death through the likeness of the cross, we [are kindled] inwardly to love of him...'[2] The third, an elaborate paean by Abbot Suger of Saint-Denis to the beauty and spiritual power of his newly rebuilt abbey church (c. 1144), implicitly counters those who saw art as a form of 'distracting materialism'.[3] Far from distracting us, Suger wrote, art draws our 'dull minds' to the sacred, 'urging [them]

---

1  'Altra cóse est aurier la painture / e altra cose est par le historie de la painture ap[re]ndre / quela cóse seit ad aurier, kar ico que la scripture aprestet / as lisanz, icó aprestet la painture as ignoranz, kar an icele veient / les ignoranz quet il deivent sivre.' Hildesheim, St Godehard Library, St Albans Psalter, fol. 68v. The same folio also contains a Latin version of the letter: 'Aliud est picturam adorare, aliud ratione[m] de pict[ur]is int[er] roganti / per picture historia[m] quid sit adorandu[m] addiscere, Nam quod legentib[us] / scriptura hoc ignotis prestat pictura, q[u]a in ipsa ignorantes vident quid / sequi debeant.'
2  Rupert of Deutz, *Anulus sive dialogus inter Christianum et Iudaeum*, ed. Rhabanus Haacke, in Maria Lodovica Arduini, *Ruperto di Deutz e la controversia tra cristiani ed ebrei nel secolo XII* (Rome: Istituto storico italiano per il Medio Evo, 1979), 232–5.
3  See Conrad Rudolph, *Artistic Change at St.-Denis: Abbot Suger's Program and the Early Twelfth-Century Controversy over Art* (Princeton: Princeton University Press, 1990).

upward from material things to the immaterial'.[4] Christian art was far from new at the time; western Christians had long enshrined the Word of God in the most beautiful possible form, and made God's majesty manifest in sumptuously decorated architecture, metalwork and ivories. But these texts nevertheless testify to an important fact: in the twelfth century, images became more central to the practice of Latin Christianity than they had ever been before.

How the images were used was as diverse as the forms they took and the people who viewed them. The three functions cited by our authors – didactic, affective, anagogic – were those most frequently evoked by medieval theologians. Yet these approaches barely begin to describe the manifold uses to which images were put. In the pages that follow, I offer a broadly chronological overview of the role of images in high medieval Christianity. Although I touch upon such traditional art-historical considerations as patronage and commission, style and iconography, my primary focus is how people viewed and used the images around them. Because most forms of image use had their origins in the eleventh and twelfth centuries, I discuss this period in some depth, and treat only significant new developments in subsequent centuries.

## Later eleventh and twelfth centuries

If the necessary preconditions for the artistic flowering of the High Middle Ages were economic revival and at least a degree of political stability, the driving impetus was religious renewal. As clerical reformers sought to elevate the status of the church and its clergy, deepen the meaning of worship, affirm the virtue of the sacraments, and draw the laity into religious life, the visual aspects of Christianity took on greater significance. The growing popularity of the cult of relics – perhaps the most noticeable symptom of the broadening and deepening of Christian faith in high medieval Europe – drew more and more people money to material objects whose sight and touch promised to provide contact with the holy.[5] When a series of church synods between 1059 and 1079 resolved the Eucharistic Controversy in favour of the doctrine

---

4 Suger of Saint Denis, *De Administratione* 27, in Erwin Panofsky, ed. and trans., *Abbot Suger on the Abbey Church of St. Denis and its Art Treasures*, 2nd edn, ed. Gerda Panofsky-Soergel (Princeton: Princeton University Press, 1979), 48.

5 On the cult of relics, see Arnold Angenendt, *Heilige und Reliquien: Die Geschichte ihres Kultes vom fruhen Christentum bis sur Gegenwart* (Munich: Verlag C. H. Beck, 1994); Patrick J. Geary, *Furta sacra: Thefts of Relics in the Central Middle Ages* (Princeton: Princeton University Press, 1978); and Barbara Abou-el-Haj, *The Medieval Cult of Saints: Formations and Transformations* (Cambridge: Cambridge University Press, 1994).

eventually known as transubstantiation, the presence in every church of the visible body of Christ was forcibly declared. And in the battle for supremacy waged between church and empire, visual splendour was almost as favoured a weapon as verbal polemic and military might.

The innovative and impressive Romanesque churches with which art historians generally begin the story of high medieval art were equally notable for the burgeoning number of ornate objects sheltered within. In addition to larger and more magnificent reliquaries, the ever-growing elaboration of the liturgy called for more, and more beautiful, liturgical vessels, vestments and utensils: chalices and patens, eucharistic doves and pyxes, croziers and combs, fans and censers, candlesticks and ewers of crystal, gold, silver, bronze, ivory and enamel crowded upon or were suspended above altar-tops. These objects, like the institutions that housed them, worked on several registers at once, simultaneously fulfilling liturgical, spiritual and practical functions, and conveying meaning through form and medium as well as subject matter. Reliquary caskets and shrines manifested the order of the spiritual realm in their symmetrical and hierarchical forms, while their precious materials represented the glory of the resurrected body.[6] Imagery on their exteriors told tales from saints' lives or Scripture, highlighted correspondences between the Old and the New Testaments, or connected the particular saint inside with the universal heavenly host. Reliquaries in the shape of body parts advertised the holy items contained within; though they could also, as scholars have recently realised, mask their contents: the arm reliquary purchased by Abbot Gauzlin of Fleury (d. 1030) contained not an arm bone but a shroud, and the arm reliquary of Peter in Binche (Hainault, Belgium) contains a leg bone.[7] In such cases, the image worked metaphorically, 'arm' signifying power and action. Many reliquaries also had ceremonial functions: the reliquary foot of St Andrew doubled as a portable altar, while arm reliquaries were used for blessing the faithful, for the swearing of oaths and to heal the sick.[8] Altar and processional crosses and crucifixes, whether gorgeous luxury items like the ivory, gold and sapphire crucifix of King Ferdinand and Queen Sancha of Castile and Leon (1063) or more modest objects like the wooden crucifix from Austria now in The Cloisters, symbolised the sacrifice at the heart of the Christian faith and recreated daily in the mass, sheltered holy relics and served as focal points for the holiest moment of the Christian year – the Good Friday

---

6 Caroline Walker Bynum, *The Resurrection of the Body in Western Christianity, 200–1336* (New York: Columbia University Press, 1995), 209–12.

7 Barbara Boehm, 'Body-Part Reliquaries: The State of Research', *Gesta* 36 (1997), 8–19.

8 Cynthia Hahn, 'The Voices of the Saints: Speaking Reliquaries', *Gesta* 36 (1997), 20–31.

liturgy culminated in the unveiling and veneration of the crucifix.[9] Chalice, paten, ewer and mitre served respectively to hold wine, wafer and water, and to adorn and exalt a bishop; but each also served more generally to catch and reflect light, to bring colour and luminescence into the church, to embody in its own beauty and luxury the inestimable preciousness of the divine.

This last, most basic function, was of course a time-honoured one – Christians had ever considered the material splendour of their sanctuaries and ceremonies to redound equally to the glory of God, the institutional church and their financial supporters. And although the influential Cistercian Abbot Bernard of Clairvaux (d. 1153) mocked monastic ostentation and urged his brothers to reduce the outward trappings of worship, most Christians, monks included, continued to regard expenditure on decoration praiseworthy acts of piety. As Cardinal Matthew of Albano (d. 1132) exclaimed in his reproach to Benedictine followers of Bernard who voted to embrace austerity, 'Beloved brothers, to whom do those honors, that reverence belong…if not to the highest and most ineffable divine majesty? Whoever sought glory from [elaborate vestments and objects], except God and the Holy Mother Church?' And although Cardinal Matthew thus sought to discount any but the most disinterested motives for such luxury, he went on to add:

> Most Christian emperors and kings and other princes…ornamented and decorated [the Church of God] with various ornaments; saints and apostolic popes and venerable abbots also did the same…and because of this they are believed to have been promised the heavenly realm.[10]

Donors too drew spiritual gain from their donations.

Sacred objects also performed what we (but probably not their original owners, to whom such distinctions were largely without meaning) might label more prosaic functions, serving as tourist attractions, spoils of war, diplomatic gifts, 'seed' money for additional donations, and as declarations of their donors' social and political aspirations. An inscription at the foot of the Ferdinand and Sancha crucifix trumpets the royal couple's piety, while the precious materials proclaim the donors' wealth and status. The sumptuous, silver-clad chest known as the Arca Santa (c. 1120), which contained a sizeable

---

9 *The Art of Medieval Spain, a.d. 500–1200* (New York: Metropolitan Museum of Art, 1993), 244.

10 Stanislaus Ceglar, 'Guillaume de Saint-Thierry et son rôle directeur aux premiers chapitres des abbés bénédictins, Reims 1131 et Soissons 1132', in M. Bur, ed., *Saint Thierry: Une abbaye du VIe au XXe siècle. Actes du Colloque international d'Histoire monastique, Reims-Saint-Thierry, 11 au 14 octobre 1976* (Saint-Thierry: Association des Amis de l'Abbaye de Saint-Thierry, 1979), 331.

relic collection, was instrumental in making Oviedo a popular stop on the pilgrimage road to Compostela, helping to elevate Oviedo's ecclesiastical privilege and prestige. When Bernard of Clairvaux wrote that monasteries coveted 'exquisite baubles' and 'gold-cased relics' in order to catch sightseers' gazes and loosen their purse strings, he was merely putting an unusually critical spin on a widely accepted practice.[11]

In the same period, such well-established forms of visual embellishment were supplemented by new kinds of images. Romanesque buildings continued and extended earlier traditions of wall painting, but they also, for the first time in the Christian West, incorporated into their architectural fabric extensive and coherent sculptural programmes; in Italy the dormant art of mosaic was revived (for example, at Montecassino in the 1070s and San Clemente, Rome, before 1128). Altars began to be faced with frontals (*antependia*) of wood, metal, enamel or stucco carved or painted with images, usually of Christ, the apostles or various saints. Crosses and crucifixes, long used in processions and displayed during mass, now came to be permanently fixed on altars. Towards the end of the eleventh century near-life-size wooden crucifixes began to be erected on the choir screen or hung from the chancel arch, according the laity a dramatically enlarged image of the saviour. Reliquary statues, which had begun to appear in the tenth century, were widespread by the end of the eleventh; in the twelfth century they were supplemented and then largely superseded by non-reliquary cult images such as the *Sedes sapientiae* (statues of the enthroned Virgin with Child) and sculpted images of saints.[12]

A variety of contemporary texts bear witness to the fact that such new kinds of images inspired some concern. The initial shock of the cleric Bernard of Angers (c. 1020) at his first encounter with the cult of the statue of Ste Foi at Conques is well known.[13] Some form of resistance apparently spurred each of the defences of art with which I opened. But most strikingly, various images themselves voice warning regarding their own misuse, while at the same time laying claim to singular merit. A titulus above a mosaic of the *Maiestas Domini*

---

11 Conrad Rudolph, *The 'Things of Greater Importance': Bernard of Clairvaux's Apologia and the Medieval Attitude toward Art* (Philadelphia: University of Pennsylvania Press, 1990).

12 Signe Horn Fuglesang, 'Christian Reliquaries and Pagan Idols', in Soren Kaspersen, ed., *Images of Cult and Devotion: Function and Reception of Christian Images in Medieval and Post-Medieval Europe* (Copenhagen: Museum Tusculanum Press, 2004), 7–32; Irene H. Forsyth, *Throne of Wisdom: Wood Sculptures of the Madonna in Romanesque France* (Princeton: Princeton University Press, 1972).

13 Bernard of Angers, *The Book of Sainte Foy*, trans. Pamela Sheingorn (Philadelphia: University of Pennsylvania Press, 1995).

in San Marco, Venice (c. 1100) asserts: 'The image teaches God, but it is not itself God. You should revere this [image], but worship with your mind that which you recognise in it.'[14] And an inscription on the north portal of the early twelfth-century Church of San Miguel, Estella cautions: 'The image that you see, is neither God nor man. But he whom the sacred image figures, is both God and man.'[15] The promise of apprehension was inherent in the image, but so was the danger of idolatry.

There was ample cause for both hope and concern. In the eleventh and twelfth centuries, sculptures and paintings seemed to absorb the holy powers traditionally attributed to relics, inspiring quite new kinds of image-based venerations.[16] Pilgrims travelled great distances to genuflect, light candles or say prayers in their presence; alternatively, images might be carried far from their homes in procession, allowing townspeople and country-dwellers to feel the presence of Mary or the saint – and also of the institution that owned them – in their own localities. In spite of the warnings, many of the faithful apparently identified the images with their prototypes, believing that the images themselves had the power 'to speak, to weep, to fly out of windows, to bring rain in time of drought, to deter invaders in time of war, or simply to box the ears of the naughty'.[17] Such confusion could only have been exacerbated by liturgical practices: the *Sedes sapientiae* are known to have played the part of Mary in mystery plays, and in the Palm Sunday liturgy of the Italian monastery of Fruttuaria a figure called the *ossana* was cast as Christ himself.[18] Exempla relating miracles worked by images, such as the crucifix that bled when mocked and struck by Jews, became increasingly popular, and must have both encouraged and guided image-based cults and devotions.[19]

14 Ragne Bugge, '*Effigiem Christi, qui transis, semper honoria*: Verses Condemning the Cult of Sacred Images in Art and Literature', *Acta archaeologiam et artium historiam pertinentia* 6 (1975), 127–39.

15 Calvin B. Kendall, *The Allegory of the Church: Romanesque Portals and their Verse Inscriptions* (Toronto: University of Toronto Press, 1998), no. 47. Nearly identical verses also appear in a manuscript of c. 1150 discussed in Jeffrey F. Hamburger, *The Visual and the Visionary: Art and Female Spirituality in Late Medieval Germany* (New York: Zone Books, 1998), 186.

16 See André Vauchez, 'L'image vivante: Quelques réflexions sur les fonctions des représentations iconographiques dans le domaine religieux en Occident aux derniers siècles du Moyen Âge', in Maurice Aymard et al., eds., *Pauvres et riches: Société et culture du Moyen Âge aux temps modernes. Mélanges offerts à Bronislaw Gesemek à l'occasion de son soixantième anniversaire* (Warsaw: Wydawnictwo Naukowe PWN, 1992), 231–41.

17 Forsyth, *Throne of Wisdom*, p. 3; David Freedberg, *The Power of Images: Studies in the History and Theory of Response* (Chicago: University of Chicago Press, 1989).

18 Forsyth, *Throne of Wisdom*; Elizabeth Lipsmeyer, 'Devotion and Decorum: Intention and Quality in Medieval German Sculpture', *Gesta* 34 (1995), 20–7.

19 Sixten Ringbom, 'Devotional Images and Imaginative Devotions: Notes on the Place of Art in Late Medieval Private Piety', *Gazette des Beaux-Arts* ser. 6.73, alt. no. 1202 (1969),

It would be a mistake, moreover, to view intense response to visual cues as an exclusively or even primarily lay phenomenon; the gap between 'elite' and 'popular' image use was probably narrower than long assumed. Certainly twelfth-century theologians such as Richard of Saint-Victor, following Augustine and Pseudo-Dionysius, ranked physical perception quite low, envisioning an ascending hierarchy that passed from corporeal sight through imagination, to image-less intellect or understanding.[20] But few aspired to, much less reached, the ultimate stage. Many monastic devotions, both male and female, revolved around visual stimuli, especially, echoing Carolingian precedent, the image of the crucified Christ. Rupert of Deutz sought to realise the monastic ideal of *imitatio Christi* through focused gazing at a crucifix, and moving and intimate *Meditations* promoting and guiding visual contemplation of the crucifix were penned by such influential figures as John of Fécamp (d. 1079), Anselm of Canterbury (d. 1109) and Aelred of Rivaulx (d. 1166) for use by monks, nuns and devout laypersons.[21] Changing devotional patterns were reflected in changing imagery: the twelfth century was a transitional period in the depiction of the Crucified. Although many crucifixes continued to accord Christ the triumphal, living aspect familiar from Carolingian and earlier art, others, such as the oaken crucifix from the church of St-Denis, Forest-lez-Bruxelles (c. 1160), which movingly depicts the sagging head and strained ribs of the dying Christ, began to reflect the new emotionalism and emphasis on Christ's humanity in their form (Figure 17.1).[22] But the relationship between outward form and devotional function is not a simple one; visual conservatism did not necessarily preclude creative responses. Rupert of Deutz, for example, was moved to a very 'modern' kind of love for and mystical union with Christ by an object that apparently adhered to traditional iconographical modes.[23] And the remarkably tender tributes to the compassionate and mournful motherhood of the Virgin composed in the period found surprisingly little

160. The miracle was mentioned in a sermon at the pro-image Seventh Council of Nicaea in 787, but only arrived in western Europe in the eleventh century, when it was commemorated in the *Passio ymaginis* office; see Michele Bacci, 'The Berardenga Antependium and the *passio ymaginis* Office', *Journal of the Warburg and Courtauld Institutes* 61 (1998), 1–16.

20 Richard de St Victor, *Liber exceptionum*, ed. J. Chatillon (Paris: J. Vrin, 1958).

21 See Rachel Fulton, *From Judgment to Passion: Devotion to Christ and the Virgin Mary, 800–1200* (New York: Columbia University Press, 2002), 336–41; Sara Lipton, 'Sweet Lean of his Head: Writing about Looking at the Crucifix', *Speculum* 80 (2005), 1172–1208.

22 *Rhein und Maas: Kunst und Kultur 800–1400* (Cologne: Schnütgen-Museum, 1973), vol. 2, 412–13, fig. 10.

23 Lipton, 'Sweet Lean of his Head'.

Fig. 17.1  Oaken crucifix. Church of St.-Denis, Forest-lez-Bruxelles, Belgium, c. 1160–80.
Copyright IRPA-KIK, Brussels. (Photo: IRPA-KIK, Brussels)

expression in art: with the exception of a handful of images, Mary continued to be depicted as the regal Queen of Heaven to the end of the twelfth century.[24]

Although illuminated manuscripts had long been known in the medieval West, the production of illustrated books – mostly Bibles and liturgical works – took a quantitative and qualitative leap forward in the years 1080–1140.[25] Sumptuous images ostentatiously announced a monastery's embrace of reform, as well as fulfilling the widespread goal of glorifying God with splendour and shine.[26] Manuscripts accordingly increased in size and expense; gold was introduced in German book art in the eleventh century and in France around the year 1100. Narrative imagery greatly expanded; illuminated saints' lives began to appear in significant numbers in the eleventh century, and extensive cycles of biblical illustration, such as that in the St Albans Psalter, in the twelfth. Despite the assertion of the St Albans scribe, it seems unlikely that the 'unlearned' were the primary audience for book art. Though some of these picture cycles may well have served as biblical handbooks, teaching sacred history to students struggling to learn Latin, or to noblemen or women who read only the vernacular, the vast majority of manuscripts were made by and for monks, who would not have resorted to images for basic instruction. Moreover, many illuminated manuscripts were far too dense and recondite to fulfill this function. The Floreffe Bible (c. 1150), for example, mingles scholarship and art in elaborate allegorical imagery that is still not fully understood (Figure 17.2).[27] Such manuscripts, which most likely formed the basis for contemplative exercises structured by both illustration and text, demonstrate the extent to which even the most learned figures of the century used images to enrich religious experience.

What, then, of that pedagogical service – teaching the unlettered the basics of their faith – so vaunted by the St Albans scribe, and long assumed by scholars to be the primary function of monumental church art? Evidence suggests that here, too, the subject is more complicated than once thought. Some of the most extensive narrative cycles, such as the biblical and hagiographical carvings that gracefully entwine the cloister capitals at the Cluniac Abbey of St Pierre in Moissac (c. 1100), as well as the majority of French

24 Fulton, From Judgment to Passion, 348.
25 Walter Cahn, Romanesque Bible Illumination (Ithaca, N.Y.: Cornell University Press, 1982), 121.
26 Cahn, Romanesque Bible, 104.
27 Anne Marie Bouché, 'The Floreffe Bible Frontispiece, London, B.L. add. ms. 17738, fol. 3v-4r, and Twelfth-Century Contemplative Theory' (PhD dissertation, Columbia University, 1997).

Fig. 17.2 Floreffe Bible frontispiece: exegesis of the opening verses of Job.
Premonstratensian Abbey of Floreffe, Meuse Valley, Belgium, c. 1150. London,
British Library add. ms. 17738, fol. 3v. (Photo: British Library)

Romanesque fresco cycles, appear in areas to which lay people had no access. Even more approachable scriptural cycles, such as the west portal of the Abbey of Santa Maria, Ripoll, Catalonia (c. 1150), which is awash in biblical imagery, or the frescoes on the nave vaults of the Cluniac priory of Saint-Savin-sur-Gartemps (c. 1100), which present a vivid pageant of biblical history from the Creation through the giving of the Law at Sinai, or the ceiling in the parish church of St Martin in Zillis, Switzerland (c. 1140–60), which boasts almost 150 panels painted with biblical scenes, seem ill-suited to serve as 'lessons for the simple'. As Laurence Duggan has pointed out, and as any visitor can attest, most such images are difficult to see and decipher, and often have to be supplemented by explanatory inscriptions.[28] Abbot Suger explicitly acknowledged that his art was accessible only to the learned, and even for them, only with the help of written descriptions.[29] Whether there has ever been such a thing as a picture that 'speaks for itself' is debatable; but it seems clear that in the Middle Ages images were not supposed to replace words, but to complement them.

The main didactic function of art, then, was not so much to teach new things, as to bring life to existing teaching, to recall lessons presented in another format, perhaps at another time.[30] This seems to be the moral of a story told about Duke Godfrey of Bouillon (d. 1100). When asked to provide examples of their master's piety, the Duke's servants reported that 'once he entered a church, he could not be lured out, even after the celebration of divine office had been completed. Rather, he demanded an explanation of every single image and picture from the priests and those who seemed to have some knowledge of such things.'[31] The duke is praised not because he looked at and learned from the images, but because he asked for help in understanding them. This account, penned by a bishop, implies that if images were the Bible of the simple, they were in the eyes of the clergy at least, like the Bible, texts in need of glossing.

Indeed, the relatively few sermons we have that refer to art approach pictorial narratives much as they approach the Bible itself – as springboards for spiritual and moralistic allegorising. A twelfth-century abbot of St Victor

---

28 Lawrence Duggan, 'Was Art Really the "Book of the Illiterate"?', *Word and Image* 5 (1989), 227–51.
29 Suger of Saint Denis, *De Administratione* 33.
30 This mnemonic function is implicit in the Pseudo-Gregorian letter to Secundinus, which praises art's ability to help people recall lessons, but it is obscured in most paraphrases of the letter, which insist on the analogy 'picture: laity::word: clergy'.
31 William of Tyre, *History of Deeds Done beyond the Sea*, trans. Emily Atwater Babcock and A. C. Krey (New York: Columbia University Press, 1943).

consistently promoted a metaphorical approach to art in his sermons, telling his canons that they should strive to imitate the saints, who 'are rightly said to be not rough but sculpted stones, because what they assert with words, they show openly with deeds, and so correct behaviour is discerned in them, just as...what they did is explained in sculpture'.[32] He is clearly not imagining a 'literal' reading of the image; Augustinian canons generally were not expected to raise the dead, cure the halt and blind, ward off demons, or perform most of the other deeds typically depicted in carvings of saints. Rather, he expected his canons to look beneath the surface of the image: to emulate the apostles in living together harmoniously, for example, or to shun temptation and vice as assiduously as Saint Anthony repulsed demons. Peter Comestor (d. 1178) explicitly condemned the literal reading of art, cautioning that, if taken literally, wall paintings of the Transfiguration could promote the mistaken opinion that Christ's body was not affected: 'for certain rays of splendour are usually painted around, but separate from, the body of the Lord ...'[33] No wonder, then, that so many church images were difficult to see – as the account about Godfrey de Bouillon suggests, images may have had greatest value when they served not to convey information but to provoke questions, which could only be answered by recourse to authority.

Of course, some images did deliver fairly straightforward messages. Bishop Hugh of Lincoln told King John of England that sculptures and pictures of the Last Judgement were placed at church doorways so that worshippers 'could truly know the terror of Hell', and a text carved along the border of the vivid Last Judgement tympanum at Ste-Foi, Conques ends with the warning: 'Sinners, if you do not reform your ways, know that you will have a dreadful fate.'[34] The location of this lesson is as pointed as its content: the portrayal of the Last Judgement on the door of a church reminds pilgrims that the clergy alone held the power to loose and to bind (as they alone could translate this Latin text for lay spectators). As a reminder, however, that art could often be used in ways unintended by its makers, let us consider King John's response to

---

32 'Qui recte non puri sed sculpti lapides esse dicuntur, quia quod verbis asserunt, operibus evidenter ostendunt, et dum in eis recta operatio cernitur, quodammodo velut in sculptura quod egerunt explanatur.' Paris, Bibliothèque nationale, ms. lat. 14, 525, fol. 95v.
33 'Ideoque tradunt splendorem illum non fuisse in corpore dominico, sed in aere circum se... Cui opinioni consonant picture in parietibus ecclesiarum, ubi depingitur transfiguratio. Solent depingi quidam radioli splendoris circa corpus dominicum seorsum a corpore dominico...' Paris, Bibliothèque nationale, ms. lat. 15,269, fol. 106v.
34 Adam of Eynsham, *Magna vita sancti Hugonis: The Life of St. Hugh of Lincoln*, 2 vols., ed. Decima L. Douie and David Hugh Farmer (Oxford: Clarendon Press, 1985), vol. 1, 138–42.

Bishop Hugh's art-based homily. Utterly uncowed, the chronicler tells us, 'John crossed over to the wall opposite and pointed out kings distinguished by splendid crowns, being joyously conducted by angels to the heavenly king. "My lord bishop," he said, "you should have shown us these!"'

Ultimately, the content of church art may well have been secondary to its sensory effect. The paintings and mosaics of Christ in Majesty that so frequently adorned Romanesque walls endowed Christ with such venerable signs of wisdom and might as alpha and omega, book and orb, but they probably impressed as much with their colour, intensity and size as with their symbolism. Much to art historians' frustration, contemporary accounts of church paintings refer more frequently to their 'brightness' and 'liveliness' than to their form or subject matter.[35] Though such visual pleasure might fall well short of Abbot Suger's anagogical apprehension of the divine, it nevertheless could serve pastoral ends: Canon Hugh of Fouilloi (d. 1172) acknowledged that art was useful in 'holding' those too simple to be delighted by subtleties of Scripture, but yet able to be delighted by pictures.[36] Even Bernard of Clairvaux conceded (with some irritation) that for many people 'that which is more colorful, is believed to be more holy'.[37]

## Thirteenth and early fourteenth centuries

In the thirteenth century leadership of religious reform passed to university-trained and city-based clerics and mendicants, who expanded their attention to encompass the entire body of the Christian faithful, addressed a broader range of human behaviour, and stressed that outward worship must be accompanied by internal dedication. These changing contexts and emphases, which led to the further erosion of clerical/lay, cloister/world contrasts, were linked to three main developments in religious imagery: a multiplication and diversification of subject matter, a trend towards emotionalism and naturalism in style, and the introduction of religious art into urban and bourgeois domestic spaces. In their aggregate, and although the basic goals of art to teach, move, inspire, exalt and/ or aggrandise did not change, these developments point to a new approach towards image function. Whereas eleventh-century art sought to capture the glory of the heavenly realm in substance, colour and form – to bring the 'elsewhere' down to the 'here' – thirteenth-century art found and highlighted

35 C. R. Dodwell, *Painting in Europe, 800 to 1200* (New Haven, Conn.: Yale University Press, 1992), 126.
36 *De claustro animae*, lb. II, c. 4, PL 176, col. 1053.
37 Rudolph, *'Things of Greater Importance'*, 280–1.

the heavenly beauty in the natural world, blurring the boundaries between 'elsewhere' and 'here'. As art endowed spiritual events with the immediacy of reality, everyday life (ideally) became infused with spiritual meaning.

Nowhere are these various trends more apparent than in the great Gothic cathedral of Notre Dame in Amiens, begun c. 1220. Its soaring vaults and pointed arches draw the eye eastward and upward, where the thin walls, delicate tracery and vast windows of the choir seem to dissolve in a sea of light, and all distinction between outside and inside is effaced (see Figure 17.3).[38] This effect is furthered by the lifelike bands of carved flora blossoming on the column capitals and above the nave arches. The profusion of sculpture on the cathedral's exterior brought a myriad of Christian images to the heart of the city. And just as the images were more visible to the city, the city was more visible in the images – in the figures' contemporary clothing and detailed settings, and in their very human gestures and expressions. Representations of the vices appear in the lowest and most visible level of the central portal of the west facade, where they are portrayed not as abstract personifications, but as familiar figures wielding commonplace objects – disobedience is a young man insulting a bishop, for example, and avarice is a miser heaping bags of money into a chest. Such images seem to echo preachers' and confessors' exhortations that their flocks train their gazes on themselves, and read their own behaviour in the light of Christian values. Higher up, the so-called Beau-Dieu sculpture of Christ on the trumeau of the central portal treads upon venerable symbols of evil and carries a book of wisdom, but in appearance he is utterly unlike the conquering Christ-Judges of Romanesque tympana. He is gentle and approachable, and also fully rounded and anatomically convincing, though more perfect than any living man.[39] The equally beautiful figure of Mary on the southern portal stretches her arm out towards the faithful in warm welcome. This increased naturalism of Gothic sculpture is sometimes explained as an expression of Aristotelian materialism or proto-Renaissance humanism, but as Paul Binski has argued, it is probably best seen as a visual articulation of the religious ethos of the period, especially the growing devotion to the human Christ.[40] Amiens, like many Gothic cathedrals and

38 Stephen Murray, *Notre-Dame, Cathedral of Amiens: The Power of Change in Gothic* (Cambridge: Cambridge University Press, 1996).
39 Wilhelm Schlink, *Der Beau-Dieu von Amiens: Das Christusbild der gotischen Kathedrale* (Frankfurt: Insel Verlag, 1991).
40 Paul Binski, *Becket's Crown: Art and Imagination in Gothic England, 1170–1300* (New Haven, Conn.: Yale University Press, 2004), and 'The Angel Choir at Lincoln and the Poetics of the Gothic Smile', *Art History* 20 (1997), 350–74.

Fig. 17.3 Cathedral of Notre-Dame, Amiens: intersection of nave and apse. Northern France, thirteenth century. (Photo: akg-images / Erich Lessing)

churches, was dedicated to the Virgin Mary, a wholly human figure, an accessible and nurturing mother, the ultimate intercessor between God and Man, who nonetheless rose to be crowned Queen of Heaven – on the Virgin portal of Amiens' own facade.

Amiens' stained glass is lost, but many contemporary windows remain to give us some idea of their appearance and effect. The gem-like, intense colours and tightly compartmentalised narratives popular earlier in the century began to give way around 1250 to lighter, more translucent glass with larger individual panels. Their detailed and vivid storytelling, the variety and profusion of characters and objects depicted, and the professional and guild insignia that so often border them highlight the interconnectedness of realms conventionally labelled 'sacred' and 'secular' – as one might expect from a building that served simultaneously as ecclesiastical headquarters and as the central meeting point of a bourgeois town.[41] (One of the few surviving thirteenth-century sermon references to stained glass demonstrates the potential risks involved in thus visually mapping sacred history onto the contemporary world: the preacher Odo of Chateauroux recalled that when he was a boy, the layman standing next to him explained that the Good Samaritan window showed the Samaritan in lay clothing and the Levite in clerical dress because 'priests have no pity for the poor and the suffering, whereas the laity have a great deal'.[42])

In Italy, where for climatic reasons thin walls and large windows were undesirable, many of the same goals were achieved through different methods. As practised first by Cimabue, and then more famously by Giotto, wall painting acquired greater naturalism and emotional immediacy through the use of individualised expressions and features, more varied colours, and the introduction of perspective. Even so traditional a figure as St Matthew is endowed with a fresh sensibility: in Cimabue's portrait of the Evangelist in the upper basilica of St Francis at Assisi (c. 1280) he rests a hand on his chest as if contemplating the sorrow of the events he narrates in his Gospel. And in frescoes depicting the lives of Christ and his mother in Padua's Arena Chapel (1305–10), Giotto created the illusion that the light pouring through the chapel's windows was actually striking the bodies of his remarkably expressive painted figures, making them and the objects they grasped seem tangible and fully present.[43] Through such images the Christian viewer, the natural world and the heavenly realm come together.

---

41 Wolfgang Kemp, *The Narratives of Gothic Stained Glass*, trans. Caroline Dobson Saltzwedel (Cambridge: Cambridge University Press, 1997); Jane W. Williams, *Bread, Wine, and Money: Windows of Trades at Chartres Cathedral* (Chicago: University of Chicago Press, 1993). There is some debate concerning whether these guild arms are indications of patronage.

42 Quoted in Kemp, *Narratives of Gothic Stained Glass*, 71.

43 Michael Camille, *Gothic Art: Glorious Visions* (New York: Harry N. Abrams, 1996), 48.

Gothic spaces and images likewise brought the inhabitants of the Christian city together, sometimes in harmony and sometimes in disorder. Stories of entire cities uniting to fund and construct their cathedrals (at Chartres enthusiastic townspeople were said to have hitched themselves to carts to help haul the stones to the site) may have been largely mythical, but they demonstrate the importance of art and architecture in symbolising civic unity and pride, but also hierarchy and power – at least for the people telling them. Nobles, burghers, workers and peasants each had their carefully orchestrated role in religious rituals activated by or involving structures and images, as in the procession organised to honour the new altarpiece painted by Duccio for the cathedral of Siena (1308–11):

> And on the day that [the painting] was carried to the Duomo the shops were shut, and the bishop conducted a great and devout company of priests and friars in solemn procession, accompanied by the nine *signiors*, and all the officers of the commune, and all the people, and one after another the worthiest with lighted candles in their hands took places near the picture, and behind came the women and children with great devotion.[44]

Where ecclesiastical and/or political authority was less accepted by the population, the cathedral became an index of division: in internally riven cities, it was often the target of violence.[45]

Within Gothic cathedrals and churches, there was a greater trend towards spectacle in the liturgy and liturgical art, and a concomitant desire to control and direct the gaze. Around the year 1200 the priest began to turn his back to the laity during mass, shielding the altar top from their view and heightening the drama when the Host was finally lifted for all to see. This theatricality was enhanced by images in the form of paintings or carved reliefs erected behind the altar (retables), which constituted literal backdrops to the ritual.[46] These

---

44 B. Kempers, 'Icons, Altarpieces and Civic Ritual in Siena Cathedral 1100–1530', in Barbara Hanawalt and Katherine L. Reyerson, eds., *City and Spectacle in Medieval Europe* (Minneapolis: University of Minnesota Press, 1994); see also Joanna Cannon and André Vauchez, *Margherita of Cortona and the Lorenzetti: Sienese Art and the Cult of the Holy Woman in Medieval Tuscany* (University Park: Pennsylvania State University Press, 1999).

45 Resistance could also be expressed through simple neglect: in Toulouse, the bishop failed to raise money to fund an ambitious Gothic reconstruction of the cathedral. See Michael T. Davis, '"Sic et Non": Recent Trends in the Study of Gothic Ecclesiastical Architecture', *The Journal of the Society of Architectural Historians* 58 (1999), 414–23.

46 In 1310 the Synod of Trier, codifying this practice, proclaimed that behind or above every altar there should be an image, sculpture, picture or even inscription showing in whose honour the altar had been constructed. Donald L. Ehresmann, 'Some Observations on the Role of Liturgy in the Early Winged Altarpiece', *Art Bulletin* 64 (1982), 368.

colourful, detailed and often crowded tableaux depicted biblical or allegorical scenes as if they were contemporary events, helping the congregation to recall, even imaginatively to relive, the key moments of sacred history. In the exquisite Westminster retable (c. 1270–80), for example, which once stood behind the high altar at Westminster Abbey, a woman witnessing one of Christ's miracles wears a pill-box hat of the very latest fashion; such an image would please the refined tastes of courtly viewers while inviting them to imagine themselves at Christ's side.[47] Screens separating the nave from the choir became higher, though they were pierced to allow for limited and controlled viewing of the space beyond, and were adorned with elaborate sculptural scenes that helped contextualise – literally framed – the mystery taking place on the other side.[48] Reliquaries, too, became more 'readable' and solicitous of the gaze: although they still sometimes used form or iconography to identify the relics within, they also increasingly displayed the relic itself through windows made of transparent crystal. Starting around 1311, when Pope Clement V ordered official adoption of the Feast of Corpus Christi, monstrances displaying the consecrated Host became increasingly common.[49]

But although images of all kinds proliferated in Gothic churches, straightforward invocations of visual narratives by preachers remained scarce, and sermons continued to promote figurative over literal readings of art. Many thirteenth-century sermons, for example, asked the faithful to 'see' in the image of the crucified Christ a rubricated parchment, a leper covered with lesions, a lover extending his arms to embrace, and a bright red military banner.[50] Preachers tended to treat the Gothic image in fragmented and piecemeal form: often it is not the narrative itself but an incidental iconographical detail that forms the springboard for a visual lesson. In a sermon delivered in Paris around 1225, Thomas of Chobham reads a message not in the deeds of the saints, but in the shape of their haloes: 'A soul ought to control itself, just as a king ought to rule himself… Therefore, it is the habit in a church, that wherever an image of any saint who ruled himself well is painted,

47 Paul Binski, 'The Earliest Photographs of the Westminster Retable', *The Burlington Magazine* 130 (1988), 128–32.

48 Jacqueline E. Jung, 'Beyond the Barrier: The Unifying Role of the Choir Screen in Gothic Churches', *Art Bulletin* 82 (2000), 622–57.

49 Miri Rubin, *Corpus Christi: The Eucharist in Late Medieval Culture* (Cambridge: Cambridge University Press, 1991), 181–5 and 290–1.

50 See Nicole Bériou, *L'avènement des maîtres de la parole: La prédication à Paris au XIIIe siècle*, 2 vols. (Paris: Institut d'Études Augustiniennes, 1998).

a round corona is drawn around his head in the form of a shield, and is called a diadem.'[51] Through such examples preachers could use external beauty to teach internal reflection – to look not with the eyes of the body, but with 'the eyes of the heart'.[52]

The pastoral potential of the image was most fully exploited in the area of manuscript illumination. Illustrated moralistic and edifying texts, such as glossed Bible commentaries, the late thirteenth-century *Somme le roi*, and illustrated miracles of the Virgin, became popular among wealthy clerics and lay elites, and were remarkable equally for their beauty and luxury, for their innovative juxtaposition of word and image, and for their polemical force. The commentary texts and illustrations of the *Bible moralisée* made for King Louis VIII of France (c. 1225), for example, apply venerable biblical and iconographic signs (including moneybags, coins, scrolls, frogs, crows and cats) to new concepts and contexts so as to construct a comprehensive catalogue of the sins and vices common to urban society (see Figure 17.4). It may have been intended primarily to induce penitence and provide instruction in Christian virtue, but it also created a visual vocabulary to mark heretics, Jews and moneylenders as antithetical to the ideal of a reformed Christendom. In doing so, the images arguably influenced royal policy towards those groups.[53]

Secular rulers were not just passive recipients of religious images, however; they too harnessed the power and beauty of Gothic art and architecture for ends simultaneously, or rather inextricably, political and religious. The surprisingly precocious appearance of French Gothic forms in the late twelfth-century cathedral and palace in Esztergom (Hungary) has been related to both the pro-French dynastic foreign policy and the Parisian-influenced reformist ecclesiastical agenda of King Bela III (d. 1196).[54] The so-called Court Style associated with King Louis IX of France (d. 1270) was first and most famously realised in the Sainte Chapelle, a delicate jewel-box of a structure made to hold

51 'Et ideo habet ecclesia in consuetudine quod ubicumque ymago alicuius sancti qui bene se rexit depingitur, describitur circa capud eius corona rotunda in modum scuti quod dicitur diadema.' Thomas of Chobham, *Sermones*, ed. Franco Morenzoni (CCCM 82A; Turnhout: Brepols, 1993), sermo 20, lines 209–13, 214–15.
52 For example, the preacher Odo of Cheriton (d. 1247) draws the following moral from an exemplum about a painting of the devil: 'Utinam quilibet faciem eius oculis cordis diligenter inspiceret, in qua cauterium et signum dampnationis comprehenderet... ' Cambridge, Gonville and Caius College, ms. 362/441, fol. 103v.
53 Sara Lipton, *Images of Intolerance: The Representation of Jews and Judaism in the Bibles moralisées* (Los Angeles and Berkeley: University of California Press, 1999).
54 Ernö Marosi, *Die Anfänge der Gotik in Ungarn: Esztergom in der Kunst des 12. – 13. Jahrhunderts* (Budapest: Akademiai Kiado, 1984).

Fig. 17.4 Detail from commentary illustration to Rev. 16.4. *Bible moralisée*, Paris, *c.* 1225. ÖNB/Vienna, picture archive, cod. 1179, fol. 236d. (Photo: Österreichische Nationalbibliothek)

two major relics of Christ.[55] In the fourteenth century, Charles IV of Bohemia likewise invested remarkable energy and expense in turning Prague's St Vitus Cathedral into a temple to royal power, and the Bohemian court into a centre of religious imagery.[56] Funerary art, too, became an important site for the joint expression of dynastic and spiritual ambitions.[57]

In regard to image-based cults and devotions, the church's official guarded stance did not change, but it came to be supplemented by more positive acknowledgments of images' legitimacy, power and importance.[58] Thomas Aquinas echoed his predecessors in praising image-less meditation as the

55 Robert Branner, *Court Style and Sainte Chapelle: St. Louis and the Court Style in Gothic Architecture* (London: A. Zwemmer, 1965).

56 Iva Rosario, *Art and Propaganda: Charles IV of Bohemia, 1346–1378* (Woodbridge: Boydell and Brewer, 2000); Paul Crossley, 'The Politics of Presentation: The Architecture of Charles IV of Bohemia', in Sarah Rees-Jones, Richard Marks and A. J. Minnis, eds., *Courts and Regions in Medieval Europe* (Woodbridge: Boydell and Brewer, 2000), 99–172.

57 Anne McGee Morganstern, *Gothic Tombs of Kinship in France, the Low Countries, and England* (University Park: Pennsylvania State University Press, 2000); Paul Binski, *Westminster Abbey and the Plantagenets* (New Haven, Conn.: Yale University Press, 1995).

58 Hamburger, *Visual and the Visionary*, 112.

highest form of contemplation, but he also held that images of Christ (though not of saints) merited the same form of veneration (*latria*) as Christ himself (in part because he recognised that it had long since become church tradition) and seemed to confirm the miraculous abilities of some images in noting that 'the blood preserved as relics in some churches did not flow from Christ's side, but is said to have flowed from some maltreated image of Christ'.[59] Pastoral texts in both Latin and the vernacular, such as the *Speculum Christiani* and the *Exemplar* of Henry Suso (d. 1366), provided instruction concerning the proper veneration of holy images. Members of both mendicant orders practised visual devotions, and helped popularise them among nuns and lay men and women; Franciscans, especially, were active promoters of imaginative meditations on the Passion and patrons of innovative passion imagery.[60]

Churches were often the setting for visual devotions, but they also increasingly came to be practised in more intimate and domestic spaces, in conjunction with an expanding number and variety of individually owned images (conventionally, though sometimes misleadingly, called *Andachstbilder*).[61] Such images generally took the form of ivory, metal or wooden statues; carved or painted panels with scenes from the Gospels or select holy figures isolated from larger narratives; or appeared in the pages of small illuminated prayer books. Many of these works depicted familiar figures and scenes – the crucifixion and the Virgin with Child remained the most common devotional images throughout the Middle Ages. But newer images privileging human tenderness also began to appear: the Christus-Johannus Group (Saint John laying his head on Jesus' breast), the Veronica (a close up of Christ's face, thought to be a true likeness or *vera icon*) and the Pietà (Mary grieving over the body of her dead son), became increasingly popular in the later thirteenth and early fourteenth centuries (see Figure 17.5). Such objects and images had a variety of uses, cultic and devotional, emotional and intellectual. They helped the faithful achieve the proper state of mind for prayer; they accorded non-ecclesiastical spaces the aura of sanctity; they allowed worshippers to approximate the actions and attitudes of a priest in their own cells or homes or during their travels; they facilitated communication with the saints; they served as mnemonic devices for advanced meditations; they assisted mystics in

---

59 Thomas Aquinas, *Summa Theologica* II.2.174, III.25.3 and III.54.3.
60 Anne Derbes, *Picturing the Passion in Late Medieval Italy: Narrative Painting, Franciscan Ideologies, and the Levant* (New York: Cambridge University Press, 1996).
61 On the origins and problematics of the term *Andachtsbilder*, and the futility of attempts to distinguish cultic from devotional images, see Kaspersen, ed., *Images of Cult and Devotion*, iv–v.

Fig. 17.5 Christus-Johannes Group (Saint John laying his head on Jesus' breast). Swabia/ Lake Constance, early fourteenth century. Munich, Bayerisches Nationalmuseum, Inv. Nr 65/38. (Photo: Andreas Praefcke; public domain)

achieving ecstatic communion with the divine.[62] Some lay people apparently considered them not just complements to but adequate substitutes for official ritual: it was believed that looking at an image of St Christopher or St Barbara on the day of your death could help you get to heaven even without last rites.[63] On the other hand, there are also reports of images acting as mouthpieces for official positions: a statue of the Virgin Mary is said to have slapped a Premonstratensian nun who indulged in excessively ascetic practices.[64]

Discussions of such images and episodes, both medieval and modern, often assume visual sensitivity to be particularly characteristic of female piety. And Jeffrey Hamburger and others have demonstrated without question the prominent role played by visual devotions in the spiritual lives of nuns and beguines. But many medieval texts indicate that clerics and lay males, too, were sensitive to art's allure: Ramon Llull experienced a passionate crucifix-inspired vision indistinguishable from those attributed to many women.[65] Responses to art probably reflected variations in spiritual preparation as well as differences in the situations and needs of the individuals concerned, rather than any simple gender differentiation.[66]

While devotional images of Christ, the Virgin and the saints proliferated, more frivolous images sprung up in less central locations of ecclesiastical structures and texts: imaginary monsters, composite beasts and grinning gargoyles decorated column capitals, cornices and water spouts; and apes, donkeys and fantasies without names frolicked in the margins of manuscript pages. These images, too, had their uses, above and beyond their primary functions of supporting arcades, channeling water and so on. At the very least, they served to draw the gaze to the far corners of the cathedral, and perhaps increased goodwill towards the church, in leavening doctrine with humour, and delighting the eye. Perhaps, too, they bore witness to the fecundity of

---

62 See Peter Dinzelbacher, 'Religiöses Erleben vor bildender Kunst in autobiographischen und biographischen Zeugnissen des Hoch- und Spätmittelalters', in Kaspersen, ed., *Images of Cult and Devotion*, 61–88. On mnemonic function and meditative guidance, see Hamburger, *Visual and the Visionary*, 78–9 and 184.

63 Henk van Os, *Art of Devotion in the Late Middle Ages in Europe, 1300–1500*, trans. Michael Hoyle (Princeton: Princeton University Press, 1994), 32.

64 Dinzelbacher, 'Religiöses Erleben', 67. Images that did not perform satisfactorily might themselves be struck or otherwise chastised in turn.

65 Ramon Llull, *Livro do amigo e do Amado*, ed. Mark D. Johnston (Warminster: Aris & Phillips, 1995), 36 (no. 91).

66 See Hamburger, *Visual and the Visionary*, 111ff. Lipton, 'Sweet Lean of his Head' provides additional texts and discussion.

God's creation. Michael Camille has argued, convincingly in some cases and less so in others, that manuscript marginalia and Gothic grotesqueries amplified, commented upon or satirised mainstream images and concepts, embodying otherwise effaced ideas and amounting to a counter-official discourse.[67] Whatever their meaning, few images better encapsulate the conceptual complexity and visual sophistication of high Gothic religious imagery than these vividly 'real' but utterly fanciful creatures perched on the peaks of the house of God.

## Later Middle Ages (c. 1330–1500)

The fourteenth and fifteenth centuries were the heyday of the religious image. Image-based devotional practices and image-inspired mystical visions penetrated all sectors of Christian society; specific images came to be associated with every important liturgical feast; pedestals, niches, tabernacles and brackets for the display of images were added to churches around the Continent; and mass-produced religious images assumed unprecedented propagandistic and commercial significance.[68] Nonetheless, as Margaret Aston has noted, 'even in this image-filled period, attitudes toward images remained ambivalent'.[69] Although clerics and the institutional church promoted and sought to profit from these trends (for example, by writing prayers to recite before images, by using prints to propagate pilgrimages and by issuing indulgences for veneration of specific sculptures and paintings), they also expressed discomfort with the emotional excesses such images often inspired, and could be suspicious of artistic innovation.[70] The laity both embraced image devotion and, in the form of the Lollard movement, spearheaded resistance to it.[71] By the late fourteenth

---

67 Michael Camille, *Image on the Edge: The Margins of Medieval Art* (Cambridge, Mass.: Harvard University Press, 1992).

68 Alison G. Stewart, 'Early Woodcut Workshops', *Art Journal* 39 (1980), 189–94.

69 Margaret Aston, 'The Use of Images', in Richard Marks and Paul Williamson, eds., *Gothic: Art for England 1400–1547* (London: Victoria and Albert Museum, 2003).

70 Ingalill Pegelow, 'Pictures of Cult and Letters of Indulgence', in Kaspersen, ed., *Images of Cult and Devotion*, 33–46; Hamburger, *Visual and the Visionary*, 348. Hamburger (p. 315) notes that an icon that had been considered appropriate for a female convent in the fourteenth century was transferred to a male convent (that is, confiscated) in the fifteenth. On resistance to innovation, see Paul Binski, 'The Crucifixion and the Censorship of Art Around 1300', in P. Linehan and J. Nelson, eds., *The Medieval World* (London and New York: Routledge, 2001), 342–60.

71 Margaret Aston, *England's Iconoclasts* (Oxford: Oxford University Press, 1988).

century, complaints that there were too many images began to be more frequently voiced.[72]

Like late medieval devotional literature, the devotional imagery of the period was characterised by intense pathos, often achieved through visual 'ugliness'.[73] A late fifteenth-century 'Coffin of Christ' from Garamszentbenedik (Hungary) not only features elaborately carved and highly dramatic scenes of the Passion, but also became the resting place for a life-sized movable corpse of Christ during Easter processions. The Man of Sorrows (a half-length figure of the wounded Christ) became the most popular of all devotional images; in contrast to the Byzantine icons on which they were based, which connected the dead body of Christ to the Glory of God, western versions emphasised Christ's very human suffering. Vulnerability and pain likewise characterised late medieval crucifixes, and in pietàs Christ's body became ever more gruesome, and Mary more deeply grief-stricken. The closely observed representation of physical and emotional suffering in such images may have helped their viewers to identify viscerally with their saintly subjects.[74] Other images mirrored other forms of late medieval anxiety: themes such as the Three Living and Three Dead, the Dance of Death (first recorded in 1423) and decomposing skeletons served as vivid reminders of the perishability of the flesh (and, by implication, the immortality of the soul).[75] Even luxurious decorative objects could have sombre undertones: a sixteenth-century ivory bead with entwined lovers on its front conceals a hideous skeleton on the back (see Figure 17.6).

The visualisation of anxiety and pain was designed to instill piety and penitence, but it also had its dark side in a concomitantly sharpened rendering of evil: late medieval art became a powerful vehicle for the conflation of religious fervour with social hatred. In representations of the Passion the tormenters of Christ became ever more hideous and cruel, and in illustrations of martyrdoms the number and ferocity of the

72 Eustache Deschamps, quoted in Michael Camille, *The Gothic Idol: Ideology and Image-Making in Medieval Art* (Cambridge: Cambridge University Press, 1989), 219.

73 See Jeffrey F. Hamburger, 'To Make Women Weep: Ugly Art as "Feminine" and the Origins of Modern Aesthetics', *Res* 31 (1997), 9–33.

74 Joanna E. Ziegler, *Sculpture of Compassion: The Pieta and the Beguines in the Southern Low Countries, c. 1300–1600* (Brussels and Rome: Institut historique belge de Rome, 1992).

75 Paul Binski, *Medieval Death: Ritual and Representation* (London: British Museum, 1996).

Fig. 17.6 Ivory rosary terminal bead with embracing lovers on the front and a hideous skeleton crawling with worms on the back. Germany, sixteenth century. New York, The Metropolitan Museum of Art, gift of J. Pierpont Morgan, 1917, 17.190.305. (Photo: © Metropolitan Museum of Art)

executioners increased.[76] Many of these evil-doers were portrayed as extravagantly dressed ribalds, gross-featured peasants, turbaned Muslims or caricatured Jews – swarthy, hook-nosed and grimacing.[77] In this period, too, libels accusing Jews of desecrating the Host and murdering Christian children began to be popular subjects for painting, prints and pamphlets.

76 James H. Marrow, *Passion Iconography in Northern European Art of the Late Middle Ages and Early Renaissance: A Study of the Transformation of Sacred Metaphor into Descriptive Narrative* (Kortrijk: Van Ghemmert, 1979).
77 Ruth Mellinkoff, *Outcasts: Signs of Otherness in Northern European Art of the Late Middle Ages* (Berkeley: University of California Press, 1993).

Such images did more than merely reflect growing anti-Jewish sentiment –
they almost certainly worked to intensify and channel it.[78]

By no means was all religious art of the period grim. Fifteenth-century
Netherlandish and Italian painting combined complex symbolism with the
latest developments in perspective and oil painting technique to create
remarkably lifelike and brilliant holy tableaux. In Jan van Eyck's painting of
the Madonna with Canon van der Paele in Bruges (1436), rich brocades, furs
and silks, and the donor himself, share centre stage with an exquisitely lovely
Madonna, an elegantly chivalrous Saint George and a luxuriously accoutred
bishop-saint Donatian; the reality of the donor's mystical vision seems to be
confirmed by the tangibility of the textiles. And many religious images
doubled as luxurious household decorations, their holy subjects embodying
the latest in elegance and style, while their vivid narratives simultaneously
entertained and edified. The remarkable Unicorn Tapestries of c. 1500 at The
Cloisters, for example, can be enjoyed as a spirited rendering of a late
medieval hunt, as an allegory of Christ's Passion, and as a paean to courtship
and fertility. So exquisite were many late medieval religious artworks that Jean
Gerson felt compelled to instruct Christians not to worship an image just for
its beauty.[79]

Image-based devotions had always had a strong tactile element, and in the
later Middle Ages art more than ever facilitated the physical expression of
religious feeling. Cribs containing sentimental images of the baby Jesus
allowed nuns to treat the figure like their own child. While on pilgrimage,
Margery Kempe would mark each important stop by reverently clothing an
image of Christ; many people left money in their wills to pay for jewellery or
clothing with which to adorn images of saints.[80] The venerable devotional
practice of embracing and kissing statues and crucifixes grew for some people
into a daily habit.[81] Genuflecting before a statue became an important demonstration of orthodoxy, and the failure to do so, cause for suspicion. Nor was
physical interaction merely one-sided: increasingly images moved too. Late
medieval northern altarpieces were furnished with moveable wings to be

78 Miri Rubin, *Gentile Tales: The Narrative Assault on Late Medieval Jews* (New Haven,
   Conn.: Yale University Press, 1999), and Sara Lipton, *Dark Mirror: Jews, Vision, and
   Witness in Medieval Christian Art* (New York: Metropolitan Books, forthcoming).
79 Quoted in Ringbom, 'Devotional images', 169 n. 50.
80 Kathleen Kamerick, *Popular Piety and Art in the Late Middle Ages: Image Worship and
   Idolatry in England, 1350–1500* (New York: Palgrave, 2002), 102.
81 Dinzelbacher, 'Religiöses Erleben'.

opened and closed during strategic moments of the liturgical year, and crucifixes and other sculpted figures were endowed with moveable limbs.[82] By the end of the Middle Ages, one no longer had to be a gifted mystic to see religious art 'come to life'.

In the High Middle Ages religious pictures and objects served a dizzying array of purposes. They were used to glorify self, family, polity or institution, to exemplify virtue and/or embody vice, to bestow authority or authenticity, to protect a city or individual, to reinforce communal cohesiveness or corporate identity or to demonstrate their breakdown, to create a mood, to work miracles, to publicise a programme or pilgrimage, to raise funds, to spawn hatred, to stimulate the imagination or to trammel it. They could serve as gifts, containers, figureheads, signs or markers. Many of these functions remained common during the entire period in question; others waxed and waned according to social and religious needs and/or the prevalent artistic forms and media. But a few basic observations hold true across the Continent and throughout the centuries of the High Middle Ages. First, there is no simple categorisation of image use according to rank, gender or spiritual status: lay people, clerics and monks, men and women were all able to learn from and be moved by images. Second, the word–image opposition implicit in the cliché 'Book of the Simple' breaks down under scrutiny: images rarely if ever 'replaced' words, many images prominently featured words, images could be 'read' allegorically, just as words were, and by the end of the Middle Ages few if any liturgical or biblical words would have been totally free of visual associations. Third, artistic, theological and social change seem to have unfolded according to a delicate oscillating rhythm. High medieval images of Christ are often regarded as the most perfect visual expressions of the Catholic conception of a loving and compassionate God-Man. But Rupert of Deutz managed to see love and compassion in a crucifix well before such feelings came to dominate artistic renderings of Christ Crucified. Thirteenth-century devotional emphases on Jesus' scars and wounds anticipated more extreme later medieval images, which then in turn inspired further devotional excesses. And sometimes viewers encountered artistic change before they were fully ready to accept it. The history of Christian imagery suggests that ideas and images, doctrine, art and society existed in a complex relationship,

---

82 Ehresmann, 'Some Observations'.

with innovation appearing in sometimes one and sometimes the other realm. Finally and most basically, the manifold, overlapping and conflicting uses of images surveyed here confirm the centrality of the religious image in the lives of high medieval Christians. This centrality was acknowledged at the close of the Middle Ages in the ritual for visiting the infirm known as *The Boke of the Crafte of Dying*.[83] Because *moriens* may be unable to hear, speak or understand, the *Boke* instructs, the priest should help him or her take solace in God's love by displaying an image of the crucifix. In the end, this text suggests, what is left to a soul deprived of all other means of access to the divine is sight. And art.

---

83 Carl Horstmann, ed., *Yorkshire Writers: Richard Rolle of Hampole, an English Father of the Church, and his Followers*, 2 vols. (New York: Macmillan, 1895–96), vol. 2, 409–10.

18

# Mary

RACHEL FULTON

Our Lady, Mother of God, Virgin of Virgins, Star of the Sea, Mother of Mercy, Seat of Wisdom, Tower of Ivory, Terror of Demons, Daughter of Jerusalem, Couch of Solomon, Garden of Delights, Mystical Rose, Blessed among women, Bride of God, Handmaid of the Trinity, heavenly Queen: these are but a few of the titles with which Mary, mother of Jesus, was addressed in the litanies and other prayers of the medieval European West.[1] They are remarkable as much for their abundance as their variety, apt witness, some might say, to the 'excesses' and 'abuses' to which the pre-Reformation Marian cult was regrettably, if not inevitably, all too prone. The earth and the heavens, the sun, moon and stars; the flowers of the garden and the fruits, spices and trees of the field; gold, silver, ivory, crystal, precious woods, gems and pearls; fountains and fortresses, temples and arks; gates, ladders, libraries and treasure-chests; mirrors and aqueducts; towers, armies and doves; the mountains and the sea: all were invoked in the art, literature and liturgies of the later Middle Ages as symbols for or attributes of the Virgin Mother of God. As the Benedictine archbishop Anselm of Canterbury (d. 1109) exclaimed in the third of his three great prayers to Mary,

> Heaven, stars, earth, waters, day and night, and whatever was in the power of use of men was guilty; they rejoice now, Lady, that they lost that glory, for a new and ineffable grace has been given them through you. They are brought back to life and give thanks…[for] by you the elements are renewed.[2]

How to explain this associative profusion of attributes, titles, privileges and symbols? One way, explicitly adverted to in certain feminist analyses but implied in much recent historical work, is to see the high and late medieval

---

1 G. G. Meersseman, *Der Hymnos Akathistos im Abendland*, 2 vols. (Spicilegium Friburgense 2–3; Fribourg: Universitätsverlag, 1958, 1960).
2 Anselm, *Oratio 7*, trans. Benedicta Ward, *The Prayers and Meditations of Saint Anselm* (Harmondsworth: Penguin, 1973), 118–19.

devotion to Mary as catalysing around a psychologically more or less inevitable 'return of the Goddess', if not necessarily to the benefit of attitudes towards other women, nevertheless arising out of deep emotional needs for maternal comfort and support. Historically, the problem then becomes simply one of explaining the local content of the universal archetypal form 'virgin-mother-daughter-bride': why 'Mary', as it were, rather than 'Ishtar', 'Cybele' or 'Isis'. This is to assume, of course, that archetypes and their attendant emotions are themselves sources of energy, capable of calling forth various expressions, the power of which, at least historically, there is arguably little reason to doubt. Thus, it has been argued, the profusion of lists. As one prominent feminist theologian has put it: '[Mary] rose [in this period] into a formidable power in her own right', as '[praise] and tribute [to her] welled up from hearts filled with loving awe'.[3] Mary, in other words, became a Goddess like God, herself an object of glorification and praise to whom the faithful might turn for protection in adversity, her powers as Queen of Heaven limited only by the relative willingness of the Judge, her Son, to give heed to her intercessory pleas.

Nevertheless, however much it might appeal to modern efforts to reconceptualise divinity as feminine, as an explanation for the devotion as it actually developed historically and theologically in Christian Europe, this reading of the late medieval image of Mary is at once both too limiting and too vague. Why should a 'poor, pious, and upright maid' (in Martin Luther's words) come to be exalted not only over all other saints, but even over the angels, as a model of and mediator for humanity's relationship with God? It is not simply that Mary, a particular historical figure, took on attributes formerly associated with the pagan goddesses of fertility, wisdom, virginity and the underworld. Rather, as Luther and his fellow reformers realised all too well, the Virgin of the high and late medieval cult challenged the very definition of the Christian godhead as articulated doctrinally both in Scripture and the creeds. If, as Luther (d. 1546) put it, 'the pope and his monks...make a god out of the Virgin Mary',[4] the problem was that they did so with reference to a particular understanding of God, not simply as Father or Son, but as Maker of Heaven and earth, Three-in-One. From this perspective, the Protestant reformers were right to argue that the invocation of Mary as mediatrix

3 Elizabeth A. Johnson, 'Marian Devotion in the Western Church', in Jill Raitt, ed., *Christian Spirituality*, vol. 2, *High Middle Ages and Reformation* (New York: Crossroad, 1987), 396, 406.
4 Beth Kreitzer, *Reforming Mary: Changing Images of the Virgin Mary in Lutheran Sermons of the Sixteenth Century* (Oxford: Oxford University Press, 2004), 31.

through the recitation of the Ave Maria as a prayer impacted upon Christ's salvific role as mediator of grace. In devotional if not theological terms, however, what they and their successors have failed to appreciate was how much removing the address to Mary from the prayers of the faithful would diminish not only Mary, but God, not, as certain feminist theologians would argue, by reinforcing the patriarchal, male-centred aspect of the divine (although, admittedly, the reformers did this, too), but, rather, by denying the very logic of the orthodox tradition upon which the late medieval image of Mary and God had been built.

Three elements of this tradition are essential to note: first, that it achieved its most developed form within the liturgical structure of the monasteries, although by the later Middle Ages with the introduction of the Book of Hours and the prayers of the rosary it was by no means strictly dependent upon such institutional support; second, that it was grounded practically as well as theologically in the liturgical use of particular passages from Scripture, including not only the explicitly Marian passages from Luke (Gabriel's 'Ave Maria' (1.28) and Mary's 'Magnificat' (1.46–55)), but also the psalms, lessons and antiphons of the Marian office, most notably, those taken from Proverbs, Ecclesiasticus, Wisdom and the Song of Songs; and third, that it developed in tandem with contemporary concerns not only about the work of salvation as accomplished by the incarnation, suffering and resurrection of Christ, but also about the work of creation as effected before and within time by all three persons of God. Whereas the reformers sought to restrict Mary's theological and devotional role to her status as human mother of Christ, high and late medieval artists, liturgists and theologians envisaged Mary as much in Trinitarian as in Christological terms, Christ-like in her compassion at his crucifixion and in the preservation of her body from corruption at her assumption into heaven, but Wisdom-like in her conception and dwelling with God 'ab initio ante saeculum' (Ecclus 24.14).

The artistic and devotional effects of these interrelated emphases are still visible throughout Europe, in the pilgrimage churches built to house the many miracle-working statues of the Virgin as the Throne of Wisdom, as well as in the many paintings and sculptures of Mary suffering under the Cross or being crowned heavenly Queen. They are perhaps most familiar as 'abuses' from the many stories told of Mary's willingness to have mercy on even the most reprobate of her devotees, particularly while interceding on their behalf with her Son (e.g. Theophilus). Extreme, even embarrassing, as these images and appeals might now seem, their origins, like Mary's, were much more modest, even boring, at least to those unaccustomed to the pitfalls and precipices of regular, liturgically structured prayer. For their practitioners, however, the recitation of these praises and prayers to the Virgin was somewhat more bracing, charged as it was with the conviction that it was not only Mary who was listening, but also hosts of many 'fiends'. As one fifteenth-century exposition on the Marian office as recited by the Birgittines of Syon Abbey (Isleworth, England) cautioned the sisters,

> we ar closed in thys holy Monastery, as knyghtes in a castell where we ar beseged wyth greate multytude of fendes that nyght and daye laboure to gette entre and pocessyon in oure soules… And therfore when we here the belle rynge to mattyns, we oughte a none as trew goddes knyghtes aryse quycly and arme vs with prayer.[5]

Like a good lord, Mary, in her turn, was expected to come to the relief of her 'trew knyghtes', and so, as miracle story after miracle story attested, she did.

Although not as old as 'Theophilus', one of the most popular of these stories, of which there were many variants, told how a clerk or a monk of otherwise dissolute life was saved by the Virgin because he never passed her altar without pausing to salute her, saying, 'Ave, Maria, gratia plena, dominus tecum'.[6] In some versions of the story, the man drowns on his way to visit his mistress, at which point a multitude of demons appears to carry off his soul. Although the angels who have likewise appeared find they are helpless against the claims of the demons, when the Virgin arrives, she reprimands the demons, saying, 'You have nothing against this soul. While it was in its body, it was my devotee; it would be wrong for me to abandon it now.'[7] The demons insist that the case be brought before the King of Heaven, who judges, nevertheless, that the man's soul should be returned to its body and the man allowed to do penance for his sins. In other versions, the cleric is murdered by his enemies. Unsure of the circumstances attending his death, the townspeople have the body buried outside the cemetery, but the Virgin appears to another cleric of the town, asking, 'Why have you treated my

---

5 John Henry Blunt, ed., *The Myroure of oure Ladye* (Early English Text Society ES 19; London: N. Trübner, 1873) 72.

6 Evelyn Faye Wilson, *The Stella maris of John of Garland* (Cambridge, Mass.: Wellesley College and The Mediaeval Academy of America, 1946), 178–9; R. W. Southern, *The Making of the Middle Ages* (New Haven, Conn.: Yale University Press, 1953), 248–9; Johannes Herolt, *Miracles of the Blessed Virgin Mary*, trans. C. C. Swinton Bland (London: George Routledge & Sons, 1928), 76–7, 100; Henry Adams, *Mont Saint Michel and Chartres* (Harmondsworth: Penguin, 1986), 249–50.

7 Gonzalo de Berceo, *Miracles of our Lady*, trans. Richard Terry Mount and Annette Grant Cash (Lexington, Ky.: University Press of Kentucky, 1997), 34. Cf. *Miracula sanctae virginis Mariae*, ed. Elise F. Dexter (University of Wisconsin Studies in the Social Sciences and History 12; Madison: University of Wisconsin Press, 1927), 17–18.

chancellor this way?' She demands that the body be given Christian burial. When the townspeople open the grave, they find a very beautiful flower blooming in the dead man's mouth and his tongue 'fresh and sound as if ready to praise God'.[8] Convinced, they move the body to the cemetery while singing *Speciosa* to the Virgin.[9]

The central point in these stories is not, as has sometimes been suggested, the capriciousness of the Virgin with respect to the demands of God's justice (the drowned cleric still had to do penance), but, rather, on the one hand, Mary's loyalty to her servants and, on the other, the great power of even the simplest liturgical prayers. The 'litel clergeon' of Chaucer's 'Prioress's Tale' could sing only *Alma redemptoris mater* as he walked to and from school, but this was sufficient both (at Satan's instigation) to provoke the Jews' ire and (with Mary's help) for the boy to go on singing the same antiphon 'fro word to word, acordynge with the note' even after his throat had been cut.[10] Saying the right words at the right time with the right pronunciation with one's full attention mattered not only to Mary, but also to God. It was, after all, with a word ('Fiat') that God had brought the world and all its creatures into being. It was, likewise, with a word ('Fiat mihi') that Mary gave her consent to the angel that she become the mother of God.

As the mellifluous Cistercian abbot Bernard of Clairvaux (d. 1153) wondered at this pressing moment, he begged the Virgin to speak:

> Virgin, you have heard what will happen, you have heard how it will happen... The angel is waiting for your reply... Give your answer quickly, my Virgin. My lady, say this word which earth and hell and heaven itself are waiting for... Only say the word and receive the Word: give yours and conceive God's... Why do you delay?[11]

The Augustinian canon William of Newburgh (d. after 1198) put the request even more forcefully in his commentary on the Song of Songs:

> Truly, [Virgin], it will not suffice [for you] simply to believe, for to believe in the heart is for justice, but to make confession by mouth is for salvation. Unless you express the faith of your heart with your mouth, the Most High

8 Dexter, ed., *Miracula*; 18–19.
9 De Berceo, *Miracles*, 37. The antiphon was one of the most ancient sung in honour of the Virgin: 'Speciosa facta es et suavis in deliciis tuis, sancta Dei Genitrix.' See Henri Barrè, 'Antiennes et répons de la Vierge', *Marianum* 29 (1967), 218.
10 Geoffrey Chaucer, *The Canterbury Tales*, Fragment 7, line 547, Oxford Text Archive no. OTA U-1678-C 1993, online at The University of Virginia Library.
11 Bernard of Clairvaux, *Homilies in Praise of the Blessed Virgin Mary*, trans. Marie-Bernard Saïd (Kalamazoo, Mich.: Cistercian Publications, 1979), 53–4.

will not take from you the sacrifice of salvation. Speak, therefore, the sweet word, say what you are about to say![12]

At stake in this exchange was far more than simply Mary's obedient willingness to become the mother of God. Rather, her speaking, like God's, was understood by her medieval devotees as a moment of creation, more properly, re-creation, contingent upon not only her assent to God's will, but, indeed, her full co-operation in allowing him into her womb. This was the mystery as Anselm of Canterbury saw it:

> Nothing equals Mary,
>> nothing but God is greater than Mary...
> All nature is created by God and God is born of Mary.
> God created all things, and Mary gave birth to God...
> He who was able to make all things out of nothing
>> refused to remake it by force,
>> but first became the Son of Mary.
> So God is the Father of all created things,
>> and Mary is the mother of all re-created things.[13]

In Jeremiah's words (31.22), 'creavit Dominus novum super terram, femina circumdabit virum', 'that is', as Bruno of Asti, bishop of Segni (d. 1123), explained, 'the Virgin Mary carried Christ in her womb, he whom the whole world could not contain'.[14]

The paradox was one on which the authors of the devotion to Mary could not help but dwell. It was a mystery greater even than that a virgin should become a mother without the intervention of a man. How was it that God, creator of heaven and earth, should enter into his own creation, not simply by taking on a material body (which would have been miracle enough), but, rather, by taking on the very flesh of one of his human creatures and doing so, moreover, by spending nine months within the likewise fleshly confines of her womb? Visually, the wonder is perhaps best expressed through the late medieval iconography of the *mappa mundi*, where, for example, in the monumental map made in the late thirteenth century for the Benedictine convent at Ebstorf in Lower Saxony, the world itself is shown as the body of Christ with his head, hands and

---

12 William of Newburgh, *Explanatio Sacri Epithalamii in Matrem Sponsi*, ed. John C. Gorman (Spicilegium Friburgense 6; Fribourg: Universitätsverlag, 1960), 200; Rachel Fulton, trans., *From Judgment to Passion: Devotion to Christ and the Virgin Mary, 800–1200* (New York: Columbia University Press, 2002), 445.

13 Anselm, *Oratio 7*, trans. Ward, 120–1.

14 Bruno, *Sententiae*, bk. 5, chap. 1, *PL* 165, col. 1022.

feet peeking just over the oceanic frame.[15] Representations of Christ as Creator such as those which appear as frontispieces for a number of the more lavishly illustrated thirteenth-century *Bibles moralisées* make a similar point: Christ, enthroned, holds the cosmos in his bosom with his left hand while he measures its dimensions with an architect's compass in his right.[16] It was in just this way, or so her devotees marvelled, that Mary carried Christ in her womb and supported him as a baby on her lap.

There were likewise suitably exquisite mysteries to follow. In the words of Ecclus 24.9–10, read as the lesson for the Saturday mass of the Virgin and as the chapter for the daily office of the Virgin at Vespers, 'From the beginning, before the ages I was created, and until the age to come I shall not cease to be; and in his holy habitation I ministered before him.'[17] The antiphons and psalms sung for the Marian office reinforced this emphasis on Mary's literally all-encompassing role with respect to creation. For example, the first antiphon *Benedicta tu* set at Matins as a frame for Psalm 8, *Domine Dominus noster*:

A. Blessed are you.

**Ps.** O Lord, our Lord, how excellent is your name in all the earth, who have set your glory above the heavens… When I consider your heavens, the work of your fingers, the moon and the stars, which you have ordained, what is man that you are mindful of him, and the son of man that you visit him? For you have made him a little lower than the angels, and you have crowned him with glory and honor… O Lord, our Lord, how excellent is your name in all the earth![18]

A. Blessed are you among women, and blessed is the fruit of your womb.

It was but a small step from here to begin to wonder how it was that God had come to choose this virgin and no other to bear the Son of Man in the first place. As the mid-twelfth-century *Speculum virginum* put it, 'how could the Mother not pre-exist with the Son, in whose conception and birth turned the hinge that opened the door for the whole rational creation to be sanctified,

---

15 David Areford, 'The Passion Measured: A Late-Medieval Diagram of the Body of Christ', in A. A. MacDonald, H. N. B. Ridderbos and R. M. Schlusemann, eds., *The Broken Body: Passion Devotion in Late-Medieval Culture* (Groningen: Egbert Forsten, 1998), plate 10; Naomi Reed Kline, *Maps of Medieval Thought* (Woodbridge: Boydell, 2001), fig. 8.4.

16 Oxford, Bodleian Library, MS Bodl. 270b, fol. IV (Kline, *Maps*, fig. 8.7); Vienna, Österreichische Nationalbibliothek, MS 1179, fol. IV (Johannes Zahlten, *Creatio mundi: Darstellungen der sechs Schöpfungstage und naturwissenschaftliches Weltbild im Mittelalter* (Stuttgart: Klett-Cotta, 1979), fig. 269); Toledo, Archivio capitular, Bible moralisée of Louis IX, fol. IV.

17 Barbara Newman, *God and the Goddesses: Vision, Poetry, and Belief in the Middle Ages* (Philadelphia: University of Pennsylvania Press, 2003), 197–8.

18 New King James translation.

unified, and restored to peace?' The short answer was that, of course, she did, 'not by quality of time but by reason of divine foreknowledge; not by the form of bodily substance but by an image of subsistence, to be revealed in her time foreordained before the ages'.[19]

God knew from the first day of creation that it was through this woman's body that he would effect his entry into the world. Accordingly, he likewise chose to fashion her who was to be his tabernacle from only the purest materials, 'gold, silver and bronze, sapphire and purple and twice-dyed scarlet', and every precious gem (cf. Exod. 25.3–7). Doctrinally, this foreknow-ing raised the thorny question of the status of Mary's soul at her conception, whether, like all other human beings since Adam and Eve, in sin or, because she was foreordained to be the mother of Christ, not. Devotionally, never-theless, matters were considerably more straightforward: Mary, mother of all re-created things, was, like creation itself, not only good, but beautiful. And like creation, she showed forth in her beauty the otherwise indescribable glory of God. 'You are all beautiful, my beloved', sang the choirs of Latin Christendom on the feast of Mary's Assumption (15 August), 'and there is no spot in you. Your lips drip honeycomb; milk and honey are under your tongue; the fragrance of your ointments is above all spices... Arise, make haste, my beloved; come from Lebanon, come, you will be crowned' (cf. Song 4.7, 11, 10; 2.10; 4.8).[20] Even the angels delighted in her beauty as they saw in her not only their Queen, but, as the Benedictine abbess Hildegard of Bingen (d. 1179) put it so lyrically, the 'shining lily on which God gazed before all creation', 'the resplendent jewel' into which the sun poured its 'unclouded beauty', 'the luminous matter through which the Word breathed forth all virtues', 'the mirror of all [God's] beauty and the embrace of his whole creation'.[21] Thus the choirs sang at her feast: 'You have been exalted, holy mother of God, above the choirs of the angels to the celestial realms.'[22]

Crystalline in its radiance as the matrix for God's incarnation, Mary's body was, nevertheless, a body, subject, it was invariably insisted, like all other human bodies to the 'law of mortality' and the 'chains of the flesh'.[23] And yet,

19 *Speculum virginum*, bk. 5, in trans., Barbara Newman, *Listen, Daughter: The* Speculum Virginum *and the Formation of Religious Women in the Middle Ages*, ed. Constant J. Mews (New York: Palgrave, 2001), 286–7.
20 Fulton, *From Judgment*, 270.
21 *Symphonia*, nos. 17, 10, 20, in Barbara Newman, ed. and trans., *Symphonia: A Critical Edition of the Symphonia armonie celestium revelationum*, 2nd edn (Ithaca, N. Y.: Cornell University Press, 1998), 123, 115, 131.
22 Barré, 'Antiennes', 224.
23 Philip of Harvengt, *Commentaria in Cantica canticorum*, PL 203, col. 349.

as one widely quoted early twelfth-century sermon on the Assumption (purportedly the work of Augustine) averred, 'the flesh of Jesus is the flesh of Mary'.[24] How could Mary's body have been allowed to disintegrate in the grave? According to stories circulating in the East from the mid-fifth century at the latest and in the West from as early as the sixth, it had not: Christ appeared with his angels at Mary's tomb only a few days after her death and invited her as his beloved to rise up from the grave. Still, there were questions: how many days after her death had Mary's body lain in the grave? How could the faithful be sure that she was already in heaven and not simply translated elsewhere to await resurrection at the coming of her Son on the Day of Judgement? Logically, or so pseudo-Augustine contended, it is not only possible, but fitting that Christ should not have allowed his mother's body, from which he took flesh without damage to her virginity, to become 'food for worms'. 'Potuit, voluit, decuit, fecit', as a good student of Anselm, possibly even Eadmer of Canterbury (d. c. 1128), might say. 'He was able, he was willing, it was fitting, so he did it.'

Others longed for more immediate reassurance, which, on occasion, the Virgin herself was willing to give. The Benedictine nun Elisabeth of Schönau (d. 1165) received one such revelation, in a series of visions which came to her over the course of three years at the feast of the Assumption. Pressed by 'one of our elders' to ask of the Virgin about the manner of her assumption, Elisabeth fell into a trance in which she saw 'in a far-away place a tomb surrounded by great light, and what looked like the form of a woman in it, with a great multitude of angels standing around. After a while, [the woman] was raised up from the tomb and, together with that multitude standing by, she was lifted up on high.' Thereupon, 'a man – glorious beyond all reckoning – came from the height of the heavens' with another great gathering of angels 'to meet her'. 'While I was watching this', Elisabeth continued, 'my Lady advanced to the door of light in which I usually saw her, and standing there she showed me her glory'. Elisabeth was subsequently given to understand that she had seen 'how our Lady was taken up into heaven in flesh as well as in spirit', and further, that this event had taken place not on 15 August, which was properly only the day of her death, but rather forty days after that, on 23 September.[25] According to what Mary later told Birgitta of Sweden (d. 1373), however, her body lay in the tomb after it was buried in the earth

---

24 *De assumptione beatae Mariae virginis*, PL 40, cols. 1141–8.
25 *Elisabeth of Schönau, The Complete Works*, trans. Anne L. Clark (New York: Paulist Press, 2000), 209–11.

only some fifteen days, 'after which it was taken up into heaven by a multitude of angels. And this number', Mary went on, 'is not without a great mystery, for in the seventh hour there shall be a general resurrection of bodies, and in the eighth hour the bliss of both souls and bodies shall be fulfilled.'[26]

Of such, then, were the Joys of Mary on which late medieval Christians meditated in their prayers: the angel's greeting at the Annunciation, the Nativity of her son, his Resurrection and Ascension, and her Assumption into heaven and Coronation as Queen.[27] There were, nevertheless, Sorrows to accompany the Joys. As Simeon had warned her: 'A sword shall pierce through your own soul' (Luke 2.35). Her soul, but also, compassionately, her body, because, as exegetes like William of Newburgh explained, it was 'bone of her bones and flesh of her flesh' (cf. Gen. 2.23) that she watched being arrested, tried, stripped, scourged, mocked, crucified, drained of blood and buried. Indeed, or so William's near contemporaries Arnold of Bonneval (d. after 1159) and Ogier of Locedio (d. 1214) would insist, the identity, by way of her maternal affection, was absolute: 'The wounds of the dying Christ were the wounds of the mother; the pains of Christ were cruel torturers in the soul of the mother.'[28] Moreover, William imagined, so wracked was she by her Son's pain that she begged to be allowed to drink the cup of his passion, 'so that just as once...I cooperated in the mystery of your holy incarnation, so even now by suffering with you...I may cooperate devotedly in the human redemption'.[29] That she did not die, it was later reasoned, was evidence enough that it was God alone who had given her strength to withstand her grief, for she 'loued her sonne god & man wyth more charite then euer myghte eny that was begotten of woman loue hymselfe or eny other'.[30] And yet, no more could she fail to suffer with her son as he died than could he allow her body to rot in the grave: 'Caro enim Jesu caro est Mariae.'

Devotionally, the identity was likewise absolute, often vividly so, as in Rogier van der Weyden's (d. 1464) famous *Descent from the Cross*, commissioned for their Lady Chapel by the Archers' Guild of Louvain. Here, just as Christ's body droops supported by Nicodemus and Joseph of Arimathea, so Mary's body collapses in the arms of the other Marys who stood with her at

26 Bridget, *Liber celestis*, bk. 6, chap. 62, in Elizabeth Spearing, trans., *Medieval Writings on Female Spirituality* (Harmondsworth: Penguin, 2002), 154.

27 *Ancrene wisse*, part 1, trans. Hugh White (Harmondsworth: Penguin, 1993), 20–1.

28 Ogier, 'Quis dabit', in Thomas Bestul, ed. and trans., *Texts of the Passion: Latin Devotional Literature and Medieval Society* (Philadelphia: University of Pennsylvania Press, 1996), 174–5.

29 William, *Explanatio*, ed. Gorman, 104–5.

30 *Myroure of oure Ladye*, ed. Blunt, 250.

the foot of the Cross and John.[31] Again, in books of hours such as that made in the 1470s for Mary of Burgundy, where miniatures of the Passion illustrate the Office of the Virgin, every hour of every day recapitulated Christ and Mary's corresponding sorrow and pain.[32] Mary's cooperation at her Son's death, such miniatures suggest, was of a piece with her cooperation at his birth: as he suffered in the garden on the night he was betrayed (Matins), so she suffered at the Annunciation, wondering if what the angel said were true; as he suffered in his trial before Pontius Pilate (Prime), so she suffered at the Visitation, knowing, even as the babe leapt in her womb, what kind of death he was to die. Sorrow, her devotees well understood, was attendant upon her every Joy, for as much as she loved her Son, so much she sorrowed at his death. And, indeed, more so than her purity at his (and her) conception, more so even than her beauty at his birth and her majesty by his side in heaven, it was, arguably, above all, her suffering hour by hour on her Son's way to Calvary that gave her such great power over other human hearts, not least because it taught them how to pray: 'Obsecro te, domina sancta Maria, dulcis mater Ihesu Christi...'[33]

Why pray to Mary, a creature, rather than directly to God? This was the question the sixteenth-century reformers asked themselves as they set about dismantling the devotion to the Virgin built up over the centuries in the hearts and minds, monasteries, Lady Chapels and pilgrimage churches of medieval Europe. It is difficult now, with the distance of centuries, to appreciate what, exactly, Europe subsequently lost, although, as Henry Adams aptly observed a century ago, it was clearly something of great power: 'All the steam in the world', he opined, 'could not, like the Virgin, build Chartres.'[34] Nevertheless, before we conclude with the sixteenth-century reformers – not to mention the majority of their successors, Catholic as well as Protestant and secular – that, for all its generative economic, artistic and architectural power, the late medieval cult of the Virgin was 'decadent', long overdue for a 'purge',[35] perhaps we might pause for a moment and ask a slightly different question: 'What does it mean to pray?'

31  Otto von Simson, 'Compassio and Co-redemptio in Roger van der Weyden's Descent from the Cross', Art Bulletin 35 (1953), 9–16.
32  Vienna, Österreichische Nationalbibliothek, Codex Vindobonensis 1857.
33  André Wilmart, 'Prières de compassion', in Auteurs spirituels et textes dévots du Moyen Âge latin: Études d'histoire littéraire (Paris: Études Augustiniennes, 1971), 526.
34  Henry Adams, Education of Henry Adams (Washington, D.C.: Printed by the author, 1907), 339.
35  Hilda Graef, Mary: A History of Doctrine and Devotion, 2 vols. in 1 (London: Sheed and Ward, 1985), vol. 1, 273, 320–2.

Modern historians of medieval devotion have tended to assume, largely, one suspects, on the basis of the stories collected at pilgrimage shrines, that for medieval people, at least, prayer was primarily a matter of asking for things: food, health, wealth, peace, help in childbirth, victory over one's enemies, release from prison, and so forth. And, to be sure, there is ample evidence in both the more literary and the strictly shrine-based miracle collections to suggest that Mary's devotees were inclined in times of crisis to make such direct requests of the 'mama' whom they hoped 'would fix everything'.[36] Nevertheless, as we have seen, by far the majority of formally attested prayers, including the Marian Offices of the books of hours and the meditations of the rosary, likewise the symbols and titles of the Virgin thereby invoked, are significantly more complex in not only their structure and their imagery, but also their theology, than such bald critiques of 'excess' would typically allow.

Prayer was potentially dangerous as well as comforting. Demons were said to have been seen lurking about the choirs, ready to collect every misspoken word and syllable as failings to be marked against the souls of the monks and nuns at Judgement. Notes sung too beautifully might tempt the singer to pride. Even more perilously, 'for god lyste not to here his prayer that hereth not hymselfe ne takyth not hede to here hys prayer', the prayer might be said or sung perfectly, and yet, only with the lips. Above all, therefore, when attempting to pray, one ought to prepare oneself at the outset, as the Birgittine *Myroure of oure Ladye* suggested, by saying with one's full attention one of the simpler prayers, for example, the Ave Maria. The 'harpe of the harte' thus having been tuned to 'the melody of our lordes praysynge', at once the sense, the words and the music of the prayers would 'serue to stirre the soulle, to loue, and to worship & to prayse god, & to haue ioye and deuocyon in hym'.[37] The words, in other words, both in form and content, mattered. We have already had occasion to note why in our reflections on God's and Mary's creative and re-creative 'Fiat'.

Could such speaking or singing ever be truly 'excessive'? Perhaps – if, that is, it were possible to praise God too much. The more usual problem, in medieval Christian terms, was always, however, how to praise him enough.

It was right to praise the Virgin Mary, or so medieval European Christians insisted in their devotions and prayers, because it was Mary who, by giving birth to him in the flesh, made the God-man visible in his human form. It was, likewise, Mary, above all, who made God the Creator visible, by reflecting in

36 Johnson, 'Marian Devotion', 411.
37 *Myroure of oure Ladye*, ed. Blunt, 39–60.

the mirror of her beauty the radiant purity of his Creation as both material and work of art. And it was Mary, in her suffering with her Son as she stood by him under his cross, who made God visible as empowering and inspiring love and in doing so taught those praying to her how they, too, might participate, through love, in both her Sorrows and her Joys. As the theologian and novelist Dorothy Sayers (d. 1957) once pointed out, citing Thomas Aquinas, but foreshadowing more recent work on the way in which our cognitive structures are embodied in metaphor,

> To forbid the making of pictures about God would be to forbid thinking about God at all, for man is so made that he has no way to think except in pictures… All language about God must…necessarily be analogical. We need not be surprised at this… The fact is, that all language about everything is analogical; we think in a series of metaphors.[38]

One such 'picture-thought' may be found in the language of the creed: 'one God the Father Almighty, Maker of Heaven and earth…one Lord Jesus Christ, the only-begotten Son…[and] the Holy Ghost the Lord, the Giver of life…who with the Father and the Son together is worshipped and glorified'. Another may be found in the late medieval so-called Shrine Madonnas, small wooden statues of the Virgin and Child which open up to reveal the Trinity depicted as the Throne of Grace, the Father supporting the crucified Son with the Holy Ghost as dove hovering in-between.[39] Here, the Virgin as the 'throne the Godhead never left' quite literally makes visible God as the Maker, Redeemer and Sustainer of Heaven and earth.[40] Yet another may be found in the *Myroure of oure Ladye*, at the exposition for the third lesson for the Sunday office of Matins, wherein is shown 'the greate loue that god had to oure lady endelessly or eny thynge was made' by way of the oil, wheat and wine provided by Abraham for Isaac before he was conceived:

> For as the fatnesse of oyle may not burne tyl a weyke or matche be put therto, ryghte so the moste feruente charite of the father shone not openly in the worlde tyl hys sonne had taken to hym a manly body that ys vnderstonded by the weyke of the O synguler chosen spouse of God… And as whete may not be made brede tyl yt be made redy wyth many instruments, ryghte so the sonne of god…appered not vnder the lykenesse of brede to the fowde of men tylle hys body was made of many members and ryghte shape in thy blessed wombe… And also as wyne may not be borne but yf vessels be fyrste made

---

38  Dorothy Sayers, *The Mind of the Maker* (repr., New York: Harper Collins, 1987), 22–3.
39  Christoph Baumer, 'Die Schreinmadonna', *Marian Library Studies* 9 (1977), 239–72.
40  Heinrich von Meissen, alias Frauenlob (d. 1318), 'Marienleich', trans. Newman, *God and the Goddesses*, 252.

redy, and lykewyse the grace of the holy gooste that is vnderstonded by the wyne oughte not to be gyuen to man to endelesse lyfe tylle the body of thy moste loued sonne…were made redy by passyon and by dethe.

Light, food and life, by way of a word: 'Fiat mihi', and the Creator of the world became the Virgin's spouse. And 'by thys holsom vessel, all swetnesse of grace ys mynystred and gyuen moste plenteously to aungels and men'.[41] How could it ever be possible to praise her, mother of all re-created things and perfect mirror of God in his creative divinity, enough?

41 *Myroure of oure Ladye*, ed. Blunt, 113.

# 19

# Mysticism and transcendence

AMY HOLLYWOOD

In the ninth book of his *Confessions*, the North African theologian Augustine of Hippo (354–430) describes life immediately after his conversion to orthodox Christianity – a conversion for which Augustine's mother, Monica, prayed from the time of his birth. In the midst of recounting the transformations wrought in his life by conversion, Augustine writes in praise of his mother and tells of an episode in which the close tie between her salvation and his own is rendered explicit.

Resting at Ostia before their long sea voyage from Italy to North Africa, Monica and Augustine lean 'from a window which overlooked the garden in the courtyard of the house' where they were staying. There they wondered together 'what the eternal life of the saints would be like' and their conversation led them to conclude 'that no bodily pleasure, however great it might be and whatever earthly light might shed luster upon it, was worthy of comparison, or even of mention, beside the happiness of the life of the saints'. As they spoke, Augustine writes, 'the flame of love burned stronger' in them both and raised them 'higher toward the eternal God'. Their thoughts ranged over all material things and up to the heavens and from thence beyond the material heavens to their own souls.

Yet 'the eternal life of the saints' lay beyond even the realm of immaterial souls, in a place of 'everlasting peace' governed by Wisdom:

> And while we spoke of the eternal Wisdom, longing for it and straining for it with all the strength of our hearts, for one fleeting instant we reached out and touched it. Then with a sigh, leaving our spiritual harvest bound to it, we returned to the sound of our own speech, in which each word has a beginning and an ending – far, far different from your Word, our Lord, who abides in himself for ever, yet never grows old and gives new life to all things.[1]

---

[1] Augustine of Hippo, *Confessions*, bk. IX, Section 10, trans. R. S. Pine-Coffin (Harmondsworth: Penguin, 1961), 197–8.

Deeply dependent on the Neoplatonic ontologies crucial to the process of his conversion, Augustine here describes a movement through the material to the immaterial and, further, from the realm of souls to that of Wisdom.

Yet where the pagan philosopher Plotinus (d. 270) writes of the individual soul's movement into, through and beyond itself into universal Soul, the Mind and the One, Augustine insists on the necessity of divine mediation for this uplifting and return to occur. Just as the mediation of the incarnate Christ is necessary to Augustine's final conversion, here Wisdom is the Word, the God become human through whom salvation becomes possible. (And whereas in Plotinus the creation of all things occurs through the emanation of the One into the Mind, the Mind into Soul, and the Soul into the realm of material creation, for Augustine creation occurs through Christ as Word and Wisdom, who 'gives new life to all things'.)

I start with Augustine because his work sets the agenda for the mysticism of the high and late Middle Ages. If the years from 1100 to 1500 are often seen as the moment of mysticism's 'flowering' in the West,[2] the foundations for this tradition are laid by Greek and Latin Christians writing in late antiquity and the early Middle Ages. For this reason, I will at times make reference to this earlier work, which provides the background against which monks, nuns, members of the new religious movements and eventually the laity lived, practised, and thought about the mystical life.

Thus, although scholars continue to debate whether or not Augustine himself was a mystic,[3] there is no doubt that this passage from the *Confessions* encapsulates themes crucial to the development of Western Christian mysticism. The episode is marked by four features that will play an important role in subsequent mystical traditions. First, Augustine and Monica strive to transcend not only the material realm, but also their own individual souls. Although primarily grounded in the use of the intellect, love – signified here by the heart – is also crucial to the process of transcendent uplifting. Secondly, in so far as they touch that transcendent Wisdom in which their souls are contained and unified, Augustine and Monica do so only fleetingly. This momentary grasp of the divine Word, thirdly, is explicitly

---

2 This is the metaphor used by Bernard McGinn for the thirteenth and fourteenth century. Yet one can easily argue, as I suggest here, that the 'flowering' begins with the Cistercian mystics of the twelfth century. See Bernard McGinn, *The Presence of God: A History of Western Christian Mysticism*, vol. 3, *The Flowering of Mysticism: Men and Women in the New Mysticism – 1200–1350* (New York: Crossroad, 1998).

3 See Bernard McGinn, *The Presence of God*, vol. 1, *The Foundations of Mysticism: Origins to the Fifth Century* (New York: Crossroad, 1992), 229–31 and the literature cited there.

contrasted to human speech. Augustine and Monica know that they no longer touch Wisdom when they return 'to the sound of [their] own speech, in which each word has a beginning and an ending'. Human speech, unlike the divine Word, occupies time, in which things have a beginning and an ending. The divine Word, on the other hand, is eternal and 'abides in himself for ever, yet never grows old'. The limitations of human speech to encompass divine Wisdom are further marked by the proliferation of metaphors – from the realms of sight, taste, touch, hearing and thought – with which Augustine attempts to articulate his and Monica's striving after and brief attainment of the divine. Finally, Augustine's experience is resolutely communal; he comes to the Word in and through his conversation with Monica. Together they 'reach out and touch' divine Wisdom and together they fall back into human speech and the 'region of unlikeness' in which creatures dwell until that time when they will come to eternal life in God.

Read in this way, Augustine provides a broadly phenomenological account of Christian mystical experience as it is articulated from the fifth to the sixteenth centuries (and in some cases, far beyond). More accurately, perhaps, his descriptions – in the *Confessions* and elsewhere – of the transcendence, transience, ineffability, and communal nature of mystical experience provide the parameters within which medieval Christians understand experiences of God and of union with God. Medieval Christian mysticism can be understood as a series of ongoing experiential, communal, and textual commentaries on and debates about the possibilities and limitations Augustine sets for the earthly encounter between God and humanity.

## Transcendence

Many of the debates about whether Augustine was a mystic circle around whether he himself claimed to have achieved an experience of the divine or of union with the divine. The *Confessions* offer clear evidence that he did, but many within the Augustinian tradition continue to be wary about claims to union with the divine. A number of crucial issues are at stake in these debates. The first, of concern more to modern scholars of mysticism than to medieval theologians, is whether mysticism – a term not available in its substantive form within the Middle Ages[4] – involves experiences simply of God's presence or of union with God. If claims are made to the latter, as they often are within

4 On the history of the terms 'mystic', 'mystical', and 'mysticism', see Louis Bouyer, 'Mysticism: An Essay on the History of the Word', in Richard Woods, ed., *Understanding*

medieval texts, is this union one in which the soul maintains its own identity or is the soul submerged into the divine? And finally, what is the best way for one to achieve union, however it is understood? Does one come to union through knowledge or love – the mind or the heart – or some combination of the two?

Claims not only to experience God's presence but also some kind of union with God occur throughout the texts of early Christianity; they are arguably found in Augustine and also in Clement (d. c. 215), Origen (c. 185–254), Gregory of Nyssa (c. 335–94), in the texts attributed to Dionysius the Areopagite (c. 500), and in a host of martyrological, hagiographical, and monastic texts. In the medieval west, the influence of Augustine and Dionysius looms largest, and both suggest – without clearly asserting – that union involves a dissolution of the self before and in God. Yet the mainstream of the Augustinian tradition, represented by the work of Bernard of Clairvaux (1090–1153) and his fellow Cistercians, as well as that of the twelfth-century Victorines and much thirteenth- and fourteenth-century Franciscan mystical writing, insists on a union of wills in which the soul maintains its identity as other than God even as it feels as if that distinction is lost.

Drawing on 1 Cor. 6.17 ('Qui autem adhaeret Domino unus spiritus est'– 'One who adheres to the Lord is one spirit with him'), Bernard of Clairvaux asks 'when will [the soul] experience this kind of love, so that the mind, drunk with divine love and forgetting itself, making itself like a broken vessel (1 Cor. 6.17), marches right into God, and, adhering to him, becomes one spirit with him?'[5] Against any who might suggest that the union of the soul's will with that of God is like that between the Father and the Son, Bernard insists that the human person and God 'do not share the same nature or substance' and so 'they cannot be said to be a unity, yet they are with complete truth and accuracy, said to be one spirit, if they cohere with the bond of love. But that unity is caused not so much by the identity of essences as by the concurrence of wills.'[6] Bernard thus both asserts that union between the soul and God is possible in this life and that this union never occurs at the expense of the continued creaturely existence of the soul. We come to be one with God

*Mysticism* (Garden City, N.Y.: Image Books, 1980), 42–55; and Michel de Certeau, "Mystique" au XVIIe siècle: Le problème du langage "mystique"', in *L'homme devant Dieu: Mélanges offerts au Père Henri de Lubac* (Paris: Aubier, 1964), vol. 2, 267–91.

5 Bernard of Clairvaux, *On Loving God*, in G. R. Evans, trans., *Selected Works* (New York: Paulist Press, 1987), X.27, 195. Translation modified.
6 Bernard of Clairvaux, *Sermons on the Song of Songs IV*, trans. Irene Edmonds (Kalamazoo, Mich: Cistercian Publications, 1980), Sermon 71, n. 7, 54.

when, through God's grace, we have so overcome our sinfulness as to have a will that fully adheres to God's will.

The notion of a union of wills remains central to the theological articulation of mystical experience throughout the Middle Ages. Yet there is a counter-trend, one first visible in northern Europe in the late thirteenth and early fourteenth centuries (although there is evidence for similar views espoused contemporaneously south of the Alps). The beguines Hadewijch (c. 1250) and Marguerite Porete (d. 1310) and the Dominican Meister Eckhart (c. 1260–1328) suggest that complete union with God occurs when the soul not only over-comes its sinfulness, but also its very creatureliness or createdness. Hadewijch hints at this view in a vision in which an angel shows her an ideal, 'full grown' Hadewijch who is enclosed within the deity and who has never fallen into sin.[7] Marguerite Porete goes further, arguing that the truly free and annihilated soul – one who has not only overcome her own sin and will, but who has also *destroyed* reason, will and desire – exists there 'where she was before she was'.[8]

Meister Eckhart provides a Neoplatonic framework for such claims. In his commentary on the Prologue to the Gospel of John, Eckhart draws out his understanding of the self-birth of the Godhead, the external emanation of all things from the divine source, and the return of all things to God. Playing on the double meaning of the Latin term *principium*, Eckhart argues that the opening of the Gospel ('In principio') refers both to the temporal beginning of all things and to their source or principle. For Eckhart, following *The Book of Causes* and other Neoplatonic sources, that which 'is produced or proceeds from anything is precontained in it' and 'it is preexistent in it as a seed in its principle'.[9] Moreover, that which proceeds not only pre-exists in its source, but also *remains* in its source 'just as it was in the beginning before it came to be'.[10] All created things, then, have their principle in another and that principle remains in the other. All of creation has both a virtual and a formal aspect – it therefore has both coeternal and temporal relations to the divine. The grounds for the return of all things to their divine source lies here, for all things have

7 Hadewijch, *The Complete Works*, trans. Mother Columba Hart (New York: Paulist Press, 1980), Vision 4, 274.
8 Marguerite Porete, *The Mirror of Simple Souls*, trans. Edmund Colledge, J. C. Marler and Judith Grant (Notre Dame: University of Notre Dame Press, 1999), ch. 135, 712. Translation modified.
9 Meister Eckhart, *Meister Eckhart: The Essential Sermons, Commentaries, Treatises, and Defense*, trans. Edmund Colledge and Bernard McGinn (New York: Paulist Press, 1981), 'Commentary on John', n. 4, 123.
10 *Ibid.*, 124.

their principle in the divine and, insofar as they remain uncreated with that divine ground, eternally participate in the self-birth of the Godhead and of all creation.

Eckhart's Latin works provide the ontological framework for his claims there and in his German sermons and treatises that human beings, insofar as they are created, are absolutely other than the Godhead, but, insofar as they are uncreated, are one with the divine ground. Eckhart's German sermons, in particular, call on his listeners to engage in a process of detachment from all creatureliness – most centrally the operations of the intellect and the will – in order to be one with the Godhead without distinction. While others debate whether knowledge or love – the intellect or the will – provide the best means to attain union with God (and hence the substance of the beatific vision),[11] Eckhart insists that the truly just human being detaches from both, insofar as they are created, in order to give birth to justice, who is the Son himself:

> The Father gives birth to his Son without ceasing; and I say more; he gives me birth, me, his Son and the same Son. I say more: he gives birth not only to me, his Son, but he gives birth to me as himself and himself as me and to me as his being and nature. In the innermost source, there I spring out in the Holy Spirit, where there is one life and one being and one work. Everything God performs is one; therefore he gives me, his Son, birth without any distinction.[12]

## Transience

Eckhart claims Augustinian warrants for his understanding of the union between the ground of the soul and the ground of the divine, yet it is unlikely that Augustine would have been comfortable with Eckhart's claims concerning the soul's ability fully to transcend its created nature. (Certainly his inquisitors were not, although in large part because of their inability to acknowledge Eckhart's distinction between former and virtual creation.)[13]

---

11  On these debates, see Bernard McGinn, 'Love, Knowledge and *Unio Mystica* in the Western Christian Tradition', in Moshe Idel and Bernard McGinn, eds., *Mystical Union in Judaism, Christianity, and Islam: An Ecumenical Dialogue* (New York: Continuum, 1996), 59–86; Bernard McGinn, *The Presence of God*, vol. 2, *The Growth of Mysticism: Gregory the Great through the Twelfth Century* (New York: Crossroad, 1994), 200–3 and 233–74; and McGinn, *The Flowering of Mysticism*, 78–87, 110–12, and 135–6.

12  Eckhart, *Essential Sermons*, German Sermon 6, 186–7. Translation slightly modified.

13  On the issue of Eckhart's condemnation, see Bernard McGinn, 'Eckhart's Condemnation Reconsidered', *The Thomist* 44 (1980), 390–414; and Bernard McGinn, *The Mystical Thought of Meister Eckhart: The Man from Whom God Hid Nothing* (New York: Herder and Herder, 2001), 14–19.

Even more clearly at odds with the Augustinian tradition is the development, in the thirteenth century, of accounts of divine union lasting not for brief moments, but for hours, days, perhaps even for a lifetime.

Bernard of Clairvaux once again sets the background against which the innovative nature of these claims becomes visible. Like Augustine in the *Confessions*, Bernard insists that any experience of union with God is exceptional and fleeting while in this life:

> I shall call him blessed and holy to whom it is given to experience even for a single instant something which is rare indeed in this life. To lose yourself as though you did not exist and to have no sense of yourself, to be emptied of yourself (Phil. 2.7) and almost annihilated, belongs to heavenly not to human love.[14]

Bernard represents the mainstream of the medieval tradition, which makes use of a specialised language to describe union with God and the heights of the contemplative life, always understood as necessarily brief.[15] As the thirteenth-century beguine Mechthild of Magdeburg insists, to remain in such a state would be 'death' to the senses and the body.[16]

Yet in the mystical hagiographies of women and men produced in the Low Countries during the thirteenth century, we begin to see accounts of ecstasies and raptures that last for days and weeks on end. James of Vitry (c. 1170–1240), for example, in his life of the beguine Marie of Oignies (1176–1213), describes her long ecstatic raptures:

> Sometimes she would gently rest with the Lord in a sweet and blessed silence for thirty-five days and she never ate any corporeal food and could utter no word except this alone: 'I want the Body of Our Lord Jesus Christ.' When she had received it, she would remain with the Lord in silence for whole days at a time. On those days she had the feeling that her spirit was separated, as it were, from her body…and…so abstracted was she from sensible things and rapt above herself in some kind of ecstasy (*excessus*). Finally, after five weeks, she returned to herself and opened her mouth and received corporeal food and she spoke to those who had been standing around her and who had been struck with wonder.[17]

---

14 Bernard of Clairvaux, *Selected Works*, 'On Loving God', X, 27, 195.
15 For the brevity of union in Gregory the Great and Bernard of Clairvaux, see McGinn, *Growth of Mysticism*, 63–70, 190–3 and 208–13.
16 Most famously, see Mechthild of Magdeburg, *The Flowing Light of the Godhead*, trans. Frank Tobin (New York: Paulist Press, 1993), Book I, ch. 44, 58–62.
17 Jacques de Vitry, *The Life of Marie d'Oignies*, trans. Margot H. King (Toronto: Peregrina Publishing, 1998), Book I, n. 25, 65–6.

As Bernard McGinn notes, James here uses language found within the contemplative monastic traditions of Gregory the Great and Bernard of Clairvaux to describe Marie's state (*'separatus a corpore, a sensibilibus abstracta, in excessu rapta'*), which lasts for days and weeks at a time.[18] Marguerite Porete again takes the position to its extreme, suggesting that the free and annihilated soul is able to remain unencumbered indefinitely. (Although it is important to recognise that, for Porète, such souls no longer are subject to the kinds of raptures and ecstasies described by James.)[19] The radicality of this claim, which implies that while on earth the soul can permanently attain a state in which it no longer requires any mediation between itself and God, may have led to her condemnation.[20]

## Ineffability

All those medieval Christians who write about union with God insist on the inability of human language ever fully to capture that experience. Yet this ineffability is enacted in innumerable ways. Bernard of Clairvaux piles biblical text upon biblical text, moving through the full range of divine revelation to suggest the experiential richness of the soul's fleeting apprehension of God. Metaphors of sight, touch, taste, smell and audition run throughout his treatises, sermons and commentaries, all meant to evoke – without claiming fully to capture – the multivalent nature of the soul's experience of God. Yet following in the tradition inaugurated by Origen, Bernard insists on the spiritual nature of the senses whose experiences are elicited and described through biblical language. In the thirteenth century, not only is the fleeting nature of these experiences called into question, but also the line between bodily and spiritual is much less sharply drawn. Hadewijch, for example, writes of the soul's multi-sensory experiences of God in ways that render unclear whether she understands them as only spiritual or as also partaking in the corporeal.[21]

---

18 McGinn, *Flowering of Mysticism*, 37–8. On William of Auvergne's (d. 1249) conflation of the language of lovesickness and mystical rapture, see Mary Wack, *Lovesickness in the Middle Ages: The 'Viaticum' and its Commentaries* (Philadelphia: University of Pennsylvania Press, 1990), 23–4.

19 Porète, *Mirror of Simple Souls*, esp. ch. 118, 142–6.

20 On Porete's condemnation and execution, see Paul Verdeyen, 'Le procès d'inquisition contre Marguerite Porète et Guiard de Cressonessart (1309–1310)', *Revue d'histoire ecclésiastique* 81 (1986), 47–94.

21 For an account that reads Hadewijch's language as at least in part somatic, see Caroline Walker Bynum, *Holy Feast and Holy Fast: The Religious Significance of Food to Medieval Women* (Berkeley: University of California Press, 1987), 153–65. For a detailed account of

In one of her most famous visions, Hadewijch describes Christ's appearance – first as a child and then as a full-grown man – in the reception of the eucharist.

> With that he came in the form and clothing of a Man, as he was on the day when he gave us his Body for the first time; looking like a Human Being and a Man, wonderful, and beautiful, and with glorious face, he came to me as humbly as anyone who wholly belongs to another. Then he gave himself to me in the shape of the Sacrament, in its outward form, as the custom is; and then he gave me to drink from the chalice, in form and taste, as the custom is. After that he came himself to me, took me entirely in his arms, and pressed me to him; and all of my members felt his in full felicity, in accordance with the desire of my heart and my humanity. So that I was outwardly satisfied and fully transported.[22]

Like the trembling and quivering of her heart and veins that proceed this vision, Hadewijch's corporeal language can easily be read as an account of experiences undergone by both the body and soul in loving union with the body and soul of Christ.

Yet even if we understand Hadewijch's language as somatic as well as spiritual, it is important to recognise the limits she places on the ability of this language and this experience to articulate fully her union with God. Thus she goes on to describe an *internal* union with the Son in which the senses are 'unsaid' and language itself finally fails.

> But soon, after a short time, I lost that manly beauty outwardly in the sight of his form. I saw him completely come to nought and so fade and all at once dissolve that I could no longer recognize or perceive him outside of me, and I could no longer distinguish him within me. Then it was to me as if we were one without difference.[23]

Whereas Augustine, Dionysius, Eckhart and other male exegetes argue for and enact the apophasis or 'unsaying' of the names of the divine (found within Scripture and philosophy), Hadewijch here uses her visionary ecstatic experience as the cataphatic base for apophasis. The ineffability of divine union is thus performatively rendered in and through her experience and her text.

---

the spiritual senses and insistence on Hadewijch's language as fully spiritual, see Gordon Rudy, *The Mystical Language of Sensation in the Later Middle Ages* (New York: Routledge, 2002).
22 Hadewijch, *Complete Works*, Vision 7, 281.
23 *Ibid.*

## Community

Arguably medieval Christian mystical traditions in the West diverge most fully from Augustine with regard to the communal nature of union. Whereas Augustine insists that he comes to touch Wisdom with his mother Monica, Hadewijch explicitly *rejects* union with Augustine. After a vision in which she sees her soul, together with Augustine's, come together to be swallowed by 'the Unity in which the Trinity dwells, wherein both [of them were] lost', Hadewijch found herself 'poor and miserable'. Angry that she must share the fruition of the Godhead with another and that God would wish her to take pleasure in union with another, Hadewijch ingeniously makes her own lowliness the basis for her audaciously high claims:

> For I am a free human creature, and also pure as to one part and I can desire freely with my will, and I can will as highly as I wish, and seize and receive from God all that he is, without objection or anger on his part – which no saint can do. For the saints have their will perfectly according to their pleasure; and they can no longer will beyond what they have. I have hated many great wonderful deeds and experiences, because I wished to belong to Love alone, and because I could not believe that any human creature loved him so passionately as I – although I know it is a fact and indubitable still I cannot believe it or feel it, so powerfully am I touched by Love.[24]

Yet despite her insistence that she cannot believe another can love God as she loves God, Hadewijch's work as a whole is directed towards communities of women with whom she wishes to share in this intransigent desire. Writing to fellow beguines (from whom she has been separated), Hadewijch calls on them to pursue the goals she here insists belong to her alone.

Hadewijch's anomalous claims suggest the tensions between the desire for a Christian mystical community and the insistence that human particularity remains within the experience of union with God. Augustine and Monica can – and perhaps inevitably must – touch Wisdom together because they exist as one in the exemplary human being who rests within Wisdom, their creator (for Augustine sees union taking place at the level of our human created nature, thus in and through the figure of Adam). For Porete and Eckhart, the loss of distinction between God and the soul occurs at an even more fundamental level; we are not only united in and through the created exemplar of our humanity, but in the uncreated source (in other words, in Wisdom itself). (It must be remembered, of course, that both Porète and

---

24 *Ibid.*, Vision II, 290–I.

Eckhart were condemned.) Here Hadewijch is much more like Bernard of Clairvaux in her insistence on the substantial nature of the created being who stands in relation to the divine. Yet unlike Bernard, who argues that union occurs only through the adherence of the human to the divine will, Hadewijch argues for a union born of desire. That desire, moreover, feels itself to be singular, even as it recognises its communal nature. Communities may exhort and support such intrepid believers, but at least for Hadewijch, her wilful desire is for Love alone.

PART V

*

# CHRISTIAN LIFE IN MOVEMENT

20

# On the margins of religious life: hermits and recluses, penitents and tertiaries, beguines and beghards

WALTER SIMONS

In the last fifty years or so, the history of medieval Christianity has cast its gaze beyond the well-known figures – the popes and bishops, emperors and kings, saints and monks – who shaped the older narratives and expressed the era's most enduring ideals. Historians now routinely consider the lowly rural priest, the industrious nun, and the masses of lay people who formed the *populus Christi* of the chronicles. The shift in perspective does more than simply expand the picture: it allows us to recognise the roles played by individuals and communities labouring in the margins of church institutions and conventional society. This essay examines a diverse but important group of people who defy easy categorisation yet were all loosely associated with religious life. As hermits and recluses, lay 'penitents', beguines and beghards, their status was ambiguous, straddling the border between the lay and monastic (or religious) categories of society. Although they identified them-selves as orthodox Christians and were indeed often praised as supremely devout, they tended to resist incorporation into the formal structures of religious life and left little trace in official records until about 1100. In the period covered by this volume, however, their numbers, influence and public prominence increased widely. The study of their *via media* or *status tertius*, as it was sometimes called in the late Middle Ages, or semi-religiosity, a term coined by modern scholars,[1] reveals a great variety of ways in which religious commitment could be expressed, and as such it illustrates both the process by which monastic ideals inspired religious life of the laity as well as the emergent questioning or even subversion of the monastic ideal.

---

1 Overview by Kaspar Elm, 'Vita regularis sine regula. Bedeutung, Rechtsstellung und Selbstverständnis des mittelalterlichen und frühneuzeitlichen Semireligiosentums', in Frantisek Smahel and Elisabeth Müller-Luckner, eds., *Häresie und vorzeitige Reformation im Spätmittelalter* (Munich: R. Oldenbourg, 1998), 239–73.

## Hermits and recluses

Antecedents to this way of life reach far back, to the sacred widowhood of early Christian women, for instance, and hermits stood of course at the basis of monasticism itself. As monastic institutions spread across the West in the early Middle Ages, setting the standards of personal perfection, the informal modes of religious life drifted into obscurity, although they certainly did not disappear. Shortly after the turn of the millennium, contemporary sources, first in central Italy and then in north-western Europe, began to report on numerous hermits and recluses who were sought out as spiritual guides or travelled the land as 'wandering preachers'. Soon hermits formed the vanguard of the new movement towards evangelical or 'apostolic' poverty, and their asceticism, preaching and personal example reinvigorated church thought from top to bottom. Peter the Hermit's role in the launching of the First Crusade is well known, but he was preceded in this capacity by another hermit, Adelelmus of La Chaise-Dieu, who in about 1080 led a Christian army in battle during the Spanish Reconquista.[2] A great many orders of monks or regular canons born in the eleventh and early twelfth centuries owe their origins to the activities of such ascetic wanderers, from the Camaldolesi (created by Romuald, d. 1027) and Vallombrosians (John Gualbert, d. 1073) to the orders of Arrouaise (Roger of Transloy, d. about 1095), Fontevraud (Robert of Arbrissel, d. 1117), Grandmont (Stephen of Muret, d. 1124), Prémontré (Norbert of Xanten, d. 1134) and of course La Grande Chartreuse (Bruno of Cologne, d. 1101) and Cîteaux (Robert of Molesme, d. 1110), to name only the most important. Indeed, rare seems to be the monastic house founded in this age that does not claim to have started as a hermitage.

It is not easy to imagine how this life was accomplished in practice. Some of the initial leaders of the movement may have been inspired by the Greek traditions of hermits with which they became personally familiar in southern Italy[3] as part of the broader pattern of intensified social and cultural contact between East and West in the eleventh century. Others exploited the

---

2  Ralph the Monk, *Vita Adelelmi Casae Dei*, ed. E. Flórez in *España Sagrada*, vol. 27 (Madrid: M. F. Rodriguez, 1772), 832–41, at 839.

3  See Jean-Marie Martin, 'L'érémitisme grec et latin en Italie méridionale (Xe–XIIIe siècle)', in André Vauchez, ed., *Ermites de France et d'Italie (XIe–XVe siècle)* (Rome: École française de Rome, 2003), 175–98; for the development of the order of Camaldoli, see Cécile Caby, *De l'érémitisme rural au monachisme urbain: Les Camaldules en Italie à la fin du Moyen Âge* (Rome: École française de Rome, 1999), and for the eremitical movement in general, Henriette Leyser, *Hermits and the New Monasticism: A Study of Religious Communities in Western Europe 1000–1150* (London: Macmillan, 1984).

opportunities for personal isolation afforded to select monks in the Western tradition, as for instance in the Rule of Benedict, where it is said that such men, 'no longer driven by the novice fervour of religious life but extensively tested within the monastery, having been trained with the help of many others to battle against the devil and well equipped, leave the battle line of the brethren for single combat in the desert'.[4] Even at Cluny, renowned for its strict and properly organised cenobitic observance, quite a few monks lived in separate cells in the woods, where Peter the Venerable would visit them during his abbacy (1122–56)[5]. The retreat to the *eremum* or *desertum*, a commonplace of ascetic history, should not always be taken literally, and few of the hermits celebrated at this time were truly solitaries – after all, the only fully successful hermit is the one who leaves no documentary record behind.[6] However, all of these men – whether originally monks, canons or laymen – shared a desire to recapture the informal asceticism associated with the primitive church, the ancient desert fathers, and of course Christ's withdrawal to the mountain and by extension his entire life, hence their occasional zeal for preaching, which may appear paradoxical to us. To achieve that ideal, they often rejected some of the norms traditionally laid down in monastic custom, like communal discipline, stability or even the concept of a rule itself. The effort to transcend the monastic model and rejoin biblical purity is memorably combined in Stephen of Muret's refusal to be called a canon, a monk or a hermit, because if he did 'glorify himself' through such titles, 'his glory was nothing' (John 8.54), and his insistence that 'there is no other rule than the gospel'.[7] The anonymous author of the remarkable *Libellus de diversis ordinibus*, writing in

---

4 *Regula Benedicti*, ch. 1, in Adalbert de Vogüé and Jean Neufville, eds., *La Règle de Saint Benoît*, vol. 1 (Paris: Éditions du Cerf, 1971–2), 436–8.

5 *Sancti Petri Venerabilis abbatis Cluniacensis vita*, ed. Martin Marrier and André Duchêne, *Bibliotheca Cluniacensis* (Paris, 1614), cols. 589–601, at 600; see Giles Constable, 'Eremitical Forms of Monastic Life', in *Istituzioni monastichi e istituzioni canonicali in Occidente (1123–1215)* (Milan: Vita e pensiero, 1980), 239–64, at 255–6, 261.

6 Such figures sometimes receive a brief mention in sources about other spiritual leaders of the period, as did Schetzelo, a hermit in the woods near Luxemburg, who for years drew on the 'food of wild pigs' for sustenance and even tried to elude St Bernard's envoys: Herbert of Clairvaux, *De miraculis Cisterciensium monachorum*, ed. PL 185, cols. 453–61, at 456. Roger, an obscure layman who first inhabited the hermitage at the Trunk of Berengar south of Arras, was joined by two clerics, Heldemar and Conon, who may be regarded as the true founders of Arrouaise after Roger's early death: Ludo Milis, *L'ordre des chanoines réguliers d'Arrouaise: Son histoire et son organisation, de la fondation de l'abbaye-mère (vers 1090) à la fin des chapitres annuels (1471)*, vol. 1 (Bruges: De Tempel, 1969), 93–113.

7 Stephen of Lecey, *Vita Stephani Muretensis*, ch. 32, and the anonymous *Liber de doctrina*, prologue, ed. Jean Becquet, *Scriptores ordinis Grandimontenses* (Turnhout: Brepols, 1968), 121 and 5, respectively. As is well known, St Francis shared these sentiments a century later.

Liège between 1121 and 1161, argued that hermits serviced and worshipped God 'gladly' in such informal fashion 'in the earliest era' (*prima aetas*), at the example of

> the just Abel, living in the shade of trees and intent on grazing sheep... For it was right that because there were few men at that time, he whom God deemed worthy to call just should serve God alone and should, as it were, establish the solitary life by grazing sheep, an animal which is without doubt a lover of quietness.

He added rather defensively that the freedom of action enjoyed by hermits in his own day thus held nothing objectionable:

> Let no one else be disturbed if a certain diversity should appear in this order and each arranges his life differently, with some living alone, some with two or three or more, living a life that is easier for some and harder for others, with a diversity such as we find among the hermits of old, and if each uses the power of his choice in order that he may attempt as much as he wishes or as much as his strength allows, and he will not be condemned by the Lord for it.[8]

Such freedom was much harder to attain for female solitaries, who tended to remain in one place, usually a cell attached to a parish church or monastery, where they might be enclosed for life. Like male hermits, female recluses or anchoresses did not always live alone, but with one or more companions – on rare occasions a male hermit,[9] yet more commonly servants or young girls who received instruction in reading and religious matters from the main recluse. Numerous variations on this model were possible, as is shown by a few intriguing sources on the earliest stages in the joint careers of the anchoress Jutta of Disibodenberg (1092–1136) and the visionary Hildegard of Bingen (1098–1179). Jutta, the daughter of the count of Sponheim in Franconia, received 'the habit of holy religion' from the local archbishop at the age of fourteen and sought out a widow, Uda, as her mentor (*magistra*), who lived with her in the residence of Jutta's widowed mother. The eight-year-old Hildegard, donated to the religious life by her parents, joined them there. Having lived together informally as recluses for some time, Jutta, Hildegard

---

8 *Libellus de diversis ordinibus et professionibus qui sunt in aecclesia*, ed. Giles Constable and Bernard Smith (Oxford: Clarendon Press, 1972), 4–6, 14–16 (with part of the translation adapted from Giles Constable, *The Reformation of the Twelfth Century* (Cambridge: Cambridge University Press, 1996), 60.

9 For instance Eve (d. 1113) and Harvey (d. 1119), who lived together near Vendôme, see Monika Otter, *Goscelin of St. Bertin, The Book of Encouragement and Consolation [Liber confortatorius]; The Letter of Goscelin to the Recluse Eva. Translated from the Latin with Introduction, Notes, and Interpretive Essay* (Cambridge: D. S. Brewer, 2004).

and another young girl were finally and solemnly walled up in an anchorhold on 1 November 1112 at the nearby Benedictine monastery of Disibodenberg, with Jutta, now twenty, serving as *magistra* and the others as 'disciples'. After her death in 1136, 'no one was judged more worthy to succeed her in the honour of her magisterium' (*in honore magisterii*) than Hildegard, who eventually became the prioress of a traditional monastic community and a famous spiritual leader in her own right.[10] The case illustrates well that an anchoress's cell formed a fertile breeding ground for monastic life, a school for young girls – a development Aelred of Rievaulx (1110–67) deplored because it impeded contemplation[11] – as well as the site of honourable traditions passed across generations from one woman to the other. By the fourteenth century, when male eremitical life began to decline, female solitaries had become a common sight in many cities and towns, primarily those of the Low Countries, England, France and Germany. Mechelen and Louvain, middle-sized cities in Brabant, had at least five and seven anchorholds in the fourteenth and early sixteenth centuries, respectively.[12] Although in a few cases anchoresses were supported by a quasi-institutional endowment, they more commonly drew on their own personal income – many came from aristocratic or patrician backgrounds – and the gifts of visitors who consulted these 'living saints' on a whole range of issues, theological and practical.[13]

## Penitents and tertiaries

If the eremitical life enjoyed a long-standing reputation, this was not the case for the other informal types of religious life that came to the fore in this age and appealed to an even larger number of people, particularly among the laity.

---

10 See Anna Silvas, ed., *Jutta and Hildegard: The Biographical Sources* (Turnhout: Brepols, 1998), 46–63; quotations are from the *Vita domnae Juttae inclusae*, ed. Franz Staab, 'Reform und Reformgruppen im Erzbistum Mainz. Vom "Libellus de Willigisi consuetudinibus" zur "Vita domnae Juttae inclusae"', in Stefan Weinfurter, ed., *Reformidee und Reformpolitik im spätsalisch-frühstaufischen Reich* (Mainz: Selbstverlag der Gesellschaft für Mittelrheinische Kirchengeschichte, 1992), 119–87, at 174, 184, 185, and Guibert of Gembloux's notes on Hildegard in his Letter 38, ed. Albert Derolez, *Guiberti Gemblacensis epistolae*, vol. 2 (Turnhout: Brepols, 1989), 375.

11 *De institutione inclusarum*, ed. Anselm Hoste and C. H. Talbot, *Aelredi Rievallenis opera omnia* (Turnhout: Brepols, 1971), 637.

12 Walter Simons, *Cities of Ladies: Beguine Communities in the Medieval Low Countries, 1200–1565* (Philadelphia: University of Pennsylvania Press, 2001), 188–9, n. 77. See also Ann K. Warren, *Anchorites and their Patrons in Medieval England* (Berkeley and Los Angeles: University of California Press, 1985), and P. L'Hermite-Leclercq, 'Le reclus dans la ville au bas Moyen Âge', *Journal des Savants* (July–December 1988), 219–62.

13 Anneke B. Mulder-Bakker, *Lives of the Anchoresses: The Rise of the Urban Recluse in Medieval Europe* (Philadelphia: University of Pennsylvania Press, 2005).

The reform-minded Benedictine and Gregorian apologist Bernold of St Blaise (d. 1100) enthusiastically commented in his chronicle that

> The common life flourished at this time [1091] in many places in the kingdom of Germany, not only among clerics and monks living most religiously but also among lay men who very devoutly offered themselves and their property to the common life and who, although they differed from clerics and monks in their habit, were considered in no way unequal to them in merits... There was not only a multitude of men, but also of women who gave themselves over to this kind of common life in obedience to clerics or monks.[14]

These were the new-style *conversi* or *conversae*, lay brothers and sisters who entered the monastery as illiterate adults and formed a distinct body alongside the monastic community, with their own habits, customs and tasks. All of the new or reformed religious orders – first those of Vallombrosa and Hirsau, then the Cistercians and others – opened their doors for lay men (and sometimes also women) practising this novel form of monastic observance and, as many other sources confirm, outnumbering in due course the choir monks and nuns.[15] But Bernold next welcomed yet another group of lay people who sought a *conversio*:

> In these villages, innumerable daughters of country stock renounced husbands and the world in order to live under the authority of a priest; even married people dedicated themselves to living religiously and to ceaselessly obey those in religion with utmost piety. This type of program flourished above all in Germany, where whole villages embraced the religious life and lay people continually supported (*praevenire*) each other by the sanctity of their ways.[16]

However much Bernold may have taken his wishes for reality in exaggerating the size of the phenomenon, he correctly identified an emerging societal trend: now that the most remote settlement had acquired its own church or chapel and all ranks of society gained access to the essentials of Christian doctrine (vividly expressed in the preaching of hermits and other reformers), some of the faithful attempted to lead a life of perfection outside the monastic

---

14 Bernold of St Blaise, *Bernoldi chronicon*, ed. Georg Pertz, in MGH, SS 5, 385–467, at 452–3, with an excerpt from a bull of Pope Urban II, confirming the arrangement, propagated by the monks of Hirsau, as one modelled after the 'distinguished pattern of the primitive Church'.

15 See Kaspar Elm, ed., *Beiträge zur Geschichte der Konversen im Mittelalter* (Berlin: Duncker & Humblot, 1980); Constable, *Reformation*, 74–82. On adult oblates, who are probably not meant by Bernold and emerge as a recognisable category of lay devotees only about one century later, see Charles de Miramon, *Les 'donnés' au Moyen Âge: Une forme de vie religieuse laïque (v. 1180–v.1500)* (Paris: Éditions du Cerf, 1999).

16 *Bernoldi chronicon*, 453.

enclosure, within their own homes, either in celibacy or as married couples. Evidence of these new efforts is at first as fragmented as it is scarce: it appears in the rural confraternity of San Desiderio of Vicenza, founded to promote religious communal life and mutual support about 1186 and whose members were considered 'penitents' from 1216 onward; it appears in the Universal Chronicle of Laon's reference, for the year 1178 or 1179, to citizens of Lombardy, possibly *Humiliati*, advocating 'a certain form of religious life' and wearing humble clothing, while living in the family; and it is also seen in the 'well-ordered phalanx' of pious church-goers of Liège led by Lambert le Bègue, a reform-minded priest, who wrote in 1175/1177 that in their homes 'they reflected upon what they heard in church and urged one another to practice it' and that he had translated into the vernacular the Acts of the Apostles (often used as a blue-print for the new religious programs), 'to assist them in their good work'.[17]

By the end of the twelfth century, this grassroots activity crystallised into a myriad of 'movements' that struggled to overcome their often tense relationship with the church. In Italy, the *Humiliati*, having fallen foul of the ecclesiastical authorities because of lay preaching, received papal recognition in 1201 as a tripartite religious order composed of branches of clerics, nuns and lay members. The 'Poor Catholics' of Lombardy, reconciled Waldensians, carried on their mission, with new limitations imposed by the church, from 1207/8 onward.[18] A great many others of northern and central Italy translated their endeavours in the idiom of penance, rooted in the ancient and canonically recognised status of penitents, or sinners whose internal conversion was displayed by such external signs as special, sober garb, observance of the seven canonical hours, rejection of military service, and stricter fasting. Groups of 'brothers and sisters of penitence' in the Romagna adopted common customs known as the *Memoriale Propositi* in 1221.[19] As lay men and women, penitents naturally came under episcopal authority, but soon supervision over them increasingly fell to the followers of St Francis, who wrote

---

17 G. G. Meersseman, *Ordo fraternitatis: Confraternite e pietà del laici nel medioevo* (Rome: Herder, 1977), 305–55; *Chronicon universale*, ed. Georg Waitz, in MGH, SS, 26, 442–57, at 449–50, and Frances Andrews, *The Early Humiliati* (Cambridge: Cambridge University Press, 1999), 39–40; Lambert le Bègue, *Epistola VI*, ed. A. Fayen, 'L'"Antigraphum Petri" et les lettres concernant Lambert le Bègue conservées dans le manuscrit de Glasgow', *Bulletin de la Commission Royale d'Histoire* 5th ser., 9 (1899), 255–356, at 351, and Simons, *Cities of Ladies*, 24–34.

18 See Andrews, *The Early Humiliati*, 64–98 and chapter 3 in this volume.

19 In G. G. Meersseman, ed., *Dossier de l'ordre de la pénitence au XIIIe siècle*, 2nd edn (Fribourg: Éditions universitaires, 1982), 91–112.

two advisory 'letters' to penitents that were regarded as regulations for an 'order of penitents'.[20] By the second half of the thirteenth century it was commonly believed that St Francis, after founding the orders of the Friars Minor and the affiliated sisters of St Clare, had also created the penitents as a 'third' order. In line with the friars' growing involvement with the penitents, Pope Nicholas IV – the first Franciscan to occupy the Holy See – approved a modified version of the *Memoriale Propositi* as an official rule for them in 1289, along with the recommendation to choose a Franciscan as their *visitator* or religious supervisor, which sealed the close bond with the Friars Minor.[21]

The new 'Third Order' remained throughout the medieval and early modern period a rather amorphous umbrella organisation that harboured many different groups and individuals, some of whom enjoyed tremendous respect locally for their saintly life or spiritual teaching, like Margaret of Cortona (d. 1297) and Angela of Foligno (d. 1309).[22] In the long run, the most widely influential of the many initiatives thus supported may have been the development, in the last decades of the thirteenth century, of a 'regular' branch within the Third Order, consisting of penitents – usually women – who formed quasi-monastic communities. The cityscape of virtually every urban centre in fifteenth-century Europe became dotted with small houses of such sisters, who adopted Pope Nicholas IV's rule as a basic set of principles flexible enough to fit every ideal, from teaching and the care of the sick in hospitals to a more cloistered life of contemplation; sisters who chose the latter eventually came to observe the strict enclosure of traditional nuns.[23]

---

20 C. Esser, ed., *Opuscula sancti patris Francisci Assisiensis* (Grottaferrata: Editiones Collegii S. Bonaventurae, 1978), 107–28; see Robert M. Stewart, *'De illis qui faciunt penitentiam': The Rule of the Secular Franciscan Order: Origins, Development, Interpretation* (Rome: Istituto Storico dei Cappuccini, 1991).

21 *Supra Montem* (18 August 1289), in J.-H. Sbaralea, ed., *Bullarium Franciscanum*, vol. 4 (Rome: Typis Sacrae Congregationis de Propaganda Fide, 1768), 94–7, no. 150.

22 Recent studies have thoroughly revised the complicated history of this Third Order. See the overview in Giovanna Casagrande, 'Il movimento penitenziale francescano nel dibattito storiografico degli ultimi 25 anni', *Analecta Tertii Ordinis Regularis Sancti Francisci* 29 (1998), 351–89, and her *Religiosità penitenziale e città al tempo dei communi* (Rome: Istituto Storico dei Cappuccini, 1995); Anna Benvenuti Papi, 'In castro poenitentiae': *Santità e società femminile nell'Italia medievale* (Rome: Herder, 1990); Daniel Bornstein and Roberto Rusconi, eds., *Women and Religion in Medieval and Renaissance Italy* (Chicago and London: University of Chicago Press, 1996).

23 Materials for the history of the 'regular' Third Order have been collected by G. Andreozzi, *Il terzo ordine regolare di San Francesco nella sua storia e nelle sue leggi*, 3 vols. (Rome: Editrice Franciscanum, 1993–5). Italian communities of Tertiaries adopted strict active enclosure from the late fourteenth century onwards; in the Low Countries, where many such convents of Tertiaries enjoyed close ties with the Modern Devout, enclosure became more common around 1410/20: Madelon van Luijk, *Bruiden van*

Meanwhile, similar organisations of penitents sprang up alongside those affiliated with Franciscans, notably the Dominican Third Order, which had local antecedents dating to the thirteenth century and whose rule received papal approval in 1405, some time after the activities of its most famous member, St Catherine of Siena (d. 1380).[24]

## Beguines and beghards

The last lay religious movement under review here, the beguines, combined many of the features noted above, but also stands out as unique because it consisted almost entirely of women. Indeed, the gendered characteristics of beguine existence, so remarkable for contemporaries and modern scholars alike, go a long way towards explaining both their successes and struggles.

The origins of the movement are diverse. Women such as Mary of Oignies (1177–1213) lived with their family – in her case, in a chaste marriage – and devoted themselves to good works, prayer and penance, much in the manner of the Italian penitents; others, like Juetta of Huy (1158–1228), served as spiritual beacons to the urban community from their anchorholds, following in the tradition of recluses. Still others, like Christine *Mirabilis* of Sint-Truiden (1150–1224), acted as ambulant miracle workers and informal preachers. Many more such women of the southern Low Countries and adjacent territories of France and Germany remained anonymous. Their clerical and lay supporters regarded them as 'religious women' (*mulieres religiosae*), even though they did not lead a monastic life or, indeed, enjoy religious status. Their lack of a monastic rule did not prevent James of Vitry (c. 1170–1240) from describing his female heroes of the diocese of Liège in terms that could have applied to cloistered women:

They scorned the temptations of the flesh for Christ, despised the riches of the world for the love of the heavenly kingdom, devoted themselves to their

---

*Christus: De tweede religieuze vrouwenbeweging in Leiden en Zwolle, 1380–1580* (Zutphen: Walburg Pers, 2004), 141–74 and Hildo van Engen, *De derde orde van Sint-Franciscus in het middeleeuwse bisdom Utrecht* (Hilversum: Verloren, 2006), 244–96.

24 The Dominican Penitents' rule is edited in Meersseman, *Dossier*, 143–56, where it is erroneously dated to 1285 and attributed to Munio de Zamora, Dominican master general from 1285 to 1291. For their Third Order, see Martina Wehrli-Johns, 'L'Osservanza dei Domenicani e il movimento penitenziale laico: Studi sulla "regola di Munio" e sul Terz'ordine domenicano in Italia e Germania', in G. Chittolini and K. Elm, eds., *Ordini religiosi e società politica in Italia e Germania nei secoli XIV e XV* (Bologna: il Mulino, 2001), 287–329; Maiju Lehmijoki-Gardner et al., *Dominican Penitent Women* (New York: Paulist Press, 2005).

heavenly bridegroom in poverty and humility, and earned a sparse meal with their hands although their families abounded in riches.[25]

For another great supporter of the early beguines, Caesarius of Heisterbach, 'they even surpass[ed] in the love of God many of those who live in the cloister. They live the eremitical life among the crowds, spiritual among the worldly and virginal among those who seek pleasure. As their battle is greater, so is their grace, and a greater crown will await them.'[26]

This concept of religious life 'in the world', without formal vows or rejection of individual property, followed naturally out of the twelfth-century emphasis on inner spirituality, personal relationships with the divine, and growing criticism of formalism. What was new, however, was that women practised it in such great numbers and gradually organised themselves without much male or clerical supervision. From about 1230 onwards, beguines who lived together informally began to acquire property jointly, elect one of their group as their superior, and make arrangements with local priests to ensure regular (and preferably exclusive) access to church services. Thus came into being the first 'beguinages', which by the 1270s encompassed entire neighbourhoods, walled off from the rest of the city, where beguines lived in small houses or larger units gathered around a church, and where they taught school, ran their textile businesses and, importantly, set up hospitals for poor or elderly women. Some of these communities in the Low Countries housed several hundred beguines at various stages of the medieval and early modern eras. The largest of all, St Catherine's of Mechelen, was home to more than 1,500 beguines in the first half of the sixteenth century.[27] In other parts of northern and central Europe, they usually resided in small convents dispersed over the city, but there, too, the total number of women who chose to live as a

25 James of Vitry, *Vita Mariae Oigniacensis*, ed. D. Papebroch in *AA.SS.*, June, vol. 5, 542–72 at 547–8. See also Anneke B. Mulder-Bakker, ed., *Mary of Oignies: Mother of Salvation* (Turnhout: Brepols, 2007); Mulder-Bakker, *Lives of the Anchoresses*, 52–77; and Barbara Newman, 'Possessed by the Spirit: Devout Women, Demoniacs, and the Apostolic Life in the Thirteenth Century', *Speculum* 73 (1998), 733–70. Other notable beguines of the early age are discussed in Ernest McDonnell, *The Beguines and Beghards in Medieval Culture: With Special Emphasis on the Belgian Scene* (New Brunswick, N.J.: Rutgers University Press, 1954), and Simons, *Cities of Ladies*, 35–48. For a systematic overview of the major texts, see Walter Simons, 'Holy Women of the Low Countries: A Survey', in Rosalynn Voaden and Alastair Minnis, eds., *The Yale Companion to Medieval Holy Women in the Christian Tradition* (New Haven, Conn.: Yale University Press, forthcoming).

26 Caesarius of Heisterbach, *Libri VIII miraculorum*, in A. Hilka, ed., *Die Wundergeschichte des Caesarius von Heisterbach*, vol. 3 (Bonn: Peter Hanstein Verlagsbuchhandlung, 1937), 26–7 (written in 1225–8).

27 For a checklist of beguine communities in the southern Low Countries, with population data, see Simons, *Cities of Ladies*, 48–60, 253–313.

beguine could be quite impressive.[28] Nevertheless, as a movement that grew largely spontaneously and in many ways resisted institutionalisation, there never was an 'order' of beguines; each local beguine community remained in principle autonomous, and few beguinages entertained close relations with each other. Communities of men who imitated the lifestyle and were called beghards (*beguini, beghardi*) developed independently but remained of modest size.

The rapid spread of the beguine ideal was in no small part the work of a few, influential clerics who promoted beguines as living examples of orthodox piety against the apparent progress of heretical movements and of Catharism in particular. James of Vitry belonged to a circle of friends who took up the priesthood or joined the new religious orders in the first decades of the thirteenth century and were keen on a vigorous apostolate among the laity. They comprised his one-time mentor, John of Nivelle (d. 1233), the latter's companion and teacher John of Liroux (d. after 1216/17), Guido of Nivelles (d. 1227) and, one generation younger, the famous hagiographer and scholar, Thomas of Cantimpré (c. 1200–c. 1272).[29] All of them studied at Paris, where they were exposed to the new pastoral theology associated with Peter the Chanter (d. 1197) and his protégés, the preacher Fulk of Neuilly (d. 1202) and the later Pope Innocent III (1198–1216); all served as priestly advisers to beguine communities in the Low Countries or wrote *vitae* recording the exploits of individual beguines. They, and quite a few other religious men (the Cistercians of Villers and various Dominican friars come to mind), legitimised beguines regionally and on an international scale, securing oral papal approval and numerous episcopal charters of support for individual beguinages.[30]

Yet the popular appeal of beguinages was also rooted in broader social and cultural changes. The burgeoning urban economies of the Low Countries and the Rhineland offered single women unprecedented avenues for employment as textile labourers, hospital workers or as teachers. City magistrates

---

28 Important regional studies are Jean-Claude Schmitt, *Mort d'une hérésie: l'Église et les clercs face aux béguines et aux beghards du Rhin supérieur du XIVe et XVe siecle* (Paris: Mouton and École des Hautes Études en Sciences Sociales, 1978); Florence Koorn, *Begijnhoven in Holland gedurende de middeleeuwen* (Assen: Van Gorcum, 1981); Andreas Wilts, *Beginen im Bodenseeraum* (Sigmaringen: Jan Thorbecke, 1994); Frank-Michael Reichstein, *Das Beginenwesen in Deutschland: Studien und Katalog* (Berlin: Koster, 2001).

29 For more on these individuals, see Simons, *Cities of Ladies*, 38–47 and 170–80.

30 In October 1216, James of Vitry wrote to his friends that Pope Honorius III had orally 'permitted religious women, not only in the diocese of Liège but also in France and the Empire, to live in the same house and to incite each other toward the good by mutual exhortations' (R. B. C. Huygens, ed., *Lettres de Jacques de Vitry (1160/1170–1240) évêque de Saint-Jean d'Acre* (Leiden: Brill, 1960), 74). John of Liroux may have sought similar assurances in Rome; written evidence of papal protection of beguines, though less explicit, is recorded from 1231 onwards (Simons, *Cities of Ladies*, 41–2, 48 and 174, n. 37).

and feudal overlords in Flanders, Brabant and Holland sometimes aided in setting up beguinages because the women fulfilled real social needs while providing cheap labour.[31] For the women, beguinages gave the promise of a safe haven in a dangerous environment, mutual support by like-minded women, and the option of expressing their religious aspirations at mass and the daily hours, in devotional exercises, in song and dance, and in writing. Hadewijch of Brabant (thirteenth century), Mechtild of Magdeburg (c. 1208–c. 1282) and Marguerite Porète (d. 1310) are the best known – but surely not the only – beguine authors of a rich, diverse mystical literature in the vernacular that originated in this milieu.[32]

Where churchmen favourable to these developments perceived a harmonious complementarity between priestly functions and lay, female devotion, opponents saw potential for heresy, *scandalum* and subversion of church authority. Popular sentiment was initially sceptical, too. The name 'beguine' was not derived, as was sometimes thought, from *Albigensis* (a Latin term for heretics in the thirteenth century) or from the name of the Liégeois priest Lambert li Bègue (erroneously considered the founding father of the movement) but rather from the root *begg-*, meaning to mumble or mutter prayers. A *beguina* thus denoted a fake devotee, a woman who claimed to be devout but whose utterances were indistinct and therefore not to be trusted. Although beguines eventually wore the insult as a badge of honour, the original meaning was kept vividly alive in controversies over the beguines' informal preaching aimed at exhortation, teaching, visionary powers and mysticism. The profound suspicion of female authority in these fields burst to the foreground in the early fourteenth century and led to the execution of Marguerite Porete for alleged heresies in 1310 and the condemnation of insubordinate beguines at the Council of Vienne (1311–12). Not coincidentally, urban economies experienced a decline in this period, reducing the need for female labour and hardening social policies. In many parts of northern Europe, beguine communities closed their doors; a few adopted an 'official' religious rule, for instance that of the Franciscan Third Order. In the Low Countries, however,

---

31 In the case of beghards or 'male beguines', fear of competition with professional guild workers limited such official support.

32 See Caroline Walker Bynum, *Holy Feast and Holy Fast: The Religious Significance of Food to Medieval Women* (Berkeley and Los Angeles: University of California Press, 1987); Amy Hollywood, *The Soul as Virgin Wife: Mechtild of Magdeburg, Marguerite Porete, and Meister Eckhart* (Notre Dame: University of Notre Dame Press, 1995); Bernard McGinn, *The Presence of God: A History of Western Christian Mysticism*, vol. 3, *The Flowering of Mysticism: Men and Women in the New Mysticism (1200–1350)* and vol. 4, *The Harvest of Mysticism in Medieval Germany (1300–1500)* (New York: Crossroad, 1998 and 2005).

the larger and well-connected beguinages survived virtually intact – some of them even until the twentieth century – while beguine forms of organisation inspired such new experiments as the *Devotio Moderna*.[33]

## Conclusion

The natural tension between institutional and informal sources of power has always been a creative source of reflection and rejuvenation in Christian religious life. In the high and late Middle Ages, that tension could easily erupt into conflict, as church and state developed more intricate machineries of government, while larger sections of the population gained access to education and writing. For the church, which placed increased emphasis on teaching by clerical *magisterium*, informal religious life posed special problems, made even more acute in the thirteenth century by the rise of beguines and female tertiaries, which added questions of gender to the complex issues of authority and orthodoxy, knowledge of the divine, and moral purity in a material world.[34] Nonetheless, some contemporaries heralded the new lay religiosity with confidence and optimism. As James of Vitry famously wrote:

> We do not consider religious only those who renounce the world and go over to a religious life, but we can also call regulars all the faithful of Christ who serve the Lord under the evangelical rule and who live in an orderly way under the one highest and supreme Abbot.[35]

In this holistic vision, unity trumped division, and mutual influence rather than dispute was the norm. Even if historians do not share that perspective, they acknowledge that the efflorescence of informal religious life in this age helped to diffuse among broad segments of society concepts and practices that once were the purview of monks alone. By the end of the Middle Ages, a penitential ideology, the principles of asceticism and voluntary poverty, meditation on the Hours of the Passion, and of course spiritual literacy had become integral parts of lay religiosity.

---

33 Elisabeth Makowski, *'A Pernicious Sort of Woman': Quasi-Religious Women and Canon Lawyers in the Later Middle Ages* (Washington, D.C.: Catholic University of America Press, 2005); Simons, *Cities of Ladies*, 109–43; see also Chapter 26.

34 These issues have been explored in a great many studies. In addition to Bynum, *Holy Feast* (still authoritative), see for instance John Coakley, *Women, Men, and Spiritual Power: Female Saints and their Collaborators* (New York: Columbia University Press, 2006), and Jeffrey Hamburger, *The Visual and the Visionary: Art and Female Spirituality in Medieval Germany* (New York: Zone Books, 1998).

35 James of Vitry, *Historia occidentalis*, ed. J. F. Hinnebusch (Fribourg: Éditions universitaires, 1972), 165–6. See also Constable, *The Reformation*, 7 and 292–3.

# 21

# Saints and pilgrimages: new and old

### ANDRÉ VAUCHEZ

The Middle Ages did not invent the cult of saints, which already, by the end of Christian Antiquity, played an important role in the religious life of the faithful, through the cult rendered to the martyrs and the confessors. Yet this devotion was boosted in the Middle Ages to the point of making it one of the keystones of human relationships with the divine, as we still see today from the innumerable works of art of this period – paintings, sculptures, gold and silver work, windows – dedicated to the menservants and maidservants of God. This cult first took the form of festivals and liturgical ceremonies, which became steadily more numerous between the ninth and the fourteenth centuries. By the Carolingian period, in every church, the clergy celebrated the feasts of the Apostles and the Evangelists and also several universal feasts such as All Saints (1 November), St John the Baptist (24 June), St Laurence (10 August), St Michael (29 September), St Martin (11 November) and the Holy Innocents (28 December), added to which were commemorations specific to each church, that is, of its dedicatee and its patron saint or saints. From the eleventh century on, the commemoration of the faithful dead (sometimes called *festum animarum* (All Souls) and celebrated on 2 November), which had been introduced at Cluny by Abbot Odilo (994–1048), was widely adopted; so was the feast of the Conception of the Virgin, which had started in Normandy and England and spread all over the Continent in the twelfth century, in spite of the protests of St Bernard, who was personally hostile to this devotion. Around 1140, the *Decretum* of Gratian contained a first official list of the feasts that were obligatory for all the faithful of the Roman Catholic Church, which was repeated more or less unchanged in the Decretal *Conquestus est* promulgated by Gregory IX on the same subject in 1232.[1] However, these two

---

[1] *Decretum Gratiani, IIIa pars, De consecratione, c.1*, and *Decretalium Gregorii papae IX compilatio, L.II, tit. IX, de feriis, c. 5 (Conquestus est nobis)*, in E. Friedberg, ed., *Corpus iuris canonici*, vol. 1 (Leipzig, 1879), c. 1353, and vol. 2 (Leipzig, 1881), cc. 272–3.

normative texts also recognised the right of the bishops to celebrate in their own dioceses other feasts of saints they believed to be important, a freedom they used so freely that the authors of all the various church reform projects that proliferated from the end of the fourteenth century demanded that the institution of new feasts should be banned, so numerous had they become. In parallel, the very wide circulation of historical martyrologies, in particular that written by Usuard in the Parisian abbey of St Germain des Prés around 875, provided the monks and canons with a basis for the composition of rhythmic offices and hagiographical texts in Latin (*Vitae et miracula*); in the most important churches these were collected into enormous legendaries *per circulum anni* covering the whole liturgical year.

## The saints at the heart of relations between this world and the next

For most Christians, sainthood was first and foremost a concrete, experiential reality, with a social dimension that was universally recognised – the most solemn oaths were sworn on the relics of saints, after all, and their relics were carried in procession whenever an epidemic raged or a calamity threatened the community. Faith in the saints was based less on theological notions accessible only to the clergy than on a set of convictions that permeated the common mindset. Important among these was belief in the permanent intervention of God in the life of humankind. The Creator might sometimes allow the forces of evil to act so as to punish sinners and unbelievers, but he also intervened in history so as to restore order in a world disrupted by sin, of which sickness, war and bad weather were the most visible consequences. However, it was rare for God, whose infinite grandeur remained inaccessible, to be approached directly. In general, people preferred to resort to intermediaries closer to humankind: the Virgin Mary or, even more, the saints, in line with the practices that governed relations between the dominant and the dominated in this world. The king of France, Louis IX (1214–70) – the future St Louis – expressed this very well:

> It is the same, he said, with the saints in Paradise as with the counsellors of kings…whoever has business with an earthly king seeks to know who he holds in high regard and who, having his ear, is able to approach him successfully. He then seeks out this favoured person and begs him to convey his request. It is the same with the saints in Paradise, who, being the friends of Our Lord and his intimates, can invoke him in all confidence, since he cannot fail to listen to them.[2]

2 Guillaume de Saint-Pathus, *Vie de Saint Louis*, ed. H.-F. Delaborde (Paris, 1899), 73.

The theme of the heavenly court, so common in the hagiographical texts and iconography of the Middle Ages, was not simply a stylistic device. It accurately expressed the way that medieval people pictured relations between God and his faithful, which they likened to those between kings and their vassals and officials. It also illustrates the importance they attached to the power of the saints and their capacity for intercession. Too extraordinary to be imitated in the eyes of simple folk, the saints were witnesses to the supernatural among ordinary humans and a potential recourse in distress, and it was in this capacity above all that they were venerated. According to a belief dating back to the first centuries of Christianity, the saints, in consideration of the merits they had acquired and the sufferings they had endured on earth, were believed to have been favoured by God with a power (*virtus*) which continued to act after their death, in their remains or in objects that had been in contact with them. This grace was manifested by signs which everyone recognised and which could not deceive: a well-preserved body and, above all, the odour of sanctity, that characteristic smell emanating from the relics of the servants of God, sometimes a seepage of oil from the side of the tomb or the altar that sheltered them. It was believed by the faithful that new or unrecognised saints expressed themselves primarily through visions in which they demanded to be honoured. If their request for a cult was not satisfied, they did not hesitate to give tangible signs of their discontent until such time as their relics were removed from the earth or place where they lay (*elevatio*), transported (*translatio*) to a more proper place – sarcophagus, stone tomb or altar – and exposed to the veneration of the faithful (*ostensio*) at great liturgical ceremonies to which great crowds flocked in search of miracles. From this anthropological perspective, sanctity appears primarily as a language of the body and as linchpin of a symbolic system based on the invigorating and healing power of relics – which did not prevent it from being at the same time, for an elite, a quality of the soul and a spiritual state.

There could be no question of opposing a devotion so deeply rooted both in the Christian tradition and in *mentalités*. The monks and the bishops of the eleventh and twelfth centuries had no scruples in exploiting the reverential awe provoked by the holy bodies they held in their churches to obtain justice or to achieve the restoration of rights or lands in the course of the innumerable disputes that arose between them and the lay aristocracy. Similarly, in the peace movements, relics played the crucial role of security for the commitments made by the lords to the church or to the weak that the church tried to protect. The great abbeys like Cluny or Sainte-Foy of Conques put the emphasis on the therapeutic efficacy and social utility of the cult of saints, drawing up *Libri miraculorum* in which they committed to writing the prodigies that occurred in their churches when the saints whose relics were venerated there were invoked; this only encouraged the faithful to make pilgrimages to them.

## Holy places and pilgrimages: the territorialisation of the sacred in the Christian West

In parallel with changes in conceptions of sainthood, there was a significant shift both in the development of the idea of sanctuary and in the geographical distribution of sanctuaries. Until the Carolingian period, there seem to have been relatively few places that were considered holy by the Christians of the West and that attracted large numbers of pilgrims. Throughout Late Antiquity and in the early Middle Ages, the most prestigious church in the Christian world was the Holy Sepulchre, built by Emperor Constantine in Jerusalem on the presumed site of the tomb and resurrection of Christ. In the eleventh century many religious edifices in the West tried to imitate the configuration of this monument, reproducing its circular plan and even sometimes its internal structure – as at St Stephen of Bologna or Neuvy-Saint-Sépulcre in France – so as to establish a privileged link with the founders of Christianity. In addition to this fundamental reference to Jerusalem and the Holy Land, which was to mark the consciousness and the imaginative world of Christians in the West for centuries to come, special importance was attached to Rome, site of the cult of the martyrs Peter and Paul and many other saints (Laurence, Agnes, Cecily, *et al.*) whose names appeared in the canon of the mass and were familiar to the faithful. Constantinople, where the Byzantine emperors had amassed a huge quantity of prestigious relics, exercised an equal fascination, even though it was less easy to visit. One can imagine, however, just how much its sacred treasures, which were to enrich the churches of Italy and France after the capture and sack of the city by the crusaders in 1204, were coveted by the Christians of the West. Apart from these three great centres of pilgrimage, mention should also be made of the great sanctuary of St Michael at Monte Sant'Angelo, in northern Apulia, which – with Monte Cassino, cradle of western monasticism – attracted many pilgrims, with its replicas, Mont-Saint-Michel in Normandy and San Michele della Chiusa, at the entry to the Alpine passes, and also St Martin of Tours.

If we skip forward two centuries of history to observe the religious geography of western Christendom at the beginning of the thirteenth century, we find a very different picture, characterised by the existence of a much larger number of sanctuaries, which were frequented by a different type of pilgrim. Certainly, Jerusalem and Rome continued to play a preponderant role: the former had never stopped attracting the Christians of the West, who had gone there in increasing numbers from the tenth century on. The number of pilgrims had grown even more after the First Crusade, when the *passagium*, that armed pilgrimage aimed at the liberation and defence of the Holy Places of Christendom, earned for all who made it the privilege of the plenary indulgence, that is, the remission of all the penalties their faults had merited. Rome, the Eternal City, benefited from the enhanced prestige of the papacy and, after the institution of the Jubilee by Boniface VIII in 1300, the plenary indulgence previously reserved to pilgrims to the Holy Land. Alongside these traditional centres of pilgrimage, however, many new sanctuaries developed in the eleventh and twelfth centuries. The most famous was St James of Compostela, whose popularity in Christendom kept pace with the progress of the Reconquista in Spain at the expense of Islam, but many other holy places, which can safely be called important even in the absence of statistical data to measure their impact, became renowned throughout Christendom. Confining ourselves to southern and central France, we may cite St Foy of Conques in Rouergue, Rocamadour in Quercy, Saint-Guilhem le Désert and Saint-Gilles in Languedoc, Le Puy-en-Velay in Auvergne, Vézelay, site of the cult of Mary Magdalene, in Burgundy, Saint-Antoine de Viennois in Dauphiné, the Trinity of Vendôme and Marmoutier in the pays de Loire among others. The same phenomenon was visible in Italy, with the growing success of the pilgrimage to Volto Santo in Lucca, St Mark's in Venice and St Nicholas in Bari. The trend spread to north-western Europe in the second half of the twelfth century with the development of the cults of the Three Kings, whose relics had been transferred from Milan to Cologne in 1164 by Frederic Barbarossa, and of St Thomas Becket, whose murder in Canterbury Cathedral in 1170 and canonisation in 1173 made the cathedral a prestigious martyr sanctuary, which attracted pilgrims from the Continent after the institution of a special jubilee.

This phenomenon was not so much a break with the past or an innovation as the acceleration of a trend that had long been under way, caused by a number of different factors which came together at this point to favour a much deeper spatial integration of Christianity. The first of these was a process of a territorialisation of the sacred that had been under way in the West since Late Antiquity and the early Middle Ages: tombs clustered round the high altar or altar of churches (*ad sanctos*) so as to be closer to the relics and to the place where the eucharistic sacrifice was offered; then, the zone around the church, designated by the expression *circuitus ecclesiae*, became the preferred place of burial of the dead, and the tombs that had previously been dispersed in necropolises out in the countryside were gradually brought closer together, giving rise to cemeteries, which, in their capacity as sacred places, enjoyed right of sanctuary. From the Carolingian period on, the bishops tried to make every church a holy place, elaborating the liturgical rite of consecration or dedication and reserving to themselves the consecration of the altars in which relics were systematically placed. Commentators on the Bible, meanwhile, compared the Christian churches to the Temple of Jerusalem, contrary to the patristic tradition that the true temple of God was not the place of worship but the assembly of the faithful gathered together for prayer and worship.

A second factor tending in the same direction was the growing importance of relics in the religious and social life of the West. In the Carolingian period only a few big abbeys and some cathedrals owned important relics, which were jealously preserved in their treasuries. Three factors then combined to encourage an increasingly rapid circulation of the remains of the servants of God through the churches of Christendom: the massive despoliation suffered by the catacombs of Rome in the Ottonian period; the dispersal of the relics held in monasteries, as a result of the Norman or Saracen invasions; and the increasing number of *furta sacra* which allowed western merchants and pirates to bring back from the Muslim East or Byzantium prestigious bodies such as those of St Mark (to Venice) or St Nicholas (to Bari). Rodulfus Glaber (985–1047) revealed himself an admiring observer of this process when he wrote:

> 'When the whole world was, as we have said, clothed in a white mantle of new churches...the relics of many saints were revealed by various signs where they had long lain hidden. It was as though they had been waiting for a brilliant resurrection and were now, by God's permission revealed to the gaze of the faithful; certainly they brought much comfort to men's minds.[3]

Another factor contributing to the proliferation of sanctuaries in the West after the year 1000 was the growing importance of pilgrimage in the religious life of the faithful. Certainly, there is evidence for Christian pilgrims in the sources for Late Antiquity and the early Middle Ages, but these journeys undertaken for devotional reasons seem, after the eleventh century, to have changed in nature and, even more, in scale. In the Carolingian period it was

---

3 J. France, ed. and trans., *Rodulfus Glaber: The Five Books of the Histories* (Oxford: Clarendon Press, 1989), 126–7.

mainly the great men of this world (bishops, abbots, monks and high lay dignitaries) who went to Jerusalem or Rome or Monte Cassino, accompanied by a small party of fellows, returning from their travels with precious objects: relics, but also oriental fabrics, ivories, phials of sacred oil and so on. After the First Crusade (1095–9), pilgrimages became much more frequent and increasingly popular in composition, even becoming meritorious acts strongly urged on the laity of both sexes, though not on the monks, as is shown by the severe injunctions addressed by St Anselm (1033–1109) to certain English abbots, and by St Bernard (1090–1153) to the Cistercians, who were reminded that the monastery was the true Jerusalem for those who had chosen a monastic life, and that it was thus pointless, even dangerous, for religious to want to visit the Holy Land.[4]

This shift can only be understood in the context of the changing role of pilgrimage within the penitential process then taking place, which made it a particularly effective means of enabling the faithful to obtain the remission of their sins. This was not altogether new, since the Irish monks had practised and advocated a form of sacred vagabondage in the early Middle Ages, which made the *peregrinus* (the Latin word for 'stranger') a penitent, and sometimes a martyr if he was murdered on his journey. By the end of the eleventh century, while the majority of the faithful who frequented the sanctuaries did so spontaneously, as a result of a vow, there were now some who took to the road because they had been enjoined to do so by ecclesiastical or even civil authorities in order to expiate their sins or evil conduct by an appropriate penance. Many sinners then embarked on a pilgrimage to Rome to get absolution from the pope for certain particularly grave sins which were reserved to the Holy See.

The canonical collections scarcely address these questions, so it is the hagiographical sources that shed most light on the evolution of beliefs and practices in this area. The most remarkable case is that of Saint-Gilles, an abbey situated on the borders of Languedoc and Provence, where the tomb of a mysterious hermit by the name of Giles, supposed to have lived there in the early Middle Ages, was venerated. His legend presents him as a particularly influential intercessor with God and even credits him with the merit of having

---

4 See the texts cited by G. Constable, 'The Opposition to Pilgrimage in the Middle Ages', in his *Religious Life and Thought (11th–12th Centuries)* (London: Variorum Reprints, 1979), vol. 4, 135–41; and by E. R. Labande, 'De saint Edouard à saint Thomas Becket: Pèlerinages anglais du XIIe siècle', in *Mediaevalia christiana, XIe-XIIIe siècles. Hommage à Raymonde Foreville* (Tournai: De Boeck Université, 1989), 315.

obtained the salvation of the soul of Charlemagne.[5] The belief that God could refuse him nothing, especially in the matter of the remission of sins, spread all over Christendom, even as far as distant Poland. His pilgrimage was hugely successful in the twelfth century, as is demonstrated by the construction by the monks of Saint-Gilles, around 1166, of a magnificent Romanesque basilica with a massive ambulatory. At the same time, the role of the saints acquired a new dimension: they were no longer asked only for cures or for prodigies, but increasingly called on to assist the living and the dead to find their salvation, by alleviating their pains on earth. The faithful began to accumulate merits, and soon indulgences granted by the pope and the bishops, by journeying to major sanctuaries; and they visited others in passing, less famous perhaps but not negligible, that were located along their route. It was at this period that the Via Francigena linking north-western Europe and Rome was joined by the 'route of the Angel', which extended it as far as the great sanctuary of St Michael at Gargano, and, most famous of all, the 'Camino francès' ('French Route') leading to Santiago de Compostela. These were true sacred itineraries, linking various sanctuaries along a route lined with hospices intended to accommodate the pilgrims, such as that of Roncevaux, at the end of a Pyrenean pass, or Altopascio, south of the Arno in Tuscany. It was one of these routes of faith that was described by the French cleric Aymery Picaud, around 1140, in his *Guide for the Pilgrim to St James of Compostella*, in which he told his readers the best route to take in order to visit the maximum number of holy places before reaching their ultimate destination.[6] Western Christendom, the *Guide* shows, was now dotted with sanctuaries of every size, forming a network, linked one to the other by special routes.

## Papal control of the making of saints

By the twelfth century, a certain unease began to be felt among certain sectors of the clergy in the face of the proliferation of cults to servants of God about whom little was known, except that their remains produced miracles in a particular place. Around 1120, for example, the monk Guibert of Nogent, in his treatise *De pigneribus sanctorum*, vehemently denounced the abuses of certain

---

5 *Galli Anonymis cronicae*, ed. K. Maleczynski, *Monumenta Poloniae historica*, n.s., vol. 2 (Krakow: Academia litterarum Poloniae, 1952) 4–7; T. Dunin-Wasowicz, 'Saint-Gilles et la Pologne aux XIe et XIIe siècles', *Annales du Midi* 82 (1970), 123–35.

6 *Le guide du pèlerin de Saint-Jacques de Compostelle*, ed. J. Vielliard (Mâcon: Protat Frères, 1963), trans. James Hogarth, *The Pilgrim's Guide: A 12th Century Guide for the Pilgrim to St James of Compostella* (London: Confraternity of St James, 1992).

ecclesiastics who were prepared to exploit popular credulity in order to increase the prestige and revenues of their sanctuary by exhibiting false relics; he expressed his amazement that three different churches in France should claim to have the head of St John Baptist.[7] This sort of critical attitude was still rare, but it was taken up at the end of the century by the papacy, which, beginning with Alexander III, tried to exert a degree of control over the cult of saints from a perspective that was in the first place disciplinary: until then, by virtue of Carolingian legislation, the institution of the cult of a saint, old or new, had been within the remit of the bishops, but had to be approved by the provincial synod to which the diocese in question belonged. In practice, the bishops acted alone, as and when they thought fit, in performing elevations and translations of holy bodies, which amounted to the authorisation of a liturgical cult; similarly, the abbots of some monasteries, both large and small, did not hesitate to introduce on their own initiative the cult of their founder or of a particular monk who had died in an odour of sanctity, even in the absence of the local bishop and without his agreement. In the wake of the Gregorian Reform and the centralisation round the Roman Church that accompanied it, the papacy intervened to impose some order on this anarchic situation. Its intervention was in general readily accepted because it gave the cults it officially recognised the sanction of its authority, guaranteeing them renown throughout western Christendom, even though the introduction of feasts of newly canonised saints into the local liturgical calendars was not obligatory and remained within the competence of each religious community. The situation was made quite clear at the juridical level with the insertion into the *Decretals* of Gregory IX, in 1234, of a letter of Alexander III, of 1172, in which the pope prohibited the celebration of the cult of a new saint without the authorisation of the Holy See.[8] In practice, however, the bishops retained up until the sixteenth century the right to institute new feasts within their dioceses.

Increased control over the cult of saints by the hierarchy was accompanied by a process of verification – and hence definition – by the papacy on behalf of the Roman Church. Here, Innocent III (1198–1216) played a decisive role by affirming, notably in the bull of canonisation of St Homobonus of Cremona (d. 1197), his desire to subject sainthood itself to detailed scrutiny:

---

7 Guibert de Nogent, *De sanctis et eorum pigneribus*, ed. R. B. C. Huygens (CCCM 127; Turnhout: Brepols, 1996).
8 *Decretalium Gregorii IX papae compilatio*, L. *III*, vol. 45, ed. E. Friedberg, *Corpus iuris canonici*, c. 650, repeating the brief *Audivimus*, taken from a letter of Alexander III to King Kol of Sweden (1171/1172) on the subject of the popular cult rendered in his country to the former king, St Eric.

Although, according to the testimony of Truth, only final perseverance is required for a soul to attain to sainthood in the Church Triumphant, since 'he who stands firm to the end will be saved', nevertheless, in the Church Militant, two things are required for someone to be deemed a saint: virtue of morals and truth of signs, that is, pious works in life and miracles after death.[9]

The pope also emphasised in this text that miracles were often ambiguous because 'Pharaoh's magicians performed them long ago and the Antichrist will perform prodigies so as to seduce into error even the elect'; it was only in cases where real and proven merits were followed by self-evident miracles that the latter constituted a sufficiently sure sign of sainthood for the church to proceed to venerate those whom God had designated in this way. These new requirements, which meant that the Holy See had to exercise a choice from among the supernatural phenomena that surrounded the servants of God and their relics, gave rise to the canonisation process. The oldest such process known – that of the hermit Galgano in Tuscany (d. 1181) – dates from 1185, but the complete juridical form was reached only after 1230. From then until the sixteenth century the procedure began with a local enquiry conducted by a bishop intended to draw the attention of the Holy See to a saint he believed deserved to be canonised, which produced a preliminary file, with the emphasis on the miracles, which was sent to the Curia. Then, if he thought fit, the pope opened an enquiry called an *inquisitio in partibus*; this was entrusted to three commissioners, usually bishops or abbots of the region concerned, who went to the places where the servants of God had lived to interrogate witnesses who had known them in life or who had benefited from their intercession. In the final – and most unpredictable – phase of the process, the complete file was scrutinised by a commission of cardinals charged with the preparation of a report which was presented to the pope and discussed in consistory. After taking advice from his cardinals, the pope gave his decision, and proceeded (or not) to the canonisation of the new saint – that is, his or her inscription into the 'catalogue of saints' of the Catholic Church – during a liturgical ceremony that was accompanied by sermons eulogising this 'friend of God'; the decision was then notified to Christendom by a solemn bull which authorised the saint's liturgical cult. The canonisation process was feared by the postulants and did, indeed, constitute a fairly effective barrier in the face of the many requests which arrived in the Holy See: out of the forty-eight

---

9 Innocent III, Bull *Quia pietas* (12 January 1199), in O. Hageneder and A. Haidacher, eds., *Das Register Innocenz'III*, vol. 1 (Graz-Cologne: Verlag der österreichischen Akademie der Wissenschaften, 1964), 761–2.

enquiries *in partibus* ordered by the papacy between 1198 and 1276 with a view to the canonisation of a saint, twenty-five – over half – came to nothing; and it was necessary for many of them to be repeated or completed because the acts in the form in which they had been transmitted to Rome by the investigators failed to satisfy the requirements now made by the papacy.

But the introduction of papal canonisation was not only or even primarily a way of stemming the flow of popular sanctity. Most of all, it was a response to the desire of the ecclesiastical hierarchy to propose to the clergy and to the faithful figures of totally virtuous and orthodox recent saints whom they might try to imitate, instead of venerating relics of doubtful authenticity or succumbing to the appeal of the ascetic behaviour and irreproachable morality of the Perfect Cathars or the itinerant Waldensian preachers. The most lucid among the clergy realised, at the end of the twelfth century and even more in the thirteenth, with the rise of the mendicant orders, that if the church wanted to Christianise in depth a population that was in part – mainly in urban areas – tending to escape its influence, it had to offer models of religious behaviour likely to win their support. So they introduced a pastoral use of sanctity, in the form of hagiographical texts devoted to persons who had often lived recently and led active lives: alongside the military saints, real or mythical, often represented on the doorways of Gothic cathedrals (Roland, let us not forget, was venerated as a martyr, as was Guillaume d'Orange, who had distinguished himself in the battle against the Saracens before becoming a monk at Gellone), there appeared artisan saints and merchant saints, especially in Italy and Flanders, where these socio-professional groups were particularly numerous and influential. Innocent III ratified this trend in 1199 by canonising St Homobonus, a former draper of Cremona who had died two years earlier and who was distinguished by his zeal in the practice of penitence and charity. It was with a similar aim that, in 1215, a French cleric, James of Vitry (d. 1240), later bishop of St John of Acre and cardinal, wrote the Life of a mystical beguine, Marie d'Oignies (d. 1213), whose spiritual director and confidant he had been, for the benefit of the female laity in the south of France who might be tempted to join the Cathars. A few decades later, in 1260, the archbishop of Pisa, Federico Visconti, did not hesitate to declare to the merchants of his city, in a sermon for the feast of St Francis of Assisi, 'That it must be agreeable to know that your brother [Francis] was a merchant and that he sanctified in our age'.[10]

---

10 N. Bériou and I. Le Masne de Chermont, eds., *Les sermons et la visite pastorale de Frédéric Visconti, archevêque de Pise (1253–1277)* (Rome: École française de Rome, 2001), 778–9.

# The revival of the sanctoral and new forms of the miraculous

The modernisation of the Roman sanctoral was one of the principal manifestations of this new attitude to the cult of saints on the part of the church. Up to the middle of the twelfth century, almost only the traditional feasts of the Apostles, the Evangelists and the martyrs of the first centuries were celebrated at St John Lateran, the pope's cathedral, and at St Peter's, together with a few great figures in the life of the church such as St Augustine, St Benedict and St Gregory the Great. From 1170 on, their liturgical calendars began to include the feasts of very contemporary saints such as Thomas Becket, whose feast spread rapidly throughout Christendom, Francis of Assisi (d. 1226) and Dominic (d. 1221), founders of the Friars Minor and Preachers, Antony of Padua (d. 1231), the Franciscan preacher and theologian, Elisabeth of Hungary (d. 1231), a princess and lay penitent who had distinguished herself in Thuringia by her love of the poor and her zeal in the service of the sick, and Peter Martyr, the Dominican inquisitor murdered near Milan in 1252 and canonised the year after. In most cases the popes were not content with canonising these persons, but intervened actively on their behalf – for example, when Gregory IX and Alexander IV affirmed the authenticity of the stigmata of St Francis, contested by his detractors – and urged local churches and the religious orders to adopt their cult. This drive to renew the sanctoral was not equally successful everywhere; it was rapid and very marked in the Mediterranean, but much less effective in countries such as Spain, northern France, the Germanic world and England, where the traditional intercessors – in particular local saints – retained all their prestige until the end of the Middle Ages, and where the new saints had difficulty in becoming established. This can be seen in the case of St Thomas Cantilupe (d. 1282), Bishop of Hereford, whose canonisation in 1320 was greeted by a great outburst of fervour in the west of England, yet whose pilgrimage soon declined, to the point of insignificance by the eve of the Reformation.[11] Yet even where the forms of sanctity that were revered remained immutable, a shift can be detected, through the medium of hagiography, in the way in which the saints were represented, and also an increase in their role in the religious life of the faithful. This change owed much to the success of the abbreviated legendaries, such as those of the Dominicans Jean de Mailly, Bartholomew of Trent and Thomas of Cantimpré,

---

11 R. C. Finucane, *Miracles and Pilgrims: Popular Belief in Medieval England* (London: J. M. Dent & Sons, 1977).

and, most influential of all, that of James of Voragine whose famous *Golden Legend*, of around 1265, survives in innumerable Latin manuscripts and was translated in the fourteenth and fifteenth centuries into every vernacular language in Christendom. It was through texts such as these, which were discussed by the clergy in their sermons and illustrated by artists in many paintings and frescoes, that the saints really penetrated the religious life of the faithful. The *exempla* – colourful and moralising stories, often taken from the Lives of saints and designed to fire the imagination of, while at the same time edifying, the listener – quoted by the clergy in their sermons helped to make them better known, if not in their historical reality at least as models of faith and piety. The saints remained, admittedly, in the majority of these works and in the hagiographical texts of the age, both astonishing and admirable persons, in their life and in their miracles, and their behaviour often went well beyond the bounds of human nature. In the thirteenth century, however, the marvellous biography tended to replace the thaumaturgic marvel: we remain always in the sphere of the marvellous (or rather the *mirabilis*) but the admirable element is found in the life of the saint (*conversatio*), which was presented as a series of heroic or extraordinary actions. This tendency strengthened in the fourteenth century, when new aspects of sanctity, such as prophesy, visions and revelations, were incorporated by the hagiographers into their writings; the image of the stigmatic St Francis, meanwhile, disseminated throughout Christendom by the Friars Minor, revealed a new expression of the supernatural in the miraculous identification of the body of a man with that of Christ crucified. By the end of this process of the popularisation of sainthood, the servants of God were still exceptional beings, gifted with abnormal merits or powers, but their persons, which had become familiar to everyone, now inspired affectionate devotion rather than reverential fear.

## From relics to images: the explosion of the Marian cult and changes in pilgrimage

Between the end of the thirteenth and the end of the fifteenth centuries, another fundamental change influenced the cult of the saints in the West: alongside relics, which retained a certain prestige, there was an increase in the power of holy images, in a mental world in which sight was beginning to play a more important role, together with touch. This belief implied recognition of both an active presence (a capacity to move and to be moved) and a passive presence (a capacity to suffer and to be offended) in certain images described as miraculous. The majority of these images, which attracted massive devotion in the fourteenth century, were sculptures, or more often paintings, that represented the Virgin Mary, whose cult assumed a quite new importance among the population in general. The criteria which caused certain images to be considered miraculous from a particular point in time remain largely unknown; any religious image, old or new, might, at a certain moment, be invested with a supernatural power which revealed itself in the full light of day in a vision, an activity – the Virgin who wept, bled or turned her head – or a miracle. The popular preference in Italy for 'exotic' images has been noted, in particular for 'alla greca' madonnas, icons of eastern origin whose manufacture was attributed to St Luke. The sacrality of the image was due less to what it represented than to its origin, seen as miraculous – for example, the statues of the Virgin found in a tree by a shepherdess, or in the ground by a peasant digging – or as supernatural – like the image of Veronica (*Vera icona*) preserved in St Peter's in Rome, or the Holy Shroud that reproduced the suffering face of the dead Christ, which began to attract attention in the mid-fourteenth century and which was venerated in the chapel of the dukes of Savoy at Chambéry and then Turin. It was this assumed divine origin that explained the supernatural power of the holy image and, in particular, its thaumaturgic capacities. The fundamental criterion for the popularity of these images was their effectiveness; the considerable success that some of them enjoyed – one thinks of the image of the Virgin *Salus Populi Romani* carried in procession every year by the confraternities through the streets of Rome – was linked, in the minds of the faithful or pilgrims, with the fact that the saints that were represented showed themselves receptive to the prayers of those who implored them; they, in their turn, thanked them for their intervention by offering them other images, the ex votos, which were both an act of gratitude and an advertisement for the sanctuary where they were displayed. The role of the place where the miracle occurred remained fundamental; in Italy the new devotions were usually to Mary. For the consumer, however, what mattered was not so much the person of the Virgin as the place where she had chosen to reveal her power. This is why these outpourings of devotion were often short-lived: in Florence, the first miraculous image seems to have been the Madonna of Orsanmichele, in 1292; however, it was soon supplanted, in the fourteenth century, by the Madonna of Impruneta, outside the city, which was itself eclipsed by the Madonna of the Annunziata, the church of the Servites, who were protected by the Medici, after the epidemics of plague. This is not to say that the original devotions disappeared; rather, after attracting, for a while, the whole population of the town, the sanctuaries which housed these miraculous images – sometimes specially constructed for the purpose – saw their influence shrink to a district or to a confraternity founded in their honour and which maintained the cult.

Historians still debate the reasons for the explosion of the Marian cult in the final centuries of the Middle Ages (in parallel with that of the eucharistic devotion). While it was particularly precocious and marked in the Mediterranean countries, it was found, with varying degrees of time-lag, all over the Christian West in the fourteenth and fifteenth centuries. It was probably encouraged by the clergy, as they preferred the devotion of the faithful to be offered to the mother of God or the eucharist than to obscure saints or relics of unknown origin. However, the initiative seems mostly to have come from the laity, who were able, through the reference to the Virgin of Mercy propagated by the confraternities, to take the initiative in new cults, in town and country alike, without needing to seek authorisation from the bishop, as was the case with the translation of relics, or even, to begin with, the collaboration of the local clergy; a Marian apparition or the revelation of the miraculous nature of a holy image to a simple believer was sometimes enough to give rise to a cult, which the church usually eventually approved, if it lasted and was accompanied by the construction of a cultic building. Thus a new more immediate relationship to the supernatural emerged, illustrated by the large number of Marian sanctuaries, the most typical of which was that of Loreto, in central Italy. There had been a rural church dedicated to the Virgin here by the end of the twelfth century, which became a local sanctuary during the thirteenth century. The devotion grew in the fourteenth century, as shown by an indulgence granted by Pope John XXII to those who made the pilgrimage. In the fifteenth century people began to talk about the presence of the house of the Holy Family in Nazareth, or 'Santa Casa', whose miraculous origins were attested by the lack of foundations of the original church, which gave rise to the legend that it had been brought there by angels. The belief in the miraculous transfer may also have been connected with the transfer to Loreto, at the time of the Turkish advance in the Balkans, of an image of the Virgin from the sanctuary of Tersatto, in Croatia, which was hardly surprising given that there had been frequent exchanges of cult and religious objects between the two shores of the Adriatic throughout the Middle Ages. By the fifteenth century the sanctuary was famous throughout the whole of Christendom; the king of France, Louis XI, was particularly devout and generous towards Our Lady of Loreto, and replicas of this sanctuary were built in a number of places outside Italy.[12]

12 F. Citterio and L. Vaccaro, eds., *Loreto crocevia religioso tra Europa, Italia e Oriente* (Brescia: Morcelliana, 1997).

At the end of the Middle Ages, both the cult of the saints and pilgrimages were changing in important ways, but they remained generally flourishing and popular. Certain devotions had declined, but others replaced them and only intellectual malcontents like Wyclif or certain Florentine humanists indulged in a few criticisms against some excesses. Never, perhaps, had Christians travelled so much as at this period, and women seem to have been particularly involved: St Bridget of Sweden went to St James of Compostela with her husband; then, after being widowed and settling in Rome, she visited most of the Italian sanctuaries; finally, before her death, she went on a great pilgrimage to the Holy Land, where she was blessed with visions, especially in Bethlehem. Another, less famous but perhaps more typical, woman, the English visionary Margery Kempe (d. 1439), also spent a large part of her time visiting sanctuaries:[13] initially in England, where she went to every holy place of any significance, from Canterbury to Bridlington, where the body of St John of Bridlington (d. 1379), who had recently been canonised, was venerated; in 1414 she reached Rome, where, in the church of the Holy Apostles, she had the vision of her mystical marriage with Christ; in 1417 she went to St James of Compostela; after which she visited Wilsnack, in north Germany, where the Holy Blood of Christ was venerated after a eucharistic miracle, and Aachen, in 1433; finally, in 1434, she crossed the North Sea with her daughter-in-law to go to Danzig, where, a few years earlier, Dorothy of Montau (d. 1394), a lay woman mystic who, like Margery, had been a wife and mother, had died (she had heard about Dorothy from her son, a merchant who frequented the Baltic ports). These two examples confirm, if confirmation is needed, the importance of the role of pilgrimage in the religious life of the faithful, but also the artificial character – at least at this period – of the distinction between popular religion and the religion of the elites, since everybody made pilgrimages, from peasants to kings, and since they provided the greatest mystics of the age with essential nourishment for their spiritual progress.

---

13  S. B. Meech and H. E. Allen, eds., *The Book of Margery Kempe* (Early English Text Society, Original Series 212; Oxford: Oxford University Press, 1940).

22

# Crusade and conquest

MARCUS BULL

The crusade is a feature of medieval Christian civilisation with a decidedly contemporary resonance. It summons up images and associations that have been routinely misunderstood and misappropriated, never more so than in the wake of 9/11. Many aspects of the medieval world have enjoyed, or endured, some sort of popular currency since the emergence of the Gothic novel and the Romantics' love affair with chivalry, but few have been as badly misrepresented as the crusades. No other event or process in medieval history, moreover, has prompted modern Christian apology, both papal and evangelical. But it is not just their lurid modern reputation which makes the crusades an important area of study, for they also impinged significantly on the medieval church and medieval culture. It is necessary, for example, to know something of the crusade movement in order to understand the functioning of papal authority between the eleventh and sixteenth centuries, changes in the ideological self-fashioning of royal governments, the ups and downs in the delicate relationship between ecclesiastical and secular authorities, the spread and influence of the international religious orders, the morphology of aristocratic culture, and expressions of popular religiosity. Itself a relative novelty, crusading nonetheless insinuated itself into the most fundamental and traditional of social relations. For example, in 1201 Pope Innocent III (1198–1216) issued a decretal stating that a crusader's vow could not be negated by a prior marriage vow. At a stroke a central tenet of the canon law treatment of marriage, an area of people's lives that the church had in fact been addressing very seriously for more than a century, was undone. The arresting stories told by writers close in time to Innocent, such as Gerald of Wales (1146–1223) and Caesarius of Heisterbach (c. 1180–c. 1240), of crusade recruits wriggling free from the despairing clutches of their wives probably say more about the sorts of made-up domestic vignettes that preachers used to spice up sermons than it does about observable reality, but they show how Innocent was responding to a real tension in society which was the direct result of crusading, its appeal and its demands.[1]

Crusading's relevance to our wider understanding of medieval life is evident in many contexts. It is sometimes said, with only a little exaggeration, that the crusades are central to the history of European taxation, because their enormous costs forced the church and secular rulers to innovate and then regularise ways of tapping into their subjects' wealth. Any history of the place of the Jews within Latin Christendom must take full account of the impact of the crusades: although there is some evidence of Christian antagonism towards Jews before the First Crusade (1095–1101), the persecutions that the preaching of this crusade triggered in northern France and the Rhineland, and the frequent correspondence between the preaching of the cross and anti-Jewish agitation in following years, reveal that the crusades represented a new and troublesome phase in Jewish history. The importance of preaching in the recruitment of crusades and the growing sophistication of the church's attention to it, in particular from the thirteenth century, are signs of the importance of the crusades to debates about medieval communication, literacy and orality, and the exchanges between elite and popular culture. The crusades are also highly relevant to current academic debates about the relationship between core and periphery in later medieval western European culture. The brainchild of the reformed papacy and dominated by inhabitants of the old Carolingian heartlands, the crusades were self-evidently the emanation of an assertive, expansionist core, yet they were for the most part played out on or beyond the margins of Latin Christendom, and in the process had to adapt to local traditions and needs.

The fact that crusade expeditions, especially the more successful ones, regularly formed the subject matter of detailed historical narratives reveals their importance to discussions of medieval commemoration and memory. It is noteworthy that the first extensive pieces of prose writing in Old French are two accounts of the Fourth Crusade (1202–4) written within a decade or so of the events they describe. The authors, Geoffrey of Villehardouin (c. 1150–c. 1212) and Robert of Cléry (d. after 1216), were eye-witnesses, part of a long tradition of participant-as-historian.[2] This is a reminder that a further interest

---

1 Gerald of Wales, *The Journey through Wales; The Description of Wales*, trans. L. Thorpe (Harmondsworth: Penguin, 1978), 76, 80, 109; Caesarius of Heisterbach, *The Dialogue on Miracles*, trans. H. von E. Scott and C. C. Swinton Bland, 2 vols. (London: Routledge, 1929), vol. 2, 191.

2 Geoffrey of Villehardouin, 'The Conquest of Constantinople', in M. R. B. Shaw, trans., *Chronicles of the Crusades* (Harmondsworth: Penguin, 1963), 27–160; Robert of Clari [Cléry], *The Conquest of Constantinople*, trans. E. H. McNeal (New York: Columbia University Press, 1936; repr. Toronto: Medieval Academy of America, 1996).

of the crusades is the way in which they break down the historiographical boundaries between observer and observed, and in the process throw up texts which purposively blur, even play with, generic distinctions – chronicle, epic song, foundation myth, grail quest, royal biography, pilgrimage guide, travel text, ethnography. Beyond this, the fascination of the crusades lies in the fact that they, perhaps uniquely and certainly to an unmatched degree, tested the boundaries of the western Christian imagination: an imagination, that is to say, which was not simply a matter of mental mapping, the extent to which the Christian world felt itself limited by geographical and religious frontiers, but also embraced the capacity of ordinary Christians to give clear expression to those notions of shared history, brotherhood and charity which might otherwise have remained amorphous and unrealised.

For all this, it is important to retain a sense of scale. The crusade was not the leitmotif for a whole civilisation, however important and pervasive it could regularly prove. The crusade was a novelty which also articulated deeply rooted ideas that pre-dated, transcended and sometimes outlived it. It involved the playing out of curious paradoxes: the creation of the Gregorian papacy, whose reform policies were grounded in the idea of clerical detachment from the secular world's contaminating influences, the crusade was also an exercise in ecclesiastical immersion in the most secular of activities, warfare, and consequently a demonstration of the church's need for the assistance of the very secular authority that its Gregorianism taught it to mistrust. Perhaps as early as the Second Crusade (1145–9), and certainly by the time of the first crusade of King Louis IX of France (1226–70) in 1248–54, the papacy was heavily reliant on the organisation and resources of kings for the prosecution of major crusades, in the process reinventing in another guise the sort of mutual dependence between popes and emperors which the Gregorians so clearly abominated, and which they originally invented the crusade precisely in order to circumvent.

The crusade was therefore an important but limited presence within medieval civilisation. It has been in the attempt to understand the complexities of the crusade's significance to the medieval church and to medieval Christian culture, in contrast to the older emphasis on simply recounting stirring narratives, that the academic study of crusading has broadened and deepened in recent decades. Much of the exciting new work done on the Middle Ages since the 1960s and 1970s has involved the examination of groups of people who were excluded from the traditional historiographical gaze: women, the poor, heretics and minorities, for example. Our understanding of old-fashioned subjects has been reanimated by new methodological approaches: the study of political conflict, for example, by insights gained from social anthropology and gender studies. But crusading is perhaps that part of the old canon of medieval history – the parts of it which go back at least as far as the invention of the academic discipline in the nineteenth century – which has reconfigured itself most profoundly in recent times. This has been in response to various changes in perspective. The most obvious, and perhaps the single most important, has been a broadening of the subject's geographical range. The traditional picture, from the first early modern historians of crusading, through *The Talisman* (1825) by Walter Scott (1771–1832), to the best-selling and much re-issued *History of the Crusades* (1951–4) by Steven Runciman (1903–2000), was straightforward: crusades were fought in the eastern Mediterranean. Indeed, they were largely defined by that basic fact. The zone of operations could be framed quite broadly in order to accommodate the strategic ebb and flow of events, thereby including Asia Minor and the north African littoral, but in essence Palestine and Syria were regarded as crusading's essential home ground, a reflection of the centrality of Jerusalem and the Holy Land to the crusaders' aspirations.

In recent decades this monolithic vision of crusading has, for most scholars at least, expanded and diversified. It is now recognised that crusades were waged in other places and consequently against other sorts of opponents than the Muslim peoples encountered in the eastern Mediterranean. Crusades were also waged against the Moorish inhabitants of Spain, political opponents of the papacy in parts of Italy, heretics, most notably the Cathars in southern France, and pagans living just beyond the north-eastern fringes of Latin Christendom in the Baltic region. As early as the Second Crusade in the 1140s an attempt was made to synchronise multiple crusade expeditions on three general fronts: in the Middle East, in Spain and in north-eastern Europe. The balance sheet of gains and losses for this particular effort was not impressive, the Christian capture of Lisbon proving the only enduring achievement, but the general sense of real interconnection persisted. In the second half of the twelfth century, one comes across simultaneous bursts of papal interest in crusading in Spain and the Baltic, for all that separated these two very different theatres; and from the pontificate of Innocent III one finds the papacy attempting a holistic direction of crusading in all its forms, so that, for example, a crusade in one area could be 'turned off' by the withdrawal of the indulgence for it in order to favour recruitment for another crusade elsewhere.

This broad vision of crusading and its purposes reflected the notion that all the specific problems identified by the papacy had a transcendental quality as threats to the whole church, understood as an emanation of the divine will, an obedience, a cultic tradition, a body of doctrine, a set of institutions, a collection of people, places with historical roles in the story of Christianity, or buildings and objects. Crusades were believed to be responses to threats against these facets of the church configured in different permutations. This helps to explain why as early as the launching of the First Crusade at the Council of Clermont in 1095, peaking with the great thirteenth-century councils of Lateran IV (1215), Lyons I (1245) and Lyons II (1274), and arguably extending as far as Trent in the sixteenth century, discussions of the crusade were bound up with wider efforts for reform, to the extent that crusading became perceived as more than just a possible collateral benefit of the renovation of the church and Christian society; it represented the validating goal of that ambition, the clinching proof that it had worked.

A corollary of the geographical broadening of crusade history has been an extension of its chronological boundaries. This has perhaps represented an equally important break from the old paradigms. The traditional story of crusading was a simple trajectory of rise and fall. The narrative, according to this view, came to its proper end in 1291, when the Mamluk sultanate took control of Acre and the other remaining Latin Christian fingerholds on the Palestinian and Syrian coastline, thereby ending the nearly two centuries of Western presence in the region which had begun with the conquests made during and soon after the First Crusade. True, the Latins were not removed from the eastern Mediterranean entirely, for they still controlled Cyprus and remnants of the short-lived Latin Empire of Constantinople (1204–61). But there seemed to be something definitive and emblematic about the panicked, scrambling flight of the last Latins to get on the last ships out of Acre – a scene akin to the frantic climbing on board the last helicopters out of Saigon in 1975. In any event, so it was argued, and this was one reason why events had come to such a critical pass, western Europe's enthusiasm for the crusades was by then in steep decline. Crusading was a finite quantity, and it had had its moment. Recently, revisionist scholars have extended the chronological range of crusading into the sixteenth century and, in certain of its institutional manifestations such as the Military Orders, beyond. The effect has been to expose the old narrative trajectory as simplistic and misleading. Yes, crusading can be said to have declined by the latter part of the thirteenth century, if by 'decline' one simply means western Europe's decreasing ability and willingness to stage reruns of the First Crusade. But this is no more realistic a benchmark than saying that castles in 1300 were somehow worse for being different from the motte-and-bailey structures of two centuries earlier, or that cathedrals should have properly continued to be Romanesque rather than Gothic in design.

Crusading constantly adapted and mutated to meet new challenges. In the fourteenth and fifteenth centuries, for example, it became more naval in emphasis to reflect the nature of warfare in the eastern Mediterranean; and it accommodated new emphases in the chivalric culture of the aristocracy. Large set-piece expeditions became fewer, as the costs of warfare rose and the growth of states' control over the activities of their warrior elites meant that crusading had sometimes to fit round the lulls in European warfare, especially the Hundred Years War. But the capture (albeit fleeting) of Alexandria by Peter I of Cyprus (1359–69) in 1365, the defence of Belgrade against the Ottomans in 1456 inspired by the preaching and leadership of John of Capistrano (1386–1456), the enthusiasm of popes committed to the cause of crusading such as Clement VI (1342–52) and Pius II (1458–64), and the widespread celebration of the victory of a Spanish-led naval coalition over the Turkish fleet off Lepanto in the Gulf of Corinth in 1571, all attest to the continuing vitality of crusading as an ideal.

What, then, was a 'crusade'? This is a contentious issue in spite of, or perhaps because of, the amount that has been written on the subject. The central problem is that modern scholarship has to work with terminology that represents a series of accommodations between the technical Latin jargon of the medieval educated elite, medieval vernacular terms which may or may not map neatly onto their Latin equivalents, concepts and categories (not least the numbering of the big crusades to the East) created by the early modern scholars who pioneered the study of the subject, and modern academic discourse. The absence of clarity and consensus in the Middle Ages is striking: evidence for vernacular terms etymologically rooted in words for 'cross', and specifically used in relation to military expeditions, only appears from the thirteenth century, already more than a century after the First Crusade. On the other hand, the absence of a precise lexis does not necessarily mean that there were not some clear ideas and images at play from the start. In recent usage, the word 'crusade' has tended to be used loosely to refer to any, and every, incidence of warfare that pitted Christians against Muslims, or at least the large subset of those wars in which there is evidence for a self-conscious religious colouration on one or both sides. The problem then becomes one of collapsing enormous variety across time and space into a single category. The study of the conflicts between Christians and Muslims in medieval Spain, for example, has until recent times been bedevilled by a reluctance to rein in the acceptations of 'crusade', which is used so loosely as to become meaningless.

At the other extreme, too precise and narrow an approach to definition can create a *pointilliste* picture of crusading history which underplays medieval people's abilities to make imaginative connections and resolve inconsistencies for themselves. Nonetheless, some attempt at definition is necessary in order to understand crusading's impact on medieval Europe: it may have been blurred around the edges, but there were core institutions, ideas, values and images which cumulatively added up to what we can satisfactorily term a crusade 'movement'. Most scholars today would single out the following main defining elements: papal authorisation of the crusade and the granting of the indulgence (the precise form of which might vary according to the underlying theology); the taking of vows, linked to but not identical to pilgrimage vows, and the wearing of crosses by participants; and an essentially reactive set of justifications, drawing on traditional Just War criteria to argue for the liberation of Christians and Christian territory or redress for harm done.

The value of some sort of clear definition is confirmed by the fact that when the First Crusade was preached, people were struck by its novelty, albeit a novelty compounded of familiar elements. The message of Pope Urban II (1088–99) in 1095–6 had many antecedents. He was responding to a request for help from the Byzantine emperor, Alexius I Comnenus (1081–1118), which was the latest in a long series of diplomatic exchanges between Rome and Constantinople. Urban's appeal for a volunteer army to liberate Jerusalem and eastern Christians living under infidel dominion had resonances in the rhetoric of the Gregorian reformers, of whom Urban was one. The emphasis upon Jerusalem and the Holy Sepulchre, and the penitential quality of the task held out to would-be crusaders, tapped into powerful currents of eleventh-century popular religiosity and the appeal of pilgrimage to the East. Urban is sometimes described as a craftsman who reassembled old material in order to make a new configuration: this probably underestimates his personal achievement, but the basic picture of creativity born of tradition is accurate. With hindsight we can see how things were building up before Clermont: radical thinkers associated with Pope Gregory VII (1073–85) had already made tentative connections between warfare and penance; Urban himself had earlier in his pontificate suggested analogies between fighting and pilgrimage. But we should not underestimate the shock of the new, which in itself does much to explain the success of the message. There is a well-known vignette towards the beginning of the history of the first crusader Tancred (c. 1076–1112) by Ralph of Caen (c. 1080–c. 1130), in which the hero is wracked by depression and anxiety. He finds himself torn between his responsibilities as a lord and warrior, which will drag him into sin, and the precepts of the Gospel, which effectively means conversion to the monastic life. He then hears about the crusade message, and his spirits suddenly and wholly revive, for he appreciates that the crusade has transformed knightly identity from an impediment hindering salvation to the vehicle for it.[3]

It is clear that the crusade message was mainly conceived with western Europe's military elites in mind. From as early as the First Crusade, Urban II's surviving utterances on the crusade speak of *milites*, knights, as the prime target, and this emphasis was to be one of the most enduring and consistent themes of crusading. In practice, however, the aristocratic quality of crusades was routinely qualified in two respects. First, no knight could function in glorious isolation from a support team of dependants that looked after him, his equipment and his horses. The image of the intrepid and lone knight errant, which became a favoured motif of imaginative literature from the twelfth century onwards, is one with no connection to the lived experience of crusaders. Second, the essentially pastoral quality of the crusade message, with its emphasis upon the remissions of sins and its co-option of pilgrimage, which was by long tradition open to people from all walks of life, meant that it was impossible to exclude the non-military majority. It has been estimated that about 10 per cent of the total numbers who went on the First Crusade were knights; and the same sort of ratio probably holds true of the other mass-participation crusades. By the thirteenth century, as it became more common for crusades to the East to travel by ship, the greater costs of sea travel acted as a social filter, accentuating crusading's aristocratic profile. It is no coincidence that from around this time, for example in 1212, 1251, 1309 and 1320, one also begins to see outbursts of popular enthusiasm for the crusade, usually triggered by official crusade preaching but also cast in some way in opposition to, and as a purer, more meritorious improvement on, the aristocratic norms. These poorer crusade enthusiasts were often described by hostile observers as 'children' or 'shepherds' as if to emphasise their misdirected innocence or subversiveness, their social marginality and their military unsuitability. The children and the shepherds could be volatile forces, given to excesses in the absence of strong leadership and a clear direction. But they at least demonstrate the enduring appeal of crusading outside the charmed circle of aristocratic culture within which crusade ideology found its immediate home.

---

3 Ralph of Caen, 'Gesta Tancredi in expeditione Hierosolymitana', in *Recueil des historiens des croisades: Historiens occidentaux*, 5 vols. (Paris: Académie des Inscriptions et Belles-Lettres, 1844–95), vol. 3, 605–6.

Because of this deliberate and persistent elitist colouring, as much to do with perceptions as actual numbers of bodies on the ground, it is principally to aristocratic society that we must look if we wish to assess crusading's impact on Christian culture as a whole. Most knights most of the time did not become crusaders, but it is striking how far the church pitched the crusade message in terms which transcended crusading's irregular rhythms and voluntary, minority-interest quality, and sought nothing less than the redefinition of knighthood itself. For example, Bernard of Clairvaux (1090–1153), one of the greatest crusade preachers and apologists, argued in his *In Praise of the New Knighthood* (c. 1130), a treatise immediately directed towards the incipient Military Order of the Templars but also full of ideas applicable to crusaders in general, that meritorious war in God's service was such a powerful instrument that it inverted the comfortable categories and assumptions that otherwise governed a knight's perception of himself and his status.[4] Playing on the similarity in Latin between *militia*, 'knighthood', and *malitia*, 'evil', Bernard argued that knights caught up in their traditional internecine struggles could not be understood as bad knights; they were not properly knights at all. Developing this startling theme, Bernard issued a further challenge: to prefer *malitia* to *militia* was to forfeit one's masculinity. This was an extraordinarily bold frontal assault on the gendering of social roles, effectively the organisational principle of male aristocratic self-fashioning. Allegations of effeminacy cut very deep. Bernard of Clairvaux's utterances were, of course, the hyperbole of a skilled rhetorician defending a new idea, but the fact that he brought issues of masculine identity to the surface of his discourse illustrates the fundamental nature of the challenge that the church wished the crusade to pose to aristocratic mores.

In the event, crusading's longevity and adaptability meant that it had to move as aristocratic culture moved. This is particularly evident in a warming towards aristocratic display and ritual as the cult of chivalry developed between the thirteenth and fifteenth centuries. Because late medieval chivalry still has an image as the triumph of form over content, and of gesture over sentiment, its close connections to crusading can easily be misinterpreted as evidence for crusading's own vacuity. This would be to underestimate chivalry's importance as a cultural force. The famously sumptuous Feast of the Pheasant staged at Lille in 1454 by Duke Philip the Good of Burgundy (1396–1467), during which the duke and many of his noble guests ostentatiously took

---

4 Bernard of Clairvaux, 'In Praise of the New Knighthood', in M. Barber and K. Bate, trans., *The Templars: Selected Sources* (Manchester: Manchester University Press, 2002), 215–27.

crusade vows, can easily be dismissed as empty frippery, but this would miss the significance that a successful and ambitious regime such as Philip's could attach to chivalry as a political and cultural tool, and by extension the value of crusading as an animating ideal of the wider value system. Chivalric display could co-exist with hard-headed dedication. It is well known that in the fourteenth century, and into the first two decades of the fifteenth, the Military Order of the Teutonic Knights attracted the nobles and knights of western Europe to its headquarters in Prussia, from which it would lead expeditions across large stretches of difficult wooded and marshy terrain against their Lithuanian enemies. These *Reisen*, 'trips', have something of the chivalric package tour about them, a sense confirmed by the panoply of ritualised feasting and heraldic display with which the trips were concluded. But these were no promenades: they had to take place in the dry heat of summer or the icy grip of midwinter for the ground to be passable, and the campaigns were directed against resourceful and increasingly well-organised opponents. In a very real way, therefore, and for all the intervening cultural and social changes that aristocrats had experienced, the demands of a Prussian *Reise* stood in straight line of descent from Urban II's idea at the time of the First Crusade that the spiritual merit of the exercise was a direct function of the dangers, the time, the cost and the sheer physical and mental effort that he shrewdly calculated the crusade would involve. This core value supplies the essential continuity in crusading's impact on aristocratic life, and explains its ability to insinuate itself within fundamental aspects of individual and group self-identity, for example in relation to ideas of gender, reputation, ritual and display.

The crusades also resonated with aristocratic culture, and to some extent with popular culture more broadly, because they were an opportunity for people to situate themselves in time in ways which their routine lives would seldom have afforded. On an intimate, domestic level this took the form of family traditions of crusading, significantly transmissible through both male and female lines. These were sufficiently to the fore in people's consciousness to be regularly exploited by preachers aiming to stir visceral, deeply emotive responses in their audiences. As early as the Second Crusade, Pope Eugenius III (1145–53) was emphasising this theme in his crusade encyclical *Quantum praedecessores*, reminding the aristocrats of his own time of the achievements of their forebears, and holding out the prospect of shameful ignominy if one generation's achievements were not replicated in the next.[5] The feeling of

---

5  L. Riley-Smith and J. S. C. Riley-Smith, *The Crusades: Idea and Reality, 1095–1274* (London: Edward Arnold, 1981), 57–9.

being part of a continuum also extended beyond domestic traditions into a broader sense of historical responsibility. When the former master general of the Dominican order, Humbert of Romans (c. 1199–1277), wrote a discussion paper for the Council of Lyons II (1274) about the current and future state of crusading, one of the possible criticisms that he tried to pre-empt was the futility of wasting Christian blood, especially the blood of revered leaders such as the recent crusade casualty St Louis. Humbert evoked the achievements of Charles Martel (684–741) and Charlemagne (747–814) in wars against the Saracens, as well as those of Godfrey of Bouillon (c. 1061–1100) on the First Crusade.[6]

One reaction to this list might be to wonder how far Humbert was reduced to scraping the barrel in an attempt to disguise the Christians' recent poor track record: two of his three exemplars had been dead for more than 450 years, and even Godfrey's achievements were nearly two centuries in the past. The fact that these figures lived for thirteenth-century aristocrats as much as anything as the heroes of epic songs further reveals the strain, to modern sensibilities at least, in Humbert's historical argument. But the bigger point is that Humbert's experience as a crusade preacher must have persuaded him that these were meaningful connections to make, and that contemporaries valued the ability to locate their own experience within a long chronological frame. Indeed, another part of Humbert's argument was to reach even further back to the time of the Old Testament, evoking parallels between crusaders and the people of Israel, which had been the stock in trade of crusade apologetics since the chronicles of the First Crusade. The biblical connection went even further: the appeal of crusading, especially to the East, presupposed a collapsing of chronological distance between the events of the Gospels and the present day. The Holy Land remained Christ's patrimony by virtue of its being the setting for his life, death and resurrection, and in this way perceived injuries visited on it and its inhabitants even more than a millennium later were to be understood as real and unmediated injuries to Christ himself, permitting him, through his mouthpiece the pope, to summon his followers to vindicate that wrong just as a secular lord would summon his knights to prosecute a vendetta. Crusades, then, ran on a heady and unique mixture of biblical, myth-historical and dynastic time.

Assessing the impact of the crusades on Christianity in the round is by no means straightforward, for we are dealing with a movement that found expression in a diverse range of institutions, habits of mind and cultural

6 *Ibid.*, 106–7.

forms. Perhaps the single most important contribution of the crusades to Christians' religious thinking, and thus to the interactions between clergy and laity in general, was the indulgence, which emerged as a benchmark against which the church could calibrate offers of spiritual reward in a wide array of circumstances. The theological bases and the popular reception of the various formulations of the crusade indulgence are both hotly debated by historians. What probably began as a generous remission of penances at the time of the First Crusade mutated by the pontificate of Innocent III into a release of the temporal penalties (in this world and in purgatory) due from sin. But popular understandings never mapped neatly onto the sometimes hesitant and ambiguous official formulations. A maximal reading of the crusade's spiritual benefits is apparent as early as the eye-witness accounts of the First Crusade, which appropriated the language of martyrdom when speaking of fallen comrades. What exactly the crusade delivered in spiritual terms was an area where the clergy and lay people largely agreed to differ, or not to ask too many awkward questions, and to this extent crusading was an exercise in the creative camouflaging of the disjunctions between educated and popular understandings of concepts such as merit and reward.

In terms of facilitating expressions of religious devotion, the most noticeable effect of the crusades was the Latin control of Jerusalem and the Holy Places between 1099 and the Muslim reconquest under Saladin in 1187. Western pilgrimage to the East had already been picking up in the eleventh century, and the success of the First Crusade made possible a veritable pilgrimage boom. Indications of the importance that this assumed are provided by the Latins' building of the magnificent church of the Holy Sepulchre and of the Knights of St John's hospital, which could accommodate many hundreds of sick and poor pilgrims. To some extent Jerusalem was an exportable quantity: relics brought back to the West by favoured pilgrims included shavings of rock from Calvary and the Sepulchre itself, as well as splinters of the True Cross and innumerable other precious objects. Mimicking the architecture of the Holy Land could be another powerful statement of pious attachment; the Temple church in London, consecrated by the patriarch of Jerusalem in 1185, is one example of this identity-through-mimesis, the extraordinary reproduction of the aedicule of the Holy Sepulchre built around 1500 in Görlitz in eastern Saxony is another. It has been argued that one effect of the opening up of the Holy Land in the twelfth century was to confirm in Western popular religiosity an attachment to the humanity of Christ and by extension to the Blessed Virgin Mary, a sensibility that the mendicant orders were able to sustain and develop from the thirteenth century onwards, even though Latin control of the Holy Land had been lost. This is an attractive thesis, but it also exposes the difficulty of isolating effects on Christian life that can be specifically and unambiguously assigned to the crusades in isolation: the interest in the humanity of Christ had many complex roots that pre-dated crusading, and the Western attachment to the Holy Land was an expression of enthusiasm for pilgrimage in general, not just the crusading subset of pilgrimage ideology.

It is often observed that, of all the events and processes played out on the big pan-European stage in the Middle Ages, mention of the crusades most frequently intrudes into annals, chronicles, miracle collections, saints' Lives, urban histories, and genealogies, that is to say the sorts of texts which were normally dominated by local affairs and very limited in their horizons. In other words, the crusades, by this index at least, did most to break down particularism and promote a sense of a joined-up Christendom. There is much to commend this view, though it should not be overstated: for the most part these texts remained resolutely local in their range, even when the crusades opened up new vistas. Equally, the many profound reorderings that took place within the cores and peripheries of Latin civilisation from the eleventh century onwards were never the result of the crusades alone. The crusades' importance lies in their being one part of a fuller picture which also includes the papal reform movement, the growth of international religious orders, changes in communication techniques such as preaching, maritime expansion, developments in military technology, and population movements towards and across frontiers in the Iberian peninsula, eastern Europe and (to a limited degree) the Middle East. The crusade asked of western Europeans that they revisit their basic identities, but it did so in terms which validated their familiar points of reference, in particular aristocratic status, the family, the values attached to property, loyalty and duty, service and reward. The crusade was an extraordinary innovation, the 'new way to attain salvation', as one historian of the First Crusade put it, but its effect was to inflect the Christian identity of later medieval European civilisation rather than to effect a radical reconfiguration.

PART VI

*

# THE CHALLENGES TO A CHRISTIAN
# SOCIETY

# 23

# Repression and power

## JOHN H. ARNOLD

It was, the annalist of the city Worms tells us, the year of Our Lord 1231:

> There came by divine permission a miserable plague and most harsh sentence. For indeed there came a certain friar called Conrad Dors, and he was completely illiterate and of the Order of Preachers, and he brought with him a certain secular man named John who was one-eyed and maimed, and in truth utterly vile. These two, beginning…firstly among the poor, said that they knew who were heretics; and they began to burn them, those who confessed their guilt and refused to leave their sect… And they condemned many who, in the hour of their death, called out with all their heart to our Lord Jesus Christ, and even in the fire strongly cried out, begging for the help of the holy Mother of God and all the saints.

Conrad Dors and John were then joined by Conrad of Marburg, a priest who had been the famously harsh confessor of St Elisabeth of Hungary (1217–31) until her recent death. Led now by this second Conrad, and backed by papal authority, the trio continued their work:

> In truth, those who confessed to heresy, as many innocent people did to stay alive, had the hair shaved from their heads above the ears, and they had to go around like this for as long as it pleased [the inquisitors]. Those who, in truth, refused [to confess] were burnt. And their will prevailed everywhere, because brother Conrad was a literate man and especially eloquent.

All three inquisitors were, the chronicler said, 'imperfect judges and without mercy', whose reported boast was that 'We would burn a hundred innocent people amongst whom there is one guilty'.[1] And burn them they did.

These events in medieval Germany, in the archdiocese of Mainz, are possibly the earliest example of inquisition into heresy in the Middle Ages. Other accounts of Conrad of Marburg's activities stress that practically nobody could escape his clutches, as freedom could be gained only through confessing

---

1 *Annales Wormatienses*, ed. G. H. Pertz, MGH, SS 17, 38–40.

to heresy, and moreover by implicating others. This fits well with a certain picture of the period: zealous inquisitors pursue hapless victims, prosecute indiscriminately, force confessions, and sentence as many as possible to death. Brutal, implacable, illogical: the dark side to an 'age of faith'. Such a time, one might well imagine, was doubtless not only characterised by this unbending demand for religious conformity, but also hostile to any cultural deviation, cared little for individual liberty, and ruthlessly enforced strict sexual and social norms. A more repressive society could scarcely be imagined.

However, before embracing too readily this popular image of medieval repression, we should look a little closer at the events around Mainz. The chronicle cited above was written around the time of the persecutions by an anonymous cleric, and it quite clearly deplores Conrad's actions. Moreover, the archbishop of Mainz wrote to the pope about Conrad's actions in very negative terms, stating that he himself had warned Conrad 'to proceed in so great a matter with more moderation and discretion, but he refused'.[2] Conrad accused various powerful noblemen of heresy, but when the case was brought before a synod of bishops and nobles at Mainz in 1233, the charges were dismissed. Three days later, Conrad was murdered, and similar fates overtook Conrad Dors and John. The pope initially wrote of Conrad as a martyr, but unlike some later murdered inquisitors, he was not canonised, probably because of the extent of his infamy. Indeed, at a church council a year after his death, one bishop 'burst out in these words, saying "Master Conrad of Marburg deserves to be dug up and burnt as a heretic"'.[3] Conrad may have had papal blessing, but that did not mean that the church as a whole welcomed his actions, nor that every ecclesiastic agreed with his views or methods, nor that the secular powers in his society supported them. As a conclusion to the 'plague', the Worms chronicler reports, a papal *nuncio* announced that in future, 'in such matters that touch upon inquisition of heretics, the succession and laws of the holy father and sacred scripture are firmly observed, now and in perpetuity'.[4] Indiscriminate persecution was to be replaced by the methodical application of law.

What was purely black now perhaps appears more confusingly grey. The picture of a dark Middle Ages remains common today, particularly in popular culture, but also affecting some historical scholarship. The image has, however, a certain history. It was forged particularly after the convulsions of the

---

2 *Chronica Albrichi monachi trium fontium*, ed. P. Scheffer-Boichorst, MGH, SS 23, 932.
3 *Annales Erfordienses*, ed. G. H. Pertz, MGH, SS 16, 29.
4 *Annales Wormatienses*, 39.

Reformation. Protestant historians, from the sixteenth century onward, sought roots for their reforms in the heresies of earlier periods, and hence associated their contemporary struggles with past persecution, depicting an all-powerful and highly repressive Catholic Church. Elements of this viewpoint continued to inform the foundational histories of medieval repression written in the late nineteenth and twentieth centuries. Recent work, however, in part informed by a greater sympathy toward medieval Catholicism, has sought to revise the image.[5] Historians have stressed the heterogeneous nature of the medieval church, argued that a degree of religious toleration can be identified in medieval intellectual thought, and – where repression is unarguably present – emphasised the extent to which medieval people saw heresies and other deviations as a profound threat to their society and salvation, and hence acted accordingly. Inquisitors, in this light, are less repressive zealots and more educated ecclesiastics working methodically in an attempt to save the souls of their flock.

Such revisions are important. The activities of Conrad of Marburg cannot and should not be taken as representative, tarring the whole medieval church with the same brush. At the same time, however, Conrad's reign of terror *did* occur, people *were* killed for perceived transgressions against the faith, and this was not the *only* occasion when a cleric led a period of fevered persecution against heterodoxy. Moreover, in substituting the rule of canon law for Conrad's zealotry, the papacy did not bestow a regime of benign religious pluralism upon Germany, but replaced unrestrained religious violence with a more subtle – but arguably more powerful – framework of doctrinal policing. The lurid picture that Protestant reformers painted of the medieval church should be abandoned. But that does not necessarily mean that we should hang in its stead a pallid watercolour of tolerance and harmony. Something that captures a more complex shadowing of dark and light is needed.

## The development of repression

R. I. Moore has developed an influential argument that, over the twelfth and thirteenth centuries, persecution of certain groups – heretics, Jews, lepers and others – became habitual and institutionalised in medieval society.[6] This was

---

5 For example G. Macy, 'Was there a "The Church" in the Middle Ages?', in R. Swanson, ed., *Unity and Diversity in the Church* (Studies in Church History 32; Oxford: Basil Blackwell, 1996), 107–16; C. J. Nederman, *Worlds of Difference: European Discourses of Toleration c. 1100–1550* (University Park: Pennsylvania State University Press, 2000).
6 R. I. Moore, *The Formation of a Persecuting Society: Power and Deviance in Western Europe 950–1250* (Oxford: Blackwell, 1987).

not because of any objective changes within those persecuted groups themselves; they were no more of a 'threat' to Christianity than they had ever been. The 'formation of a persecuting society', as Moore put it, had two interlinked causes. One was the development of nascent state bureaucracies, capable of institutionalising repression. The other was the rise of the *litterati*, a self-conscious class of educated churchmen and administrators (who largely ran the bureaucracies) who rhetorically demonised as a collective group those they deemed 'outsiders', as a means of bolstering their own elite legitimacy.

Moore's theory of the rise of the *litterati* may not tell the whole tale: one notes that whilst Conrad of Marburg's power is partially ascribed by the Worms chronicler to his literacy, Conrad Dors was described as 'totally illiterate'. However, the words used in that description – *laicus totalis* – point to the way in which clerical conceptions of the laity and their intellectual abilities informed cultural and religious change. Eleventh- and early twelfth-century sources depicting outbreaks of heresy tend to represent the laity as a rather simple, undifferentiated group: either credulous sheep easily seduced by the gilded tongue of the heresiarch, or devout believers wreaking righteous violence against the heretical sect. If such latter accounts sometimes depict a degree of reality, lay hostility towards heresy sprang not from innate antipathy to religious heterogeneity, but from attitudes taught by the church in precisely this period – and taught, most particularly, to secular authorities. The church's first weapons against heresy, and indeed against other groups, were words. In twelfth-century Languedoc, when the Cathar heresy held sway, the initial reaction was to send powerful orthodox preachers to the area, Bernard of Clairvaux (1091–1153) being the most famous of their number. In sermon collections, and in polemical texts that informed preachers, twelfth-century theologians propounded a theory of ecclesiastical dominion that encompassed not only Christianity itself, but also claimed a kind of governance over Judaism, and declared Islam to be a form of Christian heresy. Such ideas entered canon law in the thirteenth century, particularly under Innocent IV (1243–54).[7] Abstract argument was moreover supplemented with rhetoric. A variety of tropes depicting heretics became common: heretics were mad and deluded, and their heresy spread like a cancer or disease; heresy was a poison, insidious in its workings; behind a veil of false piety, the worst sexual and

---

7  D. Iogna-Prat, *Order and Exclusion: Christendom and Cluny Face Judaism, Islam and Heresy (1000–1150)*, trans. G. R. Edwards (Ithaca, N.Y.: Cornell University Press, 2002); J. Muldoon, *Popes, Lawyers and Infidels: The Church and the Non-Christian World 1250–1550* (Liverpool: Liverpool University Press, 1979).

spiritual transgressions were committed.[8] For example, heretics were accused of holding secret orgies at which children were murdered and the devil kissed on the anus – a charge made in whole or part at various times and places across the Middle Ages, including in one chronicler's report of those persecuted by Conrad of Marburg.[9]

These fantasies of evil formed a necessary preparation for the violence that followed. Rhetorics of demonisation worked to make people fear those they deemed outsiders, and hence to place them beyond the bonds of community. The hostile imagery bleeds over from one group to another: there is an obvious similarity between stories of heretical orgies and child-slaying, and the fantasies (also born in the twelfth century) of Jewish ritual murder of children; and in the fifteenth century, witchcraft too began in some areas to be associated with child murder. Heresy was a poison; Jews and lepers were feared as poisoners (particularly in 1321, when a well-poisoning plot was 'discovered' in France, the lepers supposedly paid by the Jews to administer the poison). Fear of sexual pollution – between Jews and Christians, between lepers and the healthy, between prostitutes and their clients, between sodomites and other men – was a recurrent theme. Heresy, Judaism, witchcraft, sodomy; at certain points the supposed threat was conflated, particularly in the fifteenth century, perhaps most ludicrously when certain commentators alleged that Host-desecrating Jews were joining forces with Hussite heretics. At some level, the rhetoric suggested, these transgressors were linked, conjoined in one satanic plot to attack Christendom.

The church did not dispense only rhetoric, however, but also law. One can track the institutionalisation of repression via certain legislative milestones. Responses to heresy in the eleventh century were essentially localised and specific, in both conception and practice. One bishop might write to another, asking what to do about a particular group of heretics troubling his diocese, but there was little sense of a 'church policy'; indeed, it was precisely the lack of one that prompted the search for advice. Actions thus varied from withdrawing communion but tolerating for a while the presence of heresy (advice given by Bishop Wazo of Liège around 1048), to debating with the dissenters (as at Arras in 1025), to summary execution, apparently at the hands of the laity (Monforte, around 1028). Things changed, however, in the later twelfth century. At the Third Lateran Council (1179) various named heretical groups were anathematised, using measures designed to enlist the aid of local secular

---

8 On textual representations of heresy, see further Chapter 12 (Biller).
9 *Gestorum Treverorum, continuatio IV*, ed. G. Waitz, MGH, SS 24, 401.

powers against them. The papal bulls *Ad abolendam* (1184) and *Vergentis in senium* (1199) established, respectively, that the laity had to co-operate with the church in pursuing heretics, and that heresy was in itself a kind of treason, and hence a threat to secular as well as ecclesiastical authority. Later glosses on *Ad abolendam* took Jesus' words to John as instruction on what 'condign punishment' should be meted out to heretics: 'If a man abide not in me, he is cast forth as a branch, and is withered; and men gather them, and cast them into the fire, and they are burned' (John 15.6). The Fourth Lateran Council of 1215 framed its opening definition of Christian faith with a lengthy condemnation of heresy and introduced measures symbolically separating Jewish people from the Christian communities within which they lived. Lateran IV's measures regarding heretics, Jews and the formal requirements for orthodox Christian practice (such as annual attendance at confession) were expounded and expanded in diocesan councils across Europe over the following decades and into the fourteenth century.

Measures specifically regarding religious dissent developed in the mid-thirteenth century, most notably inquisition. Inquisition against heresy first appeared in the early 1230s, making use of a new legal procedure (*inquisitio*) developed during the first years of Innocent III's papacy and formalised at the Fourth Lateran Council. The first inquisitions were, like Conrad of Marburg's efforts, ill-disciplined and unfocussed. But more refinements soon appeared. The influential canon lawyer Raymond de Peñafort (d. 1275) provided detailed definitions of heretical transgression at the council of Tarragona in 1242, the councils of Narbonne (1243) and Béziers (1246) added further instructions, the first proper inquisition manual was written around 1248, and in 1252 the bull *Ad extirpanda* gave papal blessing to the use of torture. In the early 1320s the famous Dominican inquisitor Bernard Gui compiled his *Practica inquisitionis*, which, along with the later manual by Nicholas Eymerich, formed the template for inquisitorial activities for several centuries to come. Papal inquisitors initially directed their efforts against Cathar and Waldensian heretics, principally in southern France, parts of Germany, and northern Italy. But over the following centuries, the gaze of the inquisitorial eye wandered over a wider field, suppressing the Spiritual Franciscans, harassing the beguines (lay people, particularly women, who spontaneously adopted a quasi-monastic lifestyle), famously eradicating the Templars, arguably inventing and then persecuting the so-called 'Free Spirits' in fourteenth-century Germany, and by the fifteenth century directing some of its attention to witchcraft, whilst continuing to pursue the surviving Waldensians in Germany and Piedmont. The occasional Jew, sodomite and mystic was also caught up and interrogated.

At the very end of the fifteenth century, the separate, state-sponsored Spanish Inquisition began its work against the suspect Jewish and Islamic *conversos* of the Iberian peninsula.

This crescendo of dates and practices may mislead a little, through depicting a programmatic ascent of repression. The developments were not planned that way: there was no long-term scheme to produce a persecuting society, the papacy only intermittently took the lead in directing what took place in its name, and the church remained a heterogeneous entity throughout those centuries, sometimes embracing in one area that which it prosecuted in another. Although torture was allowed (as in secular law), its use was fairly limited before the fifteenth century, not least because canonists were well aware that it could produce false confessions. There was no central institution of repression: 'The Inquisition', as a permanent papal office, was established only in the sixteenth century. Medieval inquisitors did however collaborate in their task, collate the extensive trial records that they kept, and write manuals outlining the job that they shared. Many, but not all, were drawn from the Dominican order, though inquisition into heresy was only one of their monastic tasks (Bernard Gui, for example, spent much of his time writing histories of his order). At the same time, however, other mechanisms of persecution existed beyond papal inquisition: bishops could and did use *inquisitio* against heretics in their dioceses for example, and moreover there were episcopal and archdeaconal parochial visitations that sometimes prosecuted various 'abuses' against the faith, from sexual transgression to the use of magic. Moreover, the particular instances of repression could have wider reverberations beyond the punishment of the few. Once again we may wonder whether we are looking at something clearly black-and-white, or cast in various shades of grey. It is legitimate to ask, how repressive was the medieval church? But the question might be put slightly differently: what *kind* of power did the church exercise over the currents of faith?

## Mechanisms of persecution

The most dramatic weapon in the church's armoury was crusade, wielded first against Islam in the East, but also, from the thirteenth century, within Europe against heretical regions. The attempts to subdue Languedoc between 1209 and 1229, and the crusades called against the Hussites in fifteenth-century Bohemia, were brutal attempts at repression, involving the crudest use of force and intermittently fed by feverish religious zealotry. But crusade was a blunt implement. It bludgeoned Languedoc into the loss of its political liberty (the region passing into French rule after the death of Raymond VII of Toulouse); heresy, however, was not eradicated by such measures, only displaced from the courts and towns to the woods and mountains. After the years of crusade, the Cathars drew upon their supporters in the lay population for immediate sustenance, and their loose institutional connections with Italy for spiritual support. It took the more subtle tool of inquisition to eradicate the heresy – in the main by the middle of the century, but with some remnants hanging on well into the fourteenth century (the Waldensian heresy also endured in southern Europe up to the Reformation).[10]

What inquisition did that crusade did not was to fray and eventually rend the social fabric that supported the heretical sect. When they entered an area, inquisitors preached to the people and offered them a choice: come forward of your own free will in the next fortnight, seek forgiveness for your heretical sins, and your punishment will be a light penance. But wait longer – to be cited or arrested by the inquisitors – and the punishment would be that much stronger. And when one appeared before an inquisitor, one had to name names. In stark contrast to the annual confession that Christians were enjoined to make to their parish priests, inquisitorial confession pointed outward as well as inward. Admitting one's own guilt was insufficient: the actions of others must be noted, enumerated, detailed. Such a system undermines the trust upon which community depends, particularly when that community is attempting to evade detection. Quite quickly, in the mid-thirteenth century, we find moments in the inquisitorial record of neighbours threatening or beseeching other neighbours to keep quiet about their joint activities. There is later evidence that some people used the presence of inquisitors to settle feuds, informing (whether truly or falsely) on their neighbouring enemies. Through this subtle mixture of threats and entreaties, inquisition corroded the solidarity of heretical support. On occasions, spies were used, and by the fourteenth century, inquisitors had become adept at coercing and tricking confessions from suspects. Inquisition, from the mid-thirteenth century, turned its archive of confessions into a powerful weapon that could be collated, cross-referenced and consulted by different inquisitors over decades, using the inscription of a past transgression to catch people out many years later.[11]

---

10 On both sects, see Chapter 12 (Biller).
11 J. B. Given, *Inquisition and Medieval Society: Power, Discipline and Resistance in Languedoc* (Ithaca, N.Y.: Cornell University Press, 1998), 25–51.

What must also be noted about both crusade and inquisition, however, is their limited nature. A crusade was essentially a war, and wars must at some point end. The Albigensian Crusade itself did not comprise twenty years of continuous violence, but a string of vicious conflicts spread unevenly over those two decades. Inquisition, as noted above, was not a permanent tribunal, but a particular task for a certain time and place. In the mid-thirteenth century, its reach was broad, covering much of southern France and elsewhere, and over the space of just a few years brought at least 8,000 people, and perhaps five times that many, to interrogation and sentence. But later inquisitions encompassed much smaller numbers – in the hundreds rather than the thousands – and inquisitors always operated for specific periods of time. When English bishops employed *inquisitio* against heresy in fifteenth-century England, the numbers questioned were still lower, and its use even more sporadic. Both weapons of repression also depended very much upon secular support for their effective operation – and such support was not always forthcoming. The French monarchy refused to involve itself in the crusade against the south until the final years of that conflict, and much of the legislation passed immediately following the Treaty of Paris (1229) was directed towards trying to *force* the nobility to act against heretics they had previously ignored or supported. In theory, inquisitors enjoyed wide-ranging and extraordinary powers, but in practice, without local secular support, their task was at least rendered difficult, and in the worst cases they themselves were endangered. We have seen above the fate of Conrad and his assistants; they were not the only inquisitors murdered by opponents, the same outcome befalling Guillaume Arnaud in 1242 and Peter of Verona in 1252. Lower-level intimidation, harassment and collective resistances were experienced by inquisitors in France, Italy and Germany at various times.

With regard to the fight against heresy, one might say that we can identify a persecuting society *at certain times and in certain places* – mid-thirteenth-century Languedoc and the Italian city states slightly later that century (eradicating Catharism), parts of Germany in the fourteenth century (primarily against Waldensians and supposed 'Free Spirits'), England somewhat intermittently in the fifteenth century (against Lollardy). One could say similarly of anti-semitic repression: intermittent periods of violence (to mention just a few: Germany and elsewhere in 1095–6, England sporadically in the mid-to-late twelfth century, Germany in the 1290s, France in 1320–1, Spain in the 1390s, Germany once again in the early fifteenth century) stitched together by a slew of anti-Jewish ecclesiastical legislation passed across Europe, particularly in the thirteenth century but reiterated cyclically thereafter. Recent studies have however emphasised less the constant and pathological nature of anti-Judaism and more the ways in which repressive violence against Jews was used as a political tool by various groups, from the barons struggling with the English crown in the thirteenth century (leading up to the expulsion of Jews from England in 1290) to popular political protest against taxation in fourteenth-century France.[12] It is notable also that anti-Jewish attitudes continued to perform some kind of cultural 'work' in late medieval England – in Chaucer's *Canterbury Tales* for example, and in various mystery plays – when the putative targets of this hatred had been absent from those shores for over a century. Such hatred, disconnected from its supposed target, was clearly being *used* for particular purposes. For most of our period, the same point could be made of witchcraft prosecutions: rare in any case in the earlier centuries, many cases were linked to plots against powerful figures, and were essentially part of a particular political struggle, even by the fifteenth century when the famous *Malleus maleficarum* was composed.[13] Indeed, the *Malleus* itself was written by Heinrich Institoris not as an embodiment of current attitudes and policy towards witchcraft, but in an attempt to reshape them – Heinrich having earlier been laughed out of court by the authorities at Innsbruck when he tried to persuade the authorities to prosecute the many witches he believed lurked there.[14]

Thus our opening example of repression at Mainz is, in one sense, more representative than I initially suggested: Conrad terrorised a particular area for a period of time, but the repression was conducted in politically fraught circumstances that eventually curtailed activities. There were ways in which people, individually or collectively, could resist such powers. Those interrogated by inquisitors sometimes attempted, for example, to name as accomplices only those who were already dead. Early in the years of inquisitorial deployment, various towns briefly succeeded in expelling the inquisitors from their walls. On several occasions, groups tried to steal or destroy inquisitors' documentary records. By the early fourteenth century, Cathar supporters tended to want to meet with the *perfecti* only in twos or threes, in the hope that a limited number of potential witnesses could be shrugged off more easily

---

12  R. C. Stacey, 'Antisemitism and the Medieval English State', in J. R. Maddicott and D. M. Palliser, eds., *The Medieval State* (London: Hambledon, 2000), 163–77; D. Nirenberg, *Communities of Violence: Persecution of Minorities in the Middle Ages* (Princeton: Princeton University Press, 1996).

13  R. Kieckhefer, *European Witch Trials* (London: Routledge & Kegan Paul, 1976), 10, and calendar of cases 108–47.

14  See E. Wilson, 'Institoris at Innsbruck', in R. Scribner, ed., *Popular Religion in Germany and Central Europe 1400–1800* (Houndmills: Macmillan, 1996), 87–100.

should the inquisitors come calling. The Franciscan preacher Bernard Délicieux famously led a popular and legal revolt against inquisition in southern France. He was admittedly unsuccessful – and later sentenced for witchcraft – but the fact that he was able to attempt it, and with some degree of support, illustrates that inquisitors did not possess absolute power. Thus in various ways the mechanisms of repression were prey to the vicissitudes of local politics and attitudes. One might say that the ideology was willing, but the state apparatus was, if not weak, then at best unstable. The exercise of power in these modes never possessed sufficient material resources and political support to become truly institutional or regularised. Secular opinion could be mobilised to create and expel 'outsiders' at certain times and places, but not continuously, and not always to the point of prompting violent or legal actions against them. Repression was always *located*, not endemic.

What, then, of the more subtle tools of repression? One could make some similar points about preaching. The most pointedly effective sermon campaigns against 'outsiders' – the anti-Jewish propaganda preached by Vincent Ferrer (c. 1350–1419) in late fourteenth-century Spain for example, or Bernardino da Siena's (1380–1444) denunciations of sodomy and witchcraft (among other things) in fifteenth-century Italian cities – were once again specific and located, notable precisely because they were not being repeated identically across Europe, and because the individual preachers were remarkably effective at rousing their audiences. And as much as the rhetorics of repression tended to link together the supposed enemies of Christendom into one collective threat, this did not mean that every attitude was similarly channelled. One finds, for example, at Basel in the first decade of the fifteenth century a Dominican theologian called Heinrich of Rheinfelden playing a key role in persecuting the beguine communities in that city (who were themselves defended, unsuccessfully, by the local Franciscans). The same Heinrich was, in 1416, investigated by city authorities for making 'sodomitic' advances to lay workers at the Dominican monastery. He was, however, successfully defended by his order.[15] Heresy and sodomy come together in these events, but far from in the expected mode of concatenation. The rhetoric of the 'many-headed beast' was a useful amplification of any individual threat, but it did not mean that all medieval clerics – let alone the laity – thought that Jews, heretics, lepers, homosexuals and others were continuously plotting in concert. If they had, they would scarcely have allowed any Jewish communities to

---

15 H. Puff, *Sodomy in Reformation Germany and Switzerland, 1400–1600* (Chicago: University of Chicago Press, 2003), 37–8.

live alongside them at any point, and would certainly not have given alms to the many leper houses that developed in the later Middle Ages. Even heretics could be seen in a different light, and preachers' denunciations of their crimes questioned by a lay audience. One finds, for example, various occasions of lay people, not notably connected to the Waldensian 'sect', nonetheless decrying the execution of a Waldensian preacher, believing such a figure to be clearly living a holy life and undeserving of this fate.[16]

So the church's more lurid propaganda did not always have a direct effect. Lay audiences, both popular and elite, could sometimes be swayed into repressive action by a zealous preacher, but were also capable of ignoring or even rejecting such a message. Nor did every cleric preach from the same script: the church hierarchy sought a unified Christendom in doctrine and attitudes, but in practice Christianity varied quite widely across Europe, and different strands of Christianity embodied divergent attitudes. That the Franciscans in Basel attempted to defend the beguine community from Dominican attack provides just one example among many of the tensions that could arise between different modes of Christian life, and the diversity such tension could foster. Such diversity was not, however, unlimited; and noting that the house of the medieval church had many mansions does not imply that the main edifice did not exist. It did, and it took power and authority to construct it. The cruder efforts at repression, however, do not represent in full the complex nature of those powers.

## Productions of orthodoxy

As we have seen, when people admitted their guilt, Conrad of Marburg and his associates had their heads shaved. Another source makes clear the purpose: having confessed, this was 'a sign of penance' forced upon the recipient.[17] Guilt, confession and penance focus upon the individual, and are part of a wider penitential system amplified by the papacy in the thirteenth century. At annual confession (as enjoined by Lateran IV) a lay person's confessor would assign to them a suitable penance, tailored to the sin and to the sinner's ability to perform it. The usual penances were repetitions of the Paternoster and Ave Maria prayers, making fasts, giving alms and going on pilgrimage. Such practices were usually described as 'private' penances, not meaning that

---

16 For example, Guillaume Austatz of Ornolac: J. Duvernoy, ed., *Le registre d'inquisition de Jacques Fournier, évêque de Pamiers (1318–1325)* (Toulouse: Privat, 1965), vol. I, 208–10.
17 *Gestorum Treverorum*, 401.

they were secret, but that their effects were directed inward, to the individual alone. The kind of penance imposed by Conrad, however, was of a different order: visibly public and an attempt to inculcate public shame as much as private contrition. This form of penance became a key feature in the use of inquisition against heresy, though not quite in the brutal form deployed in Mainz. Inquisitors were able to impose various penances upon those they found guilty, including long periods of imprisonment, pilgrimage to distant shrines (the pilgrim had to bring back letters proving that he or she had indeed travelled there), and hefty fines and the confiscation of property. The most common penance, however, was the imposition of crosses: two yellow ones, stitched front and back to the person's clothing, to be worn at all times for a set period – a year, two years, a decade, for life. Inquisitors are famous for having people burnt to death, and in one sense rightly so: those who 'relapsed' into heresy, or who 'obstinately' persisted in their heresy, were sent to the stake, as the church 'relinquished' the care of their soul (and set out a stark warning to others). But the death sentence was, after the Albigensian Crusade and the fall of the last Cathar castles in the 1240s, a relatively rare occurrence. The sentences handed down by Bernard Gui survive for us today: from over 600 judgments, forty-one people were sent to the stake. Many more – either immediately, or after a period of imprisonment – were to wear the yellow crosses.[18]

Burning people to death is clearly a form of repression. It silences them most effectively, and terrorises their immediate supporters. But marking people out with crosses is a rather different kind of act. Not 'kinder' – that is not what is at issue – but more complex, and more clearly directed *outward* to the society at large, as a sign to be read. Throughout the later Middle Ages, papal inquisitors handed out such sentences, and in England, too, bishops prosecuting Lollardy had those they convicted parade to church and market, sometimes carrying bundles of faggots or other penitential signs to indicate their guilt. Making transgressive bodies publicly legible is also a feature else-where: Jews were to wear distinguishing badges on their clothing, lepers had to carry a bell announcing their presence, and by the fourteenth century prostitutes were frequently ordered to dress in particular kinds of clothing such as striped hoods to mark them out. Such signs can be seen as a way of making visible 'outsiders' and thus dividing them from social embrace. But punishments of this kind had a further application which complicates the neat anthropological division of 'in-group' and 'out-group'. Across Europe, church

---

18 Given, *Inquisition and Medieval Society*, 69, table 3.1.

courts regularly sentenced people to public penances, most often for sexual sins such as fornication or adultery. Usually the guilty men and women would be beaten around the marketplace and the church, sometimes wearing only shifts and carrying a white stick or candle. Such spectacles would have been common within the medieval parish. Hence the marking out of heretics, Jews, prostitutes and lepers, and the harsher public penances enacted upon those guilty of heresy or other crimes, form part of a continuum with other regulatory aspects of communal life.

What this points to firstly is that, whilst the church's cultural weapons against heresy and other transgressions might only have gained active support on particular occasions, there was a much wider, more quiescent acceptance of the world-picture of transgressive sin, communal exclusion and hierarchical policing upon which they rested. Repression in this sense *was* largely the norm, and extended well beyond the dramatic matters of burning heretics or executing sodomites. Moreover, it has been pointed out that the development of the legal process of *inquisitio* was initially directed towards policing sexual sin (firstly among the clergy, but then more broadly). The twelfth century had seen the concept of sin becoming more aligned with that of crime, thus justifying the use of coercion in its treatment. Lateran IV's introduction of *inquisitio* allowed clerics to operate *ex officio* and search out crimes – such as sexual immorality within the parish – in the absence of any particular accuser. As Richard Fraher puts it, these developments see the formation of a prosecuting society as much as a persecuting one.[19] The church itself did not do all the prosecuting: major sexual offences, including sodomy, were frequently punished by secular authorities in Germany and northern Italy. But such matters were nonetheless strongly influenced by clerical concepts and rhetoric.

The developments over the period 1150–1350 – the consolidation of Moore's 'Persecuting Society' – did not concern only heresy, nor even the broader repression of 'outsiders'. An important background context was the slow crescendo of papal claims to authority, reaching pre-eminence under Innocent III, and the accompanying shifts in relationship between church and secular power in each European kingdom. The literate elite were part and parcel of these developments, their claim to intellectual and cultural authority underpinning the changes they sought. But two key elements lay at the heart of the shift described here, and they may prompt us to consider

19 R. M. Fraher, 'IV Lateran's Revolution in Criminal Procedure', in R. J. Castillo, ed., *Studia in honorem Eminentissimi Cardinalis Alphonsi M. Stickler* (Rome: LAS, 1992), 97–111.

how power is not simply repressive, silencing speech and eradicating action, but also *productive* – inculcating new ways of thinking, seeing, talking and behaving. The first element was a change in juridical procedure, epitomised in Innocent III's development of *inquisitio*. Inquisition, whether into heresy or clerical concubinage or lay sexual transgressions or witchcraft, provided the church with a far more hierarchical mechanism of legislative governance than the preceding procedures of *accusatio* and *denunciatio* or the trial by ordeal. The ability to act *ex officio* without local community support, the active use of bureaucratic documentation, and the increasingly cunning techniques for extracting confession made inquisition into a powerful but also delicate tool. It tackled those it governed as individuals, rather than collectivities, and inserted them into the textual machinery of governance. And here it is linked to the second element: the changed scope of the *cura animarum*. The church's interest in the spiritual lives of the laity grew over the course of the twelfth century, and entered canonical legislation particularly in the thirteenth. The universal requirement for annual confession, the provision of good parochial ministering, the expansion of preaching directed towards reforming a lay audience, all indicate a change in how the ecclesiastical elite viewed their flock. Reports of heresy in the eleventh and early twelfth century had tended to present the laity as a rather passive, easily swayed 'lump' corrupted by the small 'leaven' of the heresiarch. The use of inquisition, however, met that 'lump' in its individual components, interrogated them and found that the laity were more varied and complex in their transgressive behaviour than previously thought. This was the sharp end of a wider shift in the attempt to bring greater, more detailed and more individually tailored spiritual discipline to the people. Lay conduct – economic, sexual, spiritual – was to be policed as never before. At certain times of repression – in thirteenth-century Languedoc and in early fifteenth-century England for example – the church attempted to limit not only the activities of heretical proselytisers, but to proscribe lay discussion of the Christian faith or the dissemination of vernacular religious literature. Behaviour that might at one point have been thought simple laxity or a minor transgression could, in the later Middle Ages, take on a more sinister hue. Blaspheming, for instance, was long decried by ecclesiastical authors, but by the fifteenth century it had in some places become not merely a bad habit for which one's parishioners should be chided, but a matter of criminal legislation and even inquisitorial prosecution. The scope of *how* one could transgress had changed.

Thus the development of repression did not only silence and oppress. Over the high and later Middle Ages, it also helped to produce a new sense of what a lay person was and should be. The persecution of different 'outsiders' brought with it further productive effects, forging and mapping orthodoxy in different ways for different times and places. One chronicler, recounting more approvingly Conrad of Marburg's activities, lists the 'errors' of those he persecuted. Some are stereotypes of heretical behaviour – kissing the devil 'in the worst possible way' (probably on the anus). But others are more interestingly mundane: people who disparaged ecclesiastical authority, people who ignored clerical rules against consanguinity, people who worked on Feast Days and ate meat on Good Friday.[20] Such sins were surely not limited to members of any identifiable heretical 'sect', but were rather endemic faults within the laity. The chronicler's report on such 'crimes' was part of a wider attempt at reforming secular life, depicting what might be seen as laxity or doubt as a major transgression against the faith. A similar process was at work in other fields: anti-semitic tales of Host-desecration were used to bolster belief in, and emphasise the importance of, the miracle of transubstantiation. The grotesque display of leprosy provided a chastening example of how (sexual) sin wrote upon the body, thus encouraging people to confession and penance. Persecuting Waldensians stressed the clerical ownership of preaching, chasing so-called Free Spirits mapped the right and wrong ways of attempting mysticial communion, prosecuting Lollards bolstered the sacraments and the cult of saints (and provided the Lancastrian regime with a helpful bogeyman against which it could shore up its own legitimacy). The witch trials of the fifteenth century – which were nothing like on the scale of early-modern witch-crazes, albeit more common than in the preceding centuries – were fuelled by a belief in diabolism on the part of the prosecuting authorities rather than the general populace. For authors of witch-prosecuting manuals such as Heinrich Institoris or Johannes Nider, belief in demons bolstered belief in God and belief in the necessity of ecclesiastical authority to lead moral reform in this unsettled period. The diabolical excesses of witches were a great way to counter doubt and anticlericalism.[21]

Europe did become a persecuting society, but persecution was mostly limited to particular times and places, often when linked to other political disputes. The medieval church and secular rulers never possessed the kind of state apparatus that sustained a modern persecuting society such as Stalinist Russia, the German Democratic Republic in the later twentieth century or

20  *Gesta Treverorum*, 401.
21  W. Stephens, *Demon Lovers: Witchcraft, Sex, and the Crisis of Belief* (Chicago: University of Chicago Press, 2002); M. D. Bailey, *Battling Demons: Witchcraft, Heresy, and Reform in the Later Middle Ages* (University Park: Pennsylvania State University Press, 2003).

North Korea at the current time of writing. Nor was the link between religious identity and national governance ever as close as that produced by the bloody upheavals of the Reformation and counter-Reformation. Although the great convulsions of the sixteenth and seventeenth centuries did produce more abstract discussion of toleration, in practical terms there was a greater willingness and opportunity to repress religious difference after the Reformation than before it. Nor was medieval Europe *solely* a persecuting society: the machinery of repression was always one part of a larger mechanism for producing and refining orthodox identities. At the same time, however, in the lurid stories it told to encourage fear of 'outsiders', in the conflation of sodomy with heresy and witchcraft with diabolism, and in the development of inquisitorial procedures, it laid the groundwork for the darkness of later ages.

# 24

# Faith and the intellectuals I

## JOSEPH ZIEGLER

The history of medieval thought could be written in terms of limitations demanded from reason to make room for faith. The church would be depicted as an inherently thought-curbing institute that constantly and efficiently exerted pressure on intellectuals for the defence of orthodoxy. The oppressed intellectuals exposed to threats of ecclesiastical or university condemnations could easily become the heroes of this story.[1] But at the same time faith was subtly employed to make room for reason. From the twelfth century onwards, it became natural for scholars immersed in an academic environment (school or university) to employ reason to probe into subject areas that had not been explored before, as well as to discuss possibilities that had not previously been seriously entertained.[2]

Surely, those who applied reason to the solution of problems in theology knew that, when it came to determining the answer, reason was subordinate to faith. Yet the very idea that questioning certain articles of faith could endanger one's salvation, that vain curiosity (*vana curiositas*) particularly among theologians was undermining the academic vocation of theologians, created the need for due legal/judicial procedures that would limit or even abolish such dangerous dynamics and save faith (*salvare fidem*). The efficacy and the impact of ecclesiastical censorship apparatus (from simple verbal intimidations to condemnations, book burning and imprisonment) are still debated.[3] What is generally accepted though as far as academic

---

* This paper tremendously benefited from the comments of participants in the colloquium of the Max Plank Institut für Wissenschaftsgeschichte, Berlin, Abteilung II (3 February 2005).

1 L. Bianchi, *Censure et liberté intellectuelle à l'université de Paris (XIIIe–XIVe siècles)* (Paris: Les Belles Lettres, 1999).

2 E. Grant, *God and Reason in the Middle Ages* (Cambridge: Cambridge University Press, 2001), esp. 13–16, 182–282, 356–64.

3 J. M. M. H. Thijssen, *Censure and Heresy at the University of Paris 1200–1400* (Philadelphia: University of Pennsylvania Press, 1998), 1–39; Bianchi, *Censure et liberté*, 53–67.

condemnations are concerned is that university censures normally did not target full-fledged masters of theology, but rather members of the junior faculty, bachelors of theology and members of the inferior arts faculty. Their proneness to fall into error may be related to their young age: in their desire for fame they may have been less careful in both style and content and consequently were more in need of disciplinary guidance (or correction) on how to investigate the truth and how to discuss it in public with cautious carefulness and in a sober and honourable way. Within the University of Paris and without, doctrinal correctness was not imposed through judicial authority (bishop, prelate or pope), but through academic superiority (the masters' professional expertise and teaching authority). The theology masters, by their discursive reasoning and analytical methods demonstrated to the wayward academic that his views did not conform to faith.

It has already been shown how unhelpful and anachronistic it would be to depict the disciplinary and juridical proceedings for censuring suspect teaching as glaring signs of constraints imposed upon academic freedom.[4] In the thirteenth century and throughout the coming centuries the concept of *libertas scholastica* was interpreted in one sense only: the freedom of the university to manage its own affairs. As such neither the condemnation of 1277, nor any of the proceedings launched against individual masters in the thirteenth and fourteenth centuries threatened the academic freedom, a concept which was much narrower than ours for it neither comprised the freedom of learning for students nor the freedom to teach. Even theology masters (such as Godfrey of Fontaine) who debated in the fourteenth century the question of how to react to an episcopally condemned article which the master believes is patently true believed that academic discussion should not transgress the boundaries of faith. Only when a wrong condemnation causes an impediment to the inquiry into knowledge of the truth that concerns salvation should the theologian insist that it ought to be revoked, and he should certainly not comply with a condemnation he believes to be incorrect.

Books of natural philosophy were sometimes proscribed by ecclesiastical authority (local or papal).[5] However, there were relatively few books of natural philosophy that were of real concern to the Holy See or the local

---

4 Thijssen, *Censure and Heresy*, 90–112; Bianchi, *Censure et liberté*, 69–71; A. Boureau, *Théologie, science et censure au XIII$^e$ siècle: Le cas de Jean Peckham* (Paris: Les Belles Lettres, 1999), 335–6.

5 S. J. Williams, *The Secret of Secrets: The Scholarly Career of a Pseudo-Aristotelian Text in the Latin Middle Ages* (Ann Arbor: University of Michigan Press, 2003), 155–6; Bianchi, *Censure et liberté*, 89–127.

church official so as to instigate a ban on them. Ecclesiastical attention was directed mostly at writings that contained specifically theological errors. When works of philosophy were subjected to ecclesiastical proscription, as happened in 1210, 1215 and 1231 with Aristotle's *Libri naturales* and the commentaries on them, it was not because of magic, but because they had been implicated in the profession of heresy or specific doctrinal errors. There was no overall condemnation of the study of Aristotle's *Libri naturales*, whose teaching was prohibited but not their individual reading. Expurgations demanded in 1231 remained a dead letter, and there is ample evidence that in the 1230s and 1240s (well before the statutes of 1255 which declared the study of the entire Aristotelian corpus as a necessary precondition for entrance into the advanced faculties of medicine, law and theology) many of Aristotle's *Libri naturales* were studied within the Parisian academic space.

In the particular case of the *Secretum secretorum* (a most influential compilation of texts heavily loaded with magic, physiognomy, alchemy, astrology and medicine) it is now clear that not only did the papal court play a dominant role (together with the imperial court) in the dissemination of the text after its translation in c. 1230, but also that there was no systematic attempt to censure the text through expurgation of suspicious parts.[6] After his translation of the *Secretum secretorum*, the cleric Philip of Tripoli was rewarded with various benefices by the papacy. The text soon made its way to the academic heart of Christian Europe, the University of Paris and to other high profile institutions such as Oxford University across the Channel.

The study of the relationship between faith and reason has been overshadowed by the censorial act of the condemnation of 219 propositions in philosophy and theology by Bishop Stephen Tempier on 7 March 1277.[7] The episcopal involvement in the condemnation naturally linked the church in general to the censorial spirit underlying the document. The condemnation of

---

6  Williams, *The Secret of Secrets*, 142–82.
7  Thijssen, *Censure and Heresy*, 40–56; E. Grant, 'The Effect of the Condemnation of 1277', in N. Kretzmann, A. Kenny and J. Pinborg, eds., *The Cambridge History of Later Medieval Philosophy* (Cambridge: Cambridge University Press, 1982), 537–9; idem, *The Foundations of Modern Science in the Middle Ages: Their Religious, Institutional and Intellectual Contexts* (Cambridge: Cambridge University Press, 1996), 70–85, and *God and Reason in the Middle Ages*, 214–17; L. Bianchi and E. Randi, *Vérités dissonantes: Aristote à la fin du Moyen Âge* (Fribourg: Editions Universitaires, 1993), 50–109; Bianchi, *Censure et liberté*, 203–30; J. F. Wippel, *Mediaeval Reactions to the Encounter between Faith and Reason* (Milwaukee: Marquette University Press, 1995); pertinent are the thirty-five studies in J. A. Aertsen, K. Emery, Jr. and A. Speer, eds., *Nach der Verurteilung von 1277: Philosophie und Theologie an der Universität von Paris im letzten Viertel des 13. Jahrhunderts. Studien und Texte* (Miscellanea Mediaevalia 28; Berlin and New York: Walter de Gruyter, 2001).

1277 has often been used as a demonstration for the opposition between faith and reason, caused in that particular case by the repercussions of the introduction of the newly translated philosophical texts by Aristotle and his commentator Averroes into the arts faculty. The condemnation was portrayed as a response to the unbearable challenges to faith posed by the absorption of non-Christian philosophical learning. In cases of conflict between reason and faith, the truth was always supposed to be on the side of faith. But despite many difficulties, both theologians and natural philosophers warmly received Aristotle's natural philosophy. Theologians assigned to natural philosophy a vital role to explicate matters of faith and doctrine, and we can see no relenting of this approach after 1277. Few people could cite around 1300 the details of the document of condemnation whose actual impact may have been substantially weaker than we were led to believe. Students of medieval science seem to agree that among the more significant outcomes of the condemnation was a growing emphasis among theologians and philosophers on the reality and importance of God's absolute power (*potentia Dei absoluta*) to do whatever he pleases short of bringing about a logical contradiction. This encouraged thinkers to introduce into their philosophical debates subtle, daring and imaginative questions which generated new and interesting replies and substantially broadened the scope of scientific thought well beyond the constraints of Aristotelianism. The natural impossibilities that were explored presented additions to natural philosophy (though they did not alter its main body which remained strictly Aristotelian). And despite multiple cases of judicial condemnation of individual scholars, ideas and books, the notion of a systematic ecclesiastical repression of people and ideas does not conform to the reality characterised well into the end of the fourteenth century by an enormous, original, varied and ever more experimental intellectual output within the various scholastic institutions and disciplines.

In the context of this essay, part of the opening statement from Tempier's introductory letter should be highlighted because it suggests that among the causes motivating him to act as he did was a deep fear that some members of the arts faculty were transgressing the limits of their own faculty.[8] This fear of transgression of boundaries persisted despite the statute from April 1272 prescribing that no master or bachelor of arts shall presume to determine or

---

8 'nonnulli parisius studentes in artibus proprie facultatis limites excedentes', in D. Piché, ed., *La condamnation parisienne de 1277: Texte latin, traduction, introduction et commentaire* (Paris: Vrin, 1999), 72.

even dispute any purely theological question; that whenever a master or bachelor of arts happens to dispute a question that appears to touch on both faith and philosophy, he shall not determine it contrary to the faith; and that whenever a master or bachelor of arts happens to read or dispute a question that seems to undermine the faith, he shall either refute the arguments in so far as they are against faith, or concede that they are absolutely false.[9] The tendency to move from one discipline to the other could be enhanced by an analytic questioning technique that became widespread among the literate class and throughout all disciplines (including natural philosophy and theology). This questioning technique entailed asking hypothetical questions and facilitated the way for theologians to delve into natural philosophy and vice versa and hence rendered the disciplinary boundaries permeable. Theologians started asking questions which increasingly were drawn directly from natural philosophy. Many of these questions probed the domain of God's powers: what God could and could not do, and what God knows or does not know, and they all reflect the desires of an intellectual class that sought to know as much as they could by reason alone.

Now does this mean that one should accept the notion shared by some historians according to which theology and natural philosophy before the seventeenth century should not be regarded as distinct disciplines?[10] Whether or not one can speak of 'a Dominican version of natural philosophy' being based on Aristotle in order to counter the arguments of the Cathars, who themselves used the work of Aristotle to deny the truths of catholic Christianity; and of 'a Franciscan version of natural philosophy' (in particular optics or a *scientia perspectiva*) being based on pseudo-Dionysius (and hence on Neoplatonism) in order to promote particular spiritual practices and to study the continual creative activity of God in the universe – the fact that medieval natural philosophy was initially shaped by clerics many of whom were religious (Robert Grosseteste, Albert the Great, Thomas Aquinas, Roger Bacon, John Pecham, Jean Buridan, Nichole Oresme or Albert of Saxony, just to name the most prominent ones) invites the historian to assess the motivation of these people when studying the physical and material dimensions of the universe. Was it a direct extension of their preoccupation with God and his creation, or were they simply studying nature, as a modern

---

9 H. Denifle and H. Chatelain, eds., *Chartularium universitatis parisiensis*, 4 vols. (Paris, 1889–97), vol. I, no. 441, 499.
10 On the debate, see Grant, *God and Reason*, 185–206 who vehemently opposes the idea of no or little distinction between theology and natural philosophy in the pre-modern world.

scientist would do today?[11] The cases of Arnau de Vilanova and Galvano da Levanto, two academic physicians active around 1300 who smoothly extended their professional preoccupation to making a significant contribution to contemporary spiritual and theological discourse indicates that the first option was possible and did occasionally materialise, at least among physicians. Arnau de Vilanova was urged by Boniface VIII to practise medicine rather than mingle himself in theology and had to pay a dire personal price for not heeding this advice.[12]

But Edward Grant has shown that medieval natural philosophers largely ignored in their questions themes related to God, the faith or church doctrine, and it seems that on the whole God and faith played little role in medieval natural philosophy. This happened because the objective to provide natural explanations for natural phenomena rendered questions regarding faith irrelevant. Even those theologians who wrote treatises on natural philosophy (normally in the shape of a commentary on one of Aristotle's books) normally chose to keep the theologisation of natural philosophy to a minimum. Natural philosophy was never significantly infiltrated by theology because the two were different disciplines. It was, of course, about God's creation, but it was about that creation as a rational construction that could only be understood by reason. Hence the boundary between theology and natural philosophy was rarely blurred beyond recognition when looking from the angle of natural philosophy.

Certain natural philosophical themes as the eternity or creation of the world and the possibility of a vacuum had immediate theological consequences. Some philosophers such as Boethius of Dacia insisted that theology must be kept out of physics. Others, like Buridan, adopted a different approach.[13] Whereas Boethius of Dacia had argued that a philosopher should conclude that the world is eternal because he argues on the basis of physical principles, Buridan accepted the creation of the world in physics as in theology, resolving Aristotle's and Averroes' arguments against the possibility of a new creation.

---

11 For the ongoing debate on the topic, see the contributions of Andrew Cunningham and Edward Grant to 'Open Forum: The Nature of "Natural Philosophy"', *Early Science and Medicine* 5.3 (2000), 258–300.

12 J. Ziegler, *Medicine and Religion c. 1300: The Case of Arnau de Vilanova* (Oxford: Clarendon Press, 1998).

13 E. D. Sylla, '*Ideo quasi mendicare oportet intellectum humanum*: The Role of Theology in John Buridan's Natural Philosophy', in J. M. M. H. Thijssen and J. Zupko, eds., *The Metaphysics and Natural Philosophy of John Buridan* (Leiden: Brill, 2001), 221–45. See also J. Zupko, *John Buridan: Portrait of a Fourteenth-Century Arts Master* (Notre Dame: University of Notre Dame Press, 2003), 139–45 for the relationship of theology to philosophy.

Alternately the theological doctrine of transubstantiation forced him to admit, against Aristotle, the possibility of real accidental being. Buridan alternated his metaphysics to accommodate the separability of accidents dictated by the doctrine of faith. He reached this non-Aristotelian conclusion by Aristotelian arguments. But when offering a new definition of the notions 'substance' and 'accidents', he remained in the realm of the general level of metaphysics and refrained from giving any explanation of the mode of existence of the eucharistic accidents. As a philosopher he could not allow himself to trespass on the domain of the theologians.[14]

Things looked entirely different from the theological end: theology needed natural philosophy and was utterly dependent on it.[15] In spite of the congruity of Platonism and Christianity, Aristotelianism came to dominate speculation and scholarship at the beginning of the thirteenth century, leaving to theology its own field for scientific activity. The development of theology into a rigorous, scientific discipline was an important reason for this switch of allegiance.[16] Then, the struggle against the Cathars forced the church to resort to reason and philosophy to defend faith.[17] From the second third of the thirteenth century *Sentences* commentaries and *quodlibets* became saturated with questions and arguments taken from the realm of natural philosophy and applying reason to theology. Commentaries on book i of the *Sentences*, for example, included dense natural philosophical discussions of the infinite on all its aspects (infinite space, eternity of the world); book ii acquired dense natural philosophical discussions of the heavens (including spiritual bodies and angels), celestial bodies and light, digestion and heredity; book iii allowed the commentators to boast their detailed knowledge of embryology; and book iv encouraged theologians to use both natural philosophy and medicine to describe the bodies of Adam and Christ. Exemplary are the *Quodlibets* of John of Naples from 1315–17 (OP; d. c. 1350) which were saturated with interest in the body in all its aspects.[18]

---

14 P. J. J. M. Bakker, 'Aristotelian Metaphysics and Eucharistic Theology: John Buridan and Marsilius of Inghen on the Ontological Status of Accidental Being', in Thijssen and Zupko, eds., *The Metaphysics and Natural Philosophy of John Buridan*, 247–64.

15 Grant, *God and Reason*, 207–82; and 'What Was Natural Philosophy in the Late Middle Ages', *History of Universities* 20.2 (2005), 12–46.

16 G. Wieland, 'Plato or Aristotle – A Real Alternative in Medieval Philosophy?', in J. F. Wippel, ed., *Studies in Medieval Philosophy* (Studies in Philosophy and the History of Philosophy 17; Washington D.C.: Catholic University of America, 1987), 63–84.

17 R. French and A. Cunningham, *Before Science: The Invention of the Friars' Natural Philosophy* (Aldershot: Scholar Press, 1996), 99–145.

18 P. Biller, 'John of Naples, quodlibets and Medieval Theological Concern with the Body', in P. Biller and A. J. Minnis, eds., *Medieval Theology and the Natural Body* (York Studies in Medieval Theology 1; Woodbridge: York Medieval Press, 1997), 3–12 (4–9).

In his *Sentences* commentary from c. 1325, the Carmelite theologian John Baconthorpe discussed, like many of his colleagues, the mystery of the birth of Christ born of a woman as a result of non-seminal generation. As part of an area of thought which has acquired the name of 'divine embryology',[19] several key questions prompted theologians to long and detailed biological discussions concerning the exact role of Mary in the generation of Christ, her virginity after conception, and the primary material she supplied to the body of Christ. A detailed investigation of the role of the Holy Spirit as a substitute for the active male sperm, of the development and the life of Christ at the foetal stage (that is, whether his body was formed instantaneously or gradually), and of the possible astral influences at the moment of his conception were also part of the same trend to put the mystery of Christ in a scientific context. The answers to these questions were far more important than providing an indication for the increasingly naturalistic tendencies among thirteenth-century theologians. They had a decisive impact on the fundamental question of what made Christ belong to the human species when no male seed was involved in his generation.

Baconthorpe uniquely discussed another such question: did Christ resemble Mary?[20] The very question suggests that Baconthorpe thought of Christ biologically. The issue of resemblance between mother and her children was one of the most crucial arguments raised in debates among Galenists and Aristotelian philosophers and physicians discussing the role of women in generation.[21] For the Galenists it provided a crucial common-sensical proof for the validity of their theory which allowed the female sperm a certain active role in generation. For the positive answer to the question Baconthorpe uses two categories of similarity: *ad speciem* (which is divided into two kinds: first according to the substantial form, that is the belonging to the human species, and second, according to the individual characteristics or *signa personalia*) and accidental (*secundum aliquod accidens* – skin colour, gender, physical faults). According to Baconthorpe, the substantial form of a mixture of two animals will always be determined by the father, hence the similarity with the mother (in this case Mary) who nourishes the foetus with her blood applies only to the

---

19 M. van der Lugt, *Le ver, le démon et la vierge: Les théories médiévales de la génération extraordinaire* (Paris: Les Belles Lettres, 2004), 365–473.

20 Van der Lugt, *Le ver, le démon et la vierge*, 447–52 and esp. 449 n. 206 which transcribes parts of John Baconthorpe, *In III Sent.*, 2 vols. (Cremona, 1618), dist. 4, art. 1–4, vol. 2, 36a–39b.

21 J. Cadden, *Meaning of Sex Difference in the Middle Ages: Medicine, Science, and Culture* (Cambridge: Cambridge University Press, 1993), 34.

*signa personalia.* Here Baconthorpe introduces a zoological example which consequently becomes the foundation for a crucial analogy. The product of copulation between a dog and a fox physically resembles the feminine animal because from the mother the foetus draws its nourishment. The subject of the analogy probably taken from Aristotle, *De generatione animalium* II.7 (746a), is Jesus who is also the product of a mixture between two different species (Mary and the Holy Spirit) and should be analysed as a crossbreed between two animals. This similarity is not according to the substantial form which is always introduced by the father, but rather according to the *signa personalia* (in Christ's case Mary's humanity – *humanitas*). This resemblance is particularly strong in the case of Christ and Mary because of the lack of a male seed in the process. In Mary's case the overwhelming influence of the mother's nourishment is not hindered by the non-existent male seed. The language and style of Baconthorpe's partly Galenic explanation is purely biological, and he makes specific references to Aristotle's *De generatione animalium*. A similarly biological frame of mind applies to Baconthorpe's explanation for Christ's sex: he was born masculine because Mary, not feeling any pleasure normally felt at intercourse, emitted no superfluous humour (*humidum superfluum*) which when mixed in the menses usually is responsible for the birth of girls.

Why is this discussion pertinent to an essay on faith and the intellectuals? Because it reveals the basic trends and the subtle rules that characterised the encounter between theology and natural philosophy. While before 1240 theologians stressed the miraculous explanation of the events leading to Christ's birth (Mary received from the Holy Spirit a supernatural generative power that allowed her to generate a child without a man and without harming her virginity), after 1240 more and more theologians (Franciscans in particular, but not conclusively) stressed Mary's natural contribution to the foetus. This led to more detailed comparisons between Mary's role and the role of ordinary women (and other female animals) in the birth of their offspring. Theologians increasingly and systematically came to cite philosophical (in particular books 15 and 16 in Aristotle's *Libri de animalibus*, or the corresponding books 1 and 2 of *De generatione animalium*) and medical sources (in particular Avicenna's *Canon*).[22] The Galenic approach to women's role in the formation of the embryo (active through their seed, though not as active as the males) was here particularly helpful and in accordance with the Franciscan adoration of Mary and with Franciscan desire to elevate her prestige and solidify her cult. The more Aristotelian theologians (many of

22  Van der Lugt, *Le ver, le démon et la vierge*, 392 and 397.

whom were Dominicans) happily used Aristotle's notion of the passive woman whose menstrual blood is the main component of the embryo's flesh nourishing the embryo in its early days, whose vaginal secretion has no seminal significance but only a lubricating function facilitating coitus, who need not feel pleasure in the sexual act to conceive, and who plays no active role in the formation of the foetus, but rather supplies only the material. They linked all these characteristics to Mary's role in the formation of Christ. In many respects theological discourse underwent a process of naturalisation.

The theologians certainly did not abandon the basic mystery of Christ's birth, but they reduced the miraculous scope of the event by supplementing parts of the miraculous story with naturalistic explanations. The question of the gradual (and hence natural) formation of Christ's embryo versus its instantaneity (and hence miraculous character) was overwhelmingly determined in favour of the miraculous approach, *in order* to prevent the natural explanation from entirely taking over the miracle.[23] But by adding a scientific depth to the traditional story of Christ's birth, they reflect the intellectual needs of a milieu which was no longer satisfied with simple and supernatural explanations. This mental change allowed adding a third epistemological category to the traditional natural or supernatural things, namely preternatural things (marvels which demand natural explanations but are still a cause for wonder and admiration). Why did this change of sensitivities in relation to the miraculous take place among intellectuals in the second third of the thirteenth century is a question that still demands further study. But the obvious need to render miracles and the mysteries of faith more reasonable most probably had to do with the challenge created by the newly assimilated scientific knowledge. Its attractiveness in the eyes of the young and the bright scholars meant that, if theology was to maintain its position as the queen of all sciences, theologians had to accommodate their discourse accordingly and render it updated and relevant to the current natural philosophical issue.[24]

---

23 See, for example, Roland of Cremona, *Summa* III.20, in van der Lugt, *Le ver, le démon et la vierge*, 404–5. See J. Ziegler, 'Medicine and Immortality in Terrestrial Paradise', in P. Biller and J. Ziegler, eds., *Religion and Medicine in the Middle Ages* (York Studies in Medieval Theology 3; York and Woodbridge: York Medieval Press, 2001), 201–42 (at 232, 236–7) for the explanations of immortality in Eden that relied on natural philosophy and medicine, but did not abandon Grace as a major explanatory factor.

24 The scientific developments in the seventeenth century presented theologians with a similar challenge. They too developed naturalistic strategies to render miracles more believable. See F. Vidal, 'Extraordinary Bodies and the Physicotheological Imagination', in L. Daston and G. Pomata, eds., *The Faces of Nature in Enlightenment Europe* (Berlin: Berliner Wissenschafts-Verlag, 2003), 61–96 (at 69–74 on divine embryology).

The biological debates concerning the nature of the generation of Christ were not without limits. Thus, for example, the Galenic story of generation as the result of the mixture of the male and female seeds (adopted by many Franciscan theologians) inevitably gave rise to the question whether Mary ejaculated seed (*seminavit*) and whether this ejaculation entailed a feeling of pleasure as is normally the case with ejaculating men and women.[25] Even the hypothetical possibility that Mary could feel some pleasure at the conception of Christ has led Albert the Great to denounce the abominable ideas of Galenic theologians. There were two ways out. The first was to deny the possibility that Mary emitted seed in conception and that instead the Holy Spirit used several drops of her blood to form the body of Christ. What distinguished Mary from other women was that her blood was separated from her body by the Holy Spirit and not naturally following the physical stimulation by a male. Christ's body possessed everything necessary for his humanity through the chaste and pure blood (*ex castis et purissimis sanguinibus*) of his mother. Mary's menses remained wholly pure because no pleasure was involved in conceiving Christ under the influence of the Holy Spirit. The second way out was to define the very question of Mary's sexual excitement by the Holy Spirit and consequent ejaculation as shameful (*turpis*), as an act of curious stupidity, and as an affront to any authoritative source treating the topic. According to Bonaventure, one should avoid sliding into this unsafe territory. Instead it is enough simply to say that the Virgin supplied the matter suitable for the generation of the son of God *secundum carnem*.[26] The case of Albert the Great discussion of sodomy is another example of self-censorship that demonstrates the inability or unwillingness of intellectuals to disengage their thought from the constraints of orthodox religion. Albert consciously ignored Avicenna's physiological explanation of sodomitic inclinations (which cannot be altered and therefore should not be cured) and stuck to the traditional religious discourse that linked sin and sodomy and harshly condemned the sodomitic habitus.[27]

But despite these self-imposed restrictions, the basic inclination to reflect on all biblical stories and orthodox beliefs also through a scientific lens tremendously enriched the theological discourse from the second third of the thirteenth century onwards. This mood did not dramatically change the

25  Van der Lugt, *Le ver, le démon et la vierge*, 421–3.
26  Bonaventure, *In III Sent.*, dist. 4 art. 3, q. 1, ad 2, in van der Lugt, *Le ver, le démon et la vierge*, 422, n. 137.
27  M. Jordan, *The Invention of Sodomy in Christian Theology* (Chicago: University of Chicago Press, 1998), 114–35.

questions asked, but rather made the answers more subtle, and less simple, well anchored in up-to-date scientific theory.

The generation of Christ was not the only focus of scientific speculation among late medieval theologians. Thirteenth-century theologians were far removed from the mood accompanying the papal bull of 1567 issued by Pius V and vehemently condemning the notion that Adam's immortality was not the result of divine favour but rather the product of his natural condition.[28] They debated a series of questions such as: how should one explain Adam's immortality in *status innocentie*? Was he immortal because of God's grace, or was his body naturally endowed with physical properties which assured his immortality? How exactly can one describe the effect of eating from the Tree of Life on Adam's body? By using key terms borrowed from medical theory (complexion, *complexio equalis*, radical and nutrimental moistures, natural heat) they described Adam's body before sin as a naturally perfect body whose perfectly balanced complexion resisted any form of corruptibility and hence death. They portrayed the effect of the Tree of Life on the body's health as a substance that prevents the natural and inevitable consumption of the radical moisture (the basic explanation for the inevitability of death). By doing so they did not deny the role of grace in the explanation, they only pushed it further away and wrapped it with natural explanations. In this case medical theory (directly borrowed from medical texts) played an important auxiliary role in theological exegesis which underwent a process of medicalisation.[29] Similarly, when debating the biological transmission of original sin from Adam to his offspring, theologians wrapped a key theological concept, *veritas humane nature* (that core substance that will arise in resurrection, unique to every person and determining his/her corporeal identity) in a state-of-the-art scientific envelope using the medical/biological concept of radical moisture (*humidum radicale*).[30] This happened almost parallel to the assimilation of this key concept into medical theory.

---

28  L. Cova, 'Morte e immortalità del composto umano nella teologia francescana del XIII secolo', in C. Casagrande and S. Vecchio, eds., *Anima e corpo nella cultura medievale: Atti del V Convegno de studi della Società Italiana per lo Studio del Pensiero Medievale, Venezia, 25–28 settembre 1995* (Florence: Sismel, 1999), 107–22 (at 107, n. 1).

29  Ziegler, 'Medicine and Immortality', 201–42.

30  J. Ziegler, '*Ut dicunt medici*: Medical Knowledge and Theological Debates in the Second Half of the Thirteenth Century', *Bulletin of the History of Medicine* 73 (1999), 208–37; L. Cova, *Originale peccatum e concupiscentia in Riccardo di Mediavilla: Vizio ereditario e sessualità nell'antropologia teologica del XIII secolo* (Rome: Edizioni dell'Ateneo, 1984).

Yet another focus of scientific speculation among theologians was Christ's body during and after the crucifixion.[31] One such peculiar question, which highlights the theologians' tendency to enrich their exegesis through scientific insights, targeted the blood emitted as sweat by the suffering Christ (Luke 22.44): was the sweat of the suffering Christ on the cross natural ('utrum sudor Christi quem sudavit in agonia fuerit naturalis')?[32] This *quodlibet* question posed in 1269 by John Pecham in Oxford and then repeated by his student Roger Marston in 1284 invited a detailed explanation of why Christ's perfect complexion did not allow superfluities (such as ordinary sweat) to be formed, and therefore he could only sweat pure blood. Pecham's solution, that the sweat of blood in Christ was natural and a result of an ideal mechanism of digestion and a fully balanced complexion, includes a scientific description of the physiological effects of Christ's Passion. First, his agony affected the humoural constitution of his heart and led to the concentration of blood around it. This blood was consequently dispersed to the other organs through the action of heat and emitted in the form of sweat mixed with blood. Secondly, Christ imagined the forthcoming bloodshed and, according to the physical law that imagination moves the humours, his blood, moved by his imagination, was dispersed outside the body in the form of sweat. And thirdly, his most noble complexion was highly refined and delicate, and consequently was particularly disposed to efficient evaporation of residual humours.

All the above examples for the enrichment of theological discourse through high-level scientific information were related to the human body. But ecclesiastical interest in the human body was not only speculative. The papal court around 1300 was a leading agent in a new intellectual mood that venerated the human body and was far removed from the traditional contempt towards the inevitably corruptible cover wrapping the immortal soul. The clerical elites of the thirteenth and fourteenth centuries, and in particular within and around the papal court (Boniface VIII was their most typical representative and was reprimanded for his particular, some would say excessive, care of the body), were the main promoters (together with a few lay rulers, such as Frederick II) of the 'new sciences', namely medicine, alchemy, physiognomy and optics. All these provided important strategies for the prolongation of one's life.[33]

---

31 Boureau, *Théologie, science et censure*, 87–136.
32 Ziegler, 'Medicine and Immortality', 237–8; Van der Lugt, *Le ver, le démon et la vierge*, 468–9.
33 A. Paravicini-Bagliani, *Medicina e scienze della natura alla corte dei papi nel duecento* (Spoleto: Centro italiano di studi sull'alto medioevo, 1991), and in particular 'Federico II e la corte dei papi: Scambi culturali e scientifici', 55–84. See also his *The Pope's Body*, trans. D. S. Peterson (Chicago and London: University of Chicago Press, 1998), 171–211, 225–34.

How did the Church react to these sciences? It is now clear that the papacy did not oppose dissections for forensic or academic purposes. Dissections were regulated by papal concessions but not prohibited. At the same time that the papacy expressed its opposition to the dismemberment of corpses for funerary practices (in the famous bull from 27 September 1299, *Detestande feritatis*) we witness the first public dissections for medical or juridical purposes under papal approval. Boniface VIII who issued the bull was motivated by the notion of the overwhelming importance of the integrity of the body as well as the belief in the possibility of a smooth/direct passage from life to death and resurrection, and not by any abhorrence towards academic dissections. Therefore, to rejuvenate and consequently prolong life with the help of experimental sciences (alchemy, medicine, optics) and especially the use of potable gold was an essential precondition for approaching the final state of the resuscitated body. Such a perfect, young body was an instrument of salvation and the means to acquire it had to be cultivated.[34]

Alchemy was well received by the church in the thirteenth century, though one can detect a growing suspicion towards it from the beginning of the fourteenth century exactly when alchemy assumes mystical dimensions.[35] In the fifteenth century its critics would link it to magic and demonology. The fact that alchemy essentially deviated from the dominant characteristics of scholastic science (by denying the master–disciple relationship, eliminating the basic exercise of a commentary, and stressing the solitary dimension of the alchemist's studies) added perhaps to its suspicious status. But all this did not amount to a concerted ecclesiastical effort to curb alchemical thought in the thirteenth and fourteenth centuries. On the contrary, it seems that the religious dimension of alchemy rendered it acceptable to the ecclesiastical authorities and at the same time filled those engaged in it with a sense of religious vocation.

What did alchemy have in common with faith and religion? Alchemical discourse was suffused with the language of Christianity. From the earlier alchemical texts images of death and resurrection prefigured the dissolution of the prime matter and its reconstitution into the glorious stones. A religious and holy life was often thought a prerequisite for a successful alchemist whose knowledge was the product of divine revelation. The alchemical priest was

---

34 A. Paravicini-Bagliani, 'La papauté du XIIIe siècle et la renaissance de l'anatomie', in *Medicina e scienze*, 269–79, and 'The Corpse in the Middle Ages: The Problem of the Division of the Body', in P. Linehan and J. L. Nelson, eds., *The Medieval World* (London: Routledge, 2001), 327–41.
35 A. Boureau, 'Conclusion', *Micrologus* 3 (1995), 347–53 (at 349).

expected to be chaste, morally upright and temperate in his behaviour and habits. Alchemical knowledge was perceived to be the gift of God (*Donum dei*) and alchemical science was depicted as *partim divina*.[36] Alchemy and Christian religion thus penetrated one another as was the case with all other sciences. Nevertheless, I am not suggesting that the alchemists did not primarily aim at changes of a chemical kind, but rather used chemical language and terminology only to hide spiritual, moral or mystical processes in allegorical robe.[37] The alchemist's goals were primarily chemical, and material, but the fact that the mysteries of the Christian faith increasingly came to be depicted and explained by means of chemical analogies legitimised the study of alchemy and its practice despite its dubious scientific status. Alchemy's function as a source of tropes and imagery for rhetorical purposes or didactic exemplifications contributed to its recognition by theologians as a licit preoccupation.

When thinking about or even producing medicine which could prolong the life of humans, alchemists used the concept of *complexio equalis*, that is, a perfectly balanced complexion where the qualities of the four elements exist in a condition of perfect harmony, to describe the physical state they were seeking. The concept of *complexio equalis*, which they borrowed from medical theory, came in the second third of the thirteenth century to be heavily loaded with religious connotations.[38] Prelapsarian Adam and Christ were the only human creatures characterised by this unique complexion that assured their immortality. Such a perfect temperament would also exist in the bodies of the resurrected (both the blessed and the damned) who would be immortal. Bodily immortality was thus a natural characteristic of the human species, and thus all health defects could be repaired by natural means. Alchemy (in the form of the *elixir*) supplied an artificial means of acquiring such a body of equal complexion, which, although it would not become immortal, approached very much the final state of the resurrected body characterised also by immortality.

36  C. Crisciani, *Il papa e l'alchimia: Felice V, Guglielmo Fabri e l'elixir* (Rome: Viella, 2002), 44–5, 81. See also G. Roberts, *The Mirror of Alchemy: Alchemical Ideas and Images in Manuscripts and Books* (Toronto: University of Toronto Press, 1994), 78–82.

37  L. M. Principe and W. R. Newman, 'Some Problems with the Historiography of Alchemy', in W. R. Newman and A. Grafton, eds., *Secrets of Nature: Astrology and Alchemy in Early Modern Europe* (Cambridge Mass.: MIT Press, 2001), 385–431 (esp. 397–400). On Bacon's plea for the reliability and religious utility of the natural sciences as handmaidens of theology, see D. C. Lindberg, 'The Medieval Church Encounters the Classical Tradition: Saint Augustine, Roger Bacon and the Handmaiden Metaphor', in D. C. Lindberg and R. L. Numbers, eds., *When Science and Christianity Meet* (Chicago and London: University of Chicago Press, 2003), 7–32 (esp. 21–32).

38  Ziegler, 'Medicine and Immortality', 215–24.

Assuming this role, Roger Bacon called alchemy *instrumentum salutis* and gave it a liberating role allowing the humans to free themselves from the pessimistic views of church writers who tied original sin and corruptibility in an unbreakable knot. In his *Liber sex scientiarum* Bacon asserted that even postlapsarian man should naturally attain to a longer life span than he currently obtains.[39] His corrupted complexion arises overwhelmingly from natural causes and should therefore be capable of a natural correction restoring to the body a form of equal complexion. When such a form has been provided, the body will become balanced (*corpus equale*), old age will slow down remarkably, and all defects already accumulated by the body (through bad habits or heredity) will be removed. Aided by celestial virtue, the balanced body produced from the separated and purified humours derived from human blood would be able to propagate species which, though not incorruptible, would assure longevity characterised by extraordinary wisdom and perfect health. The neglect of a proper regimen throughout the generations is responsible for the body's swift corruptibility which neither God nor nature imposed. This neglect is due to human stupidity (*stultitia hominis*) not to sin (individual or original). Such a theology of the body was developed by the Oxford Franciscan in various texts he prepared for Pope Clement IV. But this was not a unique case: a set of thirteenth-century popes such as Innocent IV, Clement IV and Boniface VIII were the clients or commissioners of medico-alchemical treatises discussing the prolongation of life, the slowing down of the aging process and the preservation of youth.

The fact that alchemy was of little interest among Jewish thinkers is a counterfactual proof for the importance of the Christian dimension in alchemy which came to be linked to the eternal search for salvation. Thus in some pseudo-Arnaldian texts (such as *Tractatus parabolicus*) the eucharist could be matched with the philosophers' stone – the efficient but incomprehensible or even miraculous agent of nature's restructuring and change; like Christ so the stone was created miraculously, and both had to undergo physical suffering prior to acquiring curing powers; this inevitably lent a prophetic aura to the ancient authorities of alchemy who in the philosophers' stone predicted every detail of Christ's story. The search for immortality

---

39 W. R. Newman, 'An Overview of Roger Bacon's Alchemy', in J. Hackett, ed., *Roger Bacon and the Sciences: Commemorative Essays* (Leiden: Brill, 1997), 317–36 (esp. 324–8). A. Paravicini-Bagliani, 'Ruggero Bacone, Bonifacio VIII e la teoria della "Prolongatio vitae"', in *Medicina e scienze*, 329–61 and 'Ruggero Bacone e l'alchimia di lunga vita. Riflessioni sui testi', in C. Crisciani and A. Paravicini-Bagliani, eds., *Alchimia e medicina nel Medioevo* (Florence: Sismel, 2003), 33–54 (at 45–6).

through *elixir* was tightly linked to strong beliefs in the integrity of the body, and its importance in the state of glory (thus rendering it at the same time sinful and glorious) could find common grounds with the complicated alchemical transformations in which one material could have several specific forms along a period of time. The alchemical possibility for the concomitant existence of opposing qualities helped to explain the possibility of Mary's immaculate conception or the miracle of the eucharist. The salutary effect of Christ's death on the cross was metaphorically compared to theriac, the ultimate and most powerful medicine, alchemically produced and efficient against all diseases. And Christ on the cross is described as a magnet attracting to him the sins of all humankind.[40]

The papal court in the second half of the thirteenth and in the fourteenth centuries was well familiar with the religious character of the alchemical texts, some of whose manuscripts were stocked in the papal library. So there is no indication that this sliding into the religious or spiritual analogies created any suspicion among the ecclesiastical authority. Condemnations of alchemy as expressed in the decretal *Spondent* issued by John XXII in 1317, or in *Contra alchimistas* composed by the Inquisitor of Aragon, Nicholas Eymeric in 1399, targeted metallurgic alchemy and the problem of falsification of coins, but not the religious expression of alchemical discourse. In Eymeric's text the suspicion that alchemy was too magical or even demonical was a new contribution to the alchemical debates.

The flourishing of learned astrology and alchemy in the thirteenth century and beyond is yet another indication that scholastic Aristotelianism was unable to prevent scholastic and naturalistic discourse within scientific fields of knowledge outside the Aristotelian corpus. The condemnations of 1277 roundly denounced the fatalistic aspects of judicial astrology, though they left open some room for astral medicine. And the learned and semi-learned clerical milieu was impregnated with interest and curiosity in occult sciences and accommodated it with its orthodox Christian beliefs. The Dominican Albert the Great and the Franciscan Roger Bacon are just two prominent figures in the thirteenth century who represent a much larger group of clerical scientists on all levels and in all fields who were keenly interested in various aspects of the occult. Each produced his own version of fusing faith and

---

40 Boureau, 'Conclusion', 352; B. Obrist, 'Vers une histoire de l'alchimie médiévale', *Micrologus* 3 (1995), 3–43 (35–6); A. Calvet, 'À la recherche de la médicine universelle. Questions sur l'élixir et la thériaque au 14e siècle', in Crisciani and Paravicini-Bagliani, eds., *Alchimia e medicina nel Medioevo*, 177–216 (at 198–203); Ziegler, *Medicine and Religion*, 143–8; Crisciani, *Il papa e l'alchimia*, 43–5.

science and of setting the boundaries for the licit and illicit when it came to scientific speculation or practice. Thus the inevitable tensions between free scientific curiosity and the demands of faith did not undermine the clerical contribution to these sciences. Perhaps on the contrary: much of the investigation was motivated by religious concerns, or at least wrapped in thick religious or spiritual language. Once the determinism or anything hampering free will was rejected, the scope of scientific research was broad indeed. In the case of astrology or alchemy, though it was impossible artificially to change the specific form of things (a prerogative kept for God alone), it was possible to present a causal chain in which the astrological (or alchemical) cause was linked to the talisman through the instrumental agent of the artist whose art was totally subjected to natural causality and in particular to astral influences.[41]

In this context the emergence of the notion of astrological images (*imagines astronomice*), talismans used for various protective purposes and whose efficacy was explained by natural (astrological) causation, is remarkable indeed. The seeds of natural magic were sown in the thirteenth century by thinkers such as the anonymous author of *Speculum astronomie*, who envisaged a way of producing and using talismans and amulets that did not involve the invocation of other deities or supreme intelligences, but derived all their power solely from physical (mainly celestial) influences.[42] Introducing himself as *zelator fidei et philosophie*, he managed to create a subtle compromise between the demands of faith (preserving the Christian monopoly over ritual and contacts with God and his celestial agents) and the ever growing scientific interests in natural philosophy that included the more occult or marginal sciences such as astrology and other practices of divination.

A further example of a fusion between theology (and ecclesiastical career) and high-level astrological speculation without any signs of unease is provided by Pierre d'Ailly's work (d. 1420). In his writings astrology emerges as an integral part of the rational view of the world in the fourteenth and fifteenth centuries.[43] The belief that the heavenly bodies have some sort of influence on the earth below was just as pervasive as the notion that God had a plan for the

41 N. Weill-Parot, *Les 'images astrologiques' au Moyen Âges et à la Renaissance: Spéculations intellectuelles et pratiques magiques (XII<sup>e</sup>–XV<sup>e</sup> siècle)* (Paris: Honoré Champion, 2002), 877.

42 On the debate about the authorship of *Speculum astronomie* see Weill-Parot, *Les 'images astrologiques'*, 27–32 and A. Paravicini-Bagliani, *Le* Speculum Astronomiae, *une enigme? Enquête sur les manuscrits* (Turnhout: Brepols, 2001).

43 L. Ackerman Smoller, *History, Prophecy, and the Stars: The Christian Astrology of Pierre d'Ailly, 1350–1420* (Princeton: Princeton University Press, 1994).

world's destiny. He saw astrology not as a magical art by which he could manipulate the future course of the world, but rather as a rational science by which he could discern the broad patterns of earthly events. Like many people who used astrology in medicine, in making business decisions and for political advice, he believed that he was turning science for knowledge. Pierre d'Ailly's defence of astrology was motivated by his will to establish astrology as a 'natural theology', which could be used to interpret prophecy as well as to validate the chronology of religious history. And more specifically, after 1410 astrological calculations confirmed his hopeful interpretation of the schism, for they put the advent of the Antichrist in the distant future.

The renascent art and science of physiognomy provide the last decisive evidence of the rhetorical and intellectual mechanisms that allowed clerics to tolerate and even cultivate the preoccupation with a body of knowledge that potentially undermined Christian ethics and the Christian notion of free will.[44] If the external traits of the body teach us all we need to know about one's character, and since all these external traits inhere in one from birth or even from conception, then one's behaviour is determined at birth, there is little place for free will or voluntary choice, and the consequences for Christian pastoral theology are dire.

There were several strategies adopted by different intellectuals to legitimise physiognomy. First, those who accepted astronomical principles as indicators for the validity of a body of certain knowledge presented physiognomy as a reflection of the overwhelming powers of the stars over nature. For them, physiognomy therefore could not be regarded as a superstitious divinatory art.[45]

Second, authors and scribes used the proemia to physiognomic texts to explain the rationale of physiognomy in a way consonant with Christianity and to limit the scope of physiognomy thereby reducing its potential danger to Christian morality. One could claim, as did Albert the Great, that physiognomy merely shows inclinations which reflect the quality of the blood and physical spirits. But these inclinations can be, if necessary, curbed by reason.[46]

44 For a more detailed discussion of the topic, see J. Ziegler, 'Text and Context: On the Rise of Physiognomic Thought in the Later Middle Ages', in Y. Hen, ed., De Sion exibit lex et verbum domini de Hierusalem: Essays on Medieval Law, Liturgy, and Literature in Honour of Amnon Linder (Turnhout: Brepols, 2001), 159–82 (at 161–76).

45 P. Zambelli, The 'Speculum astronomiae' and its Enigma: Astrology, Theology and Science in Albertus Magnus and his Contemporaries (Boston Studies in the Philosophy of Science 17; Dordrecht, Boston and London: Kluwer, 1992), ch. 17, 272–3.

46 Albertus Magnus, De animalibus I.2.2, in De animalibus libri xxvi, ed. H. Stadler, 2 vols. (Beiträge zur Geschichte der Philosophie des Mittelalters 15; Münster: Aschendorffsche

The legend about Hippocrates' disciples who clashed with the physiognomer Phylemon over his judgment that their master was lascivious, devious and sexually compulsive was Albert's exemplary proof that one can control all negative inclinations, that philosophy is nothing but abstinence and the subjugation of lust, and that nothing is predetermined by nature. In the case of Hippocrates, it was by the love of philosophy and decency that he subdued his lust. What has been denied him by nature he received through intellectual effort (*studium*). Others stressed that the human nature decoded by the physiognomic gaze imposed no necessity and that for both humankind and beasts *nutritiva* (nourishment in the broadest sense, both spiritual and intellectual) can be stronger than nature and hence effectively change it.[47]

Sometimes a more explicit textual alteration seemed to be necessary in order to minimise the potential dangers of physiognomy. The scribe of a pastoral codex which includes a version of the *Secretum secretorum* physiognomy altered the last chapter of the text and turned it into a moral excursus about the possibility to resist and defeat the apparently innate character which nature had forced upon humanity.[48] For him the physiognomic discourse fuses smoothly with the discourse about vices and virtues. Physiognomy reveals only potential sins, so for an accurate judgement it is essential to compare the signs and their meanings with the actual deeds and behaviour of the person. Though it is difficult to obviate lust and other desires to which we are naturally inclined by virtue of our anatomy and corporeal disposition, it is still possible to do so. In this struggle, good deeds which counter the vices and a soul governed by a well-functioning rational appetite (*racionalis appetitus*) are the main means. The story of Hippocrates is again the example for this possibility to fight the natural inclinations.

Third, the scribe or an odd user would draw the reader's attention to the danger of rash physiognomic judgement and to the possibility and desirability of defeating the natural inclinations, by adding pointing fingers and other *nota bene* signs at the margins of the story of Hippocrates' disciples or the last paragraph of the *Secretum secretorum* version which warns against rash judgements based on one sign only. The scribe could add at the closing title his own remark which would underline the fact that physiognomy is about probability

Verlagsbuchhandlung, 1916), vol. 1, 46/127; *Quaestiones de animalibus*, Liber I q. 21, ed. E. Filthaut, in *Alberti magni ... Opera omnia*, vol. 12 (Aschendorff: Monasterii Westfalorum in aedibus Aschendorff, 1955), 94–5.

47 L. Ladouzy and R. Pépin, eds., *Le régime du corps du maître Aldebrandin de Sienne* (Paris: Honoré Champion, 1911), 193–202; and Ziegler, 'Text and Context', 163 n. 12.

48 Paris, BnF, MS nouv. acq. lat. 711, fol. 29<sup>r–v</sup>.

and not about necessity.[49] Another ingenious way to divert attention from the danger of physiognomy was to entitle it in a manner which turned it into a pious piece of Christian morality. Thus, in thirteenth-century Cerne Abbey (Dorset) a version of the *Secretum secretorum* Physiognomy was entitled in red: *Ypocras de contemptu mundi*.[50] By turning the story of Hippocrates' disciples and its moral lesson to the centre of the science of physiognomy, the scribe could both diffuse the danger inherent in this science and fully expose his readers to all its principles. For if the message of the text is so perfectly congruent with the monastic ideal of *contemptus mundi*, surely it can be read by all.

And fourthly, by creating a Christian physiognomic ideal type as early as the mid-thirteenth century, the users of physiognomy were led to believe that, though it is designed to teach who the humans around us really are, it can get us nearer to grasping the unfathomable, namely what Christ looked like. For the medieval physiognomer the ideal physiognomic type (characterised by a perfectly balanced complexion as attested by a perfectly proportioned body, hence perfect character and behaviour) was not an individual belonging to a specific ethnic group. It was Christ – a super-national second Adam representative of humankind in general. According to the physician Michele Savonarola, two of the foremost characteristics of the well-tempered person (*homo temperatus*) were a well-proportioned mixture of white and red colour, combined with fine, brilliant skin.[51] Savonarola linked the description of the well-tempered person who was well proportioned and characterised by *mediocritas* – the key physiognomic category for the ideal personality – to the widely disseminated thirteenth-century Latin text describing the face of Christ along what seem to be clearly physiognomic lines.[52] This description, which Savonarola fully transcribed immediately after he identified the bodily signs of the well-tempered person, included the assertion that Christ's face was without a wrinkle or any spot and that a moderate touch of red beautified it. The imaginary skin of Christ, his medium-sized and erect stature, his moderately

---

49 See for example Paris, BnF, MS lat. 6298, fols 155[rb]–156[rb], a fourteenth-century compendium of Aristotle's natural philosophy that includes a physiognomy based on the *Secretum secretorum*.

50 London, British Library, MS Egerton 843, fol. 35[v].

51 Michele Savonarola, *Speculum physonomie*, Paris, BnF, MS lat 7357, fol. 54[rb].

52 On the history of this text, see E. von Dobschütz, *Christusbilder: Untersuchungen zur christlichen Legende* (Texte und Untersuchungen zur Geschichte der Altchristlichen Literatur, vol. 3 NF; Leipzig, 1899), vol. 2, 308–30. On the physiognomic context of this literary portrait, see Ziegler, 'Text and Context', 170–2 and 'Skin and Character in Medieval and Early Renaissance Physiognomy', *Micrologus* 13 (2005), 529–30.

straight hair, and his blue, variegated and bright eyes thus became the model for the ideal body which contains the morally perfect personality. All these classical categories belonging to the best-tempered personality were Christianised and re-offered to the Western imagination as keys for deciphering the perfect personality. Physiognomy thus acquired religious legitimacy.

Despite mechanisms of ecclesiastical control and censorship, despite the overwhelming grip of Aristotelianism on natural philosophers and theologians alike, and despite the sincere reverence towards religious orthodoxy and Scripture, thirteenth- and fourteenth-century intellectuals from all fields of knowledge were engaged in vibrant dialogues with the ideas of their colleagues from other disciplines. Theologians enthusiastically interwove into their theological debates high-level, sophisticated and up-to-date scientific knowledge they borrowed directly from medical and philosophical books. In as far as experimental sciences dealing with the human body are concerned, there is no indication for a systematic repressive approach on behalf of the ecclesiastical authorities: on the contrary. And alchemists, astrologers and physiognomers adopted a series of rhetorical and doctrinal approaches to accommodate their profession to religious orthodoxy. The boundaries between the different disciplines were fixed and clear, but at no stage were they impenetrable for curious incursions by outsiders.

25

# Faith and the intellectuals II

MICHAEL STOLZ

This article concerns the persistent preoccupation with the boundaries between inquiry and faith, as they appear in the context of the liberal arts (*artes liberales*) in the high and in the later Middle Ages.[1] Since Late Antiquity the liberal arts represented the basic learning in Christian schools, where they served as a prerequisite for biblical studies. Before one considers their role on the borderline of religious and secular inquiry, a short outline of their development in the Christian world is necessary.

Christian authors such as St Augustine and St Jerome adopted the concept of the liberal arts from Greek and Roman models. In the first century CE Philon of Alexandria had defined the arts a 'circle' or 'chorus' of preliminary sophistic studies, which included grammar, rhetoric, geometry, music, but also arithmetic, dialectic and astronomy. These subjects had the inferior rank of 'intermediate learning'. For Philon the circle of studies was represented by Abraham's maid Hagar, who gave birth to Ishmael, but who was repudiated by Abraham together with her son (Gen. 16 and 21). On the other hand,

---

1 For the history of the liberal arts in the Middle Ages, see *Arts libéraux et philosophie au Moyen Âge: Actes du quatrième congrès international de philosophie médiévale. Université de Montréal, Montréal, Canada, 27 août – 2 septembre 1967* (Montréal: Institut d'études médiévales; Paris: Vrin, 1969); Detlef Illmer, 'Artes liberales', *Theologische Realenzyklopädie* 4 (1979), 156–71; David L. Wagner, ed., *The Seven Liberal Arts in the Middle Ages* (Bloomington: Indiana University Press, 1983); Uta Lindgren, *Die Artes liberales in Antike und Mittelalter: Bildungs- und wissenschaftsgeschichtliche Entwicklungslinien* (Algorismus 8; Munich: Institut für Geschichte der Naturwissenschaften, 1992); Friedrich Dechant, *Die theologische Rezeption der Artes liberales und die Entwicklung des Philosophiebegriffs in theologischen Programmschriften des Mittelalters von Alkuin bis Bonaventura* (St Ottilien: Eos, 1993); Ingrid Craemer-Ruegenberg and Andreas Speer, ed., *'Scientia' und 'ars' im Hoch- und Spätmittelalter*, 2 vols. (Miscellanea Mediaevalia 22, 1/2; Berlin and New York: Walter de Gruyter, 1994); Michael Stolz, *Artes-liberales-Zyklen: Formationen des Wissens im Mittelalter*, 2 vols. (Bibliotheca Germanica 47; Tübingen and Basel: A. Francke, 2004), 6–57. Generally many additional references to the following (including sources and editions) can be found in the latter work.

Abraham's spouse Sarah, the mother of the legitimate son Isaac, was interpreted as the figure of philosophy, virtue and wisdom.[2]

In first-century Latin culture, these disciplines became the liberal arts, conceived as preparatory to the study of moral philosophy and as leading to ethical conduct. The epithet 'liberal' means that they are worthy of a free man, that is, a man who is free both in his economic position and in his mental habits.[3] The liberal arts were treated in the lost *Disciplinarum libri* by the Roman author Varro[4] and in several treatises by Boethius, who also coined the term 'quadruvium' for the mathematical disciplines arithmetic, music, geometry and astronomy (*De institutione arithmetica* I.1).[5] As Boethius put it, their subjects are the prerequisites for philosophical knowledge, as they gradually guided the mind from the sensible to the intelligible world. Later, probably in the Carolingian era, an analogous expression for 'quadruvium' (then written 'quadrivium') arises with the term 'trivium' that stands for the linguistic disciplines grammar, dialectic and rhetoric.[6]

It is this kind of canon, composed of the *quadrivium* and the (later so-called) *trivium*, that was introduced by St Augustine into Christian learning. In his dialogue *De ordine* of 386 dealing with the topic of divine providence, Augustine referred to the disciplines of the liberal arts. A central role of these subjects, which are conceived as guiding from the sensible to the intelligible world, is attributed to dialectic (dealing with the eternal forms) and arithmetic, as the laws of forms and numbers will help to understand the order of creation. The demanding education in the liberal arts, which also includes philosophy, is equated with divine law that, although it will always stay with God, is as it were inscribed in the souls of the sages (*De ordine* II.8.25).[7] In his *De doctrina christiana* of c. 395–426/7 Augustine admits that disciplines developed in pagan antiquity may be used for biblical exegesis and, in the case of rhetoric, also for preaching (II.39 f., 58–61; IV.2.3). His main

---

2 Ilsetraut Hadot, *Arts libéraux et philosophie dans la pensée antique* (Paris: Études augustiniennes, 1984), 282–7.

3 *Ibid.*, 271–3.

4 *Ibid.*, 156–90 (critical against older attempts of reconstruction).

5 Henry Chadwick, *Boethius: The Consolations of Music, Logic, Theology, and Philosophy* (Oxford: Clarendon Press, 1981); Margaret Gibson, *Boethius: His Life, Thought and Influence* (Oxford: Basil Blackwell, 1981); Michael Masi, ed., *Boethius and the Liberal Arts: A Collection of Essays* (Utah Studies in Literature and Linguistics 18; Bern, Frankfurt a.M. and Las Vegas: Peter Lang, 1981).

6 Stolz, *Artes-liberales-Zyklen*, vol. 1, p. 12f. See also the first reference in the scholia of Horace's *Ars poetica*, Vienna, National Library of Austria, Cod. 223 [Phil. 244], fol. 1r-17v, eleventh century.

7 Henri-Irénée Marrou, *Saint Augustin et la fin de la culture antique*, new edn (Paris: Boccard 1983), esp. 184–6; Hadot, *Arts libéraux*, 101–36.

argument is that the Israelites, when they fled from Egypt, were advised by God to take foreign gold and silver vessels with them (after Exod. 3.22; 11.2; 12.35). In the same way, the Christians should learn 'for a better usage' from the pagans, as their teaching was not restricted to 'superstitious imaginings', but contained the liberal arts which indeed could be used for the investigation of truth (II.40.60).[8] A similar argument is suggested by St Jerome, who in one of his letters (nr. 70.2) refers to another passage in the Scriptures: a rule in Deuteronomy (21.10–13) reads that God authorised the Israelites to take a female captive from foreign tribes into their house and to marry her, if they respected certain hygienic measures. Likewise the Christians might take up pagan knowledge, provided that it is purged of harmful components.[9]

Justified by such arguments, the liberal arts found their way into the intellectual life of the Middle Ages. The use of secular knowledge in Christian contexts was encouraged by an influential handbook, which explains the subjects of the liberal arts by means of a mytholography: Martianus Capella's *De nuptiis Philologiae et Mercurii*.[10] Written in the later fifth century by a pagan author familiar with theurgic and mystagogic traditions, but also with Neoplatonic thought, it describes the marriage of the god Mercury and the maiden Philology. During the ceremony Mercury presents seven brides-maids as a wedding gift: the personified liberal arts; after this allegorical introduction every discipline is explained plainly and in detail. Since the Carolingian era, Martianus' *De nuptiis* serves as a basic manual of learning. Its commentators (among them John Scotus Eriugena) interpret the marriage as the synthesis of wisdom (Philology) and eloquence (Mercury).[11]

The Christian justification of the liberal arts was also supported by the sixth-century author Cassiodorus (c. 485–c. 585) who dealt with the seven disciplines, comparing them to the seven pillars of the house of wisdom (in Prov. 9.1) in the second part of his guidebook *Institutiones*. In the decades around 600 the Spanish bishop Isidore of Seville (c. 560–4 April 636) spread Cassiodorus' accounts of the liberal arts by including them in his encyclopaedic *Etymologiae* or *Origines*, which was to be used as a reference book throughout the Middle Ages.[12]

---

8 Marrou, *Saint Augustin*, 387–413; Dechant, *Die theologische Rezeption der Artes liberales*, 50–4; Stolz, *Artes-liberales-Zyklen*, vol. I, 11, and 462 n. 176.
9 J[ohn] N. D. Kelly, *Jerome: His Life, Writings and Controversies* (London: Duckworth, 1975), 43f.
10 Muriel Bovey, *Disciplinae cyclicae: L'organisation du savoir dans l'œuvre de Martianus Capella* (Polymnia 3; Trieste: Edizioni Università di Trieste, 2003); Stolz, *Artes-liberales-Zyklen*, vol. I, 19–27.
11 *Ibid.*, 27f.
12 Hadot, *Arts libéraux*, 191–214; Stolz, *Artes-liberales-Zyklen*, vol. I, 13–19.

While Cassiodorus and Isidore, as well as St Augustine, saw the liberal arts as a preparatory course for biblical studies, later authors tend to grant them a more autonomous status. This attitude is already inherent in the ninth-century commentaries of Martianus' *De nuptiis*. John Scotus Eriugena understands the term 'artes liberales' in the sense that the disciplines may be studied for their own sake ('propter se ipsas adipiscuntur et discuntur'; commentary of Martianus Capella IV.367), although this judgement refers especially to the fact that the liberal arts are 'naturally in the soul' (commentary of Martianus Capella IV.368). In contrary to the crafts, that have to be acquired by invention or imitation, the arts exist independently in the soul, giving insight into the work of the creator. This inclination towards autonomy favours science studies carried out by those who investigate natural truth (the 'fisici' or 'naturalis veritatis inquisitores'; commentary of Martianus Capella VIII.862).[13]

From the tenth century onwards this interest expands and leads to intensified studies in the field of the *quadrivium*. Gerbert of Aurillac (c. 940/59–1003), later Pope Silvester II, used the abacus, a wooden tablet equipped with stones for calculation, and he experiments with diverse astronomical instruments, such as the armillary sphere and the astrolabe.[14] The treatises on the measurements of the astrolabe written by Hermann of Reichenau (1013–54) in the early eleventh century were in use up to the fourteenth century; his writings on musical theory, the *rithmimachia* (a game on the 'battle of numbers') and the *computus* (a calendar used for the calculation of the movable date of Easter) were also in wide circulation.[15] These endeavours were influenced by achievements of learning in the Arab world, which by Gerbert's and Hermann's time were being discussed in Europe. Despite the scepticism about pagan knowledge, as it was articulated in the works of the teacher Otloh of St Emmeram in Regensburg (c. 1010–79), this process only gained momentum.[16]

New scholarly horizons were opened in the twelfth century by the 'school of Chartres', a group of French scholars loosely linked to the cathedral school of Chartres.[17] Before the great influx of Greek and Arabic texts in the following century, the 'Chartrian' scholars worked within the classical tradition yet transcended it. Among the sources that inspired them were Boethius and

13 Hadot *Arts libéraux*, 61–4; Stolz, *Artes-liberales-Zyklen*, vol. 1, 32f.
14 Lindgren, *Die Artes liberales*, 41–64.
15 Stolz, *Artes-liberales-Zyklen*, vol. 1, 34 (with further references).
16 *Ibid.*, 35.
17 R. W. Southern, *Scholastic Humanism and the Unification of Europe*, vol. 1, *Foundations* (Oxford and Cambridge, Mass.: Blackwell, 1995), 58–101.

Martianus Capella, but also the medical writings of Galen, the hermetic tradition and ancient mythology. This syncretism produced combinations of science and poetics, as it was already characteristic of Plato's *Timaios*, which is one of the main sources used by the members of the 'school of Chartres': divine creation is conceived as a work of art and poetry.

Thierry of Chartres, who since about 1142 was chancellor of the bishop of Chartres, dedicated a book to the seven liberal arts, which he calls *Heptateuchon*.[18] In this manual he gathers excerpts of ancient and medieval writings on the 'quadrivium' and the 'trivium'. The joining of the two branches, which Thierry interprets as insight and linguistic mediation, is correlated to the marriage of Philology and Mercury, designed by Martianus Capella. As Thierry states in the prologue, he has completed the assemblage of the arts (represented as personifications) for the benefit of human education. In a similar way, John of Salisbury, another author close to the 'school of Chartres', emphasised the human powers of the liberal arts. In his *Metalogicon* (from 1159)[19] he states that 'nature is the mother of the arts'. This view is justified by the fact that human beings perceive things by natural disposition in their mind, before they keep them in memory and finally judge them by means of reason. John of Salisbury saw the human mind as naturally driven by an exploratory spirit which is promoted by enthusiasm and exercise and which is the 'origin of all arts'.

From the twelfth century onwards the dominant role of the arts in the concept of knowledge, as the Chartrian authors propagate it, starts to decline. From now on, the liberal arts are incorporated in more complex systems of learning.[20] This is the case in the *Didascalicon* (c. 1127), written by the Augustinian canon Hugh of St Victor in Paris.[21] Hugh divides the overall discipline philosophy into the four branches of 'theorica', 'practica', 'mechanica' and 'logica', and includes the 'quadrivium' as a mathematical part into the 'theorica', whereas the 'trivium' appears in the field of 'logica'. For Hugh all intellectual efforts have a clearly redeeming dimension, as their aim is the restoration of a lost primary nature: after the Fall the arts may help humankind to regain a godlike status. Hugh treats the profane learning of the arts in the

---

18 Chartres, town library, cod. 497/498, destroyed in 1944 (microfilms preserved). Cf. Edouard Jeauneau, 'Le Prologus in Eptatheucon de Thierry de Chartres', *Mediaeval Studies* 16 (1954), 171–5.
19 Southern, *Scholastic Humanism*, 214–21; Stolz, *Artes-liberales-Zyklen*, vol. 1, 38f.
20 Richard William Hunt, 'The Introductions to the "Artes" in the Twelfth Century', in *Studia mediaevalia in honorem admodum Reverendi Patris Raymundi Josephi Martin* (Bruges: De Tempel, 1948), 85–112.
21 Hadot, *Arts libéraux*, 557–68; Stolz, *Artes-liberales-Zyklen*, vol. 1, 39–44.

first three books of his *Didascalicon* and dedicates the last three books to the study of the Scriptures. Both systems of knowledge are independent, but have a common goal: the restoration of divine likeness and the unification with God. In Hugh's view, the arts are no longer a prerequisite of Bible studies (as for St Augustine), but, guided by a gradual progress, they may lead humankind to redemption. This anthropological foundation, also expressed by Thierry of Chartres and John of Salisbury, is the achievement of twelfth-century humanism.[22]

Hugh's harmonising of the liberal arts with biblical studies did not endure in a world of growing knowledge and specialisation. While Hugh embodies the monastic traditions of learning with introspective methods such as 'meditatio', 'oratio' and 'contemplatio', the new dialectical techniques of 'quaestio' and 'disputatio' are practised in urban schools and universities. Beside the authority of the Bible and the classical texts stands the authority of reasoning scholars (*auctoritas magistrorum*). Peter Abelard, who in his treatise *Sic et non* (from 1123/8) confronts contradicting quotations taken from the Bible and the church fathers, is one of the most prominent representatives of this development.[23]

In the thirteenth century the polarisation of religious and secular knowledge would be enforced by the influence of Greek and Islamic learning. Now the whole Aristotelian corpus accompanied by the commentaries of Arabic philosophers becomes known throughout Europe. After a first period of translations in Spain and southern Italy, the spread of the Aristotelian writings is centred at the universities which, by the conferment of statutes, develop into the predominant intellectual institutions of the century: the statutes of Paris established in 1215–31; the statutes of Bologna, Oxford and Cambridge in the 1250s.[24]

In the university system of four faculties the liberal disciplines are taught at the lowest level in the faculty of arts. The master degree obtained after about

---

22 Southern, *Scholastic Humanism*, and C. Stephen Jaeger, *The Envy of Angels: Cathedral Schools and Social Ideals in Medieval Europe, 950–1200* (Philadelphia: University of Pennsylvania Press, 1994).

23 David C. Lindberg, *The Beginnings of Western Science: The European Scientific Tradition in Philosophical, Religious and Institutional Context, 600 B.C. to A.D. 1450* (Chicago and London: University of Chicago Press, 1992), 195–7.

24 For the translation movement and the rise of the universities, see *ibid.*, 203–13. For the history of the medieval universities, cf. (with further references) Hilde de Ridder-Symoens, ed., *A History of the University in Europe*, vol. 1, *Universities in the Middle Ages* (Cambridge: Cambridge University Press, 1992); Maarten J. F. M. Hoenen, J. H. Josef Schneider and Georg Wieland, eds., *Philosophy and Learning: Universities in the Middle Ages* (Education and Society in the Middle Ages and Renaissance 6; Leiden, New York and Cologne: Brill 1995).

six years opens the path for studies in the higher faculties of medicine, law and finally theology. But for economic reasons many students did not stay at the university after having finished (or not) the arts course. Not least for this practical reason the preparatory status attributed to the arts by Augustine was all but abandoned.

The Aristotelian writings contained in the arts curriculum included the *Logica nova* (the *Prior Analytics* and the *Posterior Analytics*, the *Topics* and the *On Sophistic Refutations*), the *Physics, On the Soul, Metaphysics*, the *Nicomachean* and *Eudemian Ethics, On Generation and Corruption, On Heaven and Earth*, and the pseudo-Aristotelian *Book of Causes*. In the second half of the thirteenth century the translator William of Moerbeke revises some of these texts and completes this Aristotelian corpus by his own work. At the same time the Arabic commentators, combining Aristotle's ideas with Neoplatonic thought, become so influential that they even start to replace the writings of the Stagirite. At the University of Paris the commentaries of Avicenna (Ibn Sina, 980–1037) and Averroes (Ibn Rushd, 1126–98) gain a status of important authority. The Aristotelian and Platonistic influences also affect the study of theology, which followed after an education in the arts faculty in an eight-year curriculum.

In Paris the gradual acceptance of the Aristotelian writings can be observed in significant stages:[25] in 1210 the council of Sens prohibits any lecture dealing with Aristotle's scientific writings and their commentaries. The statutes issued by the papal legate Robert de Courçon in 1215 confirm this interdiction, which is repeated by Pope Gregory IX in the statutes from 1228 and 1231. In 1252 the Anglo-German nation of the University of Paris introduces a bachelor curriculum that contains Aristotle's *On the Soul*. Only two years later, in 1255, a general curricular reform promotes a programme of study that now includes almost all the scientific, logical and ethical writings of Aristotle, as well as his *Metaphysics* and some inauthentic treatises such as the *Book of Causes*. By these means the Aristotelian corpus is generally accepted in the middle of the century. Almost the same can be said for Oxford, where a curriculum from 1268 equally shows the predominance of Aristotle's scientific writings.

Despite this break, Étienne Tempier, archbishop of Paris, condemns the propositions of the radical Aristotelians Siger of Brabant and Boethius of Dacia

---

25 Hadot, *Arts libéraux*, 167–70; Lindberg, *The Beginnings*, 216–23; de Ridder-Symoens, *A History of the University*, 319–22; Hoenen *et al.*, eds., *Philosophy and Learning*, 99–103.

in 1270 and 1277.[26] His prohibition is directed against naturalistic and rationalistic tendencies in philosophical and theological matters and condemns even theorems in the writings of Albert the Great and Thomas Aquinas. Frequently the proscribed opinions derive from the ideas of Aristotelian commentators, as is the case for Averroes' doctrine on the unity and uniqueness of the intellect. Other theorems proclaim the eternity of the world or deny divine providence and personal immortality.

The teaching at the universities also yielded systematic handbooks of the arts and sciences. An early version is the so-called *Guide de l'étudiant*, an anonymous students' manual written in Paris in the 1230s.[27] By its examination questions and its lists of compulsory reading it shows a predominance of logic. The Aristotelian writings on metaphysics, natural science and ethics are also named, although they are not yet part of the curriculum. From the old curriculum (as used by representatives of the 'school of Chartres') writings such as the *Timaios* and Boethius' *Consolatio philosophiae* are taken into the programme; the overall arrangement of the sciences follows Boethius' *De trinitate*.

Systematic classifications of this kind are very common in the thirteenth century. Many of them are written by members of the mendicant orders, who play an important role in university life and who, by insisting on the principle of apostolic poverty, incite the so-called dispute between the 'seculars' and the mendicants. In essence this argument concerns the relationship between philosophy and theology, but it also affects the institutional delimitation of the two faculties of arts and theology.[28]

The Dominican Robert Kilwardby, who after his education in Paris and Oxford became archbishop of Canterbury, banned the radical Aristotelian ideas in Oxford shortly after the condemnation passed by the Parisian archbishop in 1277. In his *De ortu scientiarum* (from c. 1250) Kilwardby distinguishes a 'philosophy on divine things' and a 'philosophy on human things'.[29] The 'philosophy on divine things' includes natural science, mathematics (i.e., the *quadrivium* and optics) and metaphysics. The 'philosophy on human things' comprises ethics, mechanics and the *trivium*. This is a rather unique attempt to reconcile secular and spiritual knowledge in the scope of the new learning.

---

26 Lindberg, *The Beginnings*, 234–40; David Piché, ed., *La condamnation parisienne de 1277*, nouvelle édition du texte latin, traduction, introduction et commentaire, avec la collaboration de Claude Lafleur (Sic et non) (Paris: Vrin, 1999).
27 Hoenen *et al.*, eds., *Philosophy and Learning*, 137–99.
28 *Ibid.*, 17–28.
29 *Ibid.*, 106–21.

Other attempts prove to be less inventive: in his great compilation, called *Speculum maius* (from c. 1256/9), the Dominican Vincent of Beauvais collects the knowledge of his time. Besides the parts of *Speculum naturale*, *Speculum historiale* and *Speculum morale*, the *Speculum doctrinale* treats the arts and sciences with theology at the top. Vincent's cautious attitude towards the new learning becomes obvious in a passage of the *Speculum naturale*, where he states that 'his profession would not allow him to insist in the investigation and description of such things' (prologue, chapters 10 and 18).[30] A different strategy was followed by the Franciscan scholar Bonaventura in his *De reductione artium ad theologiam*, written in Paris between 1248 and 1256. He tries to combine the Aristotelian ideas with Neoplatonic traditions and describes the different sorts of knowledge as sources of light emanating from God. These lights are the mechanical arts, sensory perception, philosophical learning (including the liberal arts) and the Scriptures.[31]

The Franciscan intellectual Roger Bacon suggested a more hierarchical view. In his *Opus maius* (from 1266/7) he uses the metaphor of a 'handmaiden' to describe the relationship between the sciences and theology: the latter is the 'mistress of the others...for which the others are integral necessities and which cannot achieve its end without them'.[32] As Roger Bacon puts it, the new learning introduced by the Aristotelian and Arabic writings must not be neglected at all, but has to be reclaimed for the faith. Whereas Augustine had suggested the use of small bits of secular learning for the help in Bible studies, Roger Bacon wants to employ this learning in its totality. This attitude is fundamental for the change of intellectual life in thirteenth-century Europe.

The great synthesis of learning and Christian theology was to be achieved by Thomas Aquinas in his *Summa theologiae* and in other writings. In his commentary on Boethius' *De trinitate* (c. 1256/7) he states that 'what is divinely taught to us by faith cannot be contrary to what we are endowed with by nature' [i.e., by philosophy] (II.3).[33] Aristotelian philosophy and Christian theology are two compatible ways for finding the truth. The one led there by the natural human faculties of sense and reason, the other by divine revelation, which goes beyond the human capacities of discovering and understanding. Though what Thomas Aquinas calls philosophy is now far from being covered by the old canon, the liberal arts. In his commentary he

---

30  Stolz, *Artes-liberales-Zyklen*, vol. 1, 52f.
31  Dechant, *Die theologische Rezeption der Artes liberales*, 182–209.
32  David C., Lindberg, 'Science as Handmaiden: Roger Bacon and the Patristic Tradition', *Isis* 78 (1987), 518–36 (at 534–6); Lindberg, *The Beginnings*, 224–7.
33  Lindberg, *The Beginnings*, 231f.

stresses that 'the liberal arts do not adequately divide theoretical philosophy' (V.1).[34]

The intellectual situation of the second half of the thirteenth century is appropriately described by this sentence. In the area of the *trivium* the part of dialectic (now mostly called logic) is prevalent and also has influence on the conception of grammar and rhetoric. The *quadrivium* is enlarged with new subjects, such as metaphysics, natural philosophy, medicine, optics and also alchemy. Towards the end of the century, the eminent universities start to distinguish themselves in certain leading fields of research. Paris excels in a philosophical and speculative orientation of the arts, especially of the *trivium*. In Oxford, where the Franciscan scholars Robert Grosseteste and Roger Bacon were active, natural science was hegemonic. In the fourteenth century the school of mathematicians at Merton College, guided by Thomas Bradwardine, plays an important role. The theories developed there are influential on members of the Parisian arts faculty, especially on the philosopher John Buridan.[35] Paris and the Anglo-Saxon universities also inspire the newly founded universities in middle Europe, such as Prague (1347/8), Vienna (1365), Heidelberg (1385) and Cologne (1388).[36]

In Paris, Oxford and Cambridge rich benefactors established autonomous colleges, which employed lecturers in the arts course. These attracted even senior scholars, and encouraged careers restricted to the arts. On the other hand, many problems treated in the arts faculty met with theological problems, especially in the domains of metaphysics, ethics, cosmology and epistemology. Increasingly, members of religious orders educated in the arts concentrated on these boundaries; during the fourteenth and fifteenth centuries they would become the leading figures in philosophical and theological questions. A central problem arose from the conception of contingency (i.e., coincidence in contrast to necessity), especially regarding the explanation of the divine work of mercy and salvation. In this context diverse topics were discussed, such as the freedom of will, the relation of human action and divine omnipotence, as well as predestination and the ways of cognition in matters of faith. The Oxford Franciscans John Duns Scotus (1265/6–1308) and William of

---

34 Stolz, *Artes-liberales-Zyklen*, vol. 1, 54f.
35 For the developments in the thirteenth and fourteenth centuries, cf. Hadot, *Arts libéraux*, 175–97, 209–13; de Ridder-Symoens, *A History of the University*, vol. 1, 323, 328–30.
36 Frank Rexroth, *Deutsche Universitätsstiftungen von Prag bis Köln: Die Intentionen des Stifters und die Wege und Chancen ihrer Verwirklichung im spätmittelalterlichen deutschen Territorialstaat* (Beihefte zum Archiv für Kulturgeschichte 34; Cologne, Weimar and Vienna: Böhlau, 1992); de Ridder-Symoens, *A History of the University*, vol. 1, 55–64, 71–4.

Occam (1285/90–c. 1348) make important contributions to these fields. They develop theories of nominalism (that denies the reality of the universals), terministic logic (that distinguishes the properties of logic terms in the sentence) and epistemological questions (e.g., on the cognition of forms and figures produced by the senses and by reason).[37]

In the fifteenth century this constellation of philosophical questions was to provoke the controversy between 'via antiqua' and 'via moderna', which temporarily split the arts faculties and caused the creation of separated chairs dedicated to the two different ways, especially at the new-founded universities of central Europe. At the arts faculties of Italian universities the humanist movement prevailed during the fourteenth and fifteenth centuries, and would then also spread to the universities and cities north of the Alps. The *Margarita philosophica* is an arts manual composed by the Carthusian prior Gregor Reisch around 1490 (first printed in Freiburg, Breisgau, in 1503).[38] This compendium itemises the seven liberal arts in seven books and complements them by books on natural science, on ethics and on the soul. Several passages show the influence of the dispute on the 'via moderna' and the one of the humanist movement (this also applies to the woodcuts opening each book, e.g., for those on logic and rhetoric). But in terms of the history of scientific and religious beliefs, the programme of the handbook is modest; its function is mainly restricted to preparation for higher education, including theology.

The measuring of the boundaries between inquiry and faith was a complex process, in which the balance of human and divine powers was constantly challenged. The continuous interplay of theology and the classical sciences meant that both spheres formed part of the mainstream of Christian culture.[39]

---

37  For the university life of the later Middle Ages (also described in the following paragraph), cf. Jozef Ijsewijn and Jacques Paquet, *The Universities in the Late Middle Ages* (Leuven: Leuven University Press, 1978); de Ridder-Symoens, *A History of the University*, vol. 1, 330–3; Hoenen *et al.*, eds., *Philosophy and Learning*, 249–386.

38  Lucia Andreini, *Gregor Reisch e la sua Margarita Philosophica* (Analecta Cartusiana 138; Salzburg: Institut für Anglistik und Amerikanistik, 1997); Stolz, *Artes-liberales-Zyklen*, vol. 1, 56f., 541–50.

39  David C. Lindberg, 'The Medieval Church Encounters the Classical Tradition', in David C. Lindberg and Ronald L. Numbers, eds., *When Science and Christianity Meet* (Chicago: University of Chicago Press, 2003), 8–32, esp. 31f.

# PART VII

# REFORM AND RENEWAL

# 26

# Empowerment through reading, writing and example: the *Devotio moderna*

KOEN GOUDRIAAN

During the last decades of the fourteenth century a movement of religious revival started in the present-day Netherlands, which came to be known as the Modern Devotion, after a term coined by Henry Pomerius in his *On the Origin of the Monastery of Groenendaal*[1] when he called Geert Grote the 'fountain and origin of the present-day devotion (*modernae devotionis*) among the regular canons'.

Geert Grote (1340–84), the son of a wealthy citizen of Deventer, studied in Paris and embarked on an ecclesiastical career, but a severe illness brought about a conversion in 1372, when he renounced his prebends and started a life of asceticism. After several years of retreat in a Carthusian monastery, he was ordained a deacon and began to preach in the diocese of Utrecht, exhorting his audience to a life of purity and spiritual renewal (1379). He fought the decadence of the church and denounced her many vices, against the background of the Western Schism. Grote criticised the secular clergy for its wealth, its multiple transgressions of the rule of celibacy and its simony. The monastic orders, too, were accused of committing simony by requiring dowers at admission. Another reproach at their address was the presence of *proprietarii* within their ranks: monks and nuns who did not take their vow of poverty seriously. Grote's intentions were wholly orthodox: his criticism sprang from reverence for the priesthood and for the monastic life. In 1383, however, he was silenced, after his severe attacks on the 'focarists' (priests living with a concubine) had thrown the whole diocesan clergy in confusion.

---

1 [Henricus Pomerius], 'De origine monasterii Viridis Vallis', *Analecta Bollandiana* 4 (1885), 288. Important primary sources on the movement can be found in Johannes Busch, *Chronicon Windeshemense und Liber de Reformatione monasteriorum*, ed. K. Grube (Halle: Hendel, 1886; repr. Farnborough: Gregg, 1968); Johannes Mauburnus, *Rosetum exercitiorum spiritualium et sacrorum meditationum*, ed. Leander de S. Martino (Douai: Bellerus, 1620) and other works listed in notes below; John Van Engen, *Devotio moderna: Basic Writings* (New York: Paulist Press, 1988) offers a selection of texts in translation.

The remaining part of his life he devoted to the translation of the *Book of Hours*. He died of the plague on 20 August 1384.

In the decades after his death, Grote's call for renewal of the church had as its main effect that the 'religious' life received an enormous impetus by the establishment of new networks of monasteries and semi-monastic institutions. In north-west Europe, the Modern Devotion was in effect the first instalment of the so-called 'Observance moment'. It branched in three main directions: the brethren and sisters of the common life, the regular canons and canonesses, and the tertiaries.

The brethren and sisters of the common life did not follow an ecclesiastically approved rule. They based their existence on voluntary application of the evangelical counsels and the return to what they considered to be the life of the apostolic church.[2] The first sister-house was 'Mr Geert's House' in Deventer, founded by Geert Grote himself. The model for the brother-houses was given by Florens' House (likewise in Deventer), a community founded in the residence of Florens Radewijns, Geert Grote's successor at the head of the movement. Here and elsewhere, the brethren counted both clerics and lay brothers among their members. In 1401 the bishop of Utrecht granted them a general licence for their way of life.

Between the sister-houses considerable differences existed, which is not surprising in view of the fact that they did not live according to a general rule but on the basis of local customs. The common life, that is, the renunciation of private property and the contribution of all personal income for the upkeep of the common household, is regarded as characteristic for these communities. In reality, quite a number of them for a long time did not introduce it. Other communities were nothing but beguine houses starting a new span of life by adhering to Grote's movement. From its cradle in the IJssel region, the brother- and sister-houses spread to the western part of the diocese of Utrecht, and across the borders of the diocese to the southern Low Countries, the Rhineland and Westphalia. In due time, the brethren adhered to one of two loose confederations, the 'Colloquies' of Zwolle and of Münster. In the second part of the fifteenth century, a 'general chapter' was founded in southern Germany, while several brother-houses were transformed into collegiate churches, the brethren adopting the status of secular canons.

---

2  The foundations of the brethren are catalogued in W. Leesch, Ernst Persoons and Anton G. Weiler, eds., *Monasticon fratrum vitae communis* (3 vols.; Brussels: Archives et bibliothèques de Belgique, 1977–2004).

The second branch of the Modern Devotion was formed by the regular canons and canonesses of St Augustine: this branch was wholly monastic from the start.[3] The first monastery, Windesheim near Zwolle, was founded in 1387. It came to lead a Congregation, which was governed in a centralised manner and eventually counted over one hundred monasteries, in large majority houses of canons. The best-known monastery of canonesses was Diepenveen near Deventer. From 1432 on, the Congregation refused further incorporation of women's convents, because it threatened to become over-burdened by the pastoral care for these houses.[4] In 1413 it had been joined by a group of seven mostly older monasteries in the province of Brabant, centred on Groenendaal, the monastery of the famous mystic John of Ruusbroec. In the middle of the fifteenth century, Windesheim extended its influence deep into the German Empire, where its members were repeatedly called to assist in the reformation of existing monasteries.

The third main category consisted of the men and women who adopted the Third Rule of Saint Francis: the tertiaries, who have become the object of more detailed research only recently.[5] A first group of houses, mainly in the western part of the diocese of Utrecht, adopted tertiary status in 1399. They received papal approval in the same year; in 1401 the Chapter (or Congregation) of Utrecht was founded. The tertiaries succeeded in maintaining their autonomy from the Franciscans, who as yet had not adopted the Observance. Secular priests as well as priests from within their own ranks and brethren of the common life assumed the pastoral care of these houses. Women's convents were in the great majority. The number of houses of tertiaries exceeded one hundred in the diocese of Utrecht alone. In due time, many of these houses conformed to the monastic life as the result of a process that could be called 'claustration'; enclosure was introduced, and the brothers or sisters often switched to the rule of St Augustine, becoming regular canons and canonesses. The tertiaries, too, spread across the borders of the diocese,

---

3 For a catalogue of houses of canons and canonesses, see Wilhelm Kohl, Ernst Persoons and Anton G. Weiler, eds., *Monasticon Windeshemense* (4 vols.; Brussels: Archives et bibliothèques de Belgique, 1976–84). For the canonesses in particular, see Wybren Scheepsma, *Medieval Religious Women in the Low Countries: The 'Modern Devotion', the Canonesses of Windesheim and their Writings* (Woodbridge: Boydell Press, 2004).

4 S. Van der Woude, *Acta Capituli Windeshemensis* (The Hague: Nijhoff, 1953), 24–5.

5 See Hildo van Engen, *De derde orde van Sint-Franciscus in het middeleeuwse bisdom Utrecht: Een bijdrage tot de institutionele geschiedenis van de Moderne Devotie* (Hilversum: Verloren, 2006), with edition of legal sources at www.bkvu.nl.

giving rise to the foundation of the Chapters of Cologne and of Zepperen (in the diocese of Liège).

The New Devout were recruited from all walks of life. In the early period, members of the nobility played a leading role, but on the whole the Modern Devotion movement did not rest upon its support. Most convents were urban or at least in geographical or social proximity to the cities in this rapidly urbanising corner of Europe. In Westphalia and the Rhineland, close contacts have been demonstrated between the convents and leading circles in the urban community.[6] The same holds true for Zwolle.[7] But the lower strata of the city population also joined the convent life of the Modern Devout. Typically, a well-to-do widow assembled a group of virgins of more humble extraction around her person.[8] For Leiden it has been argued that the population of the convents counted many recent immigrants from the countryside.[9] In their early days, the Modern Devout, and in particular the brethren and sisters of the common life, met with considerable opposition. The novelty of their way of life raised the suspicion that they transgressed the ban on *novae religiones*. The Dominican friar Matthew Grabow denounced them, but he was silenced at the Council of Constance (1416–18). The contestation occasioned several apologetic tracts. In his *On the Lifestyle of Devout Persons Living Together*, Gerard Zerbolt (1367–98) defended the lifestyle of the brethren and sisters of the common life with arguments drawn from canon law and other sources. This tract had a great influence on the later self-understanding of the movement.[10]

The leadership of the Modern Devotion took pains to remain within the confines of orthodoxy and to maintain good relations with the ecclesiastical hierarchy, with abiding results. Being as it were the successors to the beguines, the Modern Devout were acutely aware of the risk run by new religious movements of being charged with heresy: Grote had already warned his followers about it. During the first half century of the movement a strong undercurrent of mysticism existed, but the New Devout refrained from

6  G. Rehm, *Die Schwestern vom gemeinsamen Leben im nordwestlichen Deutschland: Untersuchungen zur Geschichte der Devotio Moderna und des weiblichen Religiosentums* (Berlin: Duncker & Humblot, 1985), 212–24.

7  Madelon van Luijk, *Bruiden van Christus: De tweede religieuze vrouwenbeweging in Leiden en Zwolle, 1380–1580* (Zutphen: Walburg Pers, 2004), 180–99.

8  A.G. Weiler, 'De intrede van rijke weduwen en arme meisjes in de leefgemeenschappen van de Moderne Devotie', *Ons Geestelijk Erf* 59 (1985), 403–19.

9  Van Luijk, *Bruiden van Christus*, 180–99.

10  Theo Klausmann, *Consuetudo consuetudine vincitur: Die Hausordnungen der Brüder vom gemeinsamen Leben im Bildungs- und Sozialisationsprogramm der Devotio moderna* (Frankfurt: Lang, 2003), 95–139.

speculative theology. They kept aloof from academic life and did not produce a Wyclif. No one among them challenged vested interests by formulating daring theories about *dominium* and the correct relationship between church and monarchy. Nor did they engage with public life directly. This goes far to explain why their movement did not end in catastrophe, as was the case with Wyclif's Lollards and with Hus and his followers. The Modern Devout remained part of mainstream Catholicism. In the Low Countries, the Rhineland and Westphalia they were even at the heart of it.

The Modern Devout led a life of reading, writing, meditation and prayer. Their spirituality was deeply influenced by the monastic traditions of the preceding ages. In order to find an appropriate model for their lifestyle, they reached as far back as the Fathers of the Desert; John Cassian's *Collationes patrum* were intensely studied. But the tradition of affective spirituality originating with Saint Bernard of Clairvaux and mediated by Franciscans such as Saint Bonaventure, found full reception among them as well. Both the veneration for the Virgin and the intense concentration on the earthly life of Christ, characteristic for late medieval spirituality in general, are found no less within the Modern Devotion. More recent models for the monastic life were set by the Franciscans – David of Augsburg's *Profectus religiosorum* had much influence – and by contemporary Carthusians.

The attitude of the New Devout towards mysticism was characterised by ambivalence. Speculative mysticism of the Dominican type, represented by Meister Eckhart, found no echo among them. However, the writings of Henry Suso were appreciated as were those of Ruusbroec, whose work in the vernacular dominated fourteenth-century Dutch religious literature. Ruusbroec was admired – though not without criticism – by Grote, who went to visit him in his monastery of Groenendaal. John of Schoonhoven (c. 1356–1432), himself a canon of Groenendaal and author of an important work *On the Contempt of the World*, defended Ruusbroec against accusations of heresy. Early in their history, many Devout, even those from among the leadership, were given both to mysticism and to para-mystical experiences such as heavenly raptures and visions. The primary representative of mysticism was Gerlach Petersz (1378–1411), the author of a *Soliloquium* and *Breviloquium*. Henry Mande (d. 1431) left behind a collection of *Visions*; his revelations were a topic of dispute between the Modern Devout. Towards the middle of the fifteenth century, true mysticism, which claims to possess direct and unmediated knowledge of God, came to be regarded as potentially subversive and dangerous for orderly life in the convents and was repressed. What remained was 'mystical culture', a practice of intense devotion and meditation expressing itself in terms referring to mystical union – for example in the tradition of the exegesis of the *Song of Songs* – but without actual experience of the *unio mystica*.[11]

Meditation on Christ's Passion was of paramount importance. To rethink every detail of the life of Christ and to try to conform to the model he had set filled a large part of the lives of the New Devout. The devotion towards the eucharist, a general feature of late medieval spiritual life, was intense among them. It was the goal of their lives to imitate Christ, to suffer with the Lord, to be crucified and rejected with him. In order to achieve this goal, they devised various exercises, making use of a great variety of written texts as well as of non-written, visual materials. According to Geert Grote, meditation could draw on four types of sources: Scripture, the writings of the fathers of the church, revelations to specific individuals, and one's own imagination. The use of imagination to enhance one's identification with the suffering Christ opened the way for engaging aesthetic means as tools for meditation.[12]

But it was asceticism with systematic exercise of the virtues that was at the heart of Modern Devout spirituality. Mortification of the flesh by fasting and food abstinence, frequent vigils, wearing uncomfortable and ugly clothes, and various forms of self-chastisement characterised the Modern Devotion in its early phases. Later, these exercises became more moderate. What remained was the accent placed on the sanctification of everyday life and the transformation of one's personality by systematically eradicating vices and cultivating virtues. Conversion had to be followed up by humility, obedience, charity, purity of heart and an ardent desire towards God. The fundamental works in this respect were Zerbolt's *The Reform of the Powers of the Soul* and *The Spiritual Ascensions*. Together, they constitute a complete and systematic manual for the spiritual life.

Labour was valued as a good in itself. It served to avoid idleness and its concomitant vices and to win the means necessary for the practice of charity. Though occasionally applied out of necessity in the early years, mendicancy was rejected in principle. The Devout also avoided types of labour that entailed frequent contacts with the outside world, such as nursing the sick. Women often did manual work in the textile industries, such as spinning and weaving. It had the advantage of being compatible with meditation: women

11 Th. Mertens, 'Mystieke cultuur en literatuur in de Late Middeleeuwen', in Frits van Oostrom *et al.*, eds., *Grote lijnen: Syntheses over Middelnederlandse letterkunde* (Amsterdam: Prometheus, 1995), 117–35, 205–17.

12 Kees Veelenturf, ed., *Geen povere schoonheid: Laat-middeleeuwse kunst in verband met de Moderne Devotie* (Nijmegen: Valkhof Pers, 2000).

could recite biblical texts, listen to devout lectures or sing devout songs while doing their monotonous handwork. In other words, labour functioned as an aspect of the contemplative life.

The typical work for men was the writing of books, as scribes or as authors. Writing *pro pretio* had some economic relevance; clients were found mainly among the clergy and in the many women's convents of which the brethren had pastoral care. More important, however, was writing old and new texts for one's own edification and in order to enrich the house's library. The net result was an enormous output of texts by minor writers, many of them anonymous. They show a great variety of forms and, being interconnected by multiple reciprocal borrowings, constitute a veritable 'network of texts'. The 'pragmatic literacy' of the New Devout reshaped old literary genres and created new ones, often by combining existing types of writing.[13] All these texts, however, were in one way or another subservient to the common goal of improving the lives of the houses and their inhabitants: empowerment through reading and writing. Learning, in the sense of the accumulation of knowledge for its own sake, was not much valued by the Devout, nor was the apostolate the primary motive for the attention they paid to books. As one recent historian put it, assembling rather than distribution was their pursuit.[14] Its ultimate manifestation is the 'register of Rooklooster' ('Red Cloister' near Brussels), a huge compilation of bibliographical sources on texts relevant to the monastic life, amounting to a sixteenth-century virtual library.[15] This inward-looking attitude did not prevent the Modern Devotion from giving an important impulse to late-medieval book culture in general.

One of the types of transposition and adaptation of existing genres employed by the Modern Devout to fit new contexts came in the form of translation. In this respect, too, Geert Grote led the way, being the composer of one of the most influential texts of late medieval spiritual life, the Dutch *Book of Hours*. Gerard Zerbolt defended the practice of circulating spiritual texts in the vernacular in his *On Books in the Vernacular*, the most important work on this topic produced in north-west Europe during the later Middle Ages. It was not the case, however, that the Devout opted for the vernacular out of principle. Zerbolt restricted his defence to texts that did not contain

---

13 Nikolaus Staubach, 'Pragmatische Schriftlichkeit im Bereich der Devotio moderna', *Frühmittelalterliche Studien* 25 (1991), 418–61.

14 Thomas Kock, *Die Buchkultur der Devotio moderna: Handschriftenproduktion, Literatur-versorgung und Bibliotheksaufbau im Zeitalter des Medienwechsels*, 2nd edn (Frankfurt: Lang, 2002), 323.

15 Kock, *Buchkultur*, 225–47.

'high' theological matters, for which Latin remained the appropriate vehicle. That is why Grote translated several mystical writings by Ruusbroec from the vernacular Dutch into Latin. For clerical members of the *Devotio moderna* the use of Latin remained obligatory. From the middle of the fifteenth century onward, even canonesses were obliged to read the full Office, which required them to master the Latin language.

This said, the efforts of the Devout to provide literature for the lay brothers in their monasteries and for the female majority within the movement were considerable. Expanding on Grote's translation of the *Book of Hours*, Johannes Scutken (d. 1423) translated the New Testament. Texts of instruction in the monastic life were translated as well. Several translations were made of David of Augsburg's *Profectus religiosorum*, and though it has not been established who was responsible for these translations, it is certain that they circulated among the Modern Devout, as did a vernacular translation of the *Collationes patrum* by John Cassian.[16] Wermboud of Boskoop (c. 1350–1413) translated Books V and VI of the *Vitas patrum* and probably also the *Mirror of Virgins*.[17] Another important genre were the many *Lives of Jesus*, often abridged and adapted versions of the so-called Pseudo-Bonaventura/Ludolph of Saxony *Life*.[18] Even in the field of hymnology, the Latin songs of the liturgy were combined with para-liturgical and meditational songs in the vernacular, some of which were written by leading Devout such as Dirk of Herxen and Thomas a Kempis.

Besides translations, the Devout produced new texts in a variety of genres. Life in communities not bound by a formal rule was regulated by customaries.[19] On an individual level, these were supplemented by 'Resolutions' (to convert; the term refers to Geert Grote's *Resolutions and Intentions, not Vows*) and by devout exercises, methodical programmes for the ascetic life, the practice of virtue and meditation on the Passion of Christ, such as the one ascribed to John Vos.[20]

---

16 Karl Stooker and Theo Verbeij, *Collecties op orde: Middelnederlandse handschriften uit kloosters en semi-religieuze gemeenschappen in de Nederlanden* (2 vols.; Leuven: Peeters, 1997), I, 217–18, 220, 253.

17 Stooker and Verbeij, *Collecties op orde*, 215, 221–2.

18 C. C. De Bruin, ed., *Tleven ons Heren Ihesu Christi: Het Pseudo-Bonaventura-Ludolfiaanse leven van Jesus* (Leiden: Brill, 1980). Its Latin source used to be viewed as a compilation of Pseudo-Bonaventura, *Meditationes Vitae Christi* and Ludolf of Saxony's *Vita Jesu Christi*. Although this hypothesis has now been abandoned, the clumsy title has become conventional.

19 Klausmann, *Consuetudo*, 141–331.

20 Klausmann, *Consuetudo*, 23–94.

From an early moment, the Devout developed the custom of selecting 'sayings' (*dicta*), 'good points' (*puncta*) and 'examples' (*exempla*), both from older monastic literature and from the lives and deeds of exemplary Devout.[21] The sayings, points and examples, together with excerpts of varying nature, were assembled in so-called *rapiaria*. These 'notebooks' were intended as an aid to personal meditation and therefore executed in the simplest way. Usually, they were lost after the death of the collector. But collections by famous Devout could be adopted as community literature and so start a second span of life. Gerlach Peters' *Soliloquy* is a case in point.

The points and sayings became building blocks for historiography. Historical narrative itself fell apart in diverging genres. One of these was the convent's chronicle, in which emphasis usually fell on the normative early years of the house: its function was to underscore the identification of the Devout with the house itself, its history and its values. Often it was written by or from the standpoint of the procurator (steward) and concentrated on the material wellbeing of the house. At the other end of the spectrum stood the sister-book. From the middle of the fifteenth century collections of short biographies of deceased sisters were composed, which presented their lives as models for later generations: another exhortatory genre, enabling empowerment through example.[22] Several of these genres were combined in the single most important historiographical product of the movement, the *Chronicon Windeshemense* by Johannes Busch (1399–c. 1480), who was also a great monastic reformer. Though the exemplary brothers and sisters did not receive cultic veneration, the biographies have certain traits in common with hagiography, which was practised by the New Devout as well. Collections were made of lives of older saints, the most important one by John Gielemans (1427–87) of Rooklooster. Hugo of Rugge (near Brill in Holland) wrote a *Life* of the contemporary holy woman Liduina of Schiedam (d. 1433).

Sermons originating in Modern Devout circles have also been transmitted. More characteristic, however, are the 'collations', informal addresses of a paraenetic nature for the brethren and sisters of the common life and interested outsiders, or for the students of Latin Schools entrusted to the care of the

---

21 John Van Engen, 'The Virtues, the Brothers and the Schools', *Revue Bénédictine* 98 (1988), 178–217. Idem, 'The Sayings of the Fathers: An Inside Look at the New Devout in Deventer', in Robert J. Bast and Andrew Colin Gow, eds., *Continuity and Change: The Harvest of Late Medieval and Reformation History. Essays Presented to Heiko A. Oberman on his 70th Birthday* (Leiden: Brill, 2000), 279–320.

22 Anne M. Bollmann, 'Frauenleben und Frauenliteratur in der Devotio moderna. Volkssprachige Schwesternbücher in literarhistorischer Perspektive', unpublished PhD thesis, Rijksuniversiteit Groningen, 2004.

brethren. These collations were written down afterwards in ways that still remain unclear. Important collections of them have been handed down under the names of John Brinckerinck (1359–1419) and Dirk of Herxen (1381–1457). Among the remaining genres practised by the New Devout are treatises (often in the shape of extensive letters), spiritual letters and spiritual testaments: valedictory addresses in which devout persons on their deathbed exhort their fellows to a life of virtue.

From this general background of anonymous or collective writers and of authors of minor stature, a number of important writer personalities emerge. Geert Grote, the founding father of the Modern Devotion, left behind an important oeuvre; several of his works have been mentioned above.[23] The collection of his letters finds no parallel among later Devout writers. His successor as the head of the movement, Florens Radewijns (1350–1400), was also active as a writer. His best-known work is the *Devout Treatise*, which was intended as a manual for the religious life.[24] As an author, however, he was overshadowed by his contemporary, Gerard Zerbolt.[25] Other important authors from the early decades were Gerlach Petersz, Henry Mande and John of Schoonhoven, but of course the most famous author produced by the *Devotio moderna* was Thomas a Kempis (c. 1380–1471), of Agnietenberg near Zwolle, the author of *The Imitation of Christ*.[26]

Gabriel Biel (first quarter of fifteenth century – 1495) was an exception to the rule that the *Devotio moderna* stayed aloof from university life. He entered the brotherhood later in life, became a professor in the newly established university of Tübingen and meanwhile assisted Duke Eberhard of Würtemberg in founding a series of brother-houses organised as collegiate churches. He produced theological works on a great variety of subjects and wrote apologetic works on behalf of the brotherhood.[27] Johannes Mauburnus (John Mombaer; c. 1460–1501) was born in Brussels but entered the Agnietenberg

---

23 The Titus Brandsma Instituut, affiliated with Nijmegen University, has started an edition of Grote's collected works. See R.Th. van Dijk, *Prolegomena ad Gerardi Magni opera omnia*, CCCM 192 (Turnhout: Brepols, 2003). The letters are edited in *Gerardi Magni Epistolae*, ed. W. Mulder (Antwerp: Neerlandia, 1933).

24 Florent Radewijns, *Petit manuel pour le dévot moderne: Tractatulus devotus*, ed. and trans. Francis Joseph Legrand (Turnhout: Brepols, 1999).

25 See G. H. Gerrits, *Inter timorem et spem: A Study of the Theological Thought of Gerard Zerbolt van Zutphen (1367–1398)* (Leiden: Brill, 1986).

26 *Thomae Hemerken a Kempis opera omnia*, ed. M. J. Pohl (7 vols.; Freiburg i. Br.: Herder, 1902–22).

27 See H. A. Oberman, *The Harvest of Medieval Theology: Gabriel Biel and Late Medieval Nominalism* (Cambridge, Mass.: Harvard University Press, 1963; 3rd edn, Durham, N.C.: Labyrinth Press, 1983).

monastery near Zwolle. Mombaer systematised meditation in his *Rosetum exercitiorum spiritualium* and *Scala meditationis*, which are sometimes said to have influenced Ignatius of Loyola, although this is a matter of dispute.

In addition to these male authors, the Modern Devotion knew several female authors of importance. Salome Sticken (d. 1449), the first prioress of Diepenveen, wrote a *Formula of Life*, a rule for a newly founded women's convent.[28] Alijt Bake (1415–55) produced mystical and autobiographical texts. Because her strong inclination towards mysticism was perceived as a threat, she was dismissed as prioress of the monastery of canonesses of Galilea in Ghent in 1455 and died soon afterwards.[29] Jacomijne Costers (1462/3–1503) lived in the monastery of canonesses of Facons in Antwerp; she is the author of miscellaneous religious works, including a *Vision and Example*.[30]

Grote's call for renewal of the church had touched on a broad range of topics. It had involved the clergy and the laity as well as the professed 'religious'. In the early days of the movement, such members of the leadership as Henry Voppenz, Wermboud of Boskoop and John Brinckerinck were active as popular preachers. Soon, however, Grote's followers moved in a distinctly monastic direction. Did the Devout not too readily renounce their task of reforming the 'world', unduly narrowing down their efforts to rejuvenate the church? In fact, the question of the relationship between the professed and the laity stands at the heart of the debate on the significance of the Modern Devotion to the history of Christianity.

Historiography of the Modern Devotion has long focussed on the brethren of the common life. Because these followed the evangelical counsels in complete liberty, their way of life was interpreted as non-monastic and lay. Together with an overestimation of the brethren's role as teachers in Latin Schools, this led to the interpretation of the *Devotio moderna* as a lay movement and of the Devout as precursors of the Reformation, of biblical humanism or of both.[31] This interpretation was reinforced by the tendency of Dutch scholarship to evaluate the Modern Devotion as a movement exhibiting specific 'national' qualities. It was the Catholic Nijmegen scholar R. R. Post who gave the decisive blow to this pre-Protestant, anti-monastic interpretation of

---

28 Scheepsma, *Medieval Religious Women*, 113–19.
29 Scheepsma, *Medieval Religious Women*, 197–226.
30 Scheepsma, *Medieval Religious Women*, 172–89.
31 C. Ullmann, *Reformatoren vor der Reformation*, 2nd edn (Gotha: Perthes, 1866). Albert Hyma, *The Christian Renaissance: A History of the 'Devotio Moderna'* (Grand Rapids: Reformed Press, 1924).

the Modern Devotion.[32] In recent scholarship, moreover, the focus is shifting towards the many female adherents of the Modern Devotion, which were predominant in its non-canonical branches. Still, the majority of the New Devout were neither clerical nor monastic in the technical sense of having taken the three vows of poverty, obedience and chastity. In response to a seminal article by K. Elm, published in 1985, the debate about the nature of the movement has revolved around the concept of 'semi-religiosity'.[33] Yet despite an occasional claim by the Devout to be followers of a *via media*, the one-dimensional concept of 'semi-religiosity' does not exhaust the complexities of the relationship between the Devout and the outside world.

On the one hand, a clear boundary separated the congregations from the secular world. Entering a community amounted to a conversion. Within the houses, monastic values such as poverty, chastity, obedience and humility prevailed. These could have no direct validity in the outside world. But the congregations remained part of the general society, depending on it both for recruitment and material support. Legally, too, their members belonged to the lay world. At least in the early days, the congregations lived according to secular law and were subject to the authority of the city magistrates, which for the most part treated them well and granted them various kinds of privileges. This did not prevent the congregations from seeking and often receiving recognition as ecclesiastical houses. Eventually, when the disadvantage of having an ever-growing number of exempt convents within the urban terri-tory became apparent, the cities adopted a more restrictive approach. Even then, and all through the fifteenth century, private individuals continued to favour the New Devout. In sum, although the secular world could not apply the monastic values prevalent in the convents fully within its own sphere, it recognised their validity, if only because the holiness associated with the convents reinforced their intercessional power, which benefited society as a whole.

The position of the brethren's houses was even more complex. Unlike the women's convents and the monasteries of the canons regular, the brethren regarded the apostolate as an important aspect of their duty. Except for the beginning period, they did not fulfil it by preaching publicly, a domain which they left increasingly to the Observant Mendicants. For the brethren, the main instrument of the apostolate was the 'collation', the informal pious address to

---

32 R.R. Post, *The Modern Devotion: Confrontation with Reformation and Humanism* (Leiden: Brill, 1968), 1–67.

33 Kaspar Elm, 'Die Bruderschaft vom gemeinsamen Leben. Eine geistliche Lebensform zwischen Kloster und Welt, Mittelalter und Neuzeit', *Ons Geestelijk Erf* 59 (1985), 470–96.

lay people or to pupils of the public schools on their own premises. Often, these talks resulted in new conversions to the lifestyle of the Devout. Thus, the brethren tried to reform the world by drawing it piece by piece into their own orbit. In doing so, the model of Christian life they applied was not lay, but essentially monastic. As for their production of texts, its primary objective, again, was not the apostolate. Nevertheless, activities in this field, including translation, resulted in making Scripture and devotional texts available to the outside world. The introduction of the printing press – in which the brethren played a minor role – relayed these texts further to the laity at large. All in all, it would be wrong to conclude that the *Devotio moderna* was primarily a lay movement.

The religious changes of the sixteenth century did not find much approval among the Modern Devout. True, Luther was inspired by the writings of John Pupper of Goch, a brother of the common life working in the third quarter of the fifteenth century. His works had remained unknown until they were published in the 1520s. One of them is devoted to *The Freedom of the Christian Religion*; another one deals with vows and 'factitious religion'. Generally, Pupper's ideas amounted to a rejection of the privileged position of monasticism as the Christian way of life *par excellence*. A brother-house like the one in Herford (Westphalia) joined the Reformation, and in Utrecht rector Hinne Rode was deposed from office on suspicion of heresy, but these remained exceptions. The Devout's attitudes to humanism were similar. Erasmus' philological work on the New Testament met with some interest in Modern Devout circles, but he found opposition as well. The attention to the purity of the text of the Vulgate, which the Congregation of Windesheim had displayed since the fifteenth century, had not prepared the Devout for the boldness with which Erasmus returned to the Greek original. His criticism of the medieval monastic tradition quite naturally did not find favour with them. The large majority of the Devout remained firmly Catholic and stuck to their customary way of life, insofar as the outside world allowed them to do so.

# 27

# Demons and the Christian community

ALAIN BOUREAU

The anxiety over Satan, which led, in a reciprocal relationship of cause and effect, to the relentless persecution of devil-worshippers and acolytes, took hold fully half-way through the Middle Ages. Christianity had always been conscious of the devil's presence; the earliest descriptions, found in both Genesis and the New Testament passage on Christ in the wilderness,[1] portray him as seducer and tempter. The devil[2] was the Enemy, the Foe, surrounded by demons, acolytes and other followers. The creation of the evil court, which stood in opposition to the celestial, was well known: a group of angels followed Satan in his fall and then continued to serve him. A basic dualism opposed the temptations of the flesh, ambition or despair (as with Job before his ultimate resistance) with the appeal for the love of God, compassion and hope. This dualism was dominated by the figure of Christ incarnate, unswerving and triumphant opponent of the devil and his eternal pursuance of evil works. From mid-way through the Middle Ages, devotions to Christ focused attention on the fight against demons; endeavours to imitate Jesus implied constant struggle, yet this was nothing compared with the difficulty and inequality of Christ's own battle. The extent of the evil to be confronted was such that it probably sparked the 'Cathar' heresies which appeared in the twelfth century – too easily viewed as simply one ancient and far-off error, imported and disseminated.

A number of different factors were responsible for modifying the simplicity of this dual opposition. Already, obscure forces of evil bearing no clear connection to Satan had appeared in the Old Testament, such as Asmodeus in Tobit, Lilith in Job and Isaiah, Azazel in Leviticus, and the satyrs in goat-form which occur in various books of the Bible. Christian history's centuries of

---

1  Matt. 4.1–11 and Luke 4.1–13.
2  'The Devil' representing the Greek *diabolus*, itself used to render the Hebrew *satan*, for which Jerome substituted Satan (*OED*, 2nd edn, vol. 4, 1989, 568).

spiritual guidance had created or confirmed the sense of a powerful, multi-form demonical presence either inside or close to the world of men. Yet this took place without the population being aware of any precise or organised action by the devil, who indeed held little place in the thoughts of the general community.[3] The anecdote told by Gregory the Great is well known:[4] a nun had eaten a piece of lettuce without taking the precaution of making the sign of the cross above it, and was immediately possessed by the devil, hiding inside the leaf. This 'epidemiological' notion, seemingly 'homespun', was not completely without scriptural base: in the land of the Gadarenes, Christ concealed an evil spirit called 'Legion' in a herd of 2,000 swine, and 6,000 demons were hurled into the sea.[5] Such perception of the proximity and concentration of demons, who dwelt in thick and obscure spheres of the atmosphere just above the clear earthly skies, was shared widely. Indeed, it was not incompatible with the story of the multitude of angels' fall, or, in its literal sense, with the traditional localisation of the fall, when the angels were thrown from the Empyrean – the last realm accessible to earthly creatures – all the way down to the lowest and darkest spheres surrounding the earth.

Thus the devil claims an ancient history in Christianity, but the creation of a science of the devil, a *demonology*, seems to be much more recent. Of course, St Paul had made the early distinction between spirits (evil opposed to good) one of the church's founding characteristics, which then led to the ecclesiastical office of exorcist, still in existence. Also, during Christianity's first centuries the possessed (known as *energumens*) could testify to the devil's plans and thus provide the church with useful knowledge. In addition, one can recreate a certain body of patristic and theological learning regarding the works of the devil and the bad angels. Yet nevertheless, one may only speak of a 'demonology' when an autonomous discipline concerns itself with not only the existence of demons and their actions, but above all, with the relationships devils forge with human beings, and with methods of detecting evil spirits allowing the distinction between possessed and inspired. The ancient 'gift' of recognising evil spirits came to be replaced or at least refined by more practical knowledge, an *art* based on a roughly defined doctrine. One of the tangible signs of the new discipline's emergence is seen in the specific treatises written to communicate knowledge and collective experience.

---

3 Jérôme Baschet notes that the Devil is almost completely absent from Christian imagery until the twelfth century ('Diable', in Jacques Le Goff and Jean-Claude Schmitt, eds., *Dictionnaire raisonné du Moyen Âge* (Paris: Fayard, 1999), 260).
4 Grégoire le Grand, *Dialogues*, I, 4, 7, ed. A. de Vogüé (SC 260; Paris: Cerf, 1979), 42–4.
5 Mark 5.9–13.

It is for these reasons that the birth of demonology has long been dated from the first known practical and theoretical treatise, *The Witches' Hammer*, published in 1486 by the Dominican inquisitor Henry Institoris.[6] Clearly, other handbooks for inquisitors had preceded, of which the most famous were those of Bernard Gui[7] (around 1323) and Nicholas Eymerich (around 1376), but in these the pursuit of demons and their allies the sorcerers did not play such a central role, priority being given to the hunt for heretics proper and to technical questions of procedure. This timing carried the advantage of enabling the beginnings of demonology to coincide with those of the 'demonomania' seen with the great witch-hunts.

Nevertheless, recent works, notably those by Agostino Paravicini Bagliani's group, also those by Pierrette Paravy[8] and Martine Ostorero, have shown that a fundamental moment in the formation of an earlier practical and theoretical demonology must have occurred towards the end of the 1430s. Then the first meticulous witch trials in the Valais took place and works appear on procedural doctrine, such as the report by Chancellor Johann Fründ on the Valais witches, the *Formicarius* of Dominican John Nider, the anonymous text entitled *Errores gazariorum*, and also the treatise by a judge from the Dauphine, Claude Tholosan. The Council of Basel (1431–37) would have played a vital role in the conflict between experience and doctrine.[9] In fact, only at this time does the systematic linking of the Witches' Sabbath and prosecution of devil-worshippers emerge. The doctrine was new: in its official and pastoral work the medieval church had always condemned or rejected the practice of magic, but viewed it with disdain and as no more than hollow superstition. Through trickery, the devil fooled the weak-willed into believing in his power; in reality his strength remained limited and natural ('natural' in the scholastic sense, nature encompassing all things created by God).

At this point, therefore, we must admit that the massive persecutions of devil-worshippers indeed did begin during the medieval period. The early stages were in part original in that 'sorcerers' were largely men; in the Renaissance period, women were the prime victims. Yet the beginnings of anxiety over the devil did not arise solely out of the popularisation of the

---

6 The work also gives James Springer as author, but recent historiography suggests that Henry Institoris worked alone.

7 Bernard Gui, *Manuel de l'inquisiteur*, ed. G. Mollat (Paris: Champion, 1926–7).

8 Pierrette Paravy, *De la chrétienté romaine à la Réforme en Dauphiné: Evêques, fidèle et deviants (vers 1340 – vers 1530)* (Rome: École française de Rome, 1993).

9 Martine Ostorero, Agostino Paravicini Bagliani and Kathrin Utz Tremp in collaboration with Catherine Chène, *L'Imaginaire du sabbat: Édition critique des textes les plus anciens (1430 c.–1440 c.)* (Lausanne: Université de Lausanne, 1999).

Sabbath (for both persecuted and persecutors), even if it did add to the mania by suggesting the possibility of the cult's expansion. The idea of a 'devil's synagogue' took root: a counter-church with all its ramifications and own form of 'spiritual guidance'. It is of note in passing that a picture of this disturbing assembly appears shortly after the Fourth Lateran Council (1215), among others, had regulated church observance more strictly.

Anxieties over the devil seem to have emerged prior to the discovery of these elements. The level of concern is shown in the number of trials at the beginning of the fourteenth century which were organised by the papacy and Europe's great monarchies and which involved a link with the devil. It should be noted that the new nature of the charges emanated from the very establishments which enabled the link. Indeed, it was usual to denounce an accused by likening him or her verbally to the devil, but not to particular acts – impossible without such collusion. Moreover, an important sign, not disassociated from the recent obsession, comes with John XXII's request in the autumn of 1320, asking ten theologians and canon law specialists for expertise on whether the practices of magic and invocation of the devil should qualify as heresy. It seems likely that this indicated the pope's wish to pave the way for new legislation – and the doctrinal leap for which he was preparing necessitated very serious doctrinal work.

The text of the pope's questions, with ten responses, has been conserved in the Borghese manuscript no. 428 in the Vatican Library, traced by Anneliese Maier[10] and published in its entirety by the present author.[11] Clearly, the three first questions, to which we will return, refer to various types of sorcery not explicitly linked to demonology, but the fourth question is direct: 'Should either those who make sacrifices to demons with the intention of persuading them to force someone to do what they wish, or those who invoke demons, be considered as heretics or simply practitioners of magic?' The consultation, despite the reticence of the majority of theologians asked, produced remarkable results, in that it approved the new concept of a 'heretical fact'. One of the experts, Enrico del Carretto, even sketched the outline of an effective satanic

10 Cf. Anneliese Maier in 'Eine Verfügung Johannis xxii über die Zuständigkeit der Inquisition für Zauberprozesse', *Archivum Fratrum Praedicatorum* 32 (1952), 226–46, where the Commission's first response was published. Raul Manselli later edited Enrico del Carretto's response, 'Enrico del Carretto e la consultazione sulla magia di Giovanni xxii', in Raul Manselli, ed., *Miscellanea in onore di Monsignor Martino Giusti*, vol. 2 (Vatican City: Archivo Segreto Vaticano, 1978), 97–129.

11 Alain Boureau, *Le Pape et les sorciers: Une consultation de Jean XXII sur la magie en 1320 (manuscrit B. A. V Borghese 348)* (Rome: École française de Rome, 2004).

sacrament – a description derived from the contractual theory of sacraments produced in the second half of the thirteenth century.

Such concerns with the devil's activities have solicited various explanations. R. I. Moore has stressed the repression hypothesis. Carlo Ginzburg sees the concern as stemming from the interaction between two cultures: the clerical and the popular. I propose that the process emerged out of the conjunction, revival and interaction of two ancient ideas: the pact with the devil and devil-possession. The satanic pact, an ancient notion found early in Theophilus' famous legend, took on a fresh and frightening topicality during the thirteenth century for reasons both political and theological. Following the vast movement of demographic growth and population density which marked the beginning of the first millennium, ways of organising community life had multiplied and overlapped (rural and urban communities, parishes, seigniories, principalities, kingdoms, etc.). The complex and multi-layered status of property ownership, at the heart of the feudal system, increased incidences of multi-ownership. After a period of extreme competition (which triggered a gradual reduction in fallow land and development possibilities), the thirteenth century saw a period of conflict and tension between the different types of systems. Sovereignties attempted to assert themselves with neither the institutional nor ideological means of doing so, and from the end of the century onwards the twin worlds of society and scholastic knowledge became entrenched in intense political debate – accentuated by the arrival of Aristotle's *Politics*. Secular and religious rulers alike were gripped by a fear of plots and conspiracies, demonstrated, for example, by the famous Templar persecutions at the beginning of the fourteenth century. Within theology, the gradual development of a theory of sacramental causality from the 1230s onwards focussed attention on the idea of a pact between God and humankind. Naturally enough, the ecclesiastical and ministerial theory of sacramental grace grew weaker as a consequence of this doctrine.

Possession of supernatural powers also gained new substance in the thirteenth century. Together, Cistercian concepts of the human person and Aristotelian philosophy led to an anthropological interest in the strengths and weaknesses of man's individual unity, a concept by then essential to sacramental doctrine. Those who were alienated, inspired, mad, somnambulist or euphoric acquired a particular relief,[12] like so many concave or convex mirrors of the human condition. An individual's soul and body were

---

12 The significant work by Nancy Caciola must be mentioned here (*Discerning Spirits, Divine and Demonic Possession in the Middle Ages* (Ithaca, N.Y.: Cornell University Press,

considered to be more direct receptacles for supernatural influence. The individual strength of the human gave him resistance against his fragility, yet his autonomy placed him in danger of satanic subjection.

Up to the very end of the thirteenth century, theology took little interest in demons, which presented no particular speculative problem, whereas the question of Satan and his fall provoked reflection linked to evil, predestination and divine providence. One of the more celebrated examples of this reflection was St Anselm's treatise *The Fall of the Devil* (*De casu diaboli*), composed at the end of the eleventh century. But nonetheless, it was the divine plan and its consequences for humanity which excited more interest than the devil's position. Peter Lombard's *Sentences*, written around 1140 (and providing a framework for university study) spoke only briefly of demons. Discussion was limited to the fate of demons in hell in Book IV; only one isolated comment in Book II received attention.

The situation appears to have changed quite suddenly after the 1270s. The first great work of scholastic demonology is probably the lengthy discussion of devils in Thomas Aquinas' treatise *On Evil* (*De malo*),[13] most likely published in 1272,[14] towards the end of his life. The question's twelve articles considerably updated his scattered notes in the *Summa theologiae* and the *Scriptum super sententiis* and formed a full and original body of doctrine of which historians have largely underestimated the significance.[15] The twelve articles correspond to twelve questions, which may be grouped under four headings. Firstly, a question on the nature of demons (Article 1: 'Do Demons Have Bodies Joined to them by Nature?'). Secondly, three articles discuss the circumstances of the devil's fall and that of the bad angels (Article 2: 'Are Demons Evil by their Nature or their Will?'; Article 3: 'Did the Devil in Sinning Desire Equality with God?'; Article 4: 'Did the Devil Sin, or Could he Have Sinned, at the First Moment of his Creation?'). Third, six articles follow

---

2003); also that of Dyan Elliott (*Proving Woman: Female Spirituality and Inquisitorial Culture in the Later Middle Ages* (Princeton: Princeton University Press, 2004). The authors study the feminine, non-institutional aspects of visionaries and mystics.

13 Thomas Aquinas, *De malo*, ed. Leonine Commission, *Opera omnia*, vol. 23 (Rome: Ex Typographia Polyglotta S. C. de Propaganda Fide *et al.*, 1982), 279–334.

14 For all matters of dating in Thomas Aquinas' work, and for an overview of his doctrine, I refer to the invaluable publication by J. P. Torrell, *Initiation à saint Thomas d'Aquin: Sa personne et son oeuvre* (Fribourg: Editions Universitaires; Paris: Le Cerf, 1993; rev. and expanded 2002).

15 We must note the dearth of contemporary bibliography on scholastic demonology. While almost all the subjects and ideas treated by Aquinas have been the object of continued research, the only work on demons of which I am aware is a 1940 monograph, aimed at clearing Aquinas of any responsibility in the witch-hunts at the end of the Middle Ages (Charles Edward Hopkin, *The Share of Thomas Aquinas in the Growth of Witchcraft* (Philadelphia: University of Pennsylvania Press, 1940) (several editions).

on the abilities of demons after their fall (Article 5: 'Can Demons' Free Choice Return to Good after their Sin?'; Article 6: 'Is the Devil's Intellect so Darkened after Sin that it Can Err or Be Deceived?'; Article 7: 'Do Demons Know Future Things?'; Article 8: 'Do Demons Know our Interior Thoughts?'; Article 9: 'Can Demons Alter Material Substances by Changing the Substances' Forms?'; Article 10: 'Can Demons Cause the Locomotion of Material Substances?'. Finally, the two last questions focus on the powers that demons exercise over humans (Article 11: 'Can Demons Affect the Soul's Cognitive Powers Regarding the Internal or External Senses?'; Article 12: 'Can Demons Affect Human Beings' Intellect?').

We should note that this eloquent collection of queries does not represent a simple synthesis of theological opinion on demons, but a series of reasoned and also daring stances which were to be quickly attacked by several Franciscans, in particular William de la Mare, in 1277. Shortly afterwards, another theologian, Peter de Falco, Regent Master in Paris, devoted four very lengthy disputed questions[16] to the bad angels, meticulously indicating the points where Aquinas had leant more towards *the philosophers* than the doctors of the church (particularly St Augustine). Finally, at the beginning of the 1280s, in the second book of his commentary on Peter Lombard's *Sentences*, the Franciscan Peter John Olivi wrote seven extended questions on the angels' fall.[17] It was the opposing views of Thomas Aquinas and Peter John Olivi which were to provide the basis of fresh thought with respect to demons. Yet it was not simply a question of the clash between two personalities; other theologians joined the exploration. At the beginning of the 1290s, the Dominican Master John of Paris (or Jean Quidort[18]), regarding the same passage as the *Sentences*, offered valuable additions to Thomas' doctrine. Taken together, these works which focussed on the period's main controversies constituted a rich and significant corpus and offered a solid foundation for further demonological study.[19]

The revival of scholastic interest in the devil and demons can be attributed to a number of causes. Firstly, it is possible that the continuing potency of

---

16 Peter of Falco, *Questions disputes ordinares*, ed. A. J. Gondras, vol. 3 (Louvain and Paris: Nauwelaerts, 1968), 722–842, questions 21–4.

17 Peter John Olivi, *Fr. Petrus Iohannis Olivi, o.f.m., Quaestiones in secundum librum sententiarum*, ed. Bernard Jansen, S. J., vol. 1 (Quaracchi: Collegio San Bonaventura, 1922), questions 42–8, 702–63.

18 John of Paris, *Commentaire sur les Sentences, Reportation livre I–II*, vol. 1, ed. Jean-Pierre Müller (Studia Anselmiana 47; Rome: Studia Anselmiana, 1961).

19 Notably Gilles de Rome's commentary on the second book of Peter Lombard's *Sentences*, written in the 1270s.

Cathar and other thirteenth-century dualist heresies may have driven the need for a doctrinal response to one of their basic assertions. They claimed that it was the evil demiurge, the devil, who governed the world by populating it with demons. Jacques Fournier, one of the ten experts consulted in 1320, had gained practical experience of the wide spread of dualism[20] during his scrupulous inquisitorial enquiries in the Montaillou area. As early as 1241, the University of Paris had condemned a proposition asserting that 'an evil angel has been evil from its creation and has never been other than evil'.[21] It is hard to know at whom this unattributed condemnation was aimed. Taking it literally, one might sense a heresy postulating an evil creation as opposed to divine. In his *Sentences* Peter Lombard had mentioned the opinion of some who 'say that angels had been created evil and straight away fallen. Some thought that those angels who fell had deviated towards evil not through their own free will but because God had made them evil'.[22] Thomas Aquinas signalled the mistaken proposal of 1241 in *De malo*, without seeing in it any allusion to an evil nature or creation. For Aquinas, the question turned on Satan's immediate use of free will which made him choose to sin.

> Some modern thinkers have had the audacity to assert that the devil was evil at the first moment of his creation, obviously not by nature, but by the action of free will which forced him to sin. But this position was condemned by all Masters teaching in Paris at that time.[23]

Secondly, the discovery of early pagan knowledge together with the recent prestige of ancient and Arab-Neoplatonist thinking, which viewed the world in terms of a hierarchical population of intermediary beings, led to the assimilation of demons with ancient *daimones*. These had natural and superhuman powers, and were not connected to Satan. The question of 'separate substances' took on a different slant in cosmology at the close of the thirteenth century. Angels and the souls of the dead were placed under this heading, both

---

20 Clearly the question of the reality of Cathar dualism remains fiercely debated; here only Jacques Fournier's descriptions are relevant.
21 'Quintus, quod malus angelus in principio suae creationis fuit malus, et nunquam fuit nisi malus', in H. Denifle and H. Chatelain, eds., *Cartularium universitatis parisiensis*, vol. I (Paris: Delalain, 1889), 171, no. 1218.
22 'Opinio dicentium angelos in militia creatos et sine omni mora ruisse. Putaverunt enim quidam angelos qui ceciderunt, creatos esse malos; et non libero arbitrio in malitiam declinasse.' Book II, dist. 3, Chapter 4, a. 2, vol. I, 343–4. Peter Lombard added that the tenets of his opinion were founded on two sentences by St Augustine, which he cited in the following paragraph. In fact, as Lombard's editor Ignatius Brady points out, Lombard confused two different viewpoints, one affirming an evil creation, the other, following Augustine, suggesting that the fall came immediately after creation.
23 *De malo*, in *Opera omnia*, vol. 23, 298, article 4.

stripped of their material body, and sharing their existence with heavenly bodies in supralunary space inside the first moving sphere. Notably, through the intermediary of the *Book of Causes*, Greek-Arab peripatetic cosmology embraced the notion of the Intelligences as distinct from matter and the agent Intellect. This turn presented a new challenge to Christian thought, but one can find traces of it as early as the twelfth century in the work of Bernard Silvestris, one of the few convinced Platonists in this 'renaissance' period – gives it little mention. In his treatise *De mundi universitate*,[24] Silvestris distinguishes between good demons, which live above the moon, and bad – the so-called *satellite* demons – which incite evil and inhabit obscure regions of the atmosphere. Such confusion between angels and *daimones* was maintained by the desire to see angels as descended from their heavenly empyrean and now closely participating in the world of men. Thus in about 1240, the Dominican Guerric of Saint-Quentin stated that angels had two abodes, one in the empyrean heavens, according to their nature (*ex natura*), the other in obscure regions of the atmosphere, according to their function (*ex officio*). After the fall, demons kept only the place they occupied through their function.[25]

In addition, the thirteenth century saw thinking on demons revised to take account of their potential role in the great historical setting instituted by the eschatology of the Spiritual Franciscans and based on the prophecies of Joachim of Fiore. The time was approaching when the devil would generate a new aide, the Antichrist, supported by the restructured cohort of demons. (According to John in the Apocalypse,[26] Christ delivered the group from imprisonment in the brief period preceding God's reign at the end of time.) Thus the demons were torn out of their dismal state of timelessness to become active participants in the story of salvation.

Finally, thirteenth-century scholasticism made the angels subject to significant investigation,[27] placing them at the heart of the vast paradigm which grouped ordinary and favoured human beings (notably the Virgin Mary)

---

24 Bernard Silvester, *De mundi universitate libri duo*, ed. C. S. Barach and J. Wrobel (Innsbruck: Verlag der Wagnerschen Universitäts-Buchhandlung, 1976), book II, 5, 191–5, 45–6.

25 Guerric de Saint-Quentin, *Quaestiones de quodlibet*, ed. W. H. Principe and J. Lord, introduction by J. P. Torrell (Toronto: University of Toronto Press, 2002), appendice 2 (*de aureola*), 401. Guerric was without doubt one of the first scholars to employ the important scholastic practice of quodlibetical questions. Twice a year, a scholar would respond publicly to any question posed by any individual.

26 Rev. 12.12.

27 For excellent analysis of the philosophical role of angels in scholasticism, see Tiziana Suarez-Nani, *Les anges et la philosophie: Subjectivité et fonction cosmologique des substances séparées à la fin du xiiiè siècle* (Paris: Vrin, 2002).

together with Christ-man and the angels in order to investigate humankind's limits and potential. The new categorisation brought souls and angels closer together and accorded humans, as Tiziana Suarez-Nani puts it, a 'potential angelicity'; this then fostered the need for a science of angels. Yet any question of the will or reason of an angel necessarily had to be discussed in the context of the bad angels' fall. It was perhaps the debate over the primacy of will or reason – a key area of dispute between Dominican doctor Thomas and the Franciscans – which provoked the former's desire to treat methodically of the demons, despite the awkwardness involved. In all, no doubt the scholastic interest in demons was driven primarily by the borderline case they represented rather than a fascination with diabolical powers.

Confronted by the threat from demons, it was essential to take quick and efficient action – a contradictory aim, however, since efficiency assumes the slow and difficult establishment of truth. During this period the papacy held a wide range of judicial options at its disposal, which implied differences in procedure, jurisdictional competencies and forms of enquiry. The church favoured the development of inquisitorial procedure (through enquiry) over an accusatory form. This accorded with the movement initiated by Innocent III's decretals from 1198, the final form of which is found in canon 8 of the Fourth Lateran Council (1215). It is well known that the accusatory procedure, dominant until the twelfth century, and which continued its path in British and American Common Law, leaves indictment to the prosecutor of any particular case, who may also be liable to the consequences. The judge and jury merely arbitrate. The two-part action consists of the careful construction of the case, which must be rigorously defined (in Roman terms, the *litis contestatio*) followed by deliberation. Inquisitorial procedure, on the other hand, favoured an accusation *ex officio* drawn up by a judge or prince; this followed the 'defamation' which originated in incriminating rumour. The process consisted of two successive enquiries: the first established the *fama* – an individual's reputation, good or bad, which resulted in indictment or release; the second pieced together the truth of the facts associated with the *fama*.

Various juridical bodies could deal with people who invoked demons: numerous episcopal law courts, the court of the Inquisition and ad hoc papal commissions. It is thought that the papacy created the Inquisition in about 1233 to combat heresy, and for a long time it retained that function, recruiting judges who were more theologians than jurists. Fierce controversy has tainted the image of the medieval Inquisition to the point where it is difficult to consider it rationally. Some medievalists, not without grounds, have endeavoured to refute its associations with the seemingly crazed persecutions; Edward Peters has shown how a dark myth has come to surround the Inquisition over time;[28] an impressive article by Richard Kieckhefer questions its institutional reality.[29] In fact, general opinion has often confused the implacable reality of the Roman Inquisition (established in 1542), and of, above all, the Castilian Inquisition (a state institution founded in 1481–2), with the limited and frequently confused endeavours of the medieval Inquisition. Yet it existed, and despite its weak foundations, represented a powerful institution. The Holy See appointed an inquisitor, yet the latter kept direct links with the religious order he came from (often the Dominican Order, but also the Franciscans and to a lesser extent the Carmelites). An inquisitor's daily duties placed him in direct contact with the secular authorities.

In such a context, stories of possession and invocation became more credible and more significant – and with this, we note a shift in thought on demons: belief in their limited abilities ends. The change is marked by three principal features. Firstly, demons were discovered to possess ways of behaving and relating to humans which gave them power; specifically, the pact and the satanic sacrament, where their natural powers drew together. The reassuring notion of diabolic illusion now disappeared. The demons' extended activity was confirmed by a second feature: the victims and accomplices of evil works were no longer seen as simply the *vetule* – credulous women – but, owing to their fragile constitution and susceptibility to the supernatural, as all humankind. Finally, the strong eschatological trends illustrated first signs of the demons' release into the world. Uncertainties of deciphering these were balanced by a process of enquiry and repression which the church would appear to have accepted.

Clearly, however, the witch-hunts did have a certain continuity with scholastic demonology. The follies described in *The Witches' Hammer* are largely narrative, but the doctrinal parts of the handbook remain within the boundaries of scholastic demonology. We are thus perhaps able to reject two opposing historiographical viewpoints dominating the research field. Firstly, the attempt made by some to refute the whole idea of witch-hunts in the medieval world, and secondly, the opposite notion of others that witch-hunts were the direct manifestation of church and monarchical tendencies towards repression and oppression during the Middle Ages. Scholastic rationality

28 Edward Peters, *Inquisition* (Berkeley: University of California Press, 1988).
29 Richard Kieckhefer, 'The Office of Inquisition and Medieval Heresy: The Transition from a Personal to an Institutional Jurisdiction', *Journal of Ecclesiastical History* 46 (1995) 36–61.

represented neither the principle of resistance against the insanity, nor the cause of the error; at the most one may say that the consistency of enquiry, the ongoing desire to revise traditional categories, and a growing individualisation in the search for truth had opened up troubling areas of thought – and had awoken ancient demons. The creation of a science of man, scholasticism's true innovation, came at a price.

It remains, of course, to understand the gap of a century between the formation of a new demonology and procedure, on one hand, and the beginning of the systematic persecution of magicians and witches, on the other.[30] How did the converging forces observed manifest themselves? We should note the reluctance of the civil and occasionally the ecclesiastic authorities to turn to the inquisitorial process. Anti-inquisitorial reaction is well attested, but it does not explain everything. The civil courts, so active in the sixteenth century, could have taken up the battle against demons themselves. My hypothesis is that the new demonology brought plausible arguments alone, and produced a complex and conditional concept which might be reproduced here as follows, and with which I draw together the new proposals already discussed: 'When dangerous times approach, demons are in possession of an immense potential, capable of destroying the Christian community using the individual's susceptibility to supernatural influences and peoples' readiness to form groups of heretics or sworn accomplices of Satan.' The hypothetical or temporal condition indicated by the conjunction 'when' was universally acknowledged and in keeping with common knowledge concerning the end of time. Those who believed in the proximity of the end represented a minority (the Spiritual Franciscans and beguines in particular). During the course of the fourteenth century, this state of mind might appear closer and closer to the truth; of course one must mention the Great Plague of 1348 and its various reoccurrences. Clearly it would be unwise to conclude of a single trauma following the Plague's carnage; one should think rather of a gradual accumulation of signs which rendered the proximity of the end more likely. Only present-day economists can measure the scale and duration of the upheavals in the 1310s which marked the beginning of the world's 'Little Ice Age', but these had already strewn the universe with bad signs. At the end of the century, the Great Schism in 1378 lent meaning to one of my statement's terms, with respect to the destruction of the Christian community. The West

30 Walter Stephens' significant publication, *Demon Lovers: Witchcraft, Sex and the Crisis of Belief* (Chicago: University of Chicago Press, 2002) proposes a similar chronology, with beginnings in the twelfth century and strong continuation at the start of the fourteenth century (even if the motives were different).

had experienced several papal divisions, but this one greatly affected an institution much more present in Christians' daily life than before. In addition, the support offered to one or other pope by the different national churches and monarchies gave the impression of a profound, perhaps irreparable, rupture. The hypothesis that the Councils of Constance and Basel[31] (which put an end to the schism) played an important role in the spread of a new doctrine on witchcraft (this has been suggested by Agostino Paravicini-Bagliani's group) concurs with my interpretation.

The radical renewal of the concept of the demonic pact led to the idea that heretical groups of sworn enemies of Christian unity existed, within which the witch or demon-invoker were merely examples. The idea of a threatening hidden equivalency of heresies was strengthened during the fourteenth century by a growing certainty that conversion was impossible. The Waldenses, after more than two centuries of error, spread throughout Europe. Islam endured and expanded. The Jews held on; they also became the chief victims of the recent belief in conversion's failure: it is possible that the appalling laws on the *limpieza de sangre* in fifteenth-century Spain corresponded to the conviction that the conversion of Jews was simply superficial and misleading.

Thus at the end of the Middle Ages the history of Christianity was marked deeply by the obsession with demons. The demonic invasion into scholasticism's triumph was without doubt one of the most important factors in its break-up and new collusion with the civil authorities – to which it brought too many opportunities and reasons for heavier controls. The freedom of Christian knowledge was paying dearly.

---

31  See esp. Ostoreso *et al.*, *L'Imaginaire du sabbat*, n. 9.

28

# Wycliffism and Lollardy

## KANTIK GHOSH

The title of this chapter raises a question of fundamental relevance to the study of late-medieval 'heresy' in England.[1] Commentators – both then and now – would largely be agreed in identifying the philosophical and polemical thought of John Wyclif (d. 1384),[2] and of his immediate academic followers, as integral to the formation of a dissenting *mentalité* characterised by an informed, and articulate, critical engagement (in English as well as in Latin) with the received meanings and sources of religious authority.[3] There is far less consensus as to the precise relationship of such dissent – deriving an impressive intellectual coherence from the thought of Wyclif, revealing important congruences in its implied conceptualisation of identity, and embodied in an extraordinarily diverse and voluminous textual output – to that far more diffuse, nebulous and elusive domain of what was gradually

1 The fundamental work on Wycliffism remains Anne Hudson, *The Premature Reformation: Wycliffite Texts and Lollard History* (Oxford: Clarendon Press, 1988). Also basic are Anne Hudson, *Lollards and their Books* (London: Hambledon Press, 1985); and Margaret Aston, *Lollards and Reformers: Images and Literacy in Late Medieval England* (London: Hambledon Press, 1984). See the bibliography for Lollard studies compiled by Derrick G. Pittard in Fiona Somerset, Jill C. Havens and Derrick G. Pittard, eds., *Lollards and their Influence in Late Medieval England* (Woodbridge: Boydell Press, 2003), 251–319; also maintained online at http://lollardsociety.org.
2 Recent accounts include Ian Christopher Levy, ed., *A Companion to John Wyclif, Late Medieval Theologian* (Leiden: Brill, 2006); Stephen E. Lahey, *Philosophy and Politics in the Thought of John Wyclif* (Cambridge: Cambridge University Press, 2003); Mariateresa Fumagalli Beonio Brocchieri and Stefano Simonetta, eds., *John Wyclif: logica, politica, teologia* (Florence: Galuzzo, 2003); Ian Christopher Levy, *John Wyclif: Scriptural Logic, Real Presence and the Parameters of Orthodoxy* (Milwaukee: Marquette University Press, 2003). Michael Wilks, *Wyclif: Political Ideas and Practice* (Oxford: Oxbow Books, 2000); and Anthony Kenny, ed., *Wyclif in his Times* (Oxford: Clarendon Press, 1986) remain indispensable.
3 See in particular Kantik Ghosh, *The Wycliffite Heresy: Authority and the Interpretation of Texts* (Cambridge: Cambridge University Press, 2002); also Anne Hudson, '*Peculiaris regis clericus*: Wyclif and the Issue of Authority', in M. Gosman, A. V. Vanderjagt and J. R. Veenstra, eds., *The Growth of Authority in the Medieval West* (Groningen: E. Forsten, 1999), 63–81.

perceived and defined in terms of official ecclesiastical legislation as well as in those of a burgeoning and multifarious polemic, and lived and practised, as the 'Lollard heresy'. This chapter will accordingly reopen the question of whether it might be meaningful to use 'Wycliffism' and 'Lollardy' – at least for purposes of analysis – as designating conceptually distinct phenomena, whatever their actual interrelationship may have been in late-medieval England.

In support of such an approach, one might point to the uncontroversial fact that Wyclif himself drew on and developed, in his own often idiosyncratic ways, major pre-existent traditions of criticism and dissent, pre-eminently, but not exclusively, those generally identified as pertaining to 'anticlericalism'. Various scholars have therefore emphasised the overlap, at least in the last decades of the fourteenth and the first of the fifteenth centuries, of what may be described as 'reformist' or 'radical orthodoxy' (i.e. modes of criticism which did not question the fundamental structure or raison d'être of the hierarchical church)[4] and a nascent revisionist questioning of the very foundations of medieval institutionalised Christianity as it developed in Wyclif's own thought and in that of his successors. The distinction between the two, though clear enough with hindsight, naturally often got blurred in contemporary perceptions, and the definition of the category of the 'heretical' was therefore a muddled affair. In particular, the term 'Lollard' (or, as some would prefer, 'lollard'), was used both as a synonym for followers of definitive Wycliffite lines of thought and as an imprecise polemical denigration of any aspect of religious (or indeed quasi-religious) conduct felt to be nonconformist or critical of authority.[5]

This chapter would therefore posit, as a working hypothesis, a conceptual distinction between the (as it were) 'production-end' of Wycliffite thought (Wyclif's own works, and that body of writing, both in Latin and in the vernacular, clearly identifiable as indebted to Wyclif) and the 'reception-end': emergent definitions of 'heresy' (legislation and judicial process on the one hand, and polemic, both learned and relatively unlearned, on the other); readerships of Wycliffite and related texts (of particular note here is the issue

---

4 Hudson, *Premature Reformation*, ch. 9; J. A. F. Thomson, 'Orthodox Religion and the Origins of Lollardy', *History* 74 (1989), 39–55; Lawrence M. Clopper, 'Franciscans, Lollards and Reform', in Somerset, Havens and Pittard, eds., *Lollards and their Influence*, 177–96.

5 See Andrew Cole, 'William Langland's Lollardy', and Anne Hudson, 'Langland and Lollardy?', both in *The Yearbook of Langland Studies* 17 (2003), 25–54, 93–105; also Wendy Scase, '"Heu! quanta desolatio Angliae praestatur": A Wycliffite Libel and the Naming of Heretics', and Andrew Cole, 'William Langland and the Invention of Lollardy', both in Somerset, Havens and Pittard, eds., *Lollards and their Influence*, 19–36, 37–58.

of the transmission of such texts along with religious writings of a conservative complexion, as well as the vexed question of works the ideological orientation of which is significantly unclear). It should be stressed at this point that this is not meant to constitute a resurrection of the distinction between academic Wycliffism (of notable theological, philosophical and political import) and the crude fundamentalisms of 'popular' Lollardy which, it was suggested, had rather less to do with the former.[6] A governing argument of this chapter will be that the spheres of academic speculation and extra-mural religiosity across a range of social classes affected each other in ways that disable this particular convenient polarity, and that the very shape of what emerged as 'Lollardy', as well as 'orthodoxy', was determined by the rich (though not necessarily always as satisfyingly coherent as historians might like it to be) interplay between the two.

Such an interplay was inaugurated by Wyclif himself, in his peculiar amalgamation of various intellectual and polemical traditions in his voluminous output. Wyclif's works contribute substantially to the formation of a distinctive late-medieval discourse which synthesises philosophico-theological speculation derived from the complex and differentiated specialisms of scholasticism with reformist-polemical agenda, a discourse directed outwards at a wider, extra-mural 'public'.[7] In particular, he fuses two major (distinguishable but overlapping) discursive domains: that of anticlericalism, and that comprising the massive body of academic thought engaging with the interrelationship of philosophy and theology, particularly in the aftermath of the watershed 1277 Aristotelian condemnation by Bishop Tempier of Paris.[8]

The episcopal condemnation in 1277 of 219 Aristotelian articles allegedly supported by members of the faculty of arts in the University of Paris had a long prehistory and an equally substantial posterity. It brought to a head, and

---

6 Most notably K. B. McFarlane, *John Wycliffe and the Beginnings of English Nonconformity* (London: English Universities Press, 1953); also Gordon Leff, *Heresy in the Later Middle Ages*, 2 vols. (Manchester: Manchester University Press, 1967).

7 Relevant here is the developing role of the late medieval 'public intellectual', on which see Jacques Verger, *Les gens de savoir dans l'Europe de la fin du Moyen Âge* (Paris: Presses Universitaires de France, 1997); Rita Copeland, *Pedagogy, Intellectuals and Dissent in the Later Middle Ages: Lollardy and Ideas of Learning* (Cambridge: Cambridge University Press, 2001); Fiona Somerset, *Clerical Discourse and Lay Audience in Late Medieval England* (Cambridge: Cambridge University Press, 1998); R. N. Swanson, *Universities, Academics and the Great Schism* (Cambridge: Cambridge University Press, 1979). For an account of the 'tract' as a new late-medieval scholastic genre, see Daniel Hobbins, 'The Schoolman as Public Intellectual: Jean Gerson and the Late Medieval Tract', *American Historical Review* 108 (2003), 1308–37.

8 The major edition now is David Piché, *La condamnation parisienne de 1277* (Paris: Vrin, 1999).

did so in a fashion that would resonate throughout the fourteenth century, professional, ethical and epistemological conflicts and tensions within institutionalised scholasticism, conflicts central to the very definition and meanings of scholastic vocation, and to the perceived role of various academic methodologies in the study of God.[9] The study of the Tempier condemnation constitutes a field in itself; here we may note briefly what David Piché has to say in the conclusion to his edition:

> Tout ce que l'on sait des maîtres des arts condamnés en 1277, ce qu'on peut affirmer avec certitude, c'est qu'ils ont cherché à s'aménager un territoire épistémo-institutionnel sur lequel il leur aurait été possible d'enseigner, de pratiquer et de vivre la philosophie pour elle-même, indépendamment des considerations religieuses... Que cette conception 'autonomiste' de la philosophie, autant dans sa dimension speculative que dans son 'efficace' pratique, ait heurté de front l'image unitaire de la sagesse que se faisaient les théologiens conservateurs est indubitable: la condamnation parisienne de 1277 est le fait de ces théologiens qui n'acceptaient pas la vision 'pluraliste' prônée par les artiens.[10]

The student of Wyclif will recognise in Piché's summation adumbrations of certain major, and recurrent, themes of the writings of the *doctor evangelicus*: a dismayed perception of fragmentation and conflict within intellectual discourses which ought to be aligned, or subordinate, to a univocal Christian truth; an appalled acknowledgment of the extent to which the various aspects of philosophical method (logic and dialectic in particular) had displaced an imagined purity of biblical study; and above all, a passionate engagement with the very meaning of scholastic vocation, in both its individual and its institutional forms. Wyclif's work is therefore characterised by a significant

---

9 See the various articles in Andreas Speer, Kent Emery and Jan Aertsen, eds., *Nach der Verurteilung von 1277: Philosophie und Theologie an der Universität von Paris im letzten Viertel des 13 Jahrhunderts* (Miscellanea Mediaevalia 28; Berlin: Walter de Gruyter, 2001); Jan Aertsen and Andreas Speer, eds., *Was ist Philosophie im Mittelalter?* (Miscellanea Mediaevalia 26; Berlin: Walter de Gruyter, 1998); Luca Bianchi and Eugenio Randi, *Le verità dissonanti: Aristotele alla fine del medioevo* (Rome and Bari: Laterza, 1990).

10 Piché, *La condamnation parisienne*, p. 285. 'All that we know and can affirm with any certainty about the Masters of Arts who were condemned in 1277 is that they sought to lay out for themselves an epistemological-institutional field where it would have been possible for them to teach, practise and live philosophy in its own right, independently of religious considerations...That this autonomic conception of philosophy, in its speculative dimension as well as in its efficacious realisation, collided frontally with the unitary image of wisdom held by conservative theologians is beyond doubt: the Parisian condemnation of 1277 was the achievement of those theologians who did not accept the "pluralist" vision put forward by the Artists.'

'meta-scholastic' awareness, even while he operates in terms of the discursive traditions of medieval academia.

Of equal importance in Wyclif's polemic is anticlericalism. A vast discursive field, and not confined to Latinate debate, of pan-European diffusion and diversity,[11] anticlericalism was nevertheless given what Alexander Patschovsky has called 'a vigorous theoretical basis' in Wyclif's discussion of the incompatibility of the realms of the holy and of the profane.[12] By the late Middle Ages, there were long-established lines of criticism across Europe underlining the spiritual dichotomy between the established church and the ideal *ecclesia primitiva*, with a concomitant emphasis on a return to the *vita apostolica* on the part of the individual Christian.[13] The implied endorsement of lay, extra-institutional, spiritual authority was sometimes accompanied by a questioning of the efficacy and administration of the sacraments. Disparate, and not united into a coherent doctrine or ecclesiology, such more or less dissident religiosity would be combated in a variety of ways by the church, and pre-eminently in terms of 'heresy'.[14] In Wyclif's thought, many of the persistent emphases of anticlericalism are shaped into a coherent, theoretically defensible and uncompromising programme of fundamental reform. Indeed, this distinctive synthesis of scholastic philosophical rigour and religious polemic would remain an abiding feature of Wycliffism, in both its Latin and its vernacular diffusions over a range of decades, so that even such a relatively late production as the English tract *De oblacione Iugis sacrificii* (*Of the offering of continual sacrifice*), dated by its editor from internal evidence to 1413–14,[15] can effortlessly integrate virulent anticlerical and antipapal polemic into detailed and subtle negotiations of the theology of the eucharist, including its logical and semantic aspects.

The fusion of academic speculation of considerable intellectual precision and range with focused polemical engagement with questions of religious politics was a potent one, especially when the vernacular was importantly

---

11 See Peter A. Dykema and Heiko A. Oberman, eds., *Anticlericalism in Late Medieval and Early Modern Europe* (Leiden: Brill, 1993); Wendy Scase, *Piers Plowman and the New Anticlericalism* (Cambridge: Cambridge University Press, 1989).

12 Alexander Patschovsky, 'Heresy and Society', in Caterina Bruschi and Peter Biller, eds., *Texts and the Repression of Medieval Heresy* (York: York Medieval Press, 2003), 23–41 (33).

13 See Gordon Leff, 'The Apostolic Ideal in Later Medieval Ecclesiology', *Journal of Theological Studies* n.s. 18 (1967), 58–82; 'The Making of a Myth of a True Church in the Later Middle Ages', *Journal of Mediaeval and Renaissance Studies* 1 (1971), 1–15.

14 See Robert Lerner, *The Heresy of the Free Spirit in the Later Middle Ages* (Berkeley: University of California Press, 1972).

15 Anne Hudson, ed., *The Works of a Lollard Preacher* (Early English Text Society OS 317; Oxford: Oxford University Press, 2001), 157–256; for dating, see xlix–l.

involved as the preferred language for the transmission of ideas.[16] Late-medieval scholasticism had fostered, despite recurrent papal and other condemnations, and despite increasingly sophisticated internal mechanisms of scrutiny and censorship, what has best been described by Damasus Trapp as 'a breath-taking freedom...in the intellectual field'.[17] Such freedom of questioning, of analysis, of the deconstruction of systems, when applied to the sources of religious certitude – the Bible (textuality and canonicity, language and hermeneutics, historical truth), the ecclesiastical infrastructure (the authenticity of claims to power, papal history, the history of the private religions), the sacraments (pre-eminently the eucharist) – could and did, even when confined to Latin, and to the technical specialisms of the Schools, occasion explosive controversy.[18] When exercised in the vernacular (or indeed in Latin, but with a potentially wider public than the academic)[19] and when deployed polemically in support of programmes of institutional reform, such intellectuality assumed a disruptive power which one must not underestimate. The increasingly fraught establishment response to a perceived collapse of received boundaries and structures of containment[20] (radically evidenced in the dissemination of academic learning outside the university) was not, or not only, as might appear at times, an exaggerated, disproportionate and paranoid reaction to what were 'really' minor

16 See Anne Hudson, 'Lollardy: The English Heresy?', in her *Lollards and their Books*, 141–63; also Margaret Aston, 'Wycliffe and the Vernacular', in Anne Hudson and Michael Wilks, eds., *From Ockham to Wyclif* (Studies in Church History, Subsidia 5; Oxford: Blackwell, 1987), 281–330; repr. in Margaret Aston, *Faith and Fire: Popular and Unpopular Religion, 1350–1600* (London: Hambledon Press, 1993), 27–72.

17 Damasus Trapp, 'Augustinian Theology of the 14th Century; Notes on Editions, Marginalia, Opinions and Book-Lore', *Augustiniana* 6 (1956), 146–274 (at 149).

18 See J. M. M. H. Thijssen, *Censure and Heresy at the University of Paris 1200–1400* (Philadelphia: University of Pennsylvania Press, 1998); *Théologie, science et censure au XIIIe siècle: Le cas de Jean Peckham* (Paris: Les Belles Letters, 1999); Luca Bianchi, *Censure et liberté intellectuelle à l'université de Paris (XIIIe – XIVe siècles)* (Paris: Les Belles Lettres, 1999).

19 Of relevance here is Fiona Somerset's discussion of what she calls 'radical Latin'; see her 'Expanding the Langlandian Canon: Radical Latin and the Stylistics of Reform', *The Yearbook of Langland Studies* 17 (2003), 73–92, as well as Maarten Hoenen's pointer to the growing late-medieval unease with the spread of academic specialisms and methodologies outside the university: see his 'Theology and Metaphysics: The Debate between John Wyclif and John Kenningham on the Principles of Reading the Scriptures', in Fumagalli Beonio-Brocchieri and Simonetta, eds., *John Wyclif*, 23–55 (at 53).

20 Most importantly the major pieces of legislation enshrined in *De heretico comburendo* (1401), and in Archbishop Arundel's *Constitutiones* (1407–9); see A. K. McHardy, '*De heretico comburendo*, 1401', in Margaret Aston and Colin Richmond, eds., *Lollardy and the Gentry in the Later Middle Ages* (Stroud: Sutton Publishing; New York: St Martin's Press, 1997), 112–26; Nicholas Watson, 'Censorship and Cultural Change in Late Medieval England: Vernacular Theology, the Oxford Translation Debate, and Arundel's Constitutions of 1409', *Speculum* 70 (1995), 822–64.

and marginal forms of unaccustomed dissidence, but arose out of a wholly pertinent recognition of the gravity and potential amplitude of the threat posed to the very raison d'être of institutionalised faith. Monumental pieces of fifteenth-century synthesising scholarship directed against the 'heretics', such as Thomas Netter's *Doctrinale antiquitatum fidei ecclesiae catholicae* (1420s) or, in a very different way, Reginald Pecock's vernacular *summa* (c. 1440s) begin to assume their often perplexing meaning only when placed in such a context.

The precise details of the dissemination of Wycliffite scholarship outside academia remain unclear. However, the volume and substance of textual output in the vernacular, of recurrent and major concern to the authorities, are impressive: two complete translations of the Bible (of the widest dissemination), one literal and the other idiomatic, a long sermon cycle comprising 294 sermons (again, widely disseminated), catenae of commentary known as the Glossed Gospels (several copies), encyclopaedic reference material (the *Floretum* and the *Rosarium*; many copies in Latin, one in English), and a host of other polemical and theoretical writings extant in fewer or even single copies. What is of particular note is that many of the vernacular writings (e.g. the English Wycliffite Sermons) transmit not only Wyclif's theological and ecclesiological ideas with considerable precision and eloquence (in the process introducing into English a whole range of new technical words), but also replicate his meta-disciplinary, and often complex and multivocal, engagement with the implications of scholastic methods and their teleological significance. Wyclif's work both uses and critiques the academic-rationalist tools available to medieval scholasticism. His polemic can thus appear simultaneously anti-intellectual and technical, deriving its language and partly its method from the Schools in the very process of questioning the entire raison d'être of the contemporary intellectual study of God. English Wycliffite writings therefore constitute not just 'vernacular theology' or 'vernacular philosophy' of considerable sophistication, but also, and equally radically, they incorporate a meta-discursive examination of the relationship of scholastic endeavour and 'truth'. The peculiar synthesis of the academic-rationalist, the meta-discursive and the polemical which characterises Wycliffite writings was recognised contemporaneously, most notably by Reginald Pecock, whose work, in its attempts to foster in English a lay Aristotelian philosophical engagement with the problem of morality, foregrounds a significant methodological self-awareness.[21]

---

21 See Mishtooni Bose, 'Reginald Pecock's Vernacular Voice', in Somerset, Havens and Pittard, eds., *Lollards and their Influence*, 217–36; 'Two Phases of Scholastic Self-Consciousness: Reflections on Method in Aquinas and Pecock', in Paul Van Geest,

Indeed, the dissemination of a body of philosophical and political ideas in the vernacular, provocative and inflammatory as these often were, was but one aspect of the impact of Wycliffism. An equally (indeed, arguably, more) troubling dimension of the 'heresy', and one which was recognised only gradually,[22] was its fostering, in the vernacular and outside the relatively regulated and delimited sphere of university-thought, of a distinctive intellectual attitude and of a critical methodology[23] – in other words, of a *mentalité* – not necessarily allied to any particular doctrinal bias. This mentality was characterised by what I have described elsewhere as 'intellectual literacy', that is, the ability to examine the foundations, critique the superstructures and dispute the claims of a range of crucial authoritative discourses,[24] based as these almost always were on controversial and contested readings of both the Bible and of associated patristic and scholastic traditions. The linguistic-philosophic consciousness of Wyclif's own thought (and he was very much part of the late-medieval academic milieu in this respect), and especially its defining engagement with hermeneutics, given the theoretical centrality of Scripture to medieval conceptualisations of authority, therefore played a particularly important, and destabilising, role in the operations of lay 'intellectual literacy'. Destabilising, because an examination of the linguistic and hermeneutic bases of theological and political systems – when carried out with sufficient rigour in the vernacular, with either an implied or an explicit invitation to the laity to participate in such an examination, in a society without the mechanisms to accommodate or regulate such lay intellectual

Harm Goris and Carlo Leget, eds., *Aquinas as Authority* (Leuven: Peeters, 2002), 87–107; 'Vernacular Philosophy and the Making of Orthodoxy in the Fifteenth Century', *New Medieval Literatures* 7 (2005), 73–99. Thomas Netter too showed himself acutely aware of Wycliffite methodology and its implications: see Ghosh, *Wycliffite Heresy*, 174–208; and Mishtooni Bose, 'The Opponents of John Wyclif', in Levy, ed., *Companion*, 407–55.

22 A recognition which resulted in positive (as opposed to merely punitive) attempts to inform and guide lay belief: see Margaret Aston, 'Bishops and Heresy: The Defence of the Faith', in her *Faith and Fire*, 73–93; R. M. Ball, 'Thomas Cyrcetur, a Fifteenth-Century Theologian and Preacher', *Journal of Ecclesiastical History* 37 (1986), 205–39; J. I. Catto, 'Wyclif and Wycliffism at Oxford 1356–1430', in J. I. Catto and Ralph Evans, eds., *The History of the University of Oxford, vol. 2, Late Medieval Oxford* (Oxford: Clarendon Press, 1992), 175–261 (at 254–61).

23 For a study of a particular Lollard endeavour of this nature, see Rita Copeland, 'Wycliffite Ciceronianism? The General Prologue to the Wycliffite Bible and Augustine's *De Doctrina Christiana*', in Constant J. Mews, Cary J. Nederman and Rodney M. Thomson, eds., *Rhetoric and Renewal in the Latin West 1100–1540: Essays in Honour of John O. Ward* (Turnhout: Brepols, 2003), 185–200.

24 Kantik Ghosh, 'Bishop Reginald Pecock and the Idea of "Lollardy"', in Ann Hutchison and Helen Barr, eds., *Text and Controversy from Wyclif to Bale: Essays in Honour of Anne Hudson* (Turnhout: Brepols, 2005), 251–65 (at 263–5).

initiative[25] – must result in a sense of disequilibrium, of a world turned upside down.[26]

One of the classic medieval ways of dealing with threatened disequilibrium, without large-scale precedent in England but of venerable pedigree on the Continent, was of course through the deployment of the politics of 'heresy'. Alexander Patschovsky, in a paper of far-reaching implications, has described 'heresy' as the 'necessary expression of the inner contradictions of [the medieval social] system'. 'Dogmatically speaking', he goes on to say, '[the use of heresy] is totally unspecific. It is solely for stigmatising the politico-religious opponent, nothing else'.[27] Patschovsky's insight can be of assistance in broaching the vexed question of the medieval (English) meanings and definitions of 'heresy' in general, and of Wycliffism / L/lollardy in particular. Recent scholarly debate has focused on several related subjects: how was the 'heretic' or the 'heretical' identified and defined in late-medieval England? What was the connection between such definitions and the thought of John Wyclif? What were the meanings of the term 'L/lollard', and to what extent can one postulate a sectarian, sociological or dogmatic identity for those to whom the term was applied? Was 'heresy' indeed a genuine threat to civil and ecclesiastical order, or was it a mere tool of propaganda, or a marginal phenomenon whose importance has been exaggerated by both Protestant apologists and left-leaning historians?

These are major issues which require further, nuanced, non-programmatic investigation. Ian Forrest's work has illuminated the legislative processes by means of which the late-medieval church in England sought to outline a taxonomy of heresy, and put in place procedures for its detection and extermination, and the bewilderingly complex interplay between such legis-lative and procedural initiatives and the actualities of heresy detection and reporting on the ground, these latter necessarily involving the active

---

25 A valiant, though failed attempt, was that of Reginald Pecock: see James H. Landmann, '"The Doom of Reason": Accommodating Lay Interpretation in Late Medieval England', in Barbara A. Hanawalt and David Wallace, eds., *Medieval Crime and Social Control* (Minneapolis: University of Minnesota Press, 1999), 90–123.

26 As was amply reflected in the work of contemporary poets such as John Gower, Thomas Hoccleve, John Lydgate and John Audelay: see Hudson, *Premature Reformation*, ch. 9; and James Simpson, *The Oxford English Literary History 1350–1547: Reform and Cultural Revolution* (Oxford: Oxford University Press, 2002), chs. 7 and 9.

27 Patchovsky, 'Heresy and Society', 33–5; for further discussion of the meanings and constructions of 'heresy' in the middle ages, see Monique Zerner, ed., *Inventer l'hérésie? Discours polémiques et pouvoirs avant l'inquisition* (Nice: Centre d'Études Médiévales, 1998); also Howard Kaminsky, 'The Problematics of "Heresy" and "the Reformation"', in František Šmahel and Elisabeth Müller-Luckner, eds., *Häresie und vorzeitige Reformation im Spätmittelalter* (Munich: Oldenbourg, 1998), 1–22.

cooperation of a largely non-Latinate, untrained laity.[28] Equally complex is the question of the precise relationship of the realm of ecclesiastical legislation with that of academic 'heresy', and of academic heresy with vernacular polemic: how did these diverse discursive domains in which 'heresy' featured – legislative, academic-philosophical, vernacular polemic and counter-polemic – contribute to the conceptualisation of both the human and abstract dimensions of 'heresy'? The work of Copeland, Ghosh and Somerset,[29] examining the complex negotiations of Latin and vernacular, of the (often formidable) technicalities of 'clergy' and the simplifying imperatives of religious politics, is of relevance here. 'Simplifying imperatives', or complicating ones? The question becomes acute when one comes to examine the uses of the term 'L/ lollard' (and its variants) in England, beginning in the 1380s and continuing into the next century and beyond. It is a fact often forgotten, or at least given imperfect emphasis, that the word was pervasively and diffusely used in continental religious polemic well before and during the period of the English heresy to designate a range of religious conviction and practice felt to be variously 'non-conformist'.[30] To what extent can one fix its slippery meanings, its elusive valences? How does this fundamentally equivocal word relate to a diversity of social realities?[31] And what were these 'social realities'? Can they be distinguished at all from 'imagined realities'? Paul Strohm has suggested that 'heresy' (as well as its twin, sedition) was merely a convenient antagonistic focus around which the defensive propaganda of a usurping dynasty with shaky claims to legitimacy could be more convincingly arranged.[32] Richard Rex has argued that the statistical incidence of heresy was minimal, and we (along with the medieval authorities, albeit for different reasons) are guilty of sensationalism in imagining widespread 'heresy' where there was 'in fact' very little.[33] Anne Hudson's work, on which the study of the English heresy is still largely based, provides evidence for a contrary

---

28  Ian Forrest, *The Detection of Heresy in Late Medieval England* (Oxford: Clarendon Press, 2005).

29  See nn. 3 and 7.

30  See Lerner, *Heresy of the Free Spirit*, *passim*; also Dietrich Kurze, 'Die festländischen Lollarden', *Archiv für Kulturgeschichte* 47 (1965), 48–76.

31  See Margaret Aston, 'Were the Lollards a Sect?', in Peter Biller and Barrie Dobson, eds., *The Medieval Church: Universities, Heresy and the Religious Life: Essays in Honour of Gordon Leff* (Studies in Church History, Subsidia 11; Woodbridge: Boydell Press, 1999), 163–91.

32  Paul Strohm, *England's Empty Throne: Usurpation and the Language of Legitimation, 1399– 1422* (New Haven, Conn. and London: Yale University Press, 1998), chs. 2 and 5.

33  Richard Rex, *The Lollards* (Basingstoke: Palgrave, 2002); also see Eamon Duffy, *The Stripping of the Altars: Traditional Religion in England 1400–1580* (New Haven, Conn.: Yale University Press, 1992).

interpretation; her vision of the proximate, as well as more removed, followers of Wyclif is that of a coherent 'movement', with clear and effective
ideologies of reformation (theological, ecclesiological and political being the
three main categories in *The Premature Reformation*).

The crucial question that arises here relates to identity: what constitutes
'identity', how is it formed, sustained, perceived and imagined? The question
is important as it relates not only to the definition of the 'heretical' but also to
that of the 'orthodox', and therefore, by implication, to the very geography of
the late-medieval English religio-intellectual landscape. We have, on the one
hand, from the 1380s on to at least the mid-1410s, a major body of Wycliffite
writings which give clear evidence of a doctrinally coherent and politically
vocal group of scholars, translators, pedagogues, polemicists – what Verger
would call 'les gens de savoir'[34] – and perhaps their followers and pupils, with
a remarkably unified sense of identity (reflected not only in the larger questions of ideology, but at the micro-level as well, in details of vocabulary).[35] On
the other hand, there is the ambiguous evidence – afforded by trial records, by
anti-Wycliffite polemic deriving from much older models of heretic-
slandering, by manuscripts containing texts we identify as Wycliffite – of a
far more nebulous realm of the definition, shaping and reshaping of the
meanings and boundaries of both 'heresy' and 'orthodoxy'. Identity here is
much vaguer, of shifting outlines, and can be primarily polemical, and all that
one can say with any conviction is that the *conceptual polarity* between heresy
and orthodoxy becomes more accentuated over time even if the actual
content of either side in the debate may remain protean, or be reduced to
crude simplistic formulae, amenable to being shaped into the categories of
inquisitorial terminology (as in heresy trials).[36] These processes of definition
and redefinition would continue well into the fifteenth century, and were
arguably never settled, as the heretication of Reginald Pecock's simplified
Aristotelian philosophy, or the citing of Chaucer's *Canterbury Tales* in a heresy

---

34 See n. 7.
35 For characteristic vocabulary in Wycliffite writings, see Matti Peikola, *Congregations of
the Elect: Patterns of Self-Fashioning in English Lollard Writings* (Turku: Publications of the
Department of English, University of Turku, 2000). If the Austin Canon Henry
Knighton, an acerbic contemporary observer, is to be believed, this uniformity of
vocabulary was also reflected in speech: see G. H. Martin, ed. and trans., *Knighton's
Chronicle 1337–1396* (Oxford: Clarendon Press, 1995), 302. Also see Anne Hudson, 'A
Lollard Sect Vocabulary?', in *Lollards and their Books*, 165–80.
36 For the evidence of the trial records and the problems of interpretation therein, see John
H. Arnold, 'Lollard Trials and Inquisitorial Discourse', in Chris Given-Wilson, ed.,
*Fourteenth Century England II* (Woodbridge: Boydell Press, 2002), 81–94; and Hudson,
*Premature Reformation*, 32–9.

trial, suggests.[37] Further, certain emphases of *mentalité* and methodology – for instance those relating to hermeneutics, to patristics, to the academic study of the Bible, and to speculative theology – which were initially aligned to characteristically Wycliffite positions were gradually incorporated within what presented itself as its 'orthodox' opposite.[38] Even more perplexing is the evidence of the manuscripts. Texts we perceive as ideologically remote are often found to keep company in medieval compilations – does this point to an attempt at disguise, or to a genuinely promiscuous world of reception, where scribal exigencies collaborated with devotional eclecticism?[39] And what about those texts, such as Richard Rolle's English Psalter Commentary or the *Pore Caitif*, which seem to have circulated in a variety of forms, with differing degrees of Wycliffite inflection – again, are they evidence of dissidents 'ymping [interpolating]' irreproachable writings with heresy,[40] covertly to get their point across to an unsuspecting audience, or do they indicate a domain of religiosity where neat, black-and-white markers of identity and ideology are simply irrelevant, inapplicable? Would it therefore be wisest to postulate a spectrum of non-conformist religious behaviour and conviction from the radically Wycliffite to those who engaged in non-programmatic but critically enquiring ways with questions of personal salvation, religious authority, and

37 In the trial of John Baron of Amersham in 1464; see Hudson, 'Lollardy: The English Heresy?', 142. Note also the ease with which accusations of Wycliffism could be bandied about, as for instance in the 1460 debate over that old chestnut of Christ's poverty fought out by the secular clergy and the mendicant friars. Pope Paul II deplored, in a bull dated 4 June 1465, the recrudescence in England of the Wycliffite heresy: see F. R. H. Du Boulay, 'The Quarrel between the Carmelite Friars and the Secular Clergy of London, 1464–68', *Journal of Ecclesiastical History* 5 (1954), 156–74 (at 163). On Pecock, see V. H. H. Green, *Bishop Reginald Pecock: A Study in Ecclesiastical History and Thought* (Cambridge: Cambridge University Press, 1945), and Wendy Scase, *Reginald Pecock* (Aldershot: Variorum, 1996).

38 This is one of the main claims of my *Wycliffite Heresy*.

39 Of particular relevance here is the popular late-medieval manuscript genre of the devotional miscellany, of which the 'common-profit book' constitutes a sub-genre. See Vincent Gillespie, 'Vernacular Books of Religion', in Jeremy Griffiths and Derek Pearsall, eds., *Book Production and Publishing in Britain 1375–1475* (Cambridge: Cambridge University Press; 1989), 317–44; Ralph Hanna, 'Miscellaneity and Vernacularity: Conditions of Literary Production in Late-Medieval England', in Stephen G. Nichols and Siegfried Wenzel, eds., *The Whole Book: Cultural Perspectives on the Medieval Miscellany* (Ann Arbor: University of Michigan Press, 1996), 37–51; Wendy Scase, 'Reginald Pecock, John Carpenter and John Colop's "Common-Profit" Books: Aspects of Book Ownership and Circulation in Fifteenth-Century London', *Medium Aevum* 61 (1992), 261–74. Also see Hudson, *Premature Reformation*, 421–30.

40 An accusation against the 'yuel men of Lollardry' prefacing a copy of Rolle's Psalter Commentary; printed in H. R. Bramley, ed., *The Psalter Translated by Richard Rolle of Hampole* (Oxford: Clarendon Press, 1884), 2. For discussion, see Hudson, *Premature Reformation*, 421–2; Kevin Gustafson, 'Richard Rolle's *English Psalter* and the Making of a Lollard Text', *Viator* 33 (2002), 294–309.

ecclesiastical mores, 'heresy', depending on polemical moment, being capable of location anywhere on this spectrum? And would it be plausible to identify 'lollardies'[41] with 'heresy' in this, qualified, sense – as capable of designating core Wycliffite values, as well as more diffuse questioning of authority, above all on the part of 'the lay partie' (Pecock's ubiquitous phrase to designate his misguided contemporaries)?

A profounder understanding of the phenomenon of the Wycliffite-L/lollard 'heresy' in particular, and of late-medieval English religious culture in general, would hinge on a more nuanced, subtler appreciation of the fluctuating identities of the 'heretic', and of the labile bases of identification and conceptualisation of the 'heretical'. What Wyclif, and perhaps more importantly his followers, achieved was the creation of a religio-intellectual *mentalité* which deliberately rendered problematic and porous both the real and the imagined boundaries between 'heretical' and 'orthodox', lay and clergy, English and Latin, academic speculation and religious politics, scholastic philosophical rationalities and the necessary affectivities – what Matthew Arnold would have called the 'poetry' – of organised religious practice. The intellectual examination of the bases, super-structures and sacraments – and I use the word in both its technical and non-technical senses – of faith can be destabilising at the best of times, and was always confined in the Middle Ages to a mandarin class with its own mechanisms of supervision and containment. The extra-mural dissemination of even the rudimentary tools and techniques of textual analysis, disputation and debate was from early on, and rightly, perceived as fundamentally and sensationally disruptive of a whole system of order with its conceptual centre located in a text and in the various associated traditions and institutions laying claim to hermeneutic authority. The ancient and capacious discourse of 'heresy' was therefore inevitably invoked and deployed – in a diversity of (sometimes more, sometimes less coherent) ways – to counter a challenge of far-reaching cultural implications. The story of Wycliffism-L/lollardy is in part a narrative of a society struggling to negotiate fissures and contradictions in the very warp and woof of its fabric; for 'heresy', to quote Patchovsky again, is to be located 'at the basis, not at the margin, of medieval society'.[42]

---

41  It is worth noting here the equivocal formulation of the Leicester Parliament of 1414, in its anti-heretical directives: there is a reference to the 'secte de heresie appelle Lollardrie' ('heretical sect called Lollardy'); at the same time, the civil hierarchy is directed to 'faire oustier cesser & destruir toutz man[er]s heresies & errours appellez vulgairement Lollardries' ('put out, [cause to] cease and destroy all manner of heresies and errors, commonly called lollardies'). See *The Statutes of the Realm*, 10 vols. (London: George Eyre *et al.*, 1810–28), vol. 2 (1816), 181.
42  Patchovsky, 'Heresy and Society', 41.

# 29

# Observant reform in religious orders

BERT ROEST

The period of the so-called Observant reforms (c. 1370–1500) was far more dynamic than longstanding convictions concerning the decline of religious life in the closing centuries of the Middle Ages once led us to believe. Amidst papal schisms, conciliary infighting, protracted warfare, echo-epidemics, apocalyptic expectations and heightened fears of popular heresies, many religious orders experienced a veritable renaissance, coupling aims to reclaim pristine traditions with a new pastoral and spiritual acumen. At the same time, new religious movements sprang up, whose vitality struck the imagination of contemporaries.[1]

As the name indicates, the Observance (*observantia/observantia regulae*) within the orders was first and foremost a movement to return to the rules and the lifestyle of their pristine beginnings. A major motivation for this was the conviction that the orders had succumbed to decadence, by discarding loyalty to their rules, and by giving in to pressures that had allowed them to become wealthy and influential, but through which they had lost much of the spiritual ardour to fulfil the tasks for which they had been created.

For most religious orders, the Observance constituted not the first attempt at reform. In the course of time, the call for reform had sounded repeatedly. Sometimes it had been inaugurated from within, and sometimes it had been imposed from outside, as with the 1335–9 reform statutes for the religious orders issued by Pope Benedict XII.[2] The Observance was peculiar in that it touched nearly all major religious orders, and yet cannot be relegated to one particular force driving its momentum. Rather, it was the outcome of many

---

1 The best available overview is given by Kaspar Elm, ed., *Reformbemühungen und Observanzbestrebungen im spätmittelalterlichen Ordenswesen* (Berliner historischer Studien 14, Ordensstudien 6; Berlin: Duncker & Humblot, 1989), 3–19.
2 F. J. Felten, 'Die Ordensreformen Benedikts XII. unter institutionengeschichtlichen Aspekt', in G. Melville, ed., *Institutionen und Geschichte: Theoretische Aspekte und mittelalterliche Befunde* (Cologne, Weimar and Vienna: Böhlau, 1992), 369–435.

different actions. Sometimes it was guided by order leadership, sometimes it spread outward from individual centres. It was frequently stimulated by urban and territorial rulers, local bishops, and on the whole backed up first by the reform councils of Pisa, Constance and Basel, and during the re-assertion of papal primacy by a few reform-minded popes (notably Eugenius IV in the 1440s).[3] As the following survey will show, Observant reforms touched the various orders in various ways, and could elicit different solutions to incorporate them institutionally.

Most impressive was the wave of Observant initiatives in the mendicant orders, and the Franciscan order in particular. After the clampdown on Franciscan Spiritual factions in the 1320s and 1330s, Franciscan leadership allowed remnants of these groups to retire into small hermitages, such as Brogliano, near Foligno. There, friar Paoluccio Trinci tried from 1368 onwards to reclaim pristine Franciscan ideals of evangelical poverty and Christocentric spirituality. By 1390, this movement had gained access to more than twenty Franciscan hermitages and friaries. At first, these friaries were geared towards the life of evangelical perfection, withdrawn from the world and eschewing the study houses that had made the Franciscan order one of learned clerics. Yet the second and third generation of Italian Observant friars, led by Bernardino of Siena and Giovanni of Capistrano, regained access to learning and changed into a more outward looking movement of reformers and preachers.[4] By the 1440s, this brand of the Franciscan regular Observance had reformed about 600 male and female Franciscan monasteries, and had in fact become an autonomous branch within the Franciscan order as a whole, with its own provincial and general vicars, virtually independent from the established order hierarchy, notwithstanding much opposition from the Conventuals or non-reformed friars, who saw in this an unacceptable breach of order unity.[5]

From the vicariate of Giovanni of Capistrano onwards, this regular Observance 'sub vicariis' made headway in order provinces beyond Italy, taking over or working together with already existing Observant groups in

---

3 Dieter Mertens, 'Reformkonzilien und Ordensreform im 15. Jahrhundert', in Elm, ed., *Reformbemühungen und Observanzbestrebungen*, 431–57; Katherine Walsh, 'Papsttum und Ordensreform in Spätmittelalter und Renaissance: Zur Wechselwirkung von zentraler Gewalt und lokaler Initiative', in Elm, ed., *Reformbemühungen und Observanzbestrebungen*, 411–30.

4 Mario Sensi, *Dal movimento eremitico alla regolare osservanza francescana: L'opera di fra Paoluccio Trinci* (Rome: Santa Maria degli Angeli, 1992).

5 Duncan B. Nimmo, 'The Franciscan Regular Observance: The Culmination of Medieval Franciscan Reform', in Elm, ed., *Reformbemühungen und Observanzbestrebungen*, 189–205.

these other regions, some of which had been struggling with their non-Observant provincial superiors for several decades (such as the Observants of Mirabeau (Touraine), who as early as 1415 had obtained support against their provincial superiors from the Council of Constance). Yet these were by no means the only reforming factions. Notably in France, Spain, the German lands and to some extent in England there were other Observants who tried to avoid an institutional break-up of the order. They became known as the 'Observantes sub ministris', unwilling to withdraw their obedience to the provincial ministers and the Franciscan minister general (at least officially), but nevertheless aiming to reclaim the pristine Franciscan ideals, sometimes far more radically so than the regular Observants 'sub vicariis'. Among these groups can be listed the radical eremitical *Recollectio Villacreciana* in Castile, the more moderate Coletan friars in France – started as a male support group for the Coletine reforms among the Poor Clares in France and Burgundy – and the so-called 'Martinian' friars in the German Saxony province.[6]

The second half of the fifteenth century saw an ongoing expansion of the various Observant movements within the order, in particular of the relatively moderate regular Observance 'sub vicariis', which since the times of Bernardino of Siena profited from good relations with the church hierarchy, no doubt because of its pastoral usefulness. At the same time, these Observants 'sub vicariis' not only tried to become more independent from the remaining Conventuals, but also tried to assimilate the Observants 'sub ministris', some of which were spiritually more ambitious (such as the Villacrecians and the Discalceati in Spain, or the Amadeiti and the Clareni in Italy), but nevertheless received some support from the non-reformed Franciscan provincial ministers, as these groups did not thwart the vestiges of order unity. The resulting rivalries remained unresolved until Pope Leo X ordered in 1517 all remaining Observant groups 'sub ministris' to join the regular Observance 'sub vicariis', and made the latter the official heir of the order started by Francis of Assisi, with the right to choose the Franciscan minister general. The Observant provincial vicars now officially became ministers. The remaining Conventuals became a subordinate branch (OFMConv) under a master general. That this outcome did not appease more radical Observants is shown by the foundation of the Capuchin order family around 1528.[7]

6 Brigitte Degler-Spengler, 'Observanten außerhalb der Observanz. Die franziskanischen Reformen "sub ministris"', *Zeitschrift für Kirchengeschichte* 89 (1978), 354–71.
7 Niklaus Kuster, 'Minorità e itineranza dei primi Cappucini', *Italia Francescana* 80.1 (2005), 57–74.

Observant reforms among the Augustinian hermits first made headway at the Lecceto hermitage near Siena in 1385, soon leading to the first Augustinian Observant Congregation. Between the turn of the century and the 1430s, the Augustinian Observance began to spread, mainly due to local efforts, leading to additional Observant congregations in Italy, Spain and the German lands. Between c. 1419 and the 1430s, such Observant reforms were supported by the reform Councils and stimulated by Augustinian intellectual and institutional leadership, such as the circle around Augostino Faveroni, the order's theology professor at Bologna and Florence and prior general of the order since 1419. This helped the dissemination of reforms in the various provinces. Central assistance of Observant reforms faltered temporarily when Pope Eugenius IV in the 1430s allowed the Saxony Observant congregation to elect its own vicars, a phenomenon that was not welcomed by the order hierarchy of the time. Yet this proved only a temporary lull in support. With renewed patronage by a number of Observant Augustinian priors general between 1448–60 and 1485–98, no less than eleven flourishing Observant congregations had come into existence by the end of the fifteenth century (seven in Italy, two in Spain, one in Germany and one in Ireland), making the Observance a dominant force within the Augustinian order.[8]

In the Dominican order, Observant attempts started in 1388, when Conrad of Prussia obtained permission from the general chapter of the Rome obedience to start an Observant friary, and to discard the customs and privileges that had moved the order away from its origins. The Dominican leadership and especially the order general Raymund of Capua (former confessor of Catherine of Siena) supported this development and issued in 1390 a decree in which the order was called upon to reach back to its initial ideals. Subsequent general chapters decreed that each order province should at least have one Observant friary that could be an example to others. Opposition from many friars and friaries notwithstanding, which thwarted early reform attempts in Würzburg, Colmar, Strasbourg and elsewhere, this guided effort slowly caught on after the Councils of Constance and Basel, and especially after the election of the magister general Bartholomew Texterius, who guided

---

8 Katherine Walsh, 'The Observance: Sources for a History of the Observant Reform Movement in the Order of Augustinian Friars in the Fourteenth and Fifteenth Centuries', *Rivista di Storia della Chiesa in Italia* 31 (1977), 40–67; Francis Xavier Martin, 'The Augustinian Movement', in Elm, ed., *Reformbemühungen und Observanzbestrebungen*, 325–45; Erik L. Saak, *High Way to Heaven: The Augustinian Platform between Reform and Reformation, 1292–1524* (Studies in Medieval and Reformation Thought 89; Leiden, Boston and Cologne: Brill, 2002).

moderate Observant reforms for more than twenty years between 1426 and 1449, helping to spread the Observance among male and female houses in the German Teutonia province, in the Hispania and Aragonia Provinces, as well as in the Italian Lombarda and Romana provinces, with the assistance of reform-minded provincials, priors and theologians (such as Nicholas Notel and Johann Nider).[9]

Until the 1460s the spread of moderate Dominican Observant reforms was very much a steered and moderately successful phenomenon (notwithstanding various setbacks, as several houses refused to be reformed and could react violently towards reforming parties), without granting much specific autonomy to the Observant houses. Around 1465, however, when in various provinces the number of Observant houses had grown sufficiently, it became more common that Observants elected their own provincial vicars. Ten years later, the complete Teutonia province more or less came in Observant hands, when the candidate of the Observants was elected as provincial.[10] It was a sign that the Observance was gaining the upper hand in the Dominican order throughout.

A special phenomenon was the *Congregatio Hollandiae*, a sub-branch of the Observance within the Dominican Saxonia province, which started in the Low Countries (Rotterdam, 1448; The Hague, c. 1450, etc.), but soon affected other areas within and beyond the Burgundian territories. Its growth was stimulated when the order generals Martialis Auribelli and Conrad of Asti freed its houses from provincial supervision, allowing it to become formally autonomous from normal provincial jurisdiction in 1464. Just before its dissolution during the provincial reorganisations of the order between 1514 and 1517, this congregation counted sixty-six male and nine female Observant monasteries in several provinces, from Finland in the North to Brittany in the south-west.[11]

Serious Observant reforms among the Carmelite friars started by 1413, when the provincial chapter of Tuscany confirmed the special position of the Observant friary of Le Selve. Twenty years later, the Carmelite

---

9 R. Hernandez, 'La Reforma Dominicana entre los Concilios de Constanza y Basilea', *Archivo Dominicano* 8 (1987), 5–43.

10 Benedictus M. Reichert, 'Zur Geschichte der deutschen Dominikaner und ihrer Reform', *Römische Quartalschrift* 10 (1896), 299–311; Gabriel Löhr, *Die Teutonica im 15. Jahrhundert: Studien und Texte vornehmlich zur Geschichte ihrer Reform* (Quellen und Forschungen zur Geschichte des Dominikanerordens in Deutschland 19; Leipzig: Harrassowitz, 1924); Eugen Hillebrand, 'Die Observantenbewegung in der deutschen Ordensprovinz der Dominikaner', in Elm, ed., *Reformbemühungen und Observanzbestrebungen*, 219–71.

11 Servatius Petrus Wolfs, 'Dominikanische Observanzbestrebungen: Die *Congregatio Hollandiae* (1464–1517)', in Elm, ed., *Reformbemühungen und Observanzbestrebungen*, 273–92.

Observance gained momentum, inspired by the intrepid Observant energies of Thomas Connecte, an itinerant preacher who had been burned at the stake in Rome for castigating the papal curia. His followers found refuge in the Carmelite house in Mantua, and from there initiated Observant reforms. Thus the Mantuan Congregation came into being, which reformed many friaries in Northern and Central Italy in the fifteenth century and after, obtaining a position of autonomy within the order that it was able to maintain until 1783.

There were several other Observant initiatives in Carmelite houses, notably in the Lower Germany province from the 1440s onwards. Eventually, the Observant cause reached order-wide dimensions under the prior general John Soreth (d. 1471), who from 1450 onwards systematically pushed Observant reforms (especially in provinces not yet touched by the Mantuan reform), and who promulgated Observant statutes in 1456, which received papal confirmation by Pope Calixtus III the year thereafter (making this the 'Calixtine Reform', in distinction to the older 'Mantuan Reform'). Like other Observant movements, the Carmelite Observants in this period also brought a number of female penitential and beguine communities into the Observant Carmelite fold, creating therewith a budding network of female Carmelite houses under Observant control.[12] After Soreth's death, the Observance stagnated, to be taken up again by the so-called Albi Congregation shortly before 1500 (which gained an autonomous position, not unlike the Mantuan Congregation), and more generally under the leadership of the prior general Nicolò Audet after 1523.[13]

Reform initiatives also touched the Servites of St Mary, who had seen a substantial expansion in the first half of the fourteenth century. Although the necessity of reform was less keenly felt than among other mendicants, incidental Observant reforms were initiated in individual houses such as Monte Senario in the early fifteenth century. The cause was taken up by several order officials, leading eventually to the establishment of a specific reform congregation in Lombardy and the Venice region that in the 1440s received papal approval and a measure of autonomy by Pope Eugenius IV.[14]

Observant reforms were by no means limited to the mendicant orders. The regular canons saw their first Observant attempt in the later fourteenth

---

12 Cf. A. Staring, 'The Carmelite Sisters in the Netherlands', *Carmelus* 10 (1963), 56–92.
13 Staring, 'The Carmelite Sisters'; Joachim Smet, 'Pre-Tridentine Reform in the Carmelite Order', in Elm, ed., *Reformbemühungen und Observanzbestrebungen*, 292–323.
14 Franco A. Dal Pino, 'Tentativi di riforma e movimenti di osservanza presso i servi di Maria nei secolo XIV–XV', in Elm, ed., *Reformbemühungen und Observanzbestrebungen*, 347–70.

century, in Stift Raudnitz at the Elbe (Labe, Bohemia). The congregation resulting from it counted thirteen communities before 1400. It was the earliest, but by no means the only Observant movement among the canons. Among the Premonstratensians, the Victorines and the canons of Arrouaise reform initiatives proved cumbersome. More successful were the Observant reforms after 1410 among the Friars of the Holy Cross, leading to the foundation of many new houses in the fifteenth century, notably in the Low Countries, the Rhineland and Westphalia, supported in this by noble and urban benefactors alike.[15]

Even more important were the reform movements associated with the community of regular canons of Windesheim and with the Lateran congregation that took its point of origin in Fregionaia (Lucca) and San Salvatore (Laterano). The Lateran reform congregation at first had an impact in Italy, but soon influenced many houses of regular canons in middle and eastern Europe, notably in Poland. The Observant community of Windesheim, established in 1387 near Deventer (Low Countries), and its daughter monasteries likewise had a wide-ranging impact, soon absorbing various smaller reform congregations (such as those of Neuß and Sion), and helped to establish or reform an impressive number of communities in the Low Countries, in Saxony, along the Rhine Valley and in Switzerland. Their spirituality was to a large extent shaped by the ideals of the Modern Devotion movement, which in the later fourteenth and fifteenth century also had a huge impact on male and female penitential and tertiary communities.[16]

Among the older monastic orders, there were substantial reform initiatives among the Camaldulensian and Vallombrosian monks, as well as among the Cistercians, several military orders and their late medieval offshoots. Most impressive, however, were the large reform congregations of the late medieval Benedictines. An important point of reference for several of these was the Benedictine Subiaco monastery, where Observant reforms started as early as 1362. Following this successful example, a wave of Observant reform congregations was initiated from Kastl (Oberpfaltz) in and after 1378, from San Giustina in Padua (from 1408 onwards), from Melk (c. 1415), from St Matthias in Trier (1421–39), and from Bursfeld-Klus an der Weser (c. 1430).[17]

---

15 Pieter Van den Bosch, 'Die Kreuzherrenreform des 15. Jahrhunderts', in Elm, ed., *Reformbemühungen und Observanzbestrebungen*, 71–82.

16 Wilhelm Kohl, 'Die Windesheimer Kongregation', in Elm, ed., *Reformbemühungen und Observanzbestrebungen*, 83–106; J. Van Engen, ed., *Learning Institutionalized: Teaching in the Medieval University* (Notre Dame: University of Notre Dame Press, 2000), 279–302.

17 Udo Arnold, 'Reformansätze im deutschen Orden während des Spätmittelalters', in Elm, ed., *Reformbemühungen und Observanzbestrebungen*, 139–52; Barbara Frank, 'Subiaco.

Very influential among these proved to be the reform congregations of Melk and Bursfeld. The house of Melk first had sent out monks to Subiaco for training and orientation. After the implementation of reforms in Melk itself, its initiatives led to the introduction of observant reforms in many monasteries in Austria, Swabia and Bavaria. The Bursfeld reform, in its turn, led by a number of strong Observant-minded abbots, transformed Benedictine life in Lower Saxony, Westphalia, the Rhineland, Thuringia, Denmark and the Low Countries.[18]

As the frequent reference to the Subiaco model indicates, the Benedictine Observance was a typical monastic restoration effort, trying to get rid of the crust of liturgical additions. It was an inward-looking attempt at restoring monastic spirituality for all monks, and a struggle against the monopoly position of the nobility. A possible side-effect of this was that the Benedictine reforms hardly led to new foundations. It is remarkable, however, that counter to monastic policies of previous centuries, the Observant Benedictines habitually sent young monks to local universities and recruited novices from university surroundings.[19]

The only major monastic order that seemingly steered free from Observant reforms were the contemplative Carthusians, as it was deemed that the order on the whole never had fallen from its *antiquus rigor*, thanks to the careful selection of postulants, and through the maintenance of solitude, enclosure, silence and strict visitation procedures. The call for Observance in the later fourteenth and fifteenth centuries therefore made the Carthusians very

Ein Reformkonvent des späten Mittelalters', *Quellen und Forschungen aus italienischen Archiven und Bibliotheken* 52 (1972), 526–656; Adalbert Mischlewski, *Grundzüge der Geschichte des Antoniterordens bis zum Ausgang des 15. Jahrhunderts* (Bonner Beiträge zur Kirchengeschichte 8; Cologne and Vienna: Böhlau, 1976), 17–107; Walter G. Rödel, 'Reformbestrebungen im Johanniterorden in der Zeit zwischen dem Fall Akkons und dem Verlust von Rhodos (1291–1522)', in Elm, ed., *Reformbemühungen und Observanzbestrebungen*, 109–29.

18 Albert Groiß, *Spätmittelalterliche Lebensformen der Benediktiner von der Melker Observanz vor dem Hintergrund ihrer Bräuche: Ein darstellender Kommentar zum Caeremoniale Mellicense des Jahres 1460* (Beiträge zur Geschichte des alten Mönchtums und des Benediktinertums 46; Münster: Aschendorff, 1999), xvi–xxii, 30–65.

19 Petrus Becker, 'Benediktinische Reformbewegungen im Spätmittelalter. Ansätze, Entwicklungen, Auswirkungen', in *Untersuchungen zu Kloster und Stift* (Veröffentlichungen des Max-Planck-Institut für Geschichte 68, StGS 14; Göttingen: Max-Planck-Institut für Geschichte, 1980), 167–87; Klaus Schreiner, 'Benediktiner Klosterreform als zeitgebundene Auslegung der Regel. Geistige, religiöse und soziale Erneuerung in spätmittelalterlichen Klöstern Südwestdeutschlands im Zeichen der Kastler, Melker und Bursfelder Reform', *Blätter für württembergische Kirchengeschichte* 86 (1986), 105–95; Petrus Becker, 'Erstrebte und erreichte Ziele benediktinischer Reformen im Spätmittelalter', in Elm, ed., *Reformbemühungen und Observanzbestrebungen*, 23–34.

appealing. Several other orders took over elements of Carthusian legislation (the Carthusian visitation system was partly adopted by the Bursfeld Benedictines, and the order constitutions were partly copied by the Windesheim chapter of regular canons, by Observant Cistercian houses and by the Spanish Jeronimites), and made use of the impressive Carthusian production of literature concerning matters of asceticism, discipline and spirituality. Not a few religious from other orders, frustrated by the difficulties faced by reforming parties in their own circle, opted to join the Carthusians. Not surprisingly, the Carthusians saw their greatest expansion precisely in this period. The order grew from 70 to 220 houses between c. 1300 and 1500, establishing themselves firmly in the Low Countries, England and the German lands. Quite regularly, Carthusians became actively involved with the promotion of Observant reforms in other orders, via the production of treatises directed to other religious houses, and by means of visitation journeys to implement Observant reforms elsewhere.[20]

Finally, it should be noted that this period saw the emergence of completely new orders and religious movements fuelled by the energies of Observant reform. Good examples are the lay Jesuati, the double order of Birgittines, the Minimi (the followers of Francesco of Paola), the Jeronimites in Italy and Spain, and the Brothers and Sisters of the Common life in the Low Countries (originally a form of collective religious life for lay people without formal vows, gradually developing towards a canonical lifestyle in league with the Windesheim congregation).[21]

The Observance did not simply re-invigorate the religious life of monks, canons and friars, it also had a huge impact on female religious houses and tertiary communities, especially within the Modern Devotion movement and among the mendicants. The regular Observance among the Dominicans and the Franciscans stimulated the emergence of a network of female Observant monasteries, several of which, such as the Poor Clare houses of Monteluce (Perugia) and Santa Lucia (Foligno), and Dominican convents in

---

20 Heinrich Rüthing, 'Die Kartäuser und die spätmittelalterlicher Ordensreform', in Elm, ed., *Reformbemühungen und Observanzbestrebungen*, 35–58.
21 C. C. de Bruin, E. Persoons and A. C. Weiler, *Geert Grote en de moderne devotie* (Zutphen: De Walburgpers, 1984); A. M. Galuzzi, *Origini dell' Ordine dei Minimi* (Rome: Libreria editrice della Pontificia Università Lateranense, 1967); J. R. L. Highfield, 'The Jeronomites in Spain: their Patrons and Success 1373–1516', *Journal of Ecclesiastical History* 34 (1983), 513–44; Tore Nyberg, 'Der Birgittenorden als Beispiel einer Neugründung im Zeitalter der Ordensreformen', in Elm, ed., *Reformbemühungen und Observanzbestrebungen*, 373–96.

Southern Germany themselves spread Observant reforms. The actions of abbesses in these reform houses, as well as the extraordinary activities of Birgitta of Sweden slightly earlier, who established an order of her own, tell us that the men did not have sole initiative in such matters. The foundation of new Poor Clare monasteries in France and Burgundy, for instance, owed much to Colette of Corbie, the driving force behind the Coletines and their male Coletan counterparts, both of which branches opted to remain under the obedience of the Franciscan provincial ministers rather than seeking complete autonomy. Likewise, the reform of many female tertiary houses and Observant monasteries in Italy, Spain and the German lands can hardly be envisaged without the leadership and spiritual prowess of such women as Angelina of Montegiove, Antonia of Florence, Catarina Vigri and Ursula Haider.[22]

Significant for late medieval society as a whole was the Observant interference with the religious life of the laity. After an initial inward-looking period, Observant preachers from different orders (notably the mendicants) revolutionised preaching and confession practices. The fifteenth century is the period of massive preaching rallies, in which Observant preachers toured the lands, helped by assistant preachers, translators and confessors, preaching in churches and on the market place. Thus was provided, more intensively than ever before, continuous religious instruction around all the important feasts of the liturgical year. Over and beyond religious instruction, Observant preachers interfered in intra-urban conflicts and matters of socio-economic justice, which included the promotion of so-called *Monti de pietà* and virulent protests against 'Jewish' money-lending practices. Together with accusations in Observant preaching concerning the alleged Jewish responsibility for the death of Christ, this helped to entrench antijudaic stereotypes and to condone outright persecution.[23]

---

22 Jeryldene Wood, *Women, Art and Spirituality: The Poor Clares of Early Modern Italy* (Cambridge: Cambridge University Press, 1996); Jeffrey Hamburger, *The Visual and the Visionary: Art and Female Spirituality in Late Medieval Germany* (New York: Zone Books, 1998); Nancy Bradley Warren, *Spiritual Economies: Female Monasticism in Later Medieval England* (Philadelphia: University of Pennsylvania Press, 2001); Wybren Scheepsma, *Medieval Religious Women in the Low Countries: The Modern Devotion, the Canonesses of Windesheim, and their Writings* (Woodbridge: Boydell, 2004).

23 Nirit Ben-Aryeh Debby, 'Jews and Judaism in the Rhetoric of Popular Preachers: The Florentine Sermons of Giovanni Dominici (1345–1419) and Bernardino da Siena (1380–1444)', *Jewish History* 14 (2000), 175–200; H. Martin, *Le métier du prédicateur à la fin du Moyen Âge (1350–1520)* (Paris: Cerf, 1988); Franco Mormando, *The Preacher's Demons: Bernardino of Siena and the Social Underworld of Early Renaissance Italy* (Chicago: University of Chicago Press, 1999).

Alongside the massive output of homiletic materials associated with preaching, Observant monks and friars engaged in the production of many kinds of religious instruction literature, both in Latin and in the vernacular.[24] They also produced a wealth of booklets defending and promoting the Observance (such as the *Tuitiones observantiae regulae S. Benedicti* by Martin von Senging (Melk), *De reformatione religiosorum* by John Nider OP, and *De professione monastica* by Dionysius the Carthusian). In addition, Observant congregations and houses of many orders, male and female, took up the writing of history to legitimise their programme of reform.[25]

The Observant Franciscans at first had moved away from university learning, only to return to the schools with a vengeance (if not necessarily to the degree schools, many of which for a while remained in Conventual hands) for the education of their preachers after c. 1420. This reversal was less pronounced among the Dominican and Augustinian Observants, most of whom from early on wholeheartedly subscribed to an Observant programme of learning focussed on moral theology.[26] In the monastic and canonical orders, the Observance actually led to closer contacts with university learning than before. Cases in point are the major Benedictine reform congregations, which stimulated Benedictine access to university education, as well as the Friars of the Cross, who also tapped into the intellectual resources of the university to train their friars and to recruit new postulants.

Observant learning wished to fortify faith and virtuous behaviour of religious and lay people alike against the onslaughts of Satan, seen everywhere through the spread of conflict, the Turkish threat and the spectre of popular heresy. Maybe for the first time, Observant monks and friars tended to present learning as a foundation both for their own spiritual renovation and as an intrinsic element of Christian life. This was, for instance, emphasised in the works of the Benedictine Observant Johannes Trithemius and in the *Sermo de scientiarum studiis* held before the University of Padua in 1443 by the Franciscan Observant Bernardino of Siena. Such Observant approaches to learning converged with certain strains within the Humanist movement. Although

24 For the Franciscan contribution, see Bert Roest, *Franciscan Literature of Religious Instruction before the Council of Trent* (Studies in the History of Christian Tradition 117; Leiden: Brill, 2004).

25 Bert Roest, 'Later Medieval Institutional History', in Deborah Mauskopf Deliyannis, ed., *Historiography in the Middle Ages* (Leiden and Boston: Brill, 2003), 277–315; Anne Winston-Allen, *Convent Chronicles: Women Writing about Women and Reform in the Late Middle Ages* (University Park: Pennsylvania State University Press, 2004).

26 Bert Roest, *A History of Franciscan Education (c. 1220–1517)* (Education and Society in the Middle Ages and Renaissance 11; Leiden: Brill, 2000), 153–70.

most Observants warned against undue studies of the pagans and were indifferent to matters of style and linguistic purity, there were, nevertheless, close links between discourses of Observant reform and those of humanist renewal, most clearly among the Augustinians.[27]

One side effect of all this was library formation. Early Observant communities saw the copying of texts as a valid form of ascetical labour and as an initial step in the edification of others. The Observant participation in the spiritual renovation of religious life within and beyond the religious orders added to this, leading to the emergence of substantial Observant libraries among the Friars of the Holy Cross, the Windesheim congregation, in all major mendicant orders, and in a large number of female Observant houses (such as the female Dominican houses in Nuremberg and Schlettstadt).[28]

The successes of the Observant movements were partly caused by the expectations of the laity, which took its religion very seriously, and demanded efficacious and sincere commitment from the cloisters, friaries and convents which they supported with alms and other benefits. In the aftermath of schism and conciliarism, urban authorities and territorial rulers alike sought influence over the way in which resources for religious purposes were spent. In many cases, Observant reforms freed assets from ecclesiastical control, downscaled the expenses needed for the upkeep of religious houses, and seemed to secure catechesis, schooling, pastoral and spiritual service more efficiently. One could argue, therefore, that the Observance, with all its hankering after pristine beginnings, was very much in tune with the transformations of the late medieval world.

27  D. I. Howie, 'Benedictine Monks, Manuscript Copying, and the Renaissance: Johannes Trithemius' *De Laude Scriptorum*', *Revue Bénédictine* 86 (1976), 129–54; P. O. Kristeller, 'The Contribution of Religious Orders to Renaissance Thought and Learning', *The American Benedictine Review* 21 (1970), 1–54; Kaspar Elm, 'Mendikanten und Humanisten im Florenz des Tre- und Quattrocento. Zum Problem der Legitimierung humanistischer Studien in den Bettelorden', in Otto Herding and Robert Stupperich, eds., *Die Humanisten in ihrer politischen und sozialen Umwelt* (Bonn and Bad Godesberg: Boppard, 1976), 51–85; Katherine Walsh, 'Papal Policy and Local Reform, b) Congregatio Ilicetana: The Augustinian Observant Movement in Tuscany and the Humanist Ideal', *Römische historische Mitteilungen* 22 (1980), 105–45.

28  Roest, *A History of Franciscan Education*, 212–13, 229f., 233f.; Pieter Van den Bosch, 'De bibliotheken van de Kruisherenkloosters in de Nederlanden vóór 1550', in *Studies over het boekenbezit en boekengebruik in de Nederlanden vóór 1600* (Brussels: Koninklijke Bibliotheek Albert I, 1974), 563–636; Werner Williams-Krapp, 'Die Bedeutung der reformierten Klöster des Predigerordens für das literarische Leben in Nürnberg im 15. Jahrhundert', in Falk Eisermann, Eva Schlotheuber and Volker Honemann, eds., *Studien und Texte zur literarischen und materiellen Kultur der Frauenklöster im Mittelalter: Ergebnisse eines Arbeitsgesprächs in der Herzog August Bibliothek Wolfenbüttel, 24.–26. Febr. 1999* (Studies in Medieval and Reformation Thought 99; Leiden: Brill, 2004), 311–29.

# 30

# Public purity and discipline: states and religious renewal

ROBERTO RUSCONI

## The centrality of preaching in religious and social life in the late mediaeval period

From the last decades of the fourteenth century to the first part of the sixteenth, preaching acquired a central role within the religious, social and political life of Western Europe. By the end of the fourteenth century, preachers were already at the forefront in disseminating ideas of reform, whether in England, first with John Wyclif (1320–84), and later with the Lollards, or in Bohemia, with Jan Hus (c. 1370–1415) and his followers. In the first decades of the sixteenth century, both the supporters of religious renewal and the proponents of the Reformation used preaching from the pulpit as a way of promoting their respective ideas.

A wide range of contemporary documents all attest to the fact that preaching had been established as an event which drew crowds of listeners whose sizes varied according to the fame of the preachers and the size of the town. Sometimes all commercial and manufacturing activities were suspended so that a city's population could assemble in the town square to hear a sermon; the inhabitants of the countryside were also drawn to the event.[1]

As we know from the iconographical representations of fifteenth-century preaching, pulpits were erected in the piazzas of many cities. The preachers themselves were depicted in devotional art as saints or blessed (*beati*) by virtue of their preaching. To make them recognisable to the faithful, preachers' individual attributes were developed which were associated with the devotions

---

1 For Italy, see M. G. Muzzarelli, *Pescatori di uomini: Predicatori e piazze alla fine del medioevo* (Bologna: Il Mulino, 2005); R. M. Dessì, 'La prophétie, l'Évangile et l'État. La prédication en Italie au XV$^e$ et au début du XVI$^e$ siècle', in R. M. Dessì and M. Lauwers, eds., *La parole du prédicateur V$^e$–XV$^e$ siècle* (Nice: Centre d'Études Médiévales, 1997), 395–444; and F. Bruni, *La città divisa: Le parti e il bene comune da Dante a Guicciardini* (Bologna: Il Mulino, 2003), chs. 2–5.

they promoted in their vernacular sermons: for the Friar Minor of the Observance Bernardino da Siena (1380–1444), the symbol of the Name of Jesus; for Friar Vincent Ferrer (1350–1419) of the Order of the Preachers, Christ enthroned at the Last Judgement. Giacomo della Marca (1394–1476) of the Observant Franciscans was depicted with a vial containing the blood of Christ, Giovanni da Capestrano (1386–1456) with the crusaders' banner, and Bernardino da Feltre (1439–94), with the *Christus patiens* (the emblem of the *Monti di pietà*, whose foundation he promoted).[2]

The activity of the preachers, beyond the personal charisma which many of them possessed, was characterised by an institutional holiness, which became even more marked after they were made saints by the Roman papacy. Bernardino da Siena was canonised during the Jubilee of 1450 for the Friars Minor, and Vincent Ferrer for the Order of Friars Preacher a few years later in 1458. This was preceded in 1446 by the 'retrieval' of a friar from the previous century, Nicola da Tolentino (1245–1305), for the Order of Hermits of St Augustine.

Preaching to the faithful in the vernacular, in particular by the friars of the mendicant orders, should be seen as part of a tradition towards renewal of ecclesiastical pastoral work, which began in the early thirteenth century. At this time, the friars embarked on their widespread programme of teaching Christian doctrine and devotions, and hearing confession of the laity. They preached every Sunday and on the (very numerous) feast days in their churches, and would also preach every day during Advent and Lent in the major towns (during which time every Christian was instructed to make confession and to take communion).[3]

By the fifteenth century preaching took on some distinctive characteristics of its own, and this placed it more centrally than before at the heart of the social and legal structures of late medieval society. The authorities which held power, particularly in the Italian cities, were highly aware of the effectiveness of the preachers' words (as were the preachers themselves, of course) and so preaching was politically mobilised. It was directed towards the inculcation of economic and social rules of conduct, and more broadly towards inspiring religious renewal and political reform.

---

2 See R. Rusconi, 'The Preacher Saint in Late Medieval Italian Art', in C. Muessig, ed., *Preacher, Sermon and Audience in the Middle Ages* (Leiden: Brill, 2002), 181–200.
3 See R. Rusconi, *L'ordine dei peccati: La confessione tra Medioevo ed età moderna* (Bologna: Il Mulino, 2002).

# The Christian renewal of society: the religion of 'Observance'

The institutional crisis of the Roman Church was a long drawn-out affair, and it divided Western polities into separate obediences during the papal schism of 1378–1417, first of all in Rome and Avignon, later in Pisa. This was not completely resolved even after the election of Pope Martin V at the Council of Constance, and an underlying conciliar crisis dragged on until almost the middle of the fifteenth century. Another effect of these rifts, which had a distinct effect on the faithful, was that proposals for religious reform 'in capite et in membris' moved progressively from the world of the clerics to the wider society; the preachers were instrumental in transmitting a new Christianisation of society, founded on morality rather than on doctrine.

Moral and didactic themes predominated, particularly in the preaching of the Friars Minor, the Franciscans, in the wake of the authoritative example of Bernardino da Siena.[4] This had also occurred in a more limited way in the fourteenth century with the Friars Preacher, the Dominicans, and again at the turn of the century with Giovanni Domenici (1356–1419),[5] and later with Antonino Pierozzi (1389–1459), bishop of Florence.[6] Many traces of these themes remain in the Latin books of sermons which were compiled by the friars for their own use. The content of more controversial texts (e.g. on subjects such as pacifism, propaganda in favour of the Crusade against the Turks, the foundation of the *Monti di pietà* (charitable banks) or those sermons directed against targets such as personal wealth, heretics, witches and the Jews) has also been documented by those who attended the sermons, and from chronicles of the time.

The preachers hoped to extend their religious devotional style to the whole of society. In a certain sense, it was the lay faithful's waning enthusiasm for the religious ideal which was at the root of the reforms of the mendicant friars and the monks: the 'observantia regularis'. This was a renewal based on the rigorous application of the rules – the 'regula' of the order – upon which

---

4 See F. Mormando, *The Preacher's Demons: Bernardino of Siena and the Social Underworld of Early Renaissance Italy* (Chicago and London: University of Chicago Press, 1999); and C. L. Polecritti, *Preaching Peace in Renaissance Italy: Bernardino da Siena and his Audience* (Washington, D.C.: Catholic University of America Press, 2000).

5 See N. Ben-Aryeh Debby, *Renaissance Florence in the Rhetoric of Two Popular Preachers: Giovanni Dominici (1356–1419) and Bernardino da Siena (1380–1444)* (Turnhout: Brepols, 2001).

6 See P. F. Howard, *Beyond the Written Word: Preaching and Theology in the Florence of Archbishop Antoninus, 1427–1459* (Florence: Olschki, 1995).

their identity was based. For the laity, it meant consolidating ecclesiastical pastoral care (founded on preaching in the vernacular and the hearing of confessions), which was often offered by the self-same friars, while promoting adherence to the precepts of the Ten Commandments. The reforming vision was quite traditional, based on virtues to be practised and vices to be avoided, and it placed a greater emphasis on the family and its network of internal and external connections.[7]

There were notable differences in the way in which this occurred in various areas of Western Europe, despite the shared aim of renewal and reform. This is not surprising, since power and authority were organised differently and produced differing degrees of cooperation between church and state in Europe's regions. The friar Vincent Ferrer (d. 1419) of the Order of Preachers originated from the kingdom of Valencia and was a subject of the Aragonese crown, travelled over the course of several decades through Catalonia, alpine and subalpine Italy, southern Germany and central France, and ended his days preaching in Brittany. Crowds flocked to hear him preach, first on viciously anti-Jewish themes, then later on the topic of social pacification. He finally professed himself to be a preacher of the Last Days, an image was confirmed in his papal canonisation by Pope Callistus III in 1458 and in the devotional iconography which developed around his memory and cult.[8]

In a similar way, the preaching of the Friars Minor of Observance had a social impact in Italy, beginning with Bernardino da Siena in the early fifteenth century and ending with Bernardino da Feltre in the last years of that century. This impact was first felt in those Italian territories which were progressively restoring (or even establishing) the power of the papal monarchy, while the situation was slightly different in the other states of the peninsula. Girolamo Savonarola da Ferrara (1452–98), who went from religious reformer of social mores to agent of political renewal in Florence, rose to prominence within a similar framework, in this case the political conflicts between the different factions in the city.

---

7 See R. Rusconi, 'Da Costanza al Laterano: La "calcolata devozione" del ceto mercantile-borghese nell'Italia del Quattrocento', in A. Vauchez, ed., *Storia dell'Italia religiosa*, vol. 1, *L'antichità e il Medioevo* (Rome and Bari: Laterza, 1993), 505–36.
8 See at least P. M. Cátedra García, *Sermón, sociedad y literatura en la edad media: San Vicente Ferrer en Castilla (1411–1412)* (Valladolid: Junta de Castilla y León, Consejería de Cultura y Turismo, 1994); and L. Gaffuri, '"In partibus illis ultra montanis": La missione subalpina di Vicent Ferrier (1402–1408)', in B. Hodel, O. P. and F. Morenzoni, eds., *'Mirificus Praedicator': À l'occasion du sixième centenaire du passage de saint Vicent Ferrier en pays romand* (Rome: Istituto storico domenicano, 2006), 105–20.

## Preaching to the populace and the reform of the rules

Both chronicles and regulatory documents attest that from the first decades of the fourteenth century onwards there was a growing and deliberate intervention by the Observant friars in the mechanisms of reform of city statutes. This was particularly apparent in those central Italian cities where the papal monarchy was gradually asserting its power over the local oligarchies, and took the form of preaching which explicitly condemned factional conflict and promoted peace. The presence of Franciscan preachers in Umbria and the Marches (Bernardino da Siena and Giacomo della Marca among others) can be related to a change in the power-base of cities: their presence is recorded in Perugia, Assisi, Todi and Foligno after the death of Braccio Fortebraccio in 1424, and in Ascoli Piceno and Fermo after the death of *condottiere* Niccolò Piccinino in 1444. The arrival of a well-known preacher to preach a series of sermons was never a question of chance or even of a friar's individual decision. Instead, it was generally the result of complex negotiations between the ecclesiastical authorities and local power-brokers which resulted in a prompt towards reform by one of the parties. This was true even beyond the Papal States and outside the traditional liturgical periods such as Advent and Lent, at this time and later.[9]

The impact of preaching was inevitably linked to the emotional effects produced by a preacher of charismatic reputation: hagiographical sources, domestic and city documents, and sermons recorded by their listeners are all dense with dark threats of punishment for sinners, events often confirmed by miraculous occurrences. Attempts to increase the participation of the listeners through their direct involvement are also evident. This could range from traditional processions to the new public ritual of the 'bonfire of the vanities' on which lay people forsook the values of life – gaming dice, jewellery, wigs – as a sign of inner conversion. There was a heightened emphasis on the theatrical aspects of preaching in public and this drew in laity – men and women alike.

The preachers seem, at first glance, to have been summoned to one or another city in order to facilitate those changes to the statute books which had

---

9 See R. Rusconi, "Predicò in piazza". Politica e predicazione nell'Umbria del '400', in *Signorie in Umbria tra Medioevo e Rinascimento: L'esperienza dei Trinci. Atti del Convegno. Foligno, 10–13 dicembre 1986* (Perugia: Deputazione di Storia Patria per l'Umbria, 1989), 113–41; R. M. Dessì, 'Predicare e governare nelle città dello Stato della Chiesa alla fine del Medioevo. Giacomo della Marca a Fermo', in G. Barone, L. Capo and S. Gasparri, eds., *Studi sul Medioevo per Girolamo Arnaldi* (Rome: Viella, 2000), 125–59.

been envisaged by the power-brokers who had invited them in. However, the preachers themselves became increasingly aware of this reality, and, once established in a city sought to promote their own agenda for Christian renewal, which often included a severe critique of the rulers. It is surely telling that those new laws introduced onto the statute books which went beyond merely reforming existing positions were in general extremely short-lived, and were reformed in turn not long after the departure of the preacher. Inherent in these sermons was the desire for the establishment of strong and stable government, that is to say, for forms of government in which the repressive authority of the state was exercised not only against factional violence, but also against some common social ways of behaving. For the moralist, these factors seemed in equal measure to undermine the restoration of an ordered society.

Bernardino da Siena's generation sought to obtain tangible results by preaching, and to override the apathy and concern created by the years of ecclesiastical schism and the conciliar crisis.[10] The following generation of preachers offered sermons that were ever more pointed, and some of them – thanks to the acknowledged charismatic preachers – were even used for important assignments which were directly entrusted to them by the Roman papacy. The Abruzzan friar Giovanni da Capestrano was sent to preach against the Hussites in Bohemia. He then moved from southern Germany, and he preached the crusade against the Turks, and actually 'guided' the crusader armies in the victorious battle of Belgrade in 1456. His fellow friar Giacomo della Marca carried out similar activities, operating at first within the Papal States, but then also on the other side of the Adriatic in the territories of the Hungarian crown.

Other Observant Italian Franciscans took their message to further-flung countries, benefiting from the fact that they were subjected to the same governmental authority. This was the case for Matteo d'Agrigento in the Aragonese territories, which extended from the western part of the Iberian peninsula, across the islands of the Mediterranean, Sardinia and Corsica, to the southern portion of the Italian peninsula.[11] The importance and effectiveness

---

10 J.-C. Maire-Viguer, 'Bernardin et la vie citadine', in *Bernardino predicatore e la società del suo tempo* (Atti del XVI Convegno del Centro di studi sulla spiritualità medievale; Todi: Accademia Tudertina, 1976), 253–82.

11 P. Evangelisti, 'Fede, mercato, comunità nei sermoni di un protagonista della costruzione dell'identità politica della corona catalano-aragonese. Matteo d'Agrigento (c. 1380–1450)', *Collectanea Franciscana* 73 (2003), 617–64.

of preaching was no less even in a completely different institutional and social context, such as the territory of the kingdom of France.[12]

## The 'bonfires of the vanities': against men's games and women's adornment

In the course of his preaching in southern Germany, especially in Nuremberg and Bamberg, where his words were translated into the local language by interpreters, Giovanni da Capestrano imported a ritual practice which had become a characteristic of Observant preaching in Italy. This was the 'bonfire of the vanities', which is documented from the first decades of the fifteenth century in relation to Bernardino da Siena's preaching, and after him by others, most notably his fellow Franciscan Bernardino da Feltre, and the Dominican Girolamo Savonarola in Florence, and at the beginning of the sixteenth century by another Franciscan, Giovanni da Fano.[13]

Planned as a ritual involving not only the audience, but the whole lay population, the 'bonfire' represented a forceful means of exerting pressure on the authorities towards scrutiny and control of the personal behaviour of citizens. The event was imbued with a supernatural atmosphere which would sometimes manifest itself in the spectators' conviction that they had seen the devil himself escaping through the flames. They generally burned gaming equipment and women's accessories, but in some cases they also burned weapons and the banners of the factions, which clearly demonstrates the political significance of such events. Their suppression of all forms of gaming was not motivated purely by moral considerations; it had to do with a programme of social control which had been agreed between the preachers and the authorities. The preachers linked the ideas of 'crime' and 'sin', and their critique even touched on cherished collective rituals of civic life. In Perugia, for example,

---

12  See H. Martin, 'La prédication et les masses au XV siècle: Facteurs et limites d'une réussite', in J. Delumeau, ed., *Histoire vécue du peuple chrétien* (Toulouse: Privat, 1979), vol. 2, 9–41; *Le métier du prédicateur à la fin du Moyen Âge (1350–1520)* (Paris: Cerf, 1988); 'Prédication et politique dans les provinces septentrionales de la France de la fin du XIV<sup>e</sup> à la fin du XV<sup>e</sup> siècle', in S. Gensini, ed., *Vita religiosa e identità politiche: Universalità e particolarismi nell'Europa del tardo medioevo* (Pisa: Pacini, 1998), 493–511.

13  See G. Klaniczay, 'The "Bonfire of Vanities" and the Mendicants', in Gerhard Jaritz, ed., *Emotions and Material Culture: International Round-Table Discussion. Krems an der Donau, October 7–8, 2002* (Vienna: Verlag des Österreichischen Akademie der Wissenschaften, 2003), 31–57, and also an earlier study: T. M. Izbicki, 'Pyres of Vanities: Mendicant Preaching on the Vanity of Women and its Audience', in T. L. Amos, E. A. Green and B. M. Kienzle, eds., *"De ore Domini": Preacher and Word in the Middle Ages* (Kalamazoo, Mich.: Medieval Institute Publications, 1989), 211–34.

the *sassaiola*, a battle fought with stones and wooden weapons, was prohibited. The *sassaiola* served both to defuse aggression and as a trial of prowess, but it was deemed immorally violent and so was critiqued. Elsewhere, the preacher's sermons were not so successful, precisely because of the opposition of the authorities in Venice, for example, the 'guerra dei pugni' (war of fists) continued well up to the modern period.[14]

The Observant Franciscans' vehement fight against female adornment, which corresponded with the anti-sumptuary and anti-magnate policies found in Italian towns, had a doctrinal precedent in the *Llibre de les dones* of the Catalan friar Francesc Eiximenis (1330–1409). It was also treated extensively in the *De usu cuiuscumque ornatus* of Giovanni da Capestrano, which also circulated in the vernacular for a wider readership as the *Trattato degli ornamenti specie delle donne* (*Treatise on the Different Kinds of Women's Adornment*). The arguments adopted by the preachers in the pulpit were founded on a particular reading of Christian morality: wealth represented the theft of goods from the poor, and it distorted the natural functioning of the market. The Observant friars' attention to a 'natural' working of the economy led them to consider wealth as a sort of sinful overturning of the social order. Their preaching had a substantially misogynistic tone, even though they proclaimed repeatedly the centrality of women to the family, their primary function being to promote the Christian upbringing of children. Preachers also ascribed the spread of 'sodomy' (i.e., male homosexuality) to women's adornment, since the cost of a wedding in their opinion dissuaded men from marriage. Female adornment was seen as distorting the female role in family life; it was a target which found willing adherents both among the friars and the governing elite, from whose ranks the major representative members of the religious orders were recruited.[15]

While games were suppressed, festivals were regulated, and new devotions and rituals were introduced in turn.[16] Bernardino da Siena's motion of the devotion to the Name of Jesus was particularly successful (although it was the

14  C. Cardinali, 'Il santo e la norma. Bernardino da Siena e gli statuti perugini del 1425', in G. Ortalli, ed., *Gioco e giustizia nell'Italia di Comune* (Treviso and Rome: Fondazione Benetton/Viella, 1993), 183–91.

15  On this subject, see M. G. Muzzarelli, *Gli inganni delle apparenze: Disciplina di vesti e ornamenti alla fine del Medioevo* (Turin: Scriptorium, 1996), and previously D. Owen Hughes, 'Sumptuary Law and Social Relation in Renaissance Italy', in J. Bossy, ed., *Disputes and Settlements: Law and Human Relations in the West* (Cambridge: Cambridge University Press, 1983), 69–99.

16  A. Rizzi, 'Il gioco fra norma laica e proibizione religiosa: l'azione dei predicatori fra Tre e Quattrocento', in Ortalli, ed., *Gioco e giustizia nell'Italia di Comune*, 149–82.

target of accusations of heresy from other religious orders, and even from the papacy). The intention was to create an alternative symbol to the insignias of the factions, and it finally became a cult followed in several Tuscan towns, above all, Siena. Giacomo della Marca did not succeed in creating a similar cult for the Blood of Christ (another initiative stymied for reasons of orthodox theology), but the use of the image of the *Christus patiens* for the banners of the *Monti di pietà*, promoted by Bernardino da Feltre, was more successful.

## Denunciations from the pulpit and repression of difference and diversity

Contemporary chronicles and a painted panel from the end of the fifteenth century combine to reveal the fact that the Jews were forced to listen to Giovanni da Capestrano's public preaching while he was active in Germany.[17] The infamous expulsion of the Jews from England in 1290 and France in 1306 (long before they were chased out of the reunified kingdom of Spain in 1492) meant that the Italian peninsula and the German-speaking countries were the parts of Europe with the largest Jewish communities in late medieval Europe.

Traditional anti-Jewish attitudes, encouraged by the literal tone of the Christian liturgy, were an inherent feature of preaching even when not explicitly under discussion, and they were a powerful component of the preaching of the Franciscan friars. Surprisingly, there are no visible traces of these attitudes in their representation in Italian devotional art, unlike the depictions of the Friar Preacher, Vincent Ferrer, in images made after his canonisation in 1458.

Beyond the undeniable fanaticism with which the Franciscan Bernardino da Feltre promoted the institution of the *Monti di pietà* (institutions which provided loans on the basis of small pledges) in an atmosphere of feverish anti-Judaism, it is interesting to compare the situation in different parts of the Italian peninsula.[18] In the territories of the Papal States, where the *Monti di pietà* were established – tellingly – with the backing of the local authorities, there were no major manifestations of hostility towards the Jews, probably

---

17 For the following, see R. Rusconi, 'Anti-Jewish Preaching in the Fifteenth Century and Images of Preachers in Italian Renaissance Art', in S. McMichael and S. E. Myers, eds., *Friars and Jews in the Middle Ages and Renaissance* (Leiden and Boston: Brill, 2004), 225–37.
18 See A. Toaff, *Jews, Franciscans and the First 'Monti di Pietà' in Italy (1462–1500)*, in McMichael and Myers, eds., *Friars and Jews in the Middle Ages and Renaissance*, 239–53. See also M. G. Muzzarelli, *Il denaro e la salvezza: L'invenzione del Monte di Pietà* (Bologna: Il Mulino, 2001).

because they also benefited from papal protection. This may explain the reluctance with which the Roman ecclesiastical authorities greeted the request of the bishop of Trent, Johannes Hinderbach, for the canonisation of the child Simone, the victim of a ritual murder allegedly perpetrated by Jews at Easter 1475. The Observant Franciscan preachers were strenuous advocates for this cult, as attested by the widespread diffusion of devotional iconography of the young 'martyr' in northern Italy, and in the German-speaking countries neighbouring Trent. The government of the Venetian Republic took a careful line on the subject, quickly expelling friars who did not respect the prohibition of preaching on the cult of the 'blessed' Simone within its territories. Similarly, the cult of another alleged victim of ritual murder, one Lorenzino da Marostica, never extended beyond his local land.

The hostility towards the Jews apparent in Franciscan preaching in Italy resulted from a complex blend of issues. The concept of a Christian society and a Christian economy was central to Franciscan preaching, and anything which appeared opposite was denounced and expelled. This position was already established by the second half of the thirteenth century, and was developed further as a result of the impact of the writings of the Provençal Franciscan Pierre de Jean Olieu on Bernardino da Siena. Their conception of the economy set them in direct opposition to the only group in Western society which was radically other: the Jewish communities.[19]

The Franciscans could proceed in this enterprise wherever the local authorities gave their backing. Where they enjoyed the support of town officials, friars could preach in this manner with impunity. It was much the same for another of the aims of fourteenth-century Observant preaching: the abolition of 'superstition'. The use of this term in vernacular preaching and the Latin sermons referred first to the kind of beliefs which they defined as *fatuitas* (which did not, however, contain any magical or ritual elements), but also to those practices which involved the sacrilegious use of the Christian liturgy, and to *incantamenta*, which were linked to witchcraft.[20] The difficulty of distinguishing between such practices, which were often domestic in nature and associated with feminine spheres of activity, is evident from the trial

---

19 See especially the studies by G. Todeschini, *La ricchezza degli ebrei: Merci e denaro nella riflessione ebraica e nella definizione cristiana dell'usura alla fine del Medioevo* (Spoleto: CISAM, 1989); 'Ebrei e francescani nel XV secolo. Il conflitto come verifica di un modello economico', 153–80; *Ricchezza francescana: Dalla povertà volontaria all'economia di mercato* (Bologna: Il Mulino, 2004), ch. 4: 'Il mercato come forma della società: Da Barcellona a Siena', 159–207.

20 For all this, see M. Montesano, *'Supra acqua et supra ad vento': 'Superstizioni', 'maleficia' e 'incantamenta' nei predicatori francescani osservanti (Italia, sec. XV)* (Roma: ISIME, 1999).

initiated in Rome in 1426 against a lower-class woman by the name of Finicella. An inflammatory sermon by Bernardino da Siena the previous year led to her death at the stake, when she was accused of witchcraft and numerous infanticides, allegedly caused by vampirism. This case, like that of the 'witch' Matteuccia in Todi in 1428, who met the same miserable end as a result of the work of the same friar, reveals the vulnerability of women who worked as midwives and functioned as healers.[21]

Preaching and repression of 'superstitions' and 'witchcraft' could therefore only go ahead with the support of the local authorities. It is extremely telling that when Bernardino da Siena preached in Arezzo in 1425, and wished to promote the destruction of a *fons tecta* (hidden well) which had been linked to popular beliefs, rituals and active powers, especially of female sterility, his proposals met with no support from the local officials. For broadly similar reasons, Dominican friars such as Samuele Cassini had to wait until the end of the fifteenth century before they were allowed to enact persecutions of customs that seemed to be witchcraft in mountains of Lombardy and Piedmont.

## The rise and fall of Girolamo Savonarola in Florence

The events surrounding the Dominican friar Girolamo Savonarola da Ferrara crystallised many of the characteristics and contradictions of popular preaching during the Italian Renaissance. The political significance was also accentuated by the particular situation of the Florentine Republic in the last years of the fifteenth century. Savonarola had received an entirely traditional theological and doctrinal training within the curriculum of studies prescribed by his Order, and had dedicated himself to a pastoral ministry. Prompted by the wars on Italy by Charles VIII of France's armies, Savonarola developed a personal prophetic consciousness, which allowed him to use the pulpit as a platform from which the Florentine people were urged to accept a new theocratic regime.[22]

---

21  See L. Pellegrini, 'Predicazione osservante e propaganda politica: a partire da un caso di Todi', in *La propaganda politica nel Basso Medioevo: Atti del XXXVIII convegno storico internazionale. Todi. 14–17 ottobre 2001* (Spoleto: CISAM, 2002), 511–31.

22  See D. Weinstein, *Savonarola and Florence: Prophecy and Patriotism in the Renaissance* (Princeton: Princeton University Press, 1978); and G. Garfagnini, ed., *Una città e il suo profeta: Firenze di fronte al Savonarola* (Florence: SISMEL – Edizioni del Galluzzo, 2001). See also L. Pellegrini, 'La profezia tra il pulpito e lo Stato: il caso di Girolamo Savonarola', *Annali dell'Istituto storico italo-germanico in Trento* 25 (1999), 433–56.

Savonarola's activities were fully congruous with contemporary practices of official preaching, which we have already discussed. The displays which accompanied the friar's controversial regime exhibited a marked theatricality, ranging from processions of devoted 'boys' in the streets to the 'bonfires of the vanities' in the piazzas. Printing technology was used to circulate his programme of reform, and facilitated its success. This continued the widespread use which he had made of print in previous years for circulation of his own Latin sermons and some vernacular theological and devotional works. From Lent 1494 onwards, Savonarola's sermons were immediately printed and circulated by his followers. He himself edited the text to ensure the accuracy of the report of his preached words, since this was an essential tool in the affirmation of his charismatic power as an alternative power-base to the republican institutions.[23] The tragic conclusion to the affair, brought about by his excommunication by Pope Alexander VI, which in turn led to his death at the stake in the Piazza della Signoria in Florence in 1498, was prompted by political reasons. As a result of the increasingly powerful effect of his sermons, fate inevitably overtook him as he lost the support of the traditional power elites.

Savonarola's tragic end should be seen as occurring in a rather different context to that of the itinerant penitential preachers. The presence of the latter group is documented in many city chronicles, both before him in the 1470s, and after him in his wake. They continued to operate until repressive measures were taken against them first by a decree of the Fifth Lateran Council in 1516, and then by the Florentine provincial synod in 1517, the result of the authorities' concern to avoid a political revival of Savonarolism. The itinerant preachers tended to travel alone, moving from one place to the next, particularly in central Italy, announcing the imminence of divine punishment and inciting the faithful to expiate their sins before the Last Judgement. They did not preach in churches but in the streets and the piazzas, and they sought to make their message credible not so much by simple prophecies – as did the hermit, Bernardino da Parenzo in Venice in the early decades of the sixteenth century – as by assuming the long-haired appearance of St John the Baptist, covered in animal furs and holding a large cross.[24]

---

23 See R. Rusconi, 'Le prediche di fra Girolamo da Ferrara: dai manoscritti al pulpito alle stampe', in Garfagnini, ed., *Una città e il suo profeta*, 201–34.
24 See A. Volpato, 'La predicazione penitenziale-apocalittica nell'attività di due predicatori del 1473', *Bullettino dell'Istituto Storico Italiano per il Medio Evo* 82 (1970), 114–28, and B. Nobile, '"Romiti" e vita religiosa nella cronachistica italiana fra '400 e '500', *Cristianesimo nella storia* 5 (1984), 303–40.

## Limits and contradictions of preaching in the Renaissance, exacerbated by the new era

During the period from the late fourteenth to the early sixteenth century, preaching by members of religious orders, especially the Franciscans and Dominicans, generally strengthened ecclesiastical institutions, with obvious differences from country to country. They contributed to the improvement of political institutions and acted as an agent of renewal, which heightened religious awareness and probably participation and commitment by lay people.

In the areas which had remained faithful to the religious model of the Roman Church, the preaching phenomenon had very specific origins, inspired by reform, which happened first within the mendicant orders, which preachers of both orders sought to transmit to wider society. It had also particular characteristics within the Italian peninsula, due to the close ties between the Christian renewal of society and the establishment of papal power in its territories.

In such a context, we should not emphasise the effect of mechanisms of repression and exclusion promoted by the preachers and put into practice wherever the local authorities gave their consent, without also underlining the importance of instruments of integration: the effect of preaching in the vernacular and the hearing of individual confessions. It created a common morality based on Christian ethics.[25] The promotion of confraternities by the preachers, organisations made up of devout lay people, led to further reinforcement of social solidarity within ruling and working classes. If these organisations were already in existence, the preachers encouraged them to be reactivated and enriched their spiritual activities. From the pulpits they advocated the establishment of new cults and devotions.[26]

The religious model proposed by the popular preachers became increasingly less influential from the last decades of the fifteenth century onwards, as it became subject to criticism in humanist intellectual milieux, and political opposition to the friars. Nonetheless, a religious position based on a

---

25  See J. Bossy, *Christianity in the West: 1400–1700* (Oxford: Oxford University Press 1985), ch. 3.

26  For a summary of this, see R. Rusconi, 'Confraternite, compagnie, devozioni', in G. Chittolini and G. Miccoli, eds., *La Chiesa e il potere politico* (Turin: Einaudi, 1986), 469–506; and for more detail, see C. F. Black, *Italian Confraternities in the Sixteenth Century* (Cambridge: Cambridge University Press, 1989).

homogenous morality aimed at the dominant classes in society and a behavioural ritualism which gathered a large part of the urban population was not fully undermined. It is significant that, in the years of crisis in Italian politics around the turn of the century, a whole series of female visionaries, the 'living saints' such as Lucia da Narni in Ferrara and others, drew much attention, as did hermits who prophesied the future, such as Bernardino da Parenzo in the Venetian Republic. Even the king of France, Louis XII, took a famous hermit, Francesco di Paola, back to his Parisian court.[27] However, the breaking down of the confessional and institutional unity of the church in Europe after the Reformation and the partial penetration of new religious ideas over the Alps into Italy, led to a realignment of both the power structures and the social classes which governed them, from the ecclesiastical politics of the papacy in Rome to the international hegemony of the Spanish crown. The final outcome of the process was the imposition of a new model of Catholic Christianity, which emphasised doctrinal orthodoxy. This is sometimes called Catholic Reform. If late-medieval preaching was based on the relationship between preaching in the vernacular and the hearing of confessions, so from the beginning of the modern era onwards, the role of the catechism and inculcation of correct beliefs became pre-eminent.

---

27 See G. Zarri, 'Living Saints: A Typology of Female Sanctity in the Early Sixteenth Century', in D. Bornstein and R. Rusconi, eds., *Women and Religion in Medieval and Renaissance Italy* (Chicago and London: University of Chicago Press,1996), 219–303, and 'Les prophètes de cour dans l'Italie de la Renaissance', in A. Vauchez, ed., *Les textes prophétiques et la prophétie en Occident (XIIe–XVIe siècle)* (Rome: École Française, 1990), 649–75.

# 31

# The Bible in the fifteenth century

## CHRISTOPHER OCKER

The medieval Bible was hardly a book at all, but a collection of ancient writings in translation. Even when unadorned by glosses or other commentary, which was rare, the Bible's sixty-six books and eight apocryphal writings were still difficult to separate from layers of interpretation. The translations of Jerome and others made the first layer (several books of the Vulgate were taken from the Latin version that predated Jerome; and the Vulgate's Psalms were in Jerome's second translation, from the Greek Septuagint, not the original Hebrew). Prologues made a second layer. The Old Testament prologues were taken from various of Jerome's writings. The New Testament prologues came from diverse sources but circulated under the saint's name. This rare, less adorned Vulgate was the form taken by early printed Bibles: text with prologues, often traditional but, as in the case of the German and Czech translations, sometimes new.[1] Usually the Bible was read in parts with commentary or in the form of semi-biblical narratives. It was less a book than a body of ancient literature at the core of past and present attempts to repeat, adapt, fathom and replicate its discourse, the 'base text' of 'highly imaginative commentaries, moralisations, and figures used to illumine the biblical significances'.[2]

It was also a controlled literature. Henry of Langenstein, while professor of theology at Vienna in the 1380s, lectured on Jerome's prologue to the Bible, before turning to the Pentateuch prologue and the book of Genesis. He made a fascinating observation. The meaning of biblical language involved both authorial and reading intentions. The souls of both writers and readers came to their tasks with certain interests and moral powers. This implied a textual

---

1 Christopher De Hamel, *The Book: A History of the Bible* (London: Phaidon, 2001), 22–4. Maurice Schild, *Abendländische Bibelvorreden bis zur Lutherbibel* (Gütersloh: Gerd Mohn, 1970). For the German and Czech prologues, See Walther and Kyas in note 43, below.
2 James H. Morey, *Book and Verse: A Guide to Middle English Biblical Literature* (Urbana: University of Illinois Press, 2000), 1–23, here 18.

community stretching over time and a mingling of wills subject to the agency of the Holy Spirit, who was responsible for inspiration at both ends of biblical literacy, the textual source and the human target. It was the Bible's state of continued animation that prevented its sense from being turned this way or that, thought Langenstein, manipulated like a stage prop, 'scripture does not have a wax nose but an iron and fiery nose!', he said in an uncomfortable metaphor.[3] A century later, Johannes Staupitz, Augustinian friar, mentor and friend of Martin Luther, noted that the language of God can be heard by those in whom the Spirit indwells.[4] Inspiration referred not to the mechanical production of words, but to the condition of holy writers and readers and their agreements with one another. Revelation had never ceased, as theologians learned from the fourteenth-century Franciscan William of Ockham, who enumerated the sources of Catholic truth: Scripture, apostolic oral tradition, custom, conclusions drawn from the first three, and new revelations. Late medieval theologians, whatever they thought of Ockham and the censures of the mid-fourteenth century, largely agreed on this.[5] The entire inspired series, from ancient record to the conclusion of a syllogism, occurred under or alongside or with (a debatable theological point) God's agency, the measure, check or control of the myriad possible thoughts and conclusions that might be associated with a portion of biblical writing. Even sceptics of prophecy believed in revelation, for example, the fifteenth-century chancellor of the University of Paris Jean Gerson, who listed personal inspiration with two other first-order sources of truth: Scripture and tradition.[6] Scholars

---

3 Stadtbibliothek Frankfurt am Main, HS 1449, f. 140ra. Christopher Ocker, *Biblical Poetics before Humanism and Reformation* (Cambridge: Cambridge University Press, 2002), 152–3. The prologue was Jerome's letter to the priest Paulinus, *Sancti Eusebii Hieronymi Epistulae*, ed. I. Hilberg (CSEL 54; Vienna: Verlag der Österreichischen Akademie der Wissenschaften, 1996), 442–65.

4 Markus Wriedt, *Gnade und Erwählung: Eine Untersuchung zu Johann von Staupitz und Martin Luther* (Mainz: Philipp von Zabern, 1991), 42. For additional examples, see Ocker, *Biblical Poetics*, 123–83.

5 Hermann Schüssler, *Der Primat der Heiligen Schrift als theologisches und kanonistisches Problem in Spätmittelalter* (Wiesbaden: Franz Steiner, 1977), 81–91. Guillelmus de Occam, *Dialogus de imperio et pontificia potestate*, I.ii.5, *Opera plurima* (Lyon, 1494–6; repr. Farnborough: Gregg, 1962), f. 9v. Franz Ehrle, *Der Sentenzenkommentar Peters von Candia* (Münster: Aschendorf, 1925), 141–3 n. 10. For the Ockham controversy, see J. M. M. H. Thijssen, *Censure and Heresy at the University of Paris, 1200–1400* (Philadelphia: University of Pennsylvania Press, 1998), passim, and William J. Courtenay, 'Was there an Ockhamist School?', in M. J. F. M. Hoenen, J. H. J. Schneider and G. Wieland, eds., *Philosophy and Learning: Universities in the Middle Ages* (Leiden: Brill, 1995), 276–91.

6 Schüssler, *Primat*, 87–8. Johannes Gerson, *Declaratio veritatum quae credendae sunt de necessitate salutis*, ed. Louis Ellies Du Pin, 5 vols. (Antwerp 1706; repr. Hildesheim: Georg Olms, 1987), vol. 1, 22.

provided scientific explanations of or corrections to an animist's view of the book, alive at its production, preservation and use, not by denying a supernatural view of it, but by rationalising and limiting it. In addition, the traditions of interpretation that prevailed in the church were held to be a matter of principle consistent with biblical teachings; continuity could be presupposed, as the extremely influential Franciscan theologian of the turn of the thirteenth to fourteenth century, John Duns Scotus, suggested.[7] The presumption of continuity has been observed in scholars as diverse as Marsilius of Inghen, Heinrich Totting of Oyta and John Wyclif in the late fourteenth century, and Jan Hus, Jean Gerson, Agostino Favaroni, Denys van Leeuwen and Wendelin Steinbach in the fifteenth.[8] At some point, everyone bowed to convention, even the English dissenters accused of Lollardy, in their way (more on this below), when they argued over the content and definition of conventional belief. The consensus was documented and subjected to dialectical experiments conducted by a professional class of educated men, and one could say that scholastic commentary and theology, in both Latin and vernacular adaptations, became the primary intellectual context of fifteenth-century biblical literacy.

The medieval genres of scholastic commentary and methods of interpretation completed their development before 1350.[9] The most important fifteenth-century innovation in biblical scholarship was Lorenzo Valla's philological commentary on the Greek New Testament (c. 1448), which did not become influential until its discovery and publication by Erasmus (1505).[10] Yet Valla's

---

7 Michael Seybold, *Die Offenbarung: Von der Schrift bis zum Ausgang der Scholastik* (Handbuch der Dogmengeschichte 1, fasc.1a; Freiburg: Herder, 1971), 143.

8 Schüssler, *Primat*, 91, 130–58. Albert Lang, *Die theologische Prinzipienlehre der mittelalterlichen Scholastik* (Freiburg im Breisgau: Herder, 1964), 175. For Wyclif, see G. A. Benrath, 'Traditionsbewusstsein, Schriftverständnis und Schriftprinzip bei Wyclif', in A. Zimmermann, ed., *Antiqui und Moderni* (Berlin: Walter de Gruyter, 1974), 359–82. For Jan Hus and Wendelin Steinbach (but contrast Gabriel Biel), see Helmut Feld, *Die Anfänge der modernen biblischen Hermeneutik in der spätmittelalterlichen Theologie* (Wiesbaden: Franz Steiner, 1977), 60, 69, 72–3. For Jean Gerson, see Mark S. Burrows, 'Jean Gerson on the "Traditioned Sense" of Scripture as an Argument for an Ecclesial Hermeneutic', in Mark S. Burrows and Paul Rorem, eds., *Biblical Hermeneutics in Historical Perspective* (Grand Rapids, Mich.: Eerdmans, 1991), 152–72. For Agostino Favaroni, see Willigis Eckermann, *Wort und Wirklichkeit: Das Sprachverständnis in der Theorie Gregors von Rimini und sein Weiterwirken in der Augustinerschule* (Würzburg: Augustinus-Verlag, 1978), 290. For Denys van Leeuwen, see Dionysius Carthusiensis, *Ennarratio in Genesim, Opera omnia*, 42 vols. (Montreuil: Typis Cartusiae S. M. de Pratis, 1896–1913), vol. 1, 15.

9 Gilbert Dahan, *L'exégèse chrétienne de la Bible en Occident médiéval, XIIe–XIVe siècle* (Paris: Éditions du Cerf, 1999) is the best general treatment. But see also De Hamel, *The Book*, 92–113 and the literature noted there.

10 Lorenzo Valla, *Collatio Novi Testamenti*, ed. Allesandro Perosa (Florence: Sansoni, 1970).

philology was anticipated by grammatical and rhetorical interpretation in twelfth-century monastic schools and in the early universities, although it was exercised there with limited knowledge of Hebrew, scarcely any Greek, and textual criticism, such as it was, restricted to the Vulgate without the Greek and Hebrew originals.[11]

We still know relatively little about late medieval Bible scholars, with the exception of John Wyclif, whose legacy was acknowledged among English dissenters in the aftermath of the controversy surrounding him. There has been far more interest in vernacular than in Latin religious writing, although many have pointed to the links between the two cultures.[12] Few detailed and sustained studies of fifteenth-century scholastic commentaries have appeared since 1959, when Wilfrid Werbeck published his study of the interpretation of the Psalms by an Aragonese Augustinian friar named Jamie Perez of Valencia.[13] The concluding part of Henri de Lubac's *Exégèse médiévale: les quatre sens de l'Écriture*, which was published in 1964, may have discouraged attention to this period when it characterised late medieval commentaries as 'decadent'.[14] Max Engammare included a survey of interpretations in his examination of the Song

---

11 Dahan, *L'exégèse chrétienne*, 213–62. Rita Copeland, *Rhetoric, Hermeneutics, and Translation in the Middle Ages* (Cambridge: Cambridge University Press, 1991), passim, and Rita Copeland, *Pedagogy, Intellectuals, and Dissent in the Later Middle Ages* (Cambridge: Cambridge University Press, 2001), 55–98. Suzanne Reynolds, *Medieval Reading: Grammar, Rhetoric and the Classical Text* (Cambridge: Cambridge University Press, 1996).

12 Gustav Adolf Benrath, *Wyclifs Bibelkommentar* (Berlin: Walter de Gruyter, 1966), remains a useful study of the commentaries. See also Beryl Smalley, 'The Bible and Eternity: John Wyclif's Dilemma', *Journal of the Warburg and Courtauld Institutes* 27 (1964), 73–89, reprinted in Beryl Smalley, *Studies in Medieval Thought and Learning* (London: Hambledon Press, 1981), 289ff., and G. R. Evans, 'Wyclif's *Logic* and Wyclif's Exegesis: The Context', in Diana Wood and Katherine Walsh, eds., *The Bible in the Medieval World: Essays in Memory of Beryl Smalley* (Oxford: Blackwell, 1985), 286–300. For changing perspectives on the Lollards, a good beginning is Fiona Somerset, 'Introduction', in Fiona Somerset, Jill C. Havens and Derrick G. Pitard, eds., *Lollards and their Influence in Late Medieval England* (Woodbridge: Boydell, 2003), 9–16, and the essays of the entire volume. Kantik Ghosh, *The Wycliffite Heresy: Authority and the Interpretation of Texts* (Cambridge: Cambridge University Press, 2002), 147–216, esp. 173, 201, 207–8, explores tacit hermeneutical agreements between Wycliffites and their opponents, related to tensions within scholasticism.

13 Wilfrid Werbeck, *Jacobus Perez von Valencia: Untersuchungen zu seinem Psalmenkommentar* (Tübingen: J. C. B. Mohr/Paul Siebeck, 1959).

14 Henri de Lubac, *Exégèse médiévale: Les quatre sens de l'Écriture*, 2 vols., with 2 parts each (Paris: Aubier, 1959–64), vol. 2.2, 369–91. Only volume 1 has been translated into English, Mark Sebanc, trans., *Medieval Exegesis: The Four Senses of Scripture* (Grand Rapids, Mich.: Eerdmans, 1998). See the comments of Alastair Minnis and Robert Lerner, in Alastair Minnis, 'Fifteenth-Century Versions of Thomistic Literalism', in R. E. Lerner, ed., *Neue Richtungen in der hoch- und spätmittelalterlichen Bibelexegese* (Munich: Oldenbourg, 1996), 178–79, and Lerner, 'Afterword', *ibid.*, 181–8.

of Songs in the Renaissance.[15] Salvatore I. Camporeale examined the relation of Valla's biblical work to his controversies.[16] Helmut Feld edited and studied the commentaries of the late fifteenth-century Tübingen professor Wendelin Steinbach.[17] There are a few brief studies of individuals. Jean Gerson, the outspoken chancellor of the University of Paris, produced several brief pieces on biblical interpretation, about which Karlfried Froehlich wrote an important article, but no one has as yet investigated Gerson's only complete Bible commentaries, one on the penitential Psalms and another on the Song of Songs.[18] Denys van Leeuwen, living in the Carthusian Charterhouse of Roermond, wrote forty-three Bible commentaries between 1434 and 1457.[19] Denys Turner treated his interpretation of the Song of Songs, but no one has yet devoted an entire monograph to any of the commentaries, or to much else of this Carthusian's 184 authentic writings.[20] Recent essays treat the literal exegesis of the Italian Dominican Giorgio of Siena, the literal exegesis of the Spanish secular priest Alfonso de Madrigal at mid-century and the Florentine Dominican Girolamo Savonarola near its close, and the somewhat nostalgic view of the Bible's fourfold meaning advocated by the Benedictine Johannes Trithemius.[21] A recent article uncovers the changing relation of allegorical reading to prophecy in Savonarola's sermons during the first months of the

15 Max Engammare, *Qu'il me baise des baisiers de sa bouche: Le Cantique des Cantiques à la Renaissance* (Geneva: Droz, 1993), 54–62.

16 Salvatore I. Camporeale, *Lorenzo Valla: Umanesimo e teologia* (Florence: Istituto Nazionale di Studi sul Rinascimento, 1972), 277–403.

17 Helmut Feld, *Martin Luthers und Wendelin Steinbachs Vorlesungen über den Hebräerbrief* (Wiesbaden: Franz Steiner, 1971). Feld has also produced an excellent edition of Steinbach's commentaries. Wendelin Steinbach, *Opera exegetica*, ed. H. Feld, 3 vols. (Wiesbaden: Franz Steiner, 1976–87).

18 Friedrich Stegmüller, *Repertorium biblicum*, 11 vols. (Madrid: Consejo Superior de Investigaciones Científicas, 1940–80), nos. 4484, 4485. Karlfried Froehlich, "'Always to Keep to the Literal Sense Means to Kill One's Soul': The State of Biblical Hermeneutics at the Beginning of the Fifteenth Century', in E. Miner, ed., *Literary Uses of Typology from the Late Middle Ages to the Present* (Princeton: Princeton University Press, 1977), 20–48.

19 *Dionysii Cartusiensis Opera Selecta*, ed. Kent Emery, vol. 1 *Bibliotheca manuscripta* (Turnhout: Brepols, 1991), 15–38, 218–54. Kent Emery, 'Denys the Carthusian and the Doxography of Scholastic Theology', in M. D. Jordan and K. Emery, eds., *Ad Litteram: Authoritative Texts and their Medieval Readers* (Notre Dame: University of Notre Dame Press, 1992), 327–59. A. Stoelen, 'De Chronologie van de werken van Dionysius de Karthuizer: De eerste werken en de schriftuurkommentaren', *Sacris erudiri* 5 (1953), 361–401. Lorna Shoemaker, 'Denys the Carthusian', in D. K. McKim, ed., *Historical Handbook of Major Biblical Interpreters* (Downers Grove, Ill.: Intervarsity Press, 1998), 95–9.

20 Denys Turner, *Eros and Allegory: Medieval Exegesis of the Song of Songs* (Kalamazoo, Mich.: Cistercian Publications, 1995).

21 Deeana Copeland Klepper, 'Literal versus carnal: George of Siena's Christian Reading of Jewish Exegesis', in Natalie Dohrmann and David Stern, eds., *Jewish Biblical Interpretation and Cultural Exchange: Comparative Exegesis in Context* (Philadelphia: University of Pennsylavania Press, 2008), 196–213. Minnis, 'Fifteenth-Century Versions

populist regime in Florence (1494).[22] One of the most influential commentaries was Nicholas of Lyra's *Postilla litteralis* on the entire Bible. Its reception has been studied only for Spain.[23] A Jewish convert who rose to the office of bishop, Pablo of Burgos, annotated Lyra early in the second quarter of the century in order to compensate, he said, for problems with Lyra's understanding of the original Hebrew and its Christian meaning. Burgos added his own prologue after Lyra's.[24] At mid-century, a Franciscan famous for his opposition to the expansion of observant reform in Germany, Matthias Döring, wrote corrections of Burgos in defence of Lyra. The early editions of Lyra (the first was printed by Weynheym and Pannartz at Rome in 1471–2) always included all three texts – Lyra's *Postilla litteralis*, Burgos' annotations and Döring's review – along with Lyra's *Postilla moralis*, Guilelmus Brito's exposition of the biblical prologues and short treatises by Lyra against Judaism.[25] The editions thus record a complex dialogue of views and arguments, which has only been studied in tiny bits and pieces.[26] Although the visual representation of biblical themes plays a well-known role in the production of visionary states, whatever links may have existed between visionary writings, images and devotion and scholastic methods of reading and interpretation have yet to be explored.[27]

of Thomistic Literalism', 163–80. Karlfried Froehlich, 'Johannes Trithemius on the Fourfold Sense of Scripture', in Richard A. Muller and John L. Thompson, eds., *Biblical Interpretation in the Era of the Reformation* (Grand Rapids, Mich.: Eerdmans, 1996), 23–60, for the Benedictine Johannes Trithemius' somewhat nostalgic advocacy of the fourfold meaning.

22 Michael O'Connor, 'The Ark and the Temple in Savonarola's Teaching (Winter 1494)', in Richard Griffiths, eds., *The Bible in the Renaissance: Essays on Biblical Commentary and Translation in the Fifteenth and Sixteenth Centuries* (Aldershot: Ashgate, 2001), 9–27.

23 Klaus Reinhardt, 'Das Werk des Nicolaus von Lyra im mittelalterlichen Spanien', *Traditio* 48 (1987), 321–58. But see also Ocker, *Biblical Poetics*, 179–83.

24 Nicholas of Lyra, *Postilla litteralis super bibliam cum adnotationibus et replicis* (Strasbourg: Anton Koberger, 1497), ff. 16rb-20vb for Burgos' prologue, which may strike the reader as less diametrically opposed to Lyra than Döring would suggest.

25 Karlfried Froehlich, 'The Printed Gloss', *Biblia Latina cum glossa ordinaria*, 4 vols., introduced by Margareth Gibson and Karlfried Froehlich (Turnhout: Brepols, 1992; repr. of Strasbourg: Adolph Rusch, 1480/1), vol. I, xii–xxvi, here xvi. The editor of the Venice edition of 1495, Bernardinus Gadolus, combined the Ordinary Gloss with Lyra-Burgos-Döring, and added a small treatise at the beginning on the books of the Bible and their translators, which was subsequently included in most editions of the Ordinary Gloss (*PL* 113, cols. 19-24). *Ibid.*, xvii.

26 James Samuel Preus, *From Shadow to Promise: Old Testament Interpretation from Augustine to the Young Luther* (Cambridge, Mass.: Harvard University Press, 1969). Reinhardt, 'Das Werk des Nicolaus von Lyra' (note 21 and very important). Scott H. Hendrix, *Ecclesia in via: Ecclesiological Developments in the Medieval Psalms of Martin Luther* (Leiden: Brill, 1974), 59–68, 80–2. Kenneth Hagen, *A Theology of Testament in the Young Luther: The Lectures on Hebrew* (Leiden: Brill, 1974), 16–17, 26–7, 50, 54, 75, 85, 96–7.

27 It is impossible to map here the poles of current debate in religious iconography and devotion, but these works may suggest them: Jeffrey Hamburger, *The Visual and the Visionary: Art and Female Spirituality in Late Medieval Germany* (New York: Zone Books,

This is the tip of a great iceberg. To recognise this, we must ignore Gerhard Groote (1340–84), the founder of the Modern Devotion, probably the most influential organised movement of piety in northern Europe. He once famously complained that scholastic speculation undermined the study of Scripture, and theologians seem to have often made similar charges.[28] Were this true, our labour could be brief. But the Bible continued to be studied in the schools. Bachelors and masters of theology were still required to lecture on it well into the sixteenth century, as they were also required to lecture on Peter Lombard's *Sentences* and to perform disputations.[29] In at least some places, like the University of Oxford, Bible study even increased. Earlier commentaries, like the *Historia scholastica* by Peter Comestor and the *Postilla* of Nicholas of Lyra, continued their popularity among students and teachers, and a number of Oxford commentaries produced in the fifteenth century survive.[30] Cambridge also continued to require Bible lectures, as did Paris and, given the influence of Paris' theology curriculum, probably every theology faculty in Europe's proliferating universities.[31] In central Europe, masters also gave biblical lectures until finally, at the end of the fifteenth century, professors of Bible were appointed alongside professors of theology

1998); James Marrow, *Passion Iconography in Northern European Art of the Late Middle Ages and Early Renaissance: A Study of the Transformation of Sacred Metaphor into Descriptive Narrative* (Kortrijk: Van Ghemmert, 1979); James Marrow, 'Art and Experience in Dutch Manuscript Illumination around 1400: Transcending the Boundaries', *The Journal of the Walters Art Gallery* 54 (1996), 101–17; Kurt Barstow, *The Gualenghi-d'Este Hours: Art and Devotion in Renaissance Ferrara* (Los Angeles: J. Paul Getty Museum, 2000), 117–202; and Reindert Falkenburg, *The Fruit of Devotion: Mysticism and the Imagery of Love in Flemish Paintings of the Virgin and Child, 1450–1550* (Amsterdam and Philadelphia: John Benjamins, 1994).

28 *Gerardi Magni Epistolae*, ed. Willelm Mulder (Tekstuitgaven van Ons Geestelijk Erf, 3; Antwerp: Uitgever Neerlandia, 1933), 23–36. R. R. Post, *The Modern Devotion: Confrontation with Reformation and Humanism* (Leiden: Brill, 1968), 81–2. Ocker, *Biblical Poetics*, 115–21. Compare William J. Courtenay, 'The Bible in the Fourteenth Century: Some Observations', *Church History* 54 (1985), 182. Jacques Verger, 'L'exégèse de l'Université', in Pierre Riché and Guy Lobrichon, eds., *Le Moyen Âge et la Bible* (Paris: Beauchesne, 1984), 225–6. Beryl Smalley, 'Problems of Exegesis in the Fourteenth Century', in Paul Wilpert, ed., *Antike und Orient im Mittelalter* (Miscellanea Mediaevallia 1; Berlin: Walter de Gruyter, 1962), 266–74.

29 Jacques Verger, 'Patterns', and Monika Asztalos, 'The Faculty of Theology', in H. De Ridder-Symoens, ed., *A History of the University in Europe*, vol. 1, *Universities in the Middle Ages* (Cambridge: Cambridge University Press, 1992), 35–74, 409–41.

30 J. I. Catto and R. Evans, eds. *The History of the University of Oxford*, vol. 2, *Late Medieval Oxford* (Oxford: Clarendon Press, 1992), 29–30, 196–8, 257, 267–8, 271, 279, 473. For the late medieval uses of Lyra, consider Ocker, *Biblical Poetics*, 179–83, and Klepper, 'Literal versus Carnal', passim.

31 Damian Riehl Leader, *A History of the University of Cambridge*, vol. 1, *The University to 1546* (Cambridge: Cambridge University Press, 1988), 173–4, 185–8.

(for example, the Augustinian friar Martin Luther).[32] Some of the works neglected by historians are massive. The Dominican Jacob of Soest lectured on parts of Ecclesiasticus, the Wisdom of Solomon, the Epistle to the Hebrews, and the Gospel according to Matthew at Cologne, leaving a manuscript of 639 pages.[33] The lectures are identified as the work of his baccalaureate, which seems hardly likely given their extraordinary length. They may be a later revision of the bachelor's lectures made at a Dominican school. Dietrich Kerkering, a secular priest and theologian at Cologne, who represented the university at the Council of Constance, lectured on the Bible.[34] Johannes of Dorsten, who, like several other prominent Augustinians of the fifteenth century, entered the order after attaining the degree of master of arts in a university (others include Johannes of Paltz, Johannes Nathin and Johannes Staupitz), lectured extensively on the Bible as regent master of the Augustinian school at Erfurt (his marginal notes have not been studied).[35]

Fifteenth-century theologians believed, like their predecessors, that the Bible was a coherent body of literature. It was arranged, they explained in various ways, according to a theological structure.[36] That structure represented the historical record of interactions between God and people, which progressed from promise and anticipation to fulfilment, from the Old Testament to the New.[37] The traditional division of each Testament into three parts appears in fifteenth-century commentaries (law, prophets, hagiography; Gospels, apostles and fathers; e.g. Denys van Leeuwen). Scholars would have known how to use the contrast of Testaments to structure a book, as the fourteenth-century Carmelite John Baconthorpe and the Franciscan Nicholas of Lyra did for the Gospel according to Matthew. They would have known of Pierre Aureol, a Franciscan master at Paris in the early

---

32 Erich Meuthen, *Kölner Universitätsgeschichte*, vol. 1, *Die alte Universität* (Vienna: Böhlau, 1988), 27, 142–3. Isnard Frank, *Hausstudium und Universitätsstudium der Wiener Dominikaner bis 1500* (Cologne: Böhlau, 1968), 173–4.

33 Meuthen, *Die alte Universität*, 143.

34 Meuthen, *Die alte Universität*, 163.

35 Adolar Zumkeller, *Erbsünde, Gnade, Rechtfertigung und Verdienst nach der Lehre der Erfurter Augustinertheologen des Spätmittelalters* (Würzburg: Augustinus-Verlag, 1984), 306–13.

36 Ocker, *Biblical Poetics*, 24–9.

37 Hugh of St Victor, *Didascalicon* iv, trans. Jerome Taylor (New York: Columbia, 1961), 102–19. Christopher Ocker, 'Fusion of Papal Ideology and Biblical Exegesis', in Burrows and Rorem, eds., *Biblical Hermeneutics in Historical Perspective*, 145. Beryl Smalley, 'John Baconthorpe's Postill on St. Matthew', *Medieval and Renaissance Studies* 4 (1958), 91–115, reprinted in Beryl Smalley, *Studies in Medieval Thought and Learning* (London: Hambledon Press, 1981). Dionysius Carthusiensis, *Enarratio in Genesim*, art. iv., *Opera omnia*, vol. 1, 13. Dahan, *L'exégèse chrétienne*, 268–71. Petrus Aureolus, *Compendium literalis sensus totius divine scripture* (Barcelona, Biblioteca de Universidad, Ms. 121), f. 6ra.

fourteenth century and author of a compendium of the Bible that rivaled Peter Comestor's *Historia scholastica* in scope and brevity. He distinguished eight parts by literary styles, by 'the eight methods of teaching that it assumes'. The Bible's purpose, defined as its 'final cause', was human salvation, a state of perfect humanity.[38] A stylistic paradox both betrayed and accomplished that purpose, according to Jerome's letter to the priest Paulinus, which served as a general prologue to most Bibles: biblical language was coarse and offensive, except to those with spiritual insight. For them, it was a sublime record of divine humility and conversation.[39] It belonged to a 'pragmatic literacy' documented and nurtured by the continuing history of interpretation.[40] In short, the Bible was a text entangled with subsequent Christian tradition and its subjective effects, an 'evolving text', as Gilbert Dahan has called it, and as such, it was studied in universities, increasingly preached and read in Europe's vernacular languages, repeated in church rites and private prayers, and displayed pictorially in devotional books and images, paintings and sculpture.[41]

It is relatively easy to trace biblical literacy from the privileged circles of learned priests and monks to less exclusive places. We may simply follow the books. The media of biblical knowledge multiplied in the late Middle Ages, while clergy extended efforts at religious conversion that had begun with the monastic reforms of the eleventh and twelfth centuries, which efforts reached well beyond monasteries in the next 200 years.[42] Perhaps the most important sign of the proliferation of biblical media was the production of vernacular translations of the Bible. They multiplied throughout Europe from the thirteenth century in various dialects of French, German, Dutch, English, Italian, Spanish, Czech and Polish, and they included a variety of semi-biblical genres that reflect uses of the Bible in liturgy, prayer and study: verse Gospels, passionals or other adaptations of Tatian's *Diatessaron*; evangelaries and other lectionary collections; verse and prose Psalters, some with Peter Lombard's glosses from the *Glossa ordinaria* or other commentary; Song of

---

38  Ocker, *Biblical Poetics*, 123–42.
39  De Hamel, *The Book*, 22–4. Ocker, *Biblical Poetics*, 112–23.
40  I adapt Nikolaus Staubach's phrase (Staubach stresses the link between reading and discipline in the *devotio moderna*), 'Pragmatische Schriftlichkeit im Bereich der Devotio moderna', *Frühmittelalterieche Studien* 25 (1991), 418–61.
41  Dahan, *L'exégèse chrétienne*, 65–73.
42  Ancient translations associated with the first expansion of Christianity in Europe (the Gothic Bible, Methodius' Slavonic translation, of which only fragments survive, or the Irish, Old English and Saxon verse translations of Psalms and the gospels, and the oldest vernacular glosses produced before the twelfth century) had no particular late medieval impact.

Songs; Apocalypses; and historical books or select narratives from the Old Testament.[43] A partial Bible was prepared for Louis IX, king of France, in the middle of the thirteenth century, and another appeared in Spanish about the same time. A complete French translation was completed in 1280. In the fourteenth century, complete Bibles were first translated into German (1350), Czech (c. 1357–60), Dutch (1360), and English (c. 1390), while French Bibles were recopied and re-translated and fragmentary translations in Italian were gathered into more complete versions. A Valencian translation of the entire Bible was completed in 1417.

The two most enduring commentaries to emerge from early scholasticism were the *Glossa ordinaria* and Peter Comestor's *Historia scholastica*. The *Glossa* was a standard commentary on the entire bible that circulated to all the schools of Europe from a centre of production at Paris in the thirteenth century.[44] It provided interpretations drawn from patristic literature. Although reproduction of the Latin *Glossa* dropped in the second half of the thirteenth century, the fact that parts of it were included in some of the

---

43  This and the following are based on these works. Jean Bonnard, *Les traduction de la Bible en vers français au Moyen Âge* (Geneva: Slatkine Reprints, 1967) for verse translations. G. W. H. Lampe, ed., *The Cambridge History of the Bible*, vol. 2, *The West from the Fathers to the Reformation* (Cambridge: Cambridge University Press, 1969), 362–87, 415–52, 462–91. Bettye Thomas Chambers, *Bibliography of French Bibles: Fifteenth- and Sixteenth-Century French-Language Editions of the Scriptures* (Geneva: Droz, 1983), 1–34. Amin Doumit, *Deutscher Bibeldruck von 1466–1522* (St Katharinen: Scripta Mercaturae, 1997), 10–11. Wilhelm Walther, *Die deutsche Bibelübersetzung des Mittelalters* (Nieuwkoop: B. De Graaf, 1966), cols. 741–5. J. A. A. M. Biemans, *Middelnederlandse Bijbelhandschriften* (Leiden: Brill, 1984), passim. G. C. Zieleman, *Middelnederlandse epistel- en evangeliepreken* (Leiden: Brill, 1978), 57–9. Mikel M. Kors, 'Die Bibel für Laien: Neuansatz oder Sackgasse? Der Bibelübersetzer von 1360 und Gerhard Zerbolt von Zutphen', in Nikolaus Staubach, ed., *Kirchenreform von unten: Gerhard Zerbolt von Zutphen und die Brüder vom gemeinsamen Leben* (Frankfurt am Main: Peter Lang, 2004), 243–63, here 244–8. Vladimír Kyas, 'Die alttschechische Bibelübersetzung des 14. Jahrhunderts und ihre Entwicklung im 15. Jahrhundert', in Martin of Tišov, *Kutnahorská Bible/Kuttenberger Bibel*, ed. Reinhold Olesch and Hans Rothe, 2 vols. (Paderborn: Ferdinand Schöningh, 1989), vol. 2, 9-32. *Die alttschechische Dresdener Bible/Drážd'anská anebo Leskovecká bible*, ed. Hans Rothe and Friedrich Scholz (Paderborn: Ferdinand Schöningh, 1993). Margaret Deanesly, *The Lollard Bible and other Medieval Biblical Versions* (Cambridge: Cambridge University Press, 1922), 131–55. James H. Morey, *Book and Verse: A Guide to Middle English Biblical Literature* (Urbana: University of Illinois Press, 2000). Ralph Hanna, 'English Biblical Text before Lollardy', in Fiona Somerset, Jill C. Havens and Derrick G. Pitard, eds., *Lollards and their Influence in Late Medieval England* (Woodbridge: Boydell, 2003), 141–53.

44  Christopher De Hamel, *Glossed Books of the Bible and the Origins of the Paris Booktrade* (Woodbridge: D. S. Brewer, 1984). Guy Lobrichon, 'Une nouveauté: les gloses de la Bible', in Riché and Lobrichon, eds., *Le Moyen Âge et la Bible*, 99–110. Beryl Smalley, *The Study of the Bible in the Middle Ages* (Oxford: Blackwell, 1942, 1952), 46–52. Mark A. Zier, 'The Manuscript Tradition of the *glossa ordinaria* for Daniel and Hints at a Method for a Critical Edition', *Scriptorium* 47 (1993), 3–25, esp. 3–5 remains an excellent summary of scholarship.

translations I have just noted points to its continued usefulness.[45] The *Historia scholastica* was a biblical manual whose mixture of narrative and exegesis served to coordinate diverse sources from within the Bible and between the Bible and profane history.[46] It was expanded and translated into French (1280), Catalan (1287) and Dutch (1361) and adapted piecemeal from the thirteenth century in most if not all European languages.[47] Most of these texts survive from monastic libraries. Those that were commissioned or owned by laity were usually aristocratic or royal possessions.[48] One should also consider adaptations, manuals and semi-biblical works in the vernacular, as James Morey has recently emphasised on the example of England. These include the original *Bible moralisée* prepared in Latin for King Louis VIII of France between 1220 and 1226 (a compilation of paraphrases, commentaries and interpretive images that served as the prototype of later vernacular versions), John of Caulibus' *Meditations on the Life of Christ*, which circulated widely under the name of St Bonaventure, the Carthusian Ludolf of Saxony's *Life of Christ*, the Augustinian Hermit Simon Fidati da Cascia's *Works of the Lord Savior*, selections and adaptations from the *Legenda Aurea*, a glossed *Diatessaron* in Italian from the late thirteenth century, a Dutch sermon collection with the Ordinary Gloss written before 1370, and Latin-Czech Bible dictionaries based on the *Mammotrectus*, a dictionary composed by the early fourteenth-century Franciscan Giovanni Marchesini (the Latin was published some twenty times before 1500).[49] The first complete Czech and English Bibles were also provided with new prologues.

45 On the drop in production, see Lobrichon, 'Une nouveauté: les gloses de la Bible', 101 n. 18.
46 Dahan, *L'exégèse chrétienne*, 276–7.
47 James H. Morey, 'Peter Comestor, Biblical Paraphrase, and the Medieval Popular Bible', *Speculum* 68 (1993), 6–35. James H. Morey, *Book and Verse*.
48 Examples in Walther, *Die deutsche Bibelübersetzung*, cols. 729–31, and Bonnard, Robson, Morreale, Kyas and Kors in note 43, above. The translator of the Dutch *Historiebijbel* of 1361 was responsible for a small library of religious works, several commissioned by the Brussels patrician, Jan Taye. See Kors, 'Die Bibel für Laien', 244–8.
49 Sara Lipton, *Images of Intolerance: The Representation of Jews and Judaism in the Bible moralisée* (Berkeley: University of California, 1999), 1–13, esp. 8 with n. 47. Kyas in note 43, above and Kenelm Foster, 'Vernacular Scriptures in Italy', in Lampe, ed., *Cambridge History of the Bible*, vol. 2, 452–65. For the *Mammetrectus*, see Stegmüller, *Repertorium biblicum*, nos. 4776–7. John of Caulibus, *Meditations on the Life of Christ*, trans F. X. Taney, A. Miller and C. M. Stallings-Taney (Asheville: Pegasus Press, 2000), xiv–xxvi, xxviii–xxx. Simon Fidati da Cascia, *De gestis domini salvatoris*, ed. W. Eckermann, 7 vols. (Würzburg: Cassiciacum, 1998). Walter Baier, *Untersuchungen zu den Passionsbetrachtungen in der Vita Christi des Ludolf von Sachsen: Ein quellenkritischer Beitrag zu Leben und Werk Ludolfs und zur Geschichte der Passionstheologie* (Salzburg: Analecta Cartusiana, Institut für Englische Sprache und Literatur, 1977).

All of this production – scholastic commentaries, the growing number of translations, and the variety of biblical texts and adaptations – is evidence of a thriving clerical culture that increasingly drew laity in its wake. But we should not overestimate the number and diversity of its beneficiaries. Many of these books were produced for the wealthiest people in Europe.[50] While others clearly point to a broadening readership, they could only be named 'popular' in some restricted sense. The character of the broadest readership is suggested by the famous late medieval block book, the *Biblia pauperum*, which also exists in over eighty manuscripts. It was probably written in Germany before 1300, and it circulated widely throughout central Europe. Christopher De Hamel has recently called it 'one of the most intellectually sophisticated of medieval biblical commentaries', a work clearly not written for amateurs.[51] As was also the case with the early printed copies of the Vulgate and Bible translations, most of its owners appear to have been monasteries, and many copies exist only in fragment.[52] It was designed for the trained eye, with forty pictures arranged two to the page, each consisting of two captioned scenes from the Old Testament divided vertically by scenes from the life of Christ and Mary and flanked by four small figures from the Old Testament and quotations from the Psalms or other texts. The book was obviously meant to represent the balanced parallels of the two Testaments, linked by spiritual themes. Other books followed a similar design. The *Genealogy of the Life of Christ* by Peter of Poitiers (1167–1205) circulated in manuscript and woodcut editions. It presented a pictorial life of Christ and the Blessed Virgin coordinated with Old Testament prophecies. The *Speculum humanae salvationis* (c. 1310–24) was divided into forty pictures, like the *Biblia pauperum*, each usually composed with four illustrations (some 394 manuscripts of the *Speculum* survive[53]). Books of hours, adaptations of the divine office, the monastic cycle of daily prayer, and in particular the Hours of the Blessed Virgin, a prayer office in honour of Mary, used psalms and passages from Job, the Song of Songs, and other Old Testament books, accompanied by images, some of which were identical to those of the *Biblia pauperum*.[54] In addition to these works, which documented

50 For this and the following, see De Hamel, *The Book*, 140–65. Consider also the early thirteenth-century problem of interpretation by text and image and the control of meaning. Lipton, *Images of Intolerance*, 54–81 and passim.
51 De Hamel, *The Book*, 158–63.
52 Walther, *Die deutsche Bibelübersetzung*, cols. 729–31.
53 Morey, *Book and Verse*, 112 and de Hamel, *The Book*, 158–63.
54 John Harthan, *Books of Hours and their Owners* (London: Thames and Hudson, 1977). Paul Saenger, 'Books of Hours and the Reading Habits of the Late Middle Ages', *Scrittura e Civiltà* 9 (1985), 239–69.

the past fulfilment of prophecy, Apocalypse block books advertised future prophecies. They were probably first printed in the Netherlands in the middle of the century. The majority of them circulated in the third quarter of the fifteenth century. They included pictorial representations of its prophecies. Song of Songs block books suggested allegorical interpretations.[55] Finally, a text known as the *Historia David* illustrated the ancient king's life according to the books of Kings.

Although some of these works, most obviously the Books of Hours, adapted a clerical text to a non-clerical audience, they were not designed for mass circulation, like indulgenced wood-block images of the Blessed Virgin or the *arma Christi*. They represent less a free lay religiosity than devotion tutored by clergy. Much of the increased circulation was in Latin.[56] Ecclesiastical prohibitions discouraged biblical literacy outside clergy control. To the old prohibitions of Waldensian translations came a new prohibition inspired by fear of Wycliffites and 'Lollards' and Hussites at the Council of Basel (1431–48).[57] Perhaps because of the upheaval around Wyclif and his followers, the dangers of the Hussite revolution, the coming of the printing press, and the origins of Protestantism, one tends to look to England and Germany for late medieval opposition to Bible translations, where translation and literal reading had been clearly politicised.[58] The 1407 prohibition of Bible translation and reading of Scripture in English stood among other prohibitions intended to hinder Wycliffite ideas and controversy, reflecting an association of heresy and vernacular reading that only grew at the end of the fourteenth century in England.[59] In the Holy Roman Empire, Johannes Schele, the secretary of the emperor Sigismund, and the bishop of Lübeck in 1433 prohibited translations from the Gospels, the Psalter or sacred Scripture overall, from which, they said, heresy and confusion among the *clergy* arise.[60] In 1486,

---

55  Engammare, *Qu'il me baise*, 65–7, 378–404.
56  Consider the case of Psalters: Mary Kay Duggan, 'The Psalter on the Way to the Reformation: The Fifteenth-Century Printed Psalter in the North', in Nancy Van Deusen, ed., *The Place of the Psalms in the Intellectual Culture of the Middle Ages* (Albany: State University Press of New York, 1999), 153–89.
57  Jürgen Miethke and Lorenz Weinrich, eds., *Ausgewählte Quellen zur deutschen Geschichte des Mittelalters*, 2 vols. (Darmstadt: Wisenschaftliche Buchgesellschaft, 1995), vol. 2, 44. The early legislation is summarized by Deanesly, *The Lollard Bible*, 18–57, and Morey, *Book and Verse*, 26–37.
58  Copeland, *Pedagogy*, 99–140.
59  Anne Hudson, *Lollards and their Books* (London: Hambledon Press, 1985), 146–63. Morey, *Book and Verse*, 37–44. Nicholas Watson, 'Censorship and Cultural Change in Late-Medieval England: Vernacular Theology, the Oxford Translation Debate, and Arundel's Constitutions of 1409', *Speculum* 70 (1995), 822–64.
60  Miethke and Weinrich, eds., *Ausgewählte Quellen*, vol. 2, 228.

the bishop elect of Mainz, Bertold von Henneberg, issued an edict against Bible translations from Greek and Latin, on the grounds that some language in holy texts cannot be translated into German and cannot be comprehended by the uneducated. A year later, Pope Innocent VIII ordered all bishops to control the publication of religious literature.[61] None of this amounted to overwhelming opposition. It is nothing like the politics of translation in the sixteenth century. The church's position with regard to translation was 'one of toleration in principle, and distrust in practice'.[62]

Apart from Wycliffites, no one seems to have advocated unrestricted Bible reading, and the vernacular production of theology may have declined overall in the fifteenth century.[63] The anonymous translator of the Dutch *Historia scholastica*, the *Historiebijbel* of 1361, dismissed the idea of a clerical monopoly on religious literacy, yet his patron, Jan Taye, a Brussels patrician, had to coax him repeatedly to tackle the Wisdom books, whose perils for lay readers the translator tried to navigate with a prologue that coaches one never to take these books too literally.[64] Apart from Wycliffites, the most famous late medieval advocates of lay reading were promoters of the *Devotio moderna*, who have been both praised as the forerunners of the Lutheran principle of scriptural primacy or biblical humanism and maligned as narrow-minded anti-intellectuals. The *Devotio moderna* repeated the reservations found in the prologue to the Dutch *Historiebijbel*.[65] Gerhard Zerbolt of Zutphen defended lay study in his *On Books in German* (*De libris teutonicalibus*, 1393/4). But he advocated restricted lay reading: of the Bible, the laity may only read the Gospels and the Acts of the Apostles without danger. The historical books of the Old Testament are especially perilous, because they present norms and customs that must not be imitated.[66] This was a traditional clerical

---

61  Doumit, *Deutscher Bibeldruck von 1466–1522*, 14–15. In 1496, on the basis of the papal bull, the archbishop of Cologne introduced censure in his region, threatening to excommunicate those who published any book without his permission.
62  Deanesly, *The Lollard Bible*, 372.
63  As Watson argued for England, 'Censorship and Cultural Change', 847–59. Morey also argued that there was greater tolerance of vernacular religious literature in England, until the early fourteenth century. Morey, *Book and Verse*, 37–44, 56–84.
64  Kors, 'Die Bibel für Laien', 257–8.
65  Staubach, 'Pragmatische Schriftlichkeit', 421–2.
66  Kors, 'Die Bibel für Laien', 259–63. Nikolaus Staubach, 'Gerhard Zerbolt von Zutphen und die Apologie der Laienlektüre in der Devotio moderna', in Thomas Kock and Rita Schusemann, ed., *Laienlektüre und Buchmarkt im späten Mittelalter* (Frankfurt am Main: Peter Lang, 1997), 221–89, here 237–63.

reservation over the competence of the laity in matters theological.[67] But the real goal was reading for virtue, as we will see. It has been suggested that Zerbolt's caution responded to accusations of heresy brought against the Brethren and Sisters of the Common Life at the end of the fourteenth century.[68] Fifteenth-century trends could only reinforce the cultural boundaries suggested by restricted spiritual reading: over the course of the century the Brethren and Sisters did not form the bud of a lay movement that flowered in the Reformation. Rather, they increasingly emphasised the internal life of their houses, and the character of their movement became increasingly monastic.[69]

Lay reading was, potentially, both good and bad. The fifteenth-century church knew no total censure of Bible translation. How many would agree with the German Augustinian friar, Gottschalk Hollen, who a generation after Zerbolt observed that vernacular Bible reading was as good for Germans as it was in ancient times for Greeks, Hebrews, Chaldeans, Goths, Slavs and Russians? The real danger was philosophical literature, which inspired one to glory in sophistic cleverness.[70] Many, probably, would agree, but that is not quite the same as a rush on religious books.

Biblical knowledge belonged to the society of the clergy, and it therefore implied the church's forms of government, with the sacramental economy that routinely distributed the Holy Spirit to people, and it depended on the church's cultural vanguard, who were not the same vanguard modern scholars have often admired. In the fifteenth century, the church's vanguard were not really the humanists. Nor did they belong to the Modern Devotion, often mistaken for such, which advocated controlled reading. There is little to suggest that the kind of animated text, with its time-defying presupposition of ecclesiastical consensus and the affinity of sincere minds across the centuries, was undermined anywhere by anyone, perhaps least of all by the biblicism of late medieval heretics, even though the orthodox worried that bad

---

67 Copeland, *Pedagogy*, 107–8.
68 Kors in n. 66 and Staubach and Kock in the next note.
69 Staubach, 'Pragmatische Schriftlichkeit', 424. Thomas Kock, 'Theorie und Praxis der Laienlektüre im Einflußbereich der Devotio moderna', in Kock and Schuseman, eds., *Laienlektüre und Buchmarkt*, 199–220. Theo Klausmann, *Consuetudo Consuetudine Vincitur: Die Hausordnungen der Brüder vom gemeinsamen Leben im Bildungs- und Sozialisationsprogramm der Devotio moderna* (Bern: Peter Lang, 2003), 179–80, 216, 225, 233, 246, 300, 309, and especially 273–4.
70 Volker Honemann, 'Gottschalk Hollen, De vera et falsa scriptura. Zur Rezeption des siebten Hauptstückes von Zerbolts Traktat "Super modo vivendi devotorum hominum simul commorantium"', in Staubach, ed., *Kirchenreform von unten*, 276–86.

literal readings lurked behind crises of authority.[71] The vanguard may rather have appeared to be people like Jean Gerson, disgusted with heresy, preoccupied with moral order, and insisting on the continuity of reading with tradition.[72]

Let us consider the accused. Waldensianism was a movement begun around an interpretation of the gospel and vernacular Bible reading in the late twelfth century. But in spite of periodic inquisitorial prosecutions of heretics accused of hybrid Waldensian teachings, only five writings from the entire period between 1230 and 1520 claim to be original Waldensian works, none of them biblical.[73] They were all written about 1368. If they are authentic, as scholars tend to believe, they nevertheless give us no reason to think that Waldensianism contributed to popular biblical literacy, although it is clear that theologians and inquisitors associated biblicism with the heresy.[74] When people claimed to produce books as Waldensians again, in the 1520s, the literature comprised lowbrow Catholic devotion, religious poetry and fragments of Bible translations, with some Hussite and Protestant material alongside it.[75] Apart from the Hussite and Protestant bits, it was identical with what one observes among orthodox writers. In England, the response to Wyclif raised a prolonged debate over the status of vernacular theology, whether or not Wycliffites helped erode the clerical privilege associated with theological Bible reading.[76] The opponents of Wycliffites believed that the use of

---

71 Consider Jean Gerson, Jean Petit and the assassination of the duke of Orléans by the duke of Burgundy. Froehlich, 'Always to Keep to the Literal Sense', 27–43. Ocker, *Biblical Poetics*, 165–9. Also, Ghosh, *The Wycliffite Heresy*, 215, and the association of rebellion with Lollardy as examined by Copeland, *Pedagogy*, 99–140, and the relation of biblical reading and social action, built upon the analogy of biblical characters and the contemporary church or a particular group within it, as examined by Michael P. Kuczynski, 'The Psalms and Social Action in Late Medieval England', in Van Deusen, ed., *The Place of the Psalms*, 191–214.

72 Froehlich, 'Always to Keep to the Literal Sense', 20–48. Burrows, 'Jean Gerson on the "traditioned sense of scripture"', 152–72. Ocker, *Biblical Poetics*, 119, 165–8. For Gerson's influence in his own generation and after, see Brian Patrick McGuire, *Jean Gerson and the Last Medieval Reformation* (College Park: Pennsylvania State University, 2005), chs. 7, 11.

73 Euan Cameron, *Waldenses: Rejections of Holy Church in Medieval Europe* (Oxford: Blackwell, 2000), 118–25. The manuscripts are noted in Jean Gonnet and Amedeo Molnar, *Les vaudois au Moyen Âge* (Turin: Claudiana, 1974), 447–50. Cameron adds a sixteenth-century Cambridge copy, *Waldenses*, 118–25. I am leaving out the question of the Waldensian Bible, what it was and how it circulated. See also Peter Biller, *The Waldenses, 1170–1530: Between a Religious Order and a Church* (Aldershot: Ashgate, 2001), 1–23.

74 Gonnet and Molnar, *Les vaudois*, 197–202.

75 *Ibid.*, 216–26.

76 Hudson, *Lollards and their Books*, 141–63. Copeland, *Pedagogy*, 114–40. Watson, 'Censorship and Cultural Change', 847–51.

vernacular Scriptures led to heresy and rebellion. It is still difficult to assess the extent and nature of the dissenting movement, insofar as 'Lollard' books portray a religion less dramatically singular, and they made clerical culture and its tools of biblical study more broadly accessible; they did not merely dismiss received methods and tools.[77] Wycliffite glosses argued points of doctrine, but also followed school practice, citing the Ordinary Gloss, Nicholas of Lyra and orthodox theologians.[78] Their identification of the pope as Antichrist and their allegation of the corruption of friars and the clergy were also known in Latin literature, at least some of it orthodox; the allegations against friars were widely shared. Although Wycliffite biblicism did emphasise vernacular reading, their biblical glosses and their sermons included traditional content, for example, the interpretation of passages according to the fourfold sense.[79]

This was a conservative century for the church, marked by reactions to Hussites and Wycliffites and by attempts to restore papal monarchy and adapt to the encroaching impossibility of papal temporal influence outside Italy. Biblical literacy was supposed to characterise the culture of an effective clergy, beginning at the top. According to Mattheus of Cracow's jeremiad against the papal schism, *On the Filth of the Papal Court* (*De squaloribus curie*, 1403), papal lordship over clergy was restricted by the gospel, the entire canon of Scripture, and the councils of the church.[80] Mattheus had been confessor to the electoral Prince Palatine Ruprecht III and his counsel for some years when Ruprecht was elected German king in 1400. What was true for the first bishop of Christendom in Rome was true for all other prelates everywhere. Pierre d'Ailly (1350/1–1420), the famous French conciliarist, insisted at the Council of Constance (1414–18) that high prelates cultivate spiritual, abbot-like habits. They should be elderly, discrete, spiritually minded men who care more about the church than their own lordly affairs, and 'people who study the

---

77  Copeland, *Pedagogy*, 131–40. Fiona Somerset, 'Here, There, and Everywhere? Wycliffite Conceptions of the Eucharist and Chaucer's "Other" Lollard Joke', in Somerset, Havens and Pitard, eds., *Lollards and their Influence*, 127–38. Morey, *Book and Verse*, ch. 4. Hanna, 'English Biblical Texts', 152: '[The Blackfriars condemnations of May 1382], like Arundel's later one, was surely abortive, and failed to stem the composition and the later encroachment into nonheterodox circles of Lollard vernacular scripture. Such a view – which denatures the provacateurism of the Wycliffite biblical book – would suggest that the persistent interest in Wycliffism as oppositional and revolutionary may occlude much of the historical dynamic at work.'

78  Anne Hudson, *The Premature Reformation: Wycliffite Texts and Lollard History* (Oxford: Clarendon Press, 1988), 228–77. Ghosh, *The Wycliffite Heresy*, 7–8.

79  Hudson, *Lollards and their Books*, 184–91. H. Leith Spencer, *English Preaching in the Late Middle Ages* (Oxford: Clarendon Press, 1993), 192–3.

80  Miethke and Weinrich, eds., *Ausgewählte Quellen*, vol. 1, 126.

divine scriptures and don't totally cling to the practical and legal sciences', a study intrinsic to virtue: they should be an example to the faithful. Their stoic demeanour should include modest dress and temperate eating while giving ear to Bible lessons during meals.[81] The point was not reading/hearing but the acquisition of character, a virtue-oriented version of St Augustine's view of scriptural learning as an instrument of the enjoyment of God, never an end in itself.[82] Nicholas of Cusa's advice to Pope Pius II, in his *Reformacio generalis* of 1458/9, was this: those who rise to the place of the apostles (that is, bishops) must be conformed to Christ (*Christiformes*) in order to shape others like Christ. All divinely inspired Scripture reveals desire, the desire for Christ, who is the form of virtues, immortal life and eternal happiness.[83]

Cusa adapts a scholastic commonplace, that Scripture reading produces a soul, a self of certain moral powers.[84] The *Devotio moderna* promoted this methodically, making sacred reading – with book manufacture – a central practice, just as it had been advocated as a spiritual discipline by Bernard of Clairvaux, Hugh of St Victor, William of Saint-Thiery and David of Augsburg, twelfth- and thirteenth-century monastic writers still famous in the late Middle Ages.[85] Not just any manner of reading. Florent Radewijns' *Little Book of Devotion* instructed the devout to read with the specific purpose of uprooting vices from the soul and planting virtues. 'One ought not simply to read in order to know, but to read for knowledge' (*Et non debet simpliciter studere propter scire, vel propter scienciam*). He modelled the stages of vice-eradication training on Bonaventure's scheme: reading, meditation, then prayer.[86] Florent expanded Bonaventure in a practical, if pedestrian way. Connect all sacred reading to charity and the virtues. Read whole books, not just passages. Follow a schedule. Pick out points to memorise and ruminate. Let yourself be moved and pray. Choose books that lead to a pure heart and charity. The trajectory of reading is the same as the inward trajectory of passional devotion,

---

81 Miethke and Weinrich, eds., *Ausgewählte Quellen*, vol. 1, 354-7, from Petrus de Alliaco, *De reformacione ecclesie* (October 1416, at the Council of Constance), ch. 3.

82 Margaret Gibson, 'The *De doctrina christiana* in the School of St. Victor', in E. D. English, ed., *Reading and Wisdom: The* De doctrina christiana *of Augustine in the Middle Ages* (Notre Dame: University of Notre Dame Press, 1995), 41–7.

83 Miethke and Weinrich, eds., *Ausgewählte Quellen*, vol. 2, 472.

84 Ocker, *Biblical Poetics*, 149–61.

85 Staubach, 'Pragmatische Schriftlichkeit', 428–55. For book production, see Thomas Kock's case study of the scriptorium of the Brethren's house at Wesel, 'Theorie und Praxis der Laienlektüre', 199–220.

86 Florent Radewijns, *Petit manuel pour le dévot moderne: Tractatulus devotus*, ed. and trans. Francis Joseph Legrand (Turnhout: Brepols, 1999), vii., 74–81. Bonaventure, *De triplici via*, prologue, ed. Quaracchi, 8:3.

and here too Florent is hardly original.[87] Daily meditation on Christ's Passion should follow a weekly schedule, so he listed Passion-scenes by days and included admonitory prompts for meditation.

The same purposefulness, attached to Bible reading, is apparent in the clergy's most direct effort to influence congregated people, their public oratory. Like Latin and vernacular Bibles, sermons comprised not a pure but a 'fluid genre', an 'intermediary discourse', which coincided with efforts at religious conversion and self-formation.[88] Hearing, perhaps more so than reading, was supposed to perform the union of scriptural narrative to a soul shaped by virtues. The preacher was subject to inspiration, following the presupposition of a holy and inspired continuum reaching from biblical writers to modern readers.[89] This continuum was originally a clerical presupposition, as we have seen. Preaching, together with the Bibles, commentaries and semi-biblical adaptations we have examined, had long been primarily a clerical affair, in universities, among monks in their cloisters, and at church councils and courts (the papal court was the most prestigious preaching venue). But since the thirteenth century, preaching followed the avenues of monastic influence into beguinages, hospitals, lay religious orders and confraternities.[90] Sermons occurred on Sundays and feast days, alongside rogation processions or upon the announcement of special graces, along procession routes, and in the parish churches of cities and suburbs, cathedrals, monastery churches, princely chapels, royal halls and public squares.[91] Of all the media of biblical knowledge, we can assume that more people experienced this oral one

87 Radewijns, *Petit manuel / Tractatulus devotus*, li–lvii, 159–71.
88 Beverly Mayne Kienzle, 'Introduction', in Kienzle, ed., *The Sermon* (Typologie des sources du moyen âge occidental fasc. 81–3; Turnhout: Brepols, 2000), 148–9, 153–4, 168, and Kienzle, 'Conclusion', in *The Sermon*, 964–5. Larissa Taylor, 'French Sermons, 1215–1535', in *The Sermon*, 734. Carlo Delcorno, 'Medieval Preaching in Italy (1200–1500)', in *The Sermon*, 483 n. 103, 507, 510. Mark D. Johnston, 'The *Rethorica nova* of Ramon Llull: An *Ars praedicandi* as Devotional Literature', in Thomas L. Amos, Eugene A. Green and Beverly Mayne Kienzle, eds., *De ore domini: Preacher and Word in the Middle Ages* (Studies in Medieval Culture, 27; Kalamazoo, Mich.: Western Michigan University, 1989), 119–45. Lawrence F. Hundermarck, 'Preaching the Passion: Late Medieval "Lives of Christ" as Sermon Vehicles', in Amos *et al.*, eds., *De ore domini*, 147–67.
89 Kienzle, 'Introduction', 153–4.
90 Delcorno, 'Medieval Preaching in Italy', 493, 483–6. Manuel Ambrosio Sánchez Sánchez, 'Vernacular Preaching in Spanish Portuguese and Catalan', in Kienzle, ed., *The Sermon*, 885. Hans-Jochen Schiewer, 'German Sermons in the Middle Ages', in *The Sermon*, 885–93, 922–4. J.-M. Mayeur, Ch. Pietri, A. Vauchez and M. Venard, eds., *Histoire du Christianisme des origines à nos jours*, vol. 6 (Paris: Desclée, 1995), 369-70, and for late medieval preaching in general, 369–87 and the literature noted there.
91 Anne Riising, *Danmarks middelalderlige Praediken* (Copenhagen: G. E. C. Gads, 1969), 87–115. Schiewer, 'German Sermons', 885–93. *Histoire du Christianisme*, vol. 6, 271–2.

than any other, for the simple reason that the vast majority of readers could hear, but far from all hearers could read.

The question is, what kind of biblical literacy did sermons represent or promote? As in so much of our knowledge of fifteenth-century religion in Europe, there remains a great deal to be learned, not only about sermon production, but also about the transmission and use of older collections.[92] Two general observations are permissible. First, the biblical literacy of preaching surely included a scholastic presupposition about divine speech, namely, that holy discourse, like ancient prophecy, reflected the mingling of divine and human wills and voices. But this presupposition may have become less compelling than the later idea that good sermons replicated scriptural eloquence, an idea that reflected a humanistic framework of classical rhetoric.[93] Second, the religious knowledge evident in sermons was consistent with the animated text of the Bible, as conceived in the Latin and vernacular biblical and semi-biblical literature we have considered.

This is suggested, in part, by scholastic models of the sermon. The 'modern' sermon form, promoted throughout Europe since the late thirteenth century in manuals of the *Artes praedicandi*, departed from the simple exposition of biblical narratives, phrase by phrase, which was known in ancient Christian preaching.[94] In the modern sermon, a theme was usually taken from a Gospel lesson, cited in Latin, and developed by a series of divisions or distinctions that organised the

---

92 Considerable background work on sermon texts and transmission has begun for Germany, in conjunction with the *Repertorium der ungedruckten deutschsprachigen Predigten des Mittelalters* at the Free University of Berlin. Schiewer, 'German Sermons', 885–95. Hans-Jochen Schiewer, *Die Schwarzwälder Predigten: Entstehungs- und Überlieferungsgeschichte der Sonntags- und Heiligenpredigten* (Tübingen: Max Niemeyer, 1996), 310–27. Andreas Rüther and Hans-Jochen Schiewer, 'Die Predigthandschriften des Straßburger Dominikanerinnenklosters St. Nikolaus in undis. historischer Bestand, Geschichte, Vergleich', and Monika Costard, 'Predigthandschriften der Schwestern vom gemeinsamen Leben. Spätmittelalterliche Predigtüberlieferung in der Bibliothek des Klosters Nazareth in Geldern', in Volker Mertens and Hans-Jochen Schwieger, eds., *Die deutsche Predigt im Mittelalter* (Tübingen: Max Niemeyer, 1992), 169–93, 194–222.
93 Ocker, *Biblical Poetics*, 184–213 and the literature noted there.
94 Larissa Taylor, *Soldiers of Christ: Preaching in Late Medieval and Reformation France* (New York: Oxford, 1992), 60–9. For the development of the modern sermon at Paris in the early thirteenth century, see Nicole Bériou, *L'avènement des maîtres de la Parole: La prédication à Paris au XIIIe siècle*, 2 vols. (Paris: Institut d'Études Augustiniennes, 1998), vol. 1, 133–214. Herve Martin, *Le métier de prédicateur à la fin du Moyen Âge 1350–1520* (Paris: Cerf, 1988), 235–68. Consider, too, the observations by Simon Tugwell, '*De huiusmodi sermonibus texitur omnis recta predicatio*: Changing Attitudes towards the Word of God', in Jacqueline Hamese and Xavier Hermand, eds., *De l'homélie au sermon: Histoire de la prédication médiévale* (Louvain: Université Catholique de Louvain, 1993), 159–68, here 166–7.

discourse according to a more or less dialectical architecture combining material from the Bible, church fathers, philosophers, theologians and other ancient writers.[95] Mystical sermons, which we might expect to emphasise religious subjectivity, usually followed the same kind of structure.[96] The method of interpretation in 'modern' sermons matched patterns found in scholastic Bible commentaries, which associated the words and ideas of a passage's literal sense with contemporary ideas, religious affects or moral instruction.[97] This may seem to overwhelm biblical meaning with extraneous ideas, but the Bible was the most heavily cited source in sermons, among the typical melange of scholastic authorities and moral *exempla*: 'the biblical verse is the root from which springs the tree of the sermon'.[98] The point was to connect biblical literature to religious truth and its subjective consequences. Commentaries were intended to produce the same effect.[99] Celebrity preachers intensified the subjective effect of the sermon in public spectacles before mass audiences, for example, Vincent Ferrer, John of Capistrano, Bernardino of Siena and Girolamo Savonarola, coupling their condemnations of luxury, feuding and narcissism with demands for immediate conversion in the face of apocalyptic doom, the endpoint of biblical history.[100] Perhaps their preaching had less to do with the internal re-imaging of biblical narratives, familiar in devotion to the Passion of Christ, than with the repetition of moral demands that belonged to an internalised gospel.[101] In England, at least, the modern sermon never completely

95  Mayeur, *et al.*, eds., *Histoire du Christianisme*, vol. 6, 374-6.

96  Schiewer, 'German sermons', 905–11.

97  Martin, *Le métier de prédicateur*, 261-7. Zieleman, *Middelnederlandse epistel- en evangeliepreken*, 24–9.

98  The quotation is from Delcorno, 'Medieval Preaching in Italy', 471. For citations in sermons, see Taylor, *Soldiers of Christ*, 73–6.

99  Johannes Baptist Schneyer, *Die Unterweisung der Gemeinde über die Predigt bei scholastischen Predigern: Eine Homiletik aus scholastischen Prothemen* (Munich: Ferdinand Schöningh, 1968), passim. Silvana Vecchio, 'Le prediche e l'istruzione religiosa', in *La predicazione dei Frati dalla metà desl '200 alla fine del '300* (Spoleto: Centro Italiano di Studi sull'Alto Medioevo, 1995), 301–35.

100  Delcorno, 'Medieval Preaching in Italy', 467, 479–83. Sánchez Sánchez, 'Vernacular Preaching in Spanish', 772–3. Franco Mormando, *The Preacher's Demons: Bernardino of Siena and the Social Underworld of Early Renaissance Italy* (Chicago: University of Chicago Press, 1999). For prophecy, consider also John V. Fleming, 'Christopher Columbus as a Scriptural Exegete', in Burrows and Rorem, eds., *Biblical Hermeneutics in Historical Perspective*, 173–83.

101  Thomas Lentes, '"Andacht" und "Gebärde". Das religiöse Ausdrucksverhalten', in Bernhard Jussen and Craig Koslofsky, eds., *Kulturelle Reformation* (Veröffentlichungen des Max-Planck-Instituts für Geschichte 145; Göttingen: Vandenhoeck und Ruprecht, 1999), 29–67. Sixten Ringbom, 'Devotional Images and Imaginative Devotions', *Gazette des Beaux-Arts* 73 (1969), 159–70. Peter Schmidt has suggested that printed media reduced the distance between the sacred and the viewer. Peter Schmidt, 'Bildergebrauch und Frömmigkeitspraxis. Bemerkungen zur Benutzung früher

displaced the ancient form, and the line between ancient and modern sermons should not be too sharply drawn, lest we take Wyclif's dismissal of scholastic preaching (the sophistry of friars, he said) at face value.[102] Such a dismissal reduces the variety of late medieval preachers to a false contrast, between Bible supporters and detractors. Rather, biblical literacy belonged to an animated text entangled with all manner of formal religious expression.

The sermon's coupling of diverse sources with biblical discourse is entirely consistent with the late medieval Bible as a cultural artefact. Biblical narratives, it was believed, transmitted and received meanings between the Bible, other writings and oral texts. The intentions of God, it was thought, collimated all these past and present human reflections into one bright signal of truth. This was a very idealistic view of a complicated and elusive book. It allowed interpretation to accommodate innumerable, contestable uses of Scripture, while posing as an almighty univocal voice. The fifteenth-century Bible did not cause lay rebellion or anti-clericalism, although it was sometimes associated with them, nor could the clerical hierarchy or a particular ideology entirely control interpretation. All people interested in Scripture must have agreed that its function was identical to the spiritual purpose of the church – gradually restoring human beings to an ideal form of life, salvation. Yet so benevolently disguised, the Bible could infiltrate and unsettle any region of late medieval Europe's cultural worlds.

Druckgraphik', in Andreas Curtius, ed., *Spiegel der Seligkeit: Privates Bild und Frömmigkeit im Spätmittelalter* (Nuremberg: Germanischen Nationalmuseums, 2000), 69–83, here 79. Consider also Ghosh, *The Wycliffite Heresy*, 162–4, on devout imagination and reason. For the use of images in the lay cultivation of affect, consider Frank Matthias Kammel, 'Imago pro domo. Private religiöse Bilder und ihre Benutzung im Spätmittelalter', in Curtius, ed., *Spiegel der Seligkeit*, 10–33, especially 18–25, the literature noted there, and Sixten Ringbom, *From Icon to Narrative: The Rise of the Dramatic Close-up in Fifteenth-Century Devotional Painting* (Åbo: Åbo Akademie, 1965; 2nd edn, Doornspijk: Davaco, 1984).

102 For this and the following, see Spencer, *English Preaching in the Late Middle Ages*, 143–5, 228–68, here 230. Consider also Schiewer, 'German Sermons', 911–14.

# Select bibliography

## Primary sources

*Acta Honorii III et Gregorii IX*, ed. Aloysius L. Tăutu, Pontificia Commissio ad redigendum Codicem Iuris Canonici Orientalis, ser. 3, 3, Vatican City: Typis Polyglottis Vaticanis, 1950.

Adam of Eynsham, *Magna vita sancti Hugonis: The Life of St. Hugh of Lincoln*, 2 vols., ed. Decima L. Douie and David Hugh Farmer, Oxford: Clarendon Press, 1985.

*Aelredi Rievallenis opera omnia*, ed. A. Hoste and C.H. Talbot, Turnhout: Brepols, 1971.

Alan of Lille, *Summa quadrapartita (Summa contra hereticos)*, PL 210, cols. 303–430.

Albe, E., ed. and trans., *Les miracles de Notre-Dame de Rocamadour au XIIe siècle*, rev. introduction and notes Jean Rocacher, Toulouse: Le Pérégrinateur, 1996, trans. Marcus Bull, *The Miracles of Our Lady of Rocamadour*, Woodbridge: Boydell, 1999.

Alberigo, Giuseppe, ed., *Conciliorum Oecumenicorum decreta*, 3rd edn, Bologna: Istituto per le Scienze religiose, 1973.

Albertus Magnus, *De unitate intellectus contra Averroem*, ed. A. Hufnagel, in *Alberti Magni... Opera omnia*, vol. 17.1, Münster-i-W.: Aschendorff, 1975.

Alexander IV, *Les registres d'Alexandre IV*, ed. C. Bourel de la Roncière *et al.*, 3 vols., Paris: A. Fontemoing, 1895–1953.

Alfonso X, el Sabio, *Cantigas de Santa Maria*, ed. Walter Mettmann, 3 vols., Madrid: Editorial Castalia, 1986–1989, trans. Kathleen Kulp-Hill, *Songs of Holy Mary of Alfonso X, The Wise*, Tempe, Ariz.: Arizona Center for Medieval and Renaissance Studies, 2000.

*Die alttschechische Dresdener Bibel/Drážd'anská anebo Leskovecká bible*, ed. Hans Rothe and Friedrich Scholz, Paderborn: Ferdinand Schöningh, 1993.

Amadeus of Lausanne, *De Maria virginea matre. Homiliae octo*, ed. Jean Deshusses, *Huit homélies mariales*, SC, 72, Paris: Éditions du Cerf, 1980, trans. Grace Perigo, *Eight Homilies on the Praises of Blessed Mary*, CFS 18B, Kalamazoo, Mich.: Cistercian Publications, 1979.

*Annales Erfordienses*, ed. G. H. Pertz, MGH, SS 16, 26–40.

*Annales Wormatienses*, ed. G. H. Pertz, MGH, SS 17, 34–74.

Anselm of Canterbury, *Orationes 5–7*, in *S. Anselmi Cantuariensis archiepiscopi opera omnia*, ed. F. S. Schmitt, 6 vols., Edinburgh: Thomas Nelson and Sons, 1946–1961, vol. 3, 13–25, trans. Benedicta Ward, in *The Prayers and Meditations of Saint Anselm, with the Proslogion*, Harmondsworth: Penguin, 1973.

Select bibliography

Anselm of Lucca, *Anselmi episcopi Lucensis collectio canonum una cum collectione minore*, ed. Friedrich Thaner, Innsbruck: Wagner, 1906–15.

Arnold of Bonneval, *Libellus de laudibus b. Mariae virginis*, PL 189, cols. 1725–34.

Augustine of Hippo, *Confessions*, trans. R. S. Pine-Coffin, Harmondsworth: Penguin, 1961.

*Ausgewählte Quellen zur deutschen Geschichte des Mittelalters*, ed. Jürgen Miethke and Lorenz Weinrich, 2 vols., Darmstadt: Wissenschaftliche Buchgesellschaft, 1995.

Barceló, Carmen, ed., *Un tratado Catalán medieval de derecho islámico: El llibre de la çuna e xara de los moros*, Córdoba: University of Córdoba, 1989.

Becquet, Jean, ed., *Scriptores ordinis Grandimontenses*, Turnhout: Brepols, 1978.

Berger, David, ed., *Jewish–Christian Debate in the High Middle Ages: A Critical Edition of the Nizzahon Vetus* Philadelphia: The Jewish Publication Society of America, 1979.

Bériou, N. and I. Le Masne de Chermont, eds., *Les sermons et la visite pastorale de Frédéric visconti, archevêque de Pise (1253–1277)*, Rome: École française de Rome, 2001.

Bernard of Angers, *The Book of Sainte Foy*, trans. Pamela Sheingorn, Philadelphia: University of Pennsylvania Press, 1995.

Bernard of Clairvaux, *De consideratione*, in SBO 3, 379–493, trans. John Anderson and Elizabeth Kennan, *Five Books on Consideration: Advice to a Pope*, CFS 37, Kalamazoo, Mich.: Cistercian Publications, 1976.

*In laudibus virginis matris*, in SBO 4, 13–58, trans. Marie-Bernard Saïd, *Homilies in Praise of the Blessed Virgin Mary*, CFS 18A, Kalamazoo, Mich.: Cistercian Publications, 1993.

*The Letters of St. Bernard of Clairvaux*, trans. B. S. James, new introduction by B. M. Kienzle, Stroud: Sutton Publishing, 1998, reprint of London: Burns and Oates, 1953.

*On Loving God*, in *Selected Works*, trans. G. R. Evans, New York: Paulist Press, 1987.

*On the Song of Songs, III*, trans. K. Walsh and I. M. Edmonds, CFS 31, Kalamazoo, Mich.: Cistercian Publications, 1991.

*Sancti Bernardi opera*, ed. J. Leclercq, H.-M. Rochais and C. H. Talbot, 8 vols., Rome: Editiones Cistercienses, 1957–77.

*Sermones super Cantica canticorum*, in SBO vols. 1–2.

*Sermons on the Song of Songs, IV*, trans. Irene Edmonds, CFS 40, Kalamazoo, Mich.: Cistercian Publications, 1980.

*Sermons for the Summer Season: Liturgical Sermons from Rogationtide and Pentecost*, trans. with introduction by B. M. Kienzle, additional translations by J. Jarzembowski, CFS 53, Kalamazoo, Mich.: Cistercian Publications, 1991.

*Treatises II: The Book on Loving God*, trans. M. A. Conway; *The Steps of Humility and Pride*, trans. R. Walton, CFS 13, Kalamazoo, Mich.: Cistercian Publications, 1980.

*Treatises III: In Praise of the New Knighthood*, trans. C. Greenia, CFS 19, Kalamazoo, Mich.: Cistercian Publications, 1977.

Bernard of Fontcaude, *Adversus Waldensium sectam*, PL 204, cols. 793–840.

Bernard Silvester, *De mundi universitate*, ed. C. S. Barach and J. Wrobel, Innsbruck: Wagner, 1876.

Bernardino of Siena, *Prediche volgari sul Campo di Siena, 1427*, 2 vols., ed. Carlo Delcorno, Milan: Rusconi, 1989.

Bernold of St Blaise, *Bernoldi Chronicon*, ed. Georg Pertz, in MGH, SS 5, 385–467.

495

*Biblia Latina cum glossa ordinaria*, 4 vols., introduced by Margaret Gibson and Karlfried Froehlich, Turnhout: Brepols, 1992, reprint of Strasbourg: Adolph Rusch, 1480/1.

Blamires, Alcuin, ed., *Woman Defamed and Woman Defended: An Anthology of Medieval Texts*, Oxford and New York: Oxford University Press, 1992.

Bonaventure, *De sex alis seraphim*, in *S. Bonaventurae...Opera omnia*, vol. 8, Quaracchi: Collegium S. Bonaventurae, 1898.

*Itinerarium mentis ad deum*, in *S. Bonaventurae...Opera omnia*, vol. 5, Quaracchi: Collegium S. Bonaventurae, 1891; trans. and ed. E. Cousins, *The Soul's Journey into God*, Classics of Western Spirituality, New York: Paulist Press, 1978.

Bonizo of Sutri, *Liber de vita christiana*, ed. E. Perels, Texte zur Geschichte des Römischen und kanonischen Rechts im Mittelalter, 1, Berlin: Weidmann, 1930.

Børresen, Kari, ed., *Image of God and Gender Models in the Judaeo-Christian Tradition*, Minneapolis: Fortress Press, 1994.

Boyd, Beverly, *The Middle English Miracles of the Virgin*, San Marino, Calif.: The Huntington Library, 1964.

Bozoky, E., ed. and trans., *Le livre secret des Cathares. Interrogatio Iohannis, apocryphe d'origine bogomile*, Paris: Beauchesne, 1980.

Bramley, H. R., ed., *The Psalter Translated by Richard Rolle of Hampole*, Oxford: Clarendon Press, 1884.

Bridget of Sweden. *The Liber Celestis of St. Bridget of Sweden*, ed. Roger Ellis, Early English Text Society, n.s. 291, Oxford: Oxford University Press, 1987. Excerpts trans. Elizabeth Spearing, *Medieval Writings on Female Spirituality*, 145–74, Harmondsworth: Penguin, 2002.

Brooke, R. B., ed., *The Coming of the Friars*, London: Allen & Unwin, 1975.

Bruno of Segni, *Expositio in Genesim*, PL 164, cols. 147–234.

Burchard of Worms, *Decretorum libri XX*, PL 140, cols. 557–1058.

Burkhart, Louise M., *Before Guadalupe: The Virgin Mary in Early Colonial Nahuatl Literature*, Institute for Mesoamerican Studies Monograph 13, Albany: State University of New York, 2001.

Caesarius of Heisterbach, *Dialogus miraculorum*, ed. Joseph Strange, 2 vols. Cologne: J. M. Heberle, 1851; repr., Ridgewood, N.J.: Gregg, 1966. Trans. H. von E. Scott and C. C. Swinton Bland, *The Dialogue on Miracles*, 2 vols., London: Routledge, 1929.

*Libri VIII Miraculorum*, in Alfons Hilka, ed., *Die Wundergeschichte des Caesarius von Heisterbach*, Bonn: Peter Hanstein Verlagsbuchhandlung, 1933–37.

Caracciolo, Roberto, *Opere in volgare*, ed. Enzo Esposito, Galatina: Congedo, 1993.

*Carmina burana: Die Lieder der Benediktbeurer Handschrift*, ed. B. Bishoff, Munich: Deutscher Taschenbuch Verlag, 1979.

*Chronica Albrichi monachi Trium Fontium*, ed. P. Scheffer-Boichorst, MGH, SS 23, 631–950.

*Chronicon universale*, ed. Georg Waitz, in MGH, SS 26, 442–57.

Clayton, Mary, *The Apocryphal Gospels of Mary in Anglo-Saxon England*, Cambridge: Cambridge University Press, 1998.

Colgrave, Bertram, ed. and trans., *Two Lives of Saint Cuthbert: A Life by an Anonymous Monk of Lindisfarne and Bede's Prose Life*, Cambridge: Cambridge University Press, 1940; repr. 1985.

Conrad of Saxony, *Speculum beatae Mariae virginis*, Bibliotheca Franciscana Ascetica Medii Aevi 2, Quaracchi: Collegium S. Bonaventurae, 1904, trans. Mary Emmanuel, *The*

*Mirror of the Blessed Virgin Mary and the Psalter of Our Lady*, St Louis: B. Herder Book Co., 1932.

De Bruin, C. C., ed., *Tleven ons Heren Ihesu Christi: Het Pseudo-Bonaventuria-Ludolfiaanse leven van Jesus*, Leiden: Brill, 1980.

*De vita et actibus*, ed. Peter Biller, in Caterina Bruschi and Peter Biller, eds., *Texts and the Repression of Medieval Heresy*, Medieval Theology 4, Woodbridge: Boydell and Brewer, 2003, 195–207.

Denifle H. and H. Chatelain, eds., *Chartularium universitatis parisiensis*, 4 vols., Paris: Delalain, 1889–97.

Denziger, H. and A. Schönmetzer, eds., *Enchiridion symbolorum*, 34th edn, Barcelona: Herder, 1967.

Deusdedit, *Die Kanonessammlung des Kardinals Deusdedit*, ed. Victor Wolf von Glanvell, Paderborn: Ferdinand Schöningh, 1905.

Dewick, E. S., ed., *Facsimiles of Horae de Beata Maria Virgine from English MSS. of the Eleventh Century*, Henry Bradshaw Society 21, London: Harrison and Sons, 1902.

*Dionysii Cartusiensis Opera Selecta*, vol. 1, *Bibliotheca manuscripta*, ed. Kent Emery, Turnhout: Brepols, 1991.

*Diplomatarium danicum*, ser. 1, vol. 5, ed. Niels-Skyum-Nielsen, Copenhagen: Det danske sprog- og litteraturselskab, 1957.

*Diplomatarium norvegicum*, vol. 1, ed. C. C. A. Lange and C. R. Unger, Oslo: P. T. Malling, 1849.

Dominguez Sánchez, Santiago, *Documentos de Clemente IV (1265–1268) referentes a España*, León: Universidad de León, 1996.

Dreves, Guido Maria, ed., *Psalteria rhythmica: Gereimte Psalterien des Mittelalters*, 2 vols., Analecta Hymnica Medii Aevi 35–36, Leipzig: O. R. Reisland, 1900–01.

Duparc-Quioc, Suzanne, ed., *La chanson d'Antioche*, Paris: Académie des Inscriptions et Belles-Lettres, 1977.

Durandus, William, *Rationale divinorum officiorum*, ed. A. Davril and T. M. Thibodeau, with B.-G. Guyot, 3 vols., CCCM 140, Turnhout: Brepols, 1995–2000.

Duvernoy, J., ed., *Le registre d'inquisition de Jacques Fournier, évêque de Pamiers (1318–1325)*, 3 vols., Toulouse: Privat, 1965.

Eckhart, Meister, *Meister Eckhart: The Essential Sermons, Commentaries, Treatises, and Defense*, trans. Edmund Colledge and Bernard McGinn, New York: Paulist Press, 1981.

Elisabeth of Schönau, *Libri visionum et epistolae*, in F. W. E. Roth, ed., *Die Visionen und Briefe der hl. Elisabeth sowie die Schriften der Äbte Ekbert und Emecho von Schönau*, 2nd edn, Brünn: Verlag der 'Studien aus dem Benedictiner- und Cistercienser-Orden', 1886, trans. Anne L. Clark, *Elisabeth of Schönau, Complete Works*, New York: Paulist Press, 2000.

Elliott, J. K., *The Apocryphal New Testament: A Collection of Apocryphal Christian Literature in an English Translation*, Oxford: Clarendon Press, 1993.

Esser, Caietanus, ed., *Opuscula sancti patris Francisci Assisiensis*, Grottaferrata: Collegii S. Bonaventurae Ad Claras Aquas, 1978.

*Exordium magnum cisterciense sive narratio de initio cisterciensis ordinis*, ed. B. Griesser, Rome: Editiones Cistercienses, 1961.

Fayen, A., 'L' "Antigraphum Petri" et les lettres concernant Lambert le Bègue conservées dans le manuscrit de Glasgow', *Bulletin de la Commission Royale d'Histoire* 5th s., 9 (1899), 255–356.

Febrer Romaguera, M. V., ed., *Cartas Pueblas de las Morerias Valencianas y documentacion complementaria*, vol. 1, Zaragoza: Anubar, 1991.

Fenster, T. and C. Lees, eds., *Gender in Debate from the Early Middle Ages to the Renaissance*, Basingstoke and New York: Palgrave, 2002.

France, J., ed. and trans., *Rodulfus Glaber: The Five Books of Histories*, Oxford: Clarendon Press, 1989.

Friedberg, Emil, ed., *Die Canones-Sammlungen zwischen Gratian und Bernhard von Pavia*, Leipzig: B. Tauchnitz, 1897.

*Corpus iuris canonici*, 2 vols., Leipzig: Bernhard Tauchnitz, 1879–81.

Fulbert of Chartres, *Sermones*, *PL* 141, cols. 317–40.

Gardiner, Eileen, ed., *Visions of Heaven and Hell before Dante*, New York: Italica Press, 1989.

Gautier de Coinci, *Les miracles de Nostre Dame*, ed. V. Frederic Koenig, 4 vols., Geneva: Droz, 1955–70.

Geoffrey of Auxerre, *Super Apocalypsim*, ed. F. Gastaldelli, Temi e Testi 17, Rome: Edizioni di Storia e Letteratura, 1970.

*Vita prima*, *PL* 185, cols. 301–68.

Geoffrey of Villehardouin, *La conquête de Constantinople*, ed. Edmond Faral, 2 vols., Paris: Société d'Edition 'Les belles lettres', 1961.

Gerald of Wales, *Topographia hibernica*, ed. J. S. Brewer, Rolls Series 21.5, London: Longmans, 1867.

*Gerardi Magni epistolae*, ed. Willelm Mulder, Tekstuitgaven van Ons Geestelijk Erf 3, Antwerp: Uitgeverij Neerlandia, 1933.

*Gestorum Treverorum, continuatio IV*, ed. G. Waitz, MGH, SS 24, 390–404.

Gonzalo de Berceo, *Los Milagros de Nuestra Señora*, ed. Brian Dutton, in *Obras completas*, vol. 2, London: Támesis, 1971, trans. Richard Terry Mount and Annette Grant Cash, *Miracles of Our Lady*, Lexington, Ky.: University Press of Kentucky, 1997.

Gratian, *The Treatise on Laws (Decretum DD. 1–20)*, trans. Augustine Thompson and James Gordley, Studies in Medieval and Early Modern Canon Law 2, Washington, D.C.: Catholic University of America Press, 1993.

Gray, Douglas, ed., *English Medieval Religious Lyrics*, Exeter: University of Exeter Press, 1992.

Grégoire le Grand, *Dialogues*, ed. A. de Vogüé, SC 260, Paris: Cerf, 1979.

Gregory of St Grisogono, *Polycarpus*, provisional edition by Uwe Horst with a preface by Horst Fuhrmann available at http://www.mgh.de/polycarp/.

Gregory VII, Pope, *Das Register Gregors VII*, ed. Erich Caspar, MGH, EPP, Epistolae Selectae, vol. 2, fasc. 1–2.

Guerric de Saint-Quentin, *Quaestiones de quodlibet*, ed. W. H. Principe and J. Lord, introduction by J. P. Torrell, Toronto: University of Toronto Press, 2002.

Gui, Bernard, *Manuel de l'inquisiteur*, ed. G. Mollat, Paris: Champion, 1926–7.

Guibert of Gembloux, *Guiberti Gemblacensis epistolae*, ed. Albert Derolez, Turnhout: Brepols, 1989.

Guibert of Nogent, *Dei gesta per Francos*, ed. R. B. C. Huygens, CCCM 127A, Turnhout: Brepols, 1996, trans. Robert Levine, *The Deeds of God through the Franks*, Woodbridge: Boydell Press, 1997.

Habig, Marion, ed., *St. Francis of Assisi: Writings and Early Biographies: English Omnibus of the Sources of the Life of St. Francis*, 4th rev. edn, Chicago: Franciscan Herald Press, 1983.

Hadewijch, *The Complete Works*, trans. Mother Columba Hart, New York: Paulist Press, 1980.

Haggh, Barbara, ed., *Two Offices for St Elizabeth of Hungary: Introduction and Edition*, ed. Barbara Haggh, Musicological Studies 65.1, Ottawa: Institute for Medieval Music, 1995.

Hall, J., ed., *King Horn: A Middle English Romance*, Oxford: Clarendon Press, 1901.

*Die Hannoversche Briefsammlung*, ed. C. Erdmann, in *Briefsammlungen der Zeit Heinrichs IV*, MGH, EPP, Briefe der deutschen Kaiserzeit V, Weimar: Böhlau, 1950, 1–187.

Heinrich von Meissen [Frauenlob], *Leichs, Sangsprüche, Lieder*, ed. Karl Stackmann and Karl Bertau, 2 vols., Abhandlungen der Akademie der Wissenschaften in Göttingen 119–20, Göttingen: Vandenhoeck and Ruprecht, 1981.

Heloise and Peter Abelard, 'The Letter of Heloise on Religious Life and Abelard's First Reply', ed. J. T. Muckle, *Mediaeval Studies* 17 (1955), 240–81.

[Henricus Pomerius], 'De origine monasterii Viridis Vallis', *Analecta Bollandiana* 4 (1885), 257–334.

Henry of Huntingdon, *Historia Anglorum: The History of the English People*, ed. and trans. Diana Greenaway, Oxford Medieval Texts, Oxford: Clarendon Press, 1996.

Herbert of Clairvaux, *De miraculis Cisterciensium monachorum*, PL 185, cols. 453–61.

Herman of Tournai, *The Restoration of the Monastery of Saint Martin of Tournai*, trans. Lynn H. Nelson, Washington, D.C.: The Catholic University of America Press, 1996.

Herolt, Johannes, *Miracles of the Blessed Virgin Mary*, trans. C. C. Swinton Bland, London: George Routledge and Sons, 1928.

Hervé of Bourg-Dieu, *Commentaria in epistolas divi Pauli*, PL 181, cols. 391–1692.

Hildebert of Le Mans, *Sermones*, PL 171, cols. 343–964.

Hildegard of Bingen, *Epistolarium* I, ed. L. van Acker, CCCM 91–91A, Turnhout: Brepols, 1991–93, trans. J. L. Baird and R. K. Ehrman, *The Letters of Hildegard of Bingen*, 3 vols., Oxford: Oxford University Press, 1994, 1998, 2004.

*Expositiones evangeliorum*, ed. J.-B. Pitra, in *Analecta S. Hildegardis*, in *Analecta sacra*, vol. 8, Rome, 1882, 245–327.

*Liber divinorum operum*, ed. A. Derolez and P. Dronke, CCCM 43, Turnhout: Brepols, 1996.

*Scivias*, ed. A. Führkötter and A. Carlevaris, CCCM 43, Turnhout: Brepols, 1978.

*Scivias*, trans. Columba Hart and Jane Bishop; introduction, Barbara J. Newman; preface, Caroline Walker Bynum, Classics of Western Spirituality, New York: Paulist Press, 1990.

*Symphonia: A Critical Edition of the Symphonia armonie celestium revelationum*, ed. and trans. Barbara Newman, Ithaca, N.Y.: Cornell University Press, 1998.

Honorius Augustodunensis, *Expositio in Cantica canticorum*, PL 172, cols. 347–496.

*Gemma animae*, PL 172, cols. 541–737.

*Sacramentarium*, PL 172, cols. 737–806.

Horst, Uwe, ed., *Die Kanonessammlung "Polycarpus" des Gregor von S. Grisogono: Quellen und Tendenzen*, MGH Hilfsmittel 5, Munich: Monumenta Germaniae Historica, 1980.

Horstmann, Carl, ed., *Yorkshire Writers: Richard Rolle of Hampole, an English Father of the Church, and his Followers*, 2 vols., New York: Macmillan, 1895–96.

*The Hours of Mary of Burgundy: Codex Vindobonensis 1857, Vienna, Österreichische Nationalbibliothek*, facsimile edition with commentary by Eric Inglis, London: Harvey Miller, 1995.

Hudson, Anne, ed., *The Works of a Lollard Preacher*, Early English Text Society, OS 317, Oxford: Oxford University Press, 2001.

Hugh of Rouen, *Contra haereticos sui temporis*, PL 192, cols. 1255–98.

Hugh of St Victor, *Didascalicon*, trans. Jerome Taylor, New York: Columbia University Press, 1961.

Innocent III, Pope, *Regesta sive epistolae*, PL 214–16.

    *Sermones de diversis*, trans. Corinne J. Vause and Frank C. Gardiner, *Pope Innocent III, between God and Man: Six Sermons on the Priestly Office*, Washington, D.C.: Catholic University of America Press, 2004.

    *Sermones de tempore*, PL 217, cols. 309–450.

Ivo of Chartres, *Decretum*, PL 161, cols. 47–1036.

    *Panormia*, Provisional edition by Martin Brett and Bruce C. Brasington available at http://wtfaculty.wtamu.edu/~bbrasington/panormia.html.

Jaffé, Philipp, *Regesta pontificum Romanorum*, 2nd edn, Leipzig, 1885–8.

James of Vitry, *The Historia occidentalis of Jacques de Vitry: A Critical Edition*, ed. John Frederick Hinnebusch, O. P., Fribourg: The University Press, 1972.

    *Lettres de Jacques de Vitry (1160/1170–1240) évêque de Saint-Jean d'Acre*, ed. R. B. C. Huygens, Leiden: Brill, 1960.

    *Vita Mariae Oigniacensis*, ed. D. Papebroeck, in *AA.SS., Iunius*, vol. 5 (June 23), Paris, 1867; trans. with introduction and notes M. H. King, *The Life of Marie d'Oignies*, Toronto: Peregrina Press, 1989.

Johannes Teutonicus, *Apparatus glossarum in Compilationem tertiam*, ed. K. Pennington, Vatican City: Bibliotheca Apostolica Vaticana, 1981.

Johannes Busch, *Chronicon Windeshemense und Liber de reformatione monasteriorum*, ed. K. Grube, Halle: Hendel, 1886; repr. Farnborough: Gregg, 1968.

Johannes Mauburnus, *Rosetum exercitiorum spiritualium et sacrorum meditationum*, ed. Leander de S. Martino, Douai: Bellerus, 1620.

John Beleth, *Summa de ecclesiasticis officiis*, ed. H. Douteil, 2 vols., CCCM 41, Turnhout: Brepols, 1976.

John of Caulibus, *Meditations on the Life of Christ*, trans. F. X. Taney, A. Miller and C. M. Stallings-Taney, Asheville: Pegasus Press, 2000.

John of Damascus, *Liber de haeresibus*, in P. Bonafatius Kotter, ed., *Die Schriften des Johannes von Damaskos*, 5 vols., Berlin: de Gruyter, 1969–81.

John of Garland [Giovanni di Garlandia], *Epithalamium beate virginis Marie*, ed. Antonio Saiani, Accademia Toscana di Scienze e Lettere 'La Colombaria', Studi 139, Florence: Leo S. Olschki, 1995.

John of Paris, *Commentaire sur les Sentences, Reportation livre I–II*, ed. J.-P. Müller, Rome: Studia Anselmiana, 1961.

Jordan of Saxony, *On the Beginnings of the Order of Preachers*, ed. Simon Tugwell, Dublin: Dominican Publications, 1982.

Kienzle, B. M., 'Pons of Léras', [introduction and translation] in Thomas Head, ed., *Medieval Hagiography*, New York: Garland Press, 2000, 495–513.

Kolár, Jaroslav, Anezka Vidmanová and Hana Vlhová-Wörner, eds., *Jistebnický kancional, MS Praha, Knihovna Národniho muzea, II C 7, Kritická edice/Jistebnice Kancionál, MS Prague, National Museum Library II C 7, critical edition, vol. 1: Graduale*, Monumenta liturgica bohemica 2, Brno: Marek, 2005.

Kuttner, Stephan and Antonio García y García, 'A New Eyewitness Account of the Fourth Lateran Council', *Traditio* 20 (1964), 115–78.

Lehmijoki-Gardner, Maiju, *et al.*, *Dominican Penitent Women*, New York: Paulist Press, 2005.

*Le liber pontificalis*, ed. L. Duchesne, 3 vols., Paris: E. de Boccard, 1955–7.

*Libellus de diversis ordinibus et professionibus qui sunt in aecclesia*, ed. Giles Constable and Bernard Smith, Oxford: Clarendon Press, 1972.

*Libellus de institutione morum*, ed. J. Barogh, Scriptores rerum Hungaricarum 2, Budapest: Academia Litter, Hungarica, 1938.

*Libri de iudiciorum ordine*, ed. Friedrich Christian Bergmann, Göttingen: Vandenhoeck & Ruprecht, 1842.

Limor, Osa, ed., *Die Disputationen zu Ceuta (1179) und Mallorca (1286): Zwei antijüdische Schriften aus dem mittelalterlichen Genua*, MGH, Quellen zur Geistesgeschichte des Mittelalters 15, Munich: Monumenta Germaniae Historica, 1994.

Loewenfeld, S., ed., *Epistolae pontificum romanorum ineditae*, Leipzig: Verlag Veit and Co., 1885, repr., Graz: Akademische Druck- und Verlagsanstalt, 1959.

Luchaire, Achille, ed., 'Un document retrouvé', *Journal des savants* n.s. 3 (1905), 557–68.

Machaut, Guillaume, *Oeuvres complètes*, vol. 2, ed. Leo Schrade, Monaco: L'Oiseau Lyre, 1977.

*Magnus liber organi de Notre-Dame de Paris: Les quadrupla et tripla de Paris*, ed. Edward Roesner, Monaco: L'Oiseau-Lyre, 1993.

Maimonides, Moses, *Letters and Essays of Moses Maimonides*, ed. and trans. Isaac Shailat, Jerusalem: Maliyot Press of Yeshivat Birkat Moshe Maaleh Adumim, 1987.

Mansi, Iohannes Domenicus, *Sacrorum conciliorum nova et amplissima collectio*, Florence and Venice: Antoni Zatta, 1759–98.

Marbod of Rennes, *Marbodi liber decem capitulorum*, ed. R. Leotta, Rome: Herder, 1984.

Martin, G. H., ed. and trans., *Knighton's Chronicle 1337–1396*, Oxford: Clarendon Press, 1995.

Martin of Tišov, *Kutnahorská Bible / Kuttenberger Bibel*, ed. Reinhold Olesch and Hans Rothe, 2 vols., Paderborn: Ferdinand Schöningh, 1989.

Matthew Paris, *Chronica majora*, ed. Henry Richards Luard, Rolls Series 57, pts. 1–7, London: Longman and Co., 1887.

Mechthild of Magdeburg, *The Flowing Light of the Godhead*, trans. Frank Tobin, New York: Paulist Press, 1993.

Meersseman, G. G., ed., *Der Hymnos Akathistos im Abendland*, 2 vols., Spicilegium Friburgense 2–3, Fribourg: Universitätsverlag, 1958, 1960.

*Dossier de l'ordre de la pénitence au XIIIe siècle*, 2nd edn, Fribourg: Éditions universitaires, 1982.

Menot, Michel, *Sermons choisis de Michel Menot (1508–1518)*, ed. Joseph Nève, Paris: E. Champion, 1924.

*Miracula sanctae virginis Mariae*, ed. Elise F. Dexter, University of Wisconsin Studies in the Social Sciences and History 12, Madison: University of Wisconsin Press, 1927.

Moneta of Cremona, *Adversus Catharos et Valdenses*, ed. T. A. Ricchinius, Rome: N. and M. Palearini, 1743, repr., Ridgewood, N. J.: Gregg, 1964.

*Montpellier Codex*, I, ed. Hans Tischler, Madison, Wis.: A-R Editions, 1978.

*Monumenta diplomatica S. Dominici*, ed. Vladimir J. Koudelka, Rome: Institutum Historicum Fratrum Praedicatorum, 1966.

Munch, P. A., ed., *Pavelige nuntiers regnskabs- og dagbøger førte under teinde-upkrævningen i Norden 1282–1334*, Oslo: Brögger og Christies Bogtrykkeri, 1864.

*Myroure of oure Ladye*, ed. John Henry Blunt, Early English Text Society, ES 19, London: N. Trübner, 1873.

Nelli, R., ed. and trans., *Écritures cathares*, new edn A. Brenon, Monaco Éditions du Rocher, 1995.

Nicholas of Lyra, *Postilla litteralis super bibliam cum adnotationibus et replicis*, Strasbourg: Anton Koberger, 1497.

Nigel of Canterbury, *Miracula sancta Dei genitricis virginis Marie, versifice*, ed. Jan Ziolkowski, Toronto Medieval Latin Texts 17, Toronto: Pontifical Institute of Mediaeval Studies, 1986.

Odo of Cluny, *Vita Sancti Geraldi Auriliacensis Comitis, PL* 133, cols. 639–704.

Ogier of Locedio, 'Quis dabit' ['Meditacio Bernardi de lamentacione beate virginis'], in Thomas Bestul, ed. and trans., *Texts of the Passion: Latin Devotional Literature and Medieval Society*, Philadelphia: University of Pennsylvania Press, 165–85.

Olivi, Peter John, Fr. *Petrus Iohannis Olivi, o.f.m., Quaestiones in secundum librum sententiarum*, ed. Bernard Jansen, S. J., Quaracchi: Collegium S. Bonaventurae, 1922.

Orderic Vitalis, *The Ecclesiastical History of Orderic Vitalis*, ed. Marjorie Chibnall, Oxford Medieval Texts 3, Oxford: Clarendon Press, 1972.

Ostorero, Martine, Agostino Paravicini Bagliani and Kathrin Utz Tremp in collaboration with Catherine Chène, *L'imaginaire du sabbat: Édition critique des textes les plus anciens (1430 c.–1440 c.)*, Lausanne: Université de Lausanne, 1999.

Otter, Monika, *Goscelin of St. Bertin, The Book of Encouragement and Consolation [Liber Confortatorius]; The Letter of Goscelin to the Recluse Eva. Translated from the Latin with Introduction, Notes, and Interpretive Essay*, Cambridge: D.S. Brewer, 2004.

Otto of Freising, *The Deeds of Frederick Barbarossa*, trans. Ch. Mierow, Toronto: University of Toronto Press, 1994.

Pales-Gobilliard, A., ed., *Le livre des sentences de l'inquisiteur Bernard Gui 1308–1323*, 2 vols, Paris: CNRS, 2002.

Paucapalea, *Summa über das 'Decretum Gratiani'*, ed. Johann Friedrich von Schulte, Giessen: E. Roth, 1890.

Peter Abelard, *Historia Calamitatum*, ed. J. Monfrin, Paris: Librairie Vrin, 1959; trans. Betty Radice, *The Letters of Abelard and Heloise*, rev. edn, M. T. Clanchy, Penguin: London, 2003, 3–43.

Peter Damian, *Die Briefe des Petrus Damiani*, ed. Kurt Reindel, MGH, EPP, *Die Briefe des deutsche Kaiserzeit*, vol. 4, 4 vols., Munich: MGH, 1983–93.

*Vita Beati Romualdi*, ed. Giovanni Tabacco, Fonti per la storia d'Italia 94, Rome: Istituto Storico Italiano, 1957.

Peter Lombard, *Collectanea in omnes divi Pauli epistolas, PL* 191, cols. 1297–1696; *PL* 192, cols. 9–520.

*Sententiae in IV libris distinctae*, Grottaferrata: Collegium S. Bonaventurae, 1971–81.

Peter of Falco, *Questions disputées ordinaires*, ed. A. J. Gondras, 3 vols., Louvain and Paris: Nauwelaerts, 1968.

Peter of Roissy, *Manuale de misteriis Ecclesie*, ed. M.-T. d'Alverny, in P. Gallais and Y.-J. Riou, eds., *Mélanges offerts à René Crozet à l'occasion de son soixante dixième anniversaire*, vol. 2, Poitiers: Société d'études médiévales, 1966, 1085–1104.

Peter the Venerable, *Adversus Judeorum inveteratam duritiem*, ed. Yvonne Friedman, CCCM 58, Turnhout: Brepols, 1985.

*Tractatus contra Petrobrusianos*, ed. J. Fearns, CCCM 10, Turnhout: Brepols, 1968.

Peters, Edward, ed., *The First Crusade: The Chronicler of Fulcher of Chartres and Other Source Materials*, Philadelphia: University of Pennsylvania Press, 1989.

Petrus Alfonsi, *Dialogus contra Judaeos*, PL 157, cols. 535–672.

Philip of Harvengt, *Commentaria in Cantica canticorum*, PL 203, cols. 181–490.

Piché, David, ed., *La condamnation parisienne de 1277*, Paris: J. Vrin, 1999.

Pierre des Vaux-de-Cernay, *Hystoria Albigensis*, ed. P. Guébin and E. Lyon, 3 vols., Paris: Champion, 1926–39.

Pontal, O. and J. Avril, eds., *Les statuts synodaux français du XIIIe siècle*, Collection des documents inédits sur l'histoire de France, 5 vols., Paris: C.H.T.S., 1971–2001.

Porete, Marguerite, *The Mirror of Simple Souls*, trans. Edmund Colledge, J. C. Marler and Judith Grant, Notre Dame: University of Notre Dame Press, 1999.

*Prediche del Beato Giordano da Rivalto dell'Ordine dei Predicatori*, Florence: Pietro Gaetano Viviani, 1739.

Pseudo-Augustine, *De assumptione beatae Mariae virginis*, PL 40, cols. 1141–8.

Radewijns, Florent, *Petit manuel pour le dévot moderne: Tractatulus devotus*, ed. and trans. Francis Joseph Legrand, Turnhout: Brepols, 1999.

Raimundus Martini, *Pugio fidei adversus Mauros et Judaeos*, Leipzig 1687, repr. Farnborough: Gregg, 1967.

Ramon Llull, *Livro do amigo e do Amado: Book of the Lover and the Beloved; an English translation with Latin and Old Catalan versions*, ed. Mark D. Johnston, Warminster: Aris & Phillips, 1995.

Richard de St-Victor, *Liber exceptionum*, ed. J. Chatillon, Textes philosophiques du moyen âge 5, Paris: J. Vrin, 1958.

Richard of St Laurent [pseudo-Albert], *De laudibus beatae Mariae virginis, libri duodecim*, in B. Alberti Magni Opera omnia, vol. 36, ed. A. and A. Borgnet, Paris: L. Vivès, 1898.

Rimbert, *Vita sancti Anskarii*, PL 118, cols. 959–1012.

Rufinus of Bologna, *Summa decretorum*, ed. Heinrich Singer, Paderborn: Ferdinand Schöningh, 1902.

*The Rule of St Benedict*, ed. J. C. McCann, London: Sheed and Ward, 1972.

*The Rule of St Benedict*, trans. with introduction and notes A. C. Meisel and M. L. del Mastro, New York: Doubleday Image Books, 1975.

Rupert of Deutz, *Anulus sive dialogus inter Christianum et Iudaeum*, ed. Rhabanus Haacke, in Maria Lodovica Arduini, *Ruperto di Deutz e la controversia tra cristiani ed ebrei nel secolo XII*, Rome: Istituto storico italiano per il Medio Evo, 1979, 175–242.

*Commentaria in Apocalypsim*, PL 169, cols. 825–1214.

*De sancta Trinitate et operibus eius*, ed. R. Haacke, 4 vols., CCCM 21–4, Turnhout: Brepols, 1971–2.

*In librum Ecclesiastes commentarius*, PL 168, cols. 1195–1306.

Salimbene de Adam, *Cronica*, ed. Giuseppe Scalia, 2 vols., Bari: Laterza, 1966, repr. CCCM 125–5a, Turnhout: Brepols, 1999.

Shatzmiller, Joseph, ed., *La deuxième controverse de Paris: Un chapitre dans la polémique entre chrétiens et juifs au Moyen Âge*, Collection de la Revue des Études Juives 15, Paris: Peeters, 1994.

Sicard of Cremona, *Mitrale*, PL 213, cols. 13–434.

Sigebert of Gembloux, *Apologia contra eos qui calumniantur missas coniugatorum sacerdotum*, ed. E. Sackur, MGH, Libelli de Lite Imperatorum et Pontificum 2, Hanover: Hahn, 1892, 436–48.

Silvas, Anna, trans. and annot., *Jutta and Hildegard: The Biographical Sources*, University Park: Pennsylvania State University Press, 1999.

Simon Fidati da Cascia, *De gestis domini salvatoris*, ed. Willigis Eckermann, 7 vols., Würzburg: Cassiciacum, 1998.

Simonsohn, Shlomo, ed., *The Apostolic See and the Jews*, 8 vols., Toronto: Pontifical Institute of Medieval Studies, 1988–91.

Somerville, Robert, *Papacy, Councils, and Canon Law in the 11th–12th Centuries*, Collected Studies CS 312, Aldershot: Ashgate, 1990.

*Statutes of the Realm*, 10 vols., London: George Eyre *et al.*, 1810–28.

Steinbach, Wendelin, *Opera exegetica*, ed. Helmut Feld, 3 vols., Wiesbaden: Franz Steiner, 1976–87.

Stephen of Bourbon, *Tractatus de diversis materiis praedicabilis*, in A. Lecoy de la Marche, ed., *Anecdotes historiques, légendes, et apologues tirés du recueil inédit d'Etienne de Bourbon, dominicain du XIIIe siècle*, Publications de la Société de l'histoire de France, Paris: Renouard, 1877.

Stephen of Tournai, *Die Summa Stephanus Tornacensis über das Decretum Gratiani*, ed. Johann Friedrich von Schulte, Giessen: Roth, 1891.

Suger of Saint Denis, *De administratione*, in Erwin Panofsky, ed. and trans., *Abbot Suger on the Abbey Church of St. Denis and its Art Treasures*, 2nd edn, ed. Gerda Panofsky-Soergel, Princeton: Princeton University Press, 1979.

Symeon of Durham, *Libellus de exordio atque procursu istius hoc est Dunhelmensis ecclesie: Tracts on the Origins and Progress of this the Church of Durham*, ed. and trans. David Rollason, Oxford Medieval Texts, Oxford: Clarendon Press, 2000.

Syrus, *Vita sancti Maioli*, PL 137, cols. 745–80.

Tanner, Norman, ed., *The Decrees of the Ecumenical Councils*, 2 vols., London: Sheed and Ward; Washington, D.C.: Georgetown University Press, 1990.

*Heresy Trials in the Diocese of Norwich, 1428–31*, Camden Society, 4th series, 20, London: Royal Historical Society, 1977.

Thomas Aquinas, *De aeternitate mundi contra murmurantes*, in R. M. Spiazzi, ed., *Divi Thomae Aquinatis: Opuscula philosophica*, Rome: Marietti, 1954.

*De malo*, in Leonine Commission, ed., *Opera omnia*, vol. 23.

*Opera omnia jussu Leonis XIII P. M. edita*, ed. Leonine Commission, Rome: Ex Typographia Polyglotta S.C. de Propoganda Fide *et al.*, 1882–.

*S. Thomae Aquinatis opera omnia*, ed. Robert Busa, 7 vols., Stuttgart and Bad Cannstadt: Friedrich Frommann, 1980.

*Summa theologica*, in Leonine Commission, ed., *Opera omnia*, vols. 4–12; English trans. and edn in 60 vols., London: Blackfriars, 1964–81.

Thomas of Chobham, *Sermones*, ed. Franco Morenzoni, CCCM 83A, Turnhout: Brepols, 1993.

*Thomae de Chobham: Summa confessorum*, ed. F. Broomfield, Analecta mediaevalia Namurcensia 25, Louvain and Paris: Nauwelaerts, 1968.

*Thomae Hemerken a Kempis opera omnia*, ed. M. J. Pohl, 7 vols., Freiburg i.Br.: Herder, 1902–22.

Tugwell, S., *Albert and Thomas: Selected Writings*, Classics of Western Spirituality, New York: Paulist Press, 1988.

Tugwell, S., ed., *Early Dominicans: Selected Writings*, Classics of Western Spirituality, New York: Paulist Press and London: SPCK, 1982.

Valla, Lorenzo, *Collatio Novi Testamenti*, ed. Allesandro Perosa, Florence: Sansoni, 1970.

van Dijk, R.Th. *Prolegomena ad Gerardi Magni opera omnia*, CCCM 192, Turnhout: Brepols, 2003.

Van der Woude, S., *Acta Capituli Windeshemensis*. The Hague: Nijhoff, 1953.

Van Engen, John, *Devotio Moderna: Basic Writings*, New York: Paulist Press, 1988.

Venarde, Bruce L., ed. and trans., *Robert of Arbrissel: A Medieval Religious Life*, Washington, D.C.: Catholic University of America Press, 2003.

*Vita sancti Norberti*, PL 170, cols. 1253–344.

Waddell, Chrysogonus, ed., *Hymn collections from the Paraclete*, Cistercian Liturgy Series, 8–9, Trappist, Ky.: Gethsemani Abbey, 1987–89.

*Narrative and Legislative Texts from Early Cîteaux*, Cîteaux: Commentarii Cistercienses, 1999.

*Twelfth-Century Cistercian Hymnal*, Cistercian Liturgy Series 1–2, Trappist, Ky.: Gethsemani Abbey, 1984.

Wakefield, W. L. and A. P. Evans, eds., *Heresies of the High Middle Ages*, New York: Columbia University Press, 1969, repr. Columbia: Columbia University Press, 1991.

Walter Map, *The Latin Poems Commonly Attributed to Walter Mapes*, ed. T. Wright, London: Camden Society, 1841.

Whitelock, D., M. Brett and C. N. L. Brooke, eds., *Councils and Synods with other Documents Relating to the English Church*, vol. 1, *AD 871–1204*, Oxford: Clarendon Press, 1981.

William of Newburgh, *Explanatio sacri epithalamii in matrem sponsi*, ed. John C. Gorman, Spicilegium Friburgense 6, Fribourg: Universitätsverlag, 1960.

William of Tyre, *History of Deeds Done beyond the Sea*, trans. Emily Atwater Babcock and A. C. Krey, New York: Columbia University Press, 1943.

Wilson, Evelyn Faye, *The Stella Maris of John of Garland, Edited together with a Study of Certain Collections of Mary Legends Made in Northern France in the Twelfth and Thirteenth Centuries*, Cambridge, Mass.: Wellesley College and the Mediaeval Academy of America, 1946.

Wolfram of Eschenbach, *Parzival*, ed. Karl Lachmann, Berlin: Walter de Gruyter, 1926.

# Secondary sources

Abou el-Fadl, K., 'Islamic Law and Muslim Minorities', *Islamic Law and Society* 1 (1994), 141–87.

Abulafia, David, 'The King and the Jews – the Jew in the Ruler's Service', in Christoph Cluse, ed., *The Jews of Europe in the Middle Ages (Tenth to Fifteenth Centuries)*, Turnhout: Brepols, 2004, 43–54.

*The Western Mediterranean Kingdoms 1200–1500: The Struggle for Dominion*, London: Longman, 1997.

Adams, Henry, *Mont Saint Michel and Chartres*, Harmondsworth: Penguin, 1986; first published 1904.

Aertsen, Jan and Andreas Speer, eds., *Was ist Philosophie im Mittelalter?*, Miscellanea Mediaevalia 26, Berlin: Walter de Gruyter, 1998.

Alphandéry, Paul, *La chrétienté et l'idée de croisade*, vol. 2, ed. Alphonse Dupront, Paris: Éditions Albin Michel, 1959.

d'Alverny, M.-T., 'Comment les théologiens et les philosophes voient la femme', *Cahiers de civilisation médiévale* 20 (1977), 105–29.

Amos, Thomas L., Eugene A. Green and Beverly Mayne Kienzle, eds., *De ore domini: Preacher and Word in the Middle Ages*, Studies in Medieval Culture 27, Kalamazoo, Mich.: Western Michigan University, 1989.

Amsler, Mark, 'Affective Literacy: Gestures of Reading in the Later Middle Ages', *Essays in Medieval Studies* 118 (2001), 83–110.

Andreini, Lucia, *Gregor Reisch e la sua Margarita Philosophica*, Analecta Cartusiana 138, Salzburg: Institut für Anglistik und Amerikanistik, 1997.

Andreozzi, Gabriele, *Il terzo ordine regolare di San Francesco nella sua storia e nelle sue leggi*, 3 vols., Rome: Editrice Franciscanum, 1993–95.

Andrews, Frances, *The Early Humiliati*, Cambridge: Cambridge University Press, 1999.

Angold, M. J., *The Byzantine Empire 1025–1204: A Political History*, 2nd edn, London: Longman, 1997.

*The Fourth Crusade: Event and Context*, Harlow: Longman, 2003.

Arnold, J. H., *Inquisition and Power: Catharism and the Confessing Subject in Medieval Languedoc*, Philadelphia: University of Pennsylvania Press, 2001.

'Lollard Trials and Inquisitorial Discourse', in Chris Given-Wilson, ed., *Fourteenth Century England II*, Woodbridge: Boydell Press, 2002, 81–94.

Arnold, Udo, 'Reformansätze im deutschen Orden während des Spätmittelalters', in Elm, ed., *Reformbemühingen und Observanzbestrebungen*, 139–52.

*Arts libéraux et philosophie au Moyen Âge: Actes du quatrième congrès international de philosophie médiévale. Université de Montréal, Montréal, Canada, 27 août–2 septembre 1967*, Montréal: Institut d'études médiévales; Paris: Vrin, 1969.

Asbridge, T. S., *The Creation of the Principality of Antioch, 1098–1130*, Woodbridge: Boydell Press, 2000.

Ashley, Kathleen and Robert Clark, eds., *Medieval Conduct*, Minneapolis: University of Minnesota Press, 2001.

Ashley, Kathleen and Paula Sheingorn, eds., *Interpreting Cultural Symbols: Saint Anne in Late Medieval Society*, Athens: University of Georgia Press, 1990.

Aston, Margaret, *England's Iconoclasts*, Oxford: Oxford University Press, 1988.

*Faith and Fire: Popular and Unpopular Religion, 1350–1600*, London: Hambledon Press, 1993.

*Lollards and Reformers: Images and Literacy in Late Medieval England*, London: Hambledon Press, 1984.

'The Use of Images', in Richard Marks and Paul Williamson, eds., *Gothic: Art for England 1400–1547*, London: Victoria and Albert Museum, 2003, 69–73.

'Were the Lollards a Sect?', in Peter Biller and Barrie Dobson, eds., *The Medieval Church: Universities, Heresy and the Religious Life. Essays in Honour of Gordon Leff*, Studies in Church History, Subsidia 11, Woodbridge: Boydell Press, 1999, 163–91.

'Wycliffe and the Vernacular', in Anne Hudson and Michael Wilks, eds., *From Ockham to Wyclif*, SCH, Subsidia 5, Oxford: Blackwell, 1987, 281–330; repr. in Margaret Aston, *Faith and Fire: Popular and Unpopular Religion 1350–1600*, London: Hambledon Continuum, 1984, 27–72.

Atkinson, Clarissa, *The Oldest Vocation: Christian Motherhood in the Middle Ages*, Ithaca, N.Y. and London: Cornell University Press, 1991.

Atkinson, Clarissa, Constance Buchanan and Margaret Miles, eds., *Immaculate and Powerful: The Female in Sacred Image and Reality*, Boston: Beacon Press, 1985.

Audisio, Gabriel, *The Waldensian Dissent: Persecution and Survival, c. 1170–c. 1570*, trans. Claire Davison, Cambridge and New York: Cambridge University Press, 1999.

d'Avray, D. L., *The Preaching of the Friars*, Oxford: Clarendon Press, 1985.

Bacci, Michele, 'The Berardenga Antependium and the *passio ymaginis* Office', *Journal of the Warburg and Courtauld Institutes* 61 (1998), 1–16.

Bachmann, Johannes, *Die päpstlichen Legaten in Deutschland und Skandinavien (1125–1159)*, Historische Studien 115, Berlin: Emil Ebering, 1913.

Baer, Yitzhak Fritz, *A History of the Jews in Christian Spain*, 2 vols., trans. Louis Schoffman, Philadelphia: Jewish Publication Society, 1971.

Baier, Walter, *Untersuchungen zu den Passionsbetrachtungen in der Vita Christi des Ludolf von Sachsen: Ein quellenkritischer Beitrag zu Leben und Werk Ludolfs und zur Geschichte der Passionstheologie*, Salzburg: Analecta Cartusiana, Institut für Englische Sprache und Literatur, 1977.

Bailey, M. D., *Battling Demons: Witchcraft, Heresy, and Reform in the Later Middle Ages*, University Park: Pennsylvania State University Press, 2003.

'The Feminization of Magic and the Emerging Idea of the Female Witch in the Late Middle Ages', *Essays in Medieval Studies* 19 (2002), 120–34.

Baldwin, J. W., *Masters, Princes and Merchants: The Social Views of Peter the Chanter and his Circle*, 2 vols., Princeton: Princeton University Press, 1970.

'Masters at Paris from 1179 to 1215: A Social Perspective', in Robert L. Benson, Giles Constable and Carol D. Lanham, eds., *Renaissance and Renewal in the Twelfth Century*, Cambridge, Mass.: Harvard University Press, 1982, 138–72.

Ball, R. M., 'Thomas Cyrcetur, a Fifteenth-Century Theologian and Preacher', *Journal of Ecclesiastical History* 37 (1986), 205–39.

Baltzer, Rebecca A., 'The Little Office of the Virgin and Mary's Role at Paris', in Margot E. Fassler and Rebecca A. Baltzer, eds., *The Divine Office in the Latin Middle Ages: Methodology and Source Studies, Regional Developments, Hagiography*, Oxford: Oxford University Press, 2000, 463–84.

Barber, M. C., *The Cathars: Dualist Heretics in Languedoc in the High Middle Ages*, Harlow: Longman, 2000.

'Lepers, Jews and Moslems: The Plot to Overthrow Christendom in 1321', *History* 66 (1981), 1–17.

*The New Knighthood: A History of the Order of the Temple*, Cambridge: Cambridge University Press, 1994.

*The Trial of the Templars*, Cambridge: Cambridge University Press, 1978.

Baring, Anne and Jules Cashford, *The Myth of the Goddess: Evolution of an Image*, London and New York: Viking Arkana, 1991.

Baron, Salo Wittmayer, *A Social and Religious History of the Jews*, 18 vols., 2nd edn, New York: Columbia University Press, 1952–83.

Barré, Henri, 'Antiennes et répons de la Vierge', *Marianum* 29 (1967), 153–254.

*Prières anciennes de l'occident à la mère du Sauveur des origines à saint Anselme*, Paris: P. Lethielleux, 1963.

Barstow, Anne, *Married Priests and the Reforming Papacy: The Eleventh-Century Debates*, Lewiston, N.Y.: E. Mellen Press, 1982.

Barstow, Kurt, *The Gualenghi-d'Este Hours: Art and Devotion in Renaissance Ferrara*, Los Angeles: J. Paul Getty Museum, 2000.

Bartlett, Robert, *The Making of Europe: Conquest, Colonization and Cultural Change 950–1350*, Princeton: Princeton University Press; London: Allen Lane, 1993.

Baschet, Jérôme, 'Diable', in Jacques Le Goff and Jean-Claude Schmitt, eds., *Dictionnaire raisonné du Moyen Âge*, Paris: Fayard, 1999, 260–72.

*La justice de l'au-delà: Représentations de l'enfer en France et en Italie, XIIe-XVe siècle*, Rome: École française de Rome, 1993.

Baumer, Christoph, 'Die Schreinmadonna', *Marian Library Studies* 9 (1977), 239–72.

Becker, Petrus, 'Benediktinische Reformbewegungen im Spätmittelalter. Ansätze, Entwicklungen, Auswirkungen', in *Untersuchungen zu Kloster und Stift*, Veröffentlichungen des Max-Planck-Instituts für Geschichte 68, StGS 14, Göttingen: Max-Planck-Institut für Geschichte, 1980, 167–87.

'Erstrebte und erreichte Ziele benediktinischer Reformen im Spätmittelalter', in Elm, ed., *Reformbemühungen und Observanzbestrebungen*, 23–34.

Beissel, Stephan, *Geschichte der Verehrung Marias in Deutschland während des Mittelalters: Ein Beitrag zur Religionswissenschaft und Kunstgeschichte*, Freiburg im Breisgau: Herder, 1909.

Bellomo, Manlio, *The Common Legal Past of Europe, 1000–1800*, Studies in Medieval and Early Modern Canon Law 4, Washington D.C.: Catholic University Press of America, 1995.

Belting, Hans, *The Image and its Public in the Middle Ages: Form and Function of Early Paintings of the Passion*, trans. Mark Bartusis and Raymond Meyer, New Rochelle, N.Y.: A. D. Caratzas, 1990.

*Likeness and Presence: A History of the Image before the Era of Art*, trans. Edmund Jephcott, Chicago: University of Chicago Press, 1994.

Benrath, Gustav Adolf, 'Traditionsbewusstsein, Schriftverständnis und Schriftprinzip bei Wyclif', in A. Zimmermann, ed., *Antiqui und Moderni*, Berlin: Walter de Gruyter, 1974, 359–82.

*Wyclifs Bibelkommentar*, Berlin: Walter de Gruyter, 1966.

Benson, R. L. and G. Constable with C. Lanham, eds., *Renaissance and Renewal in the Twelfth Century*, Cambridge, Mass.: Harvard University Press; repr., Toronto: University of Toronto Press, 1991.

Bent, Margaret and Andrew Wathey, eds., *Fauvel Studies: Allegory, Chronicle, Music, and Image in Paris, Bibliothèque nationale de France, MS français 146*, Oxford: Oxford University Press, 1998.

Benvenuti Papi, A., '*In castro poenitentiae': Santità e società femminile nell'Italia medievale*, Rome: Herder, 1990.

Berend, Nora, *At the Gates of Christendom: Jews, Muslims, and Pagans in Medieval Hungary, c. 1000–c. 1300*, Cambridge: Cambridge University Press, 2001.

Bériou, Nicole, *L'avènement des maîtres de la parole: La prédication à Paris au XIIIe siècle*, 2 vols., Paris: Institut d'Études Augustiniennes, 1998.

Berman, Constance Hoffman, *The Cistercian Evolution: The Invention of a Religious Order in Twelfth-Century Europe*, Philadelphia: University of Pennsylvania Press, 2000.

*Medieval Agriculture, the Southern French Countryside, and the Early Cistercians*, Transactions of the American Philosophical Society, 76.5, Philadelphia: Diana Publishing, 1986.

Berman, Harold J., *Law and Revolution: The Formation of the Western Legal Tradition*, Cambridge, Mass.: Harvard University Press, 1983.

Bernau, A., R. Evans and S. Salih, eds., *Medieval Virginities*, Toronto and Cardiff: University of Toronto Press, 2003.

Bernstein, Alan E., *The Formation of Hell: Death and Retribution in Antiquity and the Early Christian Worlds*, Ithaca, N.Y.: Cornell University Press, 1993.

'Heaven and Hell', in Maryanne Cline Horowitz, ed., *New Dictionary of the History of Ideas*, New York: Thomson/Gale, 2005, 969–73.

'The Invocation of Hell in Thirteenth-Century Paris', in J. Hankins, J. Monfasani and F. Purnell, Jr, eds., *Supplementum Festivum: Studies in Honor of Paul Oskar Kristeller*, Medieval and Renaissance Texts and Studies 49, Binghamton, N.Y.: M.R.T.S., 1987, 13–54.

'Tristitia and the Fear of Hell in Monastic Reflection from John Cassian to Hildemar of Corbie', in Robert J. Bast and Andrew C. Gow, eds., *Continuity and Change, the Harvest of Late-Medieval and Reformation History: Essays Presented to Heiko A. Oberman on his 70th Birthday*, Leiden: Brill, 2000, 183–205.

Bestul, Thomas H., *Texts of the Passion: Latin Devotional Literature and Medieval Society*, Philadelphia: University of Pennsylvania Press, 1996.

Beyer, Alfred, *Lokale Abbreviationen des 'Decretum Gratiani': Analyse und Vergleich der Dekretabbreviationen 'Omnes leges aut divine' (Bamberg), 'Humanum genus duobus regitur' (Pommersfelden) und 'De his qui intra claustra monasterii consistunt' (Lichtenthal, Baden-Baden)*, Bamberger theologische Studien 6, Frankfurt am Main: Peter Lang, 1998.

Bianchi, Luca, *Censure et liberté intellectuelle à l'université de Paris (XIIIe–XIVe siècles)*, Paris: Les Belles Lettres, 1999.

Bianchi, Luca and Eugenio Randi, *Le verità dissonanti: Aristotele alla fine del medioevo*, Rome and Bari: Laterza, 1990.

Biddick, K., 'Genders, Bodies, Borders: Technologies of the Visible', *Speculum* 68 (1993), 389–418.

Biemans, J. A. A. M., *Middelnederlandse Bijbelhandschriften*, Leiden: E. J. Brill, 1984.

Biesinger, Albert and Michael Kesseler, eds., *Himmel, Hölle, Fegefeuer: Theologisches Kontaktstudium*, Tübingen: Francke, 1995.

Biller, Peter, 'Cathars and Material Women', in Peter Biller and A. J. Minnis, eds., *Medieval Theology and the Natural Body*, York Studies in Medieval Theology 1, York: York Medieval Press, 1997, 61–108.

'The Cathars of Languedoc and Written Materials', in Peter Biller and Anne Hudson, eds., *Heresy and Literacy, 1000–1530*, Cambridge Studies in Medieval Literature 23, Cambridge: Cambridge University Press, 1994, 48–58.

'Heresy and Literacy: Earlier History of the Theme', in Peter Biller and Anne Hudson, eds., *Heresy and Literacy, 1000–1530*, Cambridge Studies in Medieval Literature 23, Cambridge: Cambridge University Press, 1994, 1–18.

*The Waldenses, 1170–1530: Between a Religious Order and a Church*, Aldershot: Ashgate, 2001.

Biller, Peter and B. Dobson, eds., *The Medieval Church: Universities, Heresy, and the Religious Life: Essays in Honour of Gordon Leff*, Studies in Church History, Subsidia 11, Woodbridge and Rochester, N.Y.: Boydell Press, 1999.

Biller, Peter and Anne Hudson, eds., *Heresy and Literacy, 1000–1530*, Cambridge Studies in Medieval Literature 23, Cambridge: Cambridge University Press, 1994.

Biller, Peter and A. J. Minnis, eds., *Medieval Theology and the Natural Body*, York: York Medieval Press, 1997.

Binski, Paul, 'The Angel Choir at Lincoln and the Poetics of the Gothic Smile', *Art History* 20 (1997), 350–74.

*Becket's Crown: Art and Imagination in Gothic England, 1170–1300*, New Haven: Yale University Press, 2004.

'The Crucifixion and the Censorship of Art around 1300', in P. Linehan and J. Nelson, eds., *The Medieval World*, London and New York: Routledge, 2001, 342–60.

'The Earliest Photographs of the Westminster Retable', *The Burlington Magazine* 130 (1988), 128–32.

Medieval Death: Ritual and Representation, London: British Museum, 1996.

Westminster Abbey and the Plantagenets, New Haven, Conn.: Yale University Press, 1995.

Birch, D. S., Pilgrimage to Rome in the Middle Ages: Continuity and Change, Woodbridge: Boydell Press, 1998.

Black, C. F., Italian Confraternities in the Sixteenth Century, Cambridge: Cambridge University Press, 1989.

Blackburn, Bonnie, 'For Whom Do the Singers Sing?', Early Music 25 (1997), 593–610.

Blackmore, J. and G. Hutcheson, eds., Queer Iberia: Sexualities, Cultures, and Crossings from the Middle Ages to the Renaissance, Durham, N.C.: Duke University Press, 1999.

Blamires, A., 'Women and Preaching in Medieval Orthodoxy, Heresy, and Saints' Lives', Viator 26 (1995), 135–52.

Blezzard, Judith, Stephen Ryle and Jonathan Alexander, 'New Perspectives on the Feast of the Crown of Thorns', Journal of the Plainsong and Mediaeval Music Society 10 (1987), 23–47.

Blumenfeld-Kosinski, R., and T. Szell, ed., Images of Sainthood in Medieval Europe, Ithaca, N.Y.: Cornell University Press, 1991.

Blumenkranz, Bernhard, Le juif médiéval au miroir de l'art chrétien, Paris: Études Augustiniennes, 1966.

Blumenthal, Uta-Renate, Papal Reform and Canon Law in the Eleventh and Twelfth Centuries, Aldershot: Ashgate Variorum, 1998.

Boehm, Barbara, 'Body-Part Reliquaries: The State of Research', Gesta 36 (1997), 8–19.

Boesch Gajano, S., La santità, Biblioteca essenziale Laterza 20, Rome: Laterza, 1999.

Boesch Gajano, S. and L. Scaraffia, eds., Luoghi sacri e spazi della santità, Sacro/Santo 1, Turin: Rosenberg & Sellier, 1990.

Bollmann, Anne M., 'Frauenleben und Frauenliteratur in der Devotio moderna. Volkssprachige Schwesternbücher in literarhistorischer Perspektive', unpublished PhD thesis, Rijksuniversiteit Groningen, 2004.

Bolton, Brenda, 'The Caravan Rests: Innocent III's Use of Itineration', in Anne J. Duggan, Joan Greatrex and Brenda Bolton, eds., Omnia disce: Medieval Studies in Memory of Leonard Boyle, O.P., Aldershot: Ashgate, 2005, 41–61.

Innocent III: Studies on Papal Authority and Pastoral Care, Aldershot: Variorum, 1995.

'Mulieres sanctae', in S. M. Stuard, ed., Women in Medieval Society, Philadelphia: University of Pennsylvania Press, 1976, 141–58.

'Poverty as Protest: Some Inspirational Groups at the Turn of the XIIth Century', in The Church in a Changing Society – Reconciliation or Adjustment?: Proceedings of the CIHEC-Conference in Uppsala, August 17–21, 1977, Uppsala: Almqvist & Wisell, 1978, 28–32.

Bolzoni, Lina, Web of Images: Vernacular Preaching from its Origins to St. Bernardino of Siena, Aldershot and Burlington, Vt.: Ashgate, 2004.

Bonnard, Jean, Les traductions de la Bible en vers français au Moyen Âge, Geneva: Slatkine Reprints, 1967.

Bornstein, Daniel, and Roberto Rusconi, eds., Women and Religion in Medieval and Renaissance Italy, Chicago and London: University of Chicago Press, 1996.

Børresen, Kari, 'Matristics: Female Godlanguage in the Middle Ages', Revue d'histoire ecclésiastique 95 (2000), 343–62.

Subordination and Equivalence: The Nature and Role of Woman in Augustine and Thomas Aquinas, Washington, D.C.: Catholic University Press of America, 1981.

Borsook, Eve and Fiorella Superbi Gioffredi, eds., *Italian Altarpieces 1250–1550: Function and Design*, Oxford: Clarendon Press, 1994.

Borst, A., *Die Katharer*, Schriften der MGH 12, Stuttgart: Anton Hiersemann, 1953.

Bose, Mishtooni, 'The Opponents of John Wyclif', in Ian Levy, ed., *A Companion to John Wyclif*, Leiden: Brill, 2006, 407–55.

'Reginald Pecock's Vernacular Voice', in Somerset, Havens and Pittard, eds., *Lollards and their Influence*, 217–36.

'Two Phases of Scholastic Self-consciousness: Reflections on Method in Aquinas and Pecock', in Paul Van Geest, Harm Goris and Carlo Leget, eds., *Aquinas as Authority*, Leuven: Peeters, 2002, 87–107.

'Vernacular Philosophy and the Making of Orthodoxy in the Fifteenth Century', *New Medieval Literatures* 7 (2005), 73–99.

Boss, Sarah Jane, *Empress and Handmaid: On Nature and Gender in the Cult of the Virgin Mary*, London: Cassell, 2000.

Bossy, J., *Christianity in the West: 1400–1700*, Oxford: Oxford University Press, 1985.

Boswell, J., *Christianity, Social Tolerance, and Homosexuality: Gay People in Western Europe from the Beginnings of the Christian Era to the Fourteenth Century*, Chicago: University of Chicago Press, 1980.

Bouchard, Constance, *'Every Valley Shall Be Exalted': The Discourse of Opposites in Twelfth-Century Thought*, Ithaca, N.Y. and London: Cornell University Press, 1991, 2003.

*Holy Entrepreneurs: Cistercians, Knights and Economic Exchange in Twelfth-Century Burgundy*, Ithaca, N.Y. and London: Cornell University Press, 1991.

Bouche, Anne-Marie, 'The Floreffe Bible Frontispiece, London, B.L. add. ms. 17738, fol. 3v–4r, and Twelfth-Century Contemplative Theory', PhD dissertation, Columbia University, 1997.

Bouet, P., G. Otranto, and A. Vauchez, eds., *Cultes et pèlerinages à saint Michel en Occident: Les trois monts dédiés à l'archange*, Rome: École française de Rome, 2003.

Boureau, A., *La légende dorée: Le système narratif de Jacques de Voragine (+1298)*, Paris: Cerf, 1984.

*Le Pape et les sorciers: Une consultation de Jean XXII sur la magie en 1320 (manuscript B.A.V Borghese 348)*, Rome: École française de Rome, 2004.

*Théologie, science et censure au XIIIe siècle: Le cas de Jean Peckham*, Paris: Les Belles Lettres, 1999.

Bouyer, Louis, 'Mysticism: An Essay on the History of the Word', in Richard Woods, ed., *Understanding Mysticism*, Garden City, N.Y.: Image Books, 1980, 42–55.

Bovey, Muriel, *Disciplinae cyclicae: L'organisation du savoir dans l'œuvre de Martianus Capella*, Polymnia 3, Trieste: Edizioni Università di Trieste, 2003.

Boyle, Leonard E., *Pastoral Care, Clerical Education and Canon Law, 1200–1400*, London: Variorum, 1981.

*The Setting of the Summa Theologiae of St Thomas*, Etienne Gilson Series 5, Toronto: Pontifical Institute of Mediaeval Studies, 1982.

*A Survey of the Vatican Archives and of its Medieval Holdings*, Toronto: Pontifical Institute of Mediaeval Studies, 1972.

Boynton, Susan, 'The Bible and the Liturgy', in Greti Dinkova-Bruun and Jennifer Harris, eds., *The Bible as a Way of Life: A Casebook*, New York: Routledge, 2006.

'From the Lament of Rachel to the Lament of Mary: A Transformation in the History of Drama and Spirituality', in Nicholas Bell, Claus Clüver and Nils Holger Petersen, eds.,

*Signs of Change: Transformations of Christian Traditions and their Representation in the Arts, 1000–2000*, Amsterdam: Rodopi, 2004, 319–40.

'Performative Exegesis in the Fleury *Interfectio Puerorum*', *Viator* 29 (1998), 39–64.

'Work and Play in Sacred Music and its Social Context, ca. 1050–1250', in R. N. Swanson, ed., *The Use and Abuse of Time in Christian History*, Studies in Church History 37, Woodbridge: Blackwell, 2002, 57–79.

Bozoky, E. and A. M. Helvétius, eds., *Les reliques: Objets cultes, symboles*, Turnhout: Brepols, 1999.

Branner, Robert, *Court Style and Sainte Chapelle: St. Louis and the Court Style in Gothic Architecture*, London: A. Zwemmer, 1965.

Brasher, Sally Mayall, *Women of the Humiliati: A Lay Religious Order in Medieval Civic Life*, New York and London: Routledge, 2003.

Brasington, Bruce C., *Ways of Mercy: The 'Prologue' of Ivo of Chartres*, Vita regularis: Ordnungen und Deutungen religiosen Lebens im Mittelalter 2, Münster: Lit Verlag, 2004.

Braun, Joseph, *Das christliche Altargerät in seinem Sein und in seiner Entwicklung*, Munich: M. Huebner, 1932.

Bredero, Adriaan, 'Jérusalem dans l'Occident médiéval', in P. Gallais and Y.-J. Riou, eds., *Mélanges offerts à René Crozet*, Poitiers: Société d'études médiévales, 1966, vol. I, 259–71.

Bremond, Claude, Jacques Le Goff and Jean-Claude Schmitt, *L'"Exemplum"*, Typologie des sources du moyen âge occidental, fasc. 40, Turnhout: Brepols, 1982.

Brenon, A., *Les femmes cathares*, Paris: Perrin, 1992.

'Fin'amors et catharisme. L'exemple de Peire Vidal en Lauragais et de Raymond de Miraval en Carcasses, avant la croisade contre les Albigeois', in V. Cognazzo and G. Mocchia di Coggiola, eds., *Peire William de Luserna e lo tems dals trobaires: Atti del convegno Storico Internazionale, 4 e 5 maggio 1991 in Luserna*, Cuneo: Ousitanio Vivo, 1994, 139–58.

'Les fonctions sacramentales du *Consolamentum*', *Heresis* 20 (1993), 33–55.

'Les hérésies de l'an mille: Nouvelles perspectives sur les origines du catharisme', *Heresis* 24 (1995), 21–36.

'La lettre d'Evervin de Steinfeld à Bernard de Clairvaux de 1143: Un document essentiel et méconnu', *Heresis* 25 (1995), 7–28.

*Le vrai visage du Catharisme*, Toulouse: Loubatières, 1990.

'The Waldensian Books', in P. Biller and A. Hudson, eds., *Heresy and Literacy, 1000–1530*, Cambridge Studies in Medieval Literature 23, Cambridge: Cambridge University Press, 1994, 137–59.

Brooke, C., *The Medieval Idea of Marriage*, Oxford: Oxford University Press, 1989.

Brooke, R. and C. Brooke, *Popular Religion in the Middle Ages: Western Europe 1000–1300*, London: Thames and Hudson, 1984.

Brown, Andrew, D., *Church and Society in England 1000–1500*, Basingstoke: Palgrave Macmillan, 2003.

*Popular Piety in Late Medieval England: The Diocese of Salisbury 1250–1550*, Oxford: Clarendon Press, 1995.

Brundage, James, *Law, Sex, and Christian Society in Medieval Europe*, Chicago: University of Chicago Press, 1987.

*Medieval Canon Law*, London and New York: Longman, 1995.

*Medieval Canon Law and the Crusader*, Madison: University of Wisconsin Press, 1969.

'Sin, Crimes and the Pleasures of the Flesh', in Peter Linehan and Janet L. Nelson, eds., *The Medieval World*, London: Routledge, 2001, 294–307.

Bruni, F., *La città divisa: Le parti e il bene comune da Dante a Guicciardini*, Bologna: Il Mulino, 2003.

Bruzelius, Caroline, *Stones of Naples: Church Building in the Angevin Kingdom, 1266–1343*, New Haven, Conn.: Yale University Press, 2004.

Bugge, Ragne, '*Effigiem Christi, qui transis, semper honora*. Verses Condemning the Cult of Sacred Images in Art and Literature', *Acta archaeologiam et artium historiam pertinentia* 6 (1975), 127–39.

Bull, M. G., *Knightly Piety and the Lay Response to the First Crusade: The Limousin and Gascony, c.970–c.1130*, Oxford: Clarendon Press, 1993.

*Thinking Medieval: An Introduction to the Study of the Middle Ages*, Basingstoke: Palgrave Macmillan, 2005.

Burger, G. and S. Kruger, eds., *Queering the Middle Ages*, Minneapolis: University of Minnesota Press, 2001.

Burman, Thomas, *Religious Polemic and the Intellectual History of the Mozarabs*, Leiden: Brill, 1994.

'Tafsīr and Translation: Robert of Ketton, Mark of Toledo, and traditional Arabic Qur'ān Exegesis', *Speculum* 73 (1998), 703–32.

Burr, D., *The Spiritual Franciscans*, University Park: Pennsylvania State University Press, 2001.

Burrows, Mark S., 'Jean Gerson on the "Traditioned Sense" of Scripture as an Argument for an Ecclesial Hermeneutic', in Mark S. Burrows and Paul Rorem, eds., *Biblical Hermeneutics in Historical Perspective*, Grand Rapids, Mich.: Eerdmans, 1991, 152–72.

Burton, Janet, *The Monastic Order in Yorkshire 1069–1215*, Cambridge Studies in Medieval Life and Thought, fourth series 40, Cambridge: Cambridge University Press, 1999.

Butterfield, Ardis, *Poetry and Music in Medieval France from Jean Renart to Guillaume de Machaut*, Cambridge: Cambridge University Press, 2002.

Buzineb, H., 'Respuestas de jurisconsultos maghrebies en torno a la inmigración de musulmanes hispánicos', *Hespéris Tamuda* 26–27 (1988), 53–66.

Bynum, Caroline Walker, *Fragmentation and Redemption: Essays on Gender and the Human Body in Medieval Religion*, New York: Zone Books, 1992.

*Holy Feast and Holy Fast: The Religious Significance of Food to Medieval Women*, Berkeley and Los Angeles: University of California Press, 1987.

*Jesus as Mother: Studies in the Spirituality of the High Middle Ages*, Berkeley, Los Angeles and London: University of California Press, 1982.

*The Resurrection of the Body in Western Christianity, 200–1336*, New York: Columbia University Press, 1995.

Bynum, Caroline Walker and Paul H. Freedman, eds., *Last Things: Death and the Apocalypse in the Middle Ages*, Philadelphia: University of Pennsylvania Press, 2000.

Bynum, C., S. Harrell and P. Richman, eds., *Gender and Religion: On the Complexity of Symbols*, Boston: Beacon Press, 1986.

Caby, Cécile, *De l'érémitisme rural au monachisme urbain: Les Camaldules en Italie à la fin du Moyen Âge*, Rome: École française de Rome, 1999.

Caciola, N., *Discerning Spirits: Divine and Demonic Possession in the Middle Ages*, Ithaca, N.Y. and London: Cornell University Press, 2003.

Cadden, J., *The Meanings of Sex Difference in the Middle Ages: Medicine, Science and Culture*, Cambridge: Cambridge University Press, 1993.

Cahn, Walter, 'Architecture and Exegesis: Richard of St-Victor's Ezekiel Commentary and its Illustrations', *Art Bulletin* 76 (1994), 53–68.

*Romanesque Bible Illumination*, Ithaca, N.Y.: Cornell University Press, 1982.

Cain van D'Elden, Stephanie, 'Black and White: Contact with the Mediterranean World in Medieval German Narrative', in Marilyn J. Chiat and Kathryn L. Reyerson, eds., *The Medieval Mediterranean: Cross-Cultural Contacts*, Minneapolis: University of Minnesota Press, 1988, 112–18.

Cameron, Euan, *Waldenses: Rejections of Holy Church in Medieval Europe*, Oxford: Blackwell, 2000.

Camille, Michael, *Gothic Art: Glorious Visions*, New York: Harry N. Abrams, 1996.

*The Gothic Idol: Ideology and Image-Making in Medieval Art*, Cambridge: Cambridge University Press, 1989.

*Image on the Edge: The Margins of Medieval Art*, Cambridge, Mass.: Harvard University Press, 1992.

Camporeale, Salvatore I., *Lorenzo Valla: Umanesimo e teologia*, Florence: Istituto Nazionale di Studi sul Rinascimento, 1972.

Candelaria, Lorenzo, '*El Cavaller de Colunya*: A Miracle of the Rosary in the Choirbooks of San Pedro Mártir de Toledo', *Viator* (2004), 221–64.

Cannon, Joanna and André Vauchez, *Margherita of Cortona and the Lorenzetti: Sienese Art and the Cult of the Holy Woman in Medieval Tuscany*, University Park: Pennsylvania State University Press, 1999.

Cardinali, C., 'Il santo e la norma. Bernardino da Siena e gli statuti perugini del 1425', in G. Ortalli, ed., *Gioco e giustizia nell'Italia di Comune*, Treviso and Rome: Fondazione Benetton/Viella, 1993, 183–91.

Carlson, C. and A. Weisl, eds., *Constructions of Widowhood and Virginity in the Middle Ages*, New York: St Martin's Press, 1999.

Carlson, Rachel Golden, 'Striking Ornaments: Complexities of Sense and Song in Aquitanian Verses', *Music & Letters* 84 (2003), 527–56.

Carozzi, Claude, *Le voyage de l'âme dans l'au-delà d'après la littérature latine (Ve–XIIIe siècle)*, Collection de l'École française de Rome 189, Rome: École française de Rome, 1994.

Carruthers, Mary J., *The Book of Memory: A Study of Memory in Medieval Culture*, Cambridge: Cambridge University Press, 1990.

Casagrande, Giovanna, 'Il movimento penitenziale francescano nel dibattito storiografico degli ultimi 25 anni', *Analecta Tertii Ordinis Regularis Sancti Francisci* 29 (1998), 351–89.

*Religiosità penitenziale e città al tempo dei communi*, Rome: Istituto Storico dei Cappuccini, 1995.

Cátedra García, P. M., *Sermón, sociedad y literatura en la edad media: San Vicente Ferrer en Castilla (1411–1412)*, Valladolid: Junta de Castilla y León, Consejería de Cultura y Turismo, 1994.

Catto, J. I., 'Wyclif and Wycliffism at Oxford 1356–1430', in J. I. Catto and Ralph Evans, eds., *The History of the University of Oxford*, vol. 2, *Late Medieval Oxford*, Oxford: Clarendon Press, 1992, 175–261.

Catto, J. I. and R. Evans, eds., *The History of the University of Oxford*, vol. 2, *Late Medieval Oxford*, Oxford: Clarendon Press, 1992.

Cavendish, Richard, *Visions of Heaven and Hell*, New York: Harmony Books, 1977.

Ceglar, Stanislaus, 'Guillaume de Saint-Thierry et son rôle directeur aux premiers chapitres des abbés bénédictins, Reims 1131 et Soissons 1132', in M. Bur, ed., *Saint Thierry: Une abbaye du VIe au XXe siècle. Actes du Colloque international d'Histoire monastique, Reims-Saint-Thierry, 11 au 14 octobre 1976*, Saint-Thierry: Association des Amis de l'Abbaye de Saint-Thierry, 1979, 299–350.

Certeau, Michel de, '"Mystique" au XVIIe siècle: Le problème du langage "mystique"', in *L'homme devant Dieu: Mélanges offerts au Père Henri de Lubac*, vol. 2, Paris: Aubier, 1964, 267–91.

Chadwick, Henry, *Boethius: The Consolations of Music, Logic, Theology, and Philosophy*, Oxford: Clarendon Press, 1981.

Chambers, Bettye Thomas, *Bibliography of French Bibles: Fifteenth- and Sixteenth-Century French-Language Editions of the Scriptures*, Geneva: Droz, 1983.

Chance, Jane, ed., *Gender and Text in the Later Middle Ages*, Gainesville, FL: University Press of Florida, 1996.

Chazan, Robert, *Barcelona and Beyond: The Disputation of 1263 and its Aftermath*, Berkeley, Los Angeles and London: University of California Press, 1992.

'The Blois Incident of 1171: A Study in Jewish Intercommunal Organization', *Proceedings of the American Academy of Jewish Research* 36 (1968), 13–32.

*Daggers of Faith: Thirteenth-Century Christian Missionizing and Jewish Response*, Berkeley and Los Angeles: University of California Press, 1989.

*European Jewry and the First Crusade*, Berkeley: University of California Press, 1987.

*Medieval Jewry in Northern France: A Political and Social History*, Baltimore and London: Johns Hopkins University Press, 1973.

Chenu, M.-D., *Introduction à l'étude de St Thomas d'Aquin*, 2nd edn, Montreal: Institut d'études médiévales, 1954; trans. A. M. Landry and D. Hughes, *Toward Understanding Saint Thomas*, Chicago: Regnery, 1964.

*Nature, Man and Society in the Twelfth Century*, ed. and trans. J. Taylor and L. K. Little, Chicago: University of Chicago Press, 1968.

*La théologie comme science au XIIIe siècle*, 3rd edn, Bibliothèque thomiste 33, Paris: Vrin, 1957.

Chiffoleau, Jacques, *La comptabilité de l'au-delà: Les hommes, la mort et la religion dans la région d'Avignon à la fin du Moyen Âge, vers 1320–vers 1480*, Collection de l'École française de Rome 47, Rome: École française de Rome, 1980.

Chodorow, Stanley, *Christian Political Theory and Church Politics in the Mid-Twelfth Century*, Publications of the Center for Medieval and Renaissance Studies, Berkeley and Los Angeles: University of California Press, 1972.

Christe, Yves, *Jugements derniers*, Saint-Léger-Vauban: Zodiaque, 2000.

Christian, William A., Jr, *Apparitions in Late Medieval and Renaissance Spain*, Princeton: Princeton University Press, 1981.

Christiansen, E., *The Northern Crusades*, 2nd edn, London: Penguin, 1997.

Citterio, F. and L. Vaccaro, eds., *Loreto crocevia religioso tra Italia, Europa e Oriente*, Brescia: Morcelliana, 1997.

Clark, Anne L., 'An Ambiguous Triangle: Jesus, Mary, and Gertrude of Helfta', *Maria: A Journal of Marian Studies* 1 (2000): 37–56.

*Elisabeth of Schönau: A Twelfth-Century Visionary*, Philadelphia: University of Pennsylvania Press, 1992.

Clark, Elizabeth A., 'Women, Gender, and the Study of Christian History', *Church History* 70 (2001), 395–426.

Clayton, Mary, *The Cult of the Virgin Mary in Anglo-Saxon England*, Cambridge: Cambridge University Press, 1990.

Clopper, Lawrence M., 'Franciscans, Lollards and Reform', in F. Somerset, J. C. Havens and D. G. Pittard, eds., *Lollards and their Influence*, Woodbridge: Boydell and Brewer, 2003, 177–96.

Cluse, Christoph, ed., *The Jews of Europe in the Middle Ages (Tenth to Fifteenth Centuries)*, Turnhout: Brepols, 2004.

Coakley, John, *Women, Men, and Spiritual Power: Female Saints and their Collaborators*, New York: Columbia University Press, 2006.

Cohen, Jeremy, *The Friars and the Jews: The Evolution of Medieval Anti-Judaism*, Ithaca, N.Y. and London: Cornell University Press, 1982.

'The Jews as the Killers of Christ in the Latin Tradition: From Augustine to the Friars', *Traditio* 39 (1983), 1–27.

*Living Letters of the Law: Ideas of the Jew in Medieval Christianity*, Berkeley, Los Angeles and London: University of California Press, 1999.

Cohen, J. and B. Wheeler, eds., *Becoming Male in the Middle Ages*, New York: Routledge, 1997.

Coing, Helmut, ed., *Handbuch der Quellen und Literatur der neueren europäischen Privatrechtsgeschichte*, vol. 1, Munich: C. H. Beck, 1973.

Cole, Andrew, 'William Langland and the Invention of Lollardy', in Somerset, Havens and Pittard, eds., *Lollards and their Influence*, 37–58.

'William Langland's Lollardy', *The Yearbook of Langland Studies* 17 (2003), 25–54.

Cole, Penny, *The Preaching of the Crusades to the Holy Land, 1095–1270*, Cambridge, Mass.: Medieval Academy of America, 1991.

Coletti, Theresa, 'Purity and Danger: The Paradox of Mary's Body and the Engendering of the Infancy Narrative in the English Mystery Cycles', in Linda Lomperis and Sarah Stanbury, eds., *Feminist Approaches to the Body in Medieval Literature*, Philadelphia: University of Pennsylvania Press, 1993, 65–95.

Colish, M., *Peter Lombard*, Brill Studies in Intellectual History 41, Leiden: Brill, 1994.

Constable, Giles. 'Eremitical Forms of Monastic Life', in *Istituzioni monastichi e istituzioni canonicali in Occidente (1123–1215)*, Milan: Vita e pensiero, 1980, 239–64.

'The Opposition to Pilgrimage in the Middle Ages', in his *Religious Life and Thought (11th–12th Centuries)*, London: Variorum Reprints, 1979, 125–46.

*The Reformation of the Twelfth Century*, Cambridge: Cambridge University Press, 1996.

'The Second Crusade as Seen by Contemporaries', *Traditio*, 9 (1953), 213–79.

Constable, Olivia Remie, *Housing the Stranger in the Mediterranean World: Lodging, Trade, and Travel in Late Antiquity and the Middle Ages*, Cambridge: Cambridge University Press, 2003.

Copeland, Rita, *Pedagogy, Intellectuals and Dissent in the Later Middle Ages: Lollardy and Ideas of Learning*, Cambridge: Cambridge University Press, 2001.

*Rhetoric, Hermeneutics, and Translation in the Middle Ages*, Cambridge: Cambridge University Press, 1991.

'Wycliffite Ciceronianism? The General Prologue to the Wycliffite Bible and Augustine's *De Doctrina Christiana*', in Constant J. Mews, Cary J. Nederman and

Rodney M. Thomson, eds., *Rhetoric and Renewal in the Latin West 1100–1540: Essays in Honour of John O. Ward*, Turnhout: Brepols, 2003, 185–200.

Corsi, Cesare and Pierluigi Petrobelli, eds., *Le polifonie primitive in Friuli e in Europa: Atti del congresso internazionale, Cividale del Friuli, 22–24 agosto 1980*, Rome: Torre d'Orfeo, 1989.

Cortese, Ennio, *Il diritto nella storia medievale*, vol. 2, *Il basso medioevo*, Rome: IL Cigno Galileo Galilei, 1995.

*Il rinascimento giuridico medievale*, 2nd edn, Rome: Bulzoni, 1996.

Courtenay, William J., 'Was There an Ockhamist School?', in M. J. F. M. Hoenen, J. H. J. Schneider and G. Wieland, eds., *Philosophy and Learning: Universities in the Middle Ages*, Leiden: Brill, 1995, 276–91.

Cowdrey, H. E. J., *Popes, Monks and Crusaders*, London: Hambledon Press, 1984.

Cracco, G., *Per una storia dei santuari cristiani in Italia: Approcci regionali*, Bologna: Il Mulino, 1999.

Craemer-Ruegenberg, Ingrid and Andreas Speer, eds., *'Scientia' und 'ars' im Hoch- und Spätmittelalter*, 2 vols., Miscellanea Mediaevalia 22, 1 / 2, Berlin and New York: Walter de Gruyter, 1994.

Crisciani C., *Il papa e l'alchimia: Felice V, Guglielmo Fabri e l'elixir*, Rome: Viella, 2002.

Crocker, Richard and David Hiley, eds., *The Early Middle Ages to 1300, New Oxford History of Music*, 2, Oxford: Oxford University Press, 1990.

Crossley, Paul, 'The Politics of Presentation: The Architecture of Charles IV of Bohemia', in Sarah Rees-Jones, Richard Marks and A. J. Minnis, eds., *Courts and Regions in Medieval Europe*, Woodbridge: Boydell and Brewer, 2000, 99–172.

Cubitt, C., 'Virginity and Misogyny in Tenth- and Eleventh-Century England', *Gender and History* 12 (2000), 1–32.

Cumming, Julie E., *The Motet in the Age of Dufay*, Cambridge: Cambridge University Press, 1999.

Cunneen, Sally, *In Search of Mary: The Woman and the Symbol*, New York: Ballantine Books, 1996.

Curtius, Andreas, ed., *Spiegel der Seligkeit: Privates Bild und Frömmigkeit im Spätmittelalter*, Nuremberg: Germanischen Nationalmuseums, 2000.

Cushing, Kathleen G., *Papacy and Law in the Gregorian Revolution: The Canonistic Work of Anselm of Lucca*, Oxford Historical Monographs, Oxford: Oxford University Press, 1998.

Dahan, Gilbert, *L'exégèse chrétienne de la Bible en Occident médiéval, XIIe-XIVe siècle*, Paris: Éditions du Cerf, 1999.

Dal Pino, Franco A., 'Tentativi di riforma e movimenti di osservanza presso i servi di Maria nei secoli XIV–XV', in Elm, ed., *Reformbemühungen und Observanzbestrebungen*, 347–70.

Davies, B., *The Thought of Thomas Aquinas*, Oxford: Clarendon Press, 1992.

Davis, Michael T., '"Sic et Non": Recent Trends in the Study of Gothic Ecclesiastical Architecture', *The Journal of the Society of Architectural Historians* 58 (1999), 414–23.

de Bruin, C. C., E. Persoons and A. C. Weiler, *Geert Grote en de moderne devotie*, Zutphen: De Walburgpers, 1984.

de Hamel, Christopher, *The Book: A History of the Bible*, London: Phaidon, 2001.

*Glossed Books of the Bible and the Origins of the Paris Booktrade*, Woodbridge: D. S. Brewer, 1984.

de Lubac, H., *Exégèse médiévale: Les quatre sens de l'écriture*, 4 vols., Louvain: Éditions Montaigne, 1959; trans. Mark Sebanc, *Medieval Exegesis: The Four Senses of Scripture*, 2 vols., Grand Rapids, Mich.: Eerdmans; Edinburgh: T&T Clark, 1988, 2000.

De Ridder-Symoens, Hilde, ed., *A History of the University in Europe*, vol. 1, *Universities in the Middle Ages*, Cambridge: Cambridge University Press, 1992.

de Wulf, M., *Histoire de la philosophie médiévale*, 6th edn, Louvain: Institut supérieur de philosophie, 1924–47; trans. Ernest C. Messenger, *History of Mediaeval Philosophy*, London: Longmans, 1926.

Deansley, Margaret, *The Lollard Bible and Other Medieval Biblical Versions*, Cambridge: Cambridge University Press, 1922.

Debby, Nirit Ben-Aryeh, 'Jews and Judaism in the Rhetoric of Popular Preachers: The Florentine Sermons of Giovanni Dominici (1345–1419) and Bernardino da Siena (1380–1444)', *Jewish History* 14 (2000), 175–200.

*Renaissance Florence in the Rhetoric of Two Popular Preachers: Giovanni Dominici (1356–1419) and Bernardino da Siena (1380–1444)*, Turnhout: Brepols, 2001.

Dechant, Friedrich, *Die theologische Rezeption der Artes liberales und die Entwicklung des Philosophiebegriffs in theologischen Programmschriften des Mittelalters von Alkuin bis Bonaventura*, St Ottilien: Eos, 1993.

Degler-Spengler, Brigitte, 'The Incorporation of Cistercian Nuns into the Order in the Twelfth and Thirteenth Century', in J. A. Nichols and L. T. Shank, eds., *Hidden Springs: Cistercian Monastic Women, Medieval Religious Women*, vol. 3.1, Cistercian Studies 113A, Kalamazoo, Mich.: Cistercian Publications, 1995, 85–134.

'Observanten außerhalb der Observanz. Die franziskanischen Reformen "sub ministris"', *Zeitschrift für Kirchengeschichte* 89 (1978), 354–71.

Delaruelle, Étienne, 'Paix de Dieu et croisade dans la chrétienté du XIIe siècle', in M.-H. Vicaire, ed., *Paix de Dieu et guerre sainte en Languedoc au XIIIe siècle*, Cahiers de Fanjeaux 4, Toulouse: Édouard Privat, 1969, 51–71.

*La piété populaire au Moyen Âge*, Turin: La Bottega d'Erasmo, 1975.

Derbes, Anne, *Picturing the Passion in Late Medieval Italy: Narrative Painting, Franciscan Ideologies, and the Levant*, New York: Cambridge University Press, 1996.

Dessì, R. M., 'Predicare e governare nelle città dello Stato della Chiesa alla fine del Medioevo. Giacomo della Marca a Fermo', in G. Barone, L. Capo and S. Gasparri, eds., *Studi sul Medioevo per Girolamo Arnaldi*, Rome: Viella, 2000, 125–54.

'La prophétie, l'Évangile et l'État. La prédication en Italie au XV$^e$ et au début du XVI$^e$ siècle', in R. M. Dessì and M. Lauwers, eds., *La parole du prédicateur V$^e$–XV$^e$ siècle*, Nice: Centre d'Études Médiévales, 1997, 395–444.

Diestelkamp, Bernhard, 'Der Vorwurf des Ritualmordes gegen Juden vor dem Hofgericht Kaiser Friedrichs II. im Jahr 1236', in Dieter Simon, ed., *Religiöse Devianz*, Frankfurt am Main: V. Klostermann, 1990, 19–39.

Dinzelbacher, Peter, *Judastraditionen*, Vienna: Selbstverlag des österreichischen Museums für Volkskunde, 1977.

'Religiöses Erleben vor bildender Kunst in autobiographischen und biographischen Zeugnissen des Hoch- und Spätmittelalters', in Soren Kaspersen, ed., *Images of Cult and Devotion: Function and Reception of Christian Images in Medieval and Post-Medieval Europe*, Copenhagen: Museum Tusculanum Press, 2004, 61–88.

*Vision und Visionsliteratur im Mittelalter*, Stuttgart: Hiersemann, 1981.

Dinzelbacher, Peter and James Lester Hogg, *Kulturgeschichte der christlichen Orden in Einzeldarstellungen*, Stuttgart: Alfred Kröner Verlag, 1997.

Dodwell, C. R., *Painting in Europe, 800 to 1200*, New Haven, Conn.: Yale University Press, 1992.

Doumit, Amin, *Deutscher Bibeldruck von 1466–1522*, St Katharinen: Scripta Mercaturae, 1997.

Du Boulay, F. R. H., 'The Quarrel between the Carmelite Friars and the Secular Clergy of London, 1464–68', *Journal of Ecclesiastical History* 5 (1954), 156–74.

Dubois, J. and J. L. Lemaître, *Sources et méthodes de l'hagiographie médiévale*, Paris: Cerf, 1993.

Dufeil, M.-M., *Guillaume de Saint-Amour et la polémique universitaire parisienne, 1250–1259*, Paris: Éditions A. et J. Picard, 1972.

Duffy, Eamon, 'Late Medieval Religion', in Richard Marks and Paul Williamson, eds., *Gothic: Art for England 1400–1547*, London: Victoria and Albert Museum, 2003, 56–67.

  *The Stripping of the Altars: Traditional Religion in England, 1400–1580*, New Haven, Conn.: Yale University Press, 1992.

Duggan, Charles, *Twelfth-Century Decretal Collections and their Importance in English History*, University of London Historical Studies 12, London: University of London, 1963.

Duggan, Lawrence G., 'Was Art Really the "Book of the Illiterate"?', *Word and Image* 5 (1989), 227–51.

Duggan, Mary Kay, 'The Psalter on the Way to the Reformation: The Fifteenth-Century Printed Psalter in the North', in Nancy Van Deusen, ed., *The Place of the Psalms in the Intellectual Culture of the Middle Ages*, Albany: State University Press of New York, 1999, 153–89.

Dumoutet, Edouard, *Le désir de voir l'hostie et les origines de la dévotion au Saint-Sacrement*, Paris: Beauchesne, 1926.

Dupront, A., *Du sacré: Croisades et pèlerinages, images et langages*, Paris: Gallimard, 1987.

Dupront, A., ed., *Saint-Jacques de Compostelle: La quête du sacré*, Turnhout: Brepols, 1985.

Duvernoy, J., *Le catharisme: La religion des cathares*, Toulouse: Privat, 1976.

  'Le catharisme: L'unité des églises', *Heresis* 21 (1993), 15–27.

  *L'histoire des cathares*, Toulouse: Privat, 1979.

Dykema, Peter A. and Heiko A. Oberman, eds., *Anticlericalism in Late Medieval and Early Modern Europe*, Leiden: Brill, 1993.

Eckermann, Willigis, *Wort und Wirklichkeit: Das Sprachverständnis in der Theorie Gregors von Rimini und sein Weiterwirken in der Augustinerschule*, Würzburg: Augustinus-Verlag, 1978.

Edbury, P. W., *The Kingdom of Cyprus and the Crusades, 1191–1374*, Cambridge: Cambridge University Press, 1991.

Edbury, P. W. and J. Rowe, *William of Tyre, Historian of the Latin East*, Cambridge: Cambridge University Press, 1988.

Edgington, Susan and Susan Lambert, eds., *Gendering the Crusades*, Cardiff: University of Wales Press, 2001.

Ehresmann, Donald L., 'Some Observations on the Role of Liturgy in the Early Winged Altarpiece', *Art Bulletin* 64 (1982), 359–69.

Ehrle, Franz, *Der Sentenzenkommentar Peters von Candia*, Münster: Aschendorf, 1925.

Ellington, Donna Spivey, *From Sacred Body to Angelic Soul: Understanding Mary in Late Medieval and Early Modern Europe*, Washington, D.C.: The Catholic University of America Press, 2001.

Elliott, D., *Fallen Bodies: Pollution, Sexuality, and Demonology in the Middle Ages*, Philadelphia: University of Pennsylvania Press, 1999.

'Mendikanten und Humanisten im Florenz des Tre- und Quattrocento. Zum Problem der Legitimierung humanistischer Studien in den Bettelorden', in Otto Herding and Robert Stupperich, eds., *Die Humanisten in ihrer politischen und sozialen Umwelt*, Bonn and Bad Godesberg: Boppard, 1976, 51–85.

*Proving Woman: Female Spirituality and Inquisitional Culture in the Later Middle Ages*, Princeton: Princeton University Press, 2004.

'Reform- und Observanzbestrebungen im spätmittelalterlichen Ordenswesen', in Elm, ed., *Reformbemühingen und Observanzbestrebungen*, 3–19.

*Spiritual Marriage: Sexual Abstinence in Medieval Wedlock*, Princeton: Princeton University Press, 1993.

Elm, Kaspar, 'Die Bruderschaft vom gemeinsamen Leben. Eine geistliche Lebensform zwischen Kloster und Welt, Mittelalter und Neuzeit', *Ons Geestelijk Erf*, 59 (1985), 470–96.

'*Vita regularis sine regula*. Bedeutung, Rechtsstellung und Selbstverständnis des mittelalterlichen und frühneuzeitlichen Semireligiosentums', in Frantisek Smahel and Elisabeth Müller-Luckner, eds., *Häresie und vorzeitige Reformation im Spätmittelalter*, Munich: Ro. Oldenbourg, 1998, 239–73.

ed., *Beiträge zur Geschichte der Konversen im Mittelalter*, Berlin: Duncker & Humblot, 1980.

*Reformbemühiingen und Observanzbestrebungen im Spätmittelalterlichen Ordenswesen*, Berliner Historischer Studien 14, Ordensstudien 6, Berlin: Duncker & Humblot, 1989.

Emery, Kent, 'Denys the Carthusian and the Doxography of Scholastic Theology', in M.D. Jordan and K. Emery, eds., *Ad Litteram: Authoritative Texts and their Medieval Readers*, eds. M. D. Jordan and K. Emery, Notre Dame: University of Notre Dame Press, 1992, 327–59.

Emmerson, Richard Kenneth, *Antichrist in the Middle Ages: A Study of Medieval Apocalypticism, Art, and Literature*, Seattle: University of Washington Press, 1981.

Engammare, Max, *Qu'il me baise des baisiers de sa bouche: Le Cantique des Cantiques à la Renaissance*, Geneva: Droz, 1993.

Epstein, Marcia, *Prions en chantant: Devotional Songs of the Trouvères*, Toronto: University of Toronto Press, 1997.

Erdmann, Carl, *Die Entstehung des Kreuzzugsgedankens*, Stuttgart: W. Kohlhammer, 1935.

Evangelisti, P., 'Fede, mercato, comunità nei sermoni di un protagonista della costruzione dell'identità politica della corona catalano-aragonese. Matteo d'Agrigento (c. 1380–1450)', *Collectanea Franciscana*, 73 (2003), 617–64.

Evans, G. R., 'Wyclif's *Logic* and Wyclif's Exegesis: The Context', in Diana Wood and Katherine Walsh, eds., *The Bible in the Medieval World: Essays in Memory of Beryl Smalley*, Oxford: Blackwell, 1985, 286–300.

Everist, Mark, *French Motets in the Thirteenth Century: Music, Poetry and Genre*, Cambridge: Cambridge University Press, 1994.

Falkenburg, Reindert, *The Fruit of Devotion: Mysticism and the Imagery of Love in Flemish Paintings of the Virgin and Child, 1450–1550*, Amsterdam and Philadelphia: John Benjamins, 1994.

Farmer, S. and C. Pasternack, eds., *Gender and Difference in the Middle Ages*, Minneapolis: University of Minnesota Press, 2003.

Farmer, S. and B. Rosenwein, eds., *Monks and Nuns, Saints and Outcasts: Religion in Medieval Society: Essays in Honor of Lester K. Little*, Ithaca, N.Y. and London: Cornell University Press, 2000.

Fassler, Margot, 'Composer and Dramatist', in Barbara Newman, ed., *Voice of the Living Light: Hildegard of Bingen and her World*, Berkeley and Los Angeles: University of California Press, 1998, 149–75.

'The Feast of Fools and *Danielis ludus*: Popular Tradition in a Medieval Cathedral Play', in Thomas Forrest Kelly, ed., *Plainsong in the Age of Polyphony*, Cambridge: Cambridge University Press, 1992, 65–99.

*Gothic Song: Victorine Sequences and Augustinian Reform in Twelfth-Century Paris*, Cambridge: Cambridge University Press, 1993.

'Mary's Nativity, Fulbert of Chartres, and the *Stirps Jesse*: Liturgical Innovation circa 1000 and its Afterlife', *Speculum* 75 (2000), 389–434.

'The Meaning of Entrance: Liturgical Commentaries and the Introit Tropes', in Paul Brainard, ed., *Reflections on the Sacred: A Musicological Perspective*, New Haven, Conn.: Yale Institute of Sacred Music, Worship, and the Arts, 1994, 8–18.

'Music and the Miraculous: Mary in the Mid-Thirteenth-Century Dominican Sequence Repertory', in Leonard Boyle and Pierre-Marie Gy, eds., *Aux origines de la liturgie dominicaine: Le manuscrit Santa Sabina XIV L1*, Rome: École française de Rome; Paris: CNRS Editions, 2004, 229–78.

Febvre, Lucien and Henri-Jean Martin, *The Coming of the Book: The Impact of Printing, 1450–1800*, trans. David Gerard, London: Verso, 1984.

Feine, Hans Erich, *Kirchliche Rechtsgeschichte*, vol. 1, *Die katholische Kirche*, Weimar: Böhlan, 1954.

Feld, Helmut, *Die Anfänge der modernen biblischen Hermeneutik in der spätmittelalterlichen Theologie*, Wiesbaden: Franz Steiner, 1977.

*Martin Luthers und Wendelin Steinbachs Vorlesungen über den Hebräerbrief*, Wiesbaden: Franz Steiner, 1971.

Felten, F. J., 'Die Ordensreformen Benedikts XII. unter institutionengeschichtlichem Aspekt', in G. Melville, ed., *Institutionen und Geschichte: Theoretische Aspekte und mittelalterliche Befunde*, Cologne, Weimar and Vienna: Böhlau, 1992, 369–435.

Ferrante, J., *Woman as Image in Medieval Literature*, New York and London: Columbia University Press, 1975.

Fichtenau, Heinrich, *Heretics and Scholars in the High Middle Ages 1000–1200*, trans. Denise A. Kaiser, University Park: Pennsylvania State University Press, 1998.

Finucane, R. C., *Miracles and Pilgrims: Popular Belief in Medieval England*, London: J. M. Dent & Sons, 1977.

Fletcher, R. A., 'Reconquest and Crusade in Spain c.1050–1150', *Transactions of the Royal Historical Society*, 5th series 37 (1987), 31–47.

Flores, N., '*Effigies amicitiae ... veritas inimicitiae*: Antifeminism in the Iconography of the Woman-Headed Serpent in Medieval and Renaissance Art and Literature', in N. Flores, ed., *Animals in the Middle Ages: A Book of Essays*, New York: Garland Publishing, 1996, 167–95.

Flori, Jean, 'La caricature de l'Islam dans l'Occident médiéval: Origine et signification de quelques stéréotypes concernant l'Islam', *Aevum* 2 (1992), 245–56.

'Réforme, *reconquista*, croisade: L'idée de reconquête dans la correspondance pontificale d'Alexandre II à Urbain II', *Cahiers de civilisation médiévale* 40 (1997), 317–35.

Flynn, William, *Medieval Music as Medieval Exegesis*, Lanham, Md. and London: Scarecrow Press, 1999.

Foreville, R., ed., *Les fonctions des saints dans le monde occidental (IIIe–XIIIe siècle)*, Rome: École française de Rome, 1991.

*Le Jubilé de saint Thomas Becket du XIIIe au XVe siècle: Études et documents*, Paris: SEVPEN, 1959.

Forey, A. J., *The Military Orders from the Twelfth to the Early Fourteenth Centuries*, Basingstoke: Macmillan, 1992.

Forrest, Ian, *The Detection of Heresy in Late Medieval England*, Oxford: Clarendon Press, 2005.

Forsyth, Irene H., *The Throne of Wisdom: Wood Sculptures of the Madonna in Romanesque France*, Princeton: Princeton University Press, 1972.

Fournié, Michelle, 'Cathédrale et liturgie des défunts: Le cas de Lavaur et de Toulouse', in *Fanjeaux: La cathédrale: XIIe–XIVe siècle*, Cahiers de Fanjeaux 30, Toulouse: Privat, 1995, 269–94.

Fournier, Paul, 'Un tournant de l'histoire du droit (1060–1140)', *Revue historique de droit français et étranger* 41 (1917), 129–80.

Fournier, Paul and Gabriel Le Bras, *Histoire des collections canoniques en Occident depuis les Fausses Décrétals jusqu'au 'Décret' de Gratien*, Paris: Recueil Sirey, 1931–32.

Fowler-Magerl, Linda, *Ordines iudiciarii and Libelli de ordine iudiciorum (From the Middle of the Twelfth to the End of the Fifteenth Century)*, Turnhout: Brepols, 1994.

Fraher, R. M., 'IV Lateran's Revolution in Criminal Procedure', in R. J. Castillo, ed., *Studia in honorem Eminentissimi Cardinalis Alphonsi M. Sticker*, Rome: LAS, 1992, 97–111.

France, J., *Victory in the East: A Military History of the First Crusade*, Cambridge: Cambridge University Press, 1994.

Frank, Barbara, 'Subiaco. Ein Reformkonvent des späten Mittelalters', *Quellen und Forschungen aus italienischen Archiven und Bibliotheken* 52 (1972), 526–656.

Frank, Isnard, *Hausstudium und Universitätsstudium der Wiener Dominikaner bis 1500*, Cologne: Böhlau, 1968.

Fransen, Gérard, *Décrétales et les collections de décrétales*, Typologie des sources du moyen âge occidental 2, Turnhout: Brepols, 1972.

Frassetto, M., *Medieval Purity and Piety: Essays on Medieval Clerical Celibacy and Religious Reform*, New York, 1998.

Freedberg, David, *The Power of Images: Studies in the History and Theory of Response*, Chicago: University of Chicago Press, 1989.

French, K., *The People of the Parish: Community Life in a Late Medieval English Diocese*, Philadelphia: University of Pennsylvania Press, 2001.

Fried, Johannes, *Die Entstehung des Juristenstandes im 12. Jahrhundert: Zur sozialen Stellung und politischen Bedeutung gelehrter Juristen in Bologna und Modena*, Forschungen zur neueren Privatrechtsgeschichte 21, Cologne: Böhlau, 1974.

Friedlander, A., *The Hammer of the Inquisitors: Brother Bernard Délicieux and the Struggle against the Inquisition in Fourteenth-Century France*, Leiden: Brill, 2000.

Froehlich, Karlfried, '"Always to Keep to the Literal Sense Means to Kill One's Soul": The State of Biblical Hermeneutics at the Beginning of the Fifteenth Century', E. Miner, ed., *Literary Uses of Typology from the Late Middle Ages to the Present*, Princeton: Princeton University Press, 1977, 20–48.

'Johannes Trithemius on the Fourfold Sense of Scripture', in Richard A. Muller and John L. Thompson, eds., *Biblical Interpretation in the Era of the Reformation*, Grand Rapids, Mich.: Eerdmans, 1996, 23–60.

Frojmovic, E., ed., *Imagining the Self, Imagining the Other: Visual Representation and Jewish–Christian Dynamics in the Middle Ages and Early Modern Period*, Leiden: Brill, 2002.

Fuglesang, Signe Horn, 'Christian Reliquaries and Pagan Idols', in Soren Kaspersen, ed., *Images of Cult and Devotion: Function and Reception of Christian Images in Medieval and Post-Medieval Europe*, Copenhagen: Museum Tusculanum Press, 2004, 7–32.

Fulton, Rachel, *From Judgment to Passion: Devotion to Christ and the Virgin Mary, 800–1200*, New York: Columbia University Press, 2002.

Fumagalli Beonio-Brocchieri, Maria-Teresa and Stefano Simonetta, eds., *John Wyclif: logica, politica, teologia*, Florence: Galuzzo, 2003.

Gaffuri, L., '"In partibus illis ultra montanis": La missione Supalpina di Vicent Ferrer (1402–1408)', in B. Hodel OP and F. Morenzoni, eds., *'Mirificus Praedicator': À l'occasion du sixième centenaire du passage de saint Vincent Ferrier en pays romand*, Rome: Istituto storico domenicano, 2006, 105–20.

Galuzzi, A. M., *Origini del'Ordini dei Minimi*, Rome: Libreria Editrice della Pontificia Universita Lateranense, 1967.

Gaposchkin, Cecilia, 'Philip the Fair, the Dominicans, and the Liturgical Office for Louis IX: New Perspectives on *Ludovicus decus regnantium*', *Plainsong and Medieval Music* 13 (2004), 33–61.

Gatti-Perrer, Maria Luisa, *La Gerusalemme celeste: Catalogo della mostra. Milano, Università Cattolica del S. Cuore 20 maggio–5 giugno 1983*, Milan: Vita e Pensiero, 1983.

Gatto, Ludovico, *Il pontificato di Gregorio X (1271–1276)*, Rome: Istituto Storico Italiano per il Medio Evo, 1959.

Gaudemet, Jean, *Église et cité: Histoire du droit canonique*, Paris: Cerf, 1994.

*Le mariage en Occident: Les mœurs et le droit*, Paris: Cerf, 1987.

*Les sources du droit canonique: VIIIe–XXe siècle*, Paris: Cerf, 1993.

Gauthier, M. M., *Les routes de la foi: reliques et reliquaires de Jérusalem à Compostella*, Fribourg and Paris: Office du Livre, 1983.

Geary, P., *Furta sacra: Thefts of Relics in the Central Middle Ages*, Princeton: Princeton University Press, 1978.

Gerrits, G. H., *Inter timorem et spem: A Study of the Theological Thought of Gerard Zerbolt van Zutphen (1367–1398)*, Leiden: Brill, 1986.

Ghosh, Kantik, 'Bishop Reginald Pecock and the Idea of "Lollardy"', in Ann Hutchison and Helen Barr, eds., *Text and Controversy from Wyclif to Bale: Essays in Honour of Anne Hudson*, Turnhout: Brepols, 2004, 251–65.

*The Wycliffite Heresy: Authority and the Interpretation of Texts*, Cambridge: Cambridge University Press, 2002.

Gibbs, Marion and Jane Lang, *Bishops and Reform 1215–1272, with Special Reference to the Lateran Council of 1215*, Oxford: Oxford University Press, 1934.

Gibson, Gail McMurray, *The Theater of Devotion: East Anglian Drama and Society in the Late Middle Ages*, Chicago: University of Chicago Press, 1989.

Gibson, J., 'Could Christ Have Been Born a Woman? A Medieval Debate', *Journal of Feminist Studies in Religion* 8 (1992), 65–82.

Gibson, Margaret, *Boethius: His Life, Thought and Influence*, Oxford: Basil Blackwell, 1981.

    'The *De doctrina christiana* in the School of St. Victor', in E. D. English, ed., *Reading and Wisdom: The De doctrina christiana of Augustine in the Middle Ages*, Notre Dame: University of Notre Dame Press, 1995, 41–7.

Gilchrist, J. T., *The Church and Economic Activity in the Middle Ages*, New York: St. Martin's Press, 1969.

Gilchrist, R., *Gender and Material Culture: The Archaeology of Religious Women*, London and New York: Routledge, 1994.

Gillespie, Vincent, 'Vernacular Books of Religion', in Jeremy Griffiths and Derek Pearsall, eds., *Book Production and Publishing in Britain 1375–1475*, Cambridge: Cambridge University Press, 1989, 317–44.

Gillingham, J., *Richard I*, New Haven, Conn.: Yale University Press, 1999.

Gilson, E., *History of Christian Philosophy in the Middle Ages*, London: Sheed and Ward, 1955.

Given, J. B., 'Factional Politics in a Medieval Society: A Case from Fourteenth-Century Foix', *Journal of Medieval History* 14 (1988), 233–50.

  *Inquisition and Medieval Society: Power, Discipline and Resistance in Languedoc*, Ithaca, N.Y.: Cornell University Press, 1998.

Glorieux, P., *Répertoire des maîtres en théologie de Paris au XIIIe siècle*, 2 vols., Paris: Vrin, 1933.

Goering, J. W., *William de Montibus (c. 1140–1213): The Schools and the Literature of Pastoral Care*, Toronto: Pontifical Institute of Mediaeval Studies, 1992.

Gonnet, Jean and Amedeo Molnar, *Les vaudois au Moyen Âge*, Turin: Claudiana, 1974.

Goodich, M., *Vita perfecta: The Ideal of Sanctity in the Thirteenth Century*, Stuttgart: Anton Hiersemann, 1982.

Górecki, Piotr, *Parishes, Tithes, and Society in Earlier Medieval Poland, ca. 1100–1250*, Philadelphia: American Philosophical Society, 1993.

Grabmann, M., *Die Geschichte der scholastischen Methode*, Freiburg.i.B.: Herder, 1909–11.

Graef, Hilda, *Mary: A History of Doctrine and Devotion*, 2 vols. in 1, London: Sheed and Ward, 1985; first published 1963, 1965.

Grant, E., *The Foundations of Modern Science in the Middle Ages: Their Religious, Institutional, and Intellectual Contexts*, Cambridge: Cambridge University Press, 1996.

  *God and Reason in the Middle Ages*, Cambridge: Cambridge University Press, 2001.

Grayzel, Solomon, *The Church and the Jews in the XIIIth Century*, Philadelphia: Dropsie College, 1933; vol. 2, ed. Kenneth Stow, New York: Jewish Theological Seminary in America, 1989.

    'The Papal Bull *Sicut Judaeis*', in Meir Ben-Horin *et al.*, eds., *Studies and Essays in Honor of Abraham A. Newman*, Leiden: Brill, 1962, 243–80.

Green, V. H. H., *Bishop Reginald Pecock: A Study in Ecclesiastical History and Thought*, Cambridge: Cambridge University Press, 1945.

Gregg, J., *Devils, Women, and Jews: Reflections of the Other in Medieval Sermon Stories*, Albany: State University of New York Press, 1997.

Grier, James, 'A New Voice in the Monastery: Tropes and Versus from Eleventh- and Twelfth-Century Aquitaine', *Speculum* 69 (1994), 1023–69.

Griffiths, Fiona, 'Brides and Dominae: Abelard's *Cura monialium* at the Augustinian Monastery of Marbach', *Viator* 34 (2003), 1–28.

'"Men's Duty to Provide for Women's Needs": Abelard, Heloise, and their Negotiation of the *cura monialium*', *Journal of Medieval History* 30 (2004), 1–24.

Gripkey, Mary Vincentine, *The Blessed Virgin Mary as Mediatrix in the Latin and Old French Legend Prior to the Fourteenth Century*, Washington, D.C.: Catholic University of America Press, 1938.

Groiß, Albert, *Spätmittelalterliche Lebensformen der Benediktiner von der Melker Observanz vor dem Hintergrund ihrer Bräuche: Ein darstellender Kommentar zum Caermoniale Mellicense des Jahres 1460*, Beiträge zur Geschichte des Alten Mönchtums und das Benediktinertums, 46, Münster: Aschendorff, 1999.

Grötecke, I., 'Representing the Last Judgement: Social Hierarchy, Gender and Sin', *Medieval History Journal* 1 (1998), 233–60.

Grundmann, Herbert, *Religious Movements in the Middle Ages: The Historical Links between Heresy, the Mendicant Orders, and the Women's Religious Movement in the Twelfth and Thirteenth Century with the Historical Foundations of German Mysticism*, trans. Steven Rowan, with an introduction by Robert Lerner, Notre Dame and London: University of Notre Dame Press, 1995.

Gujer, Regula, *Concordia discordantium codicum manuscriptorum? Die Textentwicklung von 18 Handschriften anhand der D. 16 des Decretum Gratiani*, Forschungen zur kirchlichen Rechtsgeschichte und zum Kirchenrecht 23, Cologne: Böhlau, 2004.

Gustafson, Kevin, 'Richard Rolle's *English Psalter* and the Making of a Lollard Text', *Viator* 33 (2002), 294–309.

Haas, A. and I. Kasten, eds., *Schwierige Frauen–schwierige Männer in der Literatur des Mittelalters*, Bern: Peter Lang, 1999.

Hadley, D., ed., *Masculinity in Medieval Europe: Women and Men in History*, Harlow: Addison Wesley Publishing Company, 1999.

Hadot, Ilsetraut, *Arts libéraux et philosophie dans la pensée antique*, Paris: Études augustiniennes, 1984.

Hagen, Kenneth, *A Theology of Testament in the Young Luther: The Lectures on Hebrew*, Leiden: Brill, 1974.

Haggh, Barbara, 'Foundations or Institutions? On Bringing the Middle Ages into the History of Medieval Music', *Acta musicologica* 68 (1996), 87–128.

Hagman, Ylva, 'Le catharisme, un neo-manichéisme?', in *Heresies* 21 (1993), 47–59.

'Le rite de l'initiation chrétienne chez les cathares et les bogomiles', *Heresis* 20 (1993), 13–31.

Hahn, Cynthia, 'The Voices of the Saints: Speaking Reliquaries', *Gesta* 36 (1997), 20–31.

Haller, Johannes, *Das Papsttum: Idee und Wirklichkeit*, vols. 2–5, Munich: Rowohlt, 1965.

Hamburger, Jeffrey F., *Nuns as Artists: The Visual Culture of a Medieval Convent*, Berkeley: University of California Press, 1997.

'To Make Women Weep: Ugly Art as "Feminine" and the Origins of Modern Aesthetics', *Res* 31 (1997), 9–33.

*The Visual and the Visionary: Art and Female Spirituality in Late Medieval Germany*, New York: Zone Books, 1998.

Hames, Harvey J., *The Art of Conversion: Christianity and Kabbalah in the Thirteenth Century*, Leiden: Brill, 2000.

Hamilton, Bernard, 'The Cathars and Christian Perfection', in Peter Biller and Barrie Dobson, eds., *The Medieval Church: Universities, Heresy, and the Religious Life:*

*Essays in Honour of Gordon Leff*, Studies in Church History, Subsidia II, Rochester, N.Y.: Boydell Press, 1999, 5–23.

'Introduction', in Hugh Eteriano, *Contra Patarenos*, ed. B. Hamilton, J. Hamilton and S. Hamilton, Leiden and Boston: Brill, 2004, 1–102.

*The Medieval Inquisition*, London: Edward Arnold, 1981.

'Wisdom from the East; the Reception by the Cathars of Eastern Dualist Texts', in Peter Biller and Anne Hudson, eds., *Heresy and Literacy, 1000–1530*, Cambridge Studies in Medieval Literature 23, Cambridge: Cambridge University Press, 1994, 38–60.

Hanawalt, B. and D. Wallace, eds., *Bodies and Disciplines: Intersections of Literature and History in Fifteenth-Century England*, Minneapolis: University of Minnesota Press, 1996.

Hanna, Ralph, 'Miscellaneity and Vernacularity: Conditions of Literary Production in Late-Medieval England', in Stephen G. Nichols and Siegfried Wenzel, eds., *The Whole Book: Cultural Perspectives on the Medieval Miscellany*, Ann Arbor: University of Michigan Press, 1996, 37–51.

Harper, John, *The Forms and Orders of Western Liturgy from the Tenth to the Eighteenth Century: A Historical Introduction and Guide for Students and Musicians*, Oxford: Oxford University Press, 1991.

Harris, Julie A., 'Redating the Arca Santa of Oviedo', *Art Bulletin* 77 (1995), 82–93.

Harthan, John, *Books of Hours and their Owners*, London: Thames and Hudson, 1977.

Harvey, L. P., *Islamic Spain, 1250–1500*, Chicago: University of Chicago Press, 1990.

Hasher-Burger, Ulrike, *Gesungene Innigkeit: Studien zu einer Musikhandschrift der Devotio Moderna (Utrecht, Universiteitsbibliotheek, ms. 16 H 34, olim B 113), mit einer Edition der Gesänge*, Studies in the History of Christian Thought 106, Leiden: Brill, 2002.

Haskins, Charles Homer, *The Renaissance of the Twelfth Century*, Cleveland and New York: Meridian Books, 1963.

Haug, Andreas, *Troparia tardiva: Repertorium später Tropenquellen aus dem deutschsprachigen Raum*, Kassel and New York: Bärenreiter, 1995.

Haussherr, Reiner, 'Triumphkreuz', *Lexikon der christlichen ikonographie* 4 (1972), col. 357.

Haverkamp, Alfred, 'The Jewish Quarters in German Towns during the Late Middle Ages', in R. Po-Chia Hsia and Hartmut Lehmann, eds., *In and Out of the Ghetto: Jewish–Gentile Relations in Late Medieval and Early Modern Germany*, Cambridge: Cambridge University Press, 1995, 237–53.

Helmholz, R. H., *Canon Law and the Law of England*, London: Hambledon Press, 1987.

*The Spirit of Classical Canon Law*, Athens, Ga. and London: University of Georgia Press, 1996.

Hendrix, Scott H., *Ecclesia in via: Ecclesiological Developments in the Medieval Psalms of Martin Luther*, Leiden: Brill, 1974.

Herbers, K., *Der Jakobuskult des 12. Jahrhunderts und das 'Liber sancti Jacobi'*, Wiesbaden: F. Steiner, 1984.

Hernandez, R., 'La Reforma Dominicana entre los Concilios de Constanza y Basilea', *Archivo Dominicano* 8 (1987), 5–43.

Heslop, T. A. and Veronica A. Sekules, *Medieval Art and Architecture at Lincoln Cathedral*, London: British Archaeological Association, 1986.

Highfield, J. R. L., 'The Jeronomites in Spain: Their Patrons and Success 1373–1516', *Journal of Ecclesiastical History* 34 (1983), 513–44.

Hiley, David, *Western Plainchant: A Handbook*, Oxford: Oxford University Press, 1993.

Hillebrand, Eugen, 'Die Observantenbewegung in der deutschen Ordensprovinz der Dominikaner', in Elm, ed., *Reformbemühungen und Observanzbestrebungen*, 219–71.

Hillenbrand, C., *The Crusades: Islamic Perspectives*, Edinburgh: Edinburgh University Press, 2000.

Hillgarth, Jocelyn N., *Ramon Lull and Lullism in Fourteenth-Century France*, Oxford: Clarendon Press, 1971.

Hinnebusch, W. A., *The History of the Dominican Order*, 2 vols., Staten Island, N.Y.: Alba House, 1966.

Hirn, Yrjö, *The Sacred Shrine: A Study of the Poetry and Art of the Catholic Church*, London: MacMillan and Co., 1912.

Hirschbiegel, J. and W. Paravicini, *Das Frauenzimmer: Die Frau bei Hofe in Spätmittelalter und früher Neuzeit*, Stuttgart: Thorbecke, 2000.

Hobbins, Daniel, 'The Schoolman as Public Intellectual: Jean Gerson and the Late Medieval Tract', *American Historical Review* 108 (2003), 1308–37.

Hoenen, Maarten, 'Theology and Metaphysics: The Debate between John Wyclif and John Kenningham on the Principles of Reading the Scriptures', in Fumagalli Beonio-Brocchieri and Simonetta, eds., *John Wyclif*, 23–55.

Hoenen, Maarten, Josef Schneider and Georg Wieland, eds., *Philosophy and Learning: Universities in the Middle Ages*, Education and Society in the Middle Ages and Renaissance 6, Leiden: Brill, 1995.

Hollywood, Amy, *The Soul as Virgin Wife: Mechtild of Magdeburg, Marguerite Porete, and Meister Eckhart*, Notre Dame: University of Notre Dame Press, 1995.

Hopkin, Charles Edward, *The Share of Thomas Aquinas in the Growth of Witchcraft*, Philadelphia: University of Pennsylvania Press, 1940.

Housley, N. J., *The Avignon Papacy and the Crusades, 1305–1378*, Oxford: Clarendon Press, 1986.

*The Crusaders*, Stroud: Tempus Publishing, 2002.

*The Italian Crusades: The Papal-Angevin Alliance and the Crusades against Christian Lay Powers, 1254–1343*, Oxford: Clarendon Press, 1982.

*The Later Crusades: From Lyons to Alcazar 1274–1580*, Oxford: Oxford University Press, 1992.

Howard, P. F., *Beyond the Written Word: Preaching and Theology in the Florence of Archbishop Antoninus, 1427–1459*, Florence: Olschki, 1995.

Howie, D. I., 'Benedictine Monks, Manuscript Copying, and the Renaissance: Johannes Trithemius' De Laude Scriptorum', *Revue Bénédictine* 86 (1976), 129–54.

Hudson, Anne, 'Langland and Lollardy?', *The Yearbook of Langland Studies* 17 (2003), 93–105.

*Lollards and their Books*, London: Hambledon Press, 1985.

'*Peculiaris regis clericus*: Wyclif and the Issue of Authority', in M. Gosman, A. V. Vanderjagt and J. R. Veenstra, eds., *The Growth of Authority in the Medieval West*, Groningen: E. Forsten, 1999, 63–81.

*The Premature Reformation: Wycliffite Texts and Lollard History*, Oxford: Clarendon Press, 1988.

Hughes, Andrew, 'Late Medieval Plainchant for the Divine Office', in Reinhard Strohm and Bonnie Blackburn, eds., *Music as Concept and Practice in the Late Middle Ages*, New Oxford History of Music 3.1, New York: Oxford University Press, 2001, 47–96.

Hughes, D., 'Distinguishing Signs: Ear-Rings, Jews, and Franciscan Rhetoric in the Italian Renaissance City', *Past and Present* 112 (1986), 3–59.

'Sumptuary Law and Social Relations in Renaissance Italy', in J. Bossy, ed., *Disputes and Settlements: Law and Human Relations in the West*, Cambridge: Cambridge University Press, 1983, 66–99.

Hughes, Robert, *Heaven and Hell in Western Art*, New York: Stein and Day, 1968.

Hunt, Richard William, 'The Introductions to the "Artes" in the Twelfth Century', in *Studia mediaevalia in honorem admodum Reverendi Patris Raymundi Josephi Martin*, Bruges: De Tempel, 1948, 85–112.

Huot, Sylvia, *Allegorical Play in the Old French Motet: The Sacred and the Profane in Thirteenth-Century Polyphony*, Stanford: Stanford University Press, 1997.

Hyma, Albert, *The Christian Renaissance: A History of the 'Devotio Moderna'*, Grand Rapids: Reformed Press, 1924; 2nd edn, Hamden: Archon Books, 1965.

IJsewijn, Jozeph and Jacques Paquet, eds., *The Universities in the Late Middle Ages*, Leuven: Leuven University Press, 1978.

Illmer, Detlef, 'Artes liberales', *Theologische Realenzyklopädie* 4 (1979), 156–71.

Iogna-Prat, Dominique, *Order and Exclusion: Cluny and Christendom Face Heresy, Judaism, and Islam (1000–1150)*, trans. G. R. Edwards, Ithaca, N.Y.: Cornell University Press, 2002.

Iogna-Prat, Dominique, Éric Palazzo and Daniel Russo, eds., *Marie: Le culte de la Vierge dans la société médiévale*, Paris: Beauchesne, 1996.

Izbicki, T. M., 'Pyres of Vanities: Mendicant Preaching on the Vanity of Women and its Audience', in T. L. Amos, E. A. Green and B. M. Kienzle, eds., *'De ore Domini': Preacher and Word in the Middle Ages*, Kalamazoo, Mich.: Medieval Institute Publications, 1989, 211–34.

Jackson, Peter, 'The Mongols and the Faith of the Conquered', in Reuven Amitai and Michael Biran, eds., *Mongols, Turks, and Others: Eurasian Nomads and the Sedentary World*, Leiden and Boston: Brill, 2005, 245–90.

Jaeger, C. Stephen, *The Envy of Angels: Cathedral Schools and Social Ideals in Medieval Europe, 950–1200*, Philadelphia: University of Pennsylvania Press, 1994.

James, John, *The Contractors of Chartres*, Dooralong, N.S.W.: Mandorla, 1979.

Jeauneau, Edouard, 'Le Prologus in Eptatheucon de Thierry de Chartres', *Mediaeval Studies* 16 (1954), 171–5.

Johnson, Elizabeth A., 'Marian Devotion in the Western Church', in Jill Raitt, ed., *Christian Spirituality*, vol. 2, *High Middle Ages and Reformation*, New York: Crossroad, 1987, 392–414.

Johnson, W., 'The Myth of Jewish Male Menses', *Journal of Medieval History* 24 (1998), 273–95.

Jordan, M., *The Invention of Sodomy in Christian Theology*, Chicago: University of Chicago Press, 1997.

Jordan, William Chester, *The French Monarchy and the Jews: From Philip Augustus to the Last Capetians*, Philadelphia: University of Pennsylvania Press, 1989.

*Louis IX and the Challenge of the Crusade: A Study in Rulership*, Princeton: Princeton University Press, 1979.

'Marian Devotion and the Talmud Trial of 1240', in Bernard Lewis and Friedrich Niewöhner, eds., *Religiongespräche in Mittelalter*, Wiesbaden: Harrassowitz, 1992, 67–70.

Jotischky, A., *Crusading and the Crusader States*, Harlow: Pearson Longman, 2004.

Jounel, P., *Le culte des saints dans les basiliques du Latran et du Vatican au XIIe siècle*, Rome: École française de Rome, 1977.

Jung, Jacqueline E., 'Beyond the Barrier: The Unifying Role of the Choir Screen in Gothic Churches', *Art Bulletin* 82 (2000), 622–57.

Just, Robert, 'Anti-Clericalism and National Identity: Attitudes towards the Orthodox Church in Greece', in Wendy James and Douglas H. Johnson, eds., *Vernacular Christianity: Essays in the Social Anthropology of Religion Presented to Godfrey Lienhardt*, Oxford: Jaso, 1988, 73–87.

Kaelber, L., *Schools of Asceticism: Ideology and Organization in Medieval Religious Communities*, University Park: Pennsylvania State University Press, 1998.

Kamerick, Kathleen, *Popular Piety and Art in the Late Middle Ages: Image Worship and Idolatry in England, 1350–1500*, New York: Palgrave, 2002.

Kaminsky, Howard, 'The Problematics of "Heresy" and "the Reformation"', in František Šmahel and Elisabeth Müller-Luckner, eds., *Häresie und vorzeitige Reformation im Spätmittelalter*, Munich: Oldenbourg, 1998, 1–22.

Kantorowicz, Hermann U., *Über die Entstehung der Digestenvulgata: Ergänzungen zu Mommsen*, Weimar: Böhlan, 1910.

Kantorowicz, Hermann U. and W. W. Buckland, *Studies in the Glossators of the Roman Law: Newly Discovered Writings of the Twelfth Century*, Cambridge: Scientia, 1938; repr. with 'Addenda et corrigenda' by Peter Weimar, Aalen: Scientia, 1969.

Kaplan, M., ed., *Le sacré et son inscription dans l'espace à Byzance et en Occident: Études comparées*, Paris: Publications de la Sorbonne, 2001.

Karras, R., 'Gendered Sin and Misogyny in John of Bromyard's *Summa Predicantium*', *Traditio* 47 (1992), 233–57.

'Holy Harlots: Prostitute-Saints in Medieval Legend', *Journal of the History of Sexuality* 1 (1990), 3–32.

Kaspersen, Soren, ed., *Images of Cult and Devotion: Function and Reception of Christian Images in Medieval and Post-Medieval Europe*, Copenhagen: Museum Tusculanum Press, 2004.

Kay, S. and M. Rubin, eds., *Framing Medieval Bodies*, Manchester and New York: University of Manchester Press, 1994.

Kedar, Benjamin Z., *Crusade and Mission: European Approaches towards the Muslims*, Princeton: Princeton University Press, 1984.

Kelly, John N. D., *Jerome: His Life, Writings and Controversies*, London: Duckworth, 1975.

Kemp, Eric, *Canonization and Authority in the Western Church*, London: Oxford University Press, 1948.

Kemp, Wolfgang, *The Narratives of Gothic Stained Glass*, trans. Caroline Dobson Saltzwedel, Cambridge: Cambridge University Press, 1997.

Kempers, B., 'Icons, Altarpieces and Civic Ritual in Siena Cathedral 1100–1530', in Barbara Hanawalt and Katherine L. Reyerson, eds., *City and Spectacle in Medieval Europe*, Minneapolis: University of Minnesota Press, 1994, 89–136.

Kendall, Calvin B., *The Allegory of the Church: Romanesque Portals and their Verse Inscriptions*, Toronto: University of Toronto Press, 1998.

Kennedy, H. N., *Crusader Castles*, Cambridge: Cambridge University Press, 1994.

Kenny, Anthony, ed., *Wyclif in his Times*, Oxford: Clarendon Press, 1986.

Kéry, Lotte, *Canonical Collections of the Early Middle Ages (ca. 400–1140): A Bibliographical Guide to the Manuscripts and Literature*, History of Medieval Canon Law 1, Washington, D.C.: Catholic University Press of America, 1999.

Khalil Samir, Samir and Jørgen S. Nielsen, eds., *Christian Arabic Apologetics during the Abbasid Period: 750–1258*, Leiden: Brill, 1994.

Khoury, Adel Théodore, *Polémique byzantine contre l'Islam (VIIIe–XIIIe s.)*, Leiden: Brill, 1972.

    *Les théologiens byzantins et l'Islam: Textes et auteurs (VIIIe–XIIIe s.)*, Louvain and Paris: Éditions Nauwelaerts, 1969.

Kieckhefer, Richard, *European Witch Trials*, London: Routledge & Kegan Paul, 1976.

    'Major Currents in Late Medieval Devotion', in Jill Raitt, Bernard McGinn and John Meyendorff, eds., *Christian Spirituality: High Middle Ages and Reformation*, World Spirituality 17, New York: Crossroad, 1987, 75–105.

    'The Office of Inquisition and Medieval Heresy: The Transition from a Personal to an Institutional Jurisdiction', *Journal of Ecclesiastical History* 46 (1995), 36–61.

    *The Repression of Heresy in Medieval Germany*, Liverpool: Liverpool University Press, 1979.

    *Unquiet Souls: Fourteenth-Century Saints and their Religious Milieu*, Chicago: University of Chicago Press, 1984.

Kienzle, B. M., *Cistercians, Heresy and Crusade in Occitania, 1145–1229: Preaching in the Lord's Vineyard*, Woodbridge: Boydell Press; York: York Medieval Press, 2001.

    'Holiness and Obedience: Denouncement of Twelfth-Century Waldensian Lay Preaching', in A. Ferreiro, ed., *The Devil, Heresy and Witchcraft in the Middle Ages: Essays in Honor of Jeffrey B. Russell*, Leiden, Boston and Cologne: Brill, 1998, 259–78.

    'Medieval Sermons and their Performance: Theory and Record', in C. A. Muessig, ed., *The Sermon in the Middle Ages*, Leiden: Brill, 2002, 89–124.

    'Pons of Léras', [introduction and translation] in Thomas Head, ed., *Medieval Hagiography*, New York: Garland Press, 2000, 495–513.

    'The Prostitute-Preacher: Patterns of Polemic against Waldensian Women Preachers', in B. M. Kienzle and P. J. Walker, eds., *Women Preachers and Prophets through Two Millennia of Christianity*, Berkeley, Los Angeles and London: University of California Press, 1998, 99–113.

Kienzle, B. M., ed., *The Sermon*, Typologie des sources du Moyen Âge occidental, fasc. 81–3, Turnhout: Brepols, 2000.

Kienzle, B. M. and P. Walker, eds., *Women Preachers and Prophets through Two Millennia of Christianity*, Berkeley and Los Angeles: University of California Press, 1998.

Kisch, Guido, *Forschungen zur Rechts-und Sozialgeschichte der Juden in Deutschland während des Mittelalters*, Ausgewählte Schriften 1, 2nd edn, Stuttgart: W. Kohlhammer, 1955.

    *The Jews in Medieval Germany: A Study in their Legal and Social Status*, Chicago: University of Chicago Press, 1949.

    'The Yellow Badge in History', *Historia Judaica* 19 (1957), 89–146.

Klaniczay, G., 'The "Bonfire of Vanities" and the Mendicants', in Gerhard Jaritz, ed., *Emotions and Material Culture: International Round-Table Discussion. Krems an der Donau, October 7–8, 2002*, Vienna: Verlag des Österreichischen Akademie der Wissenschaften, 2003, 31–60.

    *Holy Rulers and Blessed Princesses: Dynastic Cults in Medieval Central Europe*, Cambridge: Cambridge University Press, 2000.

Klapisch-Zuber, C., ed., *A History of Women in the West*, vol. 2, *Silences of the Middle Ages*, Cambridge, Mass.: Harvard University Press, 1992.

Klausmann, Theo, *Consuetudo consuetudine vincitur: Die Hausordnungen der Brüder vom gemeinsamen Leben im Bildungs- und Sozialisationsprogram der Devotio moderna*, Bern: Peter Lang, 2003.

Kleinberg, A. M., *Prophets in their Own Country: Living Saints and the Making of Sainthood in the Later Middle Ages*, Chicago: University of Chicago Press, 1992.

Klepper, Deeana Copeland, 'Literal versus Carnal: George of Siena's Christian Reading of Jewish Exegesis', in Natalie Dohsmann and David Stern, eds., *Jewish Biblical Interpretation and Cultural Exchange: Comparative Exegesis in Context*, Philadelphia: University of Pennsylvania Press, 2008, 196–213.

Knowles, D., *The Monastic Order in England*, Cambridge: Cambridge University Press, 1966.

*The Religious Orders in England*, vol. 1 Cambridge: Cambridge University Press, 1948.

Kock, T., *Die Buchkultur der Devotio moderna: Handschriftenproduktion, Literaturversorgung und Bibliotheksaufbau im Zeitalter des Medienwechsels*, 2nd edn, Frankfurt: Lang, 2002.

Kock, Thomas and Rita Schusemann, eds., *Laienlektüre und Buchmarkt im späten Mittelalter*, Frankfurt am Main: Peter Lang, 1997.

Kohl, Wilhelm, 'Die Windesheimer Kongregation', in Elm, ed., *Reformbemühungen und Observanzbestrebungen*, 83–106.

Kohl, Wilhelm, Ernst Persoons and Anton G. Weiler, eds., *Monasticon Windeshemense*, 4 vols., Brussels: Archives et bibliothèques de Belgique, 1976–84.

Köhler, Michael A., *Allianzen und Verträge zwischen fränkischen und islamischen Herrschern im Vorderen Orient: Eine Studie über das zwischenstaatliche Zusammenleben vom 12. bis ins 13. Jahrhundert*, Berlin: Walter de Gruyter, 1991.

Koningsveld, P. S. van, 'La Apología de Al-Kindî en la España del siglo XII: Huellas toledanas de un "animal disputax"', in *Estudios sobre Alfonso VI y la reconquista de Toledo: Actas del II congreso internacional de estudios mozárabes*, Toledo: Instituto de Estudios, 1989, 107–9.

Koningsveld, P. S. van and G. A. Wiegers, 'The Islamic Statute of the Mudejars in the Light of a New Source', *Al-Qanṭara* 17 (1996), 19–59.

'The Polemical Works of Muḥammad al-Qaysī (fl. 1309) and their Circulation in Arabic and Aljamiado among the Mudejars in the Fourteenth Century', *Al-Qanṭara* 15 (1994), 163–99.

Koorn, Florence, *Begijnhoven in Holland en Zeeland gedurende de middeleeuwen*, Assen: Van Gorcum, 1981.

Krauss, Samuel and William Horbury, *The Jewish–Christian Controversy: From the Earliest Times to 1789*, Tübingen: J. C. B. Mohr [Paul Siebeck], 1995.

Kreitzer, Beth, *Reforming Mary: Changing Images of the Virgin Mary in Lutheran Sermons of the Sixteenth Century*, Oxford: Oxford University Press, 2004.

Kretzmann, N., A. J. P. Kenny and J. Pinborg, eds., *The Cambridge History of Later Medieval Philosophy: From the Rediscovery of Aristotle to the Disintegration of Scholasticism, 1100–1600*, Cambridge: Cambridge University Press, 1982.

Kretzschmar, Robert, *Alger von Lüttichs Traktat 'De misericordia et iustitia': Ein kanonistischer Konkordanzversuch aus der Zeit des Investiturstreits*, Quellen und Forschungen zum Recht im Mittelalter 2, Sigmaringen: Thorbecke, 1985.

Kriss-Rettenbeck, L., and G. Möhlher, *Wallfahrt kennt keine Grenzen*, Munich and Zurich: Schnell & Steiner, 1984.

Kristeller, P. O., 'The Contribution of Religious Orders to Renaissance Thought and Learning', *The American Benedictine Review* 21 (1970), 1–54.

Kruckenberg, Lori, 'Some Observations on a *troparium tardivum*: The Proper Tropes in Utrecht, Universiteitsbibliotheek, 417', *Tijdschrift v.d. Kon. Vereniging voor Nederlandse Muziekgeschiedenis* 53 (2003), 151–82.

Kuhn, A., and B. Lundt, eds., *Lustgarten und Dämonenpein: Konzepte von Weiblichkeit in Mittelalter und früher Neuzeit*, Dortmund: Ebersbach, 1997.

Kupfer, Marcia, *Romanesque Wall Painting in Central France: The Politics of Narrative*, New Haven, Conn.: Yale University Press, 1993.

Kurze, Dietrich, 'Die festländischen Lollarden', *Archiv für Kulturgeschichte* 47 (1965), 48–76.

Kuster, Niklaus, 'Minorità e itineranza dei primi Cappuccini', *Italia Francescana* 80.1 (2005), 57–74.

Kuttner, Stephan, *Gratian and the Schools of Law, 1140–1234*, Collected studies CS 185, London: Variorum Reprints, 1983.

*The History of Ideas and Doctrines of Canon Law in the Middle Ages*, Collected studies CS 113, London: Variorum Reprints, 1980.

*Medieval Councils, Decretals, and Collections of Canon Law*, Collected studies CS 126, London: Variorum Reprints, 1980.

*Repertorium der Kanonistik (1140–1234): Prodromus Corporis glossarum*, vol 1, Studi e testi 71, Vatican City: Biblioteca Apostolica Vaticana, 1937.

'La réserve papale du droit de canonisation', *Revue historique de droit français et étranger* 4.17 (1938), 172–228.

*Studies in the History of Medieval Canon Law*, Collected studies CS 325, London: Variorum Reprints, 1990.

Kyas, Vladimír, 'Die alttschechische Bibelübersetzung des 14. Jahrhunderts und ihre Entwicklung im 15. Jahrhundert', in Martin of Tišov, *Kutnahorská Bible/Kuttenberger Bibel*, ed. Reinhold Olesch and Hans Rothe, 2 vols., Paderborn: Ferdinand Schöningh, 1989.

Labande, E. R., 'De saint Edouard à saint Thomas Becket: Pèlerinages anglais du XIIe siècle', in C. É. Viola, ed., *Mediaevalia christiana, XIe–XIIIe siècles. Hommage à Raymonde Foreville*, Tournai: De Boeck Université, 1989, 307–19.

ed., *Pellegrinaggi e culto dei santi in Europa fino alla prima crociata (8–11 ottobre 1961)*, Convegni del Centro di studi sulla spiritualità medievale 4, Todi: Accademia Tudertina, 1963.

Lachièzde-Rey, Marc and Jean-Pierre Luminet, *Celestial Treasury: From the Music of the Spheres to the Conquest of Space*, Cambridge: Cambridge University Press, 2001.

Lahey, Stephen E., *Philosophy and Politics in the Thought of John Wyclif*, Cambridge: Cambridge University Press, 2003.

Lambert, Malcolm D., *The Cathars*, Oxford and Malden: Blackwell, 1998.

*Franciscan Poverty: The Doctrine of the Absolute Poverty of Christ and the Apostles in the Franciscan Order 1210–1323*, London: SPCK, 1961.

*Medieval Heresy: Popular Movements from the Gregorian Reform to the Reformation*, 2nd edn, Oxford and Cambridge, Mass.: Blackwell, 1992; 3rd edn, Oxford: Blackwell, 2002.

Lamoreaux, John, 'Early Christian Responses to Islam', in John Tolan, ed., *Medieval Christian Perceptions of Islam: A Book of Essays*, New York: Garland, 1996, 3–31.

Lampe, G. W. H., ed., *The Cambridge History of the Bible*, vol. 2, *The West from the Fathers to the Reformation*, Cambridge: Cambridge University Press, 1969.

Lampert, L., *Gender and Jewish Difference from Paul to Shakespeare*, Philadelphia: University of Pennsylvania Press, 2004.

Landau, Peter, *Kanones und Dekretalen: Beiträge zur Geschichte der Quellen des kanonischen Rechts*, Bibliotheca eruditorum 2, Goldbach: Keip, 1997.

Landmann, James H., '"The Doom of Reason": Accommodating Lay Interpretation in Late Medieval England', in Barbara A. Hanawalt and David Wallace, eds., *Medieval Crime and Social Control*, Minneapolis: University of Minnesota Press, 1999, 90–123.

Lang, Albert, *Die theologische Prinzipienlehre der mittelalterlichen Scholastik*, Freiburg im Breisgau: Herder, 1964.

Langmuir, Gavin I., 'Historiographic Crucifixion', in David R. Blumenthal, ed., *Approaches to Judaism in Medieval Times*, vol. 1, Brown Judaic Studies 54, Chico, Cal.: Scholars Press, 1984, 1–26.

*History, Religion and Antisemitism*, Berkeley and Los Angeles: California University Press, 1990.

'Thomas of Monmouth: Detector of Ritual Murder', *Speculum* 59 (1984), 820–46.

*Toward a Definition of Antisemitism*, Berkeley and Los Angeles: California University Press, 1990.

Lawrence, C. H., *The Friars*, London: Longman, 1994.

*Medieval Monasticism*, London: Longman, 1989.

Le Bras, Gabriel, Charles Lefebvre and Jacqueline Rambaud, *L'âge classique 1140–1378: Sources et théories du droit*, Histoire du droit et des institutions de l'Église en Occident 7, Paris: Cujas, 1965.

Le Goff, Jacques, *The Birth of Purgatory*, Chicago: University of Chicago Press, 1984 [1981].

*Saint Louis*, Paris: Gallimard, 1996.

Lea, H. C., *A History of the Inquisition in the Middle Ages*, 3 vols., repr. New York: S. A. Russell, 1955 [1888].

*History of Sacerdotal Celibacy in the Christian Church*, 3rd edn, London: Williams and Norgate, 1907.

Leader, Damian Riehl, *A History of the University of Cambridge*, vol. 1, *The University to 1546*, Cambridge: Cambridge University Press, 1988.

Leclercq, Jean, *The Love of Learning and the Desire for God*, 3rd edn, trans. Catharine Misrahi, New York: Fordham University Press, 1982.

Lee, B., 'Men's Recollection of a Woman's Rite: Medieval English Men's Recollections Regarding the Rite of Purification of Women after Childbirth', *Gender and History* 14 (2002), 224–41.

Lees, C., ed., *Medieval Masculinities: Regarding Men in the Middle Ages*, Minneapolis: University of Minnesota Press, 1994.

Leesch, W., Ernst Persoons and Anton G. Weiler, eds., *Monasticon fratrum vitae communis*, 3 vols., Brussels: Archives et bibliothèques de Belgique, 1977–2004.

Leff, Gordon, 'The Apostolic Ideal in Later Medieval Ecclesiology', *Journal of Theological Studies* n.s. 18 (1967), 58–82.

*Heresy in the Later Middle Ages*, 2 vols., Manchester: Manchester University Press, 1967.

'The Making of the Myth of a True Church in the Later Middle Ages', *Journal of Mediaeval and Renaissance Studies* 1 (1971), 1–15.

*Paris and Oxford Universities in the Thirteenth and Fourteenth Centuries*, Huntington, N.Y.: R. E. Krieger, 1968.

Lenherr, Titus, *Die Exkommunikations- und Depositionsgewalt der Häretiker bei Gratian und den Dekretisten bis zur 'Glossa Ordinaria' des Johannes Teutonicus*, Münchener theologische Studien 3, Kanonistische Abteilung 42, Munich: Eos, 1987.

Lentes, Thomas, 'Das religiöse Ausdrucksverhalten', in Bernhard Jussen and Craig Koslofsky, eds., *Kulturelle Reformation*, Veröffentlichungen des Max-Planck-Instituts für Geschichte 145, Göttingen: Vandenhoeck & Ruprecht, 1999, 29–67.

Lerner, Robert, *The Feast of Saint Abraham: Medieval Millenarians and the Jews*, Philadelphia: University of Pennsylvania Press, 2001.

*The Heresy of the Free Spirit in the Later Middle Ages*, Berkeley: University of California Press, 1972.

Lerner, Robert E., ed., *Neue Richtungen in der hoch- und spätmittelalterlichen Bibelexegese*, Munich: Oldenbourg, 1996.

Leveleux, C., *La parole interdite: Le blasphème dans la France médiévale (XIIIe–XVIe siècles): Du péché au crime*, Paris: De Boccard, 2001.

Levy, Ian, ed., *A Companion to John Wyclif, Late Medieval Theologian*, Leiden: Brill, 2006.

Levy, Ian Christopher, *John Wyclif: Scriptural Logic, Real Presence and the Parameters of Orthodoxy*, Milwaukee: Marquette University Press, 2003.

Leyser, Henrietta, *Hermits and the New Monasticism: A Study of Religious Communities in Western Europe 1000–1150*, London: Macmillan, 1984.

L'Hermite-Leclercq, Paulette, 'Le reclus dans la ville au bas Moyen Âge', *Journal des Savants* July–December 1988, 219–62.

Lilie, R.-J., *Byzantium and the Crusader States 1096–1204*, trans. J. C. Morris and J. E. Ridings, Oxford: Clarendon Press, 1993.

Limor, O. and G. Strousma, eds., *Contra Iudaeos: Ancient and Medieval Polemics between Christians and Jews*, Tübingen: J. C. B. Mohr, 1996.

Lindberg, David C., *The Beginnings of Western Science: The European Scientific Tradition in Philosophical, Religious and Institutional Context, 600 B.C. to A.D. 1450*, Chicago and London: University of Chicago Press, 1992.

'The Medieval Church Encounters the Classical Tradition: Saint Augustine, Roger Bacon, and the Handmaiden Metaphor', in David C. Lindberg and Ronald L. Numbers, eds., *When Science and Christianity Meet*, Chicago: University of Chicago Press, 2003, 7–32.

'Science as Handmaiden: Roger Bacon and the Patristic Tradition', *Isis* 78 (1987), 518–36.

Linder, Amnon, *The Jews in the Legal Sources of the Early Middle Ages*, Detroit: Wayne State University Press, 1997.

Lindgren, Uta, *Die Artes liberales in Antike und Mittelalter: Bildungs- und wissenschaftsgeschichtliche Entwicklungslinien*, Algorismus 8, Munich: Institut für Geschichte der Naturwissenschaften, 1992.

Lipsmeyer, Elizabeth, 'Devotion and Decorum: Intention and Quality in Medieval German Sculpture', *Gesta* 34 (1995), 20–7.

Lipton, Sara, *Images of Intolerance: The Representation of Jews and Judaism in the Bibles moralisées*, Los Angeles and Berkeley: University of California Press, 1999.

'Sweet Lean of his Head: Writing about Looking at the Crucifix', *Speculum* 80 (2005), 1172–208.

Little, L. K., *Religious Poverty and the Profit Economy in Medieval Europe*, Ithaca, N.Y.: Cornell University Press, 1978.

Lloyd, S., *English Society and the Crusade 1216–1307*, Oxford: Clarendon Press, 1988.

Lochrie, K., P. McCracken and J. Schultz, eds., *Constructing Medieval Sexuality*, Minneapolis: University of Minnesota, 1997.

Logan, F. D., *A History of the Church in the Middle Ages*, London: Routledge, 2002.

Löhr, Gabriel, *Die Teutonica im 15. Jahrhundert: Studien und Texte vornehmlich zur Geschichte ihrer Reform*, Quellen and Forschungen zur Geschichte des Dominikanerordens in Deutschland 19, Leipzig: Harrassowitz, 1924.

Longère, J., *Œuvres oratoires de maîtres parisiens au XIIe siècle: Étude historique et doctrinale*, 2 vols., Paris: Études augustiniennes, 1975.

*La prédication médiévale*, Paris: Études augustiniennes, 1983.

Lotter F., 'Die Judenverfolgung des "König Rintfleisch" in Franken um 1298: Die endgültige Wende in den christlich-jüdischen Beziehungen im Deutschen Reich des Mittelalters', *Zeitschrift für Historische Forschung* 15 (1988), 385–422.

Lynch, J., *Simoniacal Entry into the Religious Life from 1000 to 1260*, Columbus: Ohio University Press, 1976.

Maccoby, Hyam, *Judaism on Trial: Jewish–Christian Disputations in the Middle Ages*, London and Toronto: Associated University Press, 1982.

*Judas Iscariot and the Myth of Jewish Evil*, London: Peter Halban, 1992.

Macy, G., 'Was there a "The Church" in the Middle Ages?', in Swanson, ed., *Unity and Diversity*, 107–16.

Maier, Anneliese, 'Eine Verfügung Johannis xxii über die Zuständigkeit der Inquisition für Zauberprozesse', *Archivum Fratrum Praedicatorum* 32 (1952), 226–46.

Maier, C. T., *Crusade Propaganda and Ideology: Model Sermons for the Preaching of the Cross*, Cambridge: Cambridge University Press, 2000.

*Preaching the Crusades: Mendicant Friars and the Cross in the Thirteenth Century*, Cambridge: Cambridge University Press, 1994.

Maire-Viguer, J.-C., 'Bernardin et la vie citadine', in *Bernardino predicatore e la società del suo tempo*, Atti del XVI Convegno del Centro di studi sulla spiritualità medievale, Todi: Accademia Tudertina, 1976, 251–82.

Maisonneuve, H., *Études sur les origines de l'inquisition*, Paris: J. Vrin, 1960.

Makowski, Elizabeth, '*A Pernicious Sort of Woman': Quasi-Religious Women and Canon Lawyers in the Later Middle Ages*, Washington D.C.: Catholic University of America Press, 2005.

Mandonnet, P., *Siger de Brabant et l'Averroisme latin au XIIIme siècle*, Louvain: Institut supérieur de philosophie, 1908–11.

Manoir, Hubert du, ed., *Maria: Études sur la sainte Vierge*, Paris: Beauchesne, 1949–61.

Manselli, Raoul, 'Enrico del Carretto e la consultazione sulla magia di Giovanni xxii', in Raul Manselli, ed., *Miscellanea in onore di Monsignor Martino Giusti*, vol. 2, (Vatican City: Archivio Segreto Vaticano, 1978, 97–129.

Marks, Richard, *Image and Devotion in Late Medieval England*, Stroud: Sutton, 2004.

Marosi, Ernö, *Die Anfänge der Gotik in Ungarn: Esztergom in der Kunst des 12.–13. Jahrhunderts*, Budapest: Akademiai Kiado, 1984.

Marrou, Henri-Irénée, *Saint Augustin et la fin de la culture antique*, new edn, Paris: Boccard 1983.

Marrow, James, 'Art and Experience in Dutch Manuscript Illumination around 1400: Transcending the Boundaries', *The Journal of the Walters Art Gallery* 54 (1996), 101–17.

    *Passion Iconography in Northern European Art of the Late Middle Ages and Early Renaissance: A Study of the Transformation of Sacred Metaphor into Descriptive Narrative*, Kortrijk: Van Ghemmert, 1979.

    'Symbol and Meaning in Northern European Art of the Late Middle Ages and the Early Renaissance', *Simiolus* 16 (1986), 150–69.

Marshall, C. J., *Warfare in the Latin East, 1192–1291*, Cambridge: Cambridge University Press, 1992.

Marti, Susan, *Malen, Schreiben und Beten: Die spätmittelalterliche Handschriftenproduktion im Doppelkloster Engelberg*, Zurich: Zurich InterPublishers, 2002.

Martin, Francis Xavier, 'The Augustinian Observant Movement', in Elm, ed., *Reformbemühungen und Observanzbestrebungen*, 325–45.

Martin, H., *Le métier du prédicateur à la fin du Moyen Âge (1350–1520)*, Paris: Cerf, 1988.

    'La prédication et les masses au XV siècle: Facteurs et limites d'une réussite', in J. Delumeau, ed., *Histoire vécue du peuple chrétien*, Toulouse: Privat, 1979, II, 9–41.

    'Prédication et politique dans les provinces septentrionales de la France de la fin du XIV$^e$ à la fin du XV$^e$ siècle', in S. Gensini, ed., *Vita religiosa e identità politiche: Universalità e particolarismi nell'Europa del tardo medioevo*, Pisa: Pacini, 1998, 493–511.

Martin, J., 'The Injustice of not Ordaining Women: A Problem for Medieval Theologians', *Theological Studies* 48 (1987), 303–16.

    'The Ordination of Women and Theologians in the Middle Ages', *Escritos del Vedat* 16 (1986), 115–77.

Martin, Jean-Marie, 'L'érémitisme grec et latin en Italie méridionale (Xe–XIIIe siècle)', in André Vauchez, ed., *Ermites de France et d'Italie (XIe–XVe siècle)*, Rome: École française de Rome, 2003, 175–98.

Masi, Michael, ed., *Boethius and the Liberal Arts: A Collection of Essays*, Utah Studies in Literature and Linguistics 18, Bern and Frankfurt a.M.: Peter Lang, 1981.

Mastnak, Tomaž, *Crusading Peace: Christendom, the Muslim World, and Western Political Order*, Berkeley: University of California Press, 2002.

Matter, E. Ann, *The Voice of My Beloved: The Song of Songs in Western Medieval Christianity*, Philadelphia: University of Pennsylvania Press, 1990.

McClanan, A. and K. Encarnación, eds., *The Material Culture of Sex, Procreation, and Marriage in Premodern Europe*, Basingstoke and New York: Palgrave, 2002.

McDannell, Colleen and Bernhard Lang, *Heaven: A History*, New Haven, Conn.: Yale University Press, 1988.

McDonnell, Ernest, *The Beguines and Beghards in Medieval Culture: With Special Emphasis on the Belgian Scene*, New Brunswick, N.J.: Rutgers University Press, 1954.

McFarlane, K. B., *John Wycliffe and the Beginnings of English Nonconformity*, London: English Universities Press, 1953.

McGinn, Bernhard, 'Eckhart's Condemnation Reconsidered', *The Thomist* 44 (1980), 390–414.

    'Love, Knowledge and *Unio Mystica* in the Western Christian Tradition', in Moshe Idel and Bernard McGinn, eds., *Mystical Union in Judaism, Christianity, and Islam: An Ecumenical Dialogue*, New York: Continuum, 1996, 59–86.

    *The Mystical Thought of Meister Eckhart: The Man from Whom God Hid Nothing*, New York: Herder and Herder, 2001.

*The Presence of God: A History of Western Christian Mysticism,* vol. 1, *The Foundations of Mysticism: Origins to the Fifth Century;* vol. 2, *The Growth of Mysticism: Gregory the Great through the Twelfth Century;* vol. 3, *The Flowering of Mysticism: Men and Women in the New Mysticism 1200–1350;* vol. 4, *The Harvest of Mysticism in Medieval Germany (1300–1500),* New York: Crossroad, 1992–2005.

McGinn, Bernard, J. Meyendorff and J. Leclercq, eds., *Christian Spirituality: Origins to the Twelfth Century,* New York: Crossroad, 1988.

McGrade, Michael, 'O rex mundi triumphator: Hohenstaufen Politics in a Sequence for Saint Charlemagne', *Early Music History* 17 (1998), 183–219.

McGuire, B. P., *Friendship and Community: The Monastic Experience 350–1250,* Cistercian Studies Series 95, Kalamazoo, Mich.: Cistercian Publications, 1988.

*Friendship and Faith: Cistercian Men, Women, and their Stories, 1100–1250,* Aldershot: Ashgate, 2002.

McHardy, A. K., *'De heretico comburendo,* 1401', in Margaret Aston and Colin Richmond, eds., *Lollardy and the Gentry in the Later Middle Ages,* Stroud: Sutton; New York: St Martin's Press, 1997, 112–26.

McInerny, M., *Eloquent Virgins from Thecla to Joan of Arc,* New York: Palgrave MacMillan, 2003.

McKim, D. K., ed., *Historical Handbook of Major Biblical Interpreters,* Downers Grove, Ill.: Intervarsity Press, 1998.

McLaughlin, M., 'Gender Paradox and the Otherness of God', *Gender and History* 3 (1991), 147–59.

McMichael, Steven J. and Susan E. Myers, eds., *Friars and Jews in the Middle Ages and Renaissance,* Leiden: Brill 2004.

McNamara, Jo Ann, *Sisters in Arms: Catholic Nuns through Two Millennia,* Cambridge, Mass.: Harvard University Press, 1996.

Meersseman, Gilles Gerard, *Ordo fraternitatis: Confraternite e pietà del laici nel medioevo,* Rome: Herder, 1977.

Mellinkoff, Ruth, *The Mark of Cain,* Berkeley, Los Angeles and London: University of California Press, 1981.

*Outcasts: Signs of Otherness in Northern European Art of the Late Middle Ages,* 2 vols., Berkeley and Los Angeles: University of California Press, 1981.

Melnikas, Anthony, *The Corpus of Miniatures in the Manuscripts of 'Decretum Gratiani',* Rome: Studia Gratiana, 1975.

Merchavia, Ch., *The Church versus Talmudic and Midrashic Literature (500–1248),* Jerusalem: The Bialik Institute, 1970 [in Hebrew].

Mertens, Dieter, 'Reformkonzilien und Ordensreform im 15. Jahrhundert', in Elm, ed., *Reformbemühungen und Observanzbestrebungen,* 431–57.

Mertens, Th., 'Mystieke cultuur en literatuur in de Late Middeleeuwen', in Frits van Oostrom *et al.,* eds., *Grote lijnen: Syntheses over Middelnederlandse letterkunde,* Amsterdam: Prometheus, 1995, 117–35; 205–17.

Meuthen, Erich, *Die alte Universität,* vol. 1, *Kölner Universitätsgeschichte,* Vienna: Böhlau, 1988.

Mews, C., *Listen, Daughter: The 'Speculum Virginum' and the Formation of Religious Women in the Middle Ages,* Basingstoke and New York: Palgrave, 2001.

Milano, Attilio, *Storia degli Ebrei in Italia,* Turin: Einaudi, 1963.

Milis, L., *L'ordre des chanoines réguliers d'Arrouaise: Son histoire et son organisation, de la fondation de l'abbaye-mère (vers 1090) à la fin des chapitres annuels (1471)*, 2 vols., Bruges: De Tempel, 1969.

Miller, Kathryn, 'Guardians of Islam: Muslim Communities in Medieval Aragon', PhD Dissertation, Yale University, 1998.

  *Religious Authority and Muslim Communities of Late Medieval Spain*, New York: Columbia University Press, 2008.

Miller, M., 'Masculinity, Reform, and Clerical Culture: Narratives of Episcopal Holiness in the Gregorian Reform', *Church History* 72 (2003), 25–52.

Mills, R., '"Whatever you Do is a Delight to Me!": Masculinity, Masochism, and Queer Play in Representations of Male Martyrdom', *Exemplaria* 13 (2001), 1–37.

Minois, Georges, *Histoire des enfers*, Paris: Fayard, 1991.

Miramon, Charles de, *Les 'donnés' au Moyen Âge: Une forme de vie religieuse laïque v.1180–v.1500*, Paris: Éditions du Cerf, 1999.

Mirrer, L., *Women, Jews, and Muslims in the Texts of Reconquest Castile*, Ann Arbor: University of Michigan Press, 1996.

Mischlewski, Adalbert, *Grundzüge der Geschichte des Antoniterordens bis zum Ausgang des 15. Jahrhunderts*, Bonner Beiträge zur Kirchengeschichte 8, Cologne and Vienna: Böhlau, 1976.

Mitchell, L., ed., *Women in Medieval Western European Culture*, New York: Garland Publishing, 1999.

Mobius, Friedrich and Ernst Schubert, eds., *Skulptur des Mittelalters: Funktion und Gestalt*, Weimar: H. Böhlaus Nachfolger, 1987.

Montesano, M., *'Supra acqua et supra ad vento': 'Superstizioni', 'maleficia' e 'incantamenta' nei predicatori francescani osservanti (Itali, sec. XV)*, Rome: ISIME, 1999.

Mooney, C., ed., *Gendered Voices: Medieval Saints and their Interpreters*, Philadelphia: University of Pennsylvania Press, 1999.

Moore, Robert I., *The Birth of Popular Heresy*, Documents of Medieval History 1, London: Edward Arnold, 1975.

  *The Formation of a Persecuting Society: Power and Deviance in Western Europe, 950–1250*, Oxford and New York: Blackwell, 1987.

  *The Origins of European Dissent*, New York: Blackwell, 1985.

Moore, S., 'The Song of Songs in the History of Sexuality', *Church History* 69 (2000), 328–49.

Moorman, John R. H., *A History of the Franciscan Order, from its Origins to the Year 1517*, Oxford: Clarendon Press, 1968.

  *Church Life in England in the Thirteenth Century*, Cambridge: Cambridge University Press, 1945.

Morey, James H., *Book and Verse: A Guide to Middle English Biblical Literature*, Urbana: University of Illinois Press, 2000.

  'Peter Comestor, Biblical Paraphrase, and the Medieval Popular Bible', *Speculum* 68 (1993), 6–35.

Morgan, Nigel, 'The Iconography of Twelfth-Century Mosan Enamels', in *Rhein und Maas: Kunst und Kultur 800–1400 II*, exhibition catalogue, Cologne: Schnütgen-Museum, 1973, 263–75.

  'Texts and Images of Marian Devotion in Fourteenth-Century England', in Nicholas Rogers, ed., *England in the Fourteenth Century: Proceedings of the 1991 Harlaxton Symposium*, Stamford: Paul Watkins, 1993, 34–57.

Morganstern, Anne McGee, *Gothic Tombs of Kinship in France, the Low Countries, and England*, University Park: Pennsylvania State University Press, 2000.

Mormando, Franco, *The Preacher's Demons: Bernardino of Siena and the Social Underworld of Early Renaissance Italy*, Chicago: University of Chicago Press, 1999.

Morris, C., *The Papal Monarchy: The Western Church from 1050–1250*, Oxford: Clarendon Press, 1989.

Muessig, Carolyn A., ed., *Medieval Monastic Preaching*, Leiden: Brill, 1998.

Mulchahey, M. M., *First the Bow is Bent in Study…: Dominican Education before 1350*, Studies and Texts, Toronto: Pontifical Institute of Mediaeval Studies, 1998.

Mulder-Bakker, Anneke, *Lives of the Anchoresses: The Rise of the Urban Recluse in Medieval Europe*, Philadelphia: University of Pennsylvania Press, 2005.

Mulder-Bakker, Anneke, ed. *Mary of Oignies: Mother of Salvation*, Turnhout: Brepols, 2007.

Muldoon, James, *Popes, Lawyers, and Infidels: The Church and the Non-Christian World*, Liverpool: Liverpool University Press, 1979.

Müller, Wolfgang P., *Huguccio: The Life, Works, and Thought of a Twelfth-Century Jurist*, Studies in Medieval and Early Modern Canon Law 3, Washington, D.C.: Catholic University of America Press, 1994.

'The Recovery of Justinian's Digest in the Middle Ages', *Bulletin of Medieval Canon Law*, n.s. 20 (1990), 1–29.

Murray, J., ed., *Conflicted Identities and Multiple Masculinities: Men in the Medieval West*, New York: Garland, 1999.

Murray, Stephen, *Notre-Dame, Cathedral of Amiens: The Power of Change in Gothic*, Cambridge: Cambridge University Press, 1996.

Muzzarelli, M. G., *Il denaro e la salvezza: L'invenzione del Monte di Pietà*, Bologna: Il Mulino, 2001.

*Gli inganni delle apparenze: Disciplina dei vesti e ornamenti alla fine del Medioevo*, Turin: Scriptorium, 1996.

*Pescatori di uomini: Predicatori e piazze alla fine del medioevo*, Bologna: Il Mulino, 2005.

Nederman, C. J., *Worlds of Difference: European Discourses of Toleration c. 1100–1550*, University Park: Pennsylvania State University Press, 2000.

Neff, Amy, 'The Pain of *Compassio*: Mary's Labor at the Foot of the Cross', *Art Bulletin* 80 (1998), 254–73.

Newman, Barbara, *From Virile Woman to WomanChrist: Studies in Medieval Religion and Literature*, Philadelphia: University of Pennsylvania Press, 1995.

*God and the Goddesses: Vision, Poetry, and Belief in the Middle Ages*, Philadelphia: University of Pennsylvania Press, 2003.

'Possessed by the Spirit: Devout Women, Demoniacs, and the Apostolic Life in the Thirteenth Century', *Speculum* 73 (1998), 733–70.

*Sister of Wisdom: St. Hildegard's Theology of the Feminine*, Berkeley and Los Angeles: University of California Press, 1987.

Newman, Martha, *The Boundaries of Charity: Cistercian Culture and Ecclesiastical Reform, 1098–1180*, Stanford: Stanford University Press, 1996.

Nichols, J. A. and L. T. Shank, ed., *Hidden Springs: Cistercian Monastic Women, Medieval Religious Women*, vol. 3.1, Cistercian Studies 113A, Kalamazoo, Mich.: Cistercian Publications, 1995.

Nicholson, H. J., *Templars, Hospitallers and Teutonic Knights: Images of the Military Orders, 1128–1291*, Leicester: Leicester University Press, 1993.

Nimmo, Duncan B., 'The Franciscan Regular Observance: The Culmination of Medieval Franciscan Reform', in Elm, ed., *Reformbemühungen und Observanzbestrebungen*, 189–205.

Nirenberg, David, *Communities of Violence: Persecution of Minorities in the Middle Ages*, Princeton: Princeton University Press, 1996.

'Varieties of Mudejar Experience: Muslims in Christian Iberia, 1000–1526', in P. Linehan and J. Nelson, eds., *The Medieval World*, London and New York: Routledge, 2001.

Nobile, B., '"Romiti" e vita religiosa nella cronachistica italiana fra '400 e '500', *Cristianesimo nella storia* 5 (1984), 303–40.

Noonan, John T., 'Gratian Slept Here: The Changing Identity of the Father of the Systematic Study of Canon Law', *Traditio* 35 (1979), 145–72.

Nyberg, Tore, 'Der Birgittenorden als Beispiel einer Neugründung im Zeitalter der Ordensreformen', in Elm, ed., *Reformbemühungen und Observanzbestrebungen*, 373–96.

Oberman, Heiko Augustinus, *The Harvest of Medieval Theology: Gabriel Biel and Late Medieval Nominalism*, 3rd edn, Durham, N.C.: Labyrinth Press, 1983.

O'Callaghan, J. F., *Crusade and Reconquest in Medieval Spain*, Philadelphia: University of Pennsylvania Press, 1992.

O'Carroll, M., *Robert Grosseteste and the Beginnings of a British Theological Tradition*, Rome: Istituto Storico dei Cappuccini, 2003.

Ocker, Christopher, *Biblical Poetics before Humanism and Reformation*, Cambridge: Cambridge University Press, 2002.

O'Connor, Michael, 'The Ark and the Temple in Savonarola's Teaching (Winter 1494)', in Richard Griffiths, ed., *The Bible in the Renaissance: Essays on Biblical Commentary and Translation in the Fifteenth and Sixteenth Centuries*, Aldershot: Ashgate, 2001, 9–27.

Østrem, Eyolf, *The Office of Saint Olav: A Study in Chant Transmission*, Acta universitatis upsaliensis, Studia musicological upsaliensia, nova series 18, Uppsala: Elanders Gotab, 2001.

Pächt, O., C. R. Dodwell and F. Wormald, *The St. Albans Psalter*, London: Warburg Institute, University of London, 1960.

Panofsky, E. '"Imago pietatis' – Ein Beitrag zur Typengeschichte des "Schmerzenmanns" und der "Maria Mediatrix"', in *Festschrift für Max J. Friedlander zum 60. Geburtstage*, Leipzig: E. A. Seemann, 1927, 261–308.

Paravicini-Bagliani, Agostino, *The Pope's Body*, Chicago: University of Chicago Press, 2000. *Medicina e scienze della natura alla corte dei papi nel duecento*, Spoleto: Centro Italiano di studi sull'alto medioevo, 1991.

Paravy, Pierrette, *De la chrétienté romaine à la Réforme en Dauphiné: Évêques, fidèles et deviants (vers 1340–vers 1530)*, Rome: École française de Rome, 1993.

Parkes, James, *The Jew in the Medieval Community*, 2nd edn, New York: Hermon Press, 1976.

Parkinson, Stephen, ed., *Cobras e son: Papers on the Text, Music and Manuscripts of the 'Cantigas de Santa Maria'*, Oxford: European Humanities Research Centre, 2000.

Parsons, J. and B. Wheeler, eds., *Medieval Mothering*, New York: Routledge, 1999.

Paterson, Linda, *The World of the Troubadours: Medieval Occitan Society, c. 1100–c. 1300*, Cambridge: Cambridge University Press, 1993.

Patschovsky, Alexander, 'Heresy and Society', in Caterina Bruschi and Peter Biller, eds., *Texts and the Repression of Medieval Heresy*, York: York Medieval Press, 2003, 23–41.

'Der "Talmudjude"': Vom mittelalterlichen Ursprung eines neuzeitlichen Themas', in Alfred Haverkamp and Franz-Josef Ziwes, eds., *Juden in der christlichen Umwelt während des späten Mittelalters*, Berlin: Duncker & Humblot, 1992, 13–27.

Payne, Thomas, '*Aurelianis civitas*: Student Unrest in Medieval France and a Conductus by Philip the Chancellor', *Speculum* 73 (2000), 589–614.

Pearson, A., 'Personal Worship, Gender, and the Devotional Portrait Diptych', *Sixteenth Century Journal* 31 (2000), 99–122.

Pegg, M. G., *The Corruption of Angels: The Great Inquisition of 1245–1246*, Princeton and Oxford: Princeton University Press, 2001.

Peikola, Matti, *Congregations of the Elect: Patterns of Self-Fashioning in English Lollard Writings*, Turku: Publications of the Department of English, University of Turku, 2000.

Pelikan, Jaroslav, *Mary through the Centuries: Her Place in the History of Culture*, New Haven, Conn.: Yale University Press, 1996.

Pellegrini, L., 'La profezia tra il pulpito e lo Stato: Il caso di Girolamo Savonarola', *Annali dell'Istituto storico italo-germanico in Trento* 25 (1999), 433–48.

'Predicazione osservante e propaganda politica: a partire da un caso di Todi', in *La propaganda politica nel Basso Medioevo: Atti del XXXVIII convegno storico internazionale. Todi. 14–17 ottobre 2001*, Spoleto: CISAM, 2002, 511–31.

Pennington, Kenneth, 'Medieval Canonists: A Bio-bibliographical Listing', in Kenneth Pennington and Wilfried Hartmann, eds., *History of Medieval Canon Law*, vol. 10, Washington, D.C.: Catholic University Press of America, forthcoming; provisionally available on the web at http://faculty.cua.edu/pennington/biobibl. htm.

*Pope and Bishops: The Papal Monarchy in the Twelfth and Thirteenth Centuries*, Philadelphia: University of Pennsylvania Press, 1984.

*Popes, Canonists, and Texts, 1150–1250*, Collected Studies CS 412, Aldershot: Ashgate, 1993.

*The Prince and the Law, 1200–1600: Sovereignty and Rights in the Western Legal Tradition*, Berkeley: University of California Press, 1993.

Peters, Edward, *Heresy and Authority in Medieval Europe*, Philadelphia: University of Pennsylvania Press, 1980.

*Inquisition*, Berkeley: University of California Press, 1988.

Petersen, Nils Holger, 'Liturgical Drama: New Approaches', in Jacqueline Hamesse, ed., *Bilan et perspectives des études médiévales (1993–1998)*, Turnhout: Brepols, 2004, 633–44.

Peuckert, Will-Erich, 'Ritualmord', in *Handwörterbuch des deutschen Aberglaubens*, Berlin: Walter de Gruyter, 1931, vol. 7, cols. 727–39.

Philippart, G., ed., *Hagiographies: Histoire internationale de la littérature hagiographique latine et vernaculaire en Occident des origines à 1550*, 4 vols., Turnhout: Brepols, 1994–2001.

Phillips, J. P., *The Crusades, 1095–1197*, Harlow: Longman, 2002.

*Defenders of the Holy Land: Relations between the Latin East and the West, 1119–1187*, Oxford: Clarendon Press, 1996.

Pixton, Paul B., *The German Episcopacy and the Implementation of the Decrees of the Fourth Lateran Council, 1216–1245: Watchmen on the Tower*, Leiden and New York: Brill, 1995.

Plöchl, Willibald, *Geschichte des Kirchenrechts*, 5 vols., Vienna: Verlag Herold, 1960–70.

Pohl-Resl, B., *Rechnen mit der Ewigkeit: Das Wiener Bürgerspital im Mittelalter*, Vienna and Munich: Böhlau, 1996.

Polecritti, C. L., *Preaching Peace in Renaissance Italy: Bernardino da Siena and his Audience*, Washington, D.C.: Catholic University of America Press, 2000.

Polzer, Joseph, 'Andrea di Bonaiuto's *Via veritatis* and Dominican Thought in Late Medieval Italy', *Art Bulletin* 77 (1995), 262–75.

Poole, Reginald, *Lectures on the History of the Papal Chancery Down to the Time of Innocent III*, Cambridge: Cambridge University Press, 1915.

Post, R. R., *The Modern Devotion: Confrontation with Reformation and Humanism*, Leiden: Brill, 1968.

Powell, James, ed., *Muslims under Latin Rule, 1100–1300*, Princeton: Princeton University Press, 1990.

Powell, J. M., *Anatomy of a Crusade, 1213–1221*, Philadelphia: University of Pennsylvania Press, 1986.

Powicke, F. M., *Stephen Langton*, Oxford: Clarendon Press, 1928.

Prawer, J., *Crusader Institutions*, Oxford: Clarendon Press, 1980.

Preus, James Samuel, *From Shadow to Promise: Old Testament Interpretation from Augustine to the young Luther*, Cambridge, Mass.: Harvard University Press, 1969.

Pryor, J. H., *Geography, Technology and War: Studies in the Maritime History of the Mediterranean, 649–1571*, Cambridge: Cambridge University Press, 1988.

Puff, H., *Sodomy in Reformation Germany and Switzerland, 1400–1600*, Chicago: University of Chicago Press, 2003.

Queller, D. E. and T. F. Madden, *The Fourth Crusade*, 2nd edn, Philadelphia: University of Pennsylvania Press, 1997.

Raban, Sandra, *Mortmain Legislation and the English Church 1279–1500*, Cambridge: Cambridge University Press, 1982.

Radding, Charles M., *The Origins of Medieval Jurisprudence: Pavia and Bologna 850–1150*, New Haven, Conn.: Yale University Press, 1988.

Raguin, V. and S. Stanbury, eds., *Women's Space: Patronage, Place, and Gender in the Medieval Church*, Albany: State University of New York, 2005.

Rankin, Susan, 'The Divine Truth of Scripture: Chant in the *Roman de Fauvel*', *Journal of the American Musicological Society* 47 (1994), 203–43.

Rashdall, H., *The Universities of Europe in the Middle Ages, New Edition*, ed. F. M. Powicke and A. B. Emden, 3 vols., Oxford: Clarendon Press, 1936; repr. 1997.

Rehm, G., *Die Schwestern vom gemeinsamen Leben im nordwestlichen Deutschland: Untersuchungen zur Geschichte der Devotio Moderna und des weiblichen Religiosentums*, Berlin: Duncker & Humblot, 1985.

Reichert, Benedictus M., 'Zur Geschichte der deutschen Dominikaner und ihrer Reform', *Römische Quartalschrift* 10 (1896), 299–311.

Reichstein, Frank-Michael, *Das Beginenwesen in Deutschland: Studien und Katalog*, Berlin: Köster, 2001.

Reinhardt, Klaus, 'Das Werk des Nicolaus von Lyra im mittelalterlichen Spanien', *Traditio* 48 (1987), 321–58.

Reinle, C., 'Exempla weibliches Stärke: Zu den Ausprägungen des mittelalterlichen Amazonenbildes', *Historiches Zeitschrift* 270 (2000), 1–38.

Remensnyder, Amy G., 'The Colonization of Sacred Architecture: The Virgin Mary, Mosques, and Temples in Medieval Spain and Early Sixteenth-Century Mexico', in Sharon Farmer and Barbara H. Rosenwein, eds., *Monks and Nuns, Saints and Outcasts*, Ithaca, N.Y. and London: Cornell University Press, 2000, 189–219.

Reuter, Timothy, 'Gifts and Simony', in Esther Cohen and Mayke B. de Jong, eds., *Medieval Transformations: Texts, Power and Gifts in Context*, Leiden: Brill, 2001, 157–68.

Rex, Richard, *The Lollards*, Basingstoke: Palgrave, 2002.

Rexroth, Frank, *Deutsche Universitätsstiftungen von Prag bis Köln: Die Intentionen des Stifters und die Wege und Chancen ihrer Verwirklichung im spätmittelalterlichen deutschen Territorialstaat*, Beihefte zum Archiv für Kulturgeschichte 34, Cologne, Weimar and Vienna: Böhlau, 1992.

Reynolds, P. L., *Marriage in the Western Church: The Christianization of Marriage During the Patristic and Early Medieval Periods*, Supplements to Vigiliae Christianae 24, Brill: Leiden, 1994.

Reynolds, Suzanne, *Medieval Reading: Grammar, Rhetoric and the Classical Text*, Cambridge: Cambridge University Press, 1996.

*Rhein und Maas: Kunst und Kultur 800–1400*, 2 vols., exhibition catalogue, Cologne: Schnütgen-Museum, 1973.

Rice, Eric, 'Music and Ritual in the Collegiate Church of St Mary in Aachen, 1300–1600', unpublished PhD thesis, Columbia University, 2002.

Richard, J., *The Crusades c.1071–c.1291*, Cambridge: Cambridge University Press, 1999.

*Les récits de voyages et de pèlerinages*, Typologie des sources du Moyen Age occidental 38, Turnhout: Brepols, 1981.

*Saint Louis, Crusader King of France*, trans. J. Birrell, Cambridge: Cambridge University Press, 1992.

Riché, Pierre and Guy Lobrichon, eds., *Le Moyen Âge et la Bible*, La Bible de tous les temps 4, Paris: Beauchesne, 1984.

Riches, S. and S. Salih, eds., *Gender and Holiness: Men, Women, and Saints in Late Medieval Europe*, London: Routledge, 2002.

Rieder, P., 'Between the Pure and the Polluted: The Churching of Women in Medieval Northern France, 1100–1500', PhD Dissertation, University of Illinois, 2000.

Riising, Anne, *Danmarks middelalderlige Praediken*, Copenhagen: G.E.C. Gads, 1969.

Riley-Smith, Jonathan S. C., *The Crusades: A Short History*, London: Athlone, 1987.

*The First Crusade and the Idea of Crusading*, London: Athlone, 1986.

*The First Crusaders, 1095–1131*, Cambridge: Cambridge University Press, 1997.

'History, the Crusades, and the Latin East: A Personal View', in M. Shatzmiller, ed., *Crusaders and Muslims in Twelfth-century Syria*, Leiden: Brill, 1993, 1–17.

*Hospitallers: The History of the Order of St John*, London: Hambledon Press, 1999.

*What Were the Crusades?*, 3rd edn, Basingstoke: Palgrave Macmillan, 2002.

Riley-Smith, Jonathan, ed., *The Atlas of the Crusades*, London: Times Books, 1991.

ed., *The Oxford Illustrated History of the Crusades*, Oxford: Oxford University Press, 1995.

Ringbom, Sixten, 'Devotional Images and Imaginative Devotions: Notes on the Place of Art in Late Medieval Private Piety', *Gazette des Beaux-Arts* Ser. 6.73, alt. no. 1202 (1969), 159–70.

*From Icon to Narrative: The Rise of the Dramatic Close-up in Fifteenth-Century Devotional Painting*, Åbo: Åbo Akademie, 1965; 2nd edn, Doornspijk: Davaco, 1984.

Rizzi, A., 'Il gioco fra norma laica e proibizione religiosa: L'azione dei predicatori fra Tre e Quattrocento', in G. Ortalli, ed., *Gioco e giustizia nell'Italia di Comune*, Treviso: Fondazione Benetton/Viella, 1993, 149–82.

Roach, Andrew P., *The Devil's World: Heresy and Society 1110–1300*, Harlow: Pearson Longman, 2005.

Robertson, Anne Walters, *Guillaume de Machaut and Reims: Context and Meaning in his Musical Works*, Cambridge: Cambridge University Press, 2002.

'The Mass of Guillaume de Machaut in the Cathedral of Reims', in Thomas Forrest Kelly, ed., *Plainsong in the Age of Polyphony*, Cambridge: Cambridge University Press, 1992, 100–39.

Robinson, I. S., *The Papacy 1073–1198: Continuity and Innovation*, Cambridge: Cambridge University Press, 1990.

Rödel, Walter G., 'Reformbestrebungen im Johanniterorden in der Zeit zwischen dem Fall Akkons und dem Verlust von Rhodos (1291–1522)', in Elm, ed., *Reformbemühungen und Observanzbestrebungen*, 109–29.

Roest, Bert, *Franciscan Literature of Religious Instruction before the Council of Trent*, Studies in the History of Christian Traditions, 117, Leiden: Brill, 2004.

*A History of Franciscan Education (c. 1220–1517)*, Education and Society in the Middle Ages and Renaissance, 11, Leiden: Brill, 2000.

'Later Medieval Institutional History', in Deborah Mauskopf Deliyannis, ed., *Historiography in the Middle Ages*, Leiden and Boston: Brill, 2003, 277–315.

Rosario, Iva, *Art and Propaganda: Charles IV of Bohemia, 1346–1378*, Woodbridge: Boydell and Brewer, 2000.

Roth, D., 'Mittelalterliche Misogynie–ein Mythos? Die antiken *molestiae nuptiarum* im *Adversus Iovinianum* und ihre Rezeption in der lateinischen Literatur des 12. Jahrhundert', *Archiv für Kulturgeschichte* 80 (1998), 39–66.

Rouse, Richard H. and Mary A. Rouse, 'The Commercial Production of Manuscript Books in Late Thirteenth-Century and Early Fourteenth-Century Paris', in L. L. Brownrigg, ed., *Medieval Book Production: Assessing the Evidence*, Los Altos Hills, Cal.: Anderson-Lovelace, 1990, 103–15.

Rousset, P., 'La notion de chrétienté aux XIe et XIIe siècles', *Le Moyen Âge* 69 (1963), 191–203.

*Les origines et les charactères de la première croisade*, Neuchâtel: Baconnière, 1945.

Rubens, Alfred, *A History of Jewish Costume*, London: Weidenfeld and Nicolson, 1973.

Rubin, Miri, *Corpus Christi: The Eucharist in Late Medieval Culture*, Cambridge: Cambridge University Press, 1991.

*Gentile Tales: The Narrative Assault on Late Medieval Jews*, New Haven, Conn.: Yale University Press, 1999.

Rudolph, Conrad, *Artistic Change at St.-Denis: Abbot Suger's Program and the Early Twelfth-Century Controversy over Art*, Princeton: Princeton University Press, 1990.

*The 'Things of Greater Importance': Bernard of Clairvaux's Apologia and the Medieval Attitude toward Art*, Philadelphia: University of Pennsylvania Press, 1990.

Rudy, Gordon, *The Mystical Language of Sensation in the Later Middle Ages*, New York: Routledge, 2002.

Ruggiero, G., *The Boundaries of Eros*, Oxford: Oxford University Press, 1985.

Rupp, Jean, *L'idée de chrétienté dans la pensée pontificale des origines à Innocent III*, Paris: Les Presses Modernes, 1939.

Rusconi, R., 'Anti-Jewish Preaching in the Fifteenth Century and Images of Preachers in Italian Renaissance Art', in S. McMichael and S. E. Myers, eds., *Friars and Jews in the Middle Ages and Renaissance*, Leiden: Brill, 2004, 225–37.

'Confraternite, compagnie, devozioni', in G. Chittolini and G. Miccoli, eds., *La Chiesa e il potere politico*, Turin: Einaudi, 1986, 467–506.

'Da Costanza al Laterano: La "calcolata devozione" del ceto mercantile-borghese nell'Italia del Quattrocento', in A. Vauchez, ed., *Storia dell'Italia religiosa*, vol. 1, *L'antichità e il Medioevo*, Rome and Bari: Laterza, 1993, 505–36.

*L'ordine dei peccati: La confessione tra Medioevo ed età moderna*, Bologna: Il Mulino, 2002.

'The Preacher Saint in Late Medieval Italian Art', in C. Muessig, ed., *Preacher, Sermon and Audience in the Middle Ages*, Leiden: Brill, 2002, 181–200.

'Le prediche di fra Girolamo da Ferrara: Ai manoscritti al pulpito alle stampe', in G. C. Garfagnini, ed., *Una città e il suo profeta: Firenze di fronte al Savonarola*, Florence: Sismel, 2001, 201–34.

'"Predicò in piazza". Politica e predicazione nell'Umbria del '400', in *Signorie in Umbria tra Medioevo e Rinascimento: L'esperienza dei Trinci. Atti del Convegno. Foligno, 10–13 dicembre 1986*, Perugia: Deputazione di Storia Patria per l'Umbria, 1989, 113–41.

Russell, Jeffrey Burton, *Dissent and Order in the Middle Ages: The Search for Legitimate Authority*, New York: Twayne Publishers; Toronto: Maxwell Macmillan Canada; New York: Maxwell Macmillan International, 1992.

*A History of Heaven: The Singing Silence*, Princeton: Princeton University Press, 1997.

Rüthing, Heinrich, 'Die Kartäuser und die spätmittelalterliche Ordensreform', in Elm, ed., *Reformbemühungen und Observanzbestrebungen*, 35–58.

Saak, Eric L., *High Way to Heaven: The Augustinian Platform between Reform and Reformation, 1292–1524*, Studies in Medieval and Reformation Thought, 89, Leiden, Boston and Cologne: Brill, 2002.

Saenger, Paul, 'Books of Hours and the Reading Habits of the Late Middle Ages', *Scrittura e Civiltà* 9 (1985), 239–69.

Sahas, Daniel, *John of Damascus on Islam: The 'Heresy' of the Ishmaelites*, Leiden: Brill, 1972.

Sánchez Sánchez, Manuel Ambrosio, 'Vernacular Preaching in Spanish, Portuguese, and Catalan', in Beverly Mayne Kienzle, ed., *The Sermon*, Typologie des sources du Moyen Âge occidental, Turnhout: Brepols, 2000, 81–3.

Sapir Abulafia, Anna, *Christians and Jews in the Twelfth-Century Renaissance*, London and New York: Routledge, 1995.

Saxon, E., *The Eucharist in Romanesque France: Iconography, and Theology*, Woodbridge: Boydell Press, 2006.

Sayers, Dorothy, *The Mind of the Maker*, New York: Harcourt Brace, 1941; repr. New York: Harper Collins, 1987.

Sayers, Jane E., *Innocent III: Leader of Europe 1198–1216*, London: Longman, 1994.

*Papal Government in England during the Pontificate of Honorius III (1216–1227)*, Cambridge: Cambridge University Press, 1984.

*Papal Judges-Delegate in the Province of Canterbury, 1198–1254: A Study in Ecclesiastical Jurisdiction and Administration*, Oxford: Oxford University Press, 1971.

Scaraffia, L. and G. Zarri, *Donna e fede: Santità e vita religiosa in Italia*, Rome: Laterza, 1994.

Scase, Wendy, '"Heu! quanta desolatio Angliae praestatur": A Wycliffite Libel and the Naming of Heretics', in Somerset, Havens and Pittard, eds., *Lollards and their Influence*, 19–36.

*Piers Plowman and the New Anticlericalism*, Cambridge: Cambridge University Press, 1989.

'Reginald Pecock, John Carpenter and John Colop's "Common-Profit" Books: Aspects of Book Ownership and Circulation in Fifteenth-Century London', *Medium Aevum* 61 (1992), 261–74.

Schäfer, Peter, *Mirror of his Beauty: Feminine Images of God from the Bible to the Early Kabbalah*, Princeton: Princeton University Press, 2002.

Scheepsma, Wybren, *Medieval Religious Women in the Low Countries: The Modern Devotion, the Canonesses of Windesheim, and their Writings*, Woodbridge: Boydell, 2004.

Schild, Maurice, *Abendländische Bibelvorreden bis zur Lutherbibel*, Gütersloh: Gerd Mohn, 1970.

Schiller, Gertrud, *Ikonographie der christlichen Kunst*, vol. 4.2, *Maria*, Gütersloh: Gütersloher Verlagshaus, 1980.

Schimmelpfennig, Bernhard, *The Papacy*, trans. James Sievert, New York: Columbia University Press, 1992.

Schlink, Wilhelm, *Der Beau-Dieu von Amiens: Das Christusbild der gotischen Kathedrale*, Frankfurt: Insel Verlag, 1991.

Schmieder, Felicitas, *Europa und die Fremden: Die Mongolen im Urteil des Abendlandes vom 13. bis in das 15. Jahrhundert*, Sigmaringen: Jan Thorbecke Verlag, 1994.

Schmitt, Jean-Claude, *Ghosts in the Middle Ages: The Living and the Dead in Medieval Society*, Chicago: University of Chicago Press, 1998 [1994].

*Le saint lévrier. Guinefort guérisseur d'enfants depuis le XIIIe siècle*, Paris: Flammarion, 1979.

*Mort d'une hérésie: L'Église et les clercs face aux béguines et aux béghards du Rhin supérier du XIVe au XVe siècle*, Paris: Mouton and École des Hautes Études en Sciences Sociales, 1978.

Schneyer, Johannes Baptist, *Die Unterweisung der Gemeinde über die Predigt bei scholastischen Predigern: Eine Homiletik aus scholastischen Prothemen*, Munich: Ferdinand Schöningh, 1968.

Schreckenberg, Heinz, *Die christlichen Adversus-Judaeos-Texte*, 3 vols., Frankfurt am Main: Peter Lang, 1982, 1988, 1994.

*The Jews in Christian Art: An Illuminated History*, New York: Continuum, 1996.

Schreiner, Klaus, 'Benediktinische Klosterreform als zeitgebundene Auslegung der Regel. Geistige, religiöse und soziale Erneuerung in spätmittelalterlichen Klöstern Südwestdeutschlands im Zeichen der Kastler, Melker und Bursfelder Reform', *Blätter für württembergische Kirchengeschichte* 86 (1986), 105–95.

*Maria: Jungfrau, Mutter, Herrscherin*, Munich: Carl Hanser, 1994.

Schuler, Carol, 'The Seven Sorrows of the Virgin: Popular Culture and Cultic Imagery in Pre-Reformation Europe', *Simiolus* 21 (1992), 5–28.

Schulte, Johann Friedrich von, *Die Geschichte der Quellen und Literatur des canonischen Rechts* I, Stuttgart: F. Enke, 1875.

Schüssler, Hermann, *Der Primat der Heiligen Schrift als theologisches und kanonistisches Problem in Spätmittelalter*, Wiesbaden: Franz Steiner, 1977.

Schwerin, Ursula, *Die Aufrufe der Päpste zur Befreiung des Heiligen Landes von den Anfängen bis zum Ausgang Innozenz IV: Ein Beitrag zur Geschichte der kurialen Kreuzzugspropaganda und der päpstlichen Epistolographie*, Berlin: Ebering, 1937.

Seiferth, Wolfgang S., *Synagogue and Church in the Middle Ages: Two Symbols in Art and Literature*, trans. Lee Chadeayne and Paul Gottwald, New York: Ungar, 1970.

Sensi, Mario, *Dal movimento eremitico alla regolare osservanza francescana: L'opera di fra Paoluccio Trinci*, Rome: Santa Maria degli Angeli, 1992.

Septimus, Bernard, '"Better under Edom than under Ishmael": The History of a Saying', *Zion* 47 (1982), 103–11 [in Hebrew].

Servatius, Viveca, *Cantus sororum: Musik- und liturgiegeschichtliche Studien zu den Antiphonen des birgittinischen Eigenrepertoires nebst 91 Transkriptionen*, Acta universitatis upsaliensis, Studia musicologica upsaliensia nova series 12, Uppsala: Almqvist & Wiksell, 1990.

Seward, D., *The Monks of War: The Military Religious Orders*, London: Penguin, 1995.

Seybold, Michael, *Die Offenbarung: Von der Schrift bis zum Ausgang der Scholastik*, Handbuch der Dogmengeschichte 1, fasc. 1a, Freiburg: Herder, 1971.

Sheils, W. and D. Wood, eds., *Women in the Church*, Studies in Church History 27, Oxford: Blackwell, 1990.

Siberry, J. E., *The New Crusaders: Images of the Crusades in the Nineteenth and Early Twentieth Centuries*, Aldershot: Ashgate, 2000.

Sigal, P., *L'homme et le miracle dans la France médiévale (XIe–XIIe siècle)*, Paris: Cerf, 1985.
*Les marcheurs de Dieu: Pèlerinages et pèlerins au Moyen Âge*, Paris: A. Colin, 1974.

Signer, Michael A., 'God's Love for Israel: Apologetic and Hermeneutical Strategies in Twelfth-Century Biblical Exegesis', in Michael A. Signer and John Van Engen, eds., *Jews and Christians in Twelfth-Century Europe*, Notre Dame: University of Notre Dame Press, 2000, 123–49.

Signer, Michael A. and John Van Engen, eds., *Jews and Christians in Twelfth-Century Europe*, Notre Dame: University of Notre Dame Press, 2000.

Signori, G., *Maria zwischen Kathedrale, Kloster und Welt*, Stuttgart: Jan Thorbecke Verlag, 1995.

Silvestre, H., 'Trois témoignages mosans du début du XIIe siècle sur le crucifix de l'arc triomphal', *Revue des archaeologues et historiens d'art de Louvain* 9 (1976), 225–31.

Simons, Walter, *Cities of Ladies: Beguine Communities in the Medieval Low Countries, 1200–1565*, Philadelphia: University of Pennsylvania Press, 2001.
'Holy Women of the Low Countries: A Survey', in Rosalynn Voaden and Alastair Minnis, eds., *The Yale Companion to Medieval Holy Women in the Christian Tradition*, New Haven, Conn.: Yale University Press, forthcoming.

Simpson, James, *The Oxford English Literary History 1350–1547: Reform and Cultural Revolution*, Oxford: Oxford University Press, 2002.

Sivan, Emmanuel, *Interpretations of Islam Past and Present*, Princeton: The Darwin Press, 1985.
*L'Islam et la Croisade: Idéologie et propagande dans les réactions musulmanes aux Croisades*, Paris: Librairie d'Amérique et d'Orient, 1968.

Slocum, Kate Brainerd, *Liturgies in Honour of Thomas Becket*, Toronto: University of Toronto Press, 2003.

Smail, R. C., *Crusading Warfare, 1097–1193*, 2nd edn, Cambridge: Cambridge University Press, 1995.

Smalley, Beryl, *The Gospels in the Schools c. 1100–c. 1280*, London: Hambledon Press, 1985.

    *Studies in Medieval Thought and Learning*, London: Hambledon Press, 1981.

    *The Study of the Bible in the Middle Ages*, 2nd edn, Oxford: Blackwell, 1952; repr. Notre Dame: University of Notre Dame Press, 1970.

Smet, Joachim, 'Pre-Tridentine Reform in the Carmelite Order', in Elm, ed., *Reformbemühungen und Observanzbestrebungen*, 293–323.

Smith, Kathryn A., 'The Neville of Hornby Hours and the Design of Literate Devotion', *Art Bulletin* 81 (1999), 72–92.

Smith, L., *Masters of the Sacred Page*, Notre Dame: University of Notre Dame Press, 2001.

Smith, R. A. L., *Canterbury Cathedral Priory: A Study in Monastic Administration*, repr., Cambridge: Cambridge University Press, 1969 [1943].

Snoeck, J., *Medieval Piety from Relics to Eucharist: A Process of Mutual Interactions*, Leiden: Brill, 1985.

Somerset, Fiona, *Clerical Discourse and Lay Audience in Late Medieval England*, Cambridge: Cambridge University Press, 1998.

    'Expanding the Langlandian Canon: Radical Latin and the Stylistics of Reform', *The Yearbook of Langland Studies* 17 (2003), 73–92.

Somerset, Fiona, Jill C. Havens and Derrik G. Pittard, eds., *Lollards and their Influence in Late Medieval England*, Woodbridge: Boydell, 2003.

Somerville, Robert and Bruce C. Brasington, *Prefaces to Canon Law Books in Latin Christianity: Selected Translations, 500–1245*, New Haven, Conn.: Yale University Press, 1998.

Somerville, Robert, with the collaboration of Stephan Kuttner, *Urban II, the "Collectio britannica," and the Council of Melfi (1089)*, Oxford: Clarendon Press, 1996.

Southern, R. W., 'The English Origins of the "Miracles of the Virgin"', *Mediaeval and Renaissance Studies* 4 (1958), 176–216.

    *Robert Grosseteste: The Growth of an English Mind in Medieval Europe*, Oxford: Clarendon Press, 1986.

    *Scholastic Humanism and the Unification of Europe*, vol. 1, *Foundations*, Oxford and Cambridge, Mass.: Blackwell, 1995.

    *Western Society and the Church in the Middle Ages*, Harmondsworth: Penguin, 1970.

Speed, Diane, 'The Saracens of King Horn', *Speculum* 65 (1990), 564–95.

Speer, Andreas, *Die entdeckte Natur: Untersuchungen zu Begründungsversuchen einer 'scientia naturalis' im 12. Jahrhundert*, Studien und Texte zur Geistesgeschichte des Mittelalters 45, Leiden, New York and Cologne: Brill, 1995.

Speer, Andreas, Kent Emery and Jan Aertsen, eds., *Nach der Verurteilung von 1277: Philosophie und Theologie an der Universität von Paris im letzten Viertel des 13 Jahrhunderts*, Miscellanea Mediaevalia 28, Berlin: Walter de Gruyter, 2001.

Spencer, H. Leith, *English Preaching in the Late Middle Ages*, Oxford: Clarendon Press, 1993.

Stacey, Robert, 'Thirteenth-Century Anglo-Jewry and the Problem of the Expulsion', in Yosef Kaplan and David S. Katz, eds., *Exile and Return: Anglo-Jewry through the Ages*, Jerusalem: The Zalman Shazar Center for Jewish History, 1993, 9–25 [in Hebrew].

Stacey, R. C., 'Antisemitism and the Medieval English State', in J. R. Maddicott and D. M. Palliser, eds., *The Medieval State*, London: Hambledon, 2000, 163–77.

Staring, A., 'The Carmelite Sisters in the Netherlands', *Carmelus* 10 (1963), 56–92.

Staubach, Nikolaus, 'Pragmatische Schriftlichkeit im Bereich der Devotio moderna', *Frühmittelalteriche Studien* 25 (1991), 418–61.

Staubach, Nikolaus, ed., *Kirchenreform von unten: Gerhard Zerbolt von Zutphen und die Brüder vom gemeinsamen Leben*, Frankfurt am Main: Peter Lang, 2004.

Stegmüller, Friedrich, *Repertorium biblicum*, 11 vols., Madrid: Consejo Superior de Investigaciones Científicas, 1940–80.

Steinberg, L., *The Sexuality of Christ in Renaissance Art and in Modern Oblivion*, 2nd edn, Chicago: University of Chicago Press, 1996.

Stephens, W., *Demon Lovers: Witchcraft, Sex, and the Crisis of Belief*, Chicago: University of Chicago Press, 2002.

Stewart, Alison G., 'Early Woodcut Workshops', *Art Journal* 39 (1980), 189–94.

Stewart, Marc and David Wulstan, eds., *The Poetic and Musical Legacy of Heloise and Abelard*, Ottawa: Institute of Mediaeval Music; Westhumble: The Plainsong and Mediaeval Music Society, 2003.

Stewart, Robert M., *'De illis qui faciunt penitentiam'. The Rule of the Secular Franciscan Order: Origins, Development, Interpretation*, Rome: Istituto Storico dei Cappuccini, 1991.

Sticca, Sandro, *The Planctus Mariae in the Dramatic Tradition of the Middle Ages*, trans. Joseph R. Berrigan, Athens: University of Georgia Press, 1988.

Stievermann, Dieter, 'Klosterreform und Territorialstaat in Süddeutschland im 15. Jahrhundert', *Rottenburger Jahrbuch für Kirchengeschichte* 11 (1992), 1149–60.

Stock, Brian, *The Implications of Literacy: Written Language and Models of Interpretation in the Eleventh and Twelfth Centuries*, Princeton: Princeton University Press, 1983.

Stoelen, A., 'De Chronologie van de werken van Dionysius de Karthuizer: De eerste werken en de schriftuurkommentaren', *Sacris erudiri* 5 (1953), 361–401.

Stolz, Michael, *Artes-liberales-Zyklen: Formationen des Wissens im Mittelalter*, 2 vols., Bibliotheca Germanica 47, Tübingen and Basel: A. Francke, 2004.

Stooker, Karl and Theo Verbeij, *Collecties op orde: Middelnederlandse handschriften uit kloosters en semi-religieuze gemeenschappen in de Nederlanden*, 2 vols., Leuven: Peeters, 1997.

Stow, Kenneth R., *Alienated Minority: The Jews of Medieval Latin Christendom*, Cambridge, Mass.: Harvard University Press, 1992.

Strayer, Joseph, *Medieval Statecraft and the Perspectives of History*, Princeton: Princeton University Press, 1971.

Strohm, Paul, *England's Empty Throne: Usurpation and the Language of Legitimation, 1399–1422*, New Haven, Conn. and London: Yale University Press, 1998.

Strohm, Reinhard, *The Rise of European Music, 1380–1500*, Cambridge: Cambridge University Press, 1993.

Strohm, Reinhard and Bonnie Blackburn, eds., *Music as Concept and Practice in the Late Middle Ages*, New Oxford History of Music 3.1, New York: Oxford University Press, 2001.

Studt, B., 'Helden und Heilige: Männlichkeitsentwürfe im frühen und hohen Mittelalter', *Historische Zeitschrift* 276 (2003), 1–36.

Suarez-Nani, Tiziana, *Les anges et la philosophie: Subjectivité et function cosmologique des substances séparées à la fin du xiiiè siècle*, Paris: Vrin, 2002.

Sumption, J., *Pilgrimage: An Image of Mediaeval Religion*, London: Faber and Faber, 1975.

Swanson, R. N., *Church and Society in Late Medieval England*, Oxford: Blackwell, 1989.

    *Universities, Academics and the Great Schism*, Cambridge: Cambridge University Press, 1979.

    ed., *Gender and Christian Religion*, Studies in Church History 34, Woodbridge: Boydell Press, 1998.

    *Unity and Diversity in the Church*, Studies in Church History 32, Oxford: Blackwell, 1994.

Szittya, P. R., *The Antifraternal Tradition in Medieval Literature*, Princeton: Princeton University Press, 1986.

Szövérffy, Joseph, *Marianische Motivik der Hymnen: Ein Beitrag zur Geschichte der marianischen Lyrik im Mittelalter*, Leiden: Classical Folia Editions, 1985.

Tangl, Georgine, *Die Teilnehmer an den allgemeinen Konzilien des Mittelalters*, Cologne: Böhlau, 1969.

Taylor, C., *Heresy in Medieval France: Dualism in Aquitaine and the Agenais, 1000–1249*, Woodbridge: Boydell and Brewer, 2005.

Taylor, Larissa, *Soldiers of Christ: Preaching in Late Medieval and Reformation France*, New York: Oxford, 1992.

Tellenbach, Gerd, *Church, State and Christian Society at the Time of the Investiture Contest*, trans. R. F. Bennett, Oxford: Basil Blackwell, 1938.

Thijssen, J. M. M. H., *Censure and Heresy at the University of Paris, 1200–1400*, Philadelphia: University of Pennsylvania Press, 1998.

Thompson, Sally, *Women Religious: The Founding of English Nunneries after the Norman Conquest*, Oxford: Clarendon Press, 1991.

Thomson, J. A. F., 'Orthodox Religion and the Origins of Lollardy', *History* 74 (1989), 39–55.

Thunoe, E. and G. Wolf, eds., *The Miraculous Image in the Late Middle Ages and Renaissance*, Rome: L'Erma di Bretschneider, 2004.

    *Uomo e spazio nell'Alto Medioevo: Atti della cinquantesima Settimana di studi sull'Alto Medio Evo (Spoleto, 4–9 aprile 2002)*, Spoleto: Centro italiano di studi sull'Alto Medioevo, 2003.

Toaff, A., *Jews, Franciscans and the First "Monti di Pietà" in Italy (1462–1500)*, in Steven J. McMichael and Susan Myers, eds., *Friars and Jews in the Middle Ages and Renaissance*, Leiden: Brill, 2004, 239–53.

Toch, Michael, *Die Juden im mittelalterlichen Reich*, Munich: R. Oldenbourg, 1998.

Todeschini, G., *La ricchezza degli ebrei: Merci e denaro nella riflessione ebraica e nella definizione cristiana dell'usura alla fine del Medioevo*, Spoleto: CISAM, 1989.

    *Ricchezza francescana: Dalla povertà volontaria all'economia di mercato*, Bologna: Il Mulino, 2004.

Tolan, John, 'Peter the Venerable, on the "Diabolical Heresy of the Saracens"', in Alberto Ferreiro, ed., *The Devil, Heresy, and Witchcraft in the Middle Ages: Essays in Honor of Jeffrey B. Russell*, Leiden: Brill, 1998, 345–68.

    *Saracens: Islam in the Medieval European Imagination*, New York: Columbia, 2002.

Torrell, J. P., *Initiation à saint Thomas d'Aquin: Sa personne et son oeuvre*, Fribourg: Editions Universitaires; Paris: Cerf, 1993 (revised and expanded 2002).

Townsend, D. and A. Taylor, eds., *The Tongue of the Fathers: Gender and Ideology in Twelfth-Century Latin*, Philadelphia: University of Pennsylvania Press, 1997.

Trachtenberg, Joshua, *The Devil and the Jew*, New Haven, Conn.: Yale University Press, 1943.

Trapp, Damasus, 'Augustinian Theology of the 14th Century; Notes on Editions, Marginalia, Opinions and Book-Lore', *Augustiniana* 6 (1956), 146–274.

Trexler, R., *Sex and Conquest: Gendered Violence, Political Order, and the European Conquest of the Americas*, Ithaca, N.Y. and London: Cornell University Press, 1995.

Tugwell, S., '*De huiusmodi sermonibus texitur omnis recta predicatio*: Changing Attitudes towards the Word of God', in Jacqueline Hamesse and Xavier Hermand, eds., *De l'homélie au sermon: Histoire de la prédication médiévale*, Louvain: Université Catholique de Louvain, 1993, 159–68.

Turner, Denys, *Eros and Allegory: Medieval Exegesis of the Song of Songs*, Kalamazoo, Mich.: Cistercian Publications, 1995.

Tyerman, C. J., *England and the Crusades, 1095–1588*, Chicago: University of Chicago Press, 1988.

*The Invention of the Crusades*, Toronto: University of Toronto Press; Basingstoke: Macmillan, 1998.

Ullmann, C., *Reformatoren vor der Reformation*, 2nd edn, Gotha: Perthes, 1866.

Ullmann, Walter, *A Short History of the Papacy in the Middle Ages*, London: Methuen and Co., 1972.

Vaccaro, L., ed., *L'Europa dei pellegrini*, Milan: Centro Ambrosiano, 2004.

Valois, N., *Guillaume d'Auvergne*, Paris: Alphonse Picard, 1880.

Van den Bosch, Pieter, 'De bibliotheken van de Kruisherenkloosters in de Nederlanden vóór 1550', in *Studies over het boekenbezit en boekengebruik in de Nederlanden vóór 1600*, Brussels: Koninklijke Bibliotheek Albert I, 1974, 563–636.

'Die Kreuzherrenreform des 15. Jahrhunderts', in Elm, ed., *Reformbemühungen und Observanzbestrebungen*, 71–82.

Van der Lugt, M., *Le ver, le démon et la vierge: Les théories médiévales de la génération extraordinaire*, Paris: Les Belles Lettres, 2004.

Van Engen, Hildo, *De derde orde van Sint-Franciscus in het middeleeuwse bisdom Utrecht: Een bijdrage tot de institutionele geschiedenis van de Moderne Devotie*, Hilversum: Verloren, 2006. With edition of legal sources: www.bkvu.nl.

Van Engen, John, 'The "Crisis of Cenobitism" Reconsidered: Benedictine Monasticism in the Years 1050–1150', *Speculum* 61 (1986), 269–304.

'The Sayings of the Fathers: An Inside Look at the New Devout in Deventer', in Robert J. Bast and Andrew Colin Gow, eds., *Continuity and Change: The Harvest of Late Medieval and Reformation History. Essays Presented to Heiko A. Oberman on his 70th Birthday*, Leiden: Brill, 2000, 279–320.

'The Virtues, the Brothers and the Schools', *Revue Bénédictine* 98 (1988), 178–217.

ed., *Learning Institutionalized: Teaching in the Medieval University*, Notre Dame, Ind.: University of Notre Dame Press, 2000.

Van Luijk, M., *Bruiden van Christus: De tweede religieuze vrouwenbeweging in Leiden en Zwolle, 1380–1580*, Zutphen: Walburg Pers, 2004.

Van Os, Henk, *The Art of Devotion in the Late Middle Ages in Europe, 1300–1500*, trans. Michael Hoyle, Princeton: Princeton University Press, 1994.

*The Way to Heaven: Relics Veneration in the Middle Ages*, Baarn: Uitgeverij de Prom, 2001.

Van Steenberghen, F., *Aristotle in the West*, 2nd edn, Louvain: Nauwelaerts, 1970.

*La Philosophie au XIII$^e$ siècle*, 2nd edn, Philosophes Médiévaux 28, Louvain: Institut supérieur de philosophie, 1991.

Vauchez, A., 'L'image vivante: Quelques réflexions sur les fonctions des représentations iconographiques dans le domaine religieux en Occident aux derniers siècles du Moyen Âge', in Maurice Aymard *et al.*, eds., *Pauvres et riches: Société et culture du Moyen Âge aux temps modernes. Mélanges offerts à Bronislaw Geremek à l'occasion de son soixantième anniversaire*, Warsaw: Wydawnictwo Naukowe PWN, 1992, 231–41.

*The Laity in the Middle Ages: Religious Beliefs and Devotional Practices*, ed. and intro. Daniel E. Bornstein; trans. Margery J. Schneider, Notre Dame: University of Notre Dame Press, 1993.

*La sainteté en Occident aux derniers siècles du Moyen Âge*, 2nd edn, Bibliothèque des Écoles françaises d'Athènes et de Rome 241, Rome: École Française de Rome, trans. Jean Birrell, *Sainthood in the Later Middle Ages*, Cambridge: Cambridge University Press, 1999.

*Saints, prophètes et visionnaires: Le pouvoir surnaturel au Moyen Âge*, Paris: Albin Michel, 1999.

Vauchez, A., ed., *Lieux sacrés, lieux de culte et sanctuaires*, Rome: École française de Rome, 2000.

Vauchez, A. and C. Caby, *L'histoire des moines, chanoines et religieux au Moyen Âge: Guide de recherche et documents*, L'atelier du médiéviste 9, Turnhout: Brepols, 2003.

Vazquez de Parga, L., J. M. Lacarra, and J. Uria Riu, *Las peregrinaciones a Santiago de Compostela*, 3 vols., Madrid: Consejo Superior de Investigaciones, 1948–49.

Vecchio, Silvana, 'Le prediche e l'istruzione religiosa', in *La predicazione dei Frati dalla metà del '200 alla fine del' 300*, Spoleto: Centro Italiano di Studi sull'Alto Medioevo, 1995, 301–35.

Venarde, B. L., *Women's Monasticism and Medieval Society: Nunneries in France and England, 890–1215*, Ithaca, N.Y.: Cornell University Press, 1997.

Verdeyen, Paul, 'Le procès d'inquisition contre Marguerite Porète et Guiard de Cressonessart (1309–1310)', *Revue d'histoire ecclésiastique* 81 (1986), 47–94.

Verger, Jacques, *Les gens de savoir dans l'Europe de la fin du Moyen Âge*, Paris: Presses Universitaires de France, 1997.

Vetulani, Adam, *Sur Gratien et les décretales: Recueil d'études*, Collected Studies CS 308, Aldershot: Ashgate, 1990.

Vicaire, M.-H., *Histoire de St Dominique*, Paris: Les Éditions du Cerf, 1957; trans. Kathleen Pond, *St Dominic and his Times*, New York, Toronto and London: McGraw Hill, 1964.

Vitz, E., 'Gender and Martyrdom', *Medievalia et Humanistica* NS 26 (1999), 79–99.

Volpato, A., 'La predicazione penitenziale-apocalittica nell'attività di due predicatori del 1473', *Bullettino dell'Istituto Storico Italiano per il Medio Evo* 82 (1970), 113–28.

Von Simson, Otto, '*Compassio* and *Co-redemptio* in Roger van der Weyden's *Descent from the Cross*', *Art Bulletin* 35 (1953), 9–16.

Vorgrimler, Herbert, *Geschichte der Hölle*, Munich: W. Fink, 1993.

Vovelle, Michel and Gaby Vovelle, *Vision de la mort et de l'au-delà en Provence, d'après les autels des âmes du purgatoire, XVe–XXe siècles*, Cahiers des Annales 29, Paris: A. Colin, 1970.

Wack, Mary, *Lovesickness in the Middle Ages: The 'Viaticum' and its Commentaries*, Philadelphia: University of Pennsylvania Press, 1990.

Waddell, Chrysogonus, 'Epithalamica: An Easter Sequence by Peter Abelard', *The Musical Quarterly* 72 (1986), 239–71.

'The Origin and Early Evolution of the Cistercian Antiphonary: Reflections on Two Cistercian Chant Reforms', in Basil Pennington, ed., *The Cistercian Spirit: A Symposium in Memory of Thomas Merton*, Washington, D.C.: Cistercian Publications, Consortium Press, 1970, 190–223.

Wagner, David L., ed., *The Seven Liberal Arts in the Middle Ages*, Bloomington: Indiana University Press, 1983.

Walsh, Katherine, 'The Observance: Sources for a History of the Observant Reform Movement in the Order of Augustinian Friars in the Fourteenth and Fifteenth Centuries', *Rivista di Storia della Chiesa in Italia* 31 (1977), 40–67.

'Papal Policy and Local Reform, a) The Beginnings of the Augustinian Observance in Tuscany, b) Congregatio Ilicetana: The Augustinian Observant Movement in Tuscany and the Humanist Ideal', *Römische historische Mitteilungen* 21 (1979), 35–72 and 22 (1980), 105–45.

'Papsttum und Ordensreform in Spätmittelalter und Renaissance: Zur Wechselwirkung von zentraler Gewalt und lokaler Initiative', in Elm, ed., *Reformbemühungen und Observanzbestrebungen*, 411–30.

Walther, Wilhelm, *Die deutsche Bibelübersetzung des Mittelalters*, Nieuwkoop: B. De Graaf, 1966.

Ward, Benedicta, *Miracles and the Medieval Mind: Theory, Record and Event, 1000–1215*, rev. edn, Philadelphia: University of Pennsylvania Press, 1987.

Warren, Ann K., *Anchorites and their Patrons in Medieval England*, Berkeley and Los Angeles: University of California Press, 1985.

Warren, Nancy Bradley, *Spiritual Economies: Female Monasticism in Later Medieval England*, Philadelphia: University of Pennsylvania Press, 2001.

Waterton, Edmund, *Pietas Mariana Britannica: A History of English Devotion to the Most Blessed Virgin Marye*, London: St. Joseph's Catholic Library, 1879.

Watson, Nicholas, 'Censorship and Cultural Change in Late Medieval England: Vernacular Theology, the Oxford Translation Debate, and Arundel's *Constitutions* of 1409', *Speculum* 70 (1995), 822–64.

Watt, John, *The Church in Medieval Ireland*, Dublin: University College Dublin Press, 1998.

Webb, D., *Patrons and Defenders: The Saints in Italian City States*, London and New York: Tauris Academic Studies, 1996.

Wegman, Rob. C., 'From Maker to Composer: Improvisation and Musical Authorship in the Low Countries, 1450–1500', *Journal of the American Musicological Society* 49 (1996), 409–79.

Wehrli-Johns, Martina, 'L'Osservanza dei Domenicani e il movimento penitenziale laico: Studi sulla "regola di Munio" e sul Terz'ordine domenicano in Italia e Germania', in Giorgio Chittolini and Kaspar Elm, eds., *Ordini religiosi e società politica in Italia e Germania nei secoli XIV e XV*, Bologna: Il Mulino, 2001, 287–329.

Wehrli-Johns, Martina and Peter Stotz, 'Der Traktat des Dominikaners Albert von Weißenstein über das Salve regina (gedruckt: Zürich um 1479/1480)', in Andreas Meyer, Constanze Rendtel and Maria Wittmer-Butsch, eds., *Päpste, Pilger, Pönitentiarie: Festschrift für Ludwig Schmugge zum 65. Geburtstag*, Tübingen: Günter Narr, 2004, 283–313.

Weigand, Rudolf, *Glossatoren des Dekrets Gratians*, Bibliotheca eruditorum 18, Goldbach: Keip, 1997.

   *Die Glossen zum 'Dekret' Gratians: Studien zu den frühen Glossen und Glossenkompositionen*, Rome: Studia Gratiana, 1991.

Weigand, Rudolf, *Liebe und Ehe im Mittelalter*, 2nd edn, Bibliotheca eruditorum, Goldbach: Keip, 1998.

Weinstein, D., *Una città e il suo profeta: Firenze di fronte al Savonarola*, ed. G. Garfagnini, Florence: SISMEL – Edizioni del Galluzzo, 2001.

   *Savonarola and Florence: Prophecy and Patriotism in the Renaissance*, Princeton: Princeton University Press, 1978.

Weinstein, Donald and Rudolph M. Bell, *Saints and Society: Two Worlds of Western Christendom, 1000–1700*, Chicago and London: University of Chicago Press, 1982.

Weisheipl, J. A., *Thomas d'Aquino and Albert his Teacher*, Toronto: Pontifical Institute of Mediaeval Studies, 1980.

Wenninger, Markus J., *Man bedarf keiner Juden mehr: Ursachen und Hintergründe ihrer Vertreibung aus den deutschen Reichsstädten im 15. Jahrhundert*, Vienna: H. Bohlaus Nachf., 1981.

Werbeck, Wilfrid, *Jacobus Perez von Valencia: Untersuchungen zu seinem Psalmenkommentar*, Tübingen: J.C.B. Mohr/Paul Siebeck, 1959.

Wettstein, Th., *Heilige vor Gericht: Das Kanonisationsverfahren im europäischen Spätmittelalter*, Cologne: Böhlau, 2004.

Wieck, Roger S., 'The Book of Hours', in Thomas J. Heffernan and E. Ann Matter, eds., *The Liturgy of the Medieval Church*, Kalamazoo, Mich.: Medieval Institute Publications, Western Michigan University Press, 2001, 473–513.

   *Time Sanctified: The Book of Hours in Medieval Art and Life*, New York: George Braziller, 1988.

Wiethaus, U., 'Sexuality, Gender and the Body in Late Medieval Spirituality: Cases from Germany and the Netherlands', *Journal of Feminist Studies in Religion* 7 (1991), 35–52.

Wiethaus, U., ed., *Maps of Flesh and Light: The Religious Experience of Medieval Women Mystics*, Syracuse, N.Y.: Syracuse University Press, 1993.

Wilkins, Eithne, *The Rose-Garden Game: The Symbolic Background to the European Prayer-Beads*, London: Victor Gollancz, 1969.

Wilks, Michael, *Wyclif: Political Ideas and Practice*, Oxford: Oxbow Books, 2000.

Williams, A. L., *Adversus Iudaeos: A Bird's-Eye View of Christian Apologiae until the Renaissance*, Cambridge: Cambridge University Press, 1935.

Williams, D. H., *The Cistercians in the Early Middle Ages*, Leominster: Gracewing, 1998.

Williams, Jane W., *Bread, Wine, and Money: Windows of Trades at Chartres Cathedral*, Chicago: University of Chicago Press, 1993.

Williams-Krapp, Werner, 'Die Bedeutung der reformierten Klöster des Predigerordens für das literarische Leben in Nürnberg im 15. Jahrhundert', in Falk Eisermann, Eva Schlotheuber and Volker Honemann, eds., *Studien und Texte zur literarischen und materiellen Kultur der Frauenklöster im Mittelalter: Ergebnisse eines Arbeitsgesprächs in der Herzog August Bibliothek Wolfenbüttel, 24.–26. Febr. 1999*, Studies in Medieval and Reformation Thought 99, Leiden: Brill, 2004, 311–29.

Wilmart, André, *Auteurs spirituels et textes dévots du Moyen Âge latin: Études d'histoire littéraire*, Paris: Études Augustiniennes, 1971 [1932].

Wilson, Blake, *Music and Merchants: The Laudesi Companies of Republican Florence*, Oxford: Oxford University Press, 1992.

Wilson, E., 'Institoris at Innsbruck', in R. Scribner, ed., *Popular Religion in Germany and Central Europe 1400–1800*, Houndmills: Macmillan, 1996, 87–100.

Winroth, Anders, *The Making of Gratian's Decretum*, Cambridge: Cambridge University Press, 2000.

Winston-Allen, Anne, *Convent Chronicles: Women Writing about Women and Reform in the Late Middle Ages*, University Park: Pennsylvania State University Press, 2004.

*Stories of the Rose: The Making of the Rosary in the Middle Ages*, University Park: Pennsylvania State University Press, 1997.

Wirth, Jean, *L'image à l'époque romane*, Paris: Éditions du Cerf, 1999.

Wolf, G., '*Salus populi romani*': Die Geschichte römischer Kultbilder im Mittelalter', Weinheim: VCH, Acta humaniora, 1990.

Wolfs, Servatius Petrus, 'Dominikanische Observanzbestrebungen: Die *Congregatio Hollandiae* (1464–1517)', in Elm, ed., *Reformbemühungen und Observanzbestrebungen*, 273–92.

Wolverton, Lisa, *Hastening toward Prague*, Philadelphia: University of Pennsylvania Press, 2001.

Wood, Jeryldene, *Women, Art and Spirituality: The Poor Clares of Early Modern Italy*, Cambridge: Cambridge University Press, 1996.

Woolf, Rosemary, *The English Religious Lyric in the Middle Ages*, Oxford: Oxford University Press, 1968.

Wriedt, Markus, *Gnade und Erwählung: Eine Untersuchung zu Johann von Staupitz und Martin Luther*, Mainz: Philipp von Zabern, 1991.

Wright, Craig, 'Dufay's *Nuper rosarum flores*, King Solomon's Temple, and the Veneration of the Virgin', *Journal of the American Musicological Society* 47 (1994), 395–441.

*The Maze and the Warrior: Symbols in Architecture, Theology, and Music*, Cambridge, Mass.: Harvard University Press, 2001.

Wulstan, David, '*Novi modulaminis melos*: The Music of Heloise and Abelard', *Plainsong and Medieval Music* 11 (2002), 1–23.

Yardley, Anne Bagnall, *Performing Piety: Musical Culture in Medieval English Nunneries*, New York: Palgrave MacMillan, 2006.

Yuval, Israel Jacob, *Two Nations in your Womb: Perceptions of Jews and Christians in Late Antiquity and the Middle Ages*, Berkeley and Los Angeles: University of California Press, 2006.

Zaleski, Carol, *Otherworld Journeys*, New York: Oxford University Press, 1987.

Zaleski, Carol and Philip Zaleski, *The Book of Heaven: An Anthology of Writings from Ancient to Modern Times*, Oxford: Oxford University Press, 2000.

Zarri, G., 'Living Saints: A Typology of Female Sanctity in the Early Sixteenth Century', in D. Bornstein and R. Rusconi, eds., *Women and Religion in Medieval and Renaissance Italy*, Chicago and London: University of Chicago Press, 1996, 219–303.

'Les prophètes de cour dans l'Italie de la Renaissance', in A. Vauchez, ed., *Les textes prophétiques et la prophétie en Occident (XIIe–XVIe siècle)*, Rome: École Française, 1990, 649–75.

*Le sante vive: Profezie di corte e devozione femminile tra '400 e 500'*, Turin: Rosenberg & Sellier, 1990.

Zerner, Monique, ed., *Inventer l'hérésie? Discours polémiques et pouvoirs avant l'inquisition*, Nice: Centre d'Études Médiévales, 1998.

Ziegler, Joanna E., *Sculpture of Compassion: The Pieta and the Beguines in the Southern Low Countries, c. 1300–1600*, Brussels and Rome: Institut historique belge de Rome, 1992.

Ziegler, J., 'Medicine and Immortality in Terrestrial Paradise', in P. Biller and J. Ziegler, eds., *Religion and Medicine in the Middle Ages*, York Studies in Medieval Theology 3, York and Woodbridge: York Medieval Press, 2001, 201–42.

*Medicine and Religion c. 1300: The Case of Arnau de Vilanova*, Oxford: Clarendon Press, 1998.

'Text and Context: On the Rise of Physiognomic Thought in the Later Middle Ages', in Y. Hen, ed., *De Sion exibit lex et verbum Domini de Hierusalem: Essays on Medieval Law, Liturgy, and Literature in Honour of Amnon Linder*, Turnhout: Brepols, 2001, 159–82.

Zieleman, G. C., *Middelnederlandse epistel- en evangeliepreken*, Leiden: Brill, 1978.

Zier, Mark A., 'The Manuscript Tradition of the *glossa ordinaria* for Daniel and Hints at a Method for a Critical Edition', *Scriptorium*, 47 (1993), 3–25.

Zumkeller, Adolar, *Erbsünde, Gnade, Rechtfertigung und Verdienst nach der Lehre der Erfurter Augustinertheologen des Spätmittelalters*, Würzburg: Augustinus-Verlag, 1984.

# Index